What the experts are saying
Choosing the Right Colle

"What more can I say? I am using *Choosing the Right College* — actively and appreciatively — as our high-school senior son contemplates colleges and universities. To parents like me, this wise and informative book is a rich blessing."

— WILLIAM MURCHISON
syndicated columnist

"Nowadays there may be no more bewildered people in this land than kids readying themselves to go to college, and no more perplexed ones than the parents who are trying to guide them. In offering this sane, civilized, and at the same time genuinely practical guide to colleges and universities, the Intercollegiate Studies Institute has performed a major service to both students and parents."

— MIDGE DECTER
author of *The Liberated Woman and Other Americans* and *Liberal Parents, Radical Children*

"The question I am probably most often asked by concerned parents is 'Where should I send my child to college?' Until now I have had to answer that question with at most one or two names. *Choosing the Right College* changes all that. At last, parents and prospective students can get an honest, in-depth account of what really awaits them at America's 100 top colleges. This book does not mince words. It provides exacting, no-nonsense assessments of academic life in both its intellectual and moral dimensions. In my opinion, *Choosing the Right College* is an indispensable guide for anyone who wants to make an informed and intelligent choice about one of the most important — and expensive — decisions most of us will ever make."

— ROGER KIMBALL
author of *Tenured Radicals: How Politics Has Corrupted Our Higher Education*

"I've got children approaching college age, so I'll be consulting this useful book. I'll even do my best to get the kids to read it."

— WILLIAM KRISTOL
editor and publisher of *The Weekly Standard*

Choosing the Right College

The Whole Truth about America's 100 Top Schools

Introduction by	WILLIAM J. BENNETT
Researched and written by	the staff of the Intercollegiate Studies Institute (ISI), T. Kenneth Cribb, Jr., President
Project Director	Jeffrey O. Nelson
Editor-in-Chief	Gregory Wolfe
Senior Editors	Winfield J. C. Myers, Jeremy Nafziger
Contributing Editors	Amy E. Fahey, Mark Johnson, Caroline Langston, Tony Mecia, Scott O. Stirling
Research Assistant	Kathryn Mullan

WILLIAM B. EERDMANS PUBLISHING COMPANY
GRAND RAPIDS, MICHIGAN / CAMBRIDGE, U.K.

© 1998 Intercollegiate Studies Institute, Inc.
P.O. Box 4431, Wilmington, Delaware 19807

Published 1998 by Wm. B. Eerdmans Publishing Co.
255 Jefferson Ave. S.E., Grand Rapids, Michigan 49503 /
P.O. Box 163, Cambridge CB3 9PU U.K.

Printed in the United States of America

03 02 01 00 99 98   7 6 5 4 3 2

Library of Congress Cataloging-in-Publication Data

Choosing the right college: the whole truth about America's 100 top schools /
    project director, Jeffrey O. Nelson; editor-in-chief, Gregory Wolfe;
    compiled by the staff of the Intercollegiate Studies Institute (ISI);
    introduction by William J. Bennett; research assistant, Kathryn Mullan.
         p.   cm.
      ISBN 0-8028-4537-1
       1. Universities and colleges — United States — Directories.
    2. College choice— United States — Handbooks, manuals, etc.
    I. Nelson, Jeffrey O. II. Wolfe, Gregory.   III. Intercollegiate Studies Institute.
    L901.C576 1998
    378.73 — dc21   98-22583
                                                              CIP

Contents

CONTENTS

Introduction

William J. Bennett

A question that I am often asked is what colleges I would recommend. It is a reasonable question. But it is also a difficult one to answer, given the vast number of colleges and universities. It simply is not possible for most people — including me — to know what is happening on all, or even most, of America's campuses. What parents and students desperately need is an intellectual road map, a commonsense guide, to help them make their way through the academy.

Choosing a college is a tremendously important — and can be an extremely expensive — undertaking. When done intelligently and thoughtfully, it can be a great investment. After all, a college education can provide graduates with the kind of high-demand skills that can serve them the rest of their lives. But college should provide much more than information and employment skills. Indeed, the undergraduate experience should be more than merely a job-training program. It can also be a time when many young people refine the convictions that will guide and mold their decisions, conduct, and character. The essence of education is, in the words of William James, to teach a person what deserves to be valued — to impart ideals as well as knowledge, to cultivate in students the ability to distinguish the true and good from their counterfeits, and the wisdom to prefer the former to the latter.

Yet despite the unparalleled resources American universities offer, there is growing evidence that many American universities are reneging on their duty to educate. The widespread abandonment of academic standards and moral discipline, the politicization of all aspects of campus life, and the deconstruction of academic disciplines have devastated the traditional mission of the liberal arts curriculum. In too many classrooms, professors teach their students that Western thought is suspect, that Enlightenment ideals are inherently oppressive, and that the basic principles of the American founding are not "relevant" to our time. The result is not education, but confusion — over the importance of knowledge, the universality of the human experience, the transcendence of ideals and principles. In the end, the central problem is not that the majority of students are being indoctrinated (although some are), but that they graduate knowing almost nothing at all. Or worse still, they graduate thinking that they know everything.

Fortunately, not all universities or professors have bought into this way of thinking. Important and impressive academic departments, professors, and universities still exist; it is simply a matter of finding them. This is no easy task, however — despite the piles of promotional information and bookstore college guides, no single publication existed that analyzed and evaluated universities, academic departments, and professors on the basis of principled instruction and intellectual rigor.

ISI's guide, *Choosing the Right College,* helps to fill that void. It offers tough-minded analysis of the quality of instruction, the level of academic standards, the campus political atmosphere, and the extent to which the liberal arts tradition is respected and cultivated. It is one of those rare books that cut through the information glut to the heart of the matter. I should add that it's been a long time since I've visited many of the colleges included in this volume — a few of them I've never visited. Nevertheless, I found this book to be authoritative, current, and extremely well written.

The organization responsible for compiling this volume — the Intercollegiate Studies Institute (ISI) — is well qualified to speak to these issues. Founded in 1953, ISI has worked tirelessly to further a better understanding of the principles that sustain a free society in American college youth. Through conferences, lectures, books, journals, and fellowships, ISI has helped to ensure that real intellectual debates — rather than one-sided indoctrination — take place in academia. In the process of compiling this book, the editors have drawn on many resources — including ISI's network of 60,000 students and faculty members — to produce thoroughly up-to-date portraits of the featured colleges.

The principle of selection in *Choosing the Right College* is eminently practical: of the one hundred institutions covered, the majority were chosen according to competitive admissions figures. In addition, the editors sought to represent the tremendous range of institutions available to the American public. The guide provides balanced and insightful reports on each of these schools.

The ISI guide illustrates and explicates the good, the bad, and the ugly in American higher education. These pages contain a number of real-life horror stories of ideological intolerance, bizarre course offerings, and absurd campus scandals. But the editors have also gone out of their way to search out what is good and commendable, from hard-working professors to dynamic departments and enriching extracurricular activities. The advice you will find in *Choosing the Right College* provides insights that may save a student from several semesters' worth of trial and error, pointing him or her in the right direction from the start. Best of all, the guide does not hesitate to name names: many of the best faculty members, departments, and special programs in each institution are specifically identified so that students can make informed education choices.

All too often, Americans treat colleges and universities with a deference that prevents them from asking hard questions and demanding real results. But if there is ever to be genuine, long-lasting education reform, parents and students will have to become shrewder and better-informed education consumers. ISI's *Choosing the Right College* is a powerful tool in this effort. It is my hope that American students will read it, learn from it, and, as a result, demand and receive a better university education.

How to Use This Guide

If you're holding this book in your hands then one thing is clear: you care about the quality of the college education you, or someone you know, will soon be receiving. We believe that this guide to 100 of America's top institutions of higher education offers a unique and valuable perspective in the high-stakes and high-stress process of choosing the right college or university.

While there are dozens of college guides on the market that convey vast amounts of information about admissions, financial aid, sports, student life, and the basics of the curriculum, few guides focus on what was once considered the essence of a sound education: the liberal arts. There is a growing recognition today, on the part of parents as well as educators, that academic specialization and technical know-how cannot provide the kind of integrated, well-rounded education that young people need to face the challenges of the wider world.

The liberal arts tradition, cultivated over centuries of educational experience, holds that students need more than technical skills or politically correct opinions to flourish in life: rather, young people need to develop the kind of wisdom and insight that is acquired by reflecting upon the classic texts of Western civilization — the civilization that has shaped our moral, political, and cultural life. As William J. Bennett writes in the introduction to this volume: "The essence of education is . . . to impart ideals as well as knowledge, to cultivate in students the ability to distinguish the true and good from their counterfeits, and the wisdom to prefer the former to the latter."

Unfortunately, the liberal arts tradition has been under attack for some time, and not just from the proponents of specialization. In the last thirty years, the greatest challenge to the liberal arts has come from the rise of political ideologies that seek to undermine the very foundation of Western learning. Many of these ideologies go well beyond revising the historical record so that it is more honest about, and just toward, various oppressed and neglected groups. Indeed, many of these radical theorists have turned the academic podium into a bully pulpit for attacks on many of the Western ideas and institutions that undergird our American order. To an extent that many parents and alumni don't fully comprehend, this politicization of the academy has a profound impact on the daily lives of millions of college students.

Choosing the Right College has a definite point of view on this subject: put simply, it is based on the conviction that the liberal arts continue to provide the broadest and most humane form of education — an education that can literally deepen and transform the lives of our young people.

The focus of this guide, then, is on where you will be able to find the liberal arts tradition at our nation's elite institutions of higher education.

Each essay in *Choosing the Right College* is divided into four sections. A brief introduction provides an overview of the history and current climate at the college or university under review. In the next section, "Academic Life," the schools' fundamental requirements are examined with an eye to how well they match up against the liberal arts ideal. In addition, this section includes information about departments and courses that are heavily politicized. But rather than concentrate on what is negative, our guide points out individual professors and departments that have demonstrated an outstanding commitment to providing a quality undergraduate education. It is our hope that by pointing out these teachers and departments, students will get more out of their educational experience. Navigating one's way through a college education can be an intimidating experience; we hope to make the sailing a little less frightening and a lot smoother.

The third part of each essay delves into the controversies and conflicts that make up a college's "Political Atmosphere." Our purpose in this section is not simply to dig up outrageous stories of politicization — although we've amassed plenty of these — but to indicate the dominant tone of a particular campus. Just as prospective students want to know whether a college is located in a city, a suburb, or a rural community, so they have a right to know the sort of political environment with which they will have to cope.

Finally, the essays in this guide conclude with a section on "Student Life." Here we pay attention to the day-to-day, extracurricular experiences on campus. Among the subjects covered in this section are campus housing, intercollegiate and intramural sports, student clubs and organizations, and the local environment, both geographical and cultural.

Above all, we have put a premium in this guide on writing that is vigorous and entertaining — writing that will absorb your attention and give you accurate and penetrating portraits of each institution covered.

Perhaps another use for this book, in addition to its immediate value for parents, students, and guidance counselors, will be as a comprehensive survey of the state of higher education in America. To read this volume from Amherst to Yale provides a panoramic view of the triumphs and tragedies of academia today.

How did we select the 100 colleges and universities included in *Choosing the Right College*? We had two basic criteria in mind: 1) academic excellence, as evidenced by competitive admissions standards, and 2) comprehensiveness, which involved an effort to include many different types of institutions from all parts of the country.

The desire to be comprehensive is based on the belief that this guide should be truly representative and offer students and parents the entire range of educational choices available to Americans. One will find, therefore, Ivy League schools and their public counterparts, large state universities from every corner of the nation, highly selective liberal arts colleges, schools with strong ties to religious communities, technical schools, and small, innovative institutions that offer opportunities not generally found elsewhere.

The information contained in this volume was compiled in a rigorous and responsible manner. At the heart of the research effort is the Intercollegiate Studies Institute, one of the oldest and most experienced organizations dedicated to upholding the liberal arts tradition on America's campuses. Relying on ISI's extensive network of campus contacts and its over 60,000 members on virtually every college campus, our researchers conducted literally hundreds of interviews with professors, students, and administrators. In addition to these interviews (many of which lasted well over an hour), researchers also employed questionnaires and site visits, as well as close scrutiny of college catalogues and web sites, and independent sources such as articles in the *Chronicle of Higher Education*.

Because the conditions in American higher education are continually changing, we invite you to help contribute your thoughts and opinions about the subjects discussed in this guide. You will find a response card in this book that asks you to tell us how helpful *Choosing the Right College* has been and to offer suggestions for improving future editions. Send e-mail to collegeguide@isi.org, or write to us at: ISI, P.O. Box 4431, Wilmington, DE 19807-0431. You can learn more about ISI's extensive educational programming and publications by visiting our web site at www.isi.org.

As William Bennett notes in his introduction, "if there is ever to be genuine, long-lasting education reform, parents and students will have to become shrewder and better-informed education consumers." It is our sincere hope that this guide will not only help you search for the right college or university but also serve in the cause of education reform in America. Only when we reward the best institutions will we have the kind of education that our nations needs — and deserves.

Gregory Wolfe,
Editor-in-Chief

AMHERST COLLEGE

P.O. Box 5000
Amherst, MA 01002-5000
(413) 542-2000
www.amherst.edu

Total enrollment: 1,610
Undergraduates: 1,610
SAT Ranges (Verbal/Math): V 650-750, M 660-750
Financial aid: 44%
Applicants: 5,208
Accepted: 20%
Enrolled: 47%
Application deadline: Dec. 31
Financial aid application deadline: Feb. 15
Tuition: $28,680 (comprehensive fee)
Core curriculum: No

Some Work for Immortality

Amherst College consistently ranks as one of the top five liberal arts colleges in the country, and thus competes with Ivy League schools for top high school students. Its student body is dedicated and studious, and is rewarded with many fine teachers and departments. As a member of a coalition of western Massachusetts colleges, Amherst also offers benefits beyond its own curriculum and social events.

Despite its liberal arts reputation, Amherst has but one general education requirement and nothing approaching a core of mandatory classes. Into this gap recently have come groups of politicized courses: the English department, for example, makes one wonder whether Emily Dickinson is safe in her own hometown. But even the departments that are politicized in comparison to the rest of the school contain good teachers and enough good courses to make the ideological ones avoidable.

The college's administration, though not always traditional in its policies, is fair, and it does not seem likely that Amherst will soon become outlandishly politicized. As long as the college can justly claim that its reputation is still deserved, it will be an excellent choice.

The college administration, while not as politicized as that at some other elite schools, is far from traditional in its policies. At best it remains on the sidelines while campus activists try to determine the school's political atmosphere.

1

Academic Life: One and Only

Only one class is required at Amherst, and it doesn't have a name. All students must take a freshman seminar, but ten to fifteen of them are offered each year, and the content is left up to the professors who teach them. No collegewide system sets the topics for these seminars. So, not only are students not guaranteed an introduction to Western thought, they aren't even guaranteed basic skills that are required for the rest of their courses.

Amherst does require thirty-two courses for graduation — and that's it.

Departments have the same lack of structure with regard to the requirements for their majors. In most cases, only one or two courses are designated as required. The remaining seven to nine are chosen by the student; just about any course in the department will count. "The students get no pressure to take certain things, but they also get no guidance," a professor says.

It should be said, however, that many of the upper-level courses are designed so as to require the more general introductory courses. "If you have any goals, you're directed to a very integrated system of requirements," says one professor. "The advisors push students into these harder things." This system works as well as it does because of the serious academic attitude of the students. According to a professor, most Amherst students are very ambitious. "Everybody comes in taking math and languages. Kids come in with a serious program. Because of the reputation, [Amherst] attracts the extraordinary: they're imaginative, energetic."

They are taught by these outstanding professors: Richard Fink and David Hansen in chemistry; Robert Hilborn in physics; Paul Ewald in biology; Walt Nicholson, Ralph Beals, Frank Westhoff, and Geoffrey Woglom in economics; William Pritchard, David Sofield, Allen Guttmann, and Richard Cody in English; N. Gordon Levin Jr. in history; Rebecca Sinos, Peter Pouncey, Frederick Griffiths, and Peter Marshall in classics; Antonio Benitez-Rojo, James Maraniss, and Ilan Stavans in Romance languages (Spanish); and Ronald Tiersky, William Taubman, and Hadley Arkes in political science.

The small size of the college (about 1,600 undergraduates) has kept most departments from the worst excesses of political correctness and multiculturalism, one instructor says. "Here, they're forced to deal with real people, and we have more cordial relationships. The chances of getting a slug are quite small. There aren't that many gut courses, and even the gut courses are pretty good." These "gut courses" are scattered race and gender courses that are still offered, as this professor notes, for an easy A, padding the transcript but not likely challenging the intellect with any rigorous or even valid content.

The natural science departments (biology, chemistry, physics, and geology) are widely praised for both teaching and research. Although Amherst is traditionally a liberal arts college, the chemistry, biology, and physics departments have as many faculty as the departments of economics, political science, and history.

Smaller humanities departments, namely, philosophy, fine arts, and Spanish (a part of the broader department of Romance languages), are also excellent in terms of teaching. One professor adds the classics department to that list, calling it "the best kept secret" at Amherst.

Of the larger departments in humanities and social sciences, economics may be the best. "They tend to be immune to a lot of the vulnerability that other departments have" in giving in to politicization, a professor says. A student points out that, at the very least, "there are no gender studies courses in economics," as there are in many other departments, including ones where they would not be expected. Enrollment in economics has recently overtaken that of English and political science despite a recent requirement of more math and statistics courses for majors. Several social science departments have joined economics in demanding tougher quantitative courses, and while "students don't love the stiffer requirements," they are still enrolling in large numbers, a professor says.

History and English have historically been Amherst's strongest, but it appears that past reputation alone is not enough to carry these departments. One professor says history is "probably not as strong" as it used to be. The outstanding professors in both English and history are senior faculty whose commitment to teaching excellence has earned them the respect of colleagues and students, regardless of political affiliation and ideology. The same cannot be said for many of the newer faculty members, the professor says.

Political science has also traditionally been one of the most popular majors at Amherst; however, both its popularity and the quality of its teaching have suffered from politicization and a tendency toward deconstructionism. But this department is faring far better than one that recently split from it, the Department of Law, Jurisprudence, and Social Thought (LJST). Though independent, LJST still draws heavily on the political science department for professors, students, and courses. Its courses often center around "critical legal theory," the academic term for a deconstructionist view of politics. A student describes it as "a warped and twisted view of political science."

LJST courses include some with fairly politicized titles: "Colonialism and Legal Theory," "Law and Social Relations: Persons, Identities, and Groups," "Re-Imagining Law: Feminist Interpretations," and "Post-Colonial Law and Culture: National, Legal, and Racial Identities." But the department also offers the most popular course in Amherst's history: "Murder." About three hundred students sign up for the course, taught by Professor Austin Sarat, one of the founders of LJST. The course's reading list includes *The Brothers Karamazov, In Cold Blood, Macbeth,* and works by Primo Levi, Hannah Arendt, Agatha Christie, and Albert Camus. "The strategy is, give them a hook — the hook is murder," Sarat told the *New York Times.* "But this is also a way to teach them the great books and moral reasoning." However, course material also includes Michel Foucault, the Marquis de Sade, and popular films like *Pulp Fiction, Natural Born Killers,* and *Psycho,* not to mention screenings of *Geraldo* and Snoop

Doggy Dogg videos. The course is rigorous, at least; students say Sarat is a notoriously difficult grader.

The most ideologically driven department at Amherst is women and gender studies (WGS), which, according to one professor, is the only department where "you lose IQ points." WGS has its own faculty, but it also borrows classes from English, political science, history, psychology, anthropology, and other departments. Cross-listed courses are exceptionally common at Amherst, and, according to some on campus, this practice has encouraged the spread of politicization across the curriculum. "[You have] difficulty finding courses not dealing with race or gender," a student says. "Even 'Science Fiction' [an English class] is cross-listed with women and gender studies."

Political Atmosphere: The Buck Stops Elsewhere

Amherst's administration tends to give in, at least on smaller issues, to a small group of radical student and faculty activists whose voices tend to be much louder than their actual numbers would indicate. Students note that the administration leaves up to student government quite a few important decisions about funding, speakers, activities, and some disciplinary matters. "The administration doesn't step in on any side," says one student. "They leave policing up to student government."

Student government consists of a variety of boards and councils, with most student members serving in more than one area. The result is a confused sort of decision making, where the personal and political prejudices of the representatives — rather than some sort of overarching vision for the college — hold sway. For example, Amherst officially recognizes and funds a variety of student publications, all of them with a liberal political point of view. The use or propriety of these funds is rarely questioned. However, the *Amherst Spectator,* the conservative alternative paper (and a rather mildly conservative one at that), recently had its funding revoked. No grounds for this action were ever stated by the student government members on the panel.

However, on some bigger issues, some feel that the administration is getting more assertive; that is, the administration is tough when it wants to be, as well as fair-minded. "The president and the dean see through some of this [political correctness]," a professor says. In 1997 the administration canceled its Early Orientation program, which brought incoming students from targeted minority groups to campus early for a series of consciousness-raising and indoctrination sessions. Despite loud protests from some campus radicals, early reports are that the administration will stand firm, and at least give a chance for "attempts at integration," as one professor puts it.

At the same time, Amherst maintains an African-American cultural dorm and an Asian house, as well as academic program houses for language study. Undergraduates seem to be highly sensitive to issues of race and gender. Consider this quotation, prominent in the college's viewbook: "For me now there's more consciousness of my background as a Latino male. Before I came to Amherst, I wasn't thinking about race or class or gender or sexual orientation. I was just thinking about people wanting to learn." One wonders whether the student didn't have the right idea in the first place. Another student is quoted in the viewbook: "When I came here, even though I thought I had no prejudice in me at all, I still saw the people of color as being outside of me and outside of my experience. I am coming to terms with the fact that there are a lot of ways to be prejudiced besides just throwing stones at people." Obviously, official Amherst gives much attention to race differences, or at least wants to be seen as doing so.

It is a safe assumption, however, that the average Amherst student spends little time worrying over these issues. There is, first of all, the amount of concentration needed for students to handle the academic workload they're coping with. Students on campus also report that the majority of their fellows view political correctness as a nuisance, not as a way of life or as anything they will take with them when they leave college. It is also apparent, however, that the college expects students to speak and act in a politically correct manner while they are enrolled.

The college does not have an official speech code, but the catalogue does contain something called the "Statement of Respect for Persons." It reads: "Respect for the rights, dignity and integrity of others is essential for the well-being of the community. Actions by any person which do not reflect such respect for others are damaging to each member of the community and hence damaging to Amherst College. Each member of the community should be free from interference, intimidation, or disparagement in the work place, the classroom and the social, recreational, and residential environment." According to some on campus, the statement is often used like a speech code, and a rather vague one at that. "Harassment and irresponsible behavior aren't defined," a student says. This gives student government and the administration a wide berth in interpreting their meaning. A professor reports that there have been cases of students disciplined for speech outside of the classroom, although he says such cases are not as common now as they were five years ago.

Student Life: Because I Could Not Stop for Socializing . . .

Amherst is not only in a college town, but in a college region, as it were. West-central Massachusetts is home to the Five Colleges Consortium (Amherst, Smith College, Mount Holyoke College, Hampshire College, and the University of Massachusetts-Amherst), whose members cooperate both academically and socially. This gives Amherst students a chance to deal with peers on other campuses and provides more cultural and musical opportunities than any one of the colleges would be able to offer alone.

Housing is guaranteed for all four years of a student's college career. Thirty-two residence halls are available (all coed), along with what the college calls "former fraternity houses." Residences are grouped into units called "demes" for the purpose of planning social events and generally getting to know the students in other dorms.

The college offers a variety of student groups, ranging from a nationally ranked debate team to religious, international, and ethnic organizations. About 15 percent of the students are members of at least one singing group — a very high percentage. There are also a number of fine instrumental groups on campus.

Amherst competes in twenty-five intercollegiate sports at the NCAA Division III level. There are also thirteen club sports. The college reports that close to 85 percent of the student body participates in the intramural program. Workout equipment and a new swimming pool are available for more casual recreation. However, western Massachusetts also offers excellent chances for hiking, canoeing, and skiing.

The college is relatively safe, but students are still appreciative of an excellent and helpful campus security squad.

AUBURN UNIVERSITY

Admissions Office
Auburn University
202 Mary Martin Hall
Auburn, AL 36849-5145
(334) 844-4080
www.auburn.edu

Total enrollment: 21,778
Undergraduates: 18,733
SAT Ranges (Verbal/Math): V 520-620, M 510-630; ACT 21-27 (composite)
Financial aid: 78%
Applicants: 9,244
Accepted: 86%
Enrolled: 40%
Application deadline: Sept. 1 (for fall)
Financial aid application deadline:
Tuition: $2,565 in-state; $7,695 out-of-state
Core curriculum: Yes

Not Just Whistling Dixie

Alabama may be one of the country's poorest states, but one of its major public universities is rich. Auburn University is certainly not rich in the material sense — teacher pay is lower than average and some departments are underfunded — but it possesses a wealth of traditions. Unlike many colleges, Auburn has managed to retain its historic character, which is imbued with a genteel Southern charm. When men open doors for women it's appreciated, not deemed "sexist" and analyzed in women's studies classes. Greek organizations generally rule the social scene, and football is king. "The politically correct stuff is kept very much at a minimum," says one instructor. "It's very different from what you experience up North."

Many of Auburn's departments concentrate on the practical needs of the state of Alabama. Agriculture, forestry, textile engineering, poultry science — these are some of the bread-and-butter departments at the university. Although not regarded as a liberal arts institution, Auburn has taken strides to improve the quality of its social science and humanities offerings. In some areas, most notably economics, the university has succeeded.

Auburn has remained largely faithful to its traditions as a land-grant university and to the culture of the Deep South. Academically, the university features a core curriculum that exposes students to several different subject areas. "Auburn is notable for the sheer goodness of its students and for the vibrancy of its cultural life," says one educator. The school seems to have found that adopting cutting-edge academic trends is not necessarily the path to true educational achievement.

When the East Alabama Male College opened its doors in Auburn, Alabama, in 1859, its timing could hardly have been worse — private liberal arts institutions had to close two years later at the outbreak of the Civil War. It reopened in 1866, though it was in financial shambles. In 1872 the Methodist church, which had run the college, transferred control to the state of Alabama, making it the first land-grant college in the South to be established apart from the state university. Several name changes later, the school became Auburn University.

Auburn now enrolls about 19,000 undergraduates and 3,000 graduate students, more than 60 percent of whom are Alabama residents. The school is consistently cited as one of the top buys in higher education. For in-state residents, tuition amounts to just more than $2,500 per year; out-of-staters pay about $7,700.

Academic Life: This Core Ain't Rotten

Auburn offers undergraduate degrees in more than 130 areas. Academically, the university is divided into eight colleges (agriculture, architecture, business, education, engineering, liberal arts, science and math, and veterinary medicine) and four schools (forestry, human sciences, nursing, and pharmacy).

Regardless of what major students choose, they must fulfill the requirements of a core curriculum. Auburn's core stresses the importance of common learning, coherence, and intellectual integration, as the university strives to ensure both that courses possess intellectual coherence and that students have a common basis of knowledge. The core, according to university literature, is designed to develop students' analytical and communications skills and to encourage them to develop a deeper appreciation of their own and other cultures.

To fulfill core requirements, students take courses in several areas. Within each area they either choose from a limited number of approved courses or take particular classes determined by their major. Specifically, students must take two English composition courses; three sequential history courses; two literature courses, "Great Books I" and "Great Books II"; two sequential science courses in biology, chemistry, geology, or physics; one math course; one philosophy course in either logic or ethics; one fine arts course; and three specific social science courses: "Society, Culture, and Environment," "Political Economy," and "Individual and Society."

Some students dislike the core curriculum, saying it forces them to take courses they have little interest in and that are irrelevant to their course of study. "A lot of people complain about those because they don't have anything to do with your major," says one senior.

The closest the core curriculum comes to advancing a professor's political agenda is the social science course called "Society, Culture, and Environment," more commonly referred to by its course number, U101. In that course professors occasionally dwell on their personal political beliefs, which include topics like overpopulation and environmentalism, students say. But few courses in the core are heavily politicized.

The shining star of Auburn's social science offerings is its department of economics, which is based in the College of Business. The department boasts solid credentials and first-rate professors. "There's not a single professor who's not a free-market man among them," says one scholar who knows the department. The department works in conjunction with the Ludwig von Mises Institute to run reading groups and other programs and provides its students with good foundations in current economic thinking so that they can excel in the workforce. However, unlike other economics departments, the one at Auburn accepts — and even welcomes — the expression of free-market ideas.

The Ludwig von Mises Institute, one of the intellectual highlights at Auburn, is an educational and scholarly center affiliated with the university's economics department. Named for an Austrian thinker who demonstrated the counterproductive nature of government intervention into the economy, the Mises Institute defends free markets, private property rights, and sound monetary policies. It publishes journals and books, awards fellowships, runs seminars and conferences, and makes the public case for limited government. Students interested in free markets and free societies would be advised to look into the institute's programs, as they provide excellent opportunities to learn from some of this country's top economists and political theorists.

Auburn selects 180 freshmen each year to participate in its honors program. Honors students live together and have their own student center. Auburn offers honors versions of the core curriculum courses as well as several upper-division courses, all of which are taught in small sections to encourage in-depth discussion. Selection of incoming freshmen is highly competitive: a 3.5 GPA and a minimum score of 1,280 on the SAT (or 29 on the ACT) are necessary for application.

Auburn has established several highly touted programs with the ROTC. The Air Force, Army, and Navy all have programs at the university, including aerospace studies, military science, and naval science. Students are eligible for ROTC scholarships that defray college costs in exchange for several years of service in the armed forces following graduation. In 1996 Auburn's Air Force ROTC program was rated the best in the nation, and the Army ROTC program ranked in the top ten of all such programs nationally.

The College of Engineering is large — fifteenth in the nation in undergraduate enrollment — and boasts an excellent reputation. A recent survey found that it supplies NASA with a large number of engineers, as nearly five hundred Auburn alumni have worked for the space agency.

Auburn boasts several outstanding programs outside of the liberal arts. Students and faculty alike cite veterinary medicine, agriculture, and forestry as tops at the university. In addition, the philosophy department is reportedly stacked with fine teachers and scholars, many of whom express liberal views in class but are receptive to opposing perspectives.

Outstanding professors at Auburn include: Robert Ekelund, David Kaserman, and Roger Garrison in economics; James Barth in finance; Wayne Flynt in history; Tibor Machan in philosophy; Craig Darch in education; Bertram Zinner in discrete and statistical sciences; Timothy Kramer in civil engineering; and Susan Fillippeli in communication.

Some departments are a little more politicized than others. The English department has some politics in its classes, though it should be noted that radicals are few and far between. Students report that many English professors and majors are left-leaning. "If you say you're an English major, people say, 'That person's liberal,' " according to one student. Most English courses cover traditional subjects but are taught in an ideological fashion. The department does offer courses in the trendy field of critical theory, which asserts that criticism of literature is more important than the literature itself, especially if the criticism gives priority to categories such as race, gender, and class.

Although most of Auburn's academic programs are fairly traditional, it has followed the lead of many other universities by offering women's studies courses, many of which prove to be vehicles for expressing strong political views. Auburn offers an interdisciplinary minor in women's studies that "examines the impact of the social construction of gender and promotes social change to improve women's, men's, and children's lives," according to university literature. When a university course pledges to bring about "social change," it has left the realm of education and entered the political arena. Fortunately, programs like this are not the norm at Auburn.

Political Atmosphere: Preppies and Politicos

Students and faculty say Auburn administrators mostly take a hands-off approach to day-to-day academic life at the school, and that faculty committees, and to a lesser extent student government, have considerable influence. They say, somewhat cynically, that the administration is mainly concerned with the two "f's": football and fund-raising.

Auburn has witnessed several high-profile controversies in recent years, some of which have ended up in lawsuits. In general the university administration has adopted a gradualist approach to change and has refrained from rushing forward with sweeping new initiatives.

Lately there has been some political jostling over who sits on Auburn's board of directors, which has a heavily conservative tilt. In 1996 Republican governor Fob James, an outspoken advocate of school prayer and the posting of the Ten Commandments in courtrooms, sought to replace two members of this board with party loyalists. The Democratic state senate refused to vote on James's choices, but the governor said he was within his rights to replace board members.

In the last few years the state government has reduced funding to higher education, resulting in what some say is the underfunding of some Auburn departments, particularly the music department. Others say the university would have all the money it needs if it reduced the number of unnecessary bureaucrats.

Another dispute was also resolved in 1996. Back in 1992 Auburn recognized a gay-student group, which cleared the way for it to seek funding from the university. In response the state legislature passed a law barring financial support to homosexual-oriented groups. But in 1996 a federal judge overturned the state law and declared the group eligible for university funding.

In 1993 Auburn settled a sex-discrimination case filed by members of the women's club soccer team, which sought varsity status. The university agreed to start a varsity team and pay the club team members $140,000. Sex discrimination was also the subject of a 1997 action in which Auburn's veterinary fraternity sued to remain all-male. The university had ordered the fraternity to open its doors to women, claiming it was a professional organization and not a social one. As this book goes to press, that lawsuit is pending.

The campus atmosphere is quite traditional. Students tend to be very polite and friendly, and dress is "preppy," says one student. Students tend to hold traditional political views — so much so that a stretch of student apartments off campus is called the "Miracle Mile" because it traditionally pulls Republicans through in elections.

Student Life: Football, Fraternities, and Other Frolics

Students say life at Auburn is serene and collegial. Many have ties, familial or emotional, to the university — perhaps their fathers attended Auburn or they cheered for the football team when they were growing up. In this state you're either an Auburn fan or an Alabama fan. There is no middle ground. "My family would have disowned me if I went to Alabama," jokes one engineering major.

Football is the major focus of energy in the fall, culminating with the yearly showdown with Alabama, or perhaps a bowl game. On football weekends more than eighty thousand fans flood the town. The cable sports network ESPN recently rated Auburn number three in the country for tailgating parties.

Even in the winter and spring, more attention is paid to football recruiting than to basketball. Both sports programs have had problems adhering to NCAA rules recently. The NCAA cited the football team for major violations in August 1993, and Auburn punished its basketball team in 1996 for recruiting violations. The basketball team forfeited two scholarships and sixteen games for infractions that included giving improper help to a player attempting to enroll in a junior college, according to the *Chronicle of Higher Education.*

Most student groups on campus tend to mind their own business. Sit-ins, rallies, and picketers are extremely rare. "The closest thing you have to a protest here is when a bunch of students get together and holler for Homecoming queen candidates," says one professor.

There is a gay and lesbian association and several self-segregating ethnic organizations, but these groups stay very quiet and keep to themselves. Auburn has many different student organizations, including a libertarian club, a growing College Republicans chapter, and a pro-life group.

Students say religious life is very active at the university. "God's really working on our campus right now," says a senior. Campus Crusade for Christ, which had around seventy-five people attending meetings a few years ago, now regularly attracts five or six hundred for a session. Numerous other religious organizations bring in Christian bands and speakers. Religious organizations also exist for Christian Scientists, Jews, Mormons, and Muslims.

Auburn's thirty-three fraternities and twenty sororities also play a large role in life at the university. Around half the undergraduates belong to the Greek system, which holds parties on weekends that are popular with many students. While there is probably some truth behind the image of the beer-guzzling, *Animal House* fraternity antics at Auburn, some fraternities have banned alcohol and claim many religious, nondrinking students as members. And some have modified their traditions to conform to '90s sensibilities. Beginning in 1993 the Auburn chapter of Kappa Alpha ended its traditional Old South parade, in which students in Confederate uniforms carried the South's Civil War battle flag. Black students had complained that the parade was racist.

Some students say there's little to do in Auburn, but others claim the town is perfectly suited for study, research, dining, and relaxation. It offers many historical sights and excellent restaurants. Take, for example, the Auburn Chapel, where the first secessionist meeting in the Deep South took place in 1851. Elsewhere in town are barbecue restaurants, Southern restaurants, barbers who sprinkle their conversation with talk about moonshine, and European-style pubs. Ten minutes from Auburn is Chewacla State Park, which has a quiet lake and relaxing picnic spots. It's a local favorite for swimming and hiking.

Auburn University provides a valuable education to students who know which classes to take and which to avoid. Its liberal arts offerings are improving, and some are already excellent. While it is a university known for its strengths in agriculture and engineering, the core curriculum ensures that all students share a fund of knowledge.

BATES COLLEGE

Office of Admissions
Lewiston, ME 04240
(207) 786-6000
www.bates.edu

Total enrollment: 1,611
Undergraduates: 1,611
SAT Ranges (Verbal/Math): V 610-690, M 600-690
Financial aid: 54%
Applicants: 3,635
Accepted: 34%
Enrolled: 37%
Application deadline: Jan. 15
Financial aid application deadline: Jan. 15
Tuition: $28,650
Core curriculum: No

Maine Events

The early history of Bates College is auspicious, even admirable. Founded in 1855 by Freewill Baptists, the school was a center of the abolition movement and admitted women and minorities from its beginning, much like its older Freewill Baptist counterpart, Hillsdale College in Michigan. It did not achieve the financial independence reached by Colby, Bowdoin, and other New England schools for many years, and even today, one faculty member notes, Bates needs to increase its endowment so that it can become less dependent on its high tuition for paying the bills. Nevertheless, the college has become increasingly selective in the past couple of decades. Today it admits only 36 percent of those who apply, although only 35 percent of those admitted enroll. Still, this is a better rate than that achieved at many better-known national universities, such as Emory, which lags in this category by 10 percentage points.

Overall, though, Bates has become less admirable in recent years. Though its 1,611 students can indeed get a very good liberal arts education, they must be aware that some majors and programs are overtly politicized. They must also cope with an administration bent on politicizing both the social life and the curriculum in its effort to win the approval of the liberal forces that now pass judgment on the suitability of colleges. It often seems that a small college wanting to rise in the popular rankings must embrace political correctness, and Bates has fallen into that trap.

While the school's history isn't as illustrious as that of nearby schools like Colby and Bowdoin, Bates does have some good things going for it. Many of these positive aspects are now overshadowed by the multicultural cudgel wielded by its president, but the school has maintained a genuine sense of community and pride. Those considering Bates should also consider the long Maine winter, which is counterbalanced by the scenic beauty of the season. If you don't like the outdoors, you might do better to stay in Boston or travel farther south. And if you don't want to be subject to a good bit of politically correct propaganda, you will find better options. The students don't always pay attention to the PC elements, but they're as much a part of this Maine scene as the lobsters, which certainly leave a better taste in the mouth.

Academic Life: The Wrong Places

It is possible to get a rounded liberal arts education at Bates, but such is not a foregone conclusion given the school's distribution requirements. These requirements do not compose a true core curriculum; rather, they ask students to take courses within several broad divisions. Students must take any three courses in the physical sciences, two of which are a department-designated set; any three courses in the social sciences, two of which are a set; any five courses from at least two humanities, including history, three of which form a coherent cluster; and one course in which "understanding and use of quantitative techniques are essential."

If this sounds rather general, it is. While Bates has made very few specific provisions for the traditional liberal arts, it is more explicit when it comes to "diversity courses." For example, there is no Western civilization requirement at Bates, but a new proposal, not yet enacted, will require a first-year seminar, as well as three physical science courses, two courses in reading and analysis of "culturally significant texts," and two multicultural courses, one dealing with a topic in the United States and one elsewhere, plus at least two courses in a foreign language. Thus, while future students will be able to graduate from Bates knowing next to nothing about U.S. or Western history, they will have under their belts two courses on multicultural topics. This fact is key to understanding the direction in which the administration hopes to take the college.

An unusual feature of the Bates calendar is a short-term unit offered at the end of spring term in late April. Lasting five weeks, these classes are often offbeat, obscure, and even silly. They include, for example, "Philosophy and *Star Trek*," "The Grail Tale: An Annotated Hypertext Version" (including Monty Python's version, of course), and "Representations of Women in Mexican Nationalism."

The most popular majors do not include philosophy or *Star Trek*, however. They are psychology, biology, English, and political science. The number of Bates students who major in biology and the life sciences is almost twice the national average for a school its size, and the number of multi/interdisciplinary studies majors is about two-and-a-half times the national average. Bates offers no business degrees or other professional majors except for education, in which 4.5 percent of students major.

Outstanding professors include Douglas Hodgkin in political science and James Leamon and John Cole in history. The philosophy department also features some excellent scholars and teachers, such as David Kolb and Mark Okrent.

The better departments at Bates are political science, English, psychology, and biology, as well as the sciences in general.

That certain departments are politicized can be surmised simply on the basis of their names. According to one professor, "the interdisciplinary programs in women's studies, African-American studies, and American cultural studies are least representative of a spectrum of views." However, this professor adds that "no department is visibly political as an advocacy group in its curriculum or activities. Although departments such as English, sociology, and political science exhibit some political tendencies, each has faculty and course offerings with more traditional orientations." As one might imagine, some of the more left-slanting faculty view the economics department as too conservative.

A close study of course offerings in selected humanities departments reveals an English department that does offer some typically politicized courses, although it is not as fad-bitten as some at other liberal arts colleges or large universities. "First-year students," as freshmen are called at Bates, are required to take two 100-level courses during their initial year, and they may select from "Colloquia in Literature" offerings, which are denoted in the catalogue as "especially appropriate for first-year students." Sections are limited to twenty students, and recent topics have included "Reading Race and Ethnicity in American Fiction," as well as courses like "Critical Theory" and "The African-American Novel." Most of the truly odd offerings, though, are found among the short-term classes. These are a telling measure of the professors, because faculty frequently use the opportunity afforded by these succinct springtime classes to teach subjects in which they are particularly interested. Since it appears that some of these classes would scarcely contain enough legitimate material to fill even a shortened class schedule, a close perusal of these courses in every department is always a good idea. In English, for example, they include "Cultural Production and Social Context, Jamaica," "Victorian Womanhood," and "Feminist Literary Criticism."

The history department has a fairly politicized list of offerings as well as a large number of courses (mostly short-term classes) on Asian history — unusually large for a small liberal arts college in Maine. Included among the former are "The Social History of the Civil War," "Topics on the Left: A History of American Radicalism," "American Protest in the Twentieth Century," "Latinos in the United States," "The United States in the Sixties and Seventies," and "Black America in the Twentieth Century." Among the short-term units offered in history are "Origins of the Cuban Revolution," "The Civil-Rights Movement," "Japanese-American 'Relocation' Camps," "Brazilian Slavery through Documents," and "Sexual Politics in Germany, 1800-1992." Also offered in this group are courses that deal with more substantial subjects, such as "Medieval Scotland," "Historical Fiction," and "Historical Archeology." However, even these should be viewed against the backdrop that Bates lacks a true core curriculum. Medieval Scotland may indeed be interesting and romantic, but, taken — as it may be — in lieu of any broader Western history or English literature offering, it is a poor substitute. It is difficult to fathom the implications of a course like "Origins of the Cuban Revolution" taking the place of, say, Plato and Aristotle in a student's education.

Since 1991 Bates has offered majors in American cultural studies and African-American studies. The fact that the two departments list an identical faculty and that the catalogue announces that race will be the primary lens through which both topics are viewed is a good indication that these are politicized departments. The American cultural studies program includes a combination English/sociology class entitled "Sexual Harassment and the U.S. Senate's Thomas-Hill Hearings."

Political Atmosphere: When Any Old Diversity Just Won't Do

For years Bates had real multiculturalism: from its founding 140 years ago, its admissions have been blind to race and gender. But that distinguished tradition wasn't sufficient for college president Donald Harward and his administration, who have decided that the only diversity worth having is one that is imposed and modeled after the strict codes in place at trendier institutions.

"The president and deans are always talking about multiculturalism and diversity," says a professor. The president, in an address titled "Higher Education in the Nineties," said of his school: "Already emerging are programmatic emphases which will bring greater attention to environmental studies, to international features of the curriculum, and to non-Western languages and culture. Continued attention will be given both to disciplinary areas, which carry the burden of the curriculum, and to interdisciplinary areas of study (such as women's studies, area studies, African American studies, and environmental studies), which complement disciplinary majors and reinforce the value of diversity." From these and other signs, it is clear that the president is determined to move as many of Bates's tents as possible into the multicultural camp. To be fair, it should be said that there has been some resistance, and the student body is hardly among the most politicized in the nation. But the fact remains that much of what the president has done, he has done in lieu of genuine efforts to improve the curriculum and faculty.

Also not unique to Bates is the presence of a multicultural center, which is featured prominently in the college's public relations materials. "The Multicultural Center celebrates and promotes the diverse cultural experiences that each member of Bates College brings to the community," announces college literature. "The Center acts as a catalyst on campus by initiating discussions about class, ethnicity, gender, nationality, race, and sexual orientation. Celebrations, workshops, and exhibits presented by both the Multicultural Center and its affiliated student organizations explore and support intellectual, social, cultural, political, and spiritual experiences."

Among the programs brought in by this center, which the administration clearly sees as a means of wedging its radical and divisive ideology into the college community, are "Black and Brown, Get Down!, a Conversation with Elizabeth Martinez and Elena Featherston," "Mix-1995/96 NY Gay/Lesbian/Bisexual Alternative Film and Video Series," and "The Personal Is Political, Art Exhibit by Marjorie Kramer." The resource room at the center is equally stimulating to the intellect, supplying students with magazines such as *Deneuve: The Lesbian Magazine, Dissident,* and *Covert Action.* Among the student organizations that emanate from the Multicultural Center is the Gay-Lesbian-Bisexual Alliance, which "serve[s] as a support group for gay, lesbian, and bisexual students" and sponsors "a play reading, parties, the Gay and Lesbian Film/Video Festival . . . and comedians." Amandla! supports "better understanding of the many communities of the African Diaspora" by bringing to campus such figures as Sister Souljah, bell hooks, and Sonia Sanchez. Women of Color "confronts issues of racism, sexism, classism, heterosexism, and other forms of prejudice that affect women of color." The group also publishes *Dialectics,* "a literary collective written and edited by women of color."

Given the administration's love affair with things chic, it isn't surprising to learn that it recently attempted to install a speech code. The effort was backed strongly by the dean of students, but a coalition of moderates and leftists defeated it. Though that proposal failed, Bates does require "sensitivity training" for freshmen during which students are told about the goodness of diversity, homosexuality, and safe sex, and an assortment of the latest politicized bromides.

Pushing any agenda on any campus is easier when the faculty backs that agenda. Thus, conservative or libertarian candidates are not given a fair shot at job openings at Bates. The administration backs the hiring of ideologically correct candidates for the same reason it created and strongly supports the Multicultural Center: having few beliefs not related to the desire to please opinion makers, it seeks to bring Bates up in the ranks of liberal arts colleges by imitating trends that originate on more prestigious campuses nationwide. A professor points out that at Bates, "There have been clear instances of hiring on the basis of affirmative action at the expense of more qualified candidates, especially recently." Another notes that when a search committee came up with a set of finalists, the dean of faculty forced the committee to reconsider on "affirmative action grounds." Says this professor: "It is difficult [for conservative scholars] to make the short list when the pool of candidates contains so few conservatives or moderates."

Campus Life: Winning the Debate

Compared to those in other schools of its class, a Bates education is among the priciest in the nation, according to U.S. Department of Education information analyzed by Memex Press. Tuition, room, and board totaled $28,650 for 1997-98. The same datum shows that the school offers the students comparatively little in the way of institutional scholarships, but does provide an unusually large amount of money for student services.

Despite the cost, Bates is generally seen as a friendly place where students and faculty know each other well. Faculty are quite accessible, and the students certainly benefit from the close contact they have with each other and with their teachers. One professor notes that the school has a "friendly atmosphere, with mostly small classes and high student-faculty contact. . . . Conservative faculty such as myself are not ostracized and continue to play a role."

There have never been any fraternities and sororities at Bates. Therefore, social life revolves around a plethora of student organizations as well as trips to nearby Portland, the ski resorts of Maine's mountains, and the Atlantic Coast. Excursions to nearby Freeport, home not only to L. L. Bean but also to numerous other outlet stores, allow students to exercise the shopping impulse. Lewiston, Bates's home, is a fairly working-class town that has seen better days. Boston is about 140 miles away.

Because of the school's location in one of the most beautiful states in the union, "Batesies," as the students are known, have access to many outdoor recreational activities. The Outing Club sponsors many excursions into the woods and is one of the most popular clubs on campus. More than seventy-five years old, this organization sponsors Winter Carnival and clambakes, and allows students to check out equipment for their own outdoor adventures.

Bates also has a long history of excellence in college debating. It and Oxford University were the first schools to hold international debates back in 1921, and its debate team is supported by the Theater and Rhetoric Department. Bates came in fourth in the North American Championships in 1992, and in 1995 won the American Parliamentary Debate Association's Second-Place Team of the Year Award.

There are, of course, numerous other student groups, including the Deansmen, a male a cappella singing group with a forty-year history; the Fencing Club; Merimanders, a student-run female a cappella singing group; the Robinson Players student theater group; and rugby, sailing, and riding clubs. The college is served by the *Bates Student,* a weekly student newspaper. WRBC Radio culls "one out of every six Batesies" for participation. There is no alternative newspaper in such a small college community, although there might be some need for one. An admittedly liberal publication notes with approval that the *Bates Student* is "known for its more liberal slant."

Other student groups are predictably political in nature, such as the Women's Action Coalition, Women of Color, Salidaridad Latina, and the Gay-Lesbian-Bisexual Alliance. These types of clubs have become an obligatory presence on America's college campuses, even at small schools such as Bates where the percentage of minority students is very small.

Lest one think that Batesies are overly serious, the college sponsors several good old-fashioned events every year that hearken back to college life before the advent of politicized student life and overly earnest extracurricular activities. The Puddle Jump allows anyone crazy enough to jump through a hole cut in the ice of Lake Andrews on St. Patrick's Day to do so. An ice cream smorgasbord is held twice yearly, as is the school's clambake (which also features lobsters, of course). The annual Harvest Dinner is a feast for the palate, and the Primal Scream is "a stress-relieving event sponsored and broadcast by WRBC held at 11:00 p.m. the Monday before finals on the Library Terrace." Then there are the Tacky Party and Pubcrawl. The former "challenges Bates students to dress their most 70s-ish and jam to the cheesiest beat around. The Salvation Army's Thrift store is a prime shopping spot for this event." Pubcrawl, held during Senior Week, allows members of the graduating class to "make coed teams of two and run to four local taverns drinking six beers as quickly as they can. The record set in '96 was less than 16 minutes."

As for more conventional sports, Bates fields thirteen men's and fourteen women's NCAA Division III sporting teams and offers intramural opportunities in all of the typical and popular sports. More than 60 percent of the student body participates in intramural competition. Recently Bates was ranked in the top thirty in a national NCAA study on how well colleges balance athletics and academics.

Most students live on campus in dorms, although some live in university-owned Victorian houses. All students eat in the Commons in Chase Hall, a fact that does much to keep the college community coherent.

BIRMINGHAM-SOUTHERN COLLEGE

Mr. Robert D. Dortch
Vice President for Admissions Services
900 Arkadelphia Road
Birmingham, AL 35254
(205) 226-4686 / (800) 523-5793
www.bsc.edu

Total enrollment: 1,526
Undergraduates: 1,410
SAT Ranges (Verbal/Math): V 540-670, M 560-650
Financial aid: 47%
Applicants: 660
Accepted: 76%
Enrolled: 55%
Application deadline: Jan. 1
Financial aid application deadline: Mar. 1
Tuition: $13,750
Core curriculum: No

Subtle Pressures

Stability should never be taken for granted in today's academic climate — there's too much pressure for change, and too many monetary reasons to accept it. But so far, at least, Birmingham-Southern College has managed to hold off the more bizarre forms of political correctness. It has a generally conservative student body with almost no history of political activism; it is situated in a traditional state and region; and it is aligned with the Methodist church. It seems financially healthy.

Most of all, there are good things about Birmingham-Southern that one hopes will be preserved. Students take small classes and have close contact with their professors. The business division has a strong free-market orientation, and more than one-third of the college's students are business majors. Southern (as it is known locally) claims to support a traditional liberal arts education, and though its core is fairly loose in construction, there is little evidence that the school opposes the traditional liberal arts. The faculty is a little shorthanded in some areas — there is only one classicist, for example, and books in those classes are in translation — but students could do much worse.

Academic Life: The Economics of Scale

Birmingham-Southern has no core curriculum to speak of. Instead, it has opted for a fairly typical set of distribution requirements. All students must take a writing course from the English department, the level of the course being determined by measurement tools like advanced placement tests, application essays, or SAT/ACT scores. Two courses in math are required, as are one lab course in astronomy, biology, chemistry, or physics; one course in philosophy and religion; one in literature; one in arts; and one in either economics, political science, psychology, or sociology. All students must also pass two units in a foreign language (or one at the 200-level or higher). These requirements apply to all students in all disciplines — an admirable policy.

There is also a requirement for one course in history, but it is very general; the catalogue actually says "any course in history." While this is not even close to a requirement in Western civilization, about 80 percent of students do fulfill their history requirement with either a U.S. history or Western civilization course. "The history faculty moans about how most students take a U.S. or Western civilization course," one faculty members says. The students' choice is encouraging, while the department's attitude is not.

The writing requirement, along with the attention paid by faculty to that skill, has been more successful at Birmingham-Southern than at other schools. Says a professor in a field not typically thought of as a strong promoter of writing skills: "I require my students to do a great deal of writing because they must know how to communicate through the written word. It's one of the real strengths of the school." The math requirement, unfortunately, has not produced such results.

Birmingham-Southern used to have a list of common readings and a seminar dedicated to that idea, but that has faded away to a nonrequired, not-for-credit "freshman reading list" and symposia throughout the year. Predictably, freshman interest is short-lived. "They're really into it the first two months, but by November the grapevine takes over and their peers become their unofficial advisors," a professor says. "You have the students only for a while." However, the college has resisted efforts by its departments to take up more and more of their students' time. "The Provost is very much committed to the idea of a general education, as opposed to concentrating just on the majors," says one educator. Different types of degrees carry additional requirements (for example, B.A. and B.S. candidates must take six courses in addition to the general requirements), and only eight courses are required for majors in B.A. and B.S. fields. A general education committee has been instrumental in protecting the core that remains, faculty say.

Recent additions to the faculty — half the current group have joined in the last ten years — have placed more emphasis on student research, and this, if allowed to expand unchecked, would also endanger the broad requirements. The research project required on a topic within each senior's major is a good idea, but more might be too much. "There is some predation on the part of the sciences and the business school," explains one professor. "At a small college this has a larger impact [than at a large university]. The faculty sometimes want a few more courses; they'll shift to a research university model if they're not careful, and that's not the model for a liberal arts college. It really comes down to the definition of what a liberal education is. Most faculty are right out of a mega-university and reflect the pedagogy of that institution and their profession."

While many professors at Birmingham-Southern pour the majority of their energy into teaching, others are quite active researchers and publishers in their fields. National trends certainly favor those who believe that publication demands should come before teaching, but the president and board of directors at Birmingham-Southern seem to know that the true strength of such a small college lies in its ability to offer good teaching to its students. After all, if students want to attend a large research university, they can usually do so for far less money than they pay at Birmingham-Southern. "If anything, we're weak on research," a professor says. "But the atmosphere of publish or perish isn't my favorite. I don't want to feel that my life is dictated by two articles or one book every six months." Professors can't think of anyone who was denied tenure for failure to publish.

"We're a private institution and we must teach well enough so that parents will continue to pay the bills," comments one teacher. To this end, the normal maximum class size is thirty-five students, though a few classes have as many as seventy. The student-teacher ratio is approximately fourteen-to-one.

One of the best times to see the faculty in action is during "Interim Term," the January session required for four years of all students at Birmingham-Southern. Faculty offer courses either in their own more specialized field of research or, at times, in a very esoteric aspect of their discipline. "A major objective of the curriculum is to encourage all students to develop their potentials for creative activity and independent research," the college catalogue states. "The January interim term provides a unique opportunity for innovation and experimentation on the part of both students and faculty." Students may choose one of the offered courses or design their own, but they are expected to "use initiative and imagination whether their project is a group endeavor or an individual effort."

During Interim Term, for example, business students might study a single industry and take field trips to living examples of that industry — perhaps Delta Airlines in Atlanta or General Motors' Saturn plant in Tennessee. Invited speakers address various elements of business and economics, and students present Harvard Business School cases before the critiquing eyes of outside experts. Other students might travel to Italy and Greece to see firsthand the material remains and cultural descendants of the ancient civilizations they study. Students in the sciences may undertake intensive laboratory experiments under the watchful eye of their professors. This program is seen by most as a resounding success, although one professor notes that "a student may resent the rigor of a lab course versus a business internship. You've got one guy working his tail off in, say, chemistry while another is being taken out for lunch."

A good bit of travel seems to accompany the Interim Term, which is the last remnant of a 1968 curricular reform at Birmingham-Southern. "There is a strong social consciousness on campus, which is reflected in the fact that every January, thirty-five students or so go off to work with the poor in a Third World country," says a professor. "The arrangement of the course allows it to be structured to the needs of the instructor and student. Scientists can live in the lab and get a great deal done. One must be self-motivated, and it leaves a lot of room for fluffy stuff, but there are lots of internships to choose from and many of them are very good. . . ." A faculty committee must approve every new January course, and the presence of some "fluffy stuff" proves that the system isn't fail-safe. Still, the Interim Term is an excellent opportunity for students to broaden their knowledge and experience in myriad fields, and students should take full opportunity of this offering.

Among the outstanding professors at Birmingham-Southern are Paul Cleveland in finance, Gary Dale in economics, Aubrey Drewry Jr. in business, Dan Holliman in biology, Mark Lester and Matthew Levey in history, Cecilia McInnis-Bowers in management and marketing, Michael McInturff in English, Samuel Pezzillo in classics, and Jane Spencer of the Spanish department.

The Division of Economics and Business Administration has four endowed chairs in business and free enterprise, and is considered one of the strongest areas of the college. It is also the most popular division on campus, as more than 35 percent of students select majors in this area — nearly four times the national average. Also very good are the departments of music, history, biology, and the fine and performing arts. Some years ago the college merged with a Birmingham conservatory, and thus the music and arts departments are much more oriented toward performance than at similar institutions.

Birmingham-Southern reflects the values and beliefs of its middle-class, Methodist constituency in that it remains a collection of scholars and not a gathering of would-be ideologues. Most course offerings are traditional at least in title, and the culture that produces most of Birmingham-Southern's students works to rein in any radicalized tendencies faculty members might have. The administration has also shown that it is willing to fight for serious courses. Solid offerings can be found in the humanities departments, always the most politicized on any campus. "There are individuals who would politicize the curriculum, but they're held in check by the rest of the faculty," notes one professor. Faculty are, for the most part, politically liberal, "but on the whole they're pretty sensible on academic matters and are committed to old fashioned standards," says another faculty member. And so far, there has been no forcible takeover by the more liberal faculty.

But while overt radicalism is not tolerated, the generational shift to a more politicized mode of thought can be detected at Southern. "There is bound to be a non-fit with the new people and what the curriculum had been," one educator explains. "For example, someone hired to teach eighteenth-century literature may have a different tack, but it is subtle and not overt." This professor tells of a colleague who has been on the faculty for a number of years. When she arrived she taught her humanities courses in a way that was "quite traditional." And yet, now "she does quite a bit of feminist theory along with it. And they [the students] still get all the material with it, so that's OK. The ones who turn it into a religion eventually grate their colleagues to the point that they [the graters] leave." Here one cannot help but be struck by the fact that philosophical dissonance between younger and older faculty is expected, and that this manifests itself in differences over how to read a book, how to conceive the past, or how to critique a poem.

The college is hardly Duke or Stanford in its level of politicization, although some courses certainly are taught with an advocate's point of view. The catalogue lists several of this type, and though many titles look traditional — okay, except for "Socialism" — the perspectives are not always so. Some examples:

- Sociology 305, "Sociology of the Family," in which one studies "the relationship between the family and the changing external environment as well as the dynamic processes within the family. Historical and cross-cultural perspectives are considered along with alternatives to the traditional family."
- Philosophy 303, "Socialism," which is "an examination of some of the philosophical, political, and economic claims of modern socialists, beginning with and emphasizing Marx, but also moving beyond Marx and Marxism into the work of contemporary socialists who stress the democratic character of socialism and the need for a socialist market economy."
- English 220, "Literature and the Social Experience," which studies "a faculty-selected topic (such as African-American Literature, War in Literature, or Androgyny in Literature) focusing on a cultural movement, a social issue, or the perspective of a social group."
- English 230-231, "Plural America I & II" (also cross-listed in History). "The intent is to recognize the aspects of other cultures appropriated into the Western tradition but often either unacknowledged or glossed over. The end should be an appreciation of the achievements and limitations of our Western heritage, and a heightened sensitivity to the cultural diversity of the world-at-large [*sic*]. Plural America I focuses on Native American and Chicano history and literature and on the European context of American society; Plural America II focuses on African-American and Asian-American history and literature and on the 1960s as a catalyst for multiculturalism."

Political Atmosphere: Slowly Circling

A few years ago some feminist faculty at Birmingham-Southern made an attempt to require so-called gender-neutral language on campus, but didn't get much support from their colleagues. Still, the use of this sort of language is unofficially enforced.

For example, if a professor brings a course description before a faculty committee for approval, an amendment will likely be forthcoming to change the wording if it is not already gender-neutral. According to one professor, a man who uses conventional English when speaking before the faculty will be politically corrected before the words are halfway out of his mouth. There seems to be little faculty opposition to this imposition, and, indeed, this is the way many radical ideas have found their place in the standard operating procedures at colleges and universities: no one stands up to them.

There was some talk of a speech code at Birmingham-Southern as far back as the Vietnam War, but nothing has been done to revive that idea recently. One administrator did say that there are "no codes, but we would be open to issues of sensitivity as needed." Whether this would include limitations on the speech of those who transgress the arbitrary boundaries of politically correct administrators is difficult to say.

Most departments at Southern host a variety of viewpoints. "There is an emphasis on diversity," a professor says. "I don't see it as much of a threat. It's the kind of diversity you actually want in an academic community. There are some multicultural types here, but the administration wouldn't let them get control of the place."

The composition of the faculty is itself controlled by several layers of administration through which any prospective faculty member must pass before receiving a job offer. "We have forty to forty-five members of the board, and a president [Neal Berte] who's a monarch," a professor says. "We still have an affiliation with the Methodist Church, which of course is itself one of the trendiest institutions in the country. But the particular Methodists who are connected with us are conservative." When a vacancy arises at Birmingham-Southern, the department head nominates three candidates to the provost. The candidates, if satisfactory to the provost, are interviewed by the president, who sometimes vetoes choices. The provost and department interview all three, as does the tenure and promotions committee.

A small school like Southern must be careful to serve its primary constituency: as one professor notes, though 45 percent of the school's budget comes from its endowment, a drop of ten to fifteen students can cause budgetary problems. The state of Alabama has cut the university system budget by $100 million recently, and the governor has said the state spends too much on higher education and not enough on kindergarten and elementary school. Alabama has quite a number of community colleges, and will soon eliminate the meager $600 grant it gives to in-state students who attend in-state private colleges like Birmingham-Southern. With all the cutbacks, public universities have been scrambling for monetary support from the same businesses that donate to private colleges. Despite this, one professor says the future at Birmingham-Southern is promising: "The academic outlook here is good. We have a good age range and mix of ages with our faculty." Another points to the $30 million worth of construction projects going on at the college now — a sign that it still has good financial support.

Student Life: A Pleasant Place

Somewhat over half of both men and women at Birmingham-Southern pledge the Greek organizations, and more than three-quarters of all students live on campus. There is no coed housing.

Southern boasts more than eighty student organizations to choose from, and enters the big-time sports arena in basketball and baseball but not football, an oddity for any Southern school. There are several academic organizations, including the American Chemical Society, a concert choir, a pre-law organization, and the *Southern Academic Review,* a scholarly journal for the college community. There seem to be very few politically active groups on campus, although the president did ask a faculty member several years ago to serve as an adviser to a gay and lesbian support group. The group is not activist compared to similar groups on other campuses; it once planned a demonstration on campus along with students from the University of Alabama-Birmingham, but according to a professor, "that was headed off before it ever began."

Birmingham itself has grown by leaps and bounds over the past few decades, and the presence of the University of Alabama-Birmingham, with its attendant hospitals and world-renowned cardiovascular center, has brought a great deal of new wealth to this city. Birmingham did not exist before the War between the States and thus has no antebellum charm, but it has turned into a dynamic place and has recovered well from the blows dealt it by the demise of most of the steel industry, which gave birth to it. It is by any measure a very pleasant place to live.

BOSTON COLLEGE

Director of Undergraduate Admissions
Devlin Hall 208
Boston College
140 Commmonwealth Avenue
Chestnut Hill, MA 02167-3809
(800) 360-2522
www.bc.edu

Total enrollment: 14,700
Undergraduates: 8,700

SAT Ranges (Verbal/Math): V 600-680, M 610-690
Financial aid: 46%
Applicants: 17,000
Accepted: 38%
Enrolled: 33%
Application deadline: Jan. 15
Financial aid application deadline: Feb. 1
Tuition: $20,760
Core curriculum: No

Holy War

Boston College (BC) was founded by the Jesuits in 1863 to "serve the sons of Boston's Irish immigrants," and although the curriculum has changed along with the character of the Jesuits, BC retains elements of a traditional liberal arts education. Though the requirements are rather broad and afflicted by passing fads like multiculturalism, they are neither as sprawling nor as trendy as those at many other colleges and universities, including some in nearby Boston neighborhoods.

BC remains a college in name only. It has all the marks of a modern university, including large graduate programs, big-time Division I athletics, and an undergraduate student body which, at around 8,500, is big for a private institution. The political trends dominant at the larger schools are catching up with both the liberal arts and Catholic aspects of BC: the 1996-97 school year saw noisy but all-too-predictable protests for more diversity.

Boston College is located six miles outside of Boston in Chestnut Hill. Much of its 115-acre campus is dominated by neo-Gothic architecture, a reminder of the rich theological and intellectual traditions that are available to Catholic schools. Boston College has done well in the raising of money, and it shows in the renovations and new buildings on campus. In the last decade alone the college has added an athletic arena, a chemistry center, four undergraduate residence halls, a new art museum, and a new central library (named for alumnus Thomas "Tip" O'Neill, former Speaker of the U.S. House of Representatives) that holds more than 1.5 million volumes and twelve thousand periodicals). But while these buildings only add to the school's reputation, BC's future will be determined by the extent to which the church's traditions will be replaced by the new ideological orthodoxies.

Academic Life: All Politics Is Local

Boston College is really a university with eleven colleges and schools, five of them dedicated to undergraduates. Fifty majors are offered in the undergraduate divisions of the College of Arts and Sciences, the Wallace E. Carroll School of Management, the School of Education, the School of Nursing, and the College of Advancing Studies (which is the continuing education school for part-time students). For the student interested in the liberal arts, the undergraduate school of choice would be the College of Arts and Sciences.

As a Jesuit university, Boston College has as its heritage a 400-year tradition of concern for the integration of the intellectual, moral, and religious development of its students. The centerpiece of Jesuit education has always been a common curriculum that emphasizes the study of the defining works of the humanities, sciences, and social sciences. But while BC claims to offer a core curriculum (and calls it "The University Core"), it really offers a set of distribution requirements — requirements that are not as loose and baggy as those at some schools, but which certainly don't amount to a true core.

The general curriculum requires these courses: one in arts, two in European history, one in literature, one in mathematics, two in the natural sciences, two in philosophy, two in social sciences, two in theology, and one in writing. In addition, there is a cultural diversity requirement that may be met with a course that also fulfills another general requirement or a requirement in the student's major. There is also the standard language proficiency requirement that all majors must complete. The school of management has further general requirements related to business, and undergrads in the School of Nursing take four natural sciences as part of their core and are not saddled with the cultural diversity requirement.

The presence of European history and theology in the general education requirements makes BC's curriculum better than many, and more religiously oriented than even some other Catholic schools. "Boston College is way above average," one professor claims. "It's not as good as Thomas Aquinas College of California or the University of Dallas, but it is one of the best." BC has over the past several years narrowed the choice of classes that may satisfy the distribution requirements, and has added a freshman writing seminar and a foreign language requirement — both moves toward a traditional liberal arts base, rather than away from it.

An average of three hundred students per year fulfill their philosophy and theology requirements through the student-run PULSE program, an interdisciplinary program that combines classroom study with hands-on social work assignments through Boston-area mental health organizations, emergency shelters, correctional facilities, and legal organizations. One professor is quick to point out that the program is not like other "social justice" programs. "PULSE is not doctrinaire liberalism; students study Dostoyevsky and Thomas Aquinas, as well as work in soup kitchens," the professor says.

All undergraduate divisions offer an honors program, open to incoming freshmen with excellent high school records, SAT scores, and recommendations, in which students take specifically designated honors courses to satisfy the distribution requirements. BC says this program provides undergraduates with "an integrated liberal arts education of a kind one can find in few colleges or universities," and, indeed, the honors program comes much closer to a true core than do the normal distribution requirements. During the first two years of the program, students take a survey of the entire Western civilization tradition entitled "Western Cultural Tradition," which fulfills the requirements in theology, philosophy, and literature. The courses use primary sources (original texts in translation) from Greek, Roman, medieval, and modern periods, and class size averages only fifteen students.

Certain faculty and departments at BC are also due honors. They include David Lowenthal, Robert Faulkner, and Christopher J. Bruell in political science; Peter Kreeft, Richard Stevens, and Joseph Flannigan in philosophy; Fred Lawrence, Ernest Fortin, Matthew Lamb, and Patrick Ryan in theology; William Kilpatrick in education; and Harold Peterson in economics.

The political science department has a reputation for offering fine classes in the liberal arts tradition, and many teachers there are influenced by the "great books"–style writing and pedagogy of Leo Strauss. Reportedly, not all the faculty in the political science department share the same understanding of the ends of a liberal arts education. Nevertheless, there is said to be a spirit of collegiality among the professors (i.e., a minimum of infighting).

The philosophy department places an emphasis on ethics and philosophy of the human person, and most of its twenty-member faculty are believing Catholics. "There is a lot of satisfaction within the department — that is to say, there is not infighting among faculty and both undergraduate and graduate students are happy with the program," says a professor.

The College of Arts and Sciences also has several politicized departments, including English, sociology, and, sadly, theology. There are also a handful of politicized minors, like black studies, women's studies, American studies, and "Faith, Peace, and Justice."

According to one BC professor, the English department spends much of its time promoting radical agendas. Such agendas are certainly apparent in the department's course listings.

- "Introduction to Feminisms." This class will introduce students to "a variety of feminist approaches to the analysis of gender. The course considers topics from women's history and experience with a sustained focus on race, class, sexuality, national identity, and ethnicity."
- "Race and Literary Studies." This class will "examine cultural representations that have been racialized as African American, Asian American, Chicano/Latino, Native American, and white." In addition, the class takes on issues of "class, gender, sexuality, and nation."

One student finds sociology to be worse than English. An introduction to sociology course investigates "race, gender, and class equalities" along with "the L.A. riots." Another sociology offering has an extensive and vivid description:

■ "Deviance and Social Control." This course, also required for the women's studies minor, "represents a social and historical inquiry into the battle between the power of a given social order and its deviant others," according to the catalogue. Not only is this the "story of control and resistance within societies organized according to economic, heterosexist, racial, and imperial hierarchies," but it's also a chronicle of "madness, religious excess, and the pornographic violence of Western Man and his most powerful social institutions." The course also claims to be "a narrative of the resistance of women, peoples of color, those who desire sex differently and those impoverished by the normal relations of a given social order of things in time. It is a story of how some of us come to know others as evil, sleazy, dirty, dangerous, sick, immoral, or crazy, and how the normative order to which we adhere is disrupted or destroyed by those who know it differently." Course requirements include the standard examinations, but also an autobiographical essay and a group field research project (which we could not begin to imagine).

With the exception of the professors listed above and perhaps a few others, the theology department — like that at many top Catholic schools — is politicized in its hiring practices and its curriculum. One professor was ousted "because she was not politically correct," according to one former colleague, and now teaches at another church school. More disturbingly, a notorious ex-Catholic who has stated that she wants to "castrate God the Father" and that she is the "anti-christ," remains in the department; she reportedly will not speak with males and laces her off-campus speeches with obscenities. Despite all that, the professor has a small following on campus who take her seriously. Her classes are described in the catalogue as covering "the interconnected atrocities perpetrated against women and nature in patriarchal society" and the "fundamental problems arising from the prevailing patriarchal myths and symbols, and the consequent reduction of women and nature to the status of objects."

American studies, taught by faculty from the departments of English, political science, sociology, history, and fine arts, focuses on "American culture past and present, specifically analyzing how American culture has been shaped by the interaction of race, class, ethnicity, and gender and other issues." Each student in the program selects a "theme," and three of the five courses required for the minor must be related to this theme. Past themes suggest that this program favors the feminist and multicultural interests of the participating faculty rather than constituting any sort of true study of all American culture. These have included race in American culture, ethnicity in American culture, media and race, media and gender, colonialism and American culture, poverty and gender, and diversity in urban culture.

Political Atmosphere: You Can't Always Get What You Want

According to one professor, the BC administration consistently takes "the typical Jesuit, inclusive, don't-piss-anyone-off approach." Overall, the administration is characterized by some on campus as primarily businesspeople who effectively manage and administer the financial affairs of the college. However, another professor compliments BC's president, Fr. William Leahy, S.J., for his strong-mindedness. Leahy is "not wishy-washy, and not afraid to engage the tough issues," this professor said. "Fr. Leahy does not want to go the way of Georgetown and betray Catholic principles," remarks another professor.

During his first few months as president, Leahy announced that if BC intended to take its Catholic nature seriously, it would also need to take seriously its stance on human sexuality and prohibit sexual activity in college dorms. Students complained that Leahy wanted to turn the college into a seminary. That policy is still informally in place — the statement was made to say it would not be tolerated, but there is no punishment for such "infractions" per se. Indeed, BC's Catholic identity is not a closely guarded secret; information on Catholic teachings is widely available. So, one may conjecture, why should students be surprised or put out by a Catholic school (which they chose to attend) promoting a Catholic point of view?

In any case, there is no reward for the just, and things only got more harried for Leahy from that point on. The spring semester of 1997 saw student protests for virtually every cause imaginable: recognition of a campus homosexual group, demands for greater diversity in the curriculum, diversity training for faculty and incoming freshmen, and more faculty in the college's minority student services office. At this writing, Leahy has held out, citing Catholic teachings as his reasons, but those on campus wonder what will happen next.

The protests began following publication of a cartoon in the campus conservative newspaper, the *Observer of Boston College*. The cartoon asked, "Which kills more Black babies?" and gave as choices the Ku Klux Klan, neo-Nazi skinheads, and a Planned Parenthood abortionist. As the paper expected, the cartoon's combination of race and the abortion issue was highly controversial. The paper pointed out that the piece had been drawn by a nationally syndicated cartoonist who had been asked to do so by an African-American minister from New Life Gospel Church in Colorado Springs. The paper's editor spoke to a protest rally on the BC quad after the paper was derided over loudspeakers as "racist." The newspaper believed the issue should be of legitimate concern to the black community. "The point of the cartoon is to show how, in our society, blacks are continuing to be oppressed because of legalized abortion," the *Observer* said in an editorial.

That didn't matter much to some students, who burned copies of the paper and organized a boycott that cost the *Observer* $4,000 in advertising. Their anger at the newspaper soon spread to loud criticisms of the alleged underrepresentation of minority students at BC — and in American society in general. The Lesbian, Gay and

Bisexual Community (LGBC), angry about Leahy's recent decision to deny it college recognition, got involved, as did other minority student groups and some nonminority supporters. The outcry culminated in a bizarre protest march that ended up at Leahy's house. During the march, the students shouted things like "We want diversity!" and then "BC unite!," finally ending with the somewhat paradoxical chant "Unify! Diversify!" The protest leader said: "We demand to be seen as students. We have earned our rights here," when in fact the protesters were distraught because they were being treated exactly as every student is treated. Unswayed by their own illogic, they kept shouting until Leahy emerged from his house to say that he was very busy, but that he would meet with protest leaders to discuss their concerns.

Leahy did just that — three meetings in the next ten days — amid what the *Observer* called "tremendous tension" on campus. At one meeting a student demanded that diversity become a major component of all core courses, complained that she was very unhappy at BC, and asked Leahy if she should leave the college. The president said that if she was unhappy, she should certainly consider leaving, just as anyone unhappy in a job should consider quitting. Leahy was then widely misquoted in signs posted on campus by activist students as having told the student, "If you don't like BC, then just leave" — which was simply not true.

Days later, Leahy met with leaders of the LGBC and was widely reviled (among the activists, anyway) for his steadfast refusal to grant them recognition. He later explained his position to the *Observer*: "Any student who is gay, lesbian, or bisexual should not be subject to harassment. They are part of Boston College. . . . However, I don't intend to do anything to compromise or undermine the mission of BC as a Jesuit and Catholic institution. It's my judgment that groups such as LGBC start as support groups for lesbian and gay students, but then become advocates for positions counter to Catholic teachings." The president said he didn't oppose organizing support systems on campus, but he could not grant the recognition the homosexual group was seeking. Leahy also indicated that he would not add sexual preference or orientation to the college's nondiscrimination clause. In turn, members of the LGBC circulated flyers on campus calling Leahy "ignorant and homophobic."

While the issues involved in that protest remain unresolved, it is certainly heartening to see an administration that refuses to be intimidated. For now at least, the president is sticking to his tradition and the college's tradition. "People get all wrought up, and I don't think it's constructive," he told the *Observer*. "Just because you want something doesn't mean the university is going to agree. There's a difference between not listening and not agreeing. . . . Life is like that: we don't always get what we want to have."

Professors have also stood up against calls to curtail freedom of expression on campus. There was a motion under faculty consideration that would have placed critical marks in professors' permanent records for violating a proposed politically correct, in-class speech code. Professors could have earned demerits for using "non-inclusive" speech or for displaying "gender bias," that is, calling on men more often than women (though we don't know if the reverse is also considered bias). In any case, the proposal was voted down by the faculty and never went into effect.

Student Life: Choice, by Lottery

We aren't sure what the protesters were asking for in regards to the diversity component of freshman orientation, since it's already there. The First Year Experience program at BC includes seven sessions held over three days and two nights. Parents of students also attend an orientation program that runs concurrently. The orientation program (at least for the students) discusses diversity themes and sexuality, along with academic requirements and campus rules. One of the recent sessions was a one-hour program entitled "Growing through Difference," in which a deputy superintendent of the Boston Police Department provided a personal account of "how his experience of diversity encouraged his personal growth." Another seminar was entitled "Reflections on Diversity," which was a series of small group discussions that focused (favorably) on multiculturalism in the BC curriculum.

Freshmen admitted to BC are assigned a number of years for which they may live in college housing. According to the college, "Most receive three years of guaranteed housing with the expectation that they will live off campus [for their] junior year." The college says it allows freshmen and sophomores "to choose, by lottery" a traditional residence hall or a suite with a living area and several bedrooms. Juniors and seniors may live in high-rise apartments or duplexes.

Campus activities include more than one hundred student-run organizations, including student government, an AM radio station, academic and language societies, performance groups, professional clubs, and service organizations. The leading organizations for traditionally minded students are the *Observer of Boston College* and the Saint Thomas More Society, whose mission is to "give students an opportunity to discover what it means to be a good Catholic in today's society." The More Society hosts orthodox Catholic speakers and sponsors on-campus debates on controversial public and theological questions.

The primary liberal groups on campus cluster under the heading AHANA, or African-American, Hispanic, Asian, and Native American students. The Office of AHANA Student Programs (OASP) is an official student services organization at BC, with a paid staff that provides numerous programs that "support and enhance the academic performance" of minority undergraduate students. Programs for these students include personal and group counseling, academic and career advising, tutorial students, and a special mentoring program. OASP also works directly with minority student organizations on campus, including the AHANA Leadership Council, the AHANA Leadership Academy, the Asian Caucus, the Black Student Forum, and the Organization of Latin American Student Affairs. Some of the benefits that

BC has handed out specifically to minority students include the AHANA Ball and the AHANA Boat Cruise, in addition to the specialized academic and professional counseling.

Boston College fields seventeen varsity teams for men and sixteen for women at the NCAA Division I level. In addition, a number of other sports-related opportunities are offered, including fencing, figure skating, scuba diving, and aerobics.

Some complain that Father Leahy's insistence on academic standards for athletes has hurt the athletic program. Recently, Leahy denied admission to two top basketball recruits because their past academic performances were not up to BC's standards. No amount of argument by the basketball coach convinced the president otherwise. Leahy's efforts come as something of a surprise to BC sports fans, since the college has been more than willing to look the other way in the past. The *Boston Globe* reported that the average SAT score for freshman basketball players from 1992 to 1995 was only 819, compared to the 1,220-1,360 range of the average applicant. Still, football fans in particular look forward to the annual "Holy War" with Catholic rival Notre Dame.

BOSTON UNIVERSITY

Office of Admissions
881 Commonwealth Avenue
Boston, MA 02215
(617) 353-2300
www.bu.edu

Total enrollment: 29,600
Undergraduates: 15,454
SAT Ranges (Verbal/Math): V 590-670, M 580-680
Financial aid: 53%
Applicants: 26,678
Accepted: 53%
Enrolled: 29%
Application deadline: Early decision, Nov. 1; regular, Jan. 15
Financial aid application deadline: Feb. 15
Tuition: $22,830
Core curriculum: Optional

The BU Revolutionaries

Boston University (BU) is a private, nonsectarian institution of some thirty thousand students occupying seventy-one acres along the south shore of the Charles River in Boston — one of America's most livable cities. The third-largest private university in the United States, BU traces its founding to 1839 in Vermont; it moved to Boston in 1867. From a small school founded to train ministers for the Methodist church, BU has grown over the decades into a massive institution with fifteen schools and colleges offering more than 250 degree programs.

BU is an urban campus — not unlike New York University and other urban schools — that substitutes sidewalks and concrete for wide-open greens and parklike expanses. Yet, what it lacks in bucolic amenities it makes up for by being situated in Boston, a town long known as one of the cultural centers of the country and which is also undergoing a tremendous economic boom. BU students have at their disposal not only the considerable resources of the institution itself, but also those of the entire city. Such an urban setting is not for everyone, but the student looking for downtown excitement, intellectual stimulation, and a solid curriculum should take a close look at this school.

BU as it exists today was decisively shaped by John Silber, who recently stepped down after many years as president of the university. Even though his current job as chancellor of BU does not put him in the day-to-day arena to the degree his presidency did, Silber's determination not to reorder the university to suit passing whims of intellectual fashion has paid off in many ways. To a greater degree than the vast majority of its peer institutions, BU employs relatively few politicized professors who'd rather indoctrinate their students than teach them. Freshmen can still take a true core curriculum in the College of Arts and Sciences, and the odds of being attacked for wanting to learn about Western history and philosophy are slimmer than one might imagine for a large private school in Boston. To top it off, BU still emphasizes teaching its undergraduates rather than throwing them into a mix of graduate students of wildly varying quality for virtually all of their first two years of coursework, as is the case at many state schools of comparable size.

BU may not start an academic revolution, but this Boston institution is not ashamed to rebel against the reigning intellectual orthodoxies of our time. BU's struggle for academic independence is a boon for any student seeking a traditional liberal arts education.

Academic Life: The Solid Core

Boston University offers its undergraduates many different tracks to earning a baccalaureate degree. According to one professor, "Some schools and colleges in the university have stronger, that is, better, requirements than others." While all of BU's programs contain excellent and dedicated faculty, several offer true core curricula. "The Core Curriculum in the College of Arts and Sciences (CAS) is splendid, but it is an option to other course work to satisfy distributive requirements," says a faculty member. "Courses that satisfy the distributive requirements are limited in number, which is a plus, and student admissions standards continue to rise progressively higher, also with good effect." This means that the best students are attracted to the best curriculum, and that the Core Curriculum in CAS is a "must" for those enrolling in that college. Students take four classes in the Core during their freshman and sophomore years.

CAS is the largest single unit of the university, enrolling over 6,500 undergraduate students. The CAS catalogue has this to say about the Core: "Core students study classics of the Western and Eastern traditions in small classes taught by full-time faculty. The focus is on discussion, understanding, and the development of critical thinking and writing skills." Discussion classes are called "the heart of the program," and enrollment is voluntary. The Core classes, which total eight, can be credited toward any major and may be taken for honors by students invited into the honors program. Satisfying the demands of the Core Curriculum will also meet the requirements of the General Education of the College of CAS. The Core classes provide a small liberal arts setting within a massive, comprehensive university, and graduates of the Core are better educated than those who miss this superb opportunity. About a third of Core students live on special residence floors in Warren Towers, and numerous opportunities for faculty-student interaction, as well as field trips to Boston's cultural riches, are part of the Core experience.

The Divisional Studies Option in the CAS is much like that found at most colleges and universities that have done away with their core curricula. The Divisional Studies Program comprises four divisions: humanities, mathematics and computer science, natural sciences, and social sciences. In brief, students majoring in a natural science must complete at least six one-semester divisional courses in the humanities and social science divisions, with at least two courses in each. Those majoring in the humanities, in mathematics and computer science, and in the social sciences must complete at least two courses in each of the three divisions outside the division of their concentration. At least one of the courses in the natural science division must include a laboratory component. Students can take very good courses through these options if they receive good advising and choose well, but the Core Curriculum is better suited to most students' needs.

A truly exciting option, the University Professors Program, consists of a selection of classes available as electives to any student as well as an invitation-only concentration for the best students at BU. It is the teaching program of the University Professors, thirty scholars "who have built their own intellectual bridges between various disciplines of the humanities, arts, and sciences." University literature says the program was designed to "respond to the necessity for rigorous and well-founded cross-disciplinary studies apparent in our cultural tradition and reflected tellingly in the work of our major academic centers. This elusive but principal objective is achieved partly by emphasizing the fundamental humanistic values inherent in all academic inquiries." Many of the program's courses are open to everyone, but it also awards both undergraduate and graduate degrees "to a select number of exceptional students. When admitted to this program as freshmen, students undertake a two-year core course program that provides a comprehensive introduction to our cultural tradition as a common foundation for future study and research. Students are expected to perform at a level of excellence comparable to that of exceptional students in normal degree programs."

The literature also says this about the program: "It is also, most importantly, an encouraging step toward the recovery of the idea of a university as the occasionally entertaining, frequently challenging, and invariably civilizing ambit of intellectual courage and responsibility, within which the noble task can best be achieved of providing a very good education for our students." Undergraduates spend their first two years taking eight core courses as well as the "ID 500 Seminar," required of everyone from newly arrived freshmen to Ph.D. students. Freshmen take core courses ranging from the great literature of the West to ethics and politics, from Plato to Augustine to Alasdair MacIntyre. Other courses cover the history of ideas, philosophy, and a foreign language (four semesters of the latter are required). This superb program, comparable to Directed Studies at Yale, should be pursued by all accomplished and intellectually ambitious students who enroll at BU.

The College of General Studies at BU offers a two-year, general education core curriculum and is, according to university literature, "oriented to the student whose traditional admissions credentials from high school may make him or her ineligible for direct admission into the University's four-year liberal arts and professional programs." This program gives both underachievers and nontraditional students a second chance at acquiring a top-notch liberal education. All courses are team taught. Each freshman faculty team consists of six professors who represent the various divisions of the undergraduate curriculum: Social Science, Science and Mathematics, and Humanities and Rhetoric. Students take classes in sections of about forty pupils, and extensive academic counseling is provided. Full-time learning specialists are also available and regularly teach classes in "learning how to learn"; weekly workshops on how to be an effective student are also offered. In the 1997-98 academic year some 800 freshmen and nearly 1,600 undergraduates were enrolled in the College of General Studies. After completing this curriculum successfully, students may proceed to baccalaureate-level studies at BU. Certainly this is one of the best programs of its kind in the nation — it is carefully thought out, offers a very real liberal education, and gives the student an opportunity for academic redemption and a better, more informed life.

The foreign language requirement depends on the school or college. CAS and the University Professors require four semesters; the College of Communications requires two; the other units of the university require none.

Outstanding professors at BU include Brian Jorgensen and Christopher Ricks in the Core; John Daverio in music (in the School of Fine Arts); Charles Griswold in philosophy; Igor Lukes in the University Professors program and International Relations; James Johnston, Merle Goldman, Clifford Backman, Dietrich Orlow, William Keylor, and John Gagliardo in history; Judy Schickedanz, Roselmina Indrisano, Mary Catherine O'Connor, Kevin Ryan, and Edwin Delattre in education; Steven Tigner in education and Core; Bonnie Costello, John Kidd, Burton Cooper, Eugene Green, Robert Levine, Robert Pinsky, and Derek Wolcott in English; Hamid Nawab in electrical and computer engineering; Alicia Borinsky in modern foreign languages; Daniel Clemens in astronomy; Robert Hefner and Peter Wood in anthropology; Elie Wiesel, Saul Bellow, Peter Berger, and Geoffrey Hill in the University Professors program; Hillel Levine in religion; Walter Clemens, Walter Connor, and Sofia Perez in political science; and Glenn Loury in economics.

Among the strongest departments at BU are the Core Curriculum, astronomy, biology, philosophy, University Professors, music (in the School of Fine Arts), biomedical engineering, anthropology, and, in education, early childhood, elementary, mathematics, and literacy education.

Political Atmosphere: Weathering the Culture Wars

BU has weathered the culture wars far better than most of its peer institutions. When one thinks of universities that still offer solid classes from faculty more concerned with imparting to their students the mind-broadening knowledge of the liberal arts and sciences than with dispensing the mind-numbing trendiness that passes for scholarship in many quarters, private schools in Massachusetts might not leap to mind. And yet, that is exactly what a student will find along the South Bank of the Charles. Says a professor: "No place is immune, but BU is less affected by such ideologies than any other university I know in depth. No one can intimidate this university or its administration and board with ideological threats, and no one prevails in argumentation here by invoking ideological clichés." This is due largely to the inspired leadership of former president John Silber, and to the many administrative and faculty allies he worked with over his more than two decades in office.

Another indication of BU's relative immunity from the politicization on so many campuses is that it has no speech code and no sensitivity training courses.

Some on campus would prefer to see BU move in a different direction, however. "Sources of influence of such ideologies include a few faculty members, some students who have been (unknowingly) subjected to ideological manipulation before coming here, and popular culture, including television, which saturates the atmosphere with ideological fashion," says a professor.

But faculty members who would turn BU into a bastion of political correctness are very few in number, and their influence is slight. Asked if candidates for hire are ever judged more on their personal politics than on their professional qualifications, a senior professor answers unequivocally: "Definitely not." Candidates who favor traditional research topics and methodology are seriously considered for academic positions at BU, as a perusal of the university's catalogue will reveal.

Asked to name some problems on the horizon for BU, a professor says poor secondary education, "especially in rigorous thinking and good writing," and grade inflation come to mind. So do the "devastating effects on academic and professional standards in schools and higher education of certain features of the Americans with Disabilities Act and the Individuals with Disabilities Education Act." Particularly dangerous are "the proliferation of putative disabilities for which there is neither scientific evidence nor any intelligible criterion for diagnosis, the readiness of courts to meddle in academic standards and requirements, and the therapeutic ethos that denies the responsibility of individuals for their conduct and themselves and the legitimacy of sanction for misconduct."

Student Life: Boston Sampler

Students at BU have access to one of the country's most interesting cities. Public transportation is readily available, and Boston's cultural attractions, including numerous museums, the Boston Symphony Orchestra, professional sports, and thousands of college students at the numerous institutions all over the area, make it unlikely that anyone will be bored at BU. Students make good use of the shopping found at Copley Square, a short streetcar ride from campus; Faneuil Hall Market Place; and more ethnic restaurants than even the hungriest undergrad could hit in four short years. Beaches and mountains are a short ride away when the need to escape the city becomes too great to resist.

Somewhat over half of all undergraduates reside on campus, and the school has not abandoned the formerly widespread tradition of *in loco parentis*. Students must sign in all guests and escort them at all times; they must show IDs to enter dorms (a practice increasingly common for security reasons); and overnight guests are allowed only for members of the same sex. Freshmen under twenty-one are required to live on campus. The dorms themselves range from small, quaint buildings to high-rises. Resident assistants live in every dorm, and faculty-in-residence live in most of the large residences and many smaller ones as well. Most dorms are coed.

Intramural and club sports are available to students, and the university fields intercollegiate teams in most major sports, although the football team has played its final game. Excellent facilities are available for all sports and recreation. The George Sherman Union (GSU) is as much of a hub as this urban school has. Located at the center of campus, it contains a lounge, student organization offices, and the like.

There are some three hundred student organizations at BU. Among these are numerous undergraduate associations in several College of Arts and Science departments, including groups for economics, English, history and international relations, modern languages, and philosophy.

Marsh Chapel offers weekly worship, and campus chaplains are available through the chapel. Hillel House provides the center for Jewish life at BU; the Catholic Center at Newman House does the same for Roman Catholic students. Many Protestant ministers other than the Methodist Chapel minister are also available on campus.

ROTC is available in all four services: Army, Navy, Air Force, and Marine Corps.

BOWDOIN COLLEGE

Office of Admissions
Brunswick, ME 04011
(207) 725-3100
www.bowdoin.edu

Total enrollment: 1,581
Undergraduates: 1,581
SAT Ranges (Verbal/Math): V 620-720, M 620-710
Financial aid: 44%
Applicants: 4,435
Accepted: 29%
Enrolled: 35%
Application deadline: Jan. 1
Financial aid application deadline: Feb. 15
Tuition: $21,750
Core curriculum: No

Liberty? Equality? Fraternity?

For starters, Bowdoin is a beautiful college, located just three miles from the sea and not far from Maine's largest city, Portland. The college has a long and venerable history, and there are some excellent classes and programs available to students. The school has a mammoth endowment of around $300 million, and, in one of those quirks of history, graduated both Nathaniel Hawthorne and Henry Wadsworth Longfellow in the same class, in 1825.

These facts might be enough to persuade a good student to spend four cold winters in Maine. However, there is some pessimism on campus regarding the college's future. This pessimism does not come from the administration, which has busily promoted itself as being at the forefront of the trend toward politicization. (Its latest claim to fame is a new policy outlawing fraternities and sororities — a rather totalitarian act for a group of people who state their commitment to freedom, choice, and individual rights.) No, the pessimism on campus comes from sources who believe in the value of a traditional liberal arts institution, and it comes *because* of the administration. To borrow an idea from a Bowdoin alum, traditionalists there might as well be wearing a scarlet letter.

A good student at Bowdoin will still be able to sort through the course offerings, choosing the good ones and ignoring the rest; however, he should expect to run into quite a bit of "the rest."

Academic Life: No Bones about It

Bowdoin requires of its students but two courses in each of three curricular divisions: natural sciences and mathematics, humanities and fine arts, and social and behavioral sciences. The college's viewbook calls this "a broad and contemporary foundation for a liberal arts education." It is certainly contemporary, but it seems like a stretch to call it broad. And it is certainly not deep enough to be called a foundation. Obviously, the college has made no attempt to implement a demanding core curriculum that would provide a common reading experience for all students.

The educational experience is further narrowed by the mandate that two of these six required courses be in "non-Eurocentric" studies. There is, of course, no Western civilization requirement. "Non-Eurocentric" is probably a new term in college catalogues, though the idea has been around for some time. Bowdoin's catalogue explains that non-Eurocentric classes do not include language courses but do include classes that "focus on a non-Eurocentric culture or society, exclusive of Europe and European Russia and their literary, artistic, musical, religious, and political traditions. The requirement is intended to introduce students to the variety of cultures and to open their minds to the different ways in which people perceive and cope with the challenges of life." Classes on North American or European topics don't count, but those on African-American, Native American, and Latin American cultures are fine — despite the fact that some of these cultures are centered in North America too.

Some of the degree programs at Bowdoin are even more proudly non-Eurocentric: Africana studies and women's studies, for example. There are more traditional disciplines, of course; the best departments include economics, chemistry, and government. More than 35 percent of Bowdoin's students major in the social sciences and history, compared to 23.5 percent nationwide at institutions of Bowdoin's class. The percentage of students who major in a foreign language (11 percent) is nearly triple the national average. Also significant are the 7.2 percent who major in a field related to conservation and natural resources, compared with only 0.6 percent nationally. This latter statistic reflects the growing popularity of Bowdoin's environmental studies major.

Among Bowdoin's best professors are Paul Nyhus in history, Carol A. N. Martin and Matthew Greenfield in English, John Fitzgerald and Andreas Ortmann in economics, John Ambrose and James Higginbotham in classics, and Richard Morgan in government and legal studies.

A large number of students choose to double-major or to take an interdisciplinary major. Another option: design your own major. And Bowdoin also allows "coordinate majors," which encourage "specialization in an area of learning within the framework of a recognized academic discipline." Currently the coordinate major is offered only in relation to the Africana studies program and the environmental studies program. This option seems little more than a backdoor attempt to get the administration to approve pet projects, eventually fund them, and make them difficult to dislodge.

One highly ideological program already in place is gay and lesbian studies, which is "an interdisciplinary analysis that both considers the specific cultural achievements of gay men and lesbians, and takes the experience of lesbians and gay men as a critical perspective on the role of sexuality in culture as a whole." Though the course of study is not formally set, the college recommends courses listed under the departments of anthropology, English (four courses), film studies, sociology (also four courses), and Spanish.

Among departments with full standing, women's studies, Africana studies, English, and religion are certainly the most politicized, according to a highly regarded professor.

Bowdoin offers many solid courses taught by highly educated professors to top-quality students. But it is very easy to find courses on esoteric subjects that reflect the patent medicines of the faculty rather than the accumulated wisdom of the West. Among the First-Year Seminars offered to freshmen (a term not used at Bowdoin) are: "Pop Art," "Power/Knowledge in Detective Fiction," "Cultural Difference and the Crime Film," "The Souls of Animals," "Racism," "The Great Soviet Experiment: Film, Art, Literature," and "Sociology of Gender and the Military." All of this comes in the first year of college, before the student has learned much of anything that might provide a deeper foundation of knowledge.

In the department of English one finds these courses among those of a more traditional bent. For example, there is "An Introduction to Literary Theory through Popular Culture," which involves "readings in structuralist, deconstructive, feminist, psychoanalytic, new historicist, African-American, and lesbian and gay theory," all of which are "paired with examples from popular or mass-cultural forms such as best-selling novels, music videos, Hollywood films, and soap operas; the 'high' and the 'abstract' will not only explain but also be explained by the 'low' and the 'concrete.'" There are, no doubt, plenty of students who find the idea of getting college credit for watching soap operas and reading pulp fiction a wonderful gift.

An English major, not wishing to mess around with Shakespeare or Wordsworth (or Bowdoin grads Hawthorne and Longfellow), can choose "The Uses of Deviance," which "explores two ways of thinking about sexuality/gender deviance — as a device for social control and as a means to expression or empowerment." Or he might enjoy "Thinking Queer," where "likely topics include the centrality or marginality of sexual practice in gay and lesbian identities; problems in constructing the history of queer sexualities and interpreting closeted texts and practices."

One Bowdoin course of study does honor a distinguished alum, Admiral Robert Peary, whose exploration led the college to start a rare Arctic studies program. The program, designated as a "special academic program," offers classes in anthropology and sociology as well as fieldwork through the geology department, both at Bowdoin and points much colder.

Political Atmosphere: The Ministry of Culture

Asked to what degree multicultural and diversity issues make themselves manifest on Bowdoin's campus, a senior professor replies with one word: "obsessively." The administration not only backs bizarre fields of study and a slew of ranting student groups, but it has gone further. In the college's public relations information, various leftist mantras are blended like the ingredients of clam chowder. We are told, for example, that a young lady featured in an attractive publication sent to prospective students is the "minister of culture" of the African-American Society and opinion editor of the *Bowdoin Orient,* the student newspaper. Most officers of student organizations settle for quaint titles like president, secretary, and so on; the appearance of the title "minister of culture" in a publication designed to attract students to Bowdoin gives some indication of the importance placed upon such undertakings by the college president and his de facto ministers of culture, whatever their official titles.

Also featured prominently in this publication are the various multicultural groups on campus, including the African-American Society, the John Brown Russwurm African-American Center, the Latin American Student Organization, the Bowdoin Women's Association, and B-GLAD (Bisexual, Gay, Lesbian Alliance for Diversity). Also celebrated is ADAPT (Awareness of Differences among People Today), whose members "receive intensive training to bring a pluralistic philosophy to other groups on campus. Student groups work together to sponsor such events as a silent dinner and a candlelight vigil to demonstrate their concern for a more diverse curriculum and community." That such atypical groups with small memberships are featured so prominently in a publication blessed by central command and offered to the inquiring public says something important about the image the administration wishes to project.

The same wish list applies to faculty hiring. "At Bowdoin, as at all similar institutions in the Northeast, there is a powerful, but always unspoken, prejudice against conservatives," says one professor. Another recalls that when a young conservative scholar came up for tenure a few years ago, she was rejected. (She now teaches at another topflight school.) Bowdoin is still not as monolithic in its liberalism as some New England schools (perhaps due in part to the rural setting of the college), but it is obvious that the Bowdoin administration equates quality with conformity to academic trends. For all its good aspects, Bowdoin is likely to remain an intellectual playground for chic intellectuals for some time to come. A politically correct catalogue such as Bowdoin's is impossible without faculty willing to teach such courses. And if those courses are afforded such a place of pride in Bowdoin's public relations material, it seems likely that those who teach them also are given preferential treatment in hiring and tenure.

Bowdoin certainly doesn't need to be politically correct in order to attract funding. Though the cost of attending is very high for a school of Bowdoin's size and rural location, the college's endowment is something in the range of $300 million (presumably, the bulk of that was raised before Bowdoin began its ideological kick). There are many new construction and renovation projects on campus, and Bowdoin has some of the finest facilities of any college in its class. A new science facility completed in the summer of 1997 replaced an aged building at a cost of no less than $20 million, a princely sum for a liberal arts college to spend on any building. The libraries are no less excellent. The Hawthorne-Longfellow Library holds nearly 850,000 volumes, a collection that places it near the top of undergraduate institutions in that category. With these impressive figures in mind, one cannot be surprised to learn that the college's expenditure per student on services (admissions, career guidance, health, etc.) is, in the words of one assessment service, "substantially in excess of the norm for institutions of its class." The college also boasts an art museum, a large Visual Arts Center, and several auditoriums used for speeches, plays, and other activities.

Bowdoin's financial future seems secure, as does its ability to draw excellent students from around the country. Nevertheless, one professor gives this assessment of its future: "I am not at all optimistic about the coming decade. . . . Almost every program and department is weaker today than it was six or seven years ago, and I don't see this being reversed. A new president with a new team could do the trick, but that person would have to be a serious academic with strong personal intellectual accomplishments. Given the tendency in recent years for places such as Bowdoin to choose non-academic managers as presidents, the prospect is not encouraging."

Student Life: Freedom's Just Another Word for Nothing Left to Lose

Bowdoin draws its approximately 1,600 students from forty-eight states and twenty-six foreign countries. It turned down more than 70 percent of applicants for the class of 2000, but enrolled only 35 percent of those accepted for admission, a moderate number. That a college in rural Maine could be this selective and attract students from so far away speaks well of Bowdoin's reputation.

Students at Bowdoin may choose from a plethora of club activities and the like. The school sponsors twelve men's and thirteen women's varsity teams, as well as coed golf and sailing. It also has excellent athletic facilities, including the new Farley Field House, which holds a sixteen-lane pool, four indoor tennis courts, and many other exercise areas. All intramural teams are coeducational, which is in keeping with the college's insistence that all students be allowed to participate in all activities, regardless of any detrimental effects this policy may have on the activities themselves.

Among the more popular student organizations is the Outing Club, which hosts excursions into Maine's ample forests and mountains. Bowdoin's debate team was a recent (1994) but welcome addition to the choices available to students. Naturally, Bowdoin also has the usual run of socially chic organizations, such as the aforementioned B-GLAD, ADAPT, African-American Society, Bowdoin Women's Association, and Latin American Student Organization, as well as the Asian Student Association, HIV/AIDS Peer Educators, Native American Interest Group, and such.

What Bowdoin no longer has, however, are fraternities and sororities. Following years of open hostility toward Greek groups, Bowdoin's Governing Board voted in May 1992 to prohibit single-sex fraternities and sororities. The policy applies to all residential and nonresidential single-sex organizations, either local or nationally affiliated. College literature describes such groups as "discriminatory social membership organizations" and proclaims that "single-sex fraternities and sororities are fundamentally inconsistent with the values of this coeducational college." Furthermore, the college has threatened disciplinary action against anyone who recruits for or joins banned organizations.

But even this policy was not draconian enough for the Governing Board. In 1997 it banned the coeducational fraternities that had been set up following the banishment of single-sex Greek letter organizations and ruled that by the year 2000 all coed fraternities will be replaced by a "non-exclusive house system" to which all students may belong. The vote followed on the heels of a report from a Governing Board commission set up to study the matter, and the language of the report can rightfully be characterized as Orwellian. Even as the report calls for the prohibition of free association among individuals of free will, it states that the commission's goals were "building a community at the College; inclusiveness; a need to revitalize the core campus; a desire to focus on the needs of the sophomore class; the importance of identification with a residence in all aspects of student life; and a return to a sense of tradition at Bowdoin." The commission also had the nerve to claim that the new policy would be successful in "fostering an environment of challenge and growth, preserving freedom of expression and inquiry, encouraging mutual respect and civility of discourse and concern for others . . . [and] friendship and fun."

The logic of this report is, well, mind-boggling: by replacing 150 years of tradition, a tradition is rejuvenated; by breaking up communities, community is ensured; and by removing freedoms, freedom of expression will thrive. That the report's words and effect could be so diametrically opposed is an irony that we hope some souls are brave enough to point out. This Orwellian Newspeak is yet another indicator that Bowdoin is in the hands of folks for whom tradition is just something to be typed over.

Under the coming house system, to be wholly owned and maintained by the college, each incoming student will be assigned (randomly) to campus dormitories. Every student will remain a member of the same house for all four years at Bowdoin, which of course will become a more friendly place open to all, make everyone feel good, and somehow make sure that all students have the right to live exactly where the college puts them. The "choices" available to students, housing-wise, will at least be above average. There is a high-rise dorm on campus but also college-owned apartments, and disciplinary and ethnic theme houses, though we wonder how these last two will be made "nondiscriminatory" come the millennium.

BRANDEIS UNIVERSITY

Office of Admissions
P.O. Box 9110
Waltham, MA 02254-9110
(617) 736-3500
(800) 622-0622 (outside Massachusetts)
www.brandeis.edu

Total enrollment: 4,219
Undergraduates: 3,020
SAT Ranges (Verbal/Math): N/A
Financial aid: 59%
Applicants: 5,520
Accepted: 53%
Enrolled: 29%
Application deadline: Feb. 1
Financial aid application deadline: Feb. 1
Tuition: $22,360
Core curriculum: No

The Justice for All

Modern principles of niche marketing have been used to package American universities into recognizable types — the small liberal arts college, the major research institution, and so on. Brandeis University, founded in 1948, has consciously chosen to make its own type. In the words of its admissions recruiters, Brandeis is "that rare type of small, undergraduate college that daily reaps the benefits of being part of a strong and energetic research university."

The good aspects of both designations apply to Brandeis. The school has a relatively small student population of about 2,900 undergraduates, and even senior faculty teach lower-level courses. But the university is also proud of its research work and its over one thousand graduate students. A university publication says Brandeis ranks ninth in the nation in the number of times the work of its faculty is cited by other researchers.

However, the school has developed a bit of a split personality, not only when it comes to liberal arts versus research, but in its relationship to its history. Brandeis was founded by the American Jewish community after the horrors of World War II. Though nonsectarian from the start, the university has moved further and further from its Jewish roots, although as many as two-thirds of the students are Jewish. And politicization has eroded somewhat the founding ideals of the school, which were based on the nineteenth-century liberal thinking of associate justice of the Supreme Court Louis Brandeis.

The education is still quite good, and students have many chances to make use of the research side of the institution as well. Even as Brandeis loses some of its distinguishing characteristics, it compensates with others.

Academic Life: Charting the Void

Brandeis has no single course that all its students must take. Instead, it offers "University Seminars in Humanistic Inquiry," an interdisciplinary program for freshmen. Each student chooses one of the forty or so seminars offered each year. Each section enrolls around twenty students, which allows for good discussions with the professor (always a senior faculty member) on the intertwining of social sciences, natural sciences, and the creative arts. The topics range from the traditional-sounding ("Human Nature, Happiness, and Good" and "Thinking with Socrates") to the suspect ("Bad Girls," "Organized Crime," "Charting the Void," and "Everyday Activity"). Regardless of topic, the seminars are said to be challenging, and each is linked to a writing lab with its own reading list and writing assignments.

There is no Western civilization requirement at Brandeis, although some seminars deal with major Western texts and, according to one professor, "our literature is overwhelmingly Western." The university did recently add a non-Western requirement — one course, possibly one that counts toward another requirement, must examine "some particular culture, society, or region of the non-Western world, or . . . systematically [make] comparisons across cultural barriers," according to the catalogue.

The freshman seminars themselves arose in the early 1990s as a replacement for what had been a rather traditional humanities core. "I think it may have been [replaced] because it was difficult to combine a focus on classical Western texts with a small class size, given the number of people available to teach it," a professor says. The school's split emphasis on the liberal arts and the research model of a university ultimately caught up with the humanities, professors say, so, while classical humanities themes are still represented, they do not predominate.

Besides the humanities seminar, each Brandeis student must complete the "Cluster Program," which is basically a well-structured distribution requirement. Students must select two clusters from two different areas of the university (creative arts, humanities, science, and social science). Each of the nearly forty multi-departmental clusters includes five to sixteen courses; students choose three. The experience is supposed to let students "share an intellectual excitement when courses connect and are related to each other," the catalogue says. Some themes are along the lines of the more politicized freshman seminars — recent examples include "Ethnicity, Race, and Culture," "Sexuality and Society," and "Colonialism and Neo-Colonialism in the Third World" — but others deal with various historical periods, philosophical questions, and scientific fields.

Brandeis also requires a quantitative reasoning course, three semesters of a foreign language, and two semesters of physical education. "This sounds like a lot of requirements," one faculty member says, "but we allow and encourage all kinds of double-dipping" — and there are certainly weaker general education requirements at other colleges. With the cluster and seminar concept, Brandeis has at least tried to preserve the linking of disciplines essential to genuine liberal education, though more than a few options are politicized.

Brandeis's founding at the end of World War II — a vastly important time for Western Judaism and the West in general — seems to have left a legacy of intellectual urgency at the institution and to have led the university toward "progressive" agendas, even as it maintains serious and rigorous academics.

Superficially, this tendency is apparent in the selection of visiting faculty. In the past couple of years, Brandeis has appointed former secretary of labor Robert Reich as a "university professor," only the fourth person so designated in the school's existence. ("They're using him as a fundraising prop," a current student says.) *Ms.* magazine founder Gloria Steinem has taught in the women's studies department, and former Texas governor Ann Richards teaches a course entitled "The Political Experience," which, typically, focuses on females in politics and multicultural issues. "I've heard very poor things," one student says of Richards's course.

At the same time, Brandeis is home to many scholars whose work is very highly regarded, both in academic circles and in mainstream society. In English, Eugene Goodheart, long associated with the *Partisan Review,* has "for decades now been a major national figure, a wide-ranging literary intellectual," as notes one of his colleagues. American studies associate professor Jacob Cohen has written widely on the "idea of conspiracy," particularly as it applies in recent contexts such as the Kennedy assassination. David Hackett Fischer, a history professor, is the author of the landmark work *Albion's Seed,* "a compelling perspective on Colonial America that explains the country's current regional differences," in the words of a university publication. That office also notes the bidding war over Fischer's latest work, *Paul Revere's Ride;* film rights were won ultimately by Paramount Pictures.

Other excellent professors include Anthony Polonsky in Near Eastern and Judaic studies, George W. Ross in sociology, and Stephen J. Whitfield in American studies.

The university's flagship program is the Philip W. Lown School of Near Eastern and Judaic Studies, which a professor from another department says "brings a lot of international savvy to the curriculum." The department covers both Jewish and Arab culture and contains various emphases on history, language, and literature, with attention as well to how Near Eastern and Jewish issues work themselves out in the United States. There are specialists in Akkadian and Hebrew language as well as courses in "Images of Jews on Film" and "The Woman's Voice in the Muslim World." Courses in the Talmud and Jewish law are also offered.

Other strong departments include politics, women's studies, economics, and history. Sciences, especially biochemistry, biology, chemistry, and physics, are outstanding, and the performing arts are considered strong. Faculty say most departments, regardless of political biases, are demanding.

The interdisciplinary premed program (not an official major but a program recommended for students hoping for medical school) is very good. Graduates' acceptance rate at medical schools is 50 percent above the national average, according to the university. Premedical studies at Brandeis are famously difficult: according to a student, "Quite a few [professors who teach premed courses] are on probation for failing too many students."

The department of economics emphasizes the free-market point of view to the point that two other departments — sociology and peace and conflict studies — have bashed it, a student says.

Those two departments, it turns out, are the ones most frequently called overly politicized by other faculty. The peace and conflict studies program has a "completely wrong philosophy," one student says, noting the department's assumption that "wars will cease to exist" and professors' subsequent refusal to "spend time [even] discussing whether war is inevitable."

The politics department occasionally strays into ideological waters, but most professors in the department will work around their personal convictions to study well the issue at hand, a student says. The English department, on the other hand, is rather trendy, offering courses like "Introduction to Gender Studies: Making Sex, Performing Gender," which announces that "gender and sexual identities are neither biologically innate nor psychologically essential." There is also a lower-level course called "Directed Studies in Current Literature," whose description asserts that "we will read books that alter one's perception towards generosity, gratitude, and perception." The course is taught by a visiting poet widely known for her lesbian activism.

However, for every "AIDS, Activism, and Representation" course in the English catalogue, there is an "Advanced Shakespeare" or "Reason and Ridicule: The Literature of Britain in the Enlightenment." The example of English seems typical of the university as well: most faculty and staff do not see politicized classes as a particular problem, although certain classes are obviously constructed on an ideological frame.

Political Atmosphere: Cast No Shadow

Though Brandeis was founded as a secular institution — "emphatically secular," one professor stresses — the student body remains one-half to two-thirds Jewish (depending on who's counting), and issues related to Judaism are at the forefront of campus discussion. "Predictably, Israeli politics are prominent, but there's never any kind of heat," one professor says.

However, the university has of late de-emphasized its Jewish roots in the interests of attracting a more diverse student body, some say. Ten years ago came the controversial introduction of pork and shellfish into campus dining halls, and about the same time the university, while not holding classes on Jewish holidays, stopped printing the names of those holidays on official campus calendars. (The university still has a kosher dining hall, it should be noted.)

On campus, many branches of Judaism are represented, from Orthodox to Reformed. Nevertheless, the heart of the university is ecumenical if not nonobservant, and this is portrayed nowhere more graphically than in the three campus chapels — Jewish, Catholic, and Protestant — designed by the famous architect Eero Saarinen. The chapels were intended to resemble the holy scriptures of each religion — the scrolls of the Jewish chapel call to mind the Torah; the shape of the Catholic and Protestant chapels resembles a Bible. However, as the viewbook says, "none of the three ever casts its shadow on either of the others, thus symbolizing the religious freedom and tolerance so valued by the university."

In addition to a diversity of religions, Brandeis has a diversity of races among its students, and the curriculum and university resources to cater to them all. "We have quite a few African-American students and broad foreign representation," one professor says, noting the campus's Intercultural Center. The same professor says the university is also concerned with the representation on the faculty of women and minorities. "We have an administrative officer [designated] for seeing we don't overlook any opportunity to enhance our diversity," the professor says. "We're not satisfied with what we've accomplished." However, such politics rarely play a role in tenure decisions, where both teaching and research are considered essential. Another faculty member says the university is definitely not under the sway of "identity politics." "I've never known of any racial incidents," this teacher says. "Brandeis is more peaceful than Berkeley or Yale."

Trouble has erupted recently at school functions, however. One student says violent incidents often occur at dances sponsored by the Brandeis African-American Student Association. "This year there was a knife fight," the student says. There are "security guards with metal detectors at every dance now. You have to line up outside whether it's cold or not and go through the metal detectors."

The university's recruiting materials feature a number of multicultural touches. One student says she came to Brandeis "less because of Judaism and more because of community and activism." Another student was worried that Brandeis would "be much less diverse" than the first school she attended, but adds that she was pleasantly surprised. The viewbook also lists the multicultural holidays celebrated on campus; the list does not include any Jewish holidays, and, truth be told, the "multicultural" events are mostly related to one minority group at a time. The university also has a speech code, and all freshmen must attend a sensitivity class given by the Anti-Defamation League.

Student Life: Louis, Louis

Brandeis students enjoy the benefits of life in Boston. Trips into the city and to Cambridge are easily accomplished with the university's free shuttle bus. The suburban location, however, is also conducive to study, and students are said to apply themselves seriously to their academic work.

On campus, two not-too-serious annual events are "not to be missed," according to the viewbook. "Louis, Louis," the name of which is apparently a rather irreverent play on the university's namesake, and similar to the title of the world's most popular party song ("Louie Louie"), comes the week before fall semester final exams. Its spring semester counterpart is "Bronstein" weekend. Both include, the viewbook says, "dances, parties, special events (including the Bronstein carnival and fireworks display), and a big-name concert." Past performers have included The Beach Boys, the Steve Miller Band, Indigo Girls, Jerry Seinfeld, Alanis Morrisette, Beck, and 10,000 Maniacs.

About 85 percent of the student body lives on campus. Besides standard dorms, there is a changing list of special-interest houses. In the past these houses have had themes such as international awareness, religious diversity, health issues, environmental awareness, music, and Jewish awareness.

The university has a variety of student organizations, including groups for the performing arts, community service, academic subjects, and students of a particular ethnic background. Students operate a twenty-four-hour radio station, WBRS. In addition to Jewish groups, other religious organizations include the Catholic Student Organization, Christian Fellowship, and the Muslim Student Association.

Among the political student groups, most are liberal rather than conservative. These include an animal rights group, a homosexual support group, Students for Environmental Action, the American Civil Liberties Union, and Amnesty International. Conservative students, such as those in the College Republicans or a group called simply the "Conservative Organization," report some discrimination directed their way. A poster for the Young America's Foundation was torn down less than thirty-six hours after being put up. A student says that during orientation, students play an icebreaker sort of game in which they identify themselves according to various characteristics, such as hair color and home state. Only the ones who identified themselves as Republicans "got booed," according to the student.

Campus publications include a conservative magazine called the *Brandeisian,* which was "somewhat controversial a couple of years ago," but more recently seems to have dropped direct political engagement for a more "pro-Brandeis," general-interest stance, a student says. The magazine has recently struggled to get its issues together, and there is some doubt as to its future. A newer conservative magazine, *Freedom,* has yet to receive funding from the university beyond "$93 from the allocations board of the Student Senate," says another student. In any case, neither publication is about to replace the main student publication, the *Justice.* There is also a liberal magazine called the *Watch.*

Despite the dominance of the political left, there is not, according to a professor, "much extremism" on campus. This professor and others credit this to the students' work ethic and the rigor of the academic program. Some still remember, however, the 1960s, when the administration building was taken over by radical students. Angela Davis, famous not only at Brandeis (her alma mater) but nationally as a Communist activist and candidate for vice president, returned to speak on campus in 1995. Editors of the *Brandeisian* posted information on Davis's background, only to have it torn down. While her speech went on as scheduled, one year earlier former U.S. ambassador to the United Nations Jeane Kirkpatrick turned down an award to be presented at the university's commencement after a small group of students protested.

For those who prefer athletics, the university has one of the largest multipurpose indoor recreation facilities in the region. The Ford Athletic and Recreation Complex includes a 70,000-square-foot field house known as the Gosman Sports and Convocation Center, which includes Red Auerbach Arena. (Fittingly, the Boston Celtics hold practices there.) The complex includes a 200-meter track, field event venues, tennis and squash courts, a volleyball court, batting cages, a fencing room, swimming and diving pools, and a variety of workout facilities. Varsity athletes compete at the NCAA Division III level in ten men's sports and ten women's sports. There are also eighteen club sports, including some rare ones like kokondo, Korean karate, Frisbee, and tae kwon do.

BROWN UNIVERSITY

Admissions Office
Brown University
Box 1876
Providence, RI 02912
(401) 863-2378
www.brown.edu

Total enrollment: 7,579
Undergraduates: 5,960
SAT Ranges (Verbal/Math): V 640-740, M 640-740
Financial aid: 38%
Applicants: 15,010
Accepted: 19%
Enrolled: 53%
Application deadline: Jan. 1
Financial aid application deadline: Jan. 20
Tuition: $23,616
Core curriculum: No

A Muddier Shade of Brown

Brown University, located in the manufacturing city of Providence, Rhode Island, is New England's third-oldest university. Founded in 1764, Brown is a member of the prestigious Ivy League, and as such, its reputation as one of the country's top universities seems secure. Brown is considered one of the least-stuffy Ivies, but also possesses one of the most liberal student bodies in the group. Its administration, on the other hand, is less dominated by the ideology of radical multiculturalism than its counterparts.

That said, Brown does little to encourage, much less guarantee, a traditional liberal arts education for its students. In fact, it has absolutely no required classes except for those taken to fulfill a major. Students are free to pick and choose the remaining classes. Moreover, they can choose the manner in which they will be graded — including the option of receiving only pass/fail grades for their entire college careers. Of course, this freedom to experiment is popular among the teenagers who arrive at Brown, but years down the road, those who have taken the paths of least resistance may find themselves wondering at the opportunities they may have missed.

The university says its mission is best summed up in the words of Henry

Merritt Wriston, Brown's president from 1937 to 1955. "The central business of the university is the increase of knowledge, the inculcation of wisdom, the refinement of emotional responses, and the development of spiritual awareness," Wriston said. The modern-day Brown has placed its own notion of freedom above all these noble pursuits; in so doing, it has compromised its educational mission.

Academic Life: Babes in Toyland

The distinguishing feature of Brown's core requirements is that there are none. Nor are there distribution requirements or general education requirements. The only required courses are those demanded by a student's major.

"A lot of people come here because of the freedom they have in choosing their classes," says one student. "Generally, people don't abuse it too much. But if you're not interested in a subject, you just don't take classes in it." The lack of requirements means that students so inclined could graduate with absolutely no education in the sciences, literature, foreign languages, or any of the other liberal arts.

Brown estimates that around 80 percent of students do take a wide array of classes, though the absence of requirements would seem to make that number or one higher a foregone conclusion. Students who have the self-discipline to take a broad range of classes — or to follow the counsel of their academic advisers — will have the most rewarding educational experience at the university, according to people on campus.

The normal courseload at Brown is four courses a semester for eight semesters. Only thirty courses are required for a degree, however, in order to "encourage risk-taking in the planning of educational programs" and to "provide a degree of flexibility" to students, according to the university catalogue. Students cannot take fewer than three courses in one semester without the permission of the dean.

With their general education requirements dispensed with upon enrollment, students must concern themselves only with completing the coursework in their concentrations. Most students stick to standard departmental concentrations, which typically require between eight and ten courses, but some devise their own concentrations (in consultation with advisers). Students must declare their concentrations by the end of their sophomore year.

Just as laid-back as the general education requirements are Brown's easy attendance and grading policies, which are also student favorites. Attendance and participation in classes are merely "encouraged." However, the catalogue states that because a student "benefits also from exercising discretion and assuming responsibility for his or her own educational progress, [they] . . . are not limited with respect to the number of absences from a course." Professors may make attendance a part of the class requirements, or, if a student abuses the privilege, may notify the dean.

As for grading, here, too, students have many options. They may take courses for letter grades: A, B, C, and "No credit." There are no D's or F's. Any grade below a C simply disappears on the way to the registrar's office — the university doesn't place any sort of notation on the student's transcript to indicate that the student even took the course. Sheila Blumstein, Brown's dean, explained the thinking behind that policy this way: "When you send in your resume, do you put down all the jobs you applied for that you didn't get?" In addition, students can elect to take all their classes pass/fail — or, in Brown's lingo, "Satisfactory/No credit." Or they can request that their instructors provide detailed, written assessments of their work in addition to their regular grades.

One recent Brown alumnus said he thought Brown's grading policy was great when he applied and first started taking classes. But after considering his future, he thought otherwise. "If you're going to go to grad school, you need grades. If you're going to get a job, you need grades," he explains. "That reality really diminishes the effect of what they're trying to accomplish."

Graduation requirements aside, Brown has some excellent and rigorous departments. The history department is considered very good. It offers a wide range of courses, from the histories of classical Greek and Roman civilizations to those of Europe, Asia, and America. Some address a particular country, others focus on a certain time or region.

The neuroscience department (part of the biology and medicine department) is also highly regarded. The department has excellent facilities for research, which is encouraged. The overall concentration of biology and medicine, which is divided into several subgroups, is also strong.

Brown's economics department offers a traditional program and has largely resisted the ideological impulses popular on other campuses. Undergraduate courses emphasize theoretical and empirical economic analyses of specific economic problems and the effect of governmental actions on the economy. "It's really a very balanced, fair department," says a student.

Geology and computer science are also noted as quality departments at Brown.

In addition to its strongest programs, Brown is home to some rare departments. The university boasts the world's only academic department in the history of mathematics, although it has just one professor. It also has North America's only Egyptology department, which has three professors. Brown's Center for Old World Archaeology and Art is an independent academic unit that encompasses a variety of disciplines. The goal of the concentration is to give students a strong background in art and archaeology, supplemented with a series of lectures and special publications. Since 1965 the department has sponsored field activities in southern Italy.

The Brown University Library is one of the largest in New England. It contains more than 2.8 million volumes and comprises five campus library buildings, the principal one being the John D. Rockefeller Jr. Library (known as "The Rock"). The university is also home to the John Carter Brown Library, a separately administered library that houses a large and excellent collection of forty thousand books and pamphlets detailing the growth of European colonies in the New World.

Politicized departments are common at Brown, as at most Ivy League schools. Not only is political science considered highly ideological in its outlook, but it is also "lacking in terms of professor quality," says a student. "They aren't the best professors compared to other departments."

The comparative literature department — working in a highly politicized field — is much taken with deconstructionism, a literary theory that holds that literary works have no fixed meaning. Instead, texts are routinely scanned for meanings to ethnic minority groups and females. Some courses are simply bizarre. Take, for example, "Vampirism." Says the course description: "From colonization to cross-dressing and from the fear of the 'new woman' to AIDS, vampirism maps, reshapes, and recycles the traumas of 20th century European history. As a focalizing point for discourses of imperialism, gender, race, and psychoanalysis, vampirism provides the building blocks for theories of border-crossings and transgression, ghosts and mourning, and new media."

Brown's department of modern culture and media offers quite a few classes with themes like imperialism, class, and exploitation. For example, a course called "(Most of) Marx's *Capital*" consists of a "rigorous and systemic reading" of that work; "the focus," the course description says, "will be intensively upon Marx's text." Other course titles in this communications department: "The British Imperial Novel," "Feminism and Poststructuralism," and one called simply "Disney."

The women's studies department offers not only feminist courses, but some with antireligious themes. An example of the latter is "Christianity, Violence and Victimization." The course description states: "While Christianity may be said to provide a remedy for evil, sin and suffering, contemporary critics, including feminist ones, argue the opposite: that Christianity has helped to create and perpetuate a culture of violence, especially against women and other dispossessed persons." Much of the women's studies curriculum is cross-referenced in other departments such as American civilization, Judaic studies, and sociology.

Political Atmosphere: New Faces, Old Problems

Brown's administration has lost eight out of its eleven senior members in the last three years. Most cited burnout as their reason for leaving. To fill their spots, lower-level administrators have been promoted and others have been brought in from the outside.

The restaffing starts at the top of the university. Vartan Gregorian, Brown's longtime, well-known president, stepped down in early 1997 to head the Carnegie Foundation. He was replaced by Gordon Gee, who most recently was the president of Ohio State University. Gee holds a bachelor's degree in history from the University of Utah and a law degree and doctorate in education from Columbia University, and has served as a law professor, law dean, and president of West Virginia University and the University of Colorado.

Recently, Brown also lost its provost, chancellor, and several vice presidents and deans. As a result, Gee is working with a fairly new team of administrators, and has been rather successful at introducing innovative solutions to problems on campus. In an address opening his first academic year in office, Gee called on students to respect the dignity of others and the variety of ideas, and to "risk asking questions. Risk putting your ideas before a group. Risk laughter. . . . Brown expects you to be engaged in your education, to abhor complacency and strive for quality in all things."

Many of the issues confronting the new president have to do with controversies that predate his term. In the early 1990s, for example, Brown fought a suit brought against it by several of its female athletes. The university, citing financial pressures, had cut four athletic teams — women's gymnastics, women's volleyball, men's golf, and men's water polo. Some members of women's teams sued, claiming that Brown discriminated against women and did not provide equal funding for men's and women's sports as required by the federal law known as Title IX. According to the suit, Brown's student body was more than 50 percent female, but only about 40 percent of its females participated in athletics. The university lost the initial decision in the case and appealed, to no avail; its options were exhausted in 1997 when the Supreme Court of the United States refused to hear the case. The appeals had cost far more than reinstating the teams would have, but the case was closely watched by universities around the country.

Brown has also grappled with the issue of sexual misconduct on campus. Several high-profile cases have raised questions about the role of Brown's student judicial boards and their adjudication of date rape cases. The most notorious case in recent memory was that of a student named Adam Lack, who faced such a charge in the fall of 1996. Lack had been at a party with a female student, and both had been drinking. The two went back to a dorm room, and the female suggested they have sex and initiated a sexual encounter. A few days later she charged that Lack had raped her, although she acknowledged suggesting that they have sex. She said Lack should have known she was drunk and declined her suggestion. The Brown student judicial board punished Lack, and his case was publicly debated on campus and in newspaper editorial pages.

More recently, in the spring of 1997, allegations surfaced that Brown had not adequately responded to accusations of sexual assault. At the urging of a professor who has done research in the country of Jordan, the university chose not to prosecute a member of that country's royal family accused of rape. It was the first time in eight years that the panel had refused to hear a rape complaint. This led to more charges that Lack, whose family raises hogs in Iowa, was treated unfairly. Also, four female students filed suit against Brown after they said they were sexually assaulted by a chemistry professor. Although Brown had received similar complaints against the professor, the pending suit alleges that the university did not fire him previously because he was black and the university needed to retain as many minority professors as it could. The professor was eventually dismissed when more women leveled similar charges.

The university's behavior code has also been at issue recently. Brown's "Tenets of Community Behavior" prohibit actions that "show flagrant disrespect for the well-being of others" or are "unreasonably disruptive of the university community." Several campus groups, including the Brown ACLU and the Brown College Republicans, have claimed the rules constitute an overly vague threat to free speech. They point to several incidents in the last few years when students have been disciplined — some expelled and some suspended for up to four years — for speech violations. Physical assaults, they say, sometimes carry lesser penalties. Students voted against the code by a nearly three-to-one margin in 1995, and a university committee that same year also recommended changes in the code — yet nothing has been altered.

To its credit, Brown and its new president have at least attempted to address issues such as these. While it may be too early to evaluate such efforts, the need to bring common sense and consistent ethical principles to bear on these issues is urgent.

The university also faces financial pressures, though many colleges and universities would gladly exchange bankbooks with Brown. The good news is that Brown has an endowment of $789 million; the bad news: that's the lowest in the Ivy League by at least $210 million. Students say that in comparison to other Ivies, the smaller endowment is holding Brown back. "They're reluctant to spend money on things," one student complains. Faculty salaries are lower than at other Ivy League colleges, and some professors have left for higher pay at more prestigious institutions. In addition, while many other colleges are "need-blind" in their admissions policies (meaning they accept or decline applications without regard to an applicant's ability to pay), Brown still considers personal finances for 5 percent of its students.

Student Life: Not Quite Divine Providence

The vast majority of Brown's students live on campus in a dormitory, fraternity or sorority, or special-interest theme house. About 10 percent of students are involved in the Greek system, which holds frequent weekend parties on campus and provides students with social bonds they wouldn't otherwise have. Most students say they are satisfied with the social environment at Brown.

In their freshman and sophomore years, students tend to stay on campus for social activities. There are always movies showing on campus, and students frequently hold parties at fraternities or in somebody's dorm room. "It was never hard getting beer before I was twenty-one," says one senior. (It should be pointed out that a Brown student group and the university's Center for Alcohol and Addiction Studies have both produced nationally recognized abuse prevention programs.) Another popular alternative is going to sporting events. Hockey games on Friday or Saturday nights during the season are always packed to the rafters, and basketball and football games are less popular but still attract fans.

Other students make the forty-five-minute trip to Boston (by bus or train) to take advantage of that city's shopping, professional sports, or other social events.

As students enter their junior or senior years, they typically look off campus for social options. Although Providence is not exactly a college town, it is also home to Providence College, a campus of the University of Rhode Island, Rhode Island College, Johnson and Wales University, and the Rhode Island School of Design, and it does have many amenities that make it attractive to college students: several good restaurants downtown (especially some Italian ones), coffee shops, bars, and clubs. The east side of town, where Brown is located, is the historic area. There are no structures still standing from 1636 (the year Roger Williams founded the city and named it Providence because he thought God guided him there), but some houses in the area are more than two hundred years old.

Although most students at Brown are politically liberal, conservative students can be found in some organizations. The College Republicans, for instance, have been very active lately and have had limited success pushing for an end to Brown's behavior code.

However, debate on campus is also controlled by political liberals, students say. "I always feel like there's a regular, vocal group of people who are much more liberal than everyone else is," says a student. The voices that seem to carry further on campus include those of feminists, who have ample resources at their disposal, including the Sarah Doyle Women's Center and the women's studies department. Also, a very sizable chapter of the International Socialist Organization holds many rallies and protests supporting Brown food service workers and other causes. Of course, many other student groups are devoted to social, academic, and athletic concerns.

The *Brown Daily Herald,* the university's daily newspaper, leans leftward but makes a genuine effort to include many perspectives on its editorial pages. During the debate on Brown's sexual harassment policy and the Lack case, the paper printed columns both attacking and defending the current policy. There is no conservative alternative paper at Brown.

Many students practice community service while enrolled at Brown. The university estimates that 25 percent undertake some sort of sustained community service project. Volunteering is coordinated by the campus's Center for Public Service, which makes opportunities known to Brown students and faculty. Each year the center awards more than $350,000 in fellowships and grants to assist with community service projects.

BRYN MAWR COLLEGE

Office of Admissions, Suite A
Bryn Mawr College
101 N. Merion Avenue
Bryn Mawr, PA 19010-2899
(610) 526-5153
www.brynmawr.edu

Total enrollment: 1,890
Undergraduates: 1,205
SAT Ranges (Verbal/Math): V 610-710, M 590-660
Financial aid: 55%
Applicants: 1,620
Accepted: 57%
Enrolled: 38%
Application deadline: Jan. 15
Financial aid application deadline: Jan. 15
Tuition: $21,020
Core curriculum: Yes

Several for the Price of One

Bryn Mawr College was founded in 1885 by Dr. Joseph Taylor, a Quaker physician who sought to found a college dedicated to the education of Quaker women. At that time an education in Greek, mathematics, philosophy, and several other fields was open only to men. The college was the first women's school to offer graduate instruction, and today it is still the only predominantly women's college with an extensive selection of graduate programs.

Although the college is no longer affiliated with the Society of Friends, it remains single-sex. However, Bryn Mawr's graduate programs are open to men, and, because many of its 1,200 undergraduates take courses at nearby Haverford College, some Bryn Mawr dorms are made coeducational by male students from Haverford. Bryn Mawr students can also take advantage of other colleges and universities in the Philadelphia area: they may enroll in classes at Swarthmore College, Villanova University, and the University of Pennsylvania, all at no additional charge.

Bryn Mawr is best known for its humanities departments, but the most popular majors are in the sciences. Ironically, those looking for a traditional education will be more likely to find it in the scientific fields; feminist theory has taken over some humanities departments, according to some at Bryn Mawr. Still, students' work in most departments is intense enough that the campus is often eerily quiet during the day, when students are in class or at the library.

Academic Life: Additional Work

Bryn Mawr's curriculum is structured to give students a broad, general education in their first two years. Specialization in one's major comes only in the junior and senior years. A bachelor's degree requires thirty-two courses, a quarter of which come in the college's distribution requirements: two courses in the social sciences and three in both the natural sciences and the humanities. Bryn Mawr requires two semesters of English composition, one semester of math, and two years of a foreign language — all of which can be bypassed with good test scores. Students must also complete eight half-semester units in physical education and pass a swimming test.

Bryn Mawr also asks students to complete "additional work" — either two advanced language courses, courses in a second foreign language, or two courses in math — outside of the distribution requirements. The college recently considered dropping the additional work requirement, but so far has not done so. Some students feel that the electives they could take if unburdened of this requirement would be more beneficial than the "additional work" courses, but others think such a step would weaken the curriculum. "You don't want to lose out on being a well-rounded student," one student says.

About one-third of the students major in math or science — a high figure compared to the number of women in those fields at other schools. Many students take science courses at Haverford, only a twenty-minute walk or one-mile bus ride away. This high number of science students is not consistent with Bryn Mawr's reputation as a powerhouse in the humanities, but, with the cross-registration possibilities at other local colleges and universities, that reputation has begun to change.

The college does have a strong record in the humanities as far as graduate academic achievement is concerned. Bryn Mawr ranks first in the nation in the percentage of its graduates to earn Ph.D.s in the humanities, and ranks third in all fields.

Bryn Mawr offers several study-abroad opportunities, both during the summer and during the regular academic year. There are college-sponsored summer programs in Avignon, France; Madrid; Florence; and Moscow, all of them requiring language proficiency. During the year students may, with the permission of their major departments and dean, take courses abroad through other universities. The majority of students who study abroad do so during their junior year.

In cooperation with the University of Pennsylvania, Bryn Mawr offers two joint-degree programs in which students take classes for five years and graduate with a double major. One is in engineering and applied science, the other in city and regional planning. Another rare program, offered exclusively by Bryn Mawr, is an interdisciplinary major in the growth and structure of cities. Students take courses in a wide variety of fields to learn about "the relationship of urban spatial organization and the built environment to politics, economics, cultures, and societies," according to the college catalogue.

One of the strongest programs at Bryn Mawr is the history of art department. This department boasts a number of outstanding professors and concentrates on Western art, students say. There are courses in the history of architecture, Western art historiography, and European painting and sculpture, and students are encouraged to spend a semester abroad to see firsthand the art they have studied in class.

Another excellent department is classical and Near Eastern archaeology, said to be one of the best in the country. Archaeology majors take courses in several different fields relating to their specialty. Students are encouraged to participate in field projects in North America and overseas, and the department helps find places for them in archaeological digs. Occasionally the department will carry out its own field projects, and undergraduates are invited to participate. Recent excavations have taken place in central Siberia, Greece, and Turkey. Two excellent professors in this department are Richard Ellis and Bryn Mawr alumna Stella Miller-Collett.

The college recently built a $12.9 million addition to its main library that provides space for the archaeology, history of art, and Growth and Structure of Cities departments and their collections.

A few departments have become politicized, at least in part. One of these is English, which, despite offering a number of courses in the foundations of literature, is home to several courses with political themes. For example, "Marginality and Transgression in Victorian Literature" focuses on "poverty, sexuality, revolution, criminality," as well as "the semiotics of transgression [and] the discourses of sexuality." (Victorian sexuality is also covered in a history course, "Topics in European Women's and Gender History," which recently devoted an entire semester to "the regulation of sexuality in Victorian Britain.") The English department also teaches courses with a feminist orientation, like " 'Womanspirit Rising': American Women Writers on Spiritual Quest." This course explores the spiritual lives of American women "with an emphasis on those who critically appropriated the religious beliefs available to them, or who challenged their exclusion from traditional religious practice." Another English course, "Lesbian and Gay Literature," is described in the catalogue as "an introduction to and rich sampling of the varieties of literary production by uncloseted, hence unfurtive, lesbian and gay writers in the U.S., the United Kingdom, and Canada, since 1969."

Another program, feminist and gender studies, does not offer a major — only a six-course "concentration." Most courses are taught by other departments (including some at Haverford). One course that can count toward the concentration is a Bryn Mawr Spanish department offering called "Gay Cinema and the Cultural Transformation in Contemporary Spanish and Spanish American Film." The course examines "the central role gay culture and more specifically gay film played in imagining and representing the cultural transformations in contemporary Spain," according to the catalogue.

Political Atmosphere: One of Those Stereotypes

Bryn Mawr recently installed a new president, Nancy J. Vickers, who took office in July 1997. Several months into her presidency, she has not made any major changes, although she intends to lead the college on an eighteen-month-long self-study and define four or five principal priorities. Although it is still too early to judge her leadership of Bryn Mawr, her track record at other schools indicates that she's probably a good fit with the college's political atmosphere.

An expert in French and Italian literature who edited a scholarly book called *Rewriting the Renaissance: The Discourses of Sexual Differences in Early Modern Europe,* Vickers spearheaded a curriculum revision at the University of Southern California (USC). Commenting recently to a Bryn Mawr publication, she described the experience as "a struggle about the nature of disciplinary and interdisciplinary — the residual pull of traditional instruction in a department or area and a sense that it needs to move somewhat beyond that."

As dean of curriculum and instruction at USC, Vickers indeed moved education "somewhat beyond" tradition and implemented new general education requirements that forced all students to take a course on diversity to help them understand people of different "age, disability, ethnicity, gender, language, race, religion, sexual orientation and social class." One course that fulfilled the requirement was called "Women's Spaces in History: Hussies, Harems, and Housewives." This politicized curriculum was a result of "some pretty committed insistence upon certain core liberal arts values that in the end we had to get behind and fight for," Vickers said in a recent interview.

Administrators insist that the college's "diversity" encompasses all voices. But it seems that there are few traditional voices left at Bryn Mawr.

The most vocal student groups include lesbian and feminist organizations, and students say these groups receive broad support and encouragement from fellow students and administrators. The most prominent group is the Rainbow Alliance, an organization of homosexual students. "Not everyone is out [of the closet] here," a Rainbow Alliance leader told a campus publication. "But it is generally easier here since the community is very comfortable and supportive." Another group leader says one of the "most important things we do" is help students come out to their parents. "The organization has all sorts of other purposes: educational, helping people with coming out issues, safe sex issues, and social issues," this student says.

Bryn Mawr also has a socialist organization whose members hang lots of posters and prod people with questions every Sunday night as they walk to dining halls. "Nobody really likes them because they're so militant," says one student. Typical issues for the socialists include labor union advocacy and opposition to the death penalty.

Some students claim that the prominence of these radical groups feeds a stereotype that has little to do with reality. "People from other schools think that I'm this militant lesbian feminist, that I'm aggressive and mean," one student says. "It's just one of those stereotypes."

Student Life: West of West Philadelphia

Bryn Mawr is only eleven miles west of Philadelphia, but the campus will make anyone forget city squalor. The 135-acre plot is full of trees and gardens, and most buildings are built of graystone in the Collegiate Gothic style. According to the college, "architects have described [the campus] as looking like a medieval English village built around an 18th-century town green." Add to that a campus food service recently named the best in the country, and it isn't hard to see that life at Bryn Mawr can be quite comfortable.

The town of Bryn Mawr, with a population of about nine thousand, is a five-minute walk from campus. Although it contains a small variety of stores and restaurants, most social life takes place on campus. Just about all students live on campus in a set of eleven dorms, two of which are coed (housing Haverford men as well as Bryn Mawr women). One dorm is set aside as a "multicultural residence for students interested in foreign languages and cultures or in the Black Cultural Center," according to the college viewbook.

But, because the academic life at the college is so intense, some students say the social life suffers. "We're not a party school," says one student. "It's not like a state school would have. Students are more concerned about their grades than their social life." A professor in the humanities agrees. "Bryn Mawr's academic environment is a serious and challenging one," she says. "Students work very hard. I suspect that students who are not really interested in their studies are in general not drawn to Bryn Mawr in the first place." The college provides learning opportunities through a wide selection of visiting speakers and performers.

College traditions remain strong at Bryn Mawr. "That's one of the things that really brings us together," says a student. For example, there's "Lantern Night," which hearkens back to a time when no buses connected the Bryn Mawr and Haverford campuses and students would walk between the institutions by the light of a lantern. On Lantern Night, each Bryn Mawr class dresses in a different color, carries lanterns, and sings songs; a big crowd always gathers to watch. The college also celebrates May Day, on which all students wear white dresses, perform medieval dances, and participate in activities such as archery contests. Administrators dress up, too.

Student groups also hold teas, which don't always involve actual tea, but are usually get-togethers with a theme. For instance, one organization recently sponsored a Kevin Bacon tea. Anyone who showed up was treated to a Kevin Bacon movie, free food, and a discussion of the actor. Sometimes, depending on the theme, students will dress up.

Despite its small size, Bryn Mawr does have a lot of student groups, including a variety of sports clubs, political organizations, and cultural groups. Many of the clubs include students from Haverford or Swarthmore. These are known as "bi-co" (bi-college, meaning Bryn Mawr and Haverford) and "tri-co" (tri-college, meaning Bryn Mawr, Haverford, and Swarthmore). Campus political groups are mostly liberal: there are the College Democrats, a "reproductive freedom" organization, and an environmental organization, as well as feminist and homosexual organizations. The College Republican group is currently dormant.

Several religious organizations exist on campus, including a Catholic Campus Ministries group, a gospel choir, a Jewish group, InterVarsity Christian Fellowship, several Protestant groups, and a Unitarian Universalist group. However, students must actively seek religion on campus because its presence is not readily apparent. "If you didn't go out looking for it, you wouldn't be able to find it," a student says.

Bryn Mawr fields varsity teams in basketball, cross-country, field hockey, lacrosse, soccer, swimming, tennis, volleyball, and badminton, which won a national title in 1995. Club teams include diving, fencing, ice hockey, rugby, sailing, squash, and track.

UNIVERSITY OF CALIFORNIA AT BERKELEY

Director of Admissions and Records
University of California at Berkeley
120 Sproul Hall
Berkeley, CA 94720
(510) 642-3175
www.berkeley.edu

Total enrollment: 29,630
Undergraduates: 21,358
SAT Ranges (Verbal/Math): V 490-640, M 610-730

Financial aid: 61%
Applicants: 27,150
Accepted: 31%
Enrolled: 42%
Application deadline: Nov. 30
Financial aid application deadline: Mar. 2
Tuition: $3,956 resident; $12,940 nonresident
Core curriculum: No

The Beginning and the End

The University of California at Berkeley began as a strong liberal arts school, rooted in a broad and humane understanding of the Western tradition. In 1855 the College of California had a curriculum based on Greek, Latin, English literature, history, mathematics, and natural science. This curriculum was maintained as the institution grew, and when the University of California was created in 1868, the school still had a strong liberal arts orientation.

But today, when Americans think of UC-Berkeley they immediately associate it with the radical movements of the 1960s. Affirmative action pilot programs started here, as did the campus free speech movement. Protesters on other campuses over the years have drawn inspiration from the actions of their fellows in Berkeley. One clear sign that UC-Berkeley has become a byword for campus radicalism is that even mainstream media commentators feel free to snicker at some of the more bizarre, politicized courses the university offers.

But even if imitation is the sincerest form of flattery, and even if that imitation has been largely harmful to traditional education, the fact remains that UC-Berkeley is one of the most prestigious universities in the world. Some even say it may be the best university in the world. At the very least, UC-Berkeley offers an exciting atmosphere and many excellent teachers and departments. It has sent more graduates on to earn their Ph.D.s than any other university in America. And even though the school is once again admitting students only on the basis of academic merit, it must turn down several thousand eminently qualified applicants every year. It may be a challenge for a student looking for a true liberal arts education to find birds of his own feather there, but the place is large enough that he can likely find most anything — a superior education and an unforgettable experience included.

Academic Life: Top of the Pops

The largest of UC-Berkeley's fourteen schools and colleges is the College of Letters and Science (L&S). This college contains more than sixty departmental majors in the fields of biological sciences, physical sciences, social sciences, and humanities. Almost 75 percent of UC-Berkeley undergraduates enroll in this college, which is also home to more than half of the university's faculty.

Like all other undergraduates at UC-Berkeley, L&S students must fulfill a very basic set of requirements. The first of these is called "Subject A," which is essentially a literacy requirement met by high school classes, test scores, or a college writing class. The State of California mandates a requirement called "American History and Institutions"; this, too, can be fulfilled with high school classes, tests, or two courses at UC-Berkeley.

The final university requirement, "American Cultures," is the most politicized of the three. Essentially a diversity requirement, it may be fulfilled with what might be described as a course on the culture of American minorities. The class, according to the catalogue, must "take substantial account of groups drawn from at least three of the following: African Americans, American Indians, Asian Americans, Chicano/Latino Americans, and European Americans." A wide range of courses will satisfy this single-course requirement, almost all of which teach that the human condition can only be understood in terms of race, class, gender, and/or sexuality.

Students in L&S have their own set of college requirements. These include a standard set of distribution requirements: one class in each of seven areas — physical science, biological science, arts and literature, historical studies, philosophy and values, international studies, and social and behavioral sciences. In meeting these requirements, students have most of the catalogue to choose from. Many options are politicized, but many are not.

Three "essential skills" requirements round out the common L&S program. Two courses must be completed in reading and composition, one as a freshman and one as a sophomore. Unfortunately, these choices often suffer from an ideological inflection; the list of departments from which these courses are drawn includes African-American studies, Asian-American studies, Chicano studies, Native American studies, and the radical departments of rhetoric and women's studies. A single course in quantitative reasoning (mathematics, computer science, or statistics) is also required, as is the study of a foreign language, either for three years in high school or for two years at UC-Berkeley. Alternately, students may take a test to prove their foreign language proficiency.

The university and L&S requirements are a pale shadow of the core curriculum UC-Berkeley had at its founding. The looseness of the current requirements does not ensure that students will graduate with the same education — either in quality or content — and does not create an intellectual community centered on the most important works of Western culture.

Though the university is known for its campus and classroom activism, one professor says things are no worse there than at many other colleges in America. "The faculty, overall, are not more liberal than any other academic institution," the professor says. "The residents of the Bay area, in my estimation, give Berkeley its left-wing reputation." Liberal or not, the faculty do teach, and despite the size of the school and the number of graduate students, teaching assistants are used primarily in remedial or language programs and to lead discussions outside the regular class period. As a rule, teaching assistants do not lecture.

Instead, fortunate students are taught by faculty like these: Kenneth T. Jowitt and Nelson W. Polsby in political science, Ann Swidler in sociology, Gerald D. Feldman, Richard M. Abrams, Thomas Brady, Robert Bretano, and David Hollinger in history, Leslie L. Threatte and Ronald S. Stroud in classics, David Vogel in business, John R. Searle in philosophy, and Arthur Quinn, a standout in the otherwise ideological rhetoric department.

UC-Berkeley boasts many high-quality departments. A recent report by the National Research Council lists thirty-five of the university's thirty-six graduate programs as among the ten best in the country in their respective fields based on "faculty competence and achievement." Since undergraduates are frequently in contact with graduate students and their professors, this study is worth noting. In L&S, departments making the top ten include classics (second), comparative literature (tenth), English (tied for first, though highly politicized), French (seventh), German (first), history (tied for sixth), mathematics (first), philosophy (fourth), and political science (second).

One professor says economics, political science, history, and — contrary to stereotype — sociology are not politicized: "In fact, they are among the best in the nation." The economics department, though not free market–oriented, promotes a variety of viewpoints with the goal of finding the greatest efficiencies in a mixed economic system. The history department's courses are remarkably devoid of the politically correct or ideological offerings so common in other history departments and in other departments at UC-Berkeley.

Those "other departments" include women's studies, English, and rhetoric, professors say.

The women's studies department literature contains a series of questions: "Although all societies make gender distinctions, how do they differ from one culture to another, how have definitions of male and female roles evolved, how are they perpetuated, and how might they be redefined?" After which, it cites a single answer to them all: The department's goal is to explain why we suffer from "sexual inequality."

A course called "Women and Work" looks at wage inequality, sexual harassment, "individual resistance strategies and collective organizing," class and race differences, and government policy. "Women in Film," another course in the department, "explores feminist approaches to the way women are represented in narrative film, focusing on the problem of how filmic representations of women work to define what it means to be gendered female in our culture."

According to one professor, "The English department has the reputation of being dominated by professors who deconstruct classic texts in order to read into them their own political agendas." The department offers several concentrations to its majors, including sexual identities/gender studies; folklore, popular culture, and cultural theory; and Anglophone and multicultural studies. (There are also concentrations in five different historical periods, ranging from medieval to contemporary literature.) While quite a few solid literature offerings are listed in the catalogue, the courses required for the trendier concentrations either ignore or attack the texts and ideas of the liberal arts tradition, a professor says. Some of the more politicized courses include "The Romantic Period," whose course description is relatively standard populist fare until its final sentence: "Why did critics come to define Romanticism as the work of six male poets?" The reading list in "Literature and Sexual Identity" includes Plato, Shakespeare, Freud, and Wilde. It is, according to the catalogue, "a course in how to do 'the' history of sexuality." The description continues: "We'll interrogate, first of all, those quotation marks: whose history is it, exactly, and for what purpose?"

But the rhetoric department surpasses both of these. "Of all the departments at Berkeley, I would say that the rhetoric department, by far, is way out in left field," a professor says. The objective of the department is to examine the "rhetorical approach of discourse of all kinds," specifically in the humanities. The fields in which this study is undertaken are diverse: film, law, literature, philosophy, and science being among them. The lenses most often used are sexuality, gender, popular culture, and race. One course offered by this department is "Introduction to the Rhetoric and Theory of Popular Culture," where "race, gender, sexuality, and acculturation, as well as economic and power dynamics are among the issues to be discussed," according to the catalogue. There are courses in "Race and Identity: Performing American Identities" and "Rhetorics of Sexual Exchange." One faculty member is the author of a book that the *Chronicle of Higher Education* credits with helping "to create queer theory."

The lesbian, gay, bisexual, and transgendered studies program at Berkeley, though not a full-fledged department, does offer a minor that includes four "core" courses and two electives. The four core courses are "Alternative Sexual Identities and Communities in Contemporary American Society," "Interpreting the Queer Past: Methods and Problems in the History of Sexuality," "Cultural Representations of Sexualities: Queer Visual Culture," and "Sexuality, Culture, and Colonialism."

Political Atmosphere: Gone, but Not Forgotten

UC-Berkeley had an affirmative action program even before there was such a term; in the early 1960s the school started something called the Educational Opportunity Program, which was designed to promote racial diversity on campus. And in thirty years of affirmative action programs, it went from an almost all-white campus to one of the country's most diverse universities. In 1994 the undergraduate student body was 39 percent Asian, 32 percent white, 14 percent Hispanic, and 6 percent black.

Affirmative action policies meant that only half of the incoming students each year were admitted solely on the basis of test scores and grades; only a tiny portion of students admitted under these criteria were black or Hispanic. The admission of another 46 percent of the 1994-95 incoming class was based on grades, test scores, essays, and "background"; Hispanic students were the largest group in this category, followed by white and Asian students. More than one hundred times as many black students were admitted in this category as were admitted when only test scores and grades were considered.

At the same time, many on campus observed very little mixing of the races, and that there was a stigma attached to black and Hispanic students. "I'm tall," a medical student told the *New York Times*. "If they decided there were not enough tall people here, I'd walk around and people would think, 'Oh, there's one of those tall admissions.' It sounds cruel, but that's how people think."

Affirmative action policies at Berkeley and other California state schools were voted out, however, in 1995 by the state universities' board of regents. The vote was encouraged by California governor Pete Wilson, who had national political ambitions at the time, and regent Ward Connerly, an African-American businessman. Though a serious blow to affirmative action, the vote still allowed university officials to admit 25 to 50 percent of freshmen based on criteria other than grades (although not on the basis of race alone).

Two years after that vote, Californians adopted Proposition 209, which officially ended all public affirmative action programs in the state. The Ninth Circuit Court of Appeals turned away a challenge to the law in August 1997, and once again UC-Berkeley is facing an overhaul of its admissions and hiring policies.

The regents' vote and the voice of the state's public has not, however, changed the administration's commitment to diversity. "I can assure you that in implementing this law, the Berkeley campus will remain fully committed to excellence through diversity in every academic and employment program," UC-Berkeley chancellor Robert Berdahl said shortly after Proposition 209 passed.

And there is legitimate reason to believe that affirmative action is not dead at Berkeley, but merely driven underground. According to the student newspaper, the *Berkeleyan*, the university administration has recently reworked its admissions policy so that it now "calls for a more personal, qualitative look at the academic and personal achievements of each student applicant." In short, the admissions office is looking for creative ways to avoid a system based strictly on merit, and to find new ways in which to evaluate applicants. According to the newspaper, one of the criteria that was recently dropped was the "academic index score," a combination of the applicant's high school GPA and SAT scores. This index has been replaced with "applicants' accomplishments and the context in which those accomplishments have been achieved." The university also considers the applicant's socioeconomic environment, as well as "leadership in non-academic areas."

Some point out that UC-Berkeley, because of the excellent applicants it attracts, will never be able to admit students purely on the basis of merit — there are simply too many students with excellent grades and test scores, and not enough spots in the freshman class. However, statistics cited by the late Peter Shaw, past chairman of the National Association of Scholars, in *National Review* indicate that doing away with affirmative action would result in a student body 55 percent Asian, 35 percent white, 5 percent Hispanic, and only 2 percent black.

What UC-Berkeley makes of the new laws and how it rearranges its admissions policies may well set the precedent for universities committed to the popular notion of diversity. Just as the university started a trend in the 1960s, it may redefine that trend in the twenty-first century.

Student Life: The Times, They Ain't A-Changin'

It is the city of Berkeley, perhaps even more than the university itself, that gives rise to the aging-hippie image of the place. To walk down Telegraph Avenue is to step into a time warp: from tie-dyed shirts and bongs to books by Herbert Marcuse, the cultural paraphernalia of the late 1960s and early 1970s are on display everywhere.

Some observers argue that nearby Stanford University is far more radical nowadays than UC-Berkeley; still, traditions die hard. According to one professor, a Louis Farrakhan–Ronald Reagan presidential race, if held at the UC-Berkeley campus, would be a dead heat.

"The people in Berkeley are totally wacked," says a San Francisco resident. "I've seen transvestites walking around in dresses during the middle of the day, and students sitting on street corners yelling out slogans at people, like 'save the animals that are being tortured to death.' " A handful of students walk around and attend classes in the nude, so loath is the university to step on their right to free expression.

The twenty thousand undergraduates and ten thousand graduate students on the Berkeley campus occupy over one thousand acres in the hills overlooking San Francisco Bay. The city of Berkeley (population about 107,000) caters principally to students. There are trendy restaurants and coffeehouses, but most notably, there are excellent bookstores. A relatively new retail bookstore, Cody's, is very popular. Within one block of campus are several excellent used bookstores, including Shakespeare and Company, Black Oak, Moe's, and Cartesian.

The Bay Area offers a combination of stunning physical beauty and a wealth of cultural attractions. San Francisco and other cities are easily accessible to UC-Berkeley students via the Bay Area Rapid Transit system (BART).

The campus can accommodate only about five thousand undergraduates, and 75 percent of the dorm space is used by freshmen. Other students live in "theme houses" centered on a language or culture. The university also assists students with finding apartments in the campus area.

Sproul Plaza is the campus landmark that perhaps best reflects the liberal and eccentric past of UC-Berkeley. The plaza was named for Robert Gordon Sproul, president of the university for thirty years starting in the 1930s, and connects the César E. Chavez Student Center and the Martin Luther King Student Union.

As early as 1961, the university regents named a fountain on Sproul Plaza for a dog named Ludwig von Schwanenberg that played in the fountain and was a favorite of students. Three years later the plaza became the center of the free speech movement. One day in 1964, student Mario Savio led a protest in the plaza against the arrest of a graduate student who was circulating brochures promoting the Congress of Racial Equality. Savio and his classmates surrounded a police car, and from its roof he delivered a famous speech, telling the protesters: "There is a time when the operation of the machine becomes so odious, makes you so sick at heart, that . . . you've got to put your bodies upon the gears and upon the wheels . . . upon all the apparatus and you've got to make it stop." The squad car was surrounded for thirty-two hours. The university has since erected a plaque in honor of the beginning of the free speech movement, and a series of Mario Savio memorial lectures began in 1997 with a speech by Boston University professor Howard Zinn, a Marxist historian.

Other speakers on campus in 1997 included Vice President Al Gore, who spoke on financial aid and in opposition to Proposition 209, and Hillary Rodham Clinton, speaking on new laws reducing parental rights relating to children in foster care.

As one might expect, conservative activism is minimal on campus. The College Republicans are active with the local party, and some conservative students publish the *Berkeley Review,* a magazine of unorthodox political opinion. The most visible conservative group on campus is the Cal Libertarians, whose goal is "to get overly intrusive government out of our lives." The Cal Libertarians host regular discussion group meetings on campus and have their own hour on Free Radio Berkeley.

These groups are outnumbered by the liberal student groups. Workers rights groups and minority rights groups have held fasts to honor the death of Cesar Chavez and to protest the abuses faced by strawberry workers in California. Several groups are organized to promote affirmative action, and the university has a Center for African Studies, described in university literature as "an interdisciplinary research center to support basic research and training of scholars."

Feminist activists at UC-Berkeley have actually called for the murder of Neil Gilbert, an otherwise liberal professor who publicly questioned feminist Mary Koss's contention that 25 percent of all American women have been raped. According to Christina Hoff Sommers's book *Who Stole Feminism?* Gilbert's reasoning so enraged some Berkeley students that "at one demonstration against Gilbert on the Berkeley campus, students chanted, 'Cut it out or cut it off,' and carried signs that read, KILL NEIL GILBERT!"

At other times, students would be satisfied if their school figuratively killed Stanford. Always an intense rivalry, the football series between the two took on legendary proportions in 1982 when UC-Berkeley beat Stanford with "The Play," a multiple-lateral kickoff return for the winning touchdown with no time left on the clock, the last fifteen yards of which were run through members of the Stanford marching band who had swarmed the field thinking that the game was over.

UC-Berkeley offers twenty-four varsity sports, as well as a number of intramural opportunities.

UNIVERSITY OF CALIFORNIA AT LOS ANGELES (UCLA)

Office of Admissions
405 Hilgard Avenue
Los Angeles, CA 90024-1438
(310) 825-3101

Total enrollment: 35,590
Undergraduates: 23,910
SAT Ranges (Verbal/Math): V 550-660, M 580-700
Financial aid: 61%
Applicants: 28,080
Accepted: 39%
Enrolled: 35%
Application deadline: Nov. 30
Financial aid application deadline: Mar. 2. Guarantees to meet demonstrated need
Tuition: $9,384 nonresident; $3,858 resident
Core curriculum: No

Large, Diverse, Competitive

"UCLA has made extraordinary accomplishments since its inception in 1928," boasts one professor, who describes the university as "an academic enterprise that can now be mentioned in the same sentence with Harvard." Another professor and administrator describes the "extraordinary diversity of choice" at UCLA, a description that may sound trendy but is particularly apt for this huge institution with thirty-five thousand students, over six hundred student organizations, and an average of three thousand undergraduate courses offered per semester. Minority enrollment at UCLA is particularly high: 35 percent of students are Asian-American, another 18 percent are Hispanic, and 6 percent are African-American. The university awards more doctoral degrees to minority students than any other college in the nation, and is proud of its wide array of ethnic studies programs. As the promotional literature notes, "UCLA maintains the only black press on the West Coast, the world's largest archive collection on Japanese Americans, the leading journal on Asian Americans and the only peer-reviewed journal devoted to Chicano studies."

Admission to UCLA is fairly competitive: more than 28,000 students apply for 3,800 freshman spots, according to recent figures. And despite recent honest efforts to help ease feelings of anonymity and alienation among undergraduates, the university is still first and foremost a research institution; large class sizes (especially for introductory courses), teaching assistants (TAs), and prestigious yet distant faculty will continue to be a part of every undergraduate's experience. But the advantages of UCLA's size — myriad opportunities for undergraduate research, access to phenomenal library resources, and the wide variety of academic, political, and social opportunities — combined with its not-quite-yet-extinguished commitment to liberal education, may be enough to persuade some bright young people to consider attending.

Academic Life: Something for Everyone

Undergraduates can enroll in the College of Letters and Science or one of four other schools offering undergraduate degrees: Arts and Architecture; Engineering and Applied Science; Nursing; and Theatre, Film, and Television. There are also five professional schools for graduate students: Education and Information Studies; Law; Management; Public Policy and Social Research; and Dentistry, Medicine and Public Health. Undergraduates thus have 112 degree programs to choose from. And, because of the dizzying number of courses offered at any given time, it is still possible to steer clear of politicized courses in favor of more traditional offerings. "You can choose to avoid race, class, and gender as the ideological agendas of your classes," confirms one student.

UCLA retains a broad set of general education course requirements all students must fulfill, including an English composition requirement, quantitative reasoning and foreign language requirements (though students can test out of these), as well as courses within the following groupings: humanities (four courses), physical sciences (three courses), social sciences (four courses), life sciences (three courses). The general education requirements receive mixed reviews from students. One student confides that he would have liked fewer of them, finding some (such as life sciences and biology) unfulfilling. Another math and economics major says that, although most of the general education classes were enjoyable, "I wish they had been more challenging." Still, many good courses can satisfy the general education requirements, and, unlike many state universities, UCLA has yet to mandate a cultural or gender diversity requirement.

In response to complaints about large class sizes, the university has developed a general education initiative that will be in place by the new millennium. "35,000 students is a lot of students," one administrator notes, adding that "undergraduate education has always been a central mission of the UC system." In order to accommodate the large number of students while maintaining a certain degree of intimacy in the educational environment, UCLA developed an "academic socialization" initiative. Every freshman will have at least one class with limited enrollment (under twenty students). This class will have some thematic connection to two other classes the student is taking, enabling him not only to experience small class size but also to make connections across the curriculum with his other general education courses. Students will take three of these "cluster courses," as they are described by one professor, during both the fall and winter terms. The subject matter will be "global," including such potential topics as "The Development of World Democracies," "The City in History," or "The Culture of Theatre."

In general, notes one professor, the majority of faculty have not remained involved in general education debates and discussions: "Those faculty who have gotten involved in it see much merit in this new program," which was arrived at after ten years of discussion. "We used to have the typical public university distribution requirement," says another faculty member. "This is a dramatic change for us." The new general education curriculum will also be residential, a feature further intended to provide students at this mammoth institution with some semblance of the small liberal arts college experience. Another salutary feature of the new program is that emeriti faculty will teach some of its requirements. These retired professors "will share their experiences and knowledge with young people," notes one excited faculty member.

UCLA is also an excellent choice for students who are interested in doing research at the undergraduate level. The university boasts one of the best research libraries in the country, with 6.4 million volumes and ninety thousand current periodicals in thirteen libraries. According to one professor, the university has a "robust program" called the Student Research Program, in which roughly 1,200 students participate in research projects with faculty each year. For students in the humanities, the program is an excellent opportunity to learn research skills that can later be used at the graduate level. Most of these research opportunities, however, are in the sciences.

Indeed, the sciences are particularly strong at UCLA. Nearly half of all freshmen intend to pursue health and medical sciences, and the university recently implemented two new science initiatives: a new core in life sciences, which will "streamline and simplify entry-level courses for pre-med students," according to one professor; and a "Science Challenge" program that provides multimedia education in the lower-division life and physical science courses. In the winter of 1998 the university is scheduled to open a National Science Learning Center with impressive facilities such as wet labs and modular workstations.

Outstanding professors at UCLA include James Q. Wilson in political science; Sebastian Edwards and Nathaniel Grossman in economics; Ed Condrin, Michael J. B. Allen, Debra K. Shuger, and George Tennyson (emeritus) in English; and Richard Rouse, Carlo Ginzburg, Patrick Geary, Ruth Bloch, Robert Burns, and Joyce Appleby in history.

UCLA's English department, with over 1,300 undergraduates, enrolls the largest number of undergraduate English majors of any university in the country. Because of its sheer size, the department is a very mixed bag. "But in spite of the differing politics of faculty, we all tend to agree on foundational studies," notes one professor, adding that students still study Chaucer, Shakespeare, and Milton and take a mandatory sophomore survey of foundational writers.

Students also recommend the biology and chemistry programs. Undergraduates are advised to treat with caution courses in "Development Studies," which has a decidedly radical political tenor. Economics is still a fairly solid choice for undergraduates, and the John E. Anderson Graduate School of Management provides students with a superior graduate education in several different areas of management and business. A significant percentage of the school's faculty respects and teaches free-market economics, and students leave it with a strong grounding in management and business theory.

The university is continually adding new programs and interdisciplinary majors in response to both political pressure and intellectual demand. More recent degree programs include interdepartmental programs in Asian studies and European studies, and a B.A. in American Literature and Culture administered through the English department. There are also interdepartmental programs in Afro-American studies and women's studies, and the recently established Cesar E. Chavez Center in Chicana and Chicano Studies. These latter programs, sadly, appear to be little more than glorified exercises in identity politics: the women's studies course objective, for instance, states that "a background in women's studies offers unique contextual validation for today's woman," while the Afro-American program offers African-Americans "a heightening of self-awareness and self-pride." Meanwhile, the objectives for the philosophy program, ranked one of the best in the nation, state: "Philosopher, translated from the Greek, literally means 'lover of wisdom'. The term has come to mean someone who seeks knowledge, enlightenment, and truth. The undergraduate program in philosophy is not directed at career objectives. . . . Philosophy is primarily taught to undergraduates as a contribution to their liberal education." The intellectual disparity between this authentic liberal arts discipline — in which members of all races and cultures can participate — and those activist programs such as women's studies is acute, and although "career objectives" may sometimes militate against pursuing a course of liberal studies, undergraduates would do well to explore the many fine opportunities in the humanities at UCLA.

Academic advising is considered patchy at best. "I never saw my advisor after the first week of my freshman year," notes one senior. One student sees a wide disparity in the limited services available to white undergraduates and those at the disposal of minority students. "There are mentoring, tutoring, and counseling programs specifically for minorities," notes this student. To supplement its advisory system, the university is developing a multimedia "Academic Instructional Enhancement Initiative" that will produce a website for every single UCLA undergraduate course — upwards of three thousand websites — to further assist students in making informed decisions about their classes.

One student complains that because of budget cuts, class sizes have gotten larger and fees have increased. "More of my classes are taught by graduate students," he notes. Most classes enroll fewer than fifty students, and even the larger classes "are not so imposing if you're motivated," counters another student. The university is generally unapologetic about its use of graduate teaching assistants; as one professor boasts, "We have some of the best trained TA's in the country . . . our graduate students are prepared to be good teachers." Students also complain about the absence of rigorous selectivity in admissions. "There was a lot of dead weight in my classes," says one student, who adds that grade inflation is also a problem. "The default grade seems to be B-. You have to work pretty hard to get less than that."

Political Atmosphere: Defusing BOMB-shells

Because it is such a large and diverse campus, UCLA is home to every conceivable form of political orientation, and there is seldom a dull moment in campus politics. "We're 60,000 individuals," explains one professor, "so there is every degree of activity and passivity you can imagine." In particular, racial and ethnic issues are continual sources of tension at the university. Earlier this decade, for instance, students agitated for the establishment of a Chicano Studies Program with a vigorous campaign that included hunger strikes and vandalism of faculty buildings. Several conservative and libertarian students organized counterprotests, but, recalls one, "We had signs ripped up and got shouted at." The end result was the establishment of the Cesar Chavez program. The program in Chicana and Chicano Studies now offers a large number of courses, including one on "Chicana Lesbian Literature."

Affirmative action also has been a flash point for controversy at UCLA, as the entire UC system decided to end race-based admissions a few months before the passage of California's Proposition 209. The decision sparked a bitter dispute between then-chancellor Charles Young and certain members of the university's board of regents. In a controversial interview with the *Los Angeles Times,* Young defended affirmative action, stating, "I can tell you if we hadn't done it, it wouldn't be an occasional uprising in South Central Los Angeles or midtown Detroit. We'd be in a battleground . . . this place would be a shambles." Students supporting Young's position, such as the political-action and education coordinator of the African Student Union, responded to calls for Young's resignation with plans for pickets and rallies, and issued statements like, "If they can come for the chancellor in the morning, they will come after us in the afternoon," according to the *Chronicle of Higher Education*. Despite the passage of Proposition 209, the issue of affirmative action is far from buried at UCLA. Chancellor Young was recently succeeded by Albert Carnesale, former provost of Harvard's Kennedy School of Government, and it remains to be seen how Chancellor Carnesale will handle minority issues at UCLA.

"There is free speech at UCLA," notes one student, "but there's also a lot of political radicalism." Consequently, as one student bemoans, the majority of the student government representatives serve as little more than advocates for liberal student groups: "It is hard to distinguish between student government and student advocacy groups." The more active political groups on campus also seem to be the more liberal ones, such as pro–affirmative action groups and Hispanic groups. "So much of our student money goes toward funding these groups," complains one undergraduate, noting that many of the more visible groups are "really vocal, organized, and obnoxious." Conservative students charge that there is "an unspoken common interest" between the administration and the radical student groups "in what they want to achieve." In response to the use of student fees to fund radical political and social organizations, a group of UCLA students and alumni founded Bruins Owed Money Back (BOMB) a couple of years ago in order to recover funds spent on such organizations. According to an October 1995 press release, "UCLA policy allows students to request refunds of part of their student fees, if they can establish that those fees went to fund religious, political, or ideological activities." Pointing out that Christian groups receive no funding because of the prohibition against supporting religious organizations, one student noted that Jewish and Muslim groups receive funding because they are considered "cultural" organizations, and added that UCLA has scores of student-funded advocacy groups that promote religious, political, and ideological positions in violation of a 1993 California Supreme Court ruling. Although few students petitioned for refunds of their student fees, BOMB at least sends a symbolic message to the student government. Which is probably all it can hope to do — one irate student reported in the *Daily Bruin* that he had to fill out ninety-six forms in order to receive money paid to eight organizations whose use of student fees he protested.

Incoming UCLA students are invited to attend a three-day student orientation, where "they [talk] a lot about diversity" and listen to skits on date rape and sexually transmitted diseases, according to one undergraduate. Also, at the start of each quarter (UCLA is on the quarter system rather than a semester schedule) numerous information tables are set up along Bruin Walk advertising every variety of student organization. "There are always lots of Christian groups," notes one student. Homosexuals have made strong political and social inroads at UCLA in recent years. The university has both a Gay and Lesbian Association and a Lesbian Bisexual Gay

Alliance. It also houses a Lesbian, Gay, Bisexual, and Transgender Resources Office, under the direction of the Division of Student and Campus Life.

Limited organizational outlets exist for conservatives, but they include the Bruin Republicans. One conservative student says "briefly, another group [besides the Bruin Republicans] would emerge," such as the Republicans for Choice or the Ayn Rand Society. "But these groups were not too hospitable to conservatives" and never really took hold at the university. There has thus been some infighting between conservatives and libertarians, but one student relates that "the political temperature here is not that high." Recent conservative speakers at UCLA include former Congressman Bob Dornan and Dinesh D'Souza.

Student Life: Microcosm in Westwood

Although it has not been around nearly as long as the perennially attractive ivy-covered halls of many universities, UCLA is described as a "pretty" to "very beautiful" campus by undergraduates. Architecturally, the campus combines the Tudor Gothic and Italian Romanesque styles of the original buildings with more modern styles. Because many of its older buildings were built without adequate earthquake protection, some of the campus is always under construction to repair existing damage or bring buildings up to current codes. The university is located in the "very safe" Westwood area of Los Angeles, within easy striking distance of shops, movie theaters, and restaurants. "There is a dying business area south of campus," relates one student, "but it doesn't cater to students very well."

The residential environment at UCLA has changed in recent years, and the university is no longer considered a commuter campus. It can accommodate about six thousand undergraduates. Almost all freshmen now live on campus, making it sometimes difficult for upperclassmen to get into the dormitories. For a variety of reasons, including convenience, cost, and social opportunities, students and faculty advise undergraduates at all levels to live in the dorms. "I strongly recommend living in the dorms," notes one student. With few exceptions, the dorms are coed. After the freshman year, upwards of 75 percent of students continue to live within a mile of campus. Still, "having a car is important," suggests one student, although on-campus parking can be difficult and the areas immediately adjacent to the university can be congested.

Despite its relative safety, the university is by no means immune from the social, political, and natural upheavals that seem to constantly plague the Los Angeles area. According to one student, several campus buildings were evacuated during the L.A. riots, and there were two small riots in Westwood, one after a movie about black gangs was released.

The Panhellenic System is fairly active at UCLA, and the university is host to more than forty-five Greek organizations. Slightly more than one-tenth of all students are members of fraternities or sororities, including a small contingent of gays and lesbians who have their own Greek organizations. And with over six hundred student groups, there is literally something for everyone at UCLA.

Not surprisingly, given its location just five miles from the Pacific Ocean, the university boasts clubs for surfing, water skiing, and windsurfing. There are also several academic clubs organized on rather esoteric and theoretical premises, including the Aesthetic Anthropology, Cultural Theory and Transnational Studies (AACTT Studies) group; the Center for Language, Interaction and Culture; and the Discourse, Identity and Representation Collective (DIRE), whose membership likely consists of trendy humanities graduate students.

There are scores of religious and political groups — everything from the International Socialist Organization to the Bruin Libertarians, from Campus Crusade for Christ to the Sri Chinmoy Meditation Group — and a host of organizations fashioned around ethnic boundaries. At least a dozen Asian and African-American groups are active on campus, as are upwards of thirty Hispanic organizations. As for the social environment, "the university is very cliquish by race," laments one student. "Iranians, blacks, Latinos, and whites pretty much stick to their own." This segregation is further exacerbated by the institutional structure of the university, which frequently maintains separate programs for minority students. Still, the biggest social event of the year is the university's annual Mardi Gras celebration — "the world's largest student-operated collegiate activity," the UCLA viewbook claims — which can serve as a brief unifying event for this disparate campus.

As befits its size and location, athletics are an enormously popular part of the UCLA experience. UCLA competes in the Pacific-Ten Conference and has excellent teams in men's football, basketball, and track and field. The women's swim team is also highly competitive. More recently, some athletic programs have suffered under the effects of Title IX, which mandates gender equity in opportunities for scholarship athletes. Certain men's teams have had their budgets greatly reduced, or have been cut altogether from the NCAA program. The men's gymnastics team, for instance, which has sent numerous competitors to the Olympics and taken home three USA Gymnastics collegiate club national championships, was recently dropped entirely from the university's roster of collegiate sports.

One professor summarizes UCLA's strongest appeal as its "youthfulness and high energy" as an institution. Another cites the "depth and breadth" available to students because of its large size. The size has an added advantage, according to one faculty member, in that it gives the faculty and students the necessary space to pursue their own studies and interests without that claustrophobic feeling often encountered at smaller institutions. "We all live far enough away from one another, so that when we do come together, we don't bring a lot of baggage with us."

The university has by no means escaped the tide of radicalization that has swept American higher education, and courses like "Sexuality and the City: Queer Los Angeles" are all too common in the curriculum. Still, many disciplines retain remnants of excellence, and discerning students can still piece together a solid liberal education while availing themselves of the many research and extracurricular opportunities on this large and truly diverse campus.

CALIFORNIA INSTITUTE OF TECHNOLOGY

Mail Code 55-63
515 South Wilson
Pasadena, CA 91125
(818) 395-6341
www.caltech.edu

Total enrollment: 1,900
Undergraduates: 880
SAT Ranges (Verbal/Math): V 680-780, M 740-800
Financial aid: 67%
Applicants: 1,990
Accepted: 26%
Enrolled: 42%
Application deadline: Jan. 1
Financial aid application deadline: Feb. 1
Tuition: $18,600
Core curriculum: Yes

Wish They All Could Be California (Institutes of Technology)

The original trustees of the California Institute of Technology laid out the school's mission in this fashion: "To train the creative type of scientist or engineer urgently needed in our educational, governmental, and industrial development." That was in 1921, but it still applies — even though no one at that time imagined the Jet Propulsion Lab (JPL) or other facilities that make Caltech the preeminent school of technology in the country and perhaps the world. The only institute in its class is another institute of technology, the one in Massachusetts. Today there are no truly weak programs at

Caltech, and its understated mission statement is just something that allows the rest of us to understand what really goes on behind the laboratory and classroom doors.

Only about a quarter of applicants can get in, and those that go must really want to go; they will be somewhat disappointed if they are looking for a traditional liberal arts education. The institute does offer majors in history, literature, philosophy, and political science, but even these students must fulfill the rigorous science, engineering, and mathematics prerequisites required of everyone else. The opposite also applies — engineers and scientists must take several humanities courses. Caltech's excellence, however, is not in the humanities but in just about every scientific field that has been conceived. Faculty and graduates have more than twenty Nobel Prizes to their credit, and students get to work with this faculty (who outnumber students only by three to one) on original research projects to an extent unmatched by any institution, in any field. As a bonus, many faculty happen to be the top experts in their disciplines.

What is now Caltech began in 1891 as a small school of arts and crafts in downtown Pasadena. It became the California Institute of Technology in 1920, and its growth thereafter was brisk. Guided by men recruited from MIT, the University of Chicago, the University of California, and many other prestigious universities, Caltech awarded its first Ph.D.s in 1924, the year after Professor Robert Millikan received the Nobel Prize in physics. The institute shed its schools of business and an academy, along with other units unnecessary for the fulfillment of its ambitious goals. It added new programs and departments only when it was certain it had the financial backing and personnel to ensure their quality. Caltech, in more ways than one, can take its students to the stars.

Academic Life: As a Matter of Fact, It *Is* Rocket Science

The only type of degree offered at Caltech is the bachelor of science, and its requirements are extremely rigorous. To put it another way, incoming students have the nation's highest average SAT scores (about 1,430), and they find the curriculum more than a little challenging.

The institute has three terms per academic year, and each course is usually worth 9 units of credit. As freshmen, students are required to take 27 units of mathematics, 27 of physics, and 18 of chemistry plus a 6-unit lab. Sophomores take 27 units of math and 27 of physics. In addition, Caltech requires a 6-unit lab, 36 units of humanities courses, 36 units of social science, 36 additional units of humanities and social sciences, and three 3-unit classes in physical education. Aptitude tests and other criteria can get the best students out of a few requirements, but this does very little to make the curriculum less demanding.

By requiring no less than 108 units (twelve courses) in the humanities and social sciences, the Caltech administration demonstrates that it believes engineers and scientists should not be culturally illiterate, and that a humane education will in fact make them better at their jobs. The institute stops short of requiring a Western civilization course, but most of the offerings in the humanities are in fact studies of Western history, literature, and arts. Two of the humanities courses must be advanced classes, and the two terms of freshman humanities courses require four thousand to six thousand words of essay writing each term.

Caltech is divided into six different academic divisions: Biology; Chemistry and Chemical Engineering; Engineering and Applied Sciences; Geological and Planetary Sciences; the Humanities and Social Sciences; and Physics, Mathematics and Astronomy. The Humanities and Social Sciences division concentrates on its well-regarded doctoral programs, and thus is probably the weakest when it comes to undergraduate education.

In the other divisions, though, the research opportunities available to undergraduates are perhaps unequaled in the university world. Beginning in their sophomore year, students are encouraged to undertake research projects that they may later expand into a senior thesis. Especially noteworthy is the selective Summer Undergraduate Research Fellowships (SURF) program, which "provides continuing undergraduate students the opportunity to work on an individual research project in a tutorial relationship with a research sponsor, usually a member of the Caltech/JPL research community," according to the catalogue.

The ten-week program is especially noteworthy for allowing students to attack complex problems early in their academic careers. About a quarter of SURF participants have their work published in scientific journals. Among the 1997 SURF projects were "Permittivity and Permeability of Ferromagnetic Nanocrystals of Different Chemical Compositions," "Visualizing the Human Body: Art and Medicine in Philadelphia, 1740-1890," "Analysis of Galactic Redshifts from the Hubble Deep Field," and "Is Nereid in Chaotic Rotation?"

Caltech has so many gifted and internationally famous faculty members that anything short of a very long list would miss more people than it includes. And the faculty really do teach the students and are famously available for consultation and — equally importantly — experiments. Most classes are small, and even large lecture sections break into small units for lab work. There are less than two thousand students — including only about nine hundred undergraduates — but there are some 280 professorial faculty members, giving Caltech an incredible student-to-faculty ratio of three-to-one. Some other impressive statistics: 74 faculty are members of the American Academy of Arts and Sciences; 63 faculty and four board members belong to the National Academy of Science; 29 faculty and 14 board members belong to the National Academy of Engineering; and 23 people associated with the institute (including 14 alumni) are Nobel Prize winners. The new president, David Baltimore, was cowinner of the 1975 Nobel Prize for medicine.

With such a faculty, it is no surprise that virtually every program at Caltech is excellent. One faculty members says it is impossible to single out the best departments: "We have so many Nobelists, National Medal Winners, and so on in all the departments." This isn't gross immodesty, just a statement of fact. It is fair to say, however, that physics, engineering, chemistry, astronomy, and biology are very strong in every respect. Departments in the humanities and social sciences are not bad, but do not equal the quality of the engineering and hard science departments.

The facilities for scientific and engineering research at Caltech are among the best in the world. As institute literature notes regarding advanced physics, "The comparatively small size of Caltech coupled with its great strength in both the pure sciences and engineering make it possible to have a faculty with a wide interest in the application of modern physics to technology, without losing close interaction with 'pure subjects.' " Students in aeronautics may use the Guggenheim Aeronautical Laboratory, the Karman Laboratory of Fluid Mechanics and Jet Propulsion, and the Firestone Flight Sciences Laboratory. For future astronomers, the observatories at Mount Palomar and Big Bear, as well as the Owens Valley Radio Observatory and the Caltech Submillimeter Observatory, "together constitute a unique and unprecedented concentration of scientific facilities in astronomy," according to the institute. Included is the 200-inch Hale Telescope on Mount Palomar, the largest reflecting telescope in the world. There are six physics labs, not including the Mount Palomar and Owens Valley telescopes, and students interested in this field may investigate particle physics, nuclear and neutrino physics, experimental high-energy astrophysics, infrared astronomy, submillimeter astronomy, computational astronomy, condensed matter physics, applied physics, quantum optics, experimental gravitational physics, neuroscience, theoretical physics, and theoretical astrophysics. There are twelve fields of study in chemical engineering. And then there is the JPL, an internationally famous facility that Caltech operates for NASA.

The list goes on and on. Suffice it to say that Caltech students don't lack the tools or expert instruction to explore just about every scientific field there is. "People who graduated from here say they did more research here as undergrads than they're doing in grad school," institute literature says. "You're not just a go-fer for the professor and his grad students; here you actually get the hands-on experience. Your adviser is guiding you along in the right direction to make sure you don't blow up anything, but for the most part, it's your project to be successful with, or to really screw up."

Most Caltech students use their undergraduate educations as a first step to learning even more. Over half of each graduating class goes on to graduate school in the sciences or engineering.

Political Atmosphere: Empirical Knowledge

Given the tremendous amount of work involved in mastering any of the fields of study at Caltech, it is no surprise that there are not enough hours in the day to spend politicizing the institute's curriculum or social life. In addition, the sciences and engineering are not very susceptible to politicization in comparison to the humanities. In other words, the faculty and students at Caltech have neither the opportunity nor, apparently, the desire to dabble in social engineering or ideological publications.

Caltech tries make sure financial constraints do not prevent any student it admits from attending and awards some merit scholarships regardless of financial need. That said, the institute does employ affirmative action in selecting its student body. It recently received $350,000 from the Andrew W. Mellon Foundation to fund its participation in the Mellon Minority Undergraduate Fellowship Program through the year 2003. When the grant was awarded, Thomas E. Everhart, then-president of the institute, said the money would further Caltech's efforts to diversify its student body. Five fellows will be selected each year. They receive year-round mentoring, stipends for conference attendance and summer research, and up to $10,000 toward their undergraduate debts if they graduate and pursue a Ph.D. in fields approved by the foundation.

Even before that grant, Caltech offered special Presidential Scholarships to minority students, and the press release that accompanied the Mellon award notes that "administrative support for minority affairs has been increased with the recent creation of an associate deanship." Caltech has an Associate Dean and Director for Minority Student Affairs. There is also a program on race, politics, and region.

The institute does not offer the same incentives to minority faculty. "All we care about is the originality of the candidate, their ability to carry out a top-notch research program, and their published record," a professor says. Minorities are, of course, sought after in all branches of university hiring, but the number of minorities and women in the Caltech engineering departments, for example, is quite small.

Caltech struggles most with its size, and how to balance enrollment with its considerable resources. "The biggest issue is to overcome the problems associated with being a small school . . . that has to remain focused," a professor says. It is almost a given, though, that very few — if any — departments and programs at Caltech will decline in the coming years. The faculty and students seem to be too excellent to permit that, and the vast majority are driven by their work.

Student Life: Chance of a Lifetime

For students attracted to Caltech, long hours of study — especially in the laboratory — are not drudgery, but the opportunity they've always dreamed of. Highly motivated and extremely bright, the average Caltech student has probably always stood out among his fellows because of a fascination with science and its application to intellectual problems. What Caltech offers these students is a chance to pursue their interests in an atmosphere fully unsatisfied with mediocrity.

Caltech gives the best students in the country the opportunity to advance as part of the community of scholars who make up the Institute. Students claim that in spite of the intense pressure to succeed, there is very little competition among students for grades. In fact, students tend to study in groups and cooperate with one another in the interest of everyone's success. The real competition, it seems, is not with fellow students, but with their own individual projects and goals.

Everyone in the Caltech community lives by the honor system, which is boiled down to: "No member shall take unfair advantage of any member of the Caltech community." It is taken for granted that students will live by the system and monitor their own behavior. Professors often give take-home exams that are both closed-book and timed. A board of control composed of elected student representatives handles suspected violations and makes recommendations to the appropriate dean.

Caltech has a number of activities that allow students to pursue hobbies apart from hard science. The institute publishes a literary magazine of students' submissions, and the student newspaper, the *California Tech*, comes out weekly. For the musically talented (or those wishing to learn), there is a wind ensemble, a jazz band, a symphony orchestra (operated with Occidental College), several choral musical groups, some small chamber ensembles, and musical programs at the college's auditoriums. Other nonscientific endeavors include men's and women's glee clubs, the Caltech Flying Team, the Motorcycle Club, the Quiz Bowl, the Folk Music Society, numerous language clubs, the usual assortment of ethnic societies, an amateur radio club, and a bridge club. The Caltech Christian Fellowship, Newman Club, and Hillel all operate on campus.

A favorite haunt is the Caltech Y, located on the upper floor of the student center and offering not merely exercise facilities, as one might expect, but also interest-free loans, economical trips and backpacking expeditions, notable speakers, meeting rooms, and a used-textbook exchange — all with no membership dues or fees. There is also a student shop in which students may build projects either for classwork or for their own use. The college catalogue notes: "Members not proficient in power tools are limited to hand tools and bench work; however, instruction in power tools is given as needed."

Naturally, among the seventy clubs and organizations are also professional societies such as the American Chemical Society and the American Society of Mechanical Engineers. Caltech sponsors numerous lectures on campus each year, and students can hear some of the best minds in science and engineering speak on their own research.

The institute competes in ten men's and seven women's sports at the NCAA Division III level. There is no football team, but Caltech does have varsity fencing, among other sports. Nearly 30 percent of undergraduates are involved in intercollegiate sports, a high number at any school, but especially high at a school so dedicated to academics. More than 80 percent are involved in some form of organized athletics, including the intramural program that pits residence halls against each other in flag football, soccer, swimming, volleyball, tennis, and softball.

Caltech is divided into seven undergraduate student houses, each of which has a separate unit with its own dining room and lounge and is home to about seventy-five students. During the first week of classes, freshmen attend parties at each house and then list their top four choices. The houses themselves list their top potential recruits, and students are assigned using both sets of rankings. Students generally remain in their assigned residential community for the entirety of their undergraduate education. These houses provide the basis for intramural sports and other rivalries, as there are no Greek organizations. The Institute also offers two apartment buildings, two dorms, and a few off-campus houses. More than 90 percent of the student body lives in university housing.

One of the newest on-campus residences is Avery House, a $16.1 million Spanish Colonial structure occupied by undergraduates, graduate students, and faculty members. Certain guests stay in the house with the residents; according to campus literature, "many of the special visitors will be entrepreneurs who have distinguished themselves in a variety of high-tech ventures and whom a young engineer or scientist-to-be would view as inspirations." Avery House allows everyone to "meet informally with entrepreneurs and Caltech guests," wherein "students, researchers, professors, visiting scholars, and industry leaders will live together and think together" and will "embody the spirit of entrepreneurship." In this way, business leaders can learn about the ideas coming out of Caltech, and students can make excellent contacts within the business community.

CALVIN COLLEGE

Office of Admissions
3201 Burton, S.E.
Grand Rapids, MI 49546
(616) 957-6000 / (800) 688-0122
www.calvin.edu

Total enrollment: 3,960
Undergraduates: 3,930
SAT Ranges (Verbal/Math): V 460-580, M 520-660
Financial aid: 90%
Applicants: 2,080
Accepted: 89%
Enrolled: 55%

Application deadline: Rolling admissions
Financial aid application deadline: Feb. 15
Tuition: $12,995
Core curriculum: No

A Reformed World

Calvin College was founded in 1876 by the Christian Reformed Church, itself a breaka-way from the Dutch Reformed Church. It traces its theological roots back to John Calvin's Geneva of the sixteenth century and still proudly declares its allegiance to the tenets of Calvinism. The seminary of the Christian Reformed Church is on Calvin's campus, and the college states that it is "a comprehensive liberal arts college in the Reformed tradition of historic Christianity. . . . We pledge fidelity to Jesus Christ, offering our hearts and lives to do God's work in God's world." Its statement of purpose says: "We study and address a world made good by God, distorted by sin, redeemed in Christ, and awaiting the fullness of God's reign." Though steeped in Reformed theology, Calvin is far from a merely pious institution; one of the central traditions of the Christian Reformed Church has been the vigorous cultivation of the intellect, as Calvin's commitment to a liberal arts education clearly demonstrates.

In the past, most of the students and faculty at Calvin have been of Dutch ancestry. But in recent years that has begun to change as Calvin actively seeks to reach a broader public. Calvin now wants to position itself as a Christian community that reaches out to all people of every nationality, and in so doing it has come face-to-face with some of the trends now sweeping secular academe — including the vexing issues surrounding multiculturalism. At some fast-approaching point, the college will have to make a decision: Will it forsake those traits and qualities that make it stand out in today's homogenous college world, or will its flirtations with ideas that have destroyed or weakened the identities of many other colleges and universities be allowed to capsize Calvin as well?

It is, at this point, a tricky balance. The effects so far have been minor, and there seems to be a feeling on campus that even secular themes can be modified to fit the Calvin system. This sort of tension is a perennial challenge for denominational schools, but while many religious institutions have succumbed to secularism, Calvin is genuinely striving for balance. For now, it remains a solid school offering a well-rounded liberal arts education.

Academic Life: Close to a Core

Calvin requires most of its students to complete a broad set of courses that conveys an appreciation for the Western tradition. The general curriculum is more of a distribution requirement (albeit a rather good one) than a true core, but the college calls it a core anyway. One professor says that although the "core" is strong, it would be even stronger if it encompassed more integration across the disciplines. The so-called core does not apply to a number of professional programs, like engineering, nursing, accounting, social work, communication disorders, recreation, medical technology, and occupational therapy. The number of liberal arts and sciences courses required for these professional degree programs varies, but it is never as many as for the traditional B.A. or B.S. degrees. Thus, although Calvin does indeed offer a very strong selection of courses, it is by no means a school along the lines of a University of Dallas or St. John's College, where all students (regardless of concentration in the case of Dallas) read a common, broad selection of great books.

Be that as it may, students in the liberal arts and sciences are required to take six courses in history, philosophy, and religion (with at least two courses in biblical studies and religion); three from mathematics and the sciences; three in literature and fine arts; one in economics or political science; and one in psychology or a social science. They must also attain competency in a foreign language and demonstrate proficiency in writing. Along with other offerings, the distribution requirements at Calvin do in fact add up to a good general education. Even education majors — a group that many state universities inexplicably permit to skip most of the liberal arts and sciences requirements — must complete the liberal arts curriculum before obtaining their professional degree. English majors must still take a course in Shakespeare, a requirement that sets Calvin apart from many places that have made study of the Bard a mere option. At least one course in Western civilization is required of all students.

Calvin is currently in the process of revising its curriculum, and one professor believes it will emerge "internationalized." The term does not mean that Calvin will have its students read modern scholarly works about other cultures, as might be the case elsewhere, but that students will likely be required to read primary sources from other cultures along with those from Western writers. "There is a Western civilization requirement now, and there will be one then," a professor says. "There will also be more common reading. The requirements in history, philosophy, world literature, and the Bible and theology are likely to stay more or less as they are."

Among the strongest departments at Calvin are communications, English, philosophy, chemistry, mathematics, and physics. Top professors include Ronald Blankespoor in chemistry; Kenneth Bratt in classics; Bill Romanowski and Quentin Schultze in communications; Edward Ericson, Dale Brown, Susan Felch, Gary Schmidt, John Timmerman, and James Vanden Bosch in English; Kurt Schaefer in economics; Kelly James Clark, Lee Hardy, and C. Stephen Evans in philosophy; Michael Stob in mathematics; and Calvin Stapert in music. The hiring practices at Calvin vary among departments, but one professor notes that "at a deeper level there is sometimes prejudice against conservative candidates. A conservative wouldn't be happy in the history department, for example. Sometimes members of a department have a bit of an anti-conservative bias in their voting on hiring." Economics is described by another teacher as the most politicized on campus. "A few of them don't call themselves socialists, but they really are," the teacher says.

Students at Calvin often benefit from conferences and seminars that grow out of the intellectual concerns of particular departments. For example, a biannual conference on literature and faith has featured some of the world's leading writers as speakers, including Annie Dillard, John Updike, Elie Wiesel, and Donald Hall.

With very few exceptions, teaching is the faculty's highest priority at Calvin. "This has not jeopardized the scholarly productivity, which is remarkably high for an institution such as ours," says a professor. "However, the lure of the prestige that comes with publication is great and there is definitely a growing tendency to expect more publication. . . . The tradition of making teaching the highest priority still remains, perhaps tenuously, in the ascendancy."

Political Atmosphere: Letting In, or Letting Out?

Calvin makes no apologies for its efforts to retain and strengthen its affiliation with the Christian Reformed Church. "When Calvin talks about being Christian, it really means that," one professor explains. The school's Christian roots are obvious in the way it presents itself to the world, and there is no doubt that Calvin is a place where most Christian students of Reformed backgrounds can find many capable professors who share their basic worldview.

Despite this unique situation, Calvin has spent a great deal of time in recent years discussing how the college might become more diverse. The 1996-97 academic year was proclaimed the "Multicultural Year," and the school devoted extra attention to multicultural themes. The hoped-for blending of multicultural ideas and Christian belief was attempted in an end-of-the-year symposium entitled "The One in the Many: Christian Identity in a Multicultural World." All of this was part of the college's "Comprehensive Plan," drawn up ten years ago with the express purpose of bringing a greater degree of diversity to the campus.

Throughout the year, the student newspaper *Chimes* devoted much space to exploring the virtues of multiculturalism and whether Calvin was sufficiently devoted to insuring that persons of different beliefs and backgrounds were made to feel welcome at the school. Among opinions printed in the newspaper were those of a Calvin dean. "Multiculturalism, once the rallying cry of those who felt excluded from the halls of academe, has become an essential ingredient in the public identity of nearly every institution," he wrote. "Without a doubt, multiculturalist principles have sometimes been invoked in defense of shoddiness and ideological distortion. . . . We must guard against the temptation to jump on the bandwagon of nonconformity and fashion our efforts for diversity on the model of everyone else's. For Calvin is in a unique position to assert, and to exemplify, something too often ignored in the contemporary debate over cultural pluralism: diversity among institutions of higher education is no less important than diversity within each of them."

These wise observations succinctly describe Calvin's dilemma: as the college and the denomination it represents and serves attempt to reach out in an evangelical manner to the world beyond their ethnic origins, the college must also attempt to adhere to those elements of its identity which made it important to begin with. It is not an easy problem, and it has wrecked more than one institution. As this dean writes toward the conclusion of his essay, "We can carry high the standard of distinctively Christian higher education that translates into a daily campus reality the vision of God's Kingdom as encompassing every people and nation. That is a far more difficult, yet far more worthwhile, endeavor than merely jumping aboard the bandwagon."

Calvin *qua* Calvin already is, and has been, a significant contribution to the diversity of American higher education, the dean correctly notes. Where else can one go for such an atmosphere and for a school with Calvin's unique history? Should Calvin prove incapable of steering the difficult course it has purposefully laid for itself, diversity in America will shrink, not increase. And should Calvin be successful in walking this border, it might very well be the first such success in the nation.

For now, the faculty is solidly committed to the school's religious tradition — a fact that will help Calvin in these contentious times. A teacher being considered for tenure at Calvin must be a practicing member of the Christian Reformed Church or an ecclesiastic body in full communion with it. Faculty must also be supportive of Christian education at all levels, and are required to send their children to a church school of any denomination. "There are some people who don't like the Dutch Christian schools and they send their kids to Catholic schools," says one faculty member. "The point is that they receive a Christian education." Also, all faculty members must accept the creedal statements underlying the Christian Reformed Church, including the Heidelberg Confession, the Confession of Faith written in 1561 by the Belgian theologian Guido de Brès, and the Canons of Dort. Faculty members who cannot comfortably sign an acknowledgment of the veracity of these statements of faith, or who do not agree to send their children to Christian schools, will not receive tenure at Calvin College.

Although Calvin recently "went through an effort to loosen up the faculty requirements involving its mission statement," according to one professor, the resulting document did little to dilute the hiring rules. "You can find a few modernish statements [now], but the college is owned by the denomination, and the mission statement was not watered down," one professor says. "We reaffirmed our distinctive Reformed Christian character. We are Calvinists." In fact, the professor continues, many of Calvin's younger faculty members are opposed to the nihilism regnant in American graduate schools, and are thus more aware of the dangers posed by political correctness than many of their predecessors.

Yet there are signs not quite so encouraging, signs that Calvin is already willing to part with some aspects of its heritage. In most cases, it seems that Calvin has borrowed a concept from the wider academic world and adapted it to fit the college's environment. Professors note that the college takes pains to seek out students from non-Dutch racial backgrounds, although about half the students on campus do have Dutch heritage. "We spend a lot of money on minorities, and most who come here are earnest Christians, so they have that in common with the community," says one professor. The college now has a Multicultural Affairs Committee, which promotes and oversees the implementation of plans to increase the diversity of the college. The same professor says such an office is not the same thing one might find on a non-Reformed campus. "Our multicultural programs aren't radicalized. It's an old fashioned notion of what multiculturalism is. We're not closed off from those influences, but everything is under the Lordship of Christ," the professor explains. "It's a strange amalgam, to be sure, but there are no ideologues here."

Multiculturalism is not the only trend to make an appearance in Calvin's camp. Soon the school plans to institute a women's studies minor, which will consist of courses in psychology, philosophy, and literature. Some of the newer ideas about literature and history — ideas that have their roots in nineteenth-century nihilism — are bantered about campus. Again, professors say such words do not carry the same meanings at Calvin as they do elsewhere. "There are some here who talk about social constructionism," says one. "There is an effort to historicize discussions of historical consciousness, for example. . . . You'll find the words used at Calvin, but not in their relativistic sense. Even those who use these words do believe in truth, objective truth." Recently, though, a professor of religious studies published in the student paper an apologia for thinking of God in feminine terms. She defended the use of inclusive language in worship and hymnody and concluded that God has no gender.

Calvin, incidentally, has a policy calling for "gender-inclusive language" to be used in publications, but does not have a speech code. And the college does not do much in the way of sensitivity training, especially when compared with other schools. "Some sort of 'sensitivity training' takes place in freshmen orientation and we occasionally have voluntary summer seminars for faculty on sensitivity toward minorities or women in the classroom," remarks one professor. "As far as I know, no 'sensitivity training' has ever been required for the alleged insensitivity of a student or faculty member."

Thus it seems that while certain trends have at least a foot in Calvin's door, the faculty and administration has — for now, and generally speaking — kept their influence at bay. The question remains whether by opening the door, Calvin has let in something worthwhile or let something even greater escape.

Campus Life: Grand, Not Rapid

The student body at Calvin is more heterogeneous than it was years ago when it drew mostly middle-class Christian Reformed students from the upper Midwest. Today Calvin's students are about two-thirds Christian Reformed, a number that has dropped quite a bit over the past decade. Calvin's "Entrada" program brings ethnic minority students to campus in an effort to meet the administration's stated goal of making Calvin "a genuinely multicultural Christian academic community and one in which a cross-cultural community is celebrated," according to the student handbook.

Many scholarships are available for students: twenty-two pages worth in the college catalogue, to be exact. This huge number makes Calvin an attractive place for anyone who shares the school's religious views and wants to apply to a school with the resources to offer so much financial aid.

All students under twenty-one years of age are required to live either on campus or at home with their parents. The college bases its code of Christian conduct (which includes prohibitions on sexual or racial harassment, underage drinking, drug use, and obscene language) on Matthew 22:37-40, "the Christian law of love," according to the student handbook. The code is enforced by judicial bodies composed of students, faculty, or both, depending on the circumstances of the allegation.

There are no fraternities or sororities at Calvin; however, there are quite a few student groups on campus, including fine arts groups like Gospel Choir, Playwright Productions, Writers' Guild, and an improvisational theater group, as well as political groups. The latter category includes both a Democratic and Republican group, as well as Amnesty International and Calvin Students for Christian Feminism, among a few others. The campus often hosts concerts by some of the many Christian alternative rock groups that have flourished in recent years. Popular sports include track and field, soccer, and women's volleyball. In 1997 Calvin had seven all-Americans at the NCAA track and field championships. The women's team finished seventh nationally. There is a full list of intramural sports as well.

To encourage students and faculty to spend time together, Calvin offers a "Take a Prof to Lunch" voucher program. Any student on the college meal plan can pick up — free of charge from the college's Student Life Division — a voucher providing a free cafeteria meal to the professor of the student's choice. "Students are encouraged to use this program as a way to get to know a particular faculty member better, to encourage a mentoring relationship, to seek additional academic advising, or to work on college committee work," the student handbook says.

CARLETON COLLEGE

Office of Admissions
100 South College Street
Northfield, MN 55057-4016
(800) 995-2275
www.carleton.edu

Total enrollment: 1,754
Undergraduates: 1,754
SAT Ranges (Verbal/Math): V 620-740, M 630-720
Financial aid: 62%
Applicants: 2,960
Accepted: 49%
Enrolled: 32%
Application deadline: Jan. 15
Financial aid application deadline: Mar. 1
Tuition: $20,171
Core curriculum: No

Trying Too Hard?

Founded over a century ago by the Congregational Church, Carleton College has established a reputation as one of the foremost liberal arts schools in the country. To some extent, this reputation is deserved: both faculty and students are dedicated to serious study. But reputations have a way of getting out of line with reality.

Carleton College tries too hard at some things and not hard enough at others. There's something self-conscious in the image the college cultivates — a place too hip for books, but which studies them and learns them so well they can afford some time off to be clever. It's the clever part where we think Carleton tries too hard — the way the portion of a recruiting package that contains campus statistics like the 95 percent of faculty with terminal degrees, the ninety-three National Merit scholars in a recent incoming class, and the half-million-volume library is followed by the noteworthy fact that there are 1.735 "Frisbees per capita" on campus.

On the other hand, the college has not tried hard enough to free its curriculum and social atmosphere of ideology. There are some strange classes in the curriculum, and this is one of the very few institutions of higher learning which sponsors a drag queen contest (which does not stem from some sort of fraternity hazing ritual). Among the stranger phenomena at Carleton: "closed" groups like fraternities are banned while "diverse" groups (like a racially segregated organization) are on the verge of getting their own dorm.

Still, say what you will about the culture on campus, there is no denying that Carleton students not only work hard and learn quite a bit, but they seem to fall in love with the life of the mind. Scores go on to graduate school, and Carleton ranks near the top of all private colleges in the percentage of graduates who obtain doctorates. The science departments are very good, and have been mostly spared the politicization that has affected the humanities side of the college. A mature student capable of withstanding the powerful forces of conformism at Carleton can obtain a fine education there.

Academic Life: Dominant Is in the Mind of the Beholder

Carleton has no core curriculum to speak of, and its distribution requirements seem to be deliberately loose — something that is in keeping with the hyper-individualism that pervades the campus. There is no Western civilization requirement, although students must take a course to fulfill the "Recognition and Affirmation of Differences Requirement." This is required because, as the college catalogue says, Carleton "defines itself as an institution that values diversity. This is reflected in the importance and pride the college places in a student body that includes a balanced number of men and women, and includes people from a variety of racial, ethnic, and economic backgrounds." What differences does the college seek to explore? "The word 'Difference' in the name of the requirement reminds us that differences do exist," the catalogue says. "And if we are to create a community that embraces diversity, we must expose ourselves to perspectives that have developed outside of, in opposition to, or in ways only dimly visible to the dominant culture in which most of us have grown up and been educated."

The term "dimly visible" might apply to the so-called dominant culture when it comes to the distribution requirements. Two courses are required in the arts and literature group, which includes art and art history, dance, English, media studies, music, theater, classical and modern literature. Since no literature classes are mandated, by name or in general, it is safe to say that Carleton makes no attempt to put its students through a systematic reading of Western classics. Two courses are also required in the humanities group, which includes history, philosophy, and religion. Again, no particular courses are set in stone, meaning a Carleton graduate could be, for the most part, ignorant of Western history.

Carleton requires students to take three courses in the social sciences (economics, educational studies, linguistics, political science, psychology, sociology, and anthropology), none of which need have anything to do with American governmental institutions. Three mathematics and natural science courses are also required from a group including biology, chemistry, geology, physics, and astronomy;

math and computer science; and certain psychology courses. All three courses can be without lab work.

The strongest part of Carleton's distribution requirements is the foreign language component: it applies to all majors (not just B.A.s, as at many places) and forces students to demonstrate fourth-term competency in a language either through classroom work or testing.

Despite these meager requirements, Carleton graduates have amassed an enviable record of achievement over the years. Carleton is first among liberal arts colleges in the number of graduates who went on to earn Ph.D.s in the laboratory sciences between 1981 and 1990, according to the National Research Council. It is among the top five undergraduate schools in terms of graduates earning doctorates in all fields of study during the same period. In fact, more than half of all Carleton alumni have earned advanced degrees, and over a quarter have earned doctorates. And, since 1980, it is one of only two undergraduate colleges whose alumni have won five Rhodes scholarships.

What these statistics reveal is a highly motivated, selective student body that receives excellent professional training from the faculty. This is especially true in the sciences, where the necessary rigor and empiricism serve to block the pernicious influences of radical and nihilistic politics. It also speaks well of the faculty's role in giving students the self-confidence and desire necessary to persevere in their chosen fields.

Carleton professors are known for permitting their students to collaborate closely with them on research projects, and students who do this are often quite well prepared for lab work or other research encountered in graduate or professional school.

Along these same lines, Carleton likes nothing more than to seem a place where the nonstandard is standard, where being an "individual" is about as important as being a good student. Much of this stems from the educational philosophy of John Dewey and his intellectual descendants, who hold that it is more important to teach students how to "think critically" than to ensure that they learn an agreed-upon body of knowledge. The irony is that without the discipline of mastering a common culture, young people have fewer resources and their individuality is of an extremely limited sort.

Even in an excellent school like Carleton, it takes little effort to find courses and departments that are a poor substitute for the more traditional, rigorous curriculum they have so often displaced. For example, English majors at Carleton must take classes from several different historical periods, yet are not required to study Shakespeare. It's hard to imagine an engineering or science program run so haphazardly — skip basic engineering, for example, and it becomes very difficult indeed to make it past later classes. It seems that the practitioners of scientific disciplines still agree on what constitutes a basic body of knowledge. This is no longer true in the humanities and, to a lesser degree, the social sciences — the hierarchy of knowledge has all but disappeared.

Here are some sample offerings from the most politicized departments at Carleton, including history, American studies, English, and women's studies. There is also a concentration in African/African-American studies that could be included on that list.

- Literary Studies 150, "Amazons, Valkyries, Naiads, Dykes: Woman-Identified and Lesbian Artists in Europe." "Questions of sexual identity and textual aesthetics will be foregrounded against the politics of cultural history an [sic] canon formation. No prerequisites."
- Sociology/Anthropology/Women's Studies 226, "Anthropology of Gender." "This course examines gender and gender relations. . . . We will discuss such key concepts as gender, status, public and private spheres, and the gendered division of labor. . . . The course will focus on . . . the impacts of colonialism and economic underdevelopment on Third World women, and the role of procreation in creating cultural notions of gender and affecting relations between genders."
- Political Science/Women's Studies 354, "Feminist Political Theory." "This seminar will cover the major developments in feminist theory as that theory relates to authority (political) relationships. Liberal, radical, Marxist and socialist-feminist critiques and their antecedents in political philosophy will be analyzed in the course."

The best departments at Carleton all end in science: political science and the hard sciences, especially chemistry, physics and astronomy, geology, and biology. Former political science professor Paul Wellstone has taken his politics to the U.S. Senate.

Political Atmosphere: There She/He Is, Miss/Mr. America . . .

Carleton is known to be generally liberal in both faculty and student leanings, and the same must be said of the administration. The public image projected by the college is one of political righteousness. The school's glossy viewbook, sent to all prospective students, includes a long section entitled "Celebrating Differences." "As in the wider world," the statement reads, "the college is not immune to the anxieties and insensitivities that grow out of racial and cultural differences. But the openness and egalitarian nature of the campus community make Carleton a more receptive place for people of different races, cultures and beliefs to get to know and understand one another."

Perhaps the most obvious example of Carleton's departure from traditional mores and beliefs is found in its energetic promotion of the gay/lesbian/bisexual/transgendered community on campus. April is "Gay and Lesbian Pride Month" at

Carleton. A few of the events sponsored by the college for this auspicious month include a lecture on "Transliberation" and the queer and women's movements by Leslie Feinberg, "a nationally renowned transgendered activist and author of 'Stone Butch Blues' and 'Transgendered Warriors,'" and a reading by a Carleton alumnus from his book called *Gay and Gaia: Ethics, Ecology and the Erotic.*

The following scene was undoubtedly the showstopper. First came this announcement: "From 8-9:00 p.m. there will be an opportunity for students to strut their stuff in a 'competition' in drag that the performers will be judging. Then, at 9:00 p.m. the show, featuring five performers from the Minneapolis club The Gay 90s, will begin."

A few students explained what happened in the next issue of a college newspaper. "It definitely pushed the limits of people's comfort zones, but that is, after all, what this month is about," one student said. "It is a way of speaking out against the repression and oppression of established social constructs. It is sexual liberation, but it's also liberation of the individual. The drag queens are expressing themselves in a way that society has forbidden them to do and in forbidding, injured them." "It really made me think about and question my preconceived notions about gender; I didn't even know what pronoun to use," said another student. The first student added, "The entire concept of transgenderism tends to blow people away. It destroys the social constructs we have about what it means to have gender and rebuilds them from a different perspective. It's a good exercise in what we're doing at Carleton as a liberal arts institution exploring the cutting edge ideas in identity politics."

It is difficult to know whether to laugh or cry at the gushing silliness of all this romanticized ideology. Whether it is truly dangerous or just a colossal waste of time, it clearly has little or nothing to do with a liberal arts education.

Carleton is also on board with a variety of so-called Shared Interest Living Areas each year, although the college recently denied such quarters for several groups that looked like shoo-ins in the early betting, including the Women's Awareness group, the African-American Awareness group, and even the Carleton Breakdance Squad. The college is reportedly reconsidering its decision on the African-American Awareness group, perhaps because efforts to segregate students by ethnicity or interests are effective marketing tools. Unfortunately, a program like this removes one of the principal arguments for dorm life: the necessity to get along with people from different backgrounds and with different interests. Meanwhile, fraternities and sororities are prohibited; a publication sent to prospective students describes these groups as "closed."

One might think that a place such as Carleton would be friendlier to liberal and chic faculty than to those who may object to the regnant orthodoxies on campus, and one would not be entirely wrong. However, one faculty member reports that "we have hired conservatives in my department regularly." Whether or not this is true for other departments is hard to tell, but this is an encouraging sign. Clearly at Carleton, as at most colleges, the degree of politicization varies from department to department, with the more humanistic programs more likely to fall prey to the ideologues.

One might also think that a place such as Carleton might be setting new legal precedent with speech codes and sensitivity training, but there one would be mostly wrong. The college does require some sensitivity training, but there is no speech code. It seems that the academic culture at Carleton is strong enough to withstand efforts to totally shut down any who oppose the liberal ethos on campus. After all, the college does not produce so many future scholars by locking them into a prescribed philosophy. Given that Carleton is such a small college in such a small town, it is clear that the threat of social ostracism plays a large role in determining just how far anyone opposed to the school's pet ideologies will go in voicing opposition.

Student Life: Smart, Hip, Grungy, Ironic?

A recruiting publication tells the story of a very unofficial campus group called "RAISE," or "Replace All International Symbols with Elvis," which stole the campus's American flag and replaced it with an Elvis banner. According to a ransom note, the flag was only to be returned after President Lewis sang, in public, at least ten seconds of an Elvis tune. The president belted out "Ain't Nothin' but a Hound Dog" at assembly one day, and the flag was returned in an attaché case by a RAISE emissary wearing dark glasses. We're pretty sure that with only 1,870 students on campus, someone must have known who he was. We're also pretty sure that he didn't know his prank would wind up as college promotional material, but we suspect he wouldn't mind.

The same publication claims that at Carleton "people laugh at pretentiousness," but the attempt by many on campus to be smart, hip, grungy, and ironic is a bit too self-conscious for some tastes. Sometimes pretentiousness creeps in the back door.

Be that as it may, students are very active out of the classroom. According to the school's reckoning, about one-third of them play at least one intercollegiate sport, and nearly three-fourths play intramurals, including snow football games that Minnesota hasn't enjoyed at the professional level since the Vikings moved indoors to the Hubert H. Humphrey Metrodome, about forty miles to the north in Minneapolis. Carleton has a Division III football team, as well as nine other sports for men and nine for women. Both sexes participate in both downhill and cross-country ski teams, and there are several other club sports. The school awards no athletic scholarships and makes a point of telling its prospective students that "Carleton coaches understand that academic coursework has priority, and athletes know that they can compete in the intercollegiate arena and still find time to study or attend afternoon laboratories."

The campus is pretty, and its 950 acres include a 400-acre arboretum and two of Minnesota's fabled ten thousand lakes. However, about 65 percent of the students leave campus for study abroad at some point during their education. They can also drive to the Twin Cities for entertainment and the wide range of cultural events held in this very underrated metropolitan area. There are also many lectures and performances on campus, including an annual visit by the excellent St. Paul Chamber Orchestra.

The approximately one hundred student groups run the gamut from the laudable to the lamentable, with far more liberal groups than conservative ones among those focused on politics. In fact, the college viewbook puts it this way: "From whatever perspective, students tend to be activists rather than bystanders on current issues and problems, ranging from AIDS to apartheid to sexual harassment." Groups on campus include choral and drama groups; *Breaking Ground,* a feminist journal; a student paper called the *Carletonian;* Carleton Christian Fellowship; the Carleton Vegans and Vegetarians; the Coalition of Women of Color; the Collective for Women's Issues; the Conservative Union; the Druids, which "celebrate a combination of many traditions with a basic reverence for nature"; Field and Stream; the Lesbian, Gay and Bisexual Community; the Newman Club for Catholic students; Pagan Studies, which "explores religions outside the Judeo-Christian tradition"; Pro-Life Organization, which "creates an awareness of the pro-life position"; and SOUL (Students Organized for Unity and Liberation), which "promotes a sense of community among African-American students."

CARNEGIE MELLON UNIVERSITY

Office of Admissions
5000 Forbes Avenue
Pittsburgh, PA 15213-3891
(412) 268-2082
www.cmu.edu

Total enrollment: 7,760
Undergraduates: 4,820
SAT Ranges (Verbal/Math): V 590-700, M 650-740
Financial aid: 62%
Applicants: 13,310
Accepted: 47%
Enrolled: 22%

Application deadline: Dec. 1
Financial aid application deadline: Feb. 15
Tuition: $21,275
Core curriculum: No

Just Achieve

In today's competitive higher education environment, many so-called liberal arts colleges lure unsuspecting students and their parents with the appeal of ivy-covered halls, an esteemed tradition, and dubious claims about their "commitment to the liberal arts." More often than not, these claims paper over the fact that many members of the administration and faculty inhabiting those halls are actively working to subvert the college's traditional mission and to transform the curriculum in ways the founders never envisioned. In this context, there is something refreshing and admirable about Carnegie Mellon's frank articulation of its rather utilitarian aims and mission, and its continued adherence to the dual interests of its founder, industrialist Andrew Carnegie.

The liberal arts are not the primary interest of Carnegie Mellon University (CMU). The university has a reputation for excellence in both the technical sciences (engineering, computer science, robotics) and the arts (especially drama). But if one word had to be chosen to define the central institutional focus, it would have to be "technology." All CMU students, regardless of the school they enter or the major they select, must take a course in computer instruction, and the university prides itself on being "one of the most progressive, intense and exciting computing environments in the world." "Andrew," the campus computer network, links over 7,500 personal computers and workstations throughout campus, enabling students to register, access grades and course material, and perform numerous other academic functions without ever having to interact with a human being. Indeed, one student looks forward to the annual spring carnival because it is "one of the few times people get out from behind their computers."

Technology has been the school's focus since its founding. Originally called the Carnegie Technical Schools, CMU was founded in 1900 to "provide the children of working families with training to move into better careers." In 1912 the school changed its name to the Carnegie Institute of Technology and launched its current reputation as a school that excels in engineering and the performing arts. In 1967 the school merged with the Mellon Institute to become Carnegie Mellon University. Despite the emphasis on computers, many CMU students do have more on their minds than information technology, and Carnegie Mellon can boast an eclectic but uniformly successful cadre of graduates, including Oscar-winning actress Holly Hunter, astronaut Judith Resnik, and artist Andy Warhol.

This college guide does not claim a person cannot be successful without a traditional education — only that such an education, in our opinion, best prepares a person to make his best efforts in his chosen field. In the case of Carnegie Mellon, we submit that the exceptions prove the rule, and that the motivation and skill of a particular student can do much to surmount whatever is lost when the student's education does not include all that we would like. Providing a liberal education has never been Carnegie Mellon's purpose; it has been enough for the school to do well the things that it does.

Academic Life: Great Skills, Not Great Books

Carnegie Mellon neither educates its students in the liberal arts tradition nor subscribes to every fad that sweeps academia. Rather, the school boldly proclaims its commitment to training individuals for highly specialized professions: "In a world which has sometimes placed too little emphasis on 'skill,'" says the undergraduate catalogue, "we take pride in educating students who display excellence in application, students who can do useful things with their learning." The cover of the catalogue is emblazoned with only one word: "Achieve." Contemplative students looking for a different type of achievement — say, a place to learn about the great books of Western civilization or to be immersed in a curriculum that prepares them for any walk of life — should go somewhere else.

The university's emphasis on doing, making, creating, and analyzing is reflected in the course requirements for undergraduates. All undergrads have two required courses, one in writing — "because sharp written communication is important to almost every field" — and one in computing, for similar reasons. The freshman English composition course is reputedly heavily politicized, and is considered by many students as one way of ensuring that all freshmen are favorably introduced to multicultural ideology early on. The students must also choose between two courses in "Argument and Interpretation." The courses are taught almost exclusively by graduate students, who, according to one student, "wield enormous power" at Carnegie Mellon.

Students at CMU enroll in one of seven colleges: Carnegie Institute of Technology (engineering); College of Fine Arts; College of Humanities and Social Sciences (H&SS); Graduate School of Industrial Administration; H. John Heinz III School of Public Policy and Management; Mellon College of Science; and the School of Computer Science. While some students complain that the administration seems largely preoccupied with fund-raising and research, and that some professors aren't as interested in teaching or advising as they should be, the university has many strong departments. According to faculty and students, these include drama, electrical engineering, computer science and robotics, the graduate business school, physics, engineering, music, and industrial management.

The university is nationally recognized as a premier institution for the study of chemical and electrical engineering, but its drama and music departments also have outstanding reputations. But while Carnegie Mellon promotes an unusual blend of science and performing arts, the humanistic disciplines seem to get lost somewhere in the shuffle. Within H&SS are a limited number of departments: economics, English, history, modern languages, philosophy, psychology, social and decision sciences, and statistics. Only about one-quarter of Carnegie Mellon's 4,820 undergraduates choose this college, which stresses "practical skills" as much as (some would say more than) traditional liberal arts studies. In keeping with its focus on the applied, analytic dimension of education, the college offers two tracks of majors in most areas: a more traditional "disciplinary" major (economics, philosophy, or political science, for instance) and a more specialized "professional" major (usually a compound description, like managerial economics, computational linguistics, or policy and management).

In addition to the writing and computing requirements is a set of general education distribution requirements that all H&SS students must complete, and again, the university has no pretensions that these resemble a traditional core. Students must choose eight courses from among the following six categories: "Cognition, Choice and Behavior," "Economic, Political, and Social Institutions," "Creative Production and Reflection," "Cultural Analysis," "Mathematical Reasoning," and "Science and Technology." There is no formal requirement in Western civilization, though the standard curriculum that all H&SS students must take includes a course in "World Culture." This course "seeks to help students to not only understand [sic] cultural differences that exist in the world, but also to value these differences." The standard H&SS curriculum also contains courses entitled "Introduction to Intelligence" and "Statistical Reasoning." To its credit, Carnegie Mellon does make an honest attempt to give students at least a glimpse of the liberal arts within the liberal/professional model of education it espouses. But because of the "progressive" nature of that model — and, of course, the general trendiness of academe — a student's transcript will likely be populated more with courses like "Debates and Controversies: Cultural Differences in Action" or "Cultural and Cross-Cultural Perspectives on the Environment" than with traditional offerings in the liberal arts.

Political Atmosphere: Noses to the Grindstone

For a variety of reasons, politics generally take a backseat to academics at Carnegie Mellon. The students' drive to achieve usually keeps political and multicultural machinations on campus to a minimum. "About 80 to 90 percent of students are mainly focused on academics," says an undergraduate. The technical nature of the school also plays a role: one professor attributes the general political neutrality, and specifically the absence of serious agitation on multicultural and diversity issues, to the general weakness of the humanities and social sciences on campus. "I think the primary thing that keeps the temperature low here . . . is the fact that the students are either in the hard sciences — where it does not appear to be a hot issue — or in the arts — where it is *de rigueur* and already exists. We do not have hoards of majors in the social sciences where this would be an issue."

Even so, things have on occasion been more than a little unsettled at Carnegie Mellon — just ask Patrick Mooney. The cautionary tale of Mooney, a political science major who repeatedly found himself in litigation against his university, is enough to give any conservative student pause before enrolling at CMU. It all began in August of 1991, when Mooney was asked to wear a triangle-shaped button, the symbol of gay and lesbian pride, as part of a "Gay, Lesbian, and Bi-Sexual Issues" session conducted as part of the training program for student residence assistants. Although he quietly attended the session, Mooney, a Roman Catholic, refused to wear the gay pride button because it conflicted with his religious beliefs. Four days later he was fired from his position, despite "receiving positive evaluations" on his performance as a residence assistant the previous semester, according to the *Western Pennsylvania Tribune-Review*. Mooney brought suit against the university, "seeking, among other things, an injunction ordering Carnegie Mellon not to discriminate on the basis of religion," according to *Campus* magazine. The suit was settled out of court.

In 1994 Mooney found himself in trouble again, this time falsely accused of harassing a gay professor and facing serious disciplinary action for removing an offensive pro-homosexual poster. The details are admittedly crude, but they illustrate the permissive attitude of Carnegie Mellon's administration toward radical groups and the general intolerance on campus for serious religious conviction. Mooney noticed a flyer with the image of Cardinal John J. O'Connor next to a condom with the message "Know Your Scumbags" printed across it. In violation of a campus policy requiring that all flyers bear the name of the sponsoring organization, this poster was unsigned, as it were, except for the pleasant reminder: "We're here. We're queer. We're funded by your student activities fees."

Mooney removed the poster in order to photocopy it and complain to the proper officials. According to Mooney, while he was noticing the poster, he approached a man nearby and asked him "if he could believe that someone would put a poster like that on campus." The man expressed support for the poster, and a brief debate ensued. Mooney later discovered that the man was a homosexual drama professor, and only then because the professor charged him with "harassment on the basis of sexual orientation." After a series of retreats by the university administration, the bogus harassment charges were dropped, but Mooney received a "disciplinary warning" for removing the poster, which turned out to have been hung by a campus gay activist group called CMU-Out.

According to one student, "Pat set a good precedent," proving that truth will win out if you make enough noise, or at least illustrating that universities hate negative press enough to stop persecuting conservative students. Still, the few Carnegie Mellon students willing to stand up for their traditional beliefs and free speech rights often fight an uphill battle. This battle often goes through the University Disciplinary Committee (UDC), which one student calls the "most horrific organization" on campus. In a recent year, according to one undergraduate, a certain female graduate student (nicknamed the "Commissar for Political Correctness") who was heavily involved in CMU-Out and the Pittsburgh Lesbian Avengers, repeatedly brought to the UDC charges against male students. In general, the 2,700 graduate students wield enormous power over campus life, reigning over what one student calls "little fiefdoms."

CMU does have a Political Speakers Forum Board. Although the speakers are predominantly liberal, the College Republicans and Young America's Foundation have, in recent years, successfully hosted such conservatives as Walter Williams and Dinesh D'Souza. Generous university funding for such events is rarely forthcoming, though "if conservatives are willing to do the work," notes one student, "they can have their fair share of the funds." But as one faculty member says, "Hardly any conservative speakers come to the campus." There is, however, a conservative newspaper, the *Phoenix,* which is published jointly with the University of Pittsburgh; yet it receives no funding from Carnegie Mellon.

Student Life: Away from the Terminal

Carnegie Mellon is located in an attractive area of Pittsburgh, within walking distance of the Oakland, Squirrel Hill, and Shadyside neighborhoods, where students can take advantage of shopping and cultural activities. The campus is bordered by the 500-acre Schenley Park, home to the Frick Fine Arts Museum and the Phipps Conservatory, which is a nice place to jog or, in the winter months, ice-skate. Pittsburgh is a thoroughly revamped steel town, partaking in elements of both Midwestern community identity and East Coast cultural activities. The Carnegie, an impressive cultural complex housing the Museum of Art (known for its Impressionist collection), the Museum of Natural History, Carnegie Music Hall, and Carnegie Library, is only a five-minute walk from campus. Although many of Pittsburgh's major cultural activities occur in the summer (the Three Rivers Arts Festival, Three Rivers Regatta, and a Shakespeare festival), CMU students will find plenty of social and cultural opportunities during the academic year.

The campus has retained some tokens of the Scottish heritage of its founder. The main cafeteria, located in Resnik House, is called the Highlander Cafe. The student newspaper is the *Tartan,* the yearbook the *Thistle,* and the drama club the Scotch 'n Soda. The university offers the world's only bagpiping major, and pipers have the opportunity to perform at campus events in the Kiltie Band. Freshmen are required to live in university housing, but they can choose from a wide range of residence halls, university apartments, special-interest houses, and Greek houses. There are a number of desirable residence hall options for first-year students, including Mudge

House, a mansion originally built by the Mudge family but now converted into a coed residence hall. Single-sex accommodations are also available: Scobell Hall houses male residents; the C and D towers of Morewood Gardens (described as what "once was a gracious apartment complex for affluent Pittsburghers") are for women only.

Although sports are not the focal point of Carnegie Mellon life, many students become involved in the thirty or so athletic groups the university offers. Carnegie Mellon competes in the NCAA Division III, comprising schools that do not offer athletic scholarships. The university is also a member of the University Athletic Association (UAA), which includes eight other private research universities. The Tartans men's football team holds the Division III record for consecutive games without being shut out, and the winning season recorded in 1995 was the team's twenty-first in a row. Women's cross-country and both men's and women's swimming are also strong.

In the spring of 1997 the board of trustees elected Dr. Jared L. Cohon as the new president of Carnegie Mellon. Cohon, who previously served as the dean of the School of Forestry at Yale University, replaced outgoing president Dr. Robert Mehrabian, known for his fund-raising skills. Cohon has also served as legislative assistant for energy and environment for Senator Daniel Patrick Moynihan (D-N.Y.), and was appointed by President Clinton in January 1997 to serve as chairman of the Nuclear Waste Technical Review Board. Although it is too soon to tell in which direction President Cohon will lead the university, many faculty speak highly of the priorities of the current administration. As one professor notes, "They have made great efforts, mostly successful, to increase the endowment and have an excellent track record in keeping the physical plant of the University in excellent condition."

Some argue that the university's two predominant interests — the hard sciences and the arts — make for a strange and sometimes volatile blend of "computer geeks" and "artsy types" on campus. One student characterizes it as a "pretty weird environment," but others think the divergent interests are an asset, not a liability. As one professor notes, "The atmosphere here is a good one because of the mix of excellent hard science and excellent arts. It's an interesting mix and makes the campus somewhat unusual."

CASE WESTERN RESERVE UNIVERSITY

P.O. Box 128016
Cleveland, OH 44112-8016
(216) 368-4450
www.cwru.edu

Total enrollment: 9,970
Undergraduates: 3,680
SAT Ranges (Verbal/Math): V 590-700, M 620-720
Financial aid: 91%
Applicants: 4,427
Accepted: 79%
Enrolled: 22%
Application deadline: Feb. 1
Financial aid application deadline: Feb. 1
Tuition: $18,500
Core curriculum: No

Taking the Case

Case Western Reserve University (CRWU) was formed in 1967 when the Case Institute of Technology (founded in 1880) got together with the liberal arts–oriented Western Reserve University (founded in 1826). Today the combined entity enrolls almost 3,700 undergraduate students and some 6,100 graduate and professional students. Both schools maintain their historic emphases; even today, the engineering core curriculum is called the Case curriculum, while the School of Arts and Sciences is considered a part of the Western Reserve side of the university. The best departments are equally divided between technology fields and the humanities.

Part of the personality of CWRU, and an important factor in its academic quality, is its location in the 600-acre University Circle area of Cleveland, about four miles from downtown. Many jokes have been told about Cleveland and its formerly burning river, but the city will probably get the last laugh: its cultural attractions are first-rate, and include a world-class symphony, museums, and the Rock and Roll Hall of Fame. All of these are not far from CWRU. These riches play an immediate and important role for students both in the enrichment they offer the curriculum and in the cultural sophistication their presence lends to campus.

The university is almost untouched by the politicization found at schools across the country, and this characteristic will likely be preserved given CWRU's hiring practices and the importance placed on undergraduate teaching there. For its neighborhood and strong infrastructure, CWRU is worth the consideration of any serious student.

Academic Life: Three Cores/One School = Distribution Requirements

Because of Case Western Reserve's unusual history as two separate institutions, the curriculum and general campus atmosphere are a bit different from that found at most other institutions. Students choose from three different degree programs that the university terms "core curricula," although they are more accurately called distribution requirements.

The Arts and Sciences Core Curriculum, which grows out of the old Western Reserve University, lays the foundation for those majoring in the humanities and arts, social and behavioral sciences, and mathematics and the natural sciences. Requirements include a freshman English course, four courses in the natural and mathematical sciences, four courses in the arts and humanities, three courses in social science, and a course in an area called "Global and Cultural Diversity." "There has been an effort to require cultural diversity," a professor says. "That's in itself good, but it is best to let the students acquire it on their own rather than having someone cram it down their throats." There are no requirements in either Western civilization or a foreign language, though good courses are available.

This core path offers a decent breadth of choices, but many courses are too specialized to be included in a broad liberal education. And some are not terribly rigorous. Says one professor: "It is possible to avoid coming to grips with the fundamental issues of civilization" in fulfilling the requirements. The specialized course options are sometimes the most academically challenging, but miss the point, the professor says; "You don't address broad and important questions in them."

The Arts and Sciences core's thirty-three hours of requirements are drawn from a relatively limited list representing a wide range of disciplines. This approach does much to teach the methodology of the chosen disciplines but little to integrate what is learned or to give students the broad knowledge that can be of use in any discipline. Students tend to learn the research skills used by professional scholars rather than a body of empirical knowledge useful to future intellectual and social growth.

The second set of distribution requirements, the Case Core Curriculum, is designed for students who major in engineering, computer science, and management science. This core provides some background in the humanities and social sciences, but as one would expect, it requires more intensive work in mathematics and science than does the Arts and Sciences core. In addition to the standard class in freshman English, all students must complete the following requirements: a four-semester sequence in calculus and differential equations; two semesters of chemistry with one term of laboratory work; three semesters of physics; one term of computer science; and seven one-semester courses in the humanities and social sciences, at least four of which must be taken in a single department or program. Students in this program are exempted from the cultural diversity requirement found in the other two curricula.

Faculty members praise the Case curriculum because it seeks to give engineers and scientists more than a merely technical education. "It does succeed, partly because the students themselves come here with the intention of getting more than just a technical or science major," a professor explains. "When the universities merged, we added a number of techies, and we decided to humanize them. We do it in a sound intellectual way."

Even with the enormous amount of assigned work, around two-thirds of the engineering and science majors earn an additional major, according to a professor. This speaks well of the students' love of learning, and shows that they have been taught to appreciate many kinds of learning.

"Most engineering students do quite well in the social sciences and humanities," a social sciences professor says. "They know how to organize their time and how to study. I'm also amazed to find them on sports teams in disproportionate numbers."

This effort to "humanize" the technical students at CWRU is analogous to a recent trend in the medical profession. For several years now, top medical schools have looked for candidates who know more than what they learned in the lab so that they can approach their human patients with both empathy and conversational English. CWRU is doing much the same thing for engineers, and one hopes that this pattern is replicated at other engineering schools.

The final core option is the Weatherhead General Education Requirements, added to the menu in 1996. Named for the Weatherhead School of Management, these requirements provide an academic foundation for those majoring in accounting and management. Among these requirements are the ubiquitous freshman English class; four courses, two with labs, in natural and mathematical sciences; three or four courses in both the arts and humanities and in the social sciences; plus the politically correct cultural diversity requirement.

The best teachers at CWRU include Christopher Cullis in biology; Roy Baumeister and Lee Thompson in psychology; Chin-Tai Kim in philosophy; William Siebenschuh, Martha Woodmansee, Suzanne Ferguson, and Thomas Bishop in English; Kenneth Grundy and Laura Tartakov in political science; Cynthia Beall in anthropology; Gary Deimling in sociology; Robert Brown, Glenn Starkman, and Lawrence Krauss in physics; Anthony Pearson in chemistry; William Pierce, Thomas Bogart, and Robert Baird in economics; Eldon Epps in religion; and Kenneth Ledford in history.

Two of the university's strongest departments, economics and accounting, are found in the Weatherhead School of Management. Art history is also very good, and makes extensive use of the resources of the Cleveland Museum of Art and the Cleveland Art Institute. History and religion are both excellent, as are biochemistry, physics, and psychology.

Among the few politicized departments at Case Western Reserve is English, which tends strongly toward deconstructionism. Anthropology is said to be deeply divided between those who specialize in medical anthropology and more traditional scholars, but, according to a professor from another department, the balance is shifting toward medical anthropology because of recent hires. "It's more tilted toward graduate education," this professor says.

Very few departments can be called politicized, says another professor. "This campus doesn't have quite that intensity that you find at some others, but in the humanities and social sciences the faculty are very much what you might call *New York Times*-oriented," the professor says. "There are a few extreme ones here and there, but none of the real academic departments are terribly politicized. The faculty who stay on seem to be pretty solid."

Political Atmosphere: Mind Meld

There have at times been signs of strain in the marriage between the two partners in this university, and today they are drifting apart, according to one source. Until a few years ago both schools were under a single dean and provost, but in 1993 Western Reserve formed the School of Arts and Sciences with a separate dean, John Bassett. "In a way it's a reversion to the old two-institution model," a professor says, an increased tendency toward the autonomy both the liberal arts institute and the technological school once emphasized when the liberal studies program was first founded. This separation is discouraged as a dominant trend for the future, however, for much emphasis is still placed on "humanizing" the science and technology majors through the Arts and Sciences school's reading and writing preparatory programs.

About 45 percent of entering students plan to major in technical subjects, but less than 30 percent end up with a technical degree printed on their diploma. The ease with which students go back and forth between the liberal arts and technical fields would seem to indicate less of a division among students; some say, in fact, that it is alumni who have never fully accepted the federation of the two schools. "There is bound to be some rivalry, some teasing that the students who are not engineers have somehow chosen an 'easier' curriculum," a professor says. "But the many students who change to the arts and humanities or who take second majors or minors in these areas appreciate the high quality faculty and the enormously rich resources of the campus."

At the very least, the two sides of CWRU share an atmosphere light on politicization. This tolerance of many philosophies is notable because of the difficulty, in today's university environment, of assembling a list of faculty candidates who are not overtly ideological and narrowly educated. Case Western has overcome this problem, and though the campus is definitely liberal, it, its faculty, and its students are not overtly ideological. "When we launch a search for a new hire, we're looking for a certain personality type, one who's open to ideas and to even arguing with us," a professor says. "We're not setting out to find people who're just like us. . . . We have faculty who reflect the ideas of their training, but we don't have many ideologues."

Many institutions have chosen to let faculty pursue pet projects (and grant money) at the expense of their teaching duties, and CWRU is certainly not blameless in this regard; junior faculty members know they must turn out publications in order to win tenure. There are, however, positive signs that Case Western Reserve is taking its teaching mission more seriously now than at any time in its recent past. "We're beginning to put our money where our mouth is and upgrade teaching," notes one professor. "New faculty must teach well, and I'm amazed at how my junior colleagues are excited about their teaching."

The president of the university, Agnar Pytte, is said by some faculty to be the only president the university has had in the last thirty years who clearly values undergraduate education. While other presidents were lawyers or engineers concerned with money and research, Pytte himself opens his door to students every Wednesday afternoon. While the university will never allow teaching to be the sole determining criterion for tenure, a professor says, "It isn't likely that someone will gain tenure if their teaching is abysmal."

All faculty candidates at CWRU must prove that they can teach before they are offered a job. While this would seem basic to the hiring process, this condition is in fact rarely imposed at other schools. "When we hire someone, we require them to teach a class of undergraduates, and then we get feedback from the students," one faculty member says. "We want to see them interact with undergraduates — to see them on their feet — and that's how you get some insight on how good they are."

The university has a Center of Innovation in Teaching and Education, which gives faculty members financial and administrative support to improve their teaching and to develop creative teaching for their courses. The university has also reduced the teaching load of some faculty from three courses per semester to two in order to protect the quality of teaching. And the people most able to recognize good teaching and most likely to bear the brunt of bad teaching — the students — have a voice in tenure decisions. "Students' and former students' opinions are routinely sought in tenure and promotion cases," a professor says. "Promotion to full professor may be delayed if there are reservations about teaching."

Some introductory courses — chemistry, for example — are taught in large auditoriums before hundreds of students. However, university statistics show that 65 percent of classes have less than thirty students, and 45 percent have less than twenty.

For more personal attention, students sometimes turn to the university's advising system. Unfortunately, the quality of faculty advising at CWRU is spotty, some on campus say. "The advising system is very uneven, which means it doesn't work all that well," complains one teacher. "The Office of Undergraduate Studies works very, very well. They already know the students' problems because they keep up with those who really need help. But some departments do their best to evade students entirely, especially those departments with large graduate programs." Some departments (history, English, political science, theater, and physics among them) have begun an open-door policy, but faculty say this idea is more a result of an individual department's culture than some university-wide initiative.

CWRU has not instituted a speech code, and the administration is strongly opposed to one, professors say. During a recent student government campaign, a poster hung by a candidate (who was a member of a racial minority) was defaced. Rather than overreacting to this wrongheaded action, several hundred people on campus signed a petition urging respect for all. The guilty student confessed, and the matter was handled by student government.

Student Life: Yes, *That* Cleveland

Cleveland, which one CWRU professor calls "the best-kept secret in the nation," offers a tremendous variety of diversions to suit every interest and taste. Students can head downtown to The Flats, an entertainment area along the Cuyahoga River filled with restaurants, nightclubs, and other necessities. The Rock and Roll Hall of Fame and Museum, which opened in 1995, is a new landmark. In the area around CWRU, known as University Circle, attractions include the Cleveland Orchestra in Severance Hall; the Cleveland Museum of Art; the Cleveland Institute of Music, which offers programs in conjunction with CWRU; the Natural History Museum; the Cleveland Botanical Gardens; and much more. A model of genuine urban renewal (as opposed to that carried out with bulldozers and dynamite), Cleveland offers its residents a very high quality of life.

The main CWRU campus encompasses 128 acres, but the university also owns a 450-acre farm in Hunting Valley and two astronomical observatories.

Because a majority of technical students nationwide are men, and about half of CWRU is technically oriented, men make up 57 percent of the undergraduate student body. The large graduate student population is 59 percent male. About two-thirds of the undergraduate student body hails from Ohio, with Pennsylvania and New York next in line but far behind. About 75 percent of CWRU graduates go on to earn advanced degrees, which is a very high percentage, and one that speaks well not only of the school's success in producing highly skilled graduates but also of the increasing demand for employees with postgraduate education. The workload at CWRU is heavy, and students are said to be studious and ambitious.

There are, of course, numerous student groups on campus offering enough variety to satisfy almost anyone. Those deemed worthy of mention by a professor include: Habitat for Humanity; Project STEP-UP, a tutoring program for middle school children; the Ballroom Dance Society; University Singers; CWRU Chamber Orchestra; and the Collegium Musicum. One should also note the various engineering societies, the Catholic Students Association, the Debate Club, InterVarsity Christian Fellowship, the Jewish Students Activity Board, College Republicans, Mortar Board, and various academic honor societies. Radical student groups include the ubiquitous Gay/ Lesbian/Bisexual Alliance, found on virtually every campus in America. And one wonders how the Students Nutrition Awareness Committee deals with what is surely the massive consumption of beer, pizza, nachos, coffee, and other staples of the college student diet.

CWRU has seventeen campus residence halls in which about three-quarters of the undergraduates reside. The university has a residency requirement, and only students who live at home and commute to campus (about 15 percent) or who are seniors and at least twenty-one years old may apply to live off campus. Most freshmen live on North Campus, which is near the art museum and other cultural attractions of Cleveland, and also closer to the arts and humanities offerings at CWRU. South Campus is near Case Quad, the area in which the science, engineering, and administration buildings are found. The entire campus is linked with fiber-optic technology, so computing at CWRU is extremely quick and easy.

As for campus safety, students should exercise caution, as is always the case in large urban areas. The university's literature recommends that students not walk alone on campus after dark and that they make use, whenever possible, of campus buses, an escort service, and well-lighted sidewalks. Dorms are locked twenty-four hours a day and can be opened only with a resident's identification card.

CWRU offers sports on the varsity, intramural, and club levels. There are eleven men's and nine women's varsity sports, including baseball, basketball, football, tennis, and wrestling for men and basketball, fencing, cross-country, softball, and track and field for women. Nineteen intramural sports are played, with teams generally organized around residence halls. Club sports, of which there are eleven, include lacrosse, ice hockey, crew, and archery.

CATHOLIC UNIVERSITY OF AMERICA

Office of Admissions
Cardinal Station
Washington, DC 20064
(202) 319-5305
www.cua.edu

Total enrollment: 6,000
Undergraduates: 2,400
SAT Ranges (Verbal/Math): V 530-640, M 570-620
Financial aid: 72%
Applicants: 2,320
Accepted: 66%
Enrolled: 31%
Application deadline: Feb. 15
Financial aid application deadline: Jan. 15
Tuition: $16,500
Core curriculum: Yes

Ex Cathedra

The Catholic University of America (CUA) is the only institution of higher education founded by the U.S. bishops; its chancellor is the archbishop of Washington, D.C., and Catholic parishes across the country donate a portion of their annual collections to the school.

Chartered in 1887 by Pope Leo XIII, the university began as a graduate research institution. In the words of the first rector, Bishop John Joseph Kane, it was anticipated that the university would be "a living embodiment and illustration of the harmony between reason and revelation, between science and religion, between the genius of America and the church of Christ."

CUA is still primarily a graduate school — less than half of the students are undergraduates. However, it offers a fine undergraduate curriculum and a solid set of general education requirements. Importantly, CUA is not afraid to stand on its foundation: all students must take courses in religion. Between 80 and 90 percent are Catholic, but the number of clerical students and faculty has dramatically diminished in the past several decades. CUA has been able to resist such trends as secularization and the lowering of standards that plague other Catholic universities, though it has had to deal with the pressure to conform to the reigning ideological fads. In remaining true to its founding principles, it adds tremendously to true diversity in American higher education.

The main difficulty facing CUA is its lack of money, caused, some say, by poor leadership. The faculty are underpaid and the library is poor. For this reason the university has developed a reputation as something of a "Catholic ghetto" rather than that of the strong liberal arts institution it continues to be.

Academic Life: Coherence of Vision

The Catholic University of America is divided into the schools of Architecture and Planning; Arts and Sciences; Engineering; Library and Information Sciences; the Columbus School of Law; the Benjamin T. Rome School of Music; Nursing; Philosophy; Religious Studies; the National Catholic School of Social Services; and the Metropolitan College, which serves adult undergraduates. Of these, the schools of law, religious studies, and social services are for graduate students only; graduate students in these and other programs make up 55 percent of the university's enrollment of 5,970.

The School of Arts and Sciences is the largest undergraduate school and is home to eighteen departments offering sixty-six majors. The core requirements in Arts and Sciences underscore the university's prevailing commitment to the liberal arts. In contrast to most general education requirements today, one professor says that "there is a coherence of vision" in the CUA undergraduate curriculum, which has remained unchanged for nearly two decades. "A lot of my friends go to public universities where the requirements are things like physical education," a student says. "Here, there's more of an emphasis on philosophy and religion."

Indeed, all undergraduates must complete four courses each in religion and philosophy. In addition, students take one course in each of these two areas: "Logic, Morality, and Action" and "Nature, Knowledge, and God." One or two courses in composition are also required, as well as three humanities courses, four in mathematics and natural science, and four in social and behavioral science. CUA has a foreign language requirement, and all students must also complete two intermediate courses in an ancient or modern language, as well as two in ancient or modern literature. The goal of the liberal arts core curriculum, according to a recent profile of the university, is to create "critical thinkers who can articulate their beliefs, make judgments, and appreciate more fully the aesthetic, moral, and religious dimensions of the Christian intellectual tradition."

Almost without exception, students and faculty rate most of Catholic University's programs of study very highly. Political science is frequently singled out as a strong department. Those interested in studying theological matters should be aware that there are two different programs, theology (which is under the aegis of

Arts and Sciences) and religious studies (under the direction of the graduate School for Religious Studies). Religious studies is slightly more orthodox than in the days of the iconoclastic theologian Charles Curran, though some students say theology is the better program. There is a separate School of Philosophy which, under the leadership of Dean Jude Dougherty, has developed a reputation for being both rigorous and orthodox. The distinguished *Review of Metaphysics* is published through the department, with considerable editorial help from CUA philosophy graduate students.

Catholic University's strength has traditionally been in medieval studies — "from Coptic to canon law," in the words of one former professor — and there are still small yet excellent programs in Greek and Latin, patristics, medieval, and Byzantine studies. The School of Music is "one of the best in the country," according to one faculty member, while the drama department is also exceptionally strong. The School of Architecture, housed in its own building, is considered first-rate and has "a lot of energy and creativity," according to one professor. The School of Nursing also receives high marks from students and faculty. Not surprising given the university's genesis as a graduate institution, graduate programs in most liberal arts disciplines also remain strong.

English literature is also an excellent department. "It is known as one of the best and most difficult departments," says a faculty member, who notes that in addition to garnering teaching awards, the department's faculty has a strong publications record. All undergraduates must complete comprehensive exams and have an option of completing a senior thesis as well. When asked whether the department had succumbed to the politicization of literature in its pedagogy, one professor insisted: "We've resisted that at every turn. Our aim has been to expose students to high quality literature — we pay attention to a work's literary and aesthetic merits." English majors receive solid grounding in English and American literature, and consequently, "we've been able to place undergraduates in first-rate graduate programs," a professor says.

History and foreign languages are among the weaker programs at CUA.

The students at CUA are described by one professor as "intelligent, though not brilliant — they are aware of what they are and are not." Students are, by and large, conscientious about their studies, though not excessively bookish. "They are a very, very friendly group," says one faculty member. According to a graduate teaching assistant, "They know things that I wish I had known as an undergraduate."

If the faculty seem generally pleased with the quality and interest of the students, the sentiment is definitely reciprocated by students, who praise their professors for their accessibility, erudition, and commitment to teaching. One professor notes that his office is open regularly and that students consistently come by for advice and conversation. Many professors receive high praise from students, including Virgil Nemoianu in comparative literature; Claes Ryn, David Walsh, Lee Edwards, and Graham Walker in political science; Eric Perl, Timothy Noone, Rev. Msgr. Robert

Sokolowski, and David Gallagher in philosophy; Robin Darling Young in theology; and Ernest Suarez in English.

Despite recent financial difficulties (see "Political Atmosphere," below), the university has completed several new buildings and has recently improved its science facilities. In 1994 CUA dedicated a $33 million law school building, which won a national design award. One professor claims that "it's as good as any I've ever seen," while a graduate student describes it as "beautiful . . . extremely impressive." The university's Life Cycle Institute recently received a half-million-dollar grant from the Lilly Endowment in order to institute a policy study on Catholic education that will culminate in the establishment of a Center for the Study of Catholic Schools.

In more recent years, Catholic University has made efforts to make its curriculum more service-oriented by instituting the "Communiversity Program." Sponsored by Campus Ministry, the program links academic and service projects that will serve the impoverished area around the northeast Washington, D.C., campus. Projects have included helping AIDS patients and the homeless, as well as tutoring and mentoring at-risk students.

The advising system at CUA is thought to be fairly strong by both students and faculty. Every student is assigned a faculty adviser, though a student says that "lots of informal advising" goes on as well, and each student meets individually with the director of undergraduate studies. Catholic University is part of a consortium of area colleges and universities, so undergraduates have the opportunity to take courses at such places as the University of Maryland and Georgetown University. They also have access to the library resources of these institutions, not to mention the Library of Congress and the Folger Shakespeare Institute. This is a welcome opportunity for students given the poor quality of the CUA library, which is plagued by poor funding and theft of materials. "Every time I've gone [to the library]," complains one student, "the books have been gone." Says another: "The library definitely needs help."

Political Atmosphere: ACT DOWN

According to one professor, the political atmosphere at CUA is "middle-of-the-road." Another describes most students as "fairly apathetic politically," noting that only a small percentage of undergraduates voted for student body president in a recent election. The undergraduate student body is considered fairly conservative, while the graduate students are even more so.

Because it is a Catholic institution, CUA is not exempt from controversy surrounding issues of abortion and homosexuality. Although the university has no pro-choice group, there is an organization for lesbian and gay student rights, and one professor argues that despite the church's stance on such issues, the university "does not shut down debate" on abortion and homosexuality.

Nonetheless, the university occasionally comes under fire for its public adherence to church teaching on controversial social issues. Most recently, it decided not to give an already announced award to actor Joseph Sicari after learning that the CUA alumnus was once a member of ACT UP, an AIDS activist group that famously disrupted a mass at St. Patrick's Cathedral in New York City in 1989. (Sicari was not a member at the time of that demonstration.) As of this writing, Sicari has threatened to sue for breach of contract and slander, pointing out that he was not a member of ACT UP at the time of the St. Patrick's disruption. According to insiders, the university would have gone ahead with the award even after learning of Sicari's involvement in ACT UP had it not been concerned about a significant outcry from alumni. In an official statement, the university defended its decision, noting that the rescinding of the award came about because of Sicari's "connection to an organization whose actions and activities are inconsistent with the university's mission and sponsorship."

Catholic University does have a very active group of pro-life students, and the university is always well represented at the annual pro-life march on Capitol Hill. Because of the university's religious orientation, social justice groups like Amnesty International are also fairly active on campus. There are chapters of both College Democrats and College Republicans, though the latter is said to be much busier. There are also other conservative groups like the CUA Conservative Union, whose mission is to "stimulate intellectual conservative thought on campus," and *Pro Veritate,* which is dedicated to a "discussion of traditional moral, social, and religious values."

By and large, the Catholic University administration has not followed academic fashion. According to one professor, the dean of Arts and Sciences, Antanas Suziedelis, is "the best single college administrator I've seen anywhere." Steve Wright, the director of undergraduate studies, is also admired by students and faculty for his individual attention to undergraduates. Unfortunately, the university's president, Brother Patrick Ellis, is not as highly praised as other administrators, and has performed poorly in the one area in which many members of the CUA community were hoping he could excel — fund-raising.

Indeed, one of the keenest sources of frustration for CUA faculty and students is the poor financial health of the school. CUA faculty are the lowest paid of any school in the District of Columbia, and, consequently, it is difficult to attract and keep good teachers. "Once the university gets a good faculty member, they often leave," says one student. "They don't have good resources in Arts and Sciences — it's so sad that it all boils down to money."

Student Life: The Crime Scene

Unlike many other Catholic colleges, including nearby Georgetown, Catholic University still retains something of its Catholic identity, probably due in no small part to its name and location. The university is adjacent to the National Shrine of the Immaculate Conception and also home to the United States Council of Bishops. The university offers daily mass, several campus prayer groups, and at least eight retreats each year. But according to one professor, although there is a definite Catholic atmosphere, "there is no pressure to conform to it — the student body is far from self-righteous or pious." One non-Catholic undergraduate says, "I don't feel much of a Catholic identity — they don't jam the faith down your throat here."

All CUA freshmen and sophomores are required to live on campus. One student suggests avoiding Spelman dormitory, where "really out of control partying" prevails. Many upperclassmen choose off-campus housing, though students are wary of living in the immediate area because of safety concerns. A gated apartment complex is located on nearby Michigan Avenue, though one student says it is "not very safe — the guards aren't there all the time." There are numerous rental opportunities in other areas of the District as well as in nearby boroughs in Maryland and Virginia, easily accessible by the Metro system. "But it is just ridiculously expensive to live here," says a graduate student.

There is no Greek system at CUA, though this does not prevent students from having "a heck of a good time," in the words of one faculty member. Some members of the CUA community have suggested that students are having too good a time in recent years, and are concerned about excessive drinking among undergraduates. The most popular bar for undergrads is Kitty's on Twelfth Street, which many freshmen and sophomores walk to and from on weekend evenings. "It's very dangerous, yet it's something Public Safety can't control," a student says. The university offers a service that will pick people up from various locations — including Kitty's — and bring them back to campus, but for obvious reasons the service does not drive students to this watering hole, and some undergraduates have been victims of crime while walking to or from the bar.

Indeed, the university's location in Washington, D.C., is a source of both vitality and vexation. Students have ready access to the myriad cultural, educational, and social opportunities available in the nation's capital, while still studying in a self-contained campus environment. "I wanted to attend a fairly small to medium size college in a big city," says one student. "Catholic University seemed ideal. It looks much more like a campus than any of the other schools in the District." Yet the university borders on an unsafe neighborhood, and crime has become a serious problem. "The area is absolutely terrible," a student says. "There is so much poverty all around, and they take it out on the students." Another student suggests that crime can be avoided if you use common sense: "Many crimes have simply been the result of irresponsible behavior."

Athletics at CUA are not enormously popular, though more than 10 percent of the undergraduate student body is involved in varsity programs. The university sponsors twenty-one NCAA Division III sports, and men's football, basketball, and baseball teams have performed well in recent years. There are club sports such as crew, ice hockey, lacrosse, rugby, ultimate Frisbee, and tae kwon do. The Raymond A. DuFour Center is home to the university's athletic facilities, which are considered less than adequate by many students.

Spiritual organizations also abound at CUA, and the university is home to a fairly active contingent of charismatic students. Organizations such as The Upper Room, a group dedicated to Marian devotion, and Fools for Jesus, a prayer and service organization, deepen the spiritual life of students.

Musical and theatrical performances are also plentiful at the university, though one student suggests that unless you are a music or drama major, "you have a slim chance of being able to participate in a performance." Susan Sarandon and Ed McMahon are both graduates of the drama program, and the university's Hartke Theatre has a national reputation for its dramatic performances.

UNIVERSITY OF CHICAGO

Office of Admissions
1116 East Fifty-ninth Street
Chicago, IL 60637
(312) 702-8650
www.uchicago.edu

Total enrollment: 12,120
Undergraduates: 3,560
SAT Ranges (Verbal/Math): V 640-740, M 640-730
Financial aid: 63%
Applicants: 5,470
Accepted: 58%
Enrolled: 31%
Application deadline: Jan. 1
Financial aid application deadline: Feb. 1
Tuition: $22,086
Core curriculum: Yes

Too Good to Live

The University of Chicago has long been a rather quirky place, even by academic standards. It has always provided a haven for those serious intellectuals for whom learning is more a vocation than a path to a career. It has been a scholar's university, a place where faculty and students alike needn't fear ridicule for their unabashed love of books and bookishness. Students really do discuss Plato with each other late into the night, and they really do spend a huge amount of time in the library studying and reading. Many would call the students nerds, and the students would not mind. Since the university's founding in 1892 by John D. Rockefeller, sixty-four students, researchers, or faculty from Chicago have been awarded a Nobel Prize. This reputation for unqualified excellence was not won easily or quickly, and it is the most treasured aspect of the Chicago legacy.

As is the case with so many institutions of higher education today, the continuation of Chicago's legacy is very much in doubt. Led by an administration that seeks to popularize the course offerings as a goad to attracting a less cerebral, more typical student body, and aided by an increasing number of younger faculty members who have little allegiance to the university or its traditions, Chicago today is in very real danger of losing its ethos. "They're trying to attract students who would be better off at another school," a student told the *Chronicle of Higher Education* in 1996. A faculty member told the magazine that the president, Hugo Sonnenschein, wants to turn the Lake Michigan–side campus into an "undergraduate playground for the golden youth of white suburbia." There has been talk of replacing Chicago's intense eleven-week quarters with a gentler semester system, and of scaling back (even further) the university's distinguishing two-year-long Common Core.

Here, as elsewhere, the demand for homogeneity (which, ironically, goes under the banner of "diversity") is reducing the choices available to students. There is a widespread notion in higher education today (more prevalent at other places than at Chicago) that to demand too much of students is somehow to stifle them, as if a serious education was like watching too much television. If the administration at Chicago has its way, it will turn what is now one of the great treasures in American higher education into just another big, rich, research university. This would be a terrible blow both to those who long for the type of education that only a school with Chicago's traditions and resources can provide, and to the nation as a whole.

Academic Life: Hurry

The Common Core at Chicago is one of the most venerable and famous of all college offerings. It is the legacy of several great leaders of the university, most notably Robert Maynard Hutchins, president from 1929 until 1951. The core was put in place in order to ensure a common reading list for all students regardless of their concentration (as majors are known at Chicago). And for many years it was a guarantee that all students could discuss the same body of works of literature, history, philosophy, and social science, as well as the natural sciences and mathematics. Even today, though somewhat diminished, the Common Core requires twenty-one courses to complete (as compared to nine to thirteen courses in the concentration and eight to twelve elective courses).

This substantial workload is no longer drawn from a strict common core, but rather from a medium-sized distribution list; the choices offered to students have increased markedly over the past couple of decades. The twenty-one quarter-long courses are drawn from a fairly wide array of classes in seven core areas: humanities (four quarters), foreign languages (three or four quarters), mathematical sciences (two quarters), natural sciences (six quarters), social sciences (a three-quarter-long sequence), civilizational studies (another three-quarter-long sequence), and physical education (three quarters). While it is still true that some students can and do take many of the same classes, Chicago can no longer claim that readings are truly common to all undergraduates regardless of concentration. In short, Chicago still offers one of the best undergraduate educations available for those who know where to look for the best professors and courses.

The quality of instruction in many courses is very high, and there are scores of dedicated teachers (see below) throughout the university community. Several of the core curriculum offerings merit special attention and deserve the serious consideration of any student interested in obtaining one of the finest educations around. But a word of caution is in order for anyone planning on attending Chicago in the not-so-distant future: given the developments there under the lead of the administration, this educational opportunity may be a limited-time offer.

But as long as the core endures, excellent courses will be offered at Chicago. According to faculty and students interviewed for this guide, the best sequences with which to fulfill the majority of the core requirements, usually within three quarters, are as follows: in humanities, take "Human Being and Citizen." To fulfill the social sciences requirement, select "Classics in Social and Political Thought." In civilizational studies, do not miss "History of Western Civilization."

In the humanities area, "Human Being and Citizen" garners the highest praise. Students read the very best works of the Western tradition, beginning with Homer and continuing into the last century. Fourteen sections of this class serve a total of nearly one thousand students, and about 40 percent of an entering class takes this class. Despite the course's popularity, however, one faculty member says it is difficult to get regular faculty to believe in it, much less teach it. "It runs on postdocs with two- or three-year appointments," the faculty member says. "They teach six sections per year. Almost nobody teaches more than one quarter of these sequences, which is very different from the way it used to be. . . . It is a great books course, and the humanities faculty would get rid of it if they could, because we read primary sources in this course rather than the secondary sources they're pushing." Students should be aware of a humanities course called "Reading Cultures: Collecting, Traveling, and Capitalist Cultures," which, according to one professor, is really a social sciences course gaining popularity "in the hands of the multicultural folks."

Speaking of the social sciences, a yearlong sequence entitled "Classics of Social and Political Thought" is superb. "Tell freshmen to take this course," says one professor. On the other hand, "Wealth, Power, and Virtue" contains "arcane cognitive psychology with no liberal education. It is no good and has only four sections," according to another faculty member.

Although Western civilization used to be required of all students, the civilizational studies element of the core can now be met with classes focusing on Latin America, Islam, Africa, Russia, South Asia, or East Asia. The "History of Western Civilization" is still "a great course on paper," says one professor, but the percentage of students taking it is down from a high of 60 percent just a few years ago to around 30 percent now. "The continuity is missing," says this teacher, lamenting the retirement of the eminent professor Karl Weintraub. Despite his official retirement, Weintraub and his wife, Katie, are the only faculty members still teaching the Western civilization courses for the entire three-quarter sequence. "But it is still a terrific course, and there are important people who care about it, so it's safe for the next half-dozen years," says this professor.

All sciences at Chicago are not created equal, so students should be particularly choosey when fulfilling the largest core requirement — the six quarters of natural sciences. "The physical scientists take teaching very seriously," says a faculty member familiar with course content. "They're extra good citizens, have some excellent courses, and don't have any trouble with staffing." Biology, however, is another matter, according to another professor. "It is budgeted through the medical school, and the College [the undergraduate unit of the university] has no leverage over it," the professor says. "They regard teaching as a burden. But they still have some very good courses, and they can attract some humanists who come there and find that they like what they see." According to a recent Chicago graduate, the natural science sequences vary in their worth. "In an attempt to interest everybody in the sciences, the university has created several rather flaky sequences in both biological and physical sciences," the graduate says. "My experience here has not been outstandingly satisfying; yet I believe the science core does accomplish the goal of providing true breadth to the liberal education at Chicago."

Classes in music and the visual arts are not stunning, but are "taught well enough," according to a faculty member.

Once finished with the core, Chicago students choose a concentration, the classes of which are selected from one of the five collegiate divisions: Biological Sciences, Humanities, New Collegiate, Physical Sciences, and Social Sciences. Recent statistics show that the most popular concentrations at Chicago are the social sciences and history, in which a whopping 40.8 percent of students major (as compared to the national average of 15.9 percent). Next in popularity are the biological and life sciences, with about 12 percent of students. Nearly 9 percent concentrate in English language and literature, compared to less than 6 percent nationally. Nearly 6 percent major in foreign languages, a rate three times the national average.

In the humanities, the classics concentration is "solid and demanding," but some new hires "are of uncertain quality," according to one professor. Philosophy, while fairly rigorous overall, is a mixed bag in terms of the quality of the classes, according to another. The newer faculty members in history have damaged that concentration's reputation; one educator calls the recent hires "just about what you'd expect." A student familiar with the situation says that "history is good, but not as good as a decade ago. The good professors have been replaced with clowns."

A cross-disciplinary major called "Fundamentals: Issues and Texts," taught through the subdivision of the College known as the New Collegiate Division, allows serious students to organize their entire major around a single large and fundamental question. Examples of such questions include: "How does telling a story shape a life?" and "Is the family a natural or a cultural institution?" The students in this program concentrate on six classic texts and must pass a senior examination on those six books. Students can choose from a huge variety of texts, as up to forty-five classes are offered each quarter on individual books. "The B.A.'s from this program go on to become M.D.'s, J.D.'s — to everything but experimental physics," says one professor. Also taught through the New Collegiate Division is another good concentration: "Law, Letters, and Society." Two other excellent interdisciplinary programs exist outside the New Collegiate Division: "General Studies in the Humanities" and "History, Philosophy and Social Studies of Science and Medicine."

As might be expected, a university with so many outstanding courses and programs is home to a long list of distinguished professors. The list, assembled from the comments of faculty and students, is almost too long to include here. Those singled out as deserving recognition include Nathan Tarcov in political science; Ralph Lerner and Leon Kass of the Committee on Social Thought; Amy Kass of the Humanities Collegiate Division; Karl Joachim Weintraub, officially retired but still teaching history, social thought, and fundamentals; James Redfield and Bert Cohler, who teach "Self, Culture, and Society"; Peter Vandervoort and Paul Sally in mathematics; David Malament, who teaches the philosophy of science; Laura Slatkin in classics; Bruce Redford in English; Michael Fishbane in Jewish studies; Lorna Straus of biology; Isaac Abella of physics; Jonathan Lear and Robert Pippin of the philosophy department and the Committee of Social Thought; President Emeritus Hannah Holborn Gray in history; Bertram Cohler, who teaches psychology and fundamentals; Jean Bethke Elshtain and Jonathan Smith of religion; Herman Sinaiko of general studies in the humanities; Tamara Trojanowska and David Powelstock in Slavic languages and literatures; and Lawrence McEnerney of the Little Red Schoolhouse writing program.

Some departments are becoming very politicized, with English chief among them. One professor says that department is "full of methodologists and ideologues." Some English faculty have even called for a reduction in the core curriculum. "English is politically correct in a big way, and they no longer believe in great texts, but only cultural studies," says a professor. "There is a committee to reevaluate the core, and it was proposed to merge the humanities and civilization courses, which are now one year each, into one one-year course . . . but it was defeated." Other politicized departments include African-American studies, gender studies, and film studies, which one professor calls "very chic."

Political Atmosphere: The Things of This World

Having heard what is best about the University of Chicago and its core, it is depressing to learn that many on campus would change both the school and the core. It becomes even more depressing when one learns that changes are being made in the names of "money" and of "fun." Yet it's true: the new administration at Chicago, led by President Sonnenschein, wants the place to be more fun, which means more people will enroll and the school will have more money.

Chicago has long been known as one of the most academically demanding and extraordinarily intellectual of the major research universities, and the very mention of it conjures up images of students poring over books, engaged in discussion of weighty ideas, and preparing for academic careers that will take them to the top of their fields. President Sonnenschein and his administration, however, believe the university should alter its ways in order to compete more fully with the Ivies and Stanford in drawing what one Chicago professor calls "merely the best and the brightest." That is, in order to garner more dollars the president wants to expand the undergraduate student enrollment by 1,000-1,500 to 4,500 over the next decade. The belief is, apparently, that there can't possibly be that many serious students available — and that the ones who are available will choose Harvard, Stanford, or Princeton, Sonnenschein's former employer. It is an idea that, if carried very far, will certainly change much of what is good about Chicago.

Here's what we mean: In a bizarre move in the fall of 1997, the university passed out flyers with a no-smoking-sign-style bar through the words "The Reg," the common name for the Regenstein Library, where students spend many hours of study. The point of the flyer was to discourage students from studying too hard or too long and, we assume, to encourage them to have more fun. As a longtime member of Chicago's faculty puts it, "The administration wants to appeal to kids who won't come here now because we require too much of them." There is a widespread fear that the administration will soon cut the number of core courses from twenty-one to fifteen. "The rumors are that they won't so much eliminate the requirements for the core as they will loosen them up," a recent graduate says. "What is given [in the core] is so useful for what I learned later [in classes in a concentration] and taught me so much that I'd hate to see it change." This graduate continues: "What the administration's running into is that when students decide to come to Chicago over one of the Ivies they're picking between attitudes about learning. . . . So you're attracting those students who love ideas and discussion, not those bent on career paths." "When you first come here for a visit you know right away whether or not you want to come here," says another student. "It's a self-selective group. The administration is now trying to attract those who aren't so sure they will fit in."

Chicago is not immune to the politicization of academia. "Today, what's best has been diluted through methodology and ideology," says a professor. "Classes are tendentious in some cases. Not everyone teaches in the spirit of liberal education.

They're not self-critical and reflective, but professionalized instead. There are some places in the curriculum where trends have crept in — less so than at most places, but more than before." As is often the case, trends have arrived in the shoulder bags of new faculty members fresh out of radical graduate programs. "The older the faculty, the more likely they'll be reasonable," says a student. "In the past ten years most of the hires have been very bad. For example, [the university] will snap up someone who writes on the history of homosexuality in America who has only one chapter of his dissertation completed." Says another student: "Many of the younger faculty are worse and are intolerant. They play favorites and reward or punish students according to whether or not they agree with their politics." Adds a third: "Most of the better known professors here came out of the Hutchins school and stayed to teach. They're getting old now, so you must hire new blood. The problem is that you can't find people who were educated like that anymore."

Recently the Law School, for long the only one of the best law schools not already in the hands of the left, offered a job to Catherine MacKinnon, who has been condemned by one of America's best-known traditionalist feminists as "the most dangerous radical feminist in America."

Despite the general decline in standards, Chicago continues to attract an excellent student body. The university is not particularly hard to get into (it accepted nearly 60 percent of applicants in 1995), but only one in three who are accepted chooses to enroll. Yet that group averages better than 1,300 on the SAT, and comes to Chicago wanting what the university now offers and expecting to work very, very hard. "There are a few goof-offs, and there are some athletes who aren't students. There are also some decadent fraternities with essay files, and plagiarism is on the rise," says a faculty member. "But we still get a lot of very serious students. There are some wonderful, wonderful people around here. They [the students] become friends in your class as a result of the class discussion. Our students are not just the best and the brightest, they're deeply intellectual."

The erosion of Chicago's proud traditions has caused a great deal of heartache among dedicated faculty members. Says one professor: "The place has been in retreat for a few decades, but the spirit survives because of a living connection to 'that' college of the Hutchins and immediate post-Hutchins era. The old timers here are a living presence who really were the university then. But the new people haven't been socialized in that way — they're not worried about the shape of the place as a whole. They're attached to their field, and their fields are trendy." It has become every professor for himself, says a senior professor. "There used to be much more of a sense of identity with the university as a whole, but now the subfield and the journal to which they contribute or edit draws their allegiance," says the professor. "They no longer consider themselves as belonging to a university community. Today one is rewarded not for teaching but for getting job offers from other places and making a big name for oneself. People are much more concerned about getting ahead in their own field."

Hostility toward the curriculum and university traditions is pretty well expected at other places by now, but is shocking at Chicago. "There is a lot of hatred for the great books among some teachers here," says a professor. "They'll warn students not to take professors who love the great books. And they become apoplectic when they discuss great books teaching." While older programs are under attack, newer, hotter ones are sailing along. One very popular program approved as recently as 1983 "might not be able to make it through [the ratification process] today," a professor says. "And yet gender studies flew through." "I'm not optimistic about the University fifteen years down the road," says a professor who has served there many years. "I am usually quite dispirited. But my students are marvelous. If you present ideas thoughtfully and seriously, they park their ideologies at the door." This professor continues, "We can hold out for another five or ten years, and that's about it. This place has had its glory, but now it's time for that mantle to pass to someone else." A professor states the problem thus: "We need a revolution in the humanities. Someone needs to come along and say, 'I have this great new idea. It's called reading a book seriously,' and present it as something new."

Only time will tell whether Chicago's traditional brand of education will survive the hostile forces that threaten it.

Campus Life: The Library as Residence Hall

Students at the University of Chicago hit their books with a degree of commitment rare in any university setting. This Chicago ethos is one of the things that has separated this sheep from every other goat in the country, and it is also the element of life the administration wants to change most. "Most undergraduates study very hard and do little else — there is very little extracurricular activity for them," says a student.

"It's a very strange place to go to school," adds another. "Undergraduates will boast of staying at the library until 1 a.m. At Chicago, there is a sense of working twice as hard to prove you're just as good. At the Ivies, a much larger proportion of the students come from old moneyed families, and the students have that to fall back on. At Chicago, many are the first or second generation in their families who have gone to college. They don't assume success here."

If any free time can be found, use some of it on the student newspaper, the *Chicago Maroon*. The College Republicans are in good shape and bring one nationally known speaker to campus each year. The Edmund Burke Society is also vigorous and offers students of the great philosopher an opportunity to meet each other and discuss ideas in the tradition of Burke. Unfortunately, the Great Books Roundtable, long a staple of Chicago life, died out about ten years ago, no doubt in part because of the increased hostility to the great books on the part of many faculty members in the humanities. The University Theater provides many opportunities, and "students do everything, from acting to directing, designing and building. Some of the most rewarding and intense learning experiences of my Chicago experience took place there," says a recent graduate. Also recommended are WHPK, the campus radio station, and DOC Films, the largest film society on campus.

Freshmen are required to live in college houses, although there is no residence hall exclusively for them. A little over two-thirds of the students enrolled in the College live in university-owned housing, and all of them eat in one of three dining commons. All housing is coed, although single-sex floors are available. Of the one-third of students who live off campus, only 4 percent reside in fraternities. There are no residential sororities at Chicago.

Chicago claims nine women's and eleven men's intercollegiate teams, known as the Maroons. Students may choose from among twenty-one intramural sports, arrayed from archery and billiards to touch football and ultimate Frisbee. No fewer than 34 club sports offer a very wide variety of activities, and every member of the university community is eligible to participate in 28 open recreation tournaments in such traditional sports as basketball, handball, tennis, and softball. The University of Chicago offers no athletic scholarships or grants-in-aid.

The university is located in Hyde Park, a few miles south of downtown Chicago. Although much of the neighborhood is in need of improvement, the area around the university is called "pretty safe" by one student, who adds, "When I walk from the library back to my apartment at 11 p.m., I don't worry about crime." Nevertheless, all students would be advised to exercise caution around the area, for, as one student says, "It's not bad here, but this isn't Ann Arbor or Cambridge." Reflecting the academic emphasis of the university, some of the best academic bookstores in the country are located in the university area.

Of course, when their eyes and minds just can't take any more reading — for a few hours, at least — students have access to Chicago, one of the most exciting cities in the country. Offering superb music and nightlife, the city also is home to some of the best museums in America. The Chicago Symphony is excellent, as is the dining and shopping, and even the most dedicated students do manage to pull themselves away from their books from time to time to have some fun — without the administration's help.

CLAREMONT McKENNA COLLEGE

Office of Admissions
890 Columbia Avenue
Claremont, CA 91711-6425
(909) 621-8088
www.mckenna.edu

Total enrollment: 954
Undergraduates: 940
SAT Ranges (Verbal/Math): V 610-700, M 630-710
Financial aid: 72%
Applicants: 2,611
Accepted: 29%
Enrolled: 32%
Application deadline: Jan. 15
Financial aid application deadline: Feb. 1
Tuition: $18,320
Core curriculum: Yes

The Liberal Arts Part of Public Policy

In the half-century that it has been in existence, Claremont McKenna College (CMC) has distinguished itself as one of the nation's top colleges for the study of government, management, and public policy. At the same time, it has become known for its commitment to the genuine liberal arts. With an enrollment of just under one thousand undergraduates, CMC certainly has many of the features of a small liberal arts college: a dedicated and accessible faculty, low student-faculty ratios, no teaching assistants, and an intimate intellectual and social community. But as part of a broader five-college undergraduate system at Claremont, CMC has a range of first-class facilities and opportunities that rivals those of much larger institutions: eight research institutions, numerous semester study programs, and myriad opportunities for undergraduate research.

William F. Buckley Jr. once called CMC the second most conservative college in the nation (next to Hillsdale College). More than half the students say they are Republicans, and the college itself supports campus visits by both conservative and liberal speakers. These leanings have kept classroom politicization to a minimum, and students are satisfied with the classical liberal educations they receive.

CMC graduates have a high acceptance rate at law and graduate school, and the college says that one of every eight CMC graduates now works in a top management position (owner, chairman, CEO, CFO, president, principal, or partner). While the college's programs in some traditional liberal arts are significantly weaker, the seriousness that characterizes CMC's flagship programs runs throughout the curriculum.

Academic Life: Public Affairs

Claremont McKenna is one of five undergraduate colleges in the Claremont system, which also includes Harvey Mudd (primarily science and engineering), Scripps (a women's liberal arts college), Pitzer (focusing on social and behavioral sciences), and Pomona (liberal arts). There is also the Claremont Graduate School, with an enrollment of about two thousand students. Although Pomona has been around longer and is perhaps better known for liberal arts than CMC, the latter college has continually gained ground on its sister school. CMC students who want to take advantage of the good faculty and courses offered at Pomona and the other Claremont colleges may cross-register throughout the five-school system.

Although it offers majors in most liberal arts disciplines, Claremont McKenna focuses on the disciplines of economics, government, and international relations. The intent of the college, according to its promotional literature, is to prepare students "for careers in management, the professions, international relations, and public affairs." The emphasis is decidedly more activist than contemplative at Claremont McKenna, and students are encouraged to become involved in a variety of academic and extracurricular activities that further develops their leadership potential.

Still, the college recognizes the importance to its students of a grounding in the liberal arts. The college proclaims the same credo it did when it opened in 1946 as the Claremont Undergraduate School for Men: "The school will require its students to complete courses in the same broad fields of human knowledge as do the social science majors in the customary liberal arts college. There is no incompatibility between an education planned for specific types of leadership and an education designed to develop a liberally informed mind."

Accordingly, the basic academic program at CMC includes a set of distribution requirements focusing on the liberal arts. All students must take one semester of either literary composition or analysis, a one-semester calculus course, and two courses in science (including one lab). The math class and one of the science requirements may be fulfilled with high school advanced placement credit or high test scores. In addition, students must take one course in three out of four social sciences fields (economics, government, history, and psychology) and a course in two of four humanities areas (foreign literature, literature, philosophy, and religious studies). CMC has a foreign language requirement that can be satisfied with a one-semester course in Western civilization. CMC has no multicultural or diversity requirement.

Many liberal arts colleges have done away with undergraduate senior theses, perhaps because they create more work for faculty already overburdened with publication pressures. But with few exceptions, all CMC students must complete a senior thesis under the guidance of a faculty reader. The catalogue describes the project as a "serious exercise in the organization and presentation of written material."

"I don't think you could graduate from here without taking courses in all of the areas of liberal education," says a student. Still, some people on campus say the college stresses the pragmatic aspects of education rather than the liberal arts. As one student writes in the alternative campus newspaper, the *Claremont Independent*, "The CMC educational experience is certainly not perfect. Our education focuses too much on practical knowledge while not ensuring that all students graduate with a rudimentary knowledge of the great works of Western civilization." But while the general education requirements are assuredly short of a traditional liberal arts core, a student who knows what he wants to take can find a solid liberal education at CMC.

Government and economics are the most highly rated departments among students and faculty. "Other departments have tended to be smaller and less ambitious," says one professor. Economics is said by one student to have "a lot of older, interesting guys from the University of Chicago." The economics course "Principles of Economic Analysis" and government's "Introduction to American Politics" are the most common choices for students looking to meet the social science sector of the general education requirements. The literature department, according to those on campus, also has some good faculty.

On the other hand, history and philosophy are considered highly politicized. A recent student poll found that every faculty member in the history department is a registered Democrat, which wouldn't be so bad if they would also teach courses on the history of ancient Greece or the Roman Empire — the catalogue shows no courses by that name, only wide surveys. Faculty hires in the department have also been excessively radical; according to one student, writing in the *Independent*, "A recent hire completed a dissertation regarding the history of menstruation." Fortunately, such politicization is confined to only a few faculty and departments at CMC.

The best faculty for CMC undergraduates includes Robert Faggen in literature, Alan Heslop in state and local government, Marc Massoud in accounting, and Charles Kesler, a government professor who also directs the Henry Salvatori Center for the Study of Individual Freedom.

Despite its public policy reputation, CMC is attracting an increasing number of science majors and premed students. The college advertises that it has first-rate facilities without the cutthroat competition present at colleges better known for scientific studies. Students have access to the labs and equipment in the massive Keck Science Center, opened in 1992 to serve Claremont McKenna, Scripps, and Pitzer Colleges. Premed and science students also use the college's government and public affairs programs to explore ethical and policy issues in the sciences.

Many students at CMC participate in undergraduate research or internships. The college supports eight research institutes, which publish on a variety of topics and offer students study opportunities with distinguished scholars. The institutes are the Salvatori Center, the Rose Institute of State and Local Government, the Institute of Decision Science for Business and Public Policy, the Keck Center for International Strategic Studies, the Lowe Institute of Political Economy, the Roberts Environmental Center, the Gould Center for Humanistic Studies, and the Henry Kravis Leadership Institute. Although all present excellent opportunities for undergraduates, the Salvatori Center — the oldest of the college's research institutes — is one of the best. The center is named for conservative entrepreneur Henry Salvatori and focuses on the study of the Constitution and "individual freedom and the economic, social, moral, political, and legal conditions essential for the preservation of that freedom."

CMC students share library facilities with the other colleges in the Claremont system. One professor describes the holdings as "very good," comparing them to those at Dartmouth College.

Faculty say CMC attracts serious students interested in true learning. Students are "getting better and better all the time," according to one professor. Typical CMC students "tend to be ambitious, they want to rise, want to do well," says another. "They are believers in the American ethic of higher learning." For the best students, the college offers the McKenna Achievement Awards. Each year the college awards approximately thirty scholarships of $2,500 each, renewable for four years. Hundreds of other scholarships are available as well.

Political Atmosphere: Athenaeum, Not Anathema

A strength of Claremont McKenna — and perhaps one of the reasons it has been able to maintain its peculiar blend of liberal arts and professional emphases — is its continuity of leadership. The college's first president, George Benson, served for twenty years, and the current officeholder, Jack Stark, has been there in some capacity since 1961. Although some students and faculty grumble that the administration is not always the educational traditionalists they would like them to be, according to one professor, the administration "has kept the place politically friendly . . . they have not gone in for authoritarian tactics."

One professor describes a "robust tradition of free speech" at Claremont McKenna. The only speech prohibited in the college's speech code is that containing threats of physical violence. The code states: "Claremont McKenna College is committed to guaranteeing to all members of the CMC community freedom of speech, because this freedom is essential to the search for truth — the central purpose of any institution of higher education."

This atmosphere of open discussion and debate is further fostered by the

Marian Miner Cook Athenaeum, site of weekly lunch and dinner meetings and lectures by prominent speakers. Students have the opportunity for a nice meal ("business attire is suggested," says a student) and an evening with a distinguished lecturer. A number of Athenaeum speakers have been conservative, including Milton Friedman, Dinesh D'Souza, Michael Novak, Ralph Reed, Jack Kemp, and David Horowitz. "These speakers are paid for out of college funds, not a third-party conservative organization that is successful at funding two token conservatives a semester," a student says. One professor describes it as a "wonderful facility," while a student rates it as "one of the nicest features of the campus." A student writing in the *Independent* describes the Athenaeum as "one of the great institutions at CMC. It is representative of all that a small college should be — intimate interaction between students, faculty, and outside speakers."

The same article, however, laments declining attendance at the Athenaeum and blames "poor speaker selection." Figures quoted in the article show that only around 65 people on average attended each event in a series called "Latino Writers on the Move" (during which one speaker removed his clothes to show the black negligee he was wearing underneath them), while sessions in series on jazz and "Taiwan, Hong Kong, China, U.S.: Conflict" averaged more than 140 attendees. A series on "Politics and Ideas" averaged about 130, and a series on the Bible, featuring Yale theologian Jaroslav Pelikan, drew about 125.

The article states that the leaders of the Athenaeum have started to move away from the college's and its students' more traditional backgrounds. "There seems to be a growing misconception on this campus that students have 'evolved' beyond the conservative roots of the college," the writer notes. This writer says that if the leaders are worried about declining attendance, they should invite speakers of intellectual worth who focus on what the college focuses on ("economics, business, law, public policy, politics, foreign affairs") and then complement those programs with ones of similar weight on "the arts, literature, music, and cultural and sociological issues."

A recent survey of the student body conducted by CMC's Rose Institute found that nearly half of CMC's students consider themselves Republican. However, when it comes to political activity, CMC has the "same apathy as you would encounter at other places," a student says. There is, of course, a greater interest in public affairs, but most students don't go in for current debates about multiculturalism and political correctness. "We're not having the same problems everyone else is," comments another student. When there is the occasional protest at CMC, it is usually students from other Claremont colleges doing the protesting.

In November of 1996, for instance, a group of individuals from within and outside the Claremont colleges gathered outside the Athenaeum to protest the speech of Latino writer Richard Rodriguez, a supporter of California's Proposition 209, which sought to end affirmative action. Protest leader Jose Calderon, an associate professor of sociology and Chicano studies at Pitzer College, was involved in a verbal exchange with CMC president Stark. Calderon later claimed — falsely, it appears — that Stark had shoved him backwards and humiliated him during a "clearly . . . peaceful and positive" protest. The next day, a theretofore unheard-of group identifying itself as the Alliance for Affirmation Action of the Claremont Colleges sent out a bogus press release on the incident from the Pitzer public relations department. Pitzer students held a walkout to support Calderon, but campus security reports indicate that Stark did not assault Calderon or any of the other protesters; rather, he was on the receiving end of antagonistic verbal and physical gestures, with some of the latter actually making contact. The event was but the most volatile in a series of incidents at Claremont surrounding the end of affirmative action in California higher education.

Sexual harassment has also been a flash point at CMC in recent years. Campus tensions rose in the spring of 1997 when a student-funded newsletter, the *Wohlford Free Press*, published sexually explicit material demeaning to women. The Women's Forum and the CMC administration met to discuss this and other incidents that had occurred on campus, including complaints against the rugby team for singing "drinking songs which made lewd references to forced group sex in public areas." Conservative students were equally outraged at the "despicable and inexcusable actions that have been committed and acquiesced to by our student body over the years." The *Independent* stated that such gross incivility should be more severely punished by the administration, and called for a more rigorous honor code for the CMC community.

The recently founded *Independent* receives no funds from the college. According to one student, because of the political allegiances of students "there was a market for a conservative paper." The paper offers an alternative to the campus paper, the *Collage,* and has featured articles on the legalization of drugs, President Clinton's performance in office, ebonics, and campus controversies such as the Calderon incident. In its own words, the paper is committed to "maintaining truth and excellence at the Claremont Colleges," and its immediate continuance is assured by the presence of several underclassmen on the editorial staff.

Student Life: Getting Along with the Neighbors

About 95 percent of all CMC students live on campus, and campus housing is abundant and adequate. One student describes the characteristics of the three main living regions: North Quad has many "jocks" and the most partyers; the midcampus area is moderate; and South Quad is quiet. The campus also owns and operates several apartment units, which are "nice living conditions . . . but kind of removed from campus life," according to a student.

There is no Greek system at Claremont McKenna. Most socializing occurs on campus, and the negligible cross-socialization among students of the five colleges is usually the result of courses with cross-registration. This general separation is agreeable to many CMC students, who feel that their commitment to academics is undermined by the presence of less serious students from an academically weaker college like Pitzer. In fact, it could be said that relations between Pitzer and CMC are not that great: as a CMC student writes in the *Independent*, "Many Pitzer students do venture down to CMC, often on a whim or the result of a bad acid trip, and find themselves experiencing a degree of intellectual rigor frowned on by the specious 60s culture. Our campuses are contiguous, and though we do our best to isolate ourselves socially from each other, there is obviously some interaction."

The Village, Claremont's town center, contains shops, restaurants, and bookstores, though the rest of the city of Claremont is considered rather boring by many students. One student describes it as inhabited mostly by retired people, which "doesn't make for a very good night life." Many students do have cars and are able to drive to West Los Angeles (forty-five minutes away), where they can enjoy the beach; to Pasadena for restaurants and movie theaters; or to the nearby San Gabriel Mountains.

One student describes CMC as a "pretty physically fit campus." The athletic resources, shared with Harvey Mudd and Scripps, are outstanding. The college recently completed a multimillion-dollar recreation facility which is open from 6 A.M. to midnight. CMC offers twenty intercollegiate sports in NCAA Division III as well as dozens of intramural sports teams. Intramural opportunities include everything from men's and women's rugby to fencing, and there are competitive ballroom dancing and cycling teams as well.

Because of its focus on management, international relations, and public affairs, performing arts are not as pronounced at Claremont McKenna as they are at the other Claremont colleges, especially Pomona and Scripps. Yet numerous musical and theater groups are available to CMC students, including a pep band, an a cappella group (Shades), the Society for the Preservation of Music (SPAM), a theater club (Under the Lights), and a comedy troupe (Without a Box).

There are also political clubs and organizations, some serving all five colleges and others exclusively for CMC students, that range from the far left to the respectable right. A five-college group supports the gay and lesbian student population, and there are campus chapters of Amnesty International, Student Association for the Environment, and both College Republicans and College Democrats.

CLEMSON UNIVERSITY

Sikes Hall
Box 345124
Clemson, SC 29634-5124
(864) 656-3311
www.clemson.edu

Total enrollment: 16,396
Undergraduates: 12,710
SAT Ranges (Verbal/Math): V 577, M 563 (avg.)
Financial aid: N/A
Applicants: 8,358
Accepted: 76%
Enrolled: 40%
Application deadline: May 1
Financial aid application deadline: Apr. 1
Tuition: $3,252 resident; $8,676 nonresident
Core curriculum: No

Landscape and History

Clemson University occupies what was once the plantation of John C. Calhoun, U.S. senator from South Carolina, vice president of the United States, and one of the most important political thinkers in American history. His house and study, located in the middle of campus, form an anchor for a school that respects the past yet presses the frontiers of technological knowledge. Calhoun's son-in-law, Thomas Greene Clemson, inherited the statesman's land and, at his own death, willed it to the state of South Carolina in order to establish a school that could help the South recover from the ravages of the Civil War. Clemson College opened in 1893 and was an all-male military school until 1955, when it went both civilian and coed. It became a university in 1964.

Today the university enrolls some 16,500 students, including 3,800 graduate students, in five colleges: Agriculture, Forestry and Life Sciences; Architecture, Arts, and Humanities; Business and Public Affairs; Engineering and Science; and Health, Education, and Human Development. Bachelor's degrees are offered in seventy-four fields of study.

The main campus occupies 1,400 acres in northwestern South Carolina, and the school owns some 17,000 acres of land around nearby Hartwell Lake as well as over 12,000 acres devoted to research throughout the state. This large investment in real estate reflects the emphasis Clemson places on agriculture, forestry, and the sciences — an emphasis that stems from Thomas Greene Clemson himself. The university also owns property used for teaching and research in Genoa, Italy, and on the Caribbean island of Dominica.

Located in a fairly isolated part of the state — an hour southwest of the Greenville-Spartanburg metropolitan area, near the Georgia border — Clemson has retained much of its Southern charm despite a steady influx of students and professors from other regions of the country, particularly the Northeast. Radical social and scholarly ideas that have come to dominate other campuses have made only modest inroads at Clemson. It's still a polite, Southern university that remains surprisingly solid in its academic standards.

Academic Life: Traditional Culture versus Trendy Ideology

All Clemson students must fulfill general education requirements that exist to ensure that graduates are "broadly educated and technically skilled." In most of the required areas, students pick from a number of approved classes. There is no core curriculum at Clemson.

Students must take four courses that improve communication and speaking skills. These include two introductory English classes, a course with an emphasis on oral communication, and one that is deemed writing intensive. Other requirements include two math courses; a course in computer skills, which gives students practical information on how to use word processors and spreadsheets; two related laboratory science classes in astronomy, biology, chemistry, geology, physical sciences, or physics; two humanities courses; and two social sciences courses, chosen from a long list of approved courses designed to "introduce students to human social and cultural diversity."

In addition, students must fulfill requirements from their major department, and some of the five academic colleges impose additional requirements. For instance, all students in the School of Humanities, which is part of the College of Architecture, Arts, and Humanities, must complete a minor field of concentration, take four humanities courses and four social science courses, and attain proficiency in a foreign language.

Overall, students and faculty seem pleased with the intellectual life of the university. One professor says, "You can get a very high quality education within a very personal atmosphere that is missing in the mega-university. Even engineers must take courses from other divisions."

For the most part, professors and students believe that the course offerings are superior and expose students to a wide range of topics. However, some caution that just because a course sounds as though it might have a traditional emphasis doesn't mean it will be taught in a traditional manner. "Some politically correct courses sound perfectly legitimate," warns one social science professor. "You may take an English course that sounds superb, only to find out too late that it has been politicized. So it's not just the department or the supposed subject of the course that's important, it's the content."

Clemson has a separate honors program, known as Calhoun College, that seeks to enrich the educational experience of some of the university's brightest students. Entering freshmen with SAT scores above 1,300 who are in the top 10 percent of their graduating class are eligible to take separate honors classes and undertake in-depth study and research. Honors students live in separate housing.

Students interested in architecture have the opportunity to study for a semester in Charleston, which is rich in beautifully constructed houses and other buildings. Clemson operates the only architectural program in South Carolina.

Among the best professors at Clemson are Ed Arnold in German; Frank Day, Harold Woodell, and Mark Winchell in English; Bill Lasser, Charles Dunn, and David Woodard in political science; Bruce Yandle in legal studies; and Robert McCormick in economics.

Clemson's department of economics offers a superior education by giving students a broad view of the discipline while focusing on its traditional values as well. Most of the professors are followers of the Chicago school of economics, which favors free markets over government intrusion in the economy. The program emphasizes environmental economics, and its undergraduate curriculum prepares students for careers in business or government by emphasizing problem-solving skills.

The political science department is said to have a strong faculty, and it receives high marks from students. Sources say it has an equitable distribution of liberals and conservatives. This provides much-needed balance to the department and ensures that students are presented with all political views. The political science faculty is also prolific: its ten members have written thirty books, a high book-to-professor ratio.

Since it is a university with a strong specialization in agriculture, some of Clemson's strongest departments lie in the hard sciences and more technical fields. Chemistry, physics, and most engineering departments are very strong, as are business-related departments such as marketing, accounting, and textile management.

Political ideologies have made their mark in some departments, however. The English department is Clemson's largest, in part because all students must take two English courses to graduate. Some of the department's older faculty members are first-rate, but many of the younger ones seem intent on politicizing the outlook of the department, some professors say. "The things I hear coming out of that department shock me," says one. "They've bought into the belief that you don't have to learn grammar in order to write well — you just write whatever you want. Nor do you have to learn how to understand the structure of a novel." Recent hiring patterns show that the department's movers and shakers are more interested in acquiring avant-garde, politicized theorists than in hiring traditional English scholars. "You have to walk around land mines there today," says another professor.

The philosophy and religion department in the School of Humanities is singled out as heavily politicized by many professors. "The department is just full of wild men — crazy old Hegelians who believe that Marx was brilliant and crazy post-modernists who can't agree on whether the sun is up these days," says one professor. One student told of attending the first day of his upper-level philosophy class. After students waited twenty minutes past the appointed hour for a professor to arrive, a man in blue jeans sitting in the back of the room revealed that he was the instructor and there would be no lectures and no reading for the class — the only assignment for the semester was to keep a journal. And as for class time? "We're just going to come in here and talk about some of the questions you've been thinking about," the instructor said. The department subsists mainly on business students who are required to take its business ethics course. Beyond that class, many offerings are limited.

Clemson has a nascent women's studies program, which offers a minor to students interested in finding out how society, history, politics, biology, and other aspects of life work to keep women "oppressed." This heavily politicized field hasn't quite caught on at Clemson as it has elsewhere; despite its advocates' best efforts to drum up interest, students aren't flocking to it. "It's not by any means growing," says one professor. Women's studies recently celebrated its tenth anniversary at Clemson. For those seeking a break from the rigor of other disciplines, the program recently unveiled a new course: Women's Studies 459, "Women's Body Image in Popular Culture." The goal of the course is to "challenge students to analyze how the influx of images from mass media serves to construct gender images, in particular women's body image."

Like English, history has some very good individual members, but it has declined in recent years because of increasing politicization. Other politicized departments include speech, which one professor calls "very weak."

Politicization on campus is thwarted, however, by several important cultural and academic influences. "Clemson has a much more conservative student body than many large state schools, and this means that the students are less likely to take political correctness seriously and are more likely to brush it off," says a professor, who sees a continuing contingent of traditionalists enter the student body.

"The culture of the institution isn't confrontational, and neither is that of South Carolina," says a faculty member. Thus, for all the efforts of some younger faculty members who would move Clemson in the direction of New England if they could, the cultural influences of the region, reflected by the students and their families, serve as tremendous impediments to rapid change. In addition, many of the departments in the liberal arts do not offer doctoral programs. That means that they tend to emphasize teaching over abstract theories that typically seek to undermine traditional values.

At Clemson, as at many other schools, faculty members are disappointed by the quality of many job applicants. "The new Ph.D.s aren't as well trained as they used to be," says a professor. "One c.v. [curriculum vitae] from a graduate of an elite university revealed that the applicant had taken only 10 courses in graduate school. That's not much time to learn what you need to know, especially if you consider the politically correct content of some of the courses."

Political Atmosphere: Sitting Squarely on the Fence

Since 1995 Clemson has been led by President Constantine W. "Deno" Curris, formerly head man at Murray State University and the University of Northern Iowa. Since arriving in South Carolina the Kentucky native has tried to lay the foundation for Clemson's goal of becoming a national university and has actively sought to hire young professors and improve technology, including wiring two thousand dormitory rooms for computer network access. He has also sought to raise money and has lobbied the state legislature for increased research funds.

Observers say Clemson's administration is politically liberal but that its main focus is fund-raising. "Their aim has more to do with survival than with changing anything," says a professor. As at most universities, Clemson's administrators are politicians, brokering compromises that make the most people happy. Since there are few protests or special-interest campaigns at Clemson, administrators have taken a live-and-let-live approach. In one sense this lack of political heavy-handedness bodes well for traditional education, since most students and state legislators, who ultimately oversee the university, have no interest in avant-garde political agendas.

Unfortunately, that style of governing also suggests that in any future political agitation, administrators will sail with the political winds. Additionally, such vacillation ensures the institutionalization of some practices. For example, Curris and his colleagues have never addressed the issue of racial preferences in university admissions, which until recently was every university's dirty little secret. Like all other competitive universities, Clemson considers race as a criterion for admission. But administrators are nervous about discussing the matter, some say. "They've never said anything about affirmative action," says one longtime faculty member. "They bend over backwards as a Southern university to show how tolerant they are."

Because most of the students come from traditional backgrounds, protests are rare. Even a January 1998 visit by Speaker of the House Newt Gingrich — a favorite target of campus agitators — drew no protests. "That's an indication of some of the freedoms we have here that we couldn't have somewhere else," says one observer. Organizers had to turn away 1,000 students from Gingrich's speech because there wasn't room in the 1,200-seat lecture hall.

Although the atmosphere at Clemson is not as politically liberal as that at other campuses, it does have an Office of Multicultural Affairs, which runs various race-based programs around the university. Many of the programs are open exclusively to minorities, drawing criticism from some who say such practices promote racial segregation. For instance, the office runs an ethnic awareness month for Hispanics (September), Native Americans (November), blacks (February), and Asian and Pacific Americans (May, but celebrated in March "because the semester ends in early May"). At the beginning of the year the office also runs what it calls a "multicultural" orientation for freshmen, although this event is restricted to minorities, thus excluding the great majority of Clemson students. Throughout the year the office also sponsors special receptions and dinners that exclude white students.

Student Life: A Tiger in Every Tank

Clemson is a small town about twenty minutes off Interstate 85, the main highway between Richmond and Atlanta. There's little in town besides the university and businesses that make a living off its 16,500 students. Some complain that there's little to do at Clemson, but others say the small, isolated nature of the place is a boon for creating a sense of community. For those who become bored, Atlanta is almost two hours south and Greenville-Spartanburg is about an hour north.

Still, Clemson does possess small-town Southern charm. There's the Esso Club, a hole-in-the-wall bar that attracts some great bands. There's Just Barbecue, the only barbecue joint in town, which offers incredible deals. Mac's Drive-In is another local landmark: a drive-in hamburger restaurant that South Carolinian politicians and Clemson sports figures have frequented for decades.

At Clemson sports is serious business, particularly football. "You have not truly experienced Clemson until you have sat on the hill during the driving rain to cheer the Tigers on to victory," says one senior. One student at North Carolina tells of the time he was driving his old Carolina blue (light blue) Volkswagen Beetle on the interstate near Clemson in the middle of football season. The car, which was adorned with numerous North Carolina window stickers, ran out of gas. By the time the student had returned to his car with help, someone had painted it bright orange, Clemson's school color.

Clemson plays in the Atlantic Coast Conference, which routinely fields some of the best college basketball teams in the country and is improving in football with the recent addition of Florida State. Clemson's football team regularly earns bids to play in postseason bowls.

Most undergraduates are natives of South Carolina, and many grew up going to Clemson football games with their families. Clemson is in these folks' blood. But an increasing number of Northerners have also sought refuge in South Carolina's temperate climate. Next to South Carolina, New Jersey sends the most students to Clemson. Students report that people from New Jersey and similar states adapt well — by their sophomore year, the Northerners are cheering just as loudly for the Tiger football team as longtime loyalists. "There's something that socializes them to the place," says one observer.

But Clemson isn't for everyone. Potential students enamored with flashy life in a cosmopolitan city should look elsewhere. "If you're a Manhattanite, you might not want to go to Clemson," advises one instructor.

Fraternities and sororities are an important part of student life. Around 20 percent of all students belong to some sort of Greek organization. Fraternities usually hold parties on the weekends, and students say joining the Greek system is a good way to meet people.

Numerous student organizations are active on campus. Religious clubs are popular with some students; a chapter of Campus Crusade for Christ, the Baptist Student Union, the Campus Ministers' Association, and several other groups for people of different faiths are present on campus.

Some students recently founded a homosexual student organization called Lambda Society, but it has few members and little campus support. Similarly, women's organizations are having problems establishing footholds on campus. A chapter of the National Organization for Women, for instance, became defunct after it failed to attract enough members.

COLBY COLLEGE

Office of Admissions–Lunder Hall
4800 Mayflower Hill
Waterville, ME 04901-8848
(207) 872-3168
(800) 723-3032
www.colby.edu

Total enrollment: 1,760
Undergraduates: 1,760
SAT Ranges (Verbal/Math): V 600-680, M 600-680
Financial aid: 43%
Applicants: 4,600
Accepted: 31%
Enrolled: 33%
Application deadline: Jan. 15

Financial aid application deadline: Feb. 1
Tuition: $20,990
Core curriculum: No

Coming Over on Mayflower Hill

Colby College is the nation's twelfth-oldest independent liberal arts college. Founded in 1813, the college was in business seven years before its home state entered the Union. Through the years, the college has developed a reputation as a solid liberal arts school. Its 1,700 students are not, however, required to take a core curriculum, but rather spend their time picking their way through a set of distribution requirements.

Although a new program of interdisciplinary seminars is a welcome return to the ideals of traditional liberal education, Colby's curriculum is dotted with politicized classes. The administration is considerably more liberal than the student body, and seems to have hired some professors who are apt to turn the podium into a pulpit.

Still, the college boasts a 700-acre campus on Mayflower Hill, near Waterville, Maine, and a median class size of only seventeen. The curriculum offers some excellent classes, and the student body seems to have good amounts of seriousness, talent, and common sense. Even with the multicultural influences, Colby remains a good liberal arts school, albeit without the liberal arts convictions it once had.

Academic Life: The Gain in Maine Is Mainly Earned without Pain

Colby students face what is nowadays the typical array of distribution requirements. These include a single course in each of six areas: the arts, historical studies, literature, quantitative reasoning, natural sciences, and social sciences. There are also requirements in English composition and a foreign language. Language proficiency may be demonstrated in a number of ways, one of which is by spending the fall semester of the freshman year at intensive language programs in Mexico or France.

Nothing in the requirements compels students to study Western civilization, but Colby does have a diversity requirement. "Students are required to take one course centrally concerned with how the diversities among peoples have contributed to the richness of human experience," the college catalogue says. "Courses that may be taken to fulfill the requirement are those that (a) focus on history, perspectives, or culture of non-Western peoples or a culture whose origins lie outside of the European traditions; (b) focus on issues and/or theories of ethnicity, gender, or class as these may be found anywhere in the world; or (c) examine the nature, history, and workings of prejudice as experienced by any group."

Some of the old physical education requirements that coerced students into playing softball, badminton, and the like with their classmates have been replaced by a "wellness" requirement, a New Age therapy session designed to massage the students' psyches rather than exercise their bodies. According to the catalogue, "The objective of the new Wellness Program is to assist in and encourage the development of self-responsibility for one's lifestyle. The program will emphasize mental, emotional, social, and spiritual fitness as well." Four credits are required, and these can be earned through varsity or club athletics, or activity and fitness courses. Another option is "wellness seminars," ten one-hour lectures that are given each semester. Attending four of them yields one wellness credit. The catalogue lists these topics: "alcohol, drugs, and sex; sexual victimization; time- and stress-management; nutrition, eating disorders and body image; spirituality and student life; and risks of student living."

The two semesters of the Colby calendar are separated by a January session. Students must attend three January terms in order to graduate. This month is a time when "topics may be pursued single-mindedly, free from the competing demands of an orthodox curriculum," the catalogue states. (It is, of course, debatable whether the college indeed has an orthodox curriculum from which to escape.) In any case, students use this term as a chance to explore career options in more of a "real world" setting than might otherwise be possible. About 80 "Jan Plan" courses are offered each year.

January courses or internships require thirty to forty hours of work per week. About eighty choices are offered each year, including trips abroad for language study or an archaeological dig or working across the United States at hospitals, laboratories, or newspapers. The college is fairly open to students' suggestions, so this session can be used by a thoughtful student for a variety of explorations.

Colby also offers two "Integrated Studies Semesters" each year in which students take several classes that explore "a brief but momentous era in world civilization from the perspective of three of four disciplines," the catalogue states. In its first year of existence — 1997 — the program drew on faculty from history, literature, music, and physics to examine the years from 1919 to 1945. The idea is a good one: such a plan of study illustrates like no single course can the interrelation of history, humanities, and science. It is in fact something of a throwback to the days of a traditional core curriculum. However, students should be aware that some of the clusters offered at Colby are rather politicized: an upcoming semester's theme will be "Sexualities East and West."

Among Colby's best professors are Sandy Maisel and G. Calvin Mackenzie in government; Thomas Longstaff in religious studies; and Joseph Roisman, Kerill O'Neill, and Hanna Roisman in classics.

Like the integrated studies semesters, the departments at Colby include the traditional and the politicized. The English department falls into the latter category. Its course titles sometimes appear to be traditional, even when their content is not. "Historical Contexts," for example, asks students to look into "some of the central political, cultural, and ideological issues occasioned by literary texts, particularly issues of race, gender, and class, through close reading and detailed analysis." Another class, "Victorian Literature I," looks at Victorian literature, but only insofar as it was formed by "the social pressures of class, religion, gender, and race."

Other English offerings don't try to hide their agendas with standard titles. Examples include "Art and Oppression: Lesbian and Gay Literature and Modern Society," "Shakespeare as Material Boy: Physical Texts and the 'Immortal' Bard," "Passionate Expression: Love, Sex, and Sexuality in Western Literature," and "Cross-dressing in Literature and Film: Transgressing Cultural Codes of Gender."

The department of religion offers many legitimate courses, but also some that examine religion as a social phenomenon or an irrational belief. There are also courses in marginal religious movements. Some course titles include "The Bible and Social Inequality"; "Contemporary Wicca: Formalists, Feminists, and Free Spirits"; and "The Goddess: A Hermeneutics in Thealogy [sic]," which offers "an exploration of some Eastern and Western visions of divinity through feminine imagery and symbolism" and "a discovering and reimagining of the Goddess's multi-dimensionality in art and literature." Three department offerings focus on the teachings of individuals: Jesus Christ, St. Paul, and radical feminist Mary Daly.

Colby has programs in African-American studies, East Asian studies, and women's studies. The women's studies menu includes courses like "Sexuality: Myth and Reality," "Women in Myth and Fairy Tale," "Gender, Race, and the Politics of Difference," and one cross-listed with history called "The History of Sexuality in the United States." That class studies topics like "abortion, birth control, fertility, and reproduction; intra- and inter-ethnic marriage; venereal disease; prostitution; and lesbian, gay, and straight cultures."

Political Atmosphere: Islands in the Mainstream

The general political atmosphere at Colby comprises a fairly mainstream student body and a more liberal faculty, all directed by a very liberal president. William R. Cotter worked for the Ford Foundation for a time before coming to Colby, and college literature notes that "his experience abroad and with developing and newly independent countries adds a special dimension to his commitment to enhancing at Colby diversity of every kind." Cotter, a Harvard-educated lawyer with an impressive resume in the legal field, recently received the Leadership Award from the Equity Institute of Maine, which "recognizes demonstrated leadership and encouragement of others to confront exclusive behavior and to value diversity." The president of the Maine Lesbian and Gay Political Alliance received the award at the same time. Cotter wrote in a 1995 issue of *Colby* magazine, "I believe that the affirmative action programs of the last thirty years have, on the whole, greatly strengthened the economy and the social fabric of the country and that whites and minorities as well as men and women have benefited substantially."

Colby, it should be noted, has historically been ahead of the curve in campus diversity. The school's Baptist founders included in the charter a religious freedom clause, and Colby admitted its first female student in 1871, making it the first New England college to become coed after starting out as an all-male institution. The first African-American to graduate from Colby did so in 1887. Alumnus Elijah Parish Lovejoy was killed in 1837 defending his newspaper from an attack by anti-abolitionists.

Today's Colby is interested in a more affirmative-action style of diversity. Its viewbook, sent to prospective students, says that since 1979 — Cotter's first year as president — "Colby took its commitment to build an increasingly diverse community a step further by establishing the Ralph J. Bunche Scholars program," which reserves scholarship money exclusively for minority students. The first page of the college catalogue proclaims: "Colby stands for diversity, without which we become parochial; for respect of various lifestyles and beliefs, without which we become mean-spirited; and for the protection of every individual against discrimination." In contemporary usage, "lifestyle" is a euphemism for sexual preference, while "belief" often denotes New Age or neopagan movements.

In 1997 Colby received a $6.25 million donation from the Oak Foundation of Geneva to endow ten scholarships for international students who have "suffered political oppression or torture, or whose family members have," according to the *Chronicle of Higher Education.* The money also establishes at Colby the Oak Institute for International Human Rights, which will "provide sabbaticals on campus for activists who work on behalf of the victims of human-rights abuses."

Certainly the number of politicized courses indicates a preference on the part of the administration for hiring and promoting faculty not afraid to teach ideologically. In such a small setting, however, most professors tend to be very accessible, and student-faculty relations are quite warm.

Student Life: I'm a Lumberjack and I'm Okay

Student life at Colby is formed by the rural location of the college. The campus is made up mostly of redbrick Georgian buildings and is perched atop a hill overlooking Waterville, a small, mostly blue-collar town of about twenty thousand residents. Since Waterville is no college town, Colby students often make use of the vast and beautiful rural areas of Maine and New Hampshire. Indeed, one of the most attractive things about going to Colby is living in one of the nation's most beautiful states. Recreational activities change with the season: cross-country and downhill skiing in the long Maine winters; hiking, fishing, and camping; or visiting Maine's spectacular coastline.

For those who need a city at least occasionally, Portland, with its restored Old Town and numerous restaurants and shops, is about an hour and a half away. Freeport, home of L. L. Bean and numerous other outlet centers, is a bit closer. And Boston, the hub of New England, is about three hours away. The campus is also occasionally visited by popular music groups, including Blues Traveler, the Spin Doctors, and Phish.

Still, the outdoors is far more popular. Almost all freshmen at Colby participate in a special program called Colby Outdoor Orientation Trip, or COOT, which occurs the week before campus orientation. It's an excellent opportunity for newly arrived students to see the state's wild places and mix with their fellow freshmen. Students are accompanied by an upperclassman with outdoor experience as well as a faculty or staff member of the college.

The college's largest student organization is the Outing Club, which offers trips into the woods for kayaking, mountain climbing, and other outdoor activities. And the "Woodsmen's Team," a student athletic club, takes on other New England colleges and universities in "old-time logging skills such as standing-block chop, log rolling, sawing, pole climbing; and newer events such as ax throw and chainsaw." The Woodsmen also host the annual "Mud Meet" each March, in which both teams and individuals, men and women, compete.

The Woodsmen are not an official athletic team, but one-third of Colby students do participate in the thirty-two teams that are. Teams include football, baseball, basketball, ice hockey, lacrosse, squash, Nordic and alpine skiing, and track and field. There are also club and intramural teams, and any student may make use of Colby's huge new athletic center.

Other student groups include Colby Christian Fellowship, the Mountaineering Club, Colby Republicans, Musician's Alliance, the Newman Council, and the Student Government Association.

The college calls itself a "residential community," and with good reason: 95 percent of the students live on campus in a system organized around what is known as the "Commons Plan." The twenty-six residence halls are organized into four commons, each with its own dining hall, gathering places, and governing body. All dorms are coed, and, according to the college, none is organized around special interests, ethnicity, or other criteria. Students in the commons work together to plan menus, parties, and other special events. Faculty are affiliated with commons as well, allowing them to develop stronger bonds with students.

The Commons Plan was instituted in 1984 by President Cotter to replace the fraternity system. The catalogue says that fraternities "had become disconsonant with Colby's values because they tended to narrow the opportunities and experiences of students rather than expand them, because they were discriminatory against women and were exclusionary by nature, and because fraternity members often engaged in disruptive and undesirable activities such as hazing and pressuring students to join." Such free association of students was rightly seen as an impediment to the administration's centralizing and leveling zeal.

COLGATE UNIVERSITY

Office of Admissions
Colgate University
Hamilton, NY 13346-1383
(315) 824-7401
www.colgate.edu

Total enrollment: 2,910
Undergraduates: 2,842
SAT Ranges (Verbal/Math): V 600-680, M 600-690
Financial aid: 44%
Applicants: 5,800
Accepted: 36%
Enrolled: 29%
Application deadline: Jan. 15
Financial aid application deadline: Feb. 1
Tuition: $22,610
Core curriculum: Yes

Not a Scandal

In the case of Colgate, the title "university" can be misleading. In essence, Colgate University is a small liberal arts college of about 2,900 undergraduates and only a few graduate students. Other contradictions can be found here, too. For example, many on campus seem to despise the fraternity system, but it remains the focus of social life on this isolated campus. There is also a contradiction within the curriculum itself: Colgate requires both a core curriculum and a set of distribution requirements, though the core is partially set up as a distribution requirement.

Despite these conflicts, it must be said that Colgate offers a fine liberal arts education, provided one takes the courses in several politicized departments with a few grains of salt. Admissions are highly selective (only 725 students are accepted each year out of more than 6,000 applications — a rate of less than 12 percent). Moreover, the setting is idyllic and the political atmosphere on campus is quiet.

Colgate was founded in 1817 as a Baptist seminary, then merged with another school in 1823 to become the Hamilton Literary and Theological Institution. After spending some years as Madison University, the school in 1890 renamed itself for a New York City soap maker, William Colgate, whose financial support had been crucial to the young institution. The university severed its church ties in 1928 and became coeducational in 1970.

147

Academic Life: A Core Sample

The general education requirements at Colgate consist of distribution choices and what the university calls the "Liberal Arts Core Curriculum." There is also a foreign language requirement that can be met with either high school or university courses.

Colgate's distribution requirements mean that a student must take two courses in each of three "divisions": humanities, natural science and mathematics, and social sciences. The two courses must come from different departments within the division; for example, the humanities requirement might be met with courses in English and religion. Any course can count toward the distribution requirement, meaning that students choose from the entire catalogue rather than a selected list.

The Liberal Arts Core Curriculum is more tightly defined. Four courses are required, with an optional fifth course available to interested students. They may be taken in any order, but are to be completed in a student's first two years.

At first glance the core curriculum appears to be outstanding. It is concerned with central, interdisciplinary, liberal arts themes — according to the catalogue, it is designed to "engage students with some of the persistent, fundamental questions of our culture as posed in classical texts and confronted today as current issues: our relationship to nature, the relationship of the temporal to the eternal and the definition of the individual within society." Professors praise the core. "Colgate has a core curriculum which is not a hollow joke," says one. "The courses are taught by a broad array of faculty, and the students are exposed to the Great Books."

One of the courses is outstanding. "Western Traditions" covers "the beginnings of Western thought and its resonance throughout the ages" in order to "give students grounding in eras crucially formative of Western traditions and provide them an enhanced appreciation of both the continuity and the diversity of these traditions," the catalogue says.

A companion course (also under the heading of "Continuity and Change in the West") can be somewhat politicized, depending on which professor teaches it. "The Challenge of Modernity," according to one professor, has a reputation for being "a bit trendy or politically correct." The course will be more rewarding if a student can get in a section led by one of the better professors listed below.

The remaining two liberal arts core courses constitute what is essentially another distribution requirement, and a politicized one at that. The "Scientific Perspectives" portion of the core is satisfied with one of eleven courses — "Psychology of Women," "Critical Analysis of Health Issues: AIDS," and "Ecology, Ethics, and Wilderness" among them. According to a student, "What Is Science?" and "Causality and Indeterminism in Science" are better choices. The former looks at the methods and practices of science, and the latter examines the history of the "idea of causality" through the works of philosophers and scientists like Aristotle, Newton, and Schrödinger.

The final requirement in the core curriculum is "Cultures of Africa, Asia and the Americas." Students must choose one course from an offering of twenty, each of which focuses on a different culture or country. "The Black Diaspora: Africans at Home and Abroad," "Women in China," and "North American Indians" are some of the options.

Interested students can take a fifth class, a seminar with coursework that includes an extensive research paper on an interdisciplinary theme. Students who complete this course successfully receive the designation "High Distinction in the Liberal Arts Core Curriculum" on their transcripts.

Classes at Colgate are usually small, especially compared to those at large state universities. The average class size is between fifteen and twenty-five students. Professors are interested in teaching, but also pursue research. "The faculty are still active researchers, and, as a result, undergraduates get unusual opportunities and greater responsibilities," a professor says. "There is a lot more one-on-one attention that the students get at Colgate than they would elsewhere." Another professor adds: "Colgate has a culture where if you are not highly regarded by students it will affect tenure, and it results in demerits even for tenured faculty. It is rumored that the university is weeding out the older faculty, which it considers deadwood, and trying to bring in a vibrant younger group. Everybody wants to be a good teacher because of the overwhelming culture."

The best professors at Colgate include Stanley Brubaker, Robert Rothstein, Barry A. Shain, and Robert Kraynak in political science; Peter Balakian and novelist Frederick M. Busch in English; Graham Hodges in history; and Michael R. Haines in economics.

"The best departments in the social sciences and the humanities at Colgate are the English, philosophy, and political science departments," one professor says. "These departments examine the classic texts of the traditional liberal arts education."

English majors must take courses in British and American literature and in the literature of the Middle Ages. The department lists two Shakespeare courses.

Political science has sixteen professors, and many are interested in American government and foreign policy. "The political science department is an unusually good department in many ways," a professor says. "The faculty are representative of a broad range of political perspectives, and all are excellent teachers." Some say political science is the best department at Colgate. Its courses cover government and international relations, but also political theory; classes are offered in constitutional law, the Enlightenment, and political thought from the ancient Greeks to modern times.

The department also has a course — "Modernity and Its Conservative American Critics" — on conservative political thought, a very rare offering in American universities. Its course description reads: "What is wrong with the modern world, especially with the political culture of liberal and progressive intellectual elites? Such questions are explored by studying the radical critique of modernity offered by philosophical, classical and Christian conservatives."

There are several politicized departments at Colgate. The sociology department bases much of its teaching on human society on race, gender, and class. Classes include "Power, Racism and Privilege," "Women and Social Change: The Women's Movement," "Gender and the Social Sciences," "Gender and Culture," and "Black Communities in Contemporary America." Another course, "Population Issues," "considers the relationship of population to a range of policy concerns including social welfare and security, the status of women, poverty and economic development, and race and ethnic relations," according to the catalogue.

Sociology also offers "Men and Masculinities," which addresses "the symbols and practices through which masculine identities are created; the evolution and forms of male dominance, patriarchy and fratriarchy; the relationship between masculinity and violence; maleness and the cultural construction of emotion; male heterosexuality and alternative modes of sexuality; the relationship between masculinity, production and social status; and the impacts of feminism on masculinity in Western societies."

Colgate's department of philosophy and religion, according to one professor, "is dominated by liberation theology and feminism — you know, all the latest trends from the Harvard Divinity School." Despite the fact that about one-third of Colgate's students are Catholic, the religion department, according to this professor, has "a strong anti-Catholic bias."

While some philosophy offerings (like "Philosophy of Nature" and "Medieval Philosophy") are in line with a traditional liberal arts education, others are of a more political nature. "Philosophy and Feminisms," according to the catalogue, "gives special attention to the categories of difference and the Other(s), as these have affected marginalized people, especially women." Topics include "oppressions (e.g. race, class, gender, ethnicity, sexual orientation), violence against women in relation to other forms of violence (e.g., militarism, contemporary colonization and rape of the earth), women's ways of knowing, friendship among women, barriers separating women [and] women's political activities."

The religion side of the department is even more ideological. "Sexuality and Human Meaning," the catalogue says, "is a critical examination of several religious and philosophical issues dealing with modes of human sexuality in relation to views of the human person." The course description says that "attitudes toward pornography, erotica, marriage, homosexuality, prostitution and abortion reflect views of the self and its relationships," and that "the perspectives of the major religious traditions and the resources of the empirical sciences" will be studied "in relation to humanizing and dehumanizing dimensions of human sexuality." Other religion courses include "Women's Lives and Religious Traditions," "Theological Themes of the Black Experience," and "Feminist and Womanist Religious Thought."

Some philosophy and religion courses overlap with the women's studies department. Women's studies is an interdisciplinary program that doesn't have its own full-time staff and therefore offers courses from other departments, including education, economics, English, history, and sociology. Six courses belong only to the women's studies department, including "Biology and Gender," which examines topics such as "evolutionary and cultural models of sexuality, bonding patterns, sex roles and parental behavior; human evolution; [and] sex role stereotypes and gender identification during childhood."

Colgate established its peace studies program in 1970 "as part of the university's response to issues raised by the escalating arms race and the war in Vietnam," according to the catalogue. Peace studies majors take ten courses and must participate in an off-campus project. Like the women's studies program, peace studies borrows courses from other departments but also has some of its own. An introductory course subtitled "Violence and Nonviolence" covers "positive and negative peace, structural and direct violence, [and] the analysis of conflict" but also attempts to link what it calls "parallel concerns": issues of race, gender, class, and international relations. Another class, "Women and Peace: War, Resistance and Justice," studies the "contributions and aspirations of women toward the creation of a more just and peaceful world."

Political Atmosphere: Fraternity-Gate

The most divisive question on Colgate's campus recently has been whether the university's nine fraternities and four sororities will survive. Over the past several years, there has been a sustained effort on the part of some faculty to break up the fraternities, and in 1996 about two-thirds of the faculty senate voted in favor of such a policy. However, alumni and students have protested, and the matter remains unresolved.

The ban on fraternities would be accomplished with a rule expelling any student who joins one. "It would basically mean that the university would revoke the charters of the fraternities," a student says. However, many fraternity houses are owned by the international foundations that govern chapter affairs. If fraternities were banned, the foundations and their alumni would be forced to rent out the fraternity house, or leave it empty between reunions. Some fear that if the university disbands the fraternities, it will rent the houses from the foundations and use the residences to set up special-interest dorms. Colgate already has twelve special-interest houses dedicated to, among other things, Asian culture, Hispanic culture, African-American cultures, and world peace.

Complaints about the fraternities include misogyny, elitism, and irresponsible behavior with respect to alcohol. "The majority of the faculty are more or less committed to destroying the Greek system," a professor says. "They think it's where all evil lies, especially because the fraternities are not quite as dormant as they were ten years ago." And because of Colgate's reputation as a party school, the administration is under pressure to develop "alternative social programs that are alcohol-free," another professor says. Reportedly, frat parties have become a little more subdued since the effort to get rid of them began.

Colgate recently suspended one chapter for three semesters (starting in November 1997) because of a party that got out of control, according to the student newspaper, *Colgate Maroon-News*. The party not only featured acts of hazing, but the acts of two "exotic dancers" from Syracuse as well. However, more than nine hundred students (about one-third of the undergraduate student body) signed a petition calling the penalty "unjustified and harsh." Other faculty and students supported the sanctions and organized a silent, candlelit march down fraternity row. "The *Maroon* even had a whole issue bashing fraternities following the event," a student says.

It still seems unlikely, however, that fraternities will be completely rousted from the Colgate campus. The university has been coed for only about twenty-five years, meaning that for a certain sector of alumni — including some faculty and members of the board of trustees — fraternity life was an important part of their experience at Colgate. "Many of the alumni are as loyal to their fraternities as they are to their alma mater," a student says. "The fraternities aren't going to just disappear."

Apart from this issue, the Colgate community is rarely given over to political activity. The students are moderately conservative, according to a professor, and though faculty are generally liberal, conservative professors are allowed to speak their minds — to a certain extent. "Conservatives are not appointed to positions of university governance," another professor says.

Most Colgate students are more interested in athletics or social activities than politics. One professor estimates that "maybe 5 percent" of students are politically active, and says non-fraternity-related demonstrations tend to be small, involving fewer than ten students. "Most students are not liberals, they are sort of mushy Republicans," a professor says. "However, conservative students receive a lot of flack in class if they're outspoken."

Student Life: Upstate — Not Uptown

Hamilton, New York, is a village of around 2,500 located in the beautiful northern tip of the Chenango Valley in upstate New York. The 1,550-acre campus is also very pretty, with some buildings dating back to the mid–nineteenth century.

Like many remote locations, Hamilton has very little to interest socially minded college students. "Hamilton is dead," a student says. "There are two bars in town . . . but most everybody goes to the fraternity parties." The two nearest cities are Syracuse and Utica, both about forty-five minutes away, but these places are also limited in social attractions and most students tend to stay on campus during their free time, further increasing the social cachet of fraternities and athletic events. "From my perspective, the Greek system is at the center of social life," says one professor. "Of course, sports and sporting events, especially hockey and basketball, are very popular."

For a smallish sort of university, Colgate has a variety of athletic opportunities and facilities. "Athletes are revered on campus," a professor says. The university fields twenty-two NCAA Division I varsity teams, eleven for women and eleven for men. (The university recently dropped intercollegiate baseball.) About two-thirds of the student body participates in intramural sports, and there are also club sports like skiing, figure skating, martial arts, weight lifting, water polo, and paintball. The university has a gymnasium with a fitness center, pool, and sauna, as well as an ice rink, trapshooting range, bowling alley, and an excellent championship golf course. On nearby Lake Moraine, the university maintains a boathouse. There is also an "outdoor education program" that offers recreational activities like backpacking, white-water rafting, and training in wilderness medicine.

The prestige of athletics has become part of the Colgate ethos, a professor says. The typical student is "clever, intelligent, extremely well-rounded," the professor says. "If you're smart and play sports, Colgate is the place for you. The kids who graduate from Colgate go on to be C.E.O.s, not Ph.D.s."

All freshmen and sophomores must live in university housing. The options include twelve college houses, eight residence halls, and three apartment complexes. Most of the facilities are coed, with men and women sharing apartments next to each other. One dorm has only single-sex floors. The college houses each carry themes around which their residents unite; most are dedicated to a particular ethnic group or political persuasion. One house, named for Nobel Peace Prize winner Ralph Bunche, is open to students interested in "world peace." Rather than using the standard university meal plan, its residents have set up a vegetarian cooperative. Another house is called an "ecological living center," where students share household tasks and promote environmental awareness.

Upperclassmen who don't live in Greek houses, which are not open to freshmen, rent apartments in Hamilton. "Apartment parties are second only to fraternity parties," according to one student.

Despite its location, Colgate has attracted several big-name speakers lately. In 1997 Mikhail Gorbachev spoke to an audience of three thousand on the future of U.S.-Russian relations. Jesse Jackson and William F. Buckley Jr. have also visited, and Governor Christine Todd Whitman of New Jersey gave the commencement address in 1997.

Of the nearly eighty student groups on campus, two are conservative: the pro-life organization "Respect Life" and the College Republicans. The university viewbook lists just four religious organizations: Colgate Jewish Union, InterVarsity Christian Fellowship, Newman Community, and the university church. The university chapel features a stunning pipe organ and is used for orchestra and choir concerts as well as services.

There are quite a few academic organizations devoted to specific disciplines such as biology or psychology. The viewbook mentions instrumental and vocal groups, as well as theater and dance troupes. The university operates an FM radio station, and there are several publications run by students, including the *Maroon,* a satire magazine, a political review, and a literary journal.

Other student groups are more politically motivated. These include the Women's Coalition; Lesbian, Gay, and Bisexual Alliance; Advocates, a group of gay and straight supporters of the homosexual community; and several multicultural groups. Students for Choice is a pro-abortion advocacy group. Students for Environmental Action (SEA) encourages members and nonmembers to recycle or to use mugs rather than Styrofoam cups — things like that. "The most I have ever seen on campus are posters from the SEA or announcements for the meetings of liberal groups," a student says. "It's not like anyone is in your face on campus. There just isn't anything like that at Colgate."

UNIVERSITY OF COLORADO AT BOULDER

Office of Admissions
Campus Box 30
Boulder, CO 80309-0030
(303) 492-6301
www.colorado.edu

Total enrollment: 24,620
Undergraduates: 18,850
SAT Ranges (Verbal/Math): V 530-630, M 540-640
Financial aid: 34%
Applicants: 14,850
Accepted: 80%
Enrolled: 33%
Application deadline: Rolling admissions
Financial aid application deadline: Apr. 1
Tuition: $2,392 resident; $14,898 nonresident
Core curriculum: No

Taking (Birken) Stock

Granola, latte, Birkenstocks — these are just some of the items that compose the grunge culture of Boulder, Colorado. The twenty-five thousand students who attend the University of Colorado at Boulder are largely satisfied with the university's laid-back atmosphere and bucolic setting. Located on a stunning 600-acre campus at the foot of the Rocky Mountains, CU-Boulder has much to recommend itself to outdoor enthusiasts.

Unfortunately, the academic landscape of the university is not as inspiring as its natural surroundings. CU-Boulder has embraced most of the deleterious trends in higher education, from radical environmentalism to a pervasive "multicultural" agenda. All students must take a course in "cultural and gender diversity," and several other requirements are also politicized. There remain pockets of excellence at this large institution, though traditional students must navigate carefully through an undergraduate curriculum littered with lightweight and politically motivated courses.

Academic Life: Lugging a Boulder up a Hill

CU-Boulder consists of eight undergraduate colleges and schools: arts and sciences, business administration, education, engineering, environmental design, journalism and mass communication, music, and pharmacy. More than two-thirds of the 18,850 undergraduates enroll in the College of Arts and Sciences, which offers more than 60 areas of study.

Students in this college must attain intermediate-level proficiency in a foreign language, pass two writing courses, and complete a course in both "critical thinking" and "quantitative reasoning and mathematics." The college also has a set of distribution requirements that eschews the standard topical names for "content areas." These include "historical context," "cultural and gender diversity," "United States context," "literature and the arts," "natural sciences," "contemporary societies," and "ideals and values." Most areas can be met with one course; however, literature and arts requires two, and natural sciences, four.

The goal of the content areas, as stated in the catalogue, usually has something to do with "critical thinking" or "critical evaluation," often with the implicit or explicit objective of undermining or questioning previously held beliefs. For example, the "ideals and values" description states that "ideals and values have usually been determined by long-standing tradition and fixed social practices." Later, the catalogue says the course in this area "will also require consideration of approaches by which value systems are constructed, justified, and applied, especially in regard to the personal, societal, and in some cases cross-cultural contexts." In the "contemporary societies" requirement, students are supposed to develop "new vantage points from which to view their own socio-cultural assumptions and traditions."

However, the curriculum seems predisposed to treat non-Western values less harshly. The general description of the "cultural and gender diversity" area centers on expanding "the range of a student's understanding" and introducing him to "the commonality and diversity of cultural responses to universal human problems."

The saving grace of these requirements is that, occasionally, courses that fulfill them do not carry the ideological impetus ascribed to the requirement. One student, for instance, says a course in "ancient and modern democracy" (which met the "ideals and values" content area) "was my favorite class." However, some politicization is inescapable: the "cultural and gender diversity" requirement can be fulfilled only with a course in non-Western culture or gender studies. "The feminists are unhappy because students tend to choose the 'culture' rather than the 'gender,' " a professor says. And the more liberal faculty are not satisfied with a single diversity requirement. As one ethnic studies professor, commenting in the campus press, said, "The curriculum is very Euro-American. . . . Students should be taking these [diversity] classes throughout their entire academic trajectory, not just one course."

With more than 1,400 courses available, picking the distribution courses can be extremely difficult, especially for those who want more traditional course offerings in order to piece together something like a genuine liberal arts education. Such a selection would be difficult even in the "United States context" area; there are few broad survey courses but quite a few specialized, politicized options like "Introduction to Asian-American History" or "Chicano History." The "critical thinking" area can be met with something like "History of Women in Progressive Social Movements."

Many CU-Boulder students rely on student evaluations posted by the university on the Internet when choosing distribution courses. Unfortunately, this process seems to push the faculty toward easy grading and pedagogical theatrics in order to get solid reviews from students. The evaluations have a decidedly political agenda: in addition to rating how much they liked the course, students also assess the professor's coverage of women's and minority issues.

Students will do well to look for these professors: E. Christian Kopff in classics, David Gross and Patricia Limerick in history, Thomas Cech in chemistry, and emeritus professor Edward Rozek in political science. Sociology chairman Gary Marx was recently named a fellow of the Woodrow Wilson Center at the Smithsonian Institution to continue his research on the social implications of new information technologies.

Despite the politicization of many departments and faculties, several departments remain solid. The sciences are generally very good at CU-Boulder, and the chemistry faculty includes Thomas Cech, winner of the 1989 Nobel Prize in that discipline. The physics department is also considered strong by several students. Some humanities faculty, however, seem unhappy with the disproportionate emphasis on the sciences at the university. "The scientists support the school with federal grants, so basically, anything they want, they get," says one professor. Humanities receive much less outside support, and thus less from the university itself, according to professors.

Among these humanities departments, few are distinguished. "There are a lot of people very committed to mainstream teaching in English and American history," says one professor. Economics is about "average," according to another. However, the most popular departments, psychology and environmental studies, are not well recommended by traditional faculty. English is described as "weak and chaotic" by one professor, though this person adds that "if you're intelligent and resourceful you can make your way through — just ask around to find good professors." Political science is considered a "radical department" by several faculty.

Even a strong department like history, which offers many Western history courses and does well in its ancient Greek and Roman classes, has courses like "Lesbian and Gay History: Culture, Politics, and Social Change in the United States." In that course students investigate "lesbian/gay identity formation, community development, politics, and 'queer' cultural resistance." The economics department has quite a few courses in traditional subdisciplines like "Theory and History of Economic Thought," "Money, Banking and Public Finance," "International Trade and Finance," "Economic History and Economic Development," and "Quantitative Economics," but also covers emerging areas such as "Natural Resources and Environmental Economics." And with more than four dozen faculty members in the English department, specialties and course offerings span the theoretical and disciplinary spectrum. The department, according to one professor, has about "a dozen good professors," but has an equal number of faculty members with specialties in gay and lesbian studies, feminist and cultural studies, and gender studies.

In general, multiculturalism affects much of the Boulder campus, particularly the School of Education, which has a strong reputation in the state but is considered a "big joke" by at least one student. The school is home to the BUENO Center for Multicultural Education, which houses a special "Equity, Diversity, and Education Library" for elementary and secondary school teachers. The goal of the center, which receives significant funding from the U.S. Department of Education, is to promote "quality education with an emphasis on cultural pluralism." The university also has programs in Afro-American, American Indian, Asian-American, and Chicano studies, all connected to the university's Center for the Study of Ethnicity and Race.

Several programs can land students in smaller, less politicized classes. One is the President's Leadership Class, a two-year program of lectures and recitations for selected students. One student, who landed an internship at the state capital through the program, notes that it serves as a "good way to have a small community in a big place." There is also a small university-wide honors program, in which classes are limited to fifteen students. An honors program member says most of the distribution requirements can be fulfilled through the program. Students can also graduate with departmental honors, which usually requires a senior thesis. There are several in-state internship opportunities, and a fair number of students also opt for programs abroad, though one student says overseas internships (rather than simply studying abroad) have become more popular of late. "You feel like you're not being frivolous," she notes.

When asked to characterize the students, one professor says that "they have a very strong commitment to looking good and skiing." But there are opportunities for solid intellectual advancement at CU-Boulder for talented and motivated students. "The best students are well taken care of," a professor says. "If you're an average student, you're on your own." According to university figures, less than a third of students ranked in the top 10 percent of their high school classes, though 70 percent were in the top quarter.

Political Atmosphere: A Rolling Boulder Gathers No Moss

Persistent, general criticism from faculty and administrators, followed by a 5-4 vote by the university board of regents against asking for her resignation, forced CU-Boulder president Judith Albino to step down in 1995. She did not take all the university's problems with her, according to some faculty. One describes the administration of the new president, John Buechner, formerly chancellor of the Denver CU campus, as "a disaster." The Boulder campus was, as of May 1997, searching for a new chancellor.

A year before the vote on Albino, the board of regents rejected the university's recommendation of tenure for an associate professor of English who specialized in erotic literature. The professor, who taught creative writing and lacked a Ph.D., had authored two books on the use of obscenity in literature. "The people that put me in office would not think that his specialty is very essential to liberal arts education," one regent told the *Chronicle of Higher Education.* "We get enough out of that from *Playboy.*" Faculty denounced the decision as a severe breach of academic freedom, and the regents, described by one professor as "Republican but spineless," ultimately reversed their decision.

The state of Colorado has not adopted anti–affirmative action measures such as California's Proposition 209, but a similar bill has been introduced by the state's attorney general and a representative. The bill would end the state's consideration of race and gender in all hiring, educational, and contracting decisions. Although some CU-Boulder students have expressed support for the bill, many more rallied outside the state capitol to protest the measure, which they say will devastate the minority student population at CU-Boulder. The university has a poor retention rate among minority students, and some of these students say they already face an uphill battle because of finances, inadequate preparation, home life, and cultural pressures on campus.

Another demonstration marked the five hundredth anniversary of Columbus's discovery of America; that one, set up by a Native American student group, lasted a full day. In addition, the Black Student Organization has lobbied the university on curriculum matters, and claims that "one of the things we worked on recently was getting the university to diversify the history requirement of the school's core curriculum, which only included courses on European history," according to the *Multicultural Student's Guide to Colleges.*

The most politically active group on the predominantly liberal campus is the Young Democrats Club. There is also an active homosexual group, the Lesbian Bisexual Gay Transgendered Alliance. Yet most students are not involved in political issues, preferring instead their academic and extracurricular pursuits. "There's definitely an individualistic tendency here," says one student.

CU-Boulder has a full calendar of campus speakers — "about three or four speakers every night," according to one student. "There are always signs all over the place." Liberal speakers outnumber conservative ones by a wide margin; recent guests include Dave Foreman, founder of Earth First!; the princess of Burma; and Secretary of the Interior Bruce Babbitt, who spoke on the threat of global warming.

Student Life: Because It's There

Founded in 1876, the CU-Boulder campus boasts many architectural attractions, including the oldest building, Old Main, and many others built in the "Italian rural style." Freshmen are required to live on campus, and about half elect to stay there for their sophomore year. Most upperclassmen move to apartments, although finding one can be frustrating. "Boulder has an ordinance so it can't grow outward," says one student. There is also a four-story height restriction on city buildings. "This is a good thing, because they want to keep the open space around the city, but it makes apartments expensive and difficult to find," the student says. "Every year, the price goes up and the quality goes down."

Even without apartment rent, Boulder is a relatively expensive city. "But the quality of living is good," says a student. Numerous restaurants and shops are within easy reach of campus, including "The Hill," an area where students can get away for a cup of coffee. There is also the Pearl Street Mall, a pedestrian area of ten blocks. But, according to one undergraduate, "students don't really hang out there — it's more for the community."

Outdoor pursuits top the list of extracurricular activities among CU-Boulder students. Hiking, mountain biking, and skiing are extremely popular. "It's about a five-minute walk to the mountains," a student says, only slightly hyperbolically. "That's probably why a lot of people come here." (About one-third of the student body is from outside of Colorado, but that group represents all remaining states plus eighty foreign countries.) There are numerous outdoor-oriented student organizations, including cycling, flying, and soaring clubs. Not surprisingly, CU-Boulder is also home to many environmental and animal rights groups, including Sinapu, a grassroots organization dedicated to reintroducing the wolf to Colorado. According to the campus press, the organization receives twenty-nine cents per student, which it uses in part to fund wilderness internships that get students involved in conservation efforts. The group has met with resistance from local ranchers, who say wolf reintroduction will devastate their cattle populations.

Those students interested in indoor social pursuits will find informal clubs for each major, as well as Mortar Board, a senior honors group that has been active in community service projects such as a children's literary festival and visits to a senior citizens' home.

When it comes to organized athletics, football is by far the most popular sport. The Buffaloes ("Buffs," to fans) compete in the Big Twelve Conference at the NCAA Division I level. The football team has gone to a bowl game in nine of the last ten seasons, and as of 1996, thirty-three alumni were on National Football League rosters. Women's basketball and volleyball have also attracted attention recently, and the university typically competes for NCAA ski championships, battling other skiing campuses like Utah and Vermont.

Greek organizations flourish on campus, often to the dismay of the administration, which doesn't care for the heavy drinking and partying that go on at some fraternities. In 1995 the fraternities banned beer at social events, but allowed members to continue to drink in their rooms. "Colorado is the first campus to go that far in combating alcohol abuse," noted an article in the *Chronicle of Higher Education*. But, apparently, alcohol abuse continued largely unabated, and in the spring of 1997 hordes of partying students in the University Hill section of town (home to fraternities, sororities, and student apartments) got out of control. Police were dispatched after fights broke out and a bonfire was started in the middle of the street. According to the *Chronicle*, police were attacked by 400 students and had to use tear gas and rubber bullets to disperse a crowd of 1,500, many of whom were "throwing bricks, looting parking meters, and setting fires."

Some students said they were protesting a recent campaign by the university to crack down on alcohol abuse at parties, while others suggested that a large percentage of the crowd were not members of fraternities or sororities, and were not even CU-Boulder students. Both the administration and the Interfraternity and Panhellenic Councils hope a new alcohol ban will help curb student drinking and preclude similar riots in the future. In an effort to reverse the university's reputation as a party school, the administration also announced it would suspend students who provide alcohol to minors. This decision outraged many students; as one undergraduate told the campus paper, "I think they've extended their bounds. . . . It's like Big Brother — they're out of their jurisdiction." Considerable cooperation between Boulder police and the university administration has resulted in scores of citations against fraternity members, although one police sergeant noted, "Drinking is not just a Greek issue; it's a student issue."

Because it is such a large and diverse campus, many of the organized campus activities revolve around multicultural celebrations (Chicano History Week or Red Nations Cultural Unity Awareness Week, for example). The university also recently began an annual "disability cultural forum" that brings together poets, writers, activists, and artists to "celebrate and raise awareness of disability culture," thus adding another element to the growing body of victimization studies.

Boulder approaches Seattle as a hotbed of grunge music, having sprouted local bands like The Samples and Big Head Todd and the Monsters. The campus has hosted the Gin Blossoms, Blind Melon, and Bush. Those with more refined musical sensibilities will not be disappointed in the university's performance opportunities, which include the Collegium Musicum (an early music group) and an English handbell choir. There are also four facilities for theater and dance productions, although the best time of year for such recitals is the summer, when the city hosts the Colorado Shakespeare Festival and Lyric Theatre Festival.

COLUMBIA UNIVERSITY

Office of Undergraduate Admissions
212 Hamilton Hall
New York, NY 10027
(212) 854-2521
www.columbia.edu

Total enrollment: 18,000
Undergraduates: 3,570
SAT Ranges (Verbal/Math): V 640-750, M 630-730
Financial aid: 56%
Applicants: 8,710
Accepted: 21%
Enrolled: 43%
Application deadline: Jan. 1
Financial aid application deadline: Feb. 1
Tuition: $22,072
Core curriculum: Yes

Roll, Columbia

Columbia's dedication to its Core curriculum sets it apart from its Ivy League peers, most of which can't seem to decide what every student should know. With its venerable Core, Columbia announces that some things must be known by those who attend college. Fellow Ivy Leaguer Brown University, for example, doesn't even impose distribution requirements on its students, let alone construct a standard set of classes on Western culture. There is a considerable difference between a university that says "learn this" and one that says "learn whatever floats your boat."

Not that Columbia is immune from multiculturalism or political correctness — its location in New York City guarantees exposure to many winds from many directions. Some politicized classes have indeed entered the curriculum. Columbia's students tend to define themselves along racial lines; gay and feminist groups dominate much of the political discourse on campus. But overall, commitment to the liberal arts tradition has survived better at Columbia than at most places, and much of this is due to the abiding Core.

Administrators constantly talk of "revising" and "updating" the Core, and a few years ago they did add a foreign cultures requirement. But the Core curriculum remains roughly as it was first conceived in 1919. At a time when many schools are desperately searching for ways to make education "relevant," Columbia can rest assured that its Core provides its students with knowledge that is both timely and *timeless*.

Academic Life: Bending but Not Breaking

The largest undergraduate unit of Columbia University is Columbia College, which enrolls approximately 3,500 students. The heart of Columbia College's curriculum — which all 3,500 students must take — is the Core.

The one constant trait of the Core is that it is always under revision — the course list has been altered several times in the last few decades. However, the current list does much to introduce students to important aspects of Western civilization. The university describes the Core as its "signature, its intellectual coat of arms." According to the catalogue, the courses in the Core "attempt to explore what it means to be human and to provide all Columbia students, regardless of their major or concentration, with a lively inheritance of Western literature, philosophy, history, music and art."

Core courses are taught in seminars limited to about two dozen students. Each course has a standard reading list, although instructors are allowed a little leeway to inject materials that fit their academic interests. Students are supposed to complete the Core by the end of their sophomore year.

"As a result, these courses are, in the best sense, the most practical that Columbia students take: the skills and habits honed by the Core — observation, analysis, argument, imaginative comparison, respect for ideas and nuances — are nothing less than a rigorous preparation for life as an intelligent citizen in today's world," the catalogue states.

"Contemporary Civilization" first appeared in Columbia's curriculum in 1919 as a course on war-and-peace issues. It has been revised extensively since then, and today this yearlong course focuses on the relation of individuals to the state and society, the problems of morality, and "the constructions of concepts like the economy, race, and gender." Students read Plato, Aristotle, Augustine, Machiavelli, Hobbes, Locke, Rousseau, Kant, Smith, Marx, Darwin, Nietzsche, and Freud.

Three Core courses are dedicated to the humanities. "Literature Humanities," also a yearlong course, was originally designed in 1937. Intensive readings range from Homer, Sophocles, and Euripides to the Bible, Dante, Goethe, and Shakespeare. "Music Humanities" and "Art Humanities," both semester courses, introduce students to the major works and movements in Western art and music. Both make use of the vast resources of New York City's museums and concert halls.

"Logic and Rhetoric" is designed to complement the four Core courses. The only text, according to the catalogue, is the students' own writing. Each section has no more than twelve students, instantly making this course preferable to the cattle call style of freshman comp classes offered at many other schools.

The Core is popular among students, mainly because they knew what they were getting into before they enrolled in Columbia. "These were all books I wanted to read," says one English major. "Very few institutions offer a type of program like this, and there aren't a lot of people walking around saying, 'This is ethnocentric. Why are we learning the canon?'"

Professors also seem to like the Core because they know that all of their students possess a certain body of knowledge. Any lecturer can allude to Dante's *Inferno*, for example, when talking about another subject and be confident that students are familiar with the work. Despite the ongoing revisions to the Core, one professor says it remains in roughly the same form it was forty years ago, though the Middle Ages get less time now and there is more emphasis on feminist topics than in the past. Some younger faculty, the professor says, resent the Core for the long, intensive hours of work it necessitates — but not for ideological reasons.

There is some movement on campus to make the Core reading lists more "inclusive" of non-European authors. An assistant professor of Spanish and Portuguese recently told a gathering of Columbia's new Latino studies program that the "Literature Humanities" list should be "flexible and elastic, constantly being revised as the nation changes." Traditionalists at Columbia and elsewhere, however, contend that making a canon "elastic" and "flexible" erodes the meaning of core courses, which are designed to provide students with timeless and lasting insight through the study of the human condition.

In addition to the Core, all students must fulfill several distribution requirements. There is a three-course science requirement, to be met with a two-term sequence plus another semester class in a different field. This requirement ensures at least some familiarity with a particular area in science or mathematics.

Additionally, students must demonstrate competency in a foreign language through the fourth-semester level, either via classes or achievement tests. The university offers courses in thirty-three languages.

Beginning with the class of 1998, Columbia instituted what it calls a "major cultures requirement." Students must complete two courses that expose them to different cultures and civilizations throughout the world. They have wide latitude in selecting which courses they will take to fulfill this requirement, added because some professors and students thought the Western emphasis of the Core was too limited. Such a requirement is not nearly as intrusive at Columbia as at other places since the university does not consider it a substitute for the thorough study of Western culture.

The final general education requirement at Columbia is nonacademic: students must take one year of general physical education courses and be able to swim seventy-five yards without resting.

Columbia has two other undergraduate entities — the School of Engineering and Applied Science, and Barnard College. Engineering students are required to take "elements of" Columbia's Core along with their own set of scientific courses, according to university literature. However, Barnard, which enrolls 2,200 women, has its own courses, admissions policies, dorms, and diplomas. Barnard women can take some courses at Columbia College, but cross-registration is neither common nor required. All students at the university are allowed to register (provided they are sufficiently prepared) for some courses in other schools, including the renowned Juilliard School of Music and other graduate programs.

Also in conjunction with its graduate and professional schools, Columbia offers accelerated paths to advanced degrees. For example, with approval students can earn a bachelor of arts degree and a law degree in six years. Similar programs exist in engineering, public policy, and international affairs.

Columbia offers qualified students the possibility of spending their junior years studying at Oxford or Cambridge. The university also operates study-abroad programs in Paris, Berlin, and Kyoto, Japan. These latter programs are taught in foreign languages, and most have a language requirement for admission.

Some of the best professors on Columbia's excellent faculty include Carol Gluck and Alan Brinkley in history; David Rosand in art history; Elaine Combs-Schilling in anthropology; George Stade, James Shapiro, and Edward Tayler in English; David Sidorsky in philosophy; Vijay Modi in mechanical engineering; Samuel Danishefsky in chemistry; and William Vickrey in economics. Another well-known professor is alumnus George Stephanopoulos, President Bill Clinton's former senior adviser, who teaches seminars on American politics in Columbia's political science department.

Among the best departments at Columbia is physics. Four graduates of this department have won Nobel Prizes in the field, and, in all, twenty-six Nobel winners have been associated with this department as students or faculty. Current professor (and Columbia alumnus) Melvin Schwartz won the Nobel Prize in 1988 and teaches some courses for undergraduates. Scientific advances made at Columbia include the invention of Formica, the smashing of the atom, FM radio, and the element deuterium, according to university literature.

Columbia's department of English and comparative literature, whose graduates include Langston Hughes, John Berryman, Allen Ginsburg, and Jack Kerouac, is very popular and well known among students for the strength of its professoriate. Because the Core familiarizes students with the great works of literature even before they get to English electives, class discussions can be conducted on a high level.

Also excellent is the history department, home to American historians Alan Brinkley and Eric Foner, as well as other strong teachers. Foner is a Marxist who specializes in labor history, but he's one of the most well-known professors in that discipline. "Aside from a few [politicized] comments in the beginning of class, he's a good professor," says one of Foner's former students.

Other departments start and end with politics. Columbia began a Latino studies department in the spring of 1996 and continues to expand it. Although departmental policies and ideology are still emerging, comments from its director printed in the *Columbia Daily News* indicate that the department's purpose is more political than academic.

Another ethnic-based department, the Institute for Research in African-American Studies, offers a major in African-American studies and other programs that bring speakers to campus. In September 1997, for instance, the institute brought in Wesleyan professor Maureen Mahon, whose talk was entitled "Jimi Hendrix Experiences: The Cultural Politics of Black Rock." Hendrix, the professor told students, "was young, black, clearly freaky, and brilliant." According to the *Columbia Daily Spectator,* she said Hendrix was "an icon of cultural freedom while not departing from the stereotype as flamboyant, obviously on drugs, and exhibitionistic." One sophomore who attended the talk was impressed. "He was treated as neither a white person or a black person because neither group really accepted him," the student told the *Spectator.* "It was interesting to hear about the dialectical nature of Hendrix."

The institute's director, Manning Marable, a self-proclaimed "democratic socialist," led a group of faculty members to Cuba in June 1997 to "examine race and gender issues" in the communist country. In a university press release, Marable spoke of Cuba in glowing terms. "Cuba has represented metaphorically the ability of an oppressed people to challenge imperialism and colonialism," Marable said. "In the political imagination of black America, Cuba represents the radical possibility of fundamental social change."

The women's and gender studies department at Columbia is also quite politicized, and its interests run to the subdiscipline of gay and lesbian studies. For example, the course "Introduction to Gay and Lesbian Studies" promises to discuss "race, class, gender, religion, and national difference . . . as part of the elaboration of homosexual/lesbian/queer identities." A course called "The Invisible Woman in Literature: The Lesbian Literary Tradition" bills itself as "an interdisciplinary exploration of the lesbian experience." "Women and Science," the course catalogue says, includes "feminist critiques of biological research and the institution of science."

Political Atmosphere: Labor Strife

The president of Columbia is George Rupp, a Presbyterian minister who holds degrees from Princeton, Yale, and Harvard and was once the dean of Harvard's divinity school. At Harvard, Rupp is credited with spearheading a drive to revise the school's curriculum to "address more directly the pluralistic character of contemporary religious life" and with implementing a women's studies program, according to a Columbia press release. Rupp became president of Columbia in 1993 and raised eyebrows soon after his arrival by replacing some of the university's top deans. Some complained that the steps were taken without proper consultation beforehand with faculty, students, and other administrators; others praised Rupp as a visionary.

More recently Rupp and his administration have faced strikes by Columbia's clerical workers and support staff. A strike in 1996 disrupted life at Barnard College for five months. Another walkout in October 1997 affected service in Columbia's dining halls, health services, and mail rooms. At issue was Columbia's elimination of many positions and the university's proposed "pay for performance" plan that would have allowed supervisors to reward outstanding employees with monetary bonuses. The union's opposition to the bonus plan was described by one striking employee, who told the *Spectator:* "I'm out here striking because I don't want to see Columbia University return to a racist, sexist, merit-pay system."

Many students and professors backed the union. Professor Foner, the specialist in labor history, and a group of faculty members began rescheduling and relocating classes to "avoid crossing the picket line," as the *Columbia Daily News* reported. Nearly three hundred classes were moved off campus to coffee shops, bars, and other locations in the city.

The strike ended after two weeks with the university raising the workers' pay by 3 percent and tabling the controversial merit-pay proposal. The money that had been set aside for bonuses is being used on worker training instead.

Certainly among those supporting the walkout was the International Socialist Organization (ISO), which has a small but aggressive chapter at Columbia. During the same month as the 1997 strike, the ISO disrupted a College Republicans barbecue celebrating Columbus Day. "The ISO came and made a circle around us. They had handbills on all the bad stuff Columbus did," one of the College Republicans said in the *Spectator.*

"What we heard from the barbecue was that it was celebrating white European roots; it was racist," an ISO organizer told the *Spectator.* "It was good for students to confront them." Campus police arrived shortly after the protest began and said they could not locate a permit for either the barbecue or the protest, although a College Republicans officer said one had been obtained two weeks earlier. Nonetheless, the police ordered both groups to go home.

Besides labor problems, Columbia has experienced some racial strife lately as well. In 1995 the president of the Black Students' Organization (BSO) set off a controversy by writing a column in the school newspaper celebrating the Million Man March and claiming that Jews' "oppression of blacks cannot go unnoticed while they disguise their evilness under the skirts and costumes of the rabbi," as quoted in the *Chronicle of Higher Education.* The column continued: "Lift up the yarmulke and what you will find is the blood of billions of Africans weighing on their heads."

One vocal campus group is the Gay, Lesbian and Bisexual Coalition (GLBC), which occasionally rallies for gay rights, often in conjunction with other homosexual advocacy groups in New York. Some members of this group formed a new gay "religious" group in the spring of 1997, calling itself "Campus Queers for Christ," which hopes to "show the campus that there are campus Queers who accept who they are, and are proud to be both gay and Christian."

Student Life: It's a Hell of a Town

What is today known as Columbia University began in 1754 as King's College, making it the first college in New York and the fifth oldest in the nation. King's College was renamed Columbia College in 1784, and that became Columbia University in 1896. The university moved in and out of several New York City locations before settling in at its current home along Broadway in the Morningside Heights neighborhood of Manhattan's Upper West Side.

Students say that if you don't like New York, you probably won't like Columbia either. A relatively large number of students transfer out of Columbia because they want out of New York City, but a large number of students transfer because they want to live in New York.

The social aspects of life at Columbia usually yield to the bright lights and big city. Students say New York mostly overrides university social events, and that life at Columbia isn't as clubbish as it is at more secluded, smaller colleges. While some students join the Greek system (twelve fraternities, six sororities, and four coed fraternities) or take advantage of on-campus movies and speakers, many others go to nearby bars and restaurants — or plays or concerts or sporting events or just about any attraction the city can provide. Students are constantly reminded that they're in a big city. "New York is a huge part of everyone's life," a student says. "Even if you try to avoid it, you're still kind of dealing with it."

Columbia has established agreements with several New York arts organizations that allow students free admission with presentation of their student IDs. Some of these organizations, including the Metropolitan Museum of Art, the Museum of Modern Art, and the Lincoln Center for the Performing Arts, also reserve internship slots for Columbia students.

Nearly all students — 90 percent — live on campus because of the high costs of renting in Manhattan. Columbia has standard dormitory accommodations, but also has "theme houses" dedicated to a particular topic or culture. Some of these include the Pan-Africa House, the Japan House, and the Art House. Dining facilities on campus are limited, students report, and most leave the university's dining plan after the first year in order to eat off campus. There is currently a space crunch on campus, and leaders of student groups say it is often difficult to find places to meet. Some of the problems should be solved in the fall of 1999, when the university is expected to open Alfred Lerner Hall, a $68 million student center now under construction.

Columbia has many different student groups, and there's something for everybody, students say. One of the largest groups on campus is the BSO, although several other ethnicity-based groups are present as well. While some say these types of groups encourage separatism among people of different backgrounds at the college, the groups' members say they are necessary to keep their cultures alive. In addition to the BSO, student groups focus on the cultures of China, Korea, the Philippines, Italy, Thailand, Vietnam, Haiti, Greece, Iran, Armenia, Hispanic countries, and Pakistan.

The most vocally politicized groups are the BSO, ISO, and GLBC discussed above. Smaller, quirkier groups are also active at Columbia. A student chapter of the National Organization for the Reform of Marijuana Laws recently asked Columbia's dorm advisers to "rethink their role" in the enforcement of Columbia's antidrug policies because the university's policies are "ineffectual and counter-productive." Columbia enforces drug laws instead of referring drug abusers to counseling, the group complained. The letter has had no apparent effect.

Another group called Conversio Virium ("exchange of power") is a university-approved organization that dedicates itself to "discussion, education, and peer support concerning BDSM [bondage, domination, sadomasochism] issues." Literature from the group assures interested parties that it "does not promote, support, or engage in violence of any sort. What it attempts to promote and support is safe, sane, and consensual BDSM play." The group says it recognizes that "these activities can become quite intense and observers may misunderstand," but that "they are actually healthy forms of sexual expression as long as they are done in a safe and mutually consensual manner." Regarding speakers the group brings to campus: "We have some very interesting and famous kinky people coming to lecture and read."

Columbia has some traditional student organizations as well. There are campus groups for people of all kinds of faith, including Baptists, Catholics, Episcopalians, Lutherans, Muslims, Methodists, Presbyterians, and members of other denominations. There are also chapters of nondenominational religious groups, such as Campus Crusade for Christ and InterVarsity Christian Fellowship. Columbia students publish a monthly nondenominational Christian newspaper, the *Columbia Standard*. The university also employs a university chaplain who coordinates events to unify the Columbia community, such as dinners with leaders of different ethnic groups on campus.

Columbia is home to twenty-two libraries, which combined hold more than

6 million volumes, nearly 4 million microforms, and more than 26 million manuscripts — the ninth-largest academic library in the country. Most students use Butler Library, the research library for humanities and history topics.

Many students take advantage of the many internship opportunities available to them in New York, and this can often help them land jobs after graduation. Economics is one of the most popular majors at the university, and the members of the 1997 graduating class took more jobs with financial institutions than with any other industry, according to Columbia's Center for Career Services.

CORNELL UNIVERSITY

Undergraduate Admissions Office
410 Thurston Avenue
Ithaca, NY 14850-2488
(607) 225-5241
www.cornell.edu

Total enrollment: 19,480
Undergraduates: 13,510
SAT Ranges (Verbal/Math): V 600-700, M 640-730
Financial aid: 68%
Applicants: 21,000
Accepted: 33%
Enrolled: 47%
Application deadline: Jan. 1
Financial aid application deadline: Feb. 15
Tuition: Privately endowed colleges, $22,874; state-assisted colleges, $9,814 resident; $18,854 nonresident
Core curriculum: No

Running the Asylum

Cornell University was founded in 1865 by Ezra Cornell (an inventor who had become rich by investing in a little company called Western Union) and his friend in the New York state legislature, Andrew Dickson White. Cornell was an earthy man-of-the-people type, while White was well traveled and elegant, educated at Yale and Oxford. Their idea was to start a school on Cornell's farm in Ithaca for all sorts of studies, and with Cornell's donation of a half-million dollars and the state support the men managed to procure, Cornell became the first school in the nation to be privately endowed and publicly supported. Even today, some of its colleges are considered public, while others are private.

Cornell grew to become a member of the elite Ivy League, and though it has never had the standing of a Harvard, a degree from Cornell is still a fine card to hold when looking for a job or a graduate school. Students who know what to watch for still get a good education, and the intellectual community at the small town in central New York State is quirky enough to be stimulating. And for in-state residents, some colleges of the university cost less than $9,000 tuition a year — a phenomenal bargain.

However, some of Cornell's approximately thirteen thousand undergraduates and an equivalent number of its graduate students have in the past sought not so much education as political satisfaction. In fact, the administration has several times had its hat handed to it by students with a strange propensity toward violent or nonviolent takeovers of campus buildings. The administration has caved in to virtually every multicultural demand, creating a fragmented campus, what amounts to segregated housing, and a badly politicized curriculum. The university even celebrates its students' activism, and is seemingly proud of its large size and "diversity" offerings, as shown in this passage from "The Big Red Book," the university's recruiting tool:

> Some courses are especially popular across the university. "Introduction to American Indians," a rural sociology course in the College of Agriculture and Life Sciences, and "Human Sexuality," a human ecology course that examines the subject's cultural and biological aspects, draw students from every college. So [does] "Psychology 101" in the arts and sciences college — so popular it's taught in a 2,000-seat concert hall.

While Cornell's reputation is worth quite a bit, a serious student must decide whether he or she can wrest an education from an institution that all too often seems to be run by the inmates.

Academic Life: Like Giving Candy to a Baby

Cornell is widely known for its fine programs in engineering and the natural sciences, but the liberal arts branch of the university, the College of Arts and Sciences, is not as distinguished. It seems as if the college is still smarting from the events of April 1969, when armed black militants took over Willard Straight Hall for three days and demanded the creation of a department of Africana studies as well as a special dormitory for black students. Both survive to this day. Since then, other groups have staged both literal and figurative takeovers, and today the College of Arts and Sciences, as well as many of the support services of the university in general, seems a hodgepodge of special-interest activities and fiefdoms.

The distribution requirements for the College of Arts and Sciences are no exception, and are similar to that found in most major colleges and universities today in that, as one professor says, they are "meaningless and arbitrary." The college, like other schools on campus, sets its own general education requirements, and though not great, they are more related to the traditional liberal arts than those at, say, the college of engineering or architecture. The general requirements at the 4,000-student college were recently revised (the first class affected was that of 1996) to include a total of nine courses from five groups: physical and biological sciences, "other science courses," quantitative and formal reasoning, social sciences and history, and humanities and the arts. Four classes must be selected from the first two groups, with at least one coming from "other sciences." If students take but one science course during their career, they are permitted to apply up to two credits of "advanced placement" high school classes toward this requirement. The other five courses come from the remaining three groups — groups that include possibilities in women's studies, Africana studies, and Asian studies.

In fact, at least one of the required courses must focus on, according to the university catalogue, "an area or people other than those of the United States, Canada, or Europe." Native American cultural classes, of course, will fulfill this requirement. Also required is one course in a historical period prior to the twentieth century. While this requirement could possibly be used to study a classical Western author like Shakespeare, Plato, or Dostoyevsky, or artists like Michelangelo or Raphael, the "diversity" requirement seems little more than a tool (though a tool as common as a hammer on campuses today) by which to ensure that the politically correct amongst the faculty will have enough students to fill their courses. There is empirical data to support that opinion: a study by the dean of faculty's office found that in 1993, 111 Cornell courses drew five or fewer students, and most of them were in women's studies, non-Western languages, and other "identity"-based areas of the curriculum. At Cornell, the diversity requirement (called a "breadth" requirement by the university) can be fulfilled with Anthropology 200, "Cultural Diversity and Contemporary Issues"; Anthropology 290, "Filming Other Cultures"; Anthropology/Women's Studies 305, "Emotion, Gender, and Culture"; "Gender and Society in the Muslim Middle East"; "Mystery Cults, Mythologies, and Religions of Iran"; or "Sex and Gender in Cross-Cultural Perspective," as well as more traditional courses.

Other general education requirements may be fulfilled with less-than-traditional classes. There is a long list of courses that will count in each category, including "Modern American Sex Roles in Historical Perspective" and "African-American Women in Slavery and Freedom." Some solid courses can be chosen, but the university makes no effort to direct students their way.

Among the outstanding professors students should try to find are Jeremy Rabkin, Thomas Christenson, and Elizabeth Sanders in government; Gail Fine in philosophy; John Najemy in history; and Patricia Carden in Russian literature.

In the College of Arts and Sciences, the departments of physics, chemistry, and biological sciences are considered excellent. Nobel Prize winner Roald Hoffman teaches in the chemistry department, but laureate Hans Bethe recently retired from the physics department and astronomer Carl Sagan has passed away. The College of Agricultural and Life Sciences, one of Cornell's three public colleges, is considered excellent for preprofessional students looking at medical school, vet school, or graduate research in the natural and applied sciences. It also houses many who wish to study engineering but are attracted by the lower tuition of the agricultural school. (The College of Engineering is private and thus has a much higher tuition.) This marriage of private and public education is one thing that makes Cornell unique: regardless of which college a student enrolls in, he is permitted to take courses in most units of the university. Thus a student may design his own program of study in engineering, the sciences, or the social sciences by enrolling in the public colleges and earning a degree in agricultural engineering, horticulture, rural sociology, industrial and labor relations, or a host of other fields while still taking many courses through the private colleges. While this mixture of private and public education presents tremendous flexibility for Cornell's students, there is an ever-present, if subtle, resentment among the students in the private colleges of engineering, arts and sciences, and architecture over sharing their classrooms with students paying the considerably cheaper public college rates.

An unusual feature of Cornell's academic program is the School of Hotel Administration, the largest and oldest program of its type in this country. Seniors from outside the program tend to take advantage of the "Wine and Beverages" course offered by the school, but the hotel administration program has a fine reputation internationally. One professor in the College of Arts and Sciences tells of traveling to Colombia for a professional meeting, where the hotel staff immediately recognized the name Cornell because the manager of the Bogota Hilton is a graduate of the hotel school. For practice, students manage the 150-room Statler Hotel and the adjoining J. Willard Marriott Center. The latter houses most of the classroom space and training facilities, while the former is a working hotel for parents, prospective students, visiting faculty or lecturers, and businessmen.

While the hotel school welcomes guests to campus, much of the rest of the campus has invited multiculturalism to take up residence, and the politicization of the traditional departments is well under way. The economics department in particular gets low marks from undergraduates and faculty, and anthropology, as at many campuses, is described as "very ideologically charged." The history department has been flooded in recent years with several younger faculty (some described as "left-wing revisionist historians"), but a recent graduate says, "History is stronger than English because they still require a lot of writing in the history department." Among the departments in the College of Arts and Sciences, none has steered clear of modern trends. "Cornell used to be strong in history and literature," a professor says. "Today, there is a scattering of good teachers throughout the arts college, but none concentrated in any one department." The good teachers must not be teaching the majority of courses, as a scan of the English, anthropology, and history departments' catalogue listings shows a bevy of courses emphasizing race, gender, ethnicity, and Third World cultures and literatures.

At the same time, Cornell's place in the lower academic half of the Ivy League does give it certain advantages. Most of the faculty are "not academic superstars," according to one professor (i.e., they are not always well known among colleagues for their research); thus, he adds: "they generally like teaching." The downside, according to the same professor, is that the lack of structure in most colleges and departments allows these faculty to "teach whatever they want," resulting in a disorganized curriculum full of marginal courses. Furthermore, when it comes to granting tenure, most departments and colleges at Cornell place little stock in teaching ability. It is publications, according to a full professor, that are given the highest consideration. Thus, even though the nature of Cornell's faculty selection process produces quality teaching, the tenure process is not designed to reward that type of excellence.

Political Atmosphere: A Little Take and Give

Cornell, like many of its peer institutions, has succumbed to the demands for more departments and programs geared toward the politically correct special interests. The lessons of April 1969 have certainly not been lost on members of other self-styled aggrieved groups. Hispanic students took over the administration building for four days in 1993 and were rewarded with both a special dormitory and a program in Latin American studies. In fact, the only missing special interest, it seems, is a department of gay and lesbian studies; however, at Cornell it is probably not needed, since the women's studies and English departments offer plenty of courses that revolve around homosexuality and sexual identity. Meanwhile, the Division of Rare and Manuscript Collections of the University Library has been working on compiling a human sexuality collection, which would bring together one hundred "historically important" erotic and pornographic films and videos so that professors and researchers could study film erotica. The collection will include such cinematic tours de force as *Caligula* and *Deep Throat,* and curators even took suggestions from a decidedly nonacademic source, "the people who own Good Vibrations, a vibrator store in San Francisco."

Not only has Cornell not repudiated the violence of April 1969 (during which one hundred armed policemen stood ready to move on the student union building, but the administration agreed not to punish the terrorists, and the faculty was forced to renounce its reprimand of the takeover leaders in order to disburse a 6,000-student demonstration), but it has actually celebrated the twenty-fifth anniversary of the takeover. On April 19, 1994, Cornell closed down Willard Straight Hall (unthreatened this time) and hung a sign outside the building: "On April 19, 1969, the Black community of Cornell University . . . seized control of Willard Straight Hall. On this day, the anniversary of that event, Willard Straight Hall is closed in commemoration of those students' courageous struggle and sacrifice." Sacrifice? Not only were the so-called crusaders not indicted (or even reprimanded), the leader of the group, who, during the takeover, said, "The time has come when the pigs are going to die too," was elected twenty-four years later to Cornell's board of trustees. Now a respected pension fund manager, he has said he wishes the incident had not occurred — and was promptly vilified by radicals now at Cornell for betraying the cause. Perhaps it was one of those radicals who telephoned a death threat to a student who tried to organize a rally protesting the university's celebration of the takeover's anniversary — another indicator that intimidation and the use of force to establish a point of view are widely accepted at Cornell.

If the arm-twisting in the curriculum doesn't give students their fill of race, class, and gender ideology, then the university is willing to supply more of the same in matters of student governance and housing. The dormitories procured by the African-American and Hispanic takeovers are just two of the university's program or theme house dorms. Native Americans have a small house, as do more traditionally academic groups interested in promoting a particular major or minor. One year prior to the Hispanic takeover of Day Hall, then-president Frank Rhodes had turned down a request for a gay and lesbian house, citing concerns over "fragmenting" the campus, and no such house exists yet — the campus gay community hasn't yet mounted an assault on a campus building. Lest you think we're being overly facetious, a student leader of the Hispanic dorm in 1994 told the *New York Times* that the reason gay students hadn't received a dorm of their own was that "they haven't presented enough of a threat to the university." In 1992 the university announced plans to assign students randomly to dorms, but that plan died because — you guessed it — students protested and voted overwhelmingly against the plan.

Cornell's policy of segregated housing has come under fire from civil rights groups, including the New York chapter of the ACLU. Cornell "must not and will not be allowed to either institute or to perpetuate a system of Jim Crow facilities on the premise that students themselves say they prefer segregation," wrote the executive director of the state's ACLU. However, the New York State Education Department ruled in 1995 that, since the houses were open to any interested student and since the university did not explicitly ask for a student's race before making a room assignment (though the information was usually apparent in the required personal essay and interview), there was no discrimination. A director of the New York Civil Rights Coalition, which filed the complaint that led to the finding, characterized the Cornell housing situation as "de facto" segregation, which is equal to the legal standard in dozens of forced busing cases at the primary and secondary education levels. And the statistics bear him out: two-thirds of Cornell's black students, at the time of the ruling, lived on the North Campus, while the West Campus has always been over-whelmingly white. Ujamaa, the black student dorm, housed only one white student that year.

Despite the university caving in to certain radical groups, both retired president Rhodes and the current president, Hunter Rawlings, have expressed misgivings about continuing the program houses, which tend to splinter students along racial lines rather than uniting them. One proposal would discontinue the practice of allowing freshmen to live in program or theme houses; that is, freshmen would be randomly assigned to housing units and then could choose to live in Ujamaa, the Latino Living Center, or Akwe:kon (the Native American dorm) in subsequent years. However, such a proposal would also affect freshmen living in fraternity and sorority houses; thus, a strange alliance of the Greek system and Ujamaa radicals has kept Rawlings from implementing this plan.

Observers say Ujamaa is really the major issue at stake. It is by far the largest program house on campus, and also has the largest percentage of freshmen in residence; thus the Rawlings proposal would cripple Ujamaa far more than the other ethnic or academic living centers by taking away its access to student housing funds. Ujamaa and the related black student groups have certainly been able to muster a protest when there are political points to be scored. In the spring of 1997 the *Cornell Review,* a conservative, student-published biweekly newspaper, published an incendiary parody (but no more politicized than some classes at Cornell) of an Africana studies department course written in ebonics, a black vernacular the Oakland School Board recently considered recognizing as a second language. More than two hundred protesters blocked the Quad to traffic for an entire afternoon, burned more than a hundred copies of the offending issue, and issued a series of demands: that the university rescind funding for the *Review* (the paper, along with just about every other student organization, including those manning the protest, receives some student government program funding); that new "racism sensitivity courses" be implemented for freshmen; that a speech code be implemented; and that Africana studies and related programs receive more funding. Dean of Students John Ford responded by praising the protesters and saying that the *Review* "performs a rather negative role on the campus." According to a student observer, Ford, watching the demonstration, snapped at one conservative student: "Are you happy with what you have done?" President Rawlings praised the student protesters as well and blamed the *Review* for inciting racial tensions — which, clearly, it had. (However, the fact that university policy doesn't force students of different races to live together, and thus perhaps understand each other better, doesn't promote racial harmony either.) Although the students who blocked traffic were in clear violation of the Student Code of Conduct, the university refused to take disciplinary action against them, and even refused an offer from the Ithaca Police Department to help control the demonstration, choosing instead to let the radicals do as they wished.

Although the administration has seemed somewhat vocal in its criticism of conservative student groups in recent years, student activists report that the administration does not administer the Code of Conduct unevenly; rather, they rarely enforce it at all. (The most notable exception was the case of a sophomoric act by a group of computer hackers who sent out a message from university computers to much of the Internet called "75 Reasons Why Women Are B*****s." The students pled guilty to abusing the campus computer system and performed many hours of community service.) One student leader says most administrators are simply "spineless." A faculty member agrees: "There is a small cadre of professional minority students, and the administration tends to cave in when they yell." But Cornell "is rather large, so one can be left alone. There is a certain freedom for conservative students."

However, campus observers report that this freedom may be slowly diminishing. The student Senate has passed a draft of a speech code, and debates about the politicization of orientation sessions seem to rage perpetually. A new yearlong orientation session for freshmen proposes to assign selected incoming students to racial, ethnic, and gender-based groupings. Orientations for peer counselors and resident assistants are already dominated by special interests, the merits of which are not up for debate. One resident assistant who complained about explicit pornographic videos shown at a housing staff orientation was told that he had to recover from latent homophobia.

It is somewhat encouraging that some university trustees have begun to voice concerns over the politicization on campus. One case that has generated considerable concern among the trustees is that of James Maas, a popular psychology professor. By all accounts, Maas was extremely friendly with many of his students; in fact, he frequently gave gifts and invited students to his home to visit him, his wife, and his children. But after four of Maas's female students took courses with a notorious feminist professor of human ecology at Cornell (human ecology?), they decided that Maas's gift giving and frequent hugs (even in the presence of his wife) constituted sexual harassment. A faculty panel found Maas guilty. He is suing because neither he nor his attorney was permitted to be present during the hearing. The suit is still pending, but the College of Arts and Sciences faculty has already weighed in, approving a new policy that gives professors greater rights to attorney representation and due process.

Student Life: Sailing to Ithaca

Those who decide that the still-considerable power of a Cornell degree on the job market outweighs the perpetual silliness and occasional hostility of the campus thought police will be rewarded with a campus and community that earn high marks from students and faculty for general aesthetic beauty. Each of the seven colleges and schools has its own classrooms, libraries, and student hangout areas. (In all, Cornell has nineteen libraries housing more than 5.5 million books.) Ithaca is located in the center of New York and borders Cayuga Lake, one of the scenic Finger Lakes.

Besides the groups prone to take over campus buildings, there are around four hundred organizations and clubs on campus, and the college viewbook claims that trying to take in all of them is like "trying to drink from a fire hydrant." Though not all groups are politically bent, Cornell seems proud of its activist heritage, even noting with pride in the viewbook the protest by La Asociacion Latina that led to the creation of the Hispanic student dorm and the picketing by the same group of a local pizzeria where immigrants were working long hours for less than minimum wage. The viewbook quotes Attorney General Janet Reno (class of 1960) as saying that "one of the joys" of her time at Cornell was that "people spoke their minds." When Reno returned to campus in 1994, she was greeted by protesters and said, "It's refreshing to see that they continue to do so." Campus events are covered by several publications: the conservative *Cornell Review*, the liberal *Cornell Perspective*, the humorous *Cornell Lunatic*, and the mainstream *Cornell Daily Sun*, the only morning paper in Ithaca and the starting point in the careers of E. B. White, Kurt Vonnegut Jr., Thomas Pynchon, and Dick Schaap.

Students are actively involved in the numerous recreational, intramural, and intercollegiate sporting activities that Ithaca and Cornell offer. Apart from the Big Red intercollegiate teams (fifteen for women and fifteen for men — all with no athletic scholarships), around six thousand students play intramural sports. The campus offers extensive recreational facilities, including an eighteen-hole golf course designed by Cornell graduate Robert Trent Jones, Sr. The university's soccer field is located atop a quarter-mile-round atom smasher.

Students are not required — or even strongly encouraged, according to the viewbook — to live on campus, though the university guarantees rooms to freshmen and to sophomores who want to keep their rooms. But three-quarters of juniors and seniors live in off-campus housing, including the fraternities and sororities that more than one-third of both men and women join.

Ithaca is a small city with around thirty thousand permanent residents, but caters to the large student population (combined, Cornell and Ithaca College double the population); thus, restaurants, coffeehouses, and shops are plentiful. As one professor observes, Cornell's real peer in the Ivy League is the University of Pennsylvania: the academic standards, faculty reputation, and degree marketability are very similar (as are the political foibles), but Cornell is located in a small upstate New York town, while Penn is located in the heart of Philadelphia. It is a bucolic setting for a very active university.

UNIVERSITY OF DALLAS

Office of Admissions
University of Dallas
1845 East Northgate Drive
Irving, TX 75062
(972) 721-5226 / (800) 628-6999
acad.udallas.edu

Total enrollment: 2,750
Undergraduates: 1,200
SAT Ranges (Verbal/Math): V 550-630, M 570-660
Financial aid: 70%
Applicants: 740
Accepted: 91%
Enrolled: 35%
Application deadline: Feb. 15
Financial aid application deadline: Jan. 15
Tuition: $11,430
Core curriculum: Yes

Wise beyond Its Years

The University of Dallas, founded in 1956, is one of the newest arrivals on the American college scene. One might be forgiven for assuming that a school with such a short institutional memory would be rather modern in its educational philosophy. A young school, you might assume, must be grounded in the modern ideology that sees higher education as little more than training for a particular career. Surely a college of this type would have little choice but to reflect the prevailing cultural values in an effort to stay afloat.

In the case of the University of Dallas, these assumptions would be incorrect. Despite the youth of the school, Dallas is closely tied to one of the most ancient institutions in the world, an institution even older than universities themselves: the Roman Catholic Church. The young age of the school is more than offset by the tradition of which it is a part; the tradition gives it not only its mission but the reason for its existence. Unlike many older Catholic universities, which have become deeply secularized, Dallas has not only refused to abandon its Catholic roots but has in fact embraced them with passion. Because of this, Dallas is one of the few genuinely countercultural universities in the nation.

This approach is successful at Dallas because the faculty who implement it believe it to be true. As one professor says, "Truth and virtue are the proper study of human life. And you sense the commitment to these beliefs when you come onto campus, which is unlike so many campuses where there are no standards." This educational philosophy underlies the way the university views its obligations to its students. Students are taught to see freedom not as the opportunity for self-aggrandizement, but as the ability to pursue truth, goodness, and beauty.

Academic Life: Hard Core

Dallas's humane and learned philosophy is taught primarily through the core curriculum, truly the heart of the university. Each of the school's 1,200 undergraduates is required to complete the core, which, in the words of a university publication,

> is designed to foster the pursuit of wisdom through formation in intellectual and moral excellence, to foster a mature understanding of the Catholic faith, and to encourage a responsible concern for shaping contemporary society. The organization and content of the Core are determined by the premise that these goals can best be achieved through a curriculum founded on the Western heritage tradition of liberal education. Within this heritage, the Christian intellectual tradition is an essential element, and the American experience merits special consideration.

This core includes these required courses: twelve credits in both philosophy and English, three to six credits in mathematics, three to six credits in fine arts, six to eight credits in science, six credits in both American and European history, three credits in politics, three credits in economics, and six credits in theology.

Additionally, a foreign language is required, the number of credits needed varying from three to fourteen, depending on how qualified the student is upon entering college. Options include both modern language and literature courses, as well as Latin and Greek. While the ancient languages are given unique emphasis for a contemporary American university, the only modern languages offered are French, German, Spanish, and Italian.

All candidates for the B.A. or B.S. degree must complete at least 120 hours of credit, or 150 hours for double majors. Core requirements are the same for both bachelor's degrees, and normally represent half the total credits needed to graduate. After completing the core, students are free to choose from among more than twenty traditional majors as well as several preprofessional programs, dual degree programs (including a B.A./M.B.A. with Dallas's Graduate School of Management), and several concentrations that may be completed in addition to a major. Credits don't come easily, either: grade inflation is almost unknown at the University of Dallas. "The B grade here is worth an A at most prestigious schools," one professor declares proudly.

In the area of philosophy, the required courses are "Philosophy and the Ethical Life," "The Philosophy of Man," "The Philosophy of Being," and a fourth course related to the major. Four English courses in "The Literary Tradition" come next on the list and include the study of ancient classical poetry, Christian epic poetry and its dissolution in the modern era, dramatic tragedies and comedies, and the nineteenth- and twentieth-century novel. Under the category of mathematics and the fine arts, students may choose either three credits of math and six of fine arts, or six of math and three of fine arts. They may choose among four math courses and six in art, drama, and music. Under science, all must take two laboratory courses, one in a life science and one in a physical science.

Also mandatory are six credits each in American and Western civilization. The two-course American sequence divides at the Civil War and includes the reading of many primary sources. The Western civilization requirement includes the works of Thucydides, Livy, St. Thomas More, John Calvin, Immanuel Kant, Edmund Burke, Karl Marx, and Pope Leo XIII.

Other categories are politics and economics, each for three credits, with one designated course in American government and another in the fundamentals of economics. Dallas is one of the few colleges in the country with a mandatory free-market economics course. Finally, the theology requirement of six credits includes two courses: "Understanding the Bible" and "Western Theological Tradition."

Students are required to spend their first two years reading a common selection of works in an order that heightens their understanding of each work. For example, Plato's *Republic* is read in its entirety in one class while, simultaneously, *The Iliad,* also read cover to cover, is required in another. That Plato advocated the banishment of Homer's work because he thought it harmful to the proper development of youth will be brought to students' attention as they read both works.

Through this system the University of Dallas disproves the current myth that the Western canon is comprised only of works supporting a particular philosophy. Dallas does not substitute one form of ideological straitjacket for another; rather, its broad, liberal education demonstrates to students that faith and reason are not enemies but allies. Professors present St. Thomas Aquinas *and* Nietzsche, Burke *and* Rousseau, Newman *and* Marx. As one professor says, "Dallas is a university, not a retreat. A retreat is a sect, and we must produce leaders. There is no Catholic sectarianism here." Recently *Omeros,* the epic poem by the West Indian poet Derrick Walcott, was introduced into the curriculum — not because of the author's ethnicity but because the poem was judged to have inherent and lasting worth. The poet himself was brought to campus to be interviewed before the decision to include his work was reached, and both he and the faculty agreed that his work confirms precisely the opposite of what is taught by the more activist multiculturalists. The University of Dallas gives no quarter to those who would use the curriculum for political ends, because such uses are themselves antithetical to true liberal education. As one professor said, "There is no pressure to read only pious literature. A move to introduce a pious textbook would be D-E-A-D. . . . We read the books [assigned] for the truth they may contain, not as propaganda."

At Dallas, then, students receive a genuinely multicultural education, one that familiarizes them with the best that has been thought and written. The common core makes possible a common language among all the students, so that during their first two years a true intellectual community is fostered: students at Dallas advance along the same paths as they read the same literature, reckon with the same mathematics, and perform the same experiments. Discussions of real intellectual weight and merit are possible, and students discover in their friends and classmates reservoirs of learning into which they can plunge at any time, anywhere. As one professor with a long tenure at Dallas puts it, "Hot button issues are discussed, but not so much in class. The principles are hammered out by the students themselves. This is not a politicized campus." Says another professor: "It has always struck me that this is one of the most open campuses in the nation. We discuss topics here that on other campuses are forbidden ground. This is extremely congenial for me, because all sides of a question can be faced, and that's very important."

Another superb offering is the Rome Program, in which, amazingly, nearly 85 percent of undergraduates participate. Available to sophomores who complete at least twelve credit hours of work and maintain a minimum GPA of 2.0, the program allows students to spend a semester at Dallas's Rome Campus. The program includes fifteen hours of study in literature, art and architecture, Italian, philosophy, theology, or history under the guidance of regular university faculty members. The Rome experience is one of the highlights of the students' experience at Dallas, and many speak of it as the best part of their education.

The faculty both in Dallas and in Rome is judged to be quite strong and very dedicated. "There are fewer stars today than there were a few years ago, but we have a very, very strong faculty," says a professor. "We are even stronger today than at any time in the past twenty years, because today there is a great deal of awareness of the problems facing the West," notes a longtime faculty member.

Although Dallas is a fairly small school, it offers doctorates in politics, philosophy, and literature. These same departments are often singled out for praise for their commitment to undergraduate teaching as well. Politics, in particular, is known to be among the best departments on campus. Excellent professors there include Glenn Thurow, Leo Paul de Alvarez, Richard Daugherty, and Tom West. In philosophy, Bob Wood, Fr. James Lehrberger, and Janet Smith excel. In English, David Davies, Fr. Robert McGuire, Scott Crider, and Scott Dupree teach overflowing classes. Other outstanding professors include Richard Olenick in physics, Judy Kelly in drama, Mark Lowery and Douglas Bushman in theology, Stephen Maddux in French, and Alexandra Wilhelmsen in Spanish. Samuel Bostaph teaches in an economics department that contains many members of the Austrian School, which eschews mathematical models in favor of a historical approach to its subject. Tom Jodziewicz is an outstanding teacher in history, and Grace Starry West stands out in classics. All of the sciences are seen as very strong, and Dallas's success rate at placing its graduates in medical school is an impressive 90 percent.

In 1997 the university became the first in the nation to be accredited by the American Academy for Liberal Education, which accredits only schools dedicated to a solid core curriculum in the tradition of a broad liberal education. The fact that Dallas embraced this accreditation where another traditional liberal arts college — Rhodes — balked at it speaks well of the university and its dedication to the liberal arts.

Two worries do cloud the beautiful education offered by the University of Dallas. The first is the school's financial woes, which stem from an endowment of only $40 million — a lot of money, true, but not enough to secure the future of a private university. Many campus buildings need renovation, but the lack of money has prevented the work from getting done. "It is very sobering," says one professor.

The other potential for trouble is significantly less worrisome for the near future, yet troubling to some faculty members: there are some rumblings, though still small, that the university should offer an undergraduate business major that exempts its students from the core curriculum. This, according to some faculty, runs counter to the university's most cherished philosophy. Notes one professor: "If a student's highest ideals at the age of eighteen are to go out and make money, then he's closed. Through the core, one obtains a nobility of the soul that one wouldn't get otherwise. Business students at other schools who don't study the liberal arts aren't unformed, they're malformed." Another says: "I would be very much afraid if the business school had an undergraduate business major." The founders of the University of Dallas did not allow an undergraduate business major for precisely these reasons, and the fact that some faculty are now a bit worried about the potential for trouble in this area must be seen as a sign that financial pressures have opened a window of opportunity to those who would abandon Dallas's insistence that its students be educated in the classical sense rather than merely trained for a career in a utilitarian mode. While this is not an immediate threat, the fact that undergraduate business majors at many public universities make up one-fourth of the student body is worrisome.

Political Atmosphere: The Trendy Need Not Apply

Given the seriousness with which the school approaches its core curriculum, it is not surprising that those who would move Dallas toward the more typical model of the American university are vastly outnumbered. There are some who would like to see the university become more committed to the multicultural curriculum found on so many other campuses, but, as one professor says, "There are zeitgeist-watchers on campus who would have a fit if anyone attempted to monkey around with the core." Indeed, the faculty and administration are firmly committed to preserving the college's curriculum because they see it as the best way to carry on a tradition that defines openness and critical inquiry. As one professor says, "We are conserving the Western intellectual tradition and the student who comes here knows that's what they get. . . . The West is about openness and that's what we do." Adds another, "Some think there is an effort to bring in non-Western courses, but the conversation about faith and culture precludes indoctrination."

About 70 percent of the students are Catholic, and Mass is said twice daily and several times on weekends. Nevertheless, students of other faiths are welcome and encouraged to attend the university. Dallas does not practice affirmative action in admissions or faculty hiring. According to former president Robert F. Sasseen, "Our policy is one of nondiscrimination and equal opportunity — *not* affirmative action" (emphasis his). As for speech codes, there are none, nor is there agitation for one. "People are willing to accept the idea that in academic life you can make controversial statements," says one professor. Another says that "as a Catholic university we have a strong history of civility and good manners." There are no militant groups making war on the university or the curriculum. At Dallas the Catholic conviction that faith is not destroyed by reason, that knowledge is a sign of faith and a means of strengthening one's understanding of religion, is manifested every day in the classroom, the dining hall, the dorm room — anywhere that students socialize.

The faculty is comprised of about 90 percent laypeople, and its religious affiliation is mixed. "There is not an oppressively Roman Catholic atmosphere," notes one professor, "but it is also not a place where Catholic topics are avoided." He also notes that "in the last two years opposition Roman Catholic groups have spoken up more. Debate here is spirited but there is no 'God-Squad' police. That was tried several years ago but didn't work. The faculty tends to side with those who advocate open debate." Non-Catholic students feel comfortable, although someone truly opposed to Catholic teaching and hostile to the Western canon might find himself engaged in many arguments. A non-Catholic professor notes that he has never been made to feel unwelcome.

Debates over hiring or tenuring decisions rarely center on anything other than scholarly qualifications. In other words, the politics of the candidate rarely carry over into the hiring process because potential hires tend to be self-selecting. All candidates for academic positions are given a copy of the school's mission statement, which explains clearly that the University of Dallas is about the business of educating students broadly in the liberal arts and with great respect for the Catholic tradition.

The problems many scholars who practice a more traditional pedagogy at other schools face are not problems at the University of Dallas. On the contrary, the fact that such professors are sometimes driven from other institutions has been to Dallas's benefit. Because so many schools refuse to hire scholars who do not share their radicalized views on teaching and research, schools such as Dallas find themselves in what one professor calls a "buyers' market." Once at Dallas, most faculty members find a happy marriage between their skills and interests and the university's needs. "People rarely leave," notes one professor. "We are able to retain them because they can't teach the curriculum elsewhere. The great pleasure in teaching here is in revisiting the great authors with colleagues who love their courses. We know the students are reading parallel texts in other departments, and that a common conversation exists. You simply don't find that at many other schools."

And teaching is indeed taken seriously at Dallas. The university does not pressure its faculty to spend their energy on publishing rather than teaching, especially prior to becoming full professors. At many smaller liberal arts colleges, including those with no graduate school, faculty are expected to teach full loads *and* to publish a book by their seventh year in order to gain tenure. Dallas's postponement of the publishing expectation to the full professor level allows its junior faculty to spend most of their time preparing for classes that, at that early date in their career, they may not have taught in graduate school or in any of their previous positions. The university's demand that its faculty learn to teach well before they spend countless hours writing a book is the most important indicator of the seriousness with which they approach their mission.

Campus Life: Other Things to Do in Dorms

A writer in the *Chronicle of Higher Education* once called the climate at the University of Dallas "reverse PC," noting that there are no free condoms, no AIDS-awareness programs, and that students must keep their dorm room doors open when a member of the opposite sex is visiting. The occasion for the article was a 1995 debate on campus over banning sex in college dormitories — something that was prohibited anyway, but which was being put into writing. Violations of the policy can result in expulsion or suspension, and the severity of the penalty was the root of some of the debate: One professor pointed out that St. Francis, St. Augustine, and St. Ignatius Loyola, all of whom spent "rather rakish" youths, could have been kicked out of the University of Dallas. Others worried that strict rules would alienate the 30 percent of Dallas students who are not Catholic. But most students didn't understand what the fuss was about. Most agreed with the university's call for students to unite their "academic and social lives with a consistent moral vision," according to the *Chronicle*.

The incident is indicative of the student culture at Dallas, where most do their best to live upright lives and are more preoccupied with academic excellence than with other pursuits. According to a Phi Beta Kappa report on the school, "Respect for one another and for the deliberative process . . . a strong dedication to maintain, for every student, at any cost, the element of a basic, shared, intellectual experience — is evident." Such endeavors, conscientiously undertaken, leave little room for trivial or destructive pursuits.

Around 70 percent of the student body is Catholic, and although attendance at Mass is not required, many students do go regularly. Other campus events and groups give students a chance to act out their faith: the university hosts a Charity Week, for example, and many student groups conduct service projects. Most groups on campus are conservative (if they are political at all), and the College Democrats are thought the most liberal group at the school. While many clubs are academic or professional in nature (Phi Beta Kappa, for example), there are also groups like Crusaders for Life, Young Conservatives of Texas, and College Republicans. Intramural and intercollegiate sports are available, and the baseball team, dropped in 1981, resumed play in 1998. There are also chess, sailing, rugby, and fencing clubs.

Although the majority (59 percent) of students are Texans, the 1,200 undergraduates at the university include students from thirty-eight states and twenty-three foreign countries. There are student organizations dedicated to several ethnic groups, including Vietnamese, Chinese, Japanese, Turkish, and Thai students. About two-thirds of the students live in university residence halls, while 7 percent live at home with their families.

DARTMOUTH COLLEGE

Dean of Admissions and Financial Aid
Dartmouth College
McNutt Hall
Hanover, NH 03775
(603) 646-2875
www.dartmouth.edu

Total enrollment: 5,500
Undergraduates: 4,300
SAT Ranges (Verbal/Math): V 660-750, M 670-760
Financial aid: 45%
Applicants: 11,400
Accepted: 20%
Enrolled: 49%
Application deadline: Jan. 1
Financial aid application deadline: Feb. 1
Tuition: $22,896
Core curriculum: No

Yet Those Who Love It

Dartmouth College was founded in 1754 as More's Indian Charity School by a graduate of Yale, the Reverend Eleazar Wheelock. The original mission of the school was to educate Native American youth, as well as English children. The school was renamed for William Legge, the earl of Dartmouth, an early contributor to the venture.

In 1818 Daniel Webster, himself a graduate of Dartmouth seventeen years earlier, went to the Supreme Court of the United States to plead against a state takeover of the college. "Sir, you may destroy this little institution; it is weak; it is in your hands! I know it is one of the lesser lights in the literary horizon of our country," Webster said. "You may put it out. But if you do so, you must carry through your work! You must extinguish, one after another, all those great lights of science which, for more than a century, have thrown their radiance over our land!"

Webster concluded his argument with these words: "It is, sir, as I have said, a small college. And yet, there are those who love it."

He won the argument. To this day, there are those who love Dartmouth, some for its past glories and some for its present achievements. Those fond of the modern Dartmouth believe it to be on the cutting edge of the academic world, making room as it does for diversity and ideological instruction in its curriculum and campus life. Those who prefer the old Dartmouth — and a large group of alumni do — fear the modern college for the same reasons: the advent of aggressive multiculturalism and politicization. At the moment it is the "new" Dartmouth that seems to have the upper hand.

Academic Life: The Dartmouth Plan

Dartmouth's basic curriculum requires that students take ten courses covering eight different sectors of the university. As such, the requirements do not force students to learn any foundational disciplines in depth. Instead, a Dartmouth student must take only a single course in art; literature; philosophical, religious, or historical analysis; international and comparative study; quantitative and deductive science; and technology or applied science; plus two courses in both social analysis and natural and physical science.

There are three additional distribution requirements known as "world culture" courses. One course is required in each of three areas, according to the college catalogue: "the culture, ideas, or institutions of the United States, of Europe, and of at least one non-Western society." According to some on campus, the non-Western courses are largely politicized and critical of the Western institutions studied in the other world culture requirements.

Dartmouth freshmen must take an English composition course within the first two quarters, but accomplished students can be exempted from this requirement.

Once the English requirement is taken care of, freshmen choose one of about seventy seminars representing thirty departments and programs. The seminars are small — the maximum size is sixteen students — and offer an introduction to the writing and scholarship required in upper-level courses, according to college materials.

All Dartmouth students must become proficient in a foreign language, although advanced achievement in high school can take the place of college coursework. The college requires three terms of physical education, and students must demonstrate the ability to swim fifty yards.

Dartmouth operates on a schedule known, not surprisingly, as the Dartmouth Plan. Adopted in 1972 when the college went coed, this calendar involves four ten-week academic terms per year. At the time the plan was implemented there were roughly one thousand male students, and rather than reducing the number of undergraduate men to five hundred, or half the university, Dartmouth chose the four-term year to make the most efficient use of its facilities. A typical student spends only two or three terms of each year on campus, but must be there for the first three terms of his freshman year and the final three of his senior year.

Faculty say the Dartmouth Plan makes it easier for students to schedule off-campus study, including terms at overseas universities and internships. The disadvantage of the plan is that students can't always get the classes they want because a particular course may be offered only during a specific term each year. "On a more personal level, a student may fall in love and they won't see their beloved for several terms," a professor says.

Dartmouth offers thirty-eight traditional majors, plus interdisciplinary majors in African and Afro-American studies, environmental studies, Native American studies, and women's studies. In addition to these choices, the college gives students considerable latitude should they choose to create their own fields of study or combine existing ones into a double major.

The best professors at Dartmouth include Edward M. Bradley and William C. Scott in classics; Michael Mastanduno and Roger Masters in government; Paul David Lagomarsino, Pamela Crossley, Kenneth E. Shewmaker, and Heide W. Whelan in history; Michael Knetter in economics; Robert Fogelin in philosophy; Charles Stinson and Ehud Benor in religion; and Peter Saccio, whose Shakespeare class is one of the best, in the English department. "Students at Dartmouth have an opportunity to be very close to their professors," a recent graduate says. "The teachers are very accessible, and it is truly amazing that undergraduate students can just walk in and talk with their professors. It is an incredible advantage."

According to professors and students, the best and most traditional departments at Dartmouth are history, government, and classics.

Three departments are considered highly politicized by students and faculty who favor the traditional liberal arts: women's studies, Latin American studies, and English.

Women's studies offers both majors and minors, and the department is very similar to its counterparts at other Ivy League schools. A course called "Roots of Feminism: A Historical, Multi-Cultural Perspective" looks at "the emergence of feminist movements around the globe . . . whether or not they would identify themselves as 'feminist,'" according to the catalogue description. "Since women's identities and the sources of domination are multiple and interconnected, resistance to women's oppression assumes multiple forms." Another course, "Feminism and Philosophy," claims students "will work on sharpening [their] critical tools for exploring a variety of issues of particular relevance to women." Among the issues to which these tools will be applied is "feminine versus masculine morality," according to the catalogue.

The Latin American, Latino, and Caribbean Studies Department does not offer a major, though many of its courses fulfill the non-Western portion of the world culture distribution requirement. One such course is "Introduction to Latin America and the Caribbean," which, after a brief introduction to the region, "examines the history of selected countries to highlight the way European conquest and colonialism have molded Latin American institutions and attitudes" before turning to "particular case studies of contemporary life and society to analyze the ongoing problems of ethnicity, inequality, and political repression engendered by the region's colonial past."

Quite a few English courses are devoted to themes of class, race, or gender. "The English department is pretty notorious for being liberal," a student says. "There are some outspoken leftists in that department." One professor reportedly has tried to intimidate those who advertise in the *Dartmouth Review* (a conservative student publication) into dropping their ads.

In many cases the politicization of the English department extends to basic survey courses. For example, the course description accompanying "American Fiction to 1900" reads: "A survey of the first century of U.S. fiction, this course focuses on historical contexts as well as social and material conditions of the production of narrative as cultural myth. We will consider selections from the so-called 'classic tradition' alongside texts by women and people of color. Issues of gender, race, and class will be emphasized."

The Nelson A. Rockefeller Center for the Social Sciences supports research into public policy questions, visiting scholars and lecturers, off-campus internships, and conferences. The center, named for the former U.S. vice president and Dartmouth alumnus, also offers a public policy minor for undergraduates. Its curriculum and some of its events have become politicized, according to students. A student organization — known as "Rocky!" — sponsored by the center has hosted panel discussions on multicultural topics as well as a recent event entitled "Environmental Racism: Does It Exist? Is It a Class Issue?"

According to one student, "It seems that the principal concern of the Rockefeller Center is bringing the social sciences to bear on environmental questions."

Political Atmosphere: The *Review* Reviewed

Over the last decade Dartmouth, like Stanford University, has been one of the prime battlegrounds on the academic front of the culture wars. This is in part because Dartmouth has had a number of outspoken conservatives on campus in recent years, including English professor emeritus (and syndicated columnist) Jeffrey Hart and various editors of the *Dartmouth Review*.

Dartmouth president James O. Freedman is singled out by Hart as the "worst college administrator" in the country. According to Hart (writing in a letter to the journal *Heterodoxy*), Freedman, who plans to retire at the end of the 1997-98 academic year, mismanaged university funds by "charging off as 'research' all sorts of things like presidential parties and limousine travel — $25,000 in a single year." He cites a university-wide poll in which 73 percent of students expressed a negative opinion of Freedman. Regarding Freedman on curricular issues, Hart writes: "He has said that requiring such authors as Shakespeare or Dante might make students miss a 'gem' like Alice Walker. Egad."

Then there is the running feud between the administration and the *Dartmouth Review*, the paper whose student staff has included Dinesh D'Souza, Benjamin Hart, Gregory Fossedal, and many others now working as scholars or journalists. While the *Review* has not always risen above the temptation to sophomoric smugness, it has received national attention for its clever spoofs of academic policies and ludicrous courses. Its subscription list includes ten thousand Dartmouth alumni.

Two books — *The Hollow Men: Politics and Corruption in Higher Education*, by Charles Sykes, and *Poisoned Ivy*, by Benjamin Hart — along with Professor Hart's letter, document the *Review*'s struggles. Students distributing the paper have been arrested, and others have been denied information by college administrators — even when the information was a matter of public record. Benjamin Hart was physically attacked by a college administrator named Samuel Smith while distributing the paper. According to Sykes's book, Smith punched and kicked Hart and tried to throw him through a plate glass door. Three days after the attack, the university faculty voted 113 to 5 against disciplinary action for Smith, but in favor of censures against the newspaper.

In another incident in the mid-1980s, a music professor named William Cole unsuccessfully sued the *Review* for libel after a reporter sat in on his class and wrote that the professor "arrived late, left class for periods of as long as ten minutes at a time, and spent at least half of his lecture on 'the race question,' referring to students as racist and sexist," according to Sykes. After the article was printed, the professor went to the reporter's dorm room and launched into an obscenity-filled, threatening tirade. He also refused to teach his class until the *Review* apologized; he relented when the administration said he could be fired for such refusal but continued to use an obscenity in his classroom references to the *Review*. He received no sanctions other than the demand that he continue to teach as he was contractually obligated to do.

Cole again was not disciplined for an attack on students in 1988, five years later. The *Review* had written another article on his class sessions as part of a story on the university's declining standards. The article included a transcript of the class session, in which, Sykes writes, "Cole was captured in a lengthy and formless ramble that included the status of Indians, his youth in Pittsburgh, nuclear waste disposal, and his thoughts on crime and poverty, salted throughout with obscenities and racial epithets." Cole hung up on *Review* reporters who wanted to ask for his side of the story, and when reporters and a photographer visited him in person, he "lunged at the photographer, breaking the flash attachment," Sykes writes.

Freedman's administration charged the students with harassment. Several groups on campus staged a rally in support of Cole, at which more than four hundred students showed up. According to Sykes, President Freedman addressed the crowd and condemned the "vexatious oral exchange," acts of "disrespect, insensitivity and personal attack," as well as "racism, sexism and other forms of ignorance" perpetrated by the *Review*. Later he said the *Review* "recklessly sets out to create a climate of intolerance and intimidation that destroys our mutual sense of community and inhibits the reasoned examination of the widest possible range of ideas." Freedman later said he supported free speech, even "speech that expresses unpopular, obnoxious, even detestable points of view." He then claimed "the issue that the *Review* presents has nothing whatever to do with freedom of the press." Instead, Freedman said, the *Review* was indecent, "irresponsible, mean-spirited, and cruel."

It was in this atmosphere, then, that three *Review* staffers were suspended and another was put on probation. However, the suspensions were overturned when a U.S. court of appeals judge — himself a Dartmouth alum — found that the disciplinary proceedings were invalid because they "took place against a backdrop of undisguised college hostility to the political views expressed in the *Dartmouth Review* as well as the polemical and excessive terms in which those opinions were sometimes cast."

Many credit alumni intervention with the survival of Dartmouth's extensive fraternity system, which was attacked recently by Dean of the College Lee Pelton, who arrived at Dartmouth having already cracked down on fraternities as an administrator at Colgate University. When Pelton came to campus in 1995, the Dartmouth administration had already banned kegs at frat parties and had ordered campus security officers to investigate and monitor the parties. Students, on the other hand, had taken to pelting the investigating officers with obscenities and cups, and to drinking hard liquor rather than beer. Pelton allowed the return of kegs with certain restrictions, but at one point more than half of the campus fraternities were on probation for violating the keg policy, according to the *Review*. Many feel that alumni support for the fraternities, despite the Greek system's many faults, kept fraternities from disappearing altogether.

Student Life: "Ivy" Seeing You in All the Old Familiar Places

The typical Dartmouth student is concerned with being well rounded, according to one recent graduate. "That's the catch word that distinguishes a Dartmouth student from his Harvard counterpart," the alumnus says. "The Harvard student is interested in being the best at one particular thing — such as a world-class violinist — and not really doing much else. The Dartmouth student is well-rounded in that he is playing a club sport like rugby, and serving as an officer in his fraternity, as well as working for a student publication or journal."

According to this graduate, the students at Dartmouth work very hard, but also play hard. "There is, as a result, a kind of anti-intellectualism," this person says. "Students are devoted to their studies, but they don't talk about them much outside of the classroom."

The center of social life is the fraternities and sororities, to which 40 percent of men and a quarter of women belong. Athletic events are the other social draw. The majority of students don't spend a great deal of time on political activism.

The presence of the *Dartmouth Review* and other conservative organizations encourages students to speak their minds — but this is not to say that conservative viewpoints are tolerated in all circles. "There is an enormous pressure for social conformity at Dartmouth," the recent graduate says. "The *Dartmouth Review* remains socially separate from the rest of the campus because they are considered the nasty conservatives. In fact, the *Dartmouth Review* is anathema on campus." A newer magazine, the *Beacon,* is closer to the political center, and is thus more socially acceptable. The *Beacon* describes itself as committed "to the following principles: Quest for good frat beer, Love of Dartmouth College, Justice and Equality, Conservatism 'n' stuff." It contains student critiques of general cultural and national politics, as well as articles on Dartmouth issues like student activity funding, affirmative action, and the university's alcohol policy.

Other student groups include the Dartmouth Coalition for Life, which promotes alternatives to abortion, and the Conservative Union, which most recently worked to ensure the continuation of the university ROTC program. In 1997 Dartmouth hosted the Ivy League Conference for Life, which included pro-lifers Olivia Gans, Pam Smith (president of Pro-Life Obstetricians and Gynecologists), and former U.S. ambassador to the United Nations Alan Keyes.

Dartmouth alumni interested in preserving university liberal arts traditions and standards have founded the Hopkins Institute, an unofficial alumni organization based in Arlington, Virginia. "Dartmouth students are no longer required to read Shakespeare, Dante, Plato or even to know the basic facts of American history," says one alumnus associated with the group. The organization has brought speakers to campus, including William F. Buckley Jr., Jack Kemp, and former U.S. treasury secretary William Simon, and provides scholarship money to selected students. The institute is named for former Dartmouth president Ernest Martin Hopkins, in honor of his commitment to the traditional liberal arts and to open dialogue on campus. For example, Hopkins, president for more than thirty years starting in 1916, once invited a leading communist to campus — even though he strongly disagreed with the man's ideology — and later said he would have invited Lenin or Trotsky had they been available.

Among the seventy or so student groups at Dartmouth are several multicultural organizations. The Movimiento Estudiantil Chicano de Aztlan works for Latino and Chicano interests at Dartmouth. Another group, the African-American Society, hosted a talk recently by former Black Panther leader Elaine Brown. In a speech entitled "Resolving Problems of Racism, Gender Oppression, and Class Disparity," Brown said racism was apparent in the fact that 60 percent of Gulf War soldiers were black, and also alleged that the CIA had purposely caused the drug problems in America's inner cities. The university officially recognizes an Afrocentric publication called *Black Praxis*.

Another group, Students for Choice, works for abortion rights. A prohomosexual organization called Men's Group was started to "discuss the social and personal issues of gender socialization, sexism, sexual violence, homophobia, and racism," according to the group. The Dartmouth Rainbow Alliance, according to its web page, is an "organization for gays, lesbians, bi and trans individuals, as well as straight allies." The Rainbow Alliance maintains an office and a library in the university student center. Finally, a left-wing publication called *Stet* promotes Marxist and feminist agendas in its pages, and has praised the Nicaraguan and Angolan revolutions.

The university also has student groups dedicated to service projects, literary or academic endeavors, the arts, and social events.

One social outlet is intramural sports; the more than twenty-five options are divided into male-only, female-only, and coed leagues. The university also has thirty-three intercollegiate sports teams that compete at the NCAA Division I level.

The campus and the area around it are lovely. "Dartmouth is a great place if you like the outdoors — it is fantastically beautiful," a recent graduate says. Hanover, New Hampshire, is a small New England rural town near the upper valley of the Connecticut River. The 200-acre campus is surrounded by forests and mountain ranges, providing students with a beautiful setting for their studies and outdoor activities. The Dartmouth Outing Club, the nation's oldest collegiate outing club, runs outdoor activities for about 1,500 students (about a third of the undergraduate student body) each year.

The campus includes the Collis Center, a red-and-white brick building with large white Roman columns at its entrance, which houses student meeting areas and offices. The center includes the "Common Ground" room, which can hold up to 250 people, as well as a restaurant and tavern.

Dartmouth also has the Hood Museum of Art, one of the oldest college museums in the country. It houses more than sixty thousand objects, mostly non-Western and modern art.

The main venue for the performing arts is the Hopkins Center, used for movies, art exhibitions, drama and dance performances, and the occasional seminar. "The Hop," as it is known, was designed by Wallace K. Harrison, who also designed the Metropolitan Opera House in New York City. The largest auditorium seats nine hundred people, and the building contains a whopping six acres of floor space.

The Baker Library, one of the oldest in the United States, is accessible to all students via the personal computers with which all of them are provided. Dormitory rooms and faculty offices are all on the university computer network, meaning that the library and other information are easy to reach from about any place on campus.

DAVIDSON COLLEGE

Office of Admissions
P.O. Box 1737
Davidson, NC 28036
(704) 892-2230
web.davidson.edu

Total enrollment: 1,610
Undergraduates: 1,610
SAT Ranges (Verbal/Math): V 630-730, M 640-720
Financial aid: 34%
Applicants: 3,182
Accepted: 37%
Enrolled: 42%
Application deadline: Jan. 15
Financial aid application deadline: Feb. 15
Tuition: $21,395
Core curriculum: No

Holding Out

Davidson College was founded by Presbyterians in 1837 as a liberal arts college, and over the many years of its existence it has maintained its informal ties to the church while remaining true to its tradition as a place in which teaching excellence is expected and rewarded. Although never formally connected with the Presbyterian church, Davidson still sees itself as related to the church and, as its statement of purpose says, "intends that this vital relationship be continued to the mutual benefit of church and school." This statement continues: "The primary purpose of Davidson College is to assist students in developing humane instincts and disciplined and creative minds for lives of leadership and service." This same statement notes that the college "emphasizes those studies, disciplines and activities that are mentally, spiritually and physically liberating."

In general, the school complies quite closely with its mission statement. Classes are small and students receive individualized attention. Davidson has no plans to grow into a large university with graduate programs, and for this the college community is to be thanked. There is a greater need in this country for good liberal arts colleges than for yet more schools of graduate studies.

To its credit, Davidson stresses teaching over research, still attracts a fairly conservative student body, and offers many excellent teachers who are deeply concerned about the well-being and development of their students. Students tend to love the college because of the close friendships formed there, and they tend to believe that they receive a very good education.

Academic Life: Coming Close

The basic curriculum at Davidson consists of ten courses chosen from among the arts and sciences (including literature, history, religion, philosophy, fine arts, the sciences, and mathematics), plus a "cultural diversity requirement." There is no Western civilization requirement, although enough humanities-related courses are required that it would be difficult for any student to graduate without some exposure to Western culture. Nevertheless, the presence of the "cultural diversity requirement" indicates a bowing, however slight, to those demanding a "more inclusive" curriculum. Even if the requirement were fulfilled with a perfectly aboveboard and rigorous course, it is disturbing that such a course is mandated while a Western civilization course is not. It seems strange for the college to insist on exposure to other cultures while not making sure students are taught the fundamentals of the culture that gave birth to the university itself and to their own country. While other cultures should be studied in their own right and for the perspective they can give, no student can fully appreciate other cultures until he learns a fair amount of the history and literature of his own.

The core of courses is better than that found at many state universities, but it is rather weak when compared to the rigorous requirements found at colleges which place more importance on reading that is both broad and deep. Davidson's core requires that students satisfy distribution requirements rather than read a common set of works, and thus there is less chance that the student body will be able to communicate in a common language gained through its classes.

Although Davidson's requirements prevent the more egregious lapses in liberal education often found in institutions that adopt even looser requirements, one cannot help but lament the lost opportunity this open core presents. As a college that rightly prides itself on its commitment to broad liberal learning, Davidson could, with a stricter core requirement, bolster the shrinking ranks of colleges and universities that insist that their students obtain a better, more comprehensive, liberal arts education. Instead, Davidson has chosen merely to come close.

Some of what is missing from the college's core requirements is made up by a dedicated group of professors. Since Davidson seriously values teaching, and considers it when making hiring and tenure decisions, there are many highly motivated, excellent teachers on campus. Professors mentioned time and again by their colleagues as being among the best include Price Zimmerman in history, Peter Ahrensdorf in political science, and Lance Stell and Al Mele in philosophy. Particularly strong departments include philosophy, political science, history, mathematics, chemistry, and economics. Other sciences are also widely praised.

Students interested in eliminating the weaknesses of their core education should consider the outstanding Humanities Program, an interdisciplinary offering modeled on a great books approach. Both teachers and students in the program are enthusiastic about their work. The program takes up a minimum of two years, and its classes meet en masse for lectures before breaking into smaller sections of sixteen students each for discussions with individual instructors. The result, for students who choose to enroll in the program, is a thorough liberal education.

Unfortunately, the Humanities Program has many enemies on campus, and, at this writing, there is a chance it will not live more than a few more academic years. The criticism comes from those quarters opposed to any traditional approach to learning in which crucial books are read closely by a self-selecting group of students who crave intellectual stimulation. It is both unfortunate and ironic that, at a college founded by religious people, it would be members of the religion department leading the charge against this program. But that is indeed the case at Davidson. As one professor puts it, "There are fewer faculty members today who want to teach [the Humanities Program], because they think it's too traditional. There are some who want the program to die. Religion is most hostile to it, because they see it as too Western and too much like a Great Books program." Thus, a very unique and intellectually exciting program may be sacrificed to those who prefer teaching what is hot to teaching what is true. Should this sacrifice come to pass, students looking for something more than Davidson's requirements will need to look elsewhere.

Political Atmosphere: All Politics Is Local

Davidson has long been associated with a reasonably genteel, polite element of Southern society whose code of conduct frowns upon unwarranted personal attack or radical politics. This legacy of Southern manners continues to play a significant role on campus, where, as one teacher notes, "there is a kind of Southern preference for a consensual approach. If someone is too combative they're thought of as rude and are shunned." Says one transplant who praises Davidson: "Being here may take away some of the intellectual liveliness, but at such a small place things would otherwise be fratricidal, so I appreciate the influence of Southern culture. You don't hear the type of snide remarks here that you might hear at other places. Politics is not the most important element on campus."

Yet the degree to which this mannerly atmosphere will continue is uncertain. One professor notes that Davidson is still a "relatively depoliticized place where teaching is taken seriously," but also claims that "there is here a creeping influence of the left, and I wonder if it isn't only a matter of time before we become a Stanford or a Williams," rife with institutionalized, radical politics. Notes another professor: "The move toward politicization here is not dramatic but it is not glacial, either. There is a definite tendency in that direction. It won't happen merely in five years, but maybe ten to fifteen years."

Politicization, at this point, varies widely from department to department. The religion department is, not surprisingly in light of its stance on the Humanities Program, one of the most politicized on campus. Davidson also now has what are called "concentrations" in both gender studies and ethnic studies. A concentration does not have departmental standing and is not a major, but operates like a minor at other schools in that it may be used to complement one's major field of studies. Initially there was an effort to create a women's studies concentration, but enough faculty members at that time opposed singling out one sex for study that the proponents had to settle for gender studies instead. Nevertheless, the gender studies offerings overwhelmingly deal with women, rendering the victory of that concentration's opponents little more than semantic. Within the ethnic studies concentration a student may choose from several tracks, including Africana, Native American, and Latino, but should not assume that any of the choices will lead to a well-rounded education. One professor notes that, in both gender and ethnic studies, "there is no pretense of a variety of viewpoints." Says another: "There is a degree of struggling with multicultural experiences here, because in this day nobody knows what the hell that means."

As is often the case, the faculty are by and large not so much radicalized as open to intimidation by radicals, who make up a minority at Davidson. "Many faculty can be cowed," says one professor. "You state your case to someone, and if they're PC, they say 'Why don't you like women?' " Another faculty member estimates that around 95 percent of the faculty are liberal Democrats, although most are "more traditional than they realize. Some of them are friendlier with conservative students, and some can't stand them. It is not monolithic."

A greater concern for some faculty involves the quality — even more than the political leanings — of newer faculty members: Some longtime Davidson faculty members see their new colleagues as less rigorously educated than the older generation. "One of the depressing things about the younger people isn't political, it's just that they haven't read the really difficult material and they don't know it," says one professor. "It's too hard for them. It is easier to read twentieth-century scholarly criticism than the real thing." Sadly, some of the newer appointments, especially those made by the office of the dean, seem to be based on factors other than academic excellence. Says one professor: "It is possible for Davidson to slide down hill. I worry about some of our newer appointments because they were made by a dean who sees race and gender quotas as legitimate goals." Notes another: "Even though there is considerable pressure here for affirmative action hiring, if women candidates haven't worked out, they've been refused tenure." And yet, this same professor continues, "There is a kind of steady pressure in that [affirmative action, politicized] direction. Describing it can be complicated, but still there is an uneasy sense here, and the students feel it, too."

Despite the range of political convictions on campus, Davidson students are not battered by radical propaganda, as students are at other schools — although the trend is in that direction, according to a faculty member. There is at Davidson both a sexual harassment code and sensitivity training for incoming freshmen. The harassment code is similar to those found at many universities today in that it seeks to institutionalize the victimization of some members of society. But, just as typically, its results are often as undesirable as its existence. According to one professor, the chief result of the harassment code has been an increase in the perceived risk to male professors dealing with coeds. "Whose behavior is affected by the code? Women! The jerks [targeted by the code] won't change their behavior, but you don't see as many women in faculty offices discussing problems with their professors because [the code] discourages working with them," the professor says.

The sensitivity training begins when all incoming freshmen, as part of their freshman seminar, are required to read a novel "on the evils of the white male European civilization and the importance of recognizing the hegemonic discourse present in Western literature," says one professor. Notes another faculty member: "The presence of sensitivity training makes me sick. The people who do it are heavy-handed and shouldn't be working in the college community — they should be fired. They are not consultants from the outside, but are support staff who are brought in from the dean's office." The idea, which has beset Davidson for about five years, is "the worst kind of fad," says a professor. "A lot of lives can be ruined by these people, and we are hemorrhaging countless dollars over this stupid idea."

Sensitivity, it seems, is not a two-way street at Davidson. The list of recent speakers includes Maya Angelou, Spike Lee, Hodding Carter III, and Tom Wicker. But when a speaker from the other side of the spectrum, Christina Hoff Sommers, the prominent feminist critic of radical feminism, lectured on campus recently, one faculty member called her — to her face, during a public discussion following the speech — an "intellectual thug," and there was widespread faculty complaint that she was invited to campus. Additionally, faculty in the humanities have received memos from the administration urging them to use gender-neutral language in their classes, although there seems to be a strong resentment among teachers to this type of intrusion. Says one: "The faculty would be pretty darned resistant to the PC police." And yet it is from the faculty that much of the pressure to politicize has come, and one might say there was more resentment over the fact that the memos had come from the administration than to the memos' contents per se.

These incidents notwithstanding, Davidson has certainly maintained a more open community than many of those covered in this guide. But still, anyone who values the integrity of thought, the free expression of ideas, and the importance of an education that is based upon the Western tradition should be concerned about recent events and increasingly strong radical trends at this venerable North Carolina college.

At the same time, some signs are heartening. Pressure to turn Davidson into a research-oriented college where teaching is devalued has thus far not prevailed. There is no doubt that teaching is taken very seriously by the administration, faculty, and students, and that it still counts for a great deal when decisions regarding hiring or tenure are made. One professor tells of the campus interview conducted as part of the hiring process. "When I was here to be interviewed I went out to lunch with the professors, and they were all talking about their students by their first names," the professor says. "I was taken aback by this and thought it patronizing, but after being here a while I know that they were sincere. There is a very strong rapport between the faculty and students, and the administration encourages it." This same professor notes that newer faculty, in particular, have a hard time trusting the administration when it assures them teaching is of paramount importance. "Junior faculty are properly nervous because of their graduate school experience [in which teaching is rarely mentioned]. They're nervous to teach and teach alone, because it's going to decrease productivity in the first six to eight years, and that's when they're being evaluated for tenure. Davidson makes it clear they will reward you for great teaching, but believing that takes a lot of trust."

At the same time, professors are expected to be "professionally active," as one professor puts it, which means that publishing is expected. "If you go back thirty years there has been a significant change. Before the 1970s, publishing was not a significant part of a faculty member's life." This professor sees the encouragement of publishing as a good development, because "the number one criterion is excellence in teaching. The ethos here is very different from a large research university. Our time spent with students is highly prized, but we're looking for people who are active in their fields."

Campus Life: An Honorable Community

Davidson students tend to praise their college very highly because of the friendly atmosphere that prevails, the accessibility of the faculty, the college's commitment to teaching, and the generally high quality of life on campus. Of particular note is the honor code, which is taken very seriously and is rigorously enforced by the students themselves. The code proscribes all dishonest behavior as it relates to classwork or college business, and stipulates that anyone knowing of any violation of the code is "honor bound" to report it immediately, under penalty of violating the code oneself. The penalty for any violation is harsh: "Every student found guilty of a violation shall ordinarily be dismissed from the College." Says a student: "I would turn in a friend, but I've never been faced with that situation."

This code is reportedly enforced with some vigor and helps maintain what is by all accounts a very safe campus, although suburban encroachment from nearby Charlotte has increased petty crime somewhat in recent years. One female senior reports that she sleeps with her dorm room unlocked and that most other students do the same. While this seems unwise, it does indicate the degree of security students feel on campus. A professor notes that "I'm continually surprised at how hard the students are on each other" in enforcing the code. Thus, the "Davidson ethos" spoken of so often is not simply a marketing tool but is grounded in a very real feeling of pride shared by both faculty and students.

Davidson places great importance on maintaining a residence community, and to that end it is able to house from 90 to 95 percent of its student body on campus. This is an extraordinarily high percentage these days, when so many colleges are little more than commuter schools because so many students live off campus in private apartments or houses. Most students are required to live on campus all four years, a move sure to increase the closeness and permanence of the Davidson community. Students choose to take their meals from among several fraternities, women's houses, and other local clubs. None of the clubs or fraternities offers living accommodations, and all must open their doors to diners even though membership in national fraternities is by invitation. No student may be discouraged from joining any of the eating houses.

Davidson is very active on the collegiate athletic scene, fielding eleven men's and ten women's intercollegiate teams at the NCAA Division I varsity level, an extraordinary number for a small liberal arts college. The intramural program is also very strong, with over 90 percent of the student body participating in six sports. There are also eleven club sports in which Davidson teams play other colleges. Thus, Davidson students are nothing if not physically active, at least during their teams' competitive seasons.

DUKE UNIVERSITY

Director of Undergraduate Admissions
2138 Campus Drive
Durham, NC 27706
(919) 684-3214
www.duke.edu

Total enrollment: 11,590
Undergraduates: 6,330
SAT Ranges (Verbal/Math): V 640-730, M 700-750
Financial aid: 44%
Applicants: 12,810
Accepted: 32%
Enrolled: 41%
Application deadline: Jan. 2
Financial aid application deadline: Nov. 1
Tuition: $23,220
Core curriculum: No

The Duke of PC

The Quaker and Methodist farmers who founded Union College in 1838 never imagined that what they had started would become Duke University. The question is,
had they known, would they have still done it? For their idea of a small college
intended to educate teachers has evolved to become not only a modern research
university, but a university nationally known for both the best and worst that academe
has to offer.

Classes at today's Duke University can range from extremely good to nonscholarly and worse. Like many universities, Duke seems willing to pursue the trendiest, most nontraditional programs in an effort to boost its national recognition —
in that pursuit, it has perhaps achieved a Pyrrhic victory. While Duke has attained
the recognition it seeks, it has performed poorly when it comes to the basic task of
a university: providing students with a liberal education.

The university has chosen to offer a wide array of truly strange classes, to use
faddish criteria in making tenure decisions, and to embrace quota-based hiring programs so as to look more diverse. Free speech has been compromised on campus in
some instances, and the school is not at all interested in any curriculum that even
approximates a solid core of liberal learning. Good professors and programs can be
found if one searches, but the chances are good that political correctness and its

various manifestations will make the search difficult, and that in the coming years these things will further obscure the values of this liberal arts university.

Academic Life: This Is Silly Stuff

Students looking for a strong core curriculum at Duke will be disappointed, while those who come to college in search of a wide range of silly political rants posing as college courses will be overjoyed. In providing outrageous topics to its students, Duke is probably ahead of most institutions (i.e., worse than), but its general education requirements are what one might expect from a school that personifies trendiness.

That is to say, there is no true core curriculum at Duke. Students must instead choose a B.A. or B.S. degree in one of thirty-five majors (called "Program I"), or design their own major ("Program II"). Program I is much like that found at other colleges and universities, in that students must fulfill concentration requirements rather than a broad common reading program. This type of setup benefits teachers, both full-time and teaching assistants, rather than students, because it allows departments to fill their introductory classes with warm bodies who are required to be there.

Thus, the 85 percent of undergraduates not majoring in engineering (which has its own requirements) and enrolled in Trinity College, the undergraduate division of arts and sciences, choose courses from five of six areas of knowledge: civilizations, arts and literature, social sciences, quantitative reasoning, natural sciences, and foreign languages. Students must take at least two classes in one of these areas and three in each of the other four, including at least one upper-level course in each of those four. Most students will end up in a few good classes even if they don't try to pick them, but in order to avoid mediocre classes and choose the best, a student must be savvy and well informed — traits that can hardly be expected of eighteen-year-olds. As one undergraduate says, "It is fully possible to get by without reading any of the great works of Western literature, but you'd probably have to read some of the philosophy or political theory and vice versa. If you really tried hard, you could probably get by without any of them, but it would be very difficult."

Program II students design their own curricula and can therefore tailor their studies more specifically to suit their own interests. Recent Program II topics include: Arabic studies, bioethics, human development, Judaic studies, literature and the media, and computer-aided design.

A special option, called the FOCUS Interdisciplinary Programs, is available to incoming freshmen who apply before they arrive in Durham and covers their first semester at the school. FOCUS students choose from among fourteen theme-oriented programs. Each unit is taught by faculty in small classes, and students live in the same freshman residential hall and participate in weekly dinner discussions with their program faculty. The programs that are somewhat traditionalist in content

— and not all are — should provide excellent opportunities for incoming students to learn in a more intimate setting. Faculty speak highly of the FOCUS programs.

Duke does have many outstanding teachers, and serious students should seek them out rather than rely on the curricular structure to land them in classes taught by these professors. According to faculty and students, the best teachers at Duke include Victor Strandberg, Tom Ferraro, Kenny Williams, Reynolds Price, and Michael Moses in English; Bruce Kuniholm in history; Carol Flatch in Russian; Michael Gillespie, Michael Shirley, Peter Feaver, Christopher Gelpi, Albert Eldridge, Peter Lange, John Aldridge, and Allen Kornberg in political science; Diskin Clay and Francis Newton in classics; Sarah Cormack in art history; Alasdair MacIntyre in philosophy; Thomas Pfau in Romance languages; Steve Knowicki in biology; Crawford Goodwin and Neil Demarchi in economics; Ellis Page in educational psychology; John Staddon in psychology; Edna Andrews in Slavic languages; and Ronald Perkins in geology. The departments and programs noted for excellence include political science, economics, Slavic languages and literature, and classical studies.

With careful planning, it is certainly possible for a student to get a good education at Duke. But even a conscientious student cannot escape all of the worst things offered by the university. Duke embraces a huge variety of bizarre and pedagogically useless courses whose principal purpose is to advance and sustain the pseudo-scholarly enterprise that can only thrive when no one calls its bluff. Even by the standards of today's universities, Duke's offerings are notable for their sheer quantity and silliness. If it's weird, it sells at Duke, regardless of whether significant numbers of students are interested. The lack of structure in the curriculum means that, as one student put it, "whatever a student's major, he is going to have at least a couple of very liberal teachers . . . [and] some students do graduate after having taken four years of pure and total nonsense."

The nonsense includes, for starters, several of the areas in which Duke offers certificates, which are awarded in addition to a major. One of these, called "Marxism and Society," announces that it "deals with the contribution of Marxist theory to human studies." The university catalogue goes on to say: "Students learn that scholars of Marxian thought, following the example of Marx himself, have sought to break down the boundaries between disciplines which they feel are obstacles to an appreciation of the wholeness and unity of social life." Students can also pick up a certificate in the "Study of Sexualities." This new program, unveiled in 1996, reviews sexualities past and present from around the world. Says the program's brochure: "Such expressions encompass a wide range from heterosexuality to homosexuality, and include other erotic desires, sexual relationships, and gender roles."

Several departments have also chosen to part ways with traditional scholarship. The Program in Literature, which is different from the English department and is for graduate students only, is littered with Marxists. The chairman of the department, Frederic Jameson, once told *Commentary* magazine that preparing students for the "struggles of the future" was "the supreme mission of a Marxist pedagogy."

Like many trendy universities, Duke offers both a major and minor in women's studies. The department is designed to raise the political awareness of women and, some say, to give high grades, attracting all sorts of unmotivated people into its classes. Other politicized departments, by everyone's reckoning, include cultural anthropology, public policy, African and African-American studies, and drama. And the history department, although it contains some excellent scholars, has taken a turn "toward oppression studies and labor history," according to one faculty member.

Sadly, the religion department is also on the list of departments preferring politics over substance. Duke, long affiliated with the Methodist church, employs some scholars of religion who are better at attacking the Christian tradition than teaching it. "My roommate and I both took Old Testament, each from a different professor," says one student. "Mine was an old, near-retiring man and hers was a middle-aged woman. I learned what I expected to learn: about Scripture. My roommate's class was totally based upon subjectivity, not what was actually written. Her professor took the course to be grounds for teaching how the Bible was unfair to women, and how it opposed her own personal beliefs."

Duke's English department has been for over a decade among the most eager to ape the latest trend in scholarship, regardless of its lack of merit or intellectual weight. Stanley Fish, after being hired away from Johns Hopkins University to be chairman of English, hired as many high-profile Marxists (including Jameson) and assorted poststructuralists as his lavish budget would allow. Fish, who has published a book of essays entitled *There's No Such Thing as Free Speech . . . and It's a Good Thing, Too,* and who once told an audience that he was "fascinated by my own will," was publicly humiliated when he was caught in a lie in his efforts to smear members of Duke's chapter of the National Association of Scholars (NAS). Although he denied passing around a memo calling for blackballing all members from hiring and tenure committees on the basis of their alleged "racism, sexism, and homophobia," his letter calling for just that was published alongside his letter of denial. Although he has left English, he continues to play a major role in the intellectual life of the university through both his work at the university's School of Law and his leadership of Duke University Press, which under his direction has almost ceased publishing scholarly works in favor of the writings of America's foremost nihilists.

In Fish's absence, the English department continues his ideology. As one professor noted, "The English department has invested a lot of appointments in gay and lesbian studies, and they are very politicized." Certain courses from the department stand out as gems of the genre: "Machos, Martyrs, and Mothers of Revenge"; "Unholy Passion? Fictional Representations of Illicit Desire"; and "Adult Pleasures," whose course description states that "from sexuality's most radical limits, this course will develop a vocabulary to analyze both literature and film. . . . Sadomasochism and fetishism will be studied in both media. . . . Loosely speaking, queer politics will motivate this study of sexual arenas that society often dismisses as 'perverse.'" Topics of discussion in "Cultural Studies" include "identifications and desires that cross normative gender/sexual distinctions; drag and other gender performances (particularly the role of the diva); . . . sadomasochism and leather culture." The director of undergraduate studies in the department of English, along with the director of English graduate studies, are coeditors of a book titled *Displacing Homophobia: Gay Male Perspectives in Literature and Culture.*

Theory has emerged supreme in literary studies over the past decade and a half, and we are now faced with a generation of scholars who are largely unfamiliar with the primary texts of their own field. This result is illustrated in the case of a student who, like many others at Duke, was taught by faculty more fascinated with methodology and secondary, scholarly literature than with the literature itself. While being interviewed for a very prestigious national academic award, the student was asked to recite a favorite poem of the literary figure who was the subject of his senior thesis. And yet no poem was known to the student, who had not read the works that made this literary figure famous, but only theoretical secondary works written by and for scholars.

Political Atmosphere: Seeking the Heat

Many of the curricular and political problems at Duke stem from the university's attempt to buy its way into the academic upper crust through the wholesale purchase of other universities' most visible purveyors of the school of thought commonly known as postmodernism. These professors, who usually draw higher salaries and more perks than the regular faculty, come to Duke with the understanding that they can hire their own kind and develop programs conducive to the advancement of their own reputations and ideologies. Duke plays the ratings game as well as any school in the country, and it is richly rewarded by those self-regarding judges of higher education who publish commercialized annual surveys purporting to tell which schools are hot and which are cool. Duke, by this measure, is aflame.

At Duke the process of politicization begins with the students' arrival on campus. There are the usual (they're common on most campuses) orientation meetings on racism and sexism and rape and homophobia, but, as one student notes, "there's no real force involved." The next installment is the "University Writing" course, the only course at Duke required of all students, which, according to another student, "is pretty much filled with English department graduate students who are usually very liberal."

As a student's time at Duke progresses, wildly liberal professors become even more unavoidable. Many of Duke's younger faculty members are more willing to politicize their courses than are their older colleagues. "The younger members of the faculty are much more liberal [than their elders]," says one student. "However, the older ones are often scared to be bold in their more conservative views and often present certain things that may oppose their normal ideas. They are simply scared that they will not be thought to be open-minded. In other words, the older members of the faculty are over-compensating to the left-wing agenda."

In 1988 the faculty senate voted to require all fifty-six departments to hire at least one more black professor by 1993. The result? Over the next five years the university hired nineteen black professors, but lost fourteen of those already on staff when the hiring demand was made. Duke wound up with only a handful more black professors than it had in 1988. Duke's explicit quota-hiring program failed because similar minority-hiring pushes all over the country attenuated the pool of black scholars. Says one senior scholar: "It is extremely difficult to hire minority faculty, and those who do come want more money."

Politicization at Duke is not limited to the faculty. Several student groups, with administration support, also push the concepts of multiculturalism. Among these are ethnic organizations that complain constantly about a perceived "lack of diversity." These include: Spectrum, the Black Student Alliance, and Mi Gente (a Hispanic group). The Mary Lou Williams Center promotes black culture. Spectrum is also given prime living space on Duke's West Campus, so that people who want to de-emphasize Western culture can all live together.

Duke has a speakers' program that often hosts forums on multiculturalism, imperialism, and the evils of Western civilization. The administration gingerly avoids the appearance of disagreeing with any radical or minority group. In 1997 the *Duke Review,* the monthly student newspaper considered much more conservative than its daily counterpart, the *Chronicle,* ran an article in which the laziness of some Duke employees was criticized. The story was accompanied by photographs of several university employees lounging rather than working, and some of the employees pictured were black. About the same time, two white university police officers arrested a black student who was later exonerated of the charges against him. An uproar ensued in which the *Review* as well as the officers was accused of racism and insensitivity. Duke president Nan Keohane offered a public apology and stated that both officers were punished, even though an internal investigation exonerated them of racial intent. Several years earlier, three hundred copies of the *Review* were stolen from a pickup point on campus. A black student was caught and found guilty of the theft, but his conviction was overturned by Duke vice president Janet Dickerson, thus signaling that it is permissible to steal others' property and to deny students the opportunity to read a conservative newspaper. Free speech, it seems, exists on a sliding scale at Duke.

Despite all this, some members of the Duke community believe the academic climate has improved a bit in recent years. "I don't feel personally threatened by political correctness on campus," says a senior professor. Another states that "the general atmosphere is extremely open, frank, and tolerant." Still, the professor who doesn't feel threatened also advises untenured colleagues to avoid joining any group, such as the NAS, that is viewed as hostile to the so-called progressive professoriate that upholds the new orthodoxies. One might conclude that while senior faculty who are firmly entrenched in the university may indeed be able to speak their minds at will, younger scholars who hope to join them on the high ground called tenure would do well to keep any heterodox thoughts to themselves.

The cost of finding oneself in just such a predicament became painfully clear several years ago when Timothy Lomperis, a Duke Ph.D. who was up for tenure in the political science department, was denied tenure despite a reputation as an outstanding teacher and an excellent publication record that included three books, numerous articles, and a fourth book accepted by Yale University Press. In a bitter fight that split the department, Lomperis lost on appeal and is today chairman of the political science department at St. Louis University. Published accounts note that members of the NAS split their vote evenly, three for and three against, which indicates a level of personal disagreement as well as, on the part of some, political differences. The story made the editorial page of the *Wall Street Journal* when it broke, and still receives attention at Duke, where some faculty members are researching the case.

Perhaps the most effective way to gauge the influence of politicization is to check with those most likely to be affected: the students. Though many students are young enough to be impressionable, some of the better ones — and Duke can attract some talented young people — resent the sheer silliness of the PC police and ignore them.

Student Life: Enough to Go Around

A few years ago the accomplished Southern author Reynolds Price, who teaches at Duke, said in an interview with the *Atlanta Journal* that he wished Duke's student body were more studious and intellectually oriented. So many students, Price noted, are so hungover on Fridays that carrying on a normal class is difficult. These charges, coming as they did from a respected author, North Carolina native, and James B. Duke Professor of English, stung the university because they punctured its carefully cultivated image as an intellectual powerhouse equal to any college found in the North. Spurred by such criticism, the administration has taken several steps in recent years to curb students' drinking habits. Kegs and open parties are now banned during the Greek system's rush period, for example, and the Greeks must now hire an expensive university-approved bartender for all parties at which alcohol is served.

In any case, many students at Duke enjoy their educational experience because it is still possible to find dedicated faculty in their fields of interest. A student who finds these professors tends to stick with them, and a close mentor-pupil relationship may develop. One student notes that many students, especially those from the South, tend to have fairly traditional views. According to the student, those who come to Durham from the Northeast bring with them more liberal views, generally speaking. And the two groups generally tolerate each other. "Duke is comfortable for conservative students who are strong in their beliefs and willing to challenge those who oppose them," the student says. "There is usually somebody who agrees with me on certain topics and who will help to back me up."

At the same time, many students, with faculty and administrative backing, are very vocal and are always willing to attack students such as the one quoted above. "Generally, the students are more conservative than the faculty, but there's a large contingent of left-of-centers here. That means everyone from the radical feminists to the simply socially and economically tenderhearted," another student says. "I have never had much of a problem speaking in class when I think something needs to be said, but there have certainly been times when I was glad looks couldn't kill."

Regardless of the student body's diverse political leanings, all hold at least one thing in common: the Duke Blue Devils. The university's first-class athletic program is exceptional because it successfully balances sports with academics — a difficult feat in an age of rampant NCAA violations and double standards for scholarship athletes. The university is properly proud of its scholar-athletes, who not only display prowess in competition but also achieve a remarkable 95 percent on-time graduation rate, a percentage that embarrasses most of Duke's rivals. Duke's stellar sports program is spearheaded by its men's basketball team (cheered on by the no-holds-barred "Cameron Crazies" in the student section), and includes superb competitors in men's and women's soccer and women's tennis. All of these teams regularly rank near the top of their respective divisions. Baseball, field hockey, football, fencing, golf, and wrestling are also popular. Duke boasts more than thirty club sports, including ice hockey, water polo, and skydiving, but some students complain that not enough attention is paid to average athletes, and that, compared to the glamorous varsity players, "mere mortals get overcrowded gyms and mediocre equipment," in the words of one student. University facilities, nevertheless, are impressive in their variety and include a recently renovated football stadium, two gymnasiums, indoor and outdoor swimming pools, a golf course, nearly forty tennis courts, a track, and acres of athletic and recreational fields. Students can also stroll the trails of the 7,500-acre Duke Forest.

The undergraduate population at Duke exceeds six thousand, but the university states that it will fund the entire demonstrated financial need of each student, and that admissions decisions are made with no consideration for the student's ability to pay. Less than 15 percent of the student body is from North Carolina, and students come to Duke from all fifty states plus forty foreign lands. About one-quarter of a recent incoming class were "students of color," according to the university. About two-thirds of Duke students attended public high schools, with the remaining third graduating from private or parochial high schools. Nearly 90 percent ranked in the top tenth of their high school classes, and 98 percent of Duke freshmen indicated on a survey that they considered themselves to be of "superior" academic ability.

Each student at Duke should be able to find something that matches his interests. "Duke is good at providing something for everyone. No matter what your interests, you can find a place to do it here, and usually you can find other people who want to do it, too," one student says. "You can live pretty much unmolested, or you can make yourself a nuisance and/or a target. Some Dukies take themselves way too seriously, others are happy to take their studies seriously. This place is what you make of it."

EMORY UNIVERSITY

Office of Admissions
Boisfeuillet Jones Center
Atlanta, GA 30322
(404) 727-6036
www.eckerd.edu

Total enrollment: 11,109
Undergraduates: 5,996
SAT Ranges (Verbal/Math): V 630-700, M 650-710
Financial aid: 73%
Applicants: 9,781
Accepted: 46%
Enrolled: 28%
Application deadline: Jan. 15
Financial aid application deadline: Feb. 15
Tuition: $20,870
Core curriculum: Yes

The Real Thing?

The Methodist church leaders who founded Emory College in 1836 had certainly never heard of Coca-Cola. It was, however, a fortune created by this soft drink company that has permitted the Atlanta college to compete nationwide for professors, programs, and renown. In 1979 a $105 million gift from Emory alumnus Robert Woodruff, then CEO of Atlanta-based Coca-Cola Inc., vaulted Emory to a national prominence it had not previously enjoyed.

Whether Emory becomes "the real thing" in terms of educational quality remains to be seen. The university enrolls only 28 percent of the students it accepts, indicating that for most students it is a second or third choice. Add to the equation the fact that the Emory administration has vowed in the past to make the institution "a model of multicultural diversity," and the result is: mostly second-tier students being taught by professors who are becoming increasingly radical. However, the student body is, by most measures, better today than in the past.

Emory certainly began as a traditional liberal arts school. The institution was founded to provide for the education of clergymen and civic leaders. For many decades afterward, Emory provided Southern parents a place to send their children to establish contacts in the professional world or become United Methodist ministers. After moving to its present campus in the upper-middle-class Druid Hills region of Atlanta in 1919, it boasted some excellent faculty and maintained a decent medical school, hospital, and school of theology, but made no pretensions to being a national university along the lines of Columbia or Princeton. This is not to say that it did not give its students a good general education in a pleasant setting. As a small liberal arts college, it succeeded in producing generations of successful graduates, including literally hundreds of Methodist church leaders. Yet it rarely cast a shadow beyond its home in the Deep South.

Now, with an endowment well over $4 billion (the sixth largest in the nation), Emory University can buy whatever it likes, and the changes of the past two decades have brought increasing fame and prestige to its pretty but increasingly crowded campus. Emory has plucked famous faculty from universities across the country by offering better salaries, a hospitable climate, and a home in one of the most economically dynamic cities in the nation. Perhaps the most notable changes have come in the sciences and medical school. Drawing strength from the Centers for Disease Control and Prevention and the American Cancer Society, both of which are located on campus, the medical school and hospital set the standard against which health care in Georgia is measured. The university is closely associated with the Jimmy Carter Center and owns the Yerkes Regional Primate Research Center. Departments that once employed a dozen or so faculty have doubled in size, and new buildings filled with the latest scientific equipment have sprung up all over campus. Indeed, a visitor returning to campus after several years' absence might well feel discombobulated to find much of the college's green space now filled with buildings.

While the facilities may be wonderful, the university seems determined to use its wealth to tilt for national ratings and publicity. These contests, driven by identification with the latest intellectual fad, are for sale, and Emory, more than most universities, can afford the price. Emory does offer much that is positive and valuable to anyone seeking a good liberal arts education: it is a dynamic campus in a fast-growing city, has established a huge endowment, and employs many excellent professors in numerous fields of study. And yet, the administration maintains that the true measure of education is not a search for truth or the formation of well-rounded individuals, but an adherence to fashions and fads that blow continually through the academic world. Without a measure against which the quality of ideas can be determined, higher education becomes politicized and ephemeral.

Academic Life: National Rankings at What Cost?

While Emory does employ many dedicated, excellent teachers and writers, the current ethos in higher education rewards not a traditional approach to liberal learning but one that recognizes and seizes temporal intellectual trends. Excellence in humanities and social science departments relies less on new buildings, equipment, and research grants than on the visions of those employed to research and write about history, literature, languages, and the other divisions of liberal learning. Thus, the impact of the Woodruff gift on these areas is more mixed, despite expenditures on a scale similar to that spent on the sciences.

The Emory administration's status-conscious approach has resulted in policies that often attack traditional learning openly and, at other times, subvert the curriculum through quieter yet more effective means. Yet these policies have not always taken root. A recent attempt to reform the core curriculum began on a very somber note but has, surprisingly, taken a turn for the better. The old curriculum, inasmuch as it had a core of any type, simply required students to choose from a variety of disciplines and was designed more to fulfill departmental wishes for students than to insure that Emory's graduates received a well-rounded liberal arts education. Although the plan for revamping the curriculum was, as one professor put it, an "absolute abomination," it was presented to the university community and the public as a return to a more traditional curriculum. As supporting evidence, the new plan noted that the so-called cafeteria approach to higher education found in the previous core curriculum was a failure because it was instituted in the 1960s and 1970s when faculty and administrators were loath to assign values to courses or disciplines.

The new plan was billed as a resurrection of the pre-1960s curricular structure, but in reality it had a 1990s twist: the plan judiciously employed such code words as "diversity," "pluralistic," "complex," "global," and "ethnicity." Ultimately, the more egregious defects in the original proposal were omitted in favor of a fairly rigorous set of courses that, when completed, will provide the student with some, if not all, of the ingredients of liberal learning. The new curriculum, while not perfect, is certainly a positive step away from the system of education through distribution requirements enacted in the 1960s.

Fulfilling the distribution requirements at Emory entails completing courses from six different areas of study: (1) "Tools of Learning," which consists of English composition and the writing of a major research paper in each of the following years of study as well as a selection from mathematics followed by economics or other social science or humanities courses; (2) "Natural Science and Mathematics"; (3) "Historical Perspective of the Western World," which includes offerings from many humanities and social science departments; (4) "The Individual and Society"; (5) "Aesthetics and Values"; and (6) "Health and Physical Education." These requirements are a bit more ambitious than those found at many other universities. While they do not add up to anything approaching a core curriculum, they force the student to take a reasonable load of courses while offering many excellent choices. Some of the classes are politicized, but many are not, and the discerning student can choose a set of courses that imparts a broad range of knowledge.

As is the case at many schools, there is at Emory a sizable though shrinking coterie of senior faculty who, whatever their personal politics, still believes in objective scholarship and rigorous teaching. As older professors retire, however, they are being replaced by young Ph.D.s from universities with very radicalized graduate programs. These professors, along with the members of the '60s generation to whom they look for guidance, are gaining strength on campus, and their influence on Emory's intellectual life is already making itself known through the enforcement of speech and harassment codes that hinder the free exchange of ideas, which is essential to true academic debate.

While most departments contain some radicalism, some stand out as particularly scornful of traditional teaching. The women's studies, African-American studies, and Romance languages departments, along with the Institute for Liberal Arts, harbor a number of trendy intellectuals who revel in denouncing the evils of Western culture, male hegemony, and ethnocentrism. Rather than academic departments, they are, in the words of one professor, "mere political parties."

Particularly egregious — especially in a school founded by and for Methodists — is the politicization found in the religion department and the Candler School of Theology, both of which employ numerous professors for whom religion is little more than a social construct peculiar to a specific time and place. Along with traditional courses on Christian history, ethics, and world religions, students may choose from a broad selection of topics that place less emphasis on traditional approaches to the study of religion than on gender, class, race, disabilities, and social activism. The religion department expects all students and faculty to adhere to a statement on inclusive language that forbids the use of "man," "mankind," or "he" to denote all persons.

The school of theology and the religion department, which are separate entities, have reputations as two of the more politicized elements on campus. But amidst an increasingly homogeneous crew of activists posing as academics are quite a few respectable, dedicated, and even distinguished faculty members and departments. Among the former are Elizabeth Fox-Genovese, Ken Stein, Patrick Allitt, and Thomas Burns of the history department; Merle Black, Harvey Klehr, Randy Strayham, and Steve Couts of the political science department; Donald Livingston, Philip Verene, James Gouinlock, and Ann Hartel of the philosophy department; and Luke Timothy Johnson and James Gustafson of the school of theology. Among the strongest departments are history, political science, and many of the sciences, which benefited most from the large sums of money spent in recent years. Psychology is also said to be excellent.

The work ethic at Emory is probably more developed than at many universities. Many students, aiming at prestigious graduate schools, are quite serious, yet the overall atmosphere is relaxed and Southern. Class sizes are generally small, and professors are available for private meetings. Most teachers consider class discussions as important as written work, and the many guided research projects and reading programs further encourage professor-student relationships. A bright student can still obtain a very good education at Emory, but he will need foresight, a strong character, and a bit of luck. While excellent professors are available, it is impossible to graduate without encountering many classes taught by ideologues whose mediocrity is masked by their adherence to trendy fields of study.

Political Atmosphere: Speak at Your Own Risk

A few years ago a group of students launched a campaign against Emory's speech code — which demonstrated that they were "much braver than the faculty," as one member of that group put it. Despite their bravery, the effort failed to overturn the code, which bans "discriminatory harassment," defined as "conduct (oral, written, graphic, or physical) directed against any person or group . . . that has the purpose or reasonably foreseeable effect of creating an offensive, demeaning, intimidating, or hostile environment." The result has been that when students and faculty broach controversial issues — if they do so at all — they broach them with trepidation. As one professor notes, speaking one's mind on academic matters involving gender and race is "just too damn risky." "People keep their mouths shut," says another, adding that to exercise one's First Amendment rights to free speech is to invite social and professional ostracism, ridicule, and even legal trouble.

The survival of the speech code is not the only event to deter all but the boldest faculty from taking public stances against new ideologues. Recently a nationally prominent scholar of women's issues faced a spurious charge after she dared to criticize her fellow feminists for their ahistorical scholarship and professional ax grinding. When the book *The Bell Curve* was published in 1994 by Charles Murray and the late Richard Herrnstein, a panel of four Emory professors from fields related to the book's topic of race and intelligence was convened; all four adopted the accepted position that the work was so viciously racist that it could not be taken as serious scholarship. Yet in the heated debate that ensued, two of the four professors admitted that they had not read the work, a fact that is hardly comforting to those who still think of colleges as places where the key issues of our day are settled by informed and dispassionate scholars.

Only the judicious intervention of a wise administrator saved another professor from being sued for sexual harassment. His crime? He noted that a prominent social critic had paid insufficient attention to the congenital differences between men and women. To suggest that men and women differ from one another was to invite a lawsuit on the nebulous charge of sexual harassment. "If I was younger, I'd be dismayed," a senior faculty member says. "Bright young people are dismayed because of the intolerance that abounds. There is a lack of opportunity for them."

A similar level of intolerance reigns in the speakers program. When Associate Supreme Court Justice Clarence Thomas was invited to speak on campus in 1990, the dean of the law school refused to meet with him, just as he had refused to see Attorney General Edwin Meese in 1988. In the fall of 1996, campus Young Republicans attempted to obtain university funds to bring to campus Starr Parker, a black woman and former welfare recipient who is now an entrepreneur and spokeswoman for black conservatism. Although the student council voted overwhelmingly to sponsor the event, the council president, a student, vetoed her appearance because Mrs. Parker was rumored to be critical of homosexuality. University president William Chase, the former president of Wesleyan College in Connecticut who has vowed to make Emory a model of multicultural education, refused to allot any of his discretionary funds for Parker's appearance, which was eventually sponsored by sources outside the university community. Yet Emory has hosted recently a large number of controversial speakers, including rap singer Sister Souljah, Patricia Ireland of the National Organization for Women, former surgeon general Joycelyn Elders, former Communist Party vice presidential candidate Angela Davis, and radical feminist June Jordan.

Curiously, the strongest opposition to these actions has come not from the faculty but from students. Given the threat of legal action outlined above, it is somewhat understandable that many faculty members would be loath to risk home and savings in the defense of scholarly integrity, although one could wish for a stronger stand. Yet many faculty are cowed by a different fear, one known to adolescents everywhere: social ostracism. Beyond the actions of a few brave souls who, in fact, are often thanked privately by colleagues too fearful to speak up in public, the defense of freedom of speech on campus often falls to students, who by their nature are more fearless and transient than their teachers.

That the exercise of clear thinking and common sense will result in controversy is a fact driven home to freshmen as soon as they arrive on campus. All new students must take a freshman seminar during which they are often exposed to a barrage of propaganda on sexuality — propaganda that assaults the values and beliefs of the majority of students. This seminar, which one professor termed a "failure," is to be replaced with a course that offers more opportunity for good faculty to teach in a more traditional setting, although it will not prevent radicals from propagandizing in their own sections. Until that new program is instituted, however, many students will continue to find that their first exposure to the life of the mind as promulgated by Emory faculty is designed less to educate than to indoctrinate. A Southern woman, who termed her freshman seminar her "worst experience at Emory," was asked by her seminar leader whether her father was her mother's brother. That the student's brother, she was told, suffered from mental problems was obvious by his choice of college (not Emory), while an illness from which she suffered her freshman year demonstrated that she was the physically sickly child of the family — both facts of which, taken together, suggested incest. While many Emory students hail from other regions of the country, those born closer to Atlanta may find themselves quite unwelcome by such professors. The welcome may be even ruder should they choose to think for themselves.

Student Life: Metropolitan Choices

Naturally, campus life is not all work and no play. Although Emory does not field a varsity football team, students enthusiastically support nine intercollegiate teams for men and eight for women, and forty intramural teams for each sex. There are no athletic scholarships, and sports stars are not idolized on campus. But the sports facilities are excellent: tennis courts, a huge new gymnasium, and an Olympic-sized swimming pool. Nature lovers enjoy Lullwater, a park that adjoins the campus and features walking trails, fields, and a small lake.

The 630-acre campus is itself an attraction, with its gentle hills, spreading trees, and pretty — though shrinking — green space. Buildings are colorful and rather grand, with marble facades and red roofs. The Woodruff money has generated a rush of new construction, including a library and new residential halls. Other impressive facilities have also sprouted recently, most notably a large research/science center, a student center, and an art and archaeology museum.

All this expansion has enabled Emory to inject new vitality into campus life. There are two hundred groups and organizations, including Amnesty International; College Republicans; Young Democrats; Alternative Spring Break (which sends students on service-oriented projects); various religious, ethnic, and cultural groups; and Emory's Amazing Throwing Up Society, a juggling club.

Emory has twenty-five fraternities and sororities, to which about half the students belong. The Greeks lead the social scene but don't dominate it; there are simply too many attractive alternatives. When students want a break from campus life, downtown Atlanta is only five miles away. There they find myriad cultural attractions, as well as a multitude of cinemas, malls, gardens, bars, and restaurants. The Metropolitan Atlanta Rapid Transportation System (MARTA) goes to all parts of the city. Students can also find many amenities within walking distance of the university. Crime is not a major problem at Emory, and the campus security system is excellent. Drug use stays in the closet; alcohol use does not.

Housing at Emory has been in shorter supply recently because freshman classes have been getting larger. Many students prefer to live in apartments or fraternities, however, and almost all students who desire university housing receive it. Freshmen must live on campus; upperclassmen's housing is determined by lottery. All dormitories are coed except for one allotted to women. Comfort levels range from doubles with no sink to small apartments with kitchens.

FLORIDA STATE UNIVERSITY

Office of Admissions
A2500 University Center
Florida State University
Tallahassee, FL 32306-1009
(904) 644-6200
www.fsu.edu

Total enrollment: 30,519
Undergraduates: 22,850
SAT Ranges (Verbal/Math): V 460-570, M 520-630
Financial aid: 60%
Applicants: 16,402
Accepted: 73%
Enrolled: 30%
Application deadline: Mar. 1
Financial aid application deadline: Mar. 1
Tuition: resident, $1,987.80; nonresident, $7,904.40
Core curriculum: No

Party On?

Florida State University (FSU) has already topped the list in one college guide: *Rolling Stone* magazine, with its tongue only partially in its cheek, recently named FSU the number one party school in the nation. Since the priorities in this college guide are somewhat different from those of *Rolling Stone,* we can't be as generous in our evaluation of FSU. Unfortunately, FSU is not as strong in terms of a traditional liberal arts education, unless one pursues a major in classics or takes classes in the economics department, which recently received a $10 million gift earmarked for the teaching of market economics.

FSU is a public institution, part of the State University System of Florida, which was founded in 1857. What is now FSU began as the Florida State College for Women, and went coeducational in 1947; many of the first men on campus came via the GI Bill. With a main campus on 418 acres in the state capital, Tallahassee, the university operates a smaller extension campus in Panama City, as well as a Seminole Reservation recreational facility; a Marine Laboratory on the Gulf Coast; and facilities at Innovation Park in Tallahassee, which include the Florida A & M University/FSU College of Engineering, the university computing center, the Division of Research, the National High Magnetic Field Laboratory, and the university radio and television studios. More than thirty thousand students (about three-quarters of which are undergraduates) enjoy the four-season climate of the Florida panhandle — a climate different from that of West Palm Beach or Sarasota, for example. They also love their football team.

Academic Life: The Illiberal Arts

In its promotional materials, the FSU administration informs prospective students that the university wants to provide an education broader than one "narrowly focused on acquisition of skills needed to secure your first job." Consequently, the university encourages students to take courses in the liberal arts. But the administration at FSU, like so many across America, has a rather muddled understanding of what constitutes the liberal arts tradition. Indeed, FSU sees the liberal arts through the clouded lens of multiculturalism.

The university has not so much required a certain number of multicultural courses as it has incorporated the ideology across the entire undergraduate curriculum. Undergraduate students are required to undertake a comparative study of Western and non-Western traditions, thinking not only about their own culture but how it relates to every existing stream of thought, including ethnic and gender-based interpretations of human history. It doesn't sound so bad, until one realizes that the curriculum at FSU doesn't live up to the more enlightened sense of multiculturalism, and that most courses there shortchange Western culture for trendier brands of indoctrination.

FSU has sixteen major academic divisions, including Arts and Sciences, Business, Communication, Education, Engineering, Human Sciences, Law, Social Sciences, Criminology and Criminal Justice, Film (Motion Picture, Television, and Recording Arts), Information Studies, Music, Nursing, Social Work, Theatre, and Visual Arts and Dance.

The College of Arts and Sciences comprises nineteen departments, six institutes, and ten interdisciplinary programs. Departmental majors include most traditional disciplines, along with the more unusual majors in meteorology, English with an emphasis in business, and Latin and Caribbean studies, both with and without an emphasis in business.

The College of Social Sciences, a separate college since 1973, is home to twelve departments, including the very fine department of economics, both a Black Studies Program and a center for African-American culture, and other departments dedicated to urban planning and public policy. In keeping with Florida's position as the state with the oldest population, this college also maintains the Pepper Institute on Aging.

FSU students in these two colleges, like those in the other divisions of the university, are required to come up with 120 credit hours in order to graduate. Each student must also pass the College Level Academic Skills Test (which includes sections on algebra and vocabulary, among others) in order to return to FSU as a junior. General education requirements, however, are determined by a student's major, meaning that not only does FSU lack a common core curriculum, it even lacks a list of distribution requirements that would at least be common to all students. The major-determined distribution requirements are also said to be among the easiest courses offered by the university. For what they're worth, the requirements generally include two math courses and two English courses (each set completed with a C-minus or better), one history course, one social science course, a literature course, a fine arts course, and two natural sciences (one with an associated lab). Students seeking a B.A. degree must display proficiency in a foreign language at the intermediate level.

Then there are the two multicultural requirements. The first, one class designated as a "cross cultural course," is known as "the X requirement." The second, also one class, comes from a group called "Diversity in Western Culture," and is known as "the Y requirement." If these sound like concessions to current academic trends, they are. "The X and Y requirements are nothing more than indoctrination courses," says a student. "We have to take classes like women's studies, African-American studies, and other courses taught from an ideological point of view."

FSU also has an unusual requirement known as "The Gordon Rule." This rule demands that each student write twenty-four thousand words in English, history, and humanities classes during his time as a student. Half the words must be committed to paper in English classes, while the other half must come from history and the humanities; courses from which writing will count toward the Gordon Rule must be completed with a C-minus or better. Obviously, this requirement is intended to improve the writing skills of FSU undergraduates, but there is some question on campus as to whether this objective is regularly achieved.

Freshmen and sophomores meet in very large classes, which shrink only in the third and fourth years (or fifth year — 60 percent of incoming freshmen graduate in five years). Likewise, very few student-faculty relationships become close until the students' junior and senior years.

One professor notes that "if a serious student comes to FSU, he can get a good education." This would be not because of the university's curricular structure, but in spite of it. Certain teachers are excellent, and the departments of classics and economics are well thought of by traditional scholars. In the economics department, look for professors Bruce L. Benson, James D. Gwartney, and Randall G. Holcombe. In classics, find Leon Golden for classes on classical Greek thought, or Joseph Plescia, who specializes in Roman law. Other departments boast very good faculty as well, including Thomas R. Dye and Charles E. Billings in government, Edward F. Keuchel in history, and Douglas R. Fowler in English.

The economics department is open-minded enough (a rare trait in today's academe) to represent several economic theories, including the Chicago School (the monetarist theories of Milton Friedman), the Austrian School of Friedrich Hayek and

Ludwig von Mises, and the Keynesian School. The department provides under-graduates with an education in free-market economics, another rarity these days. The breadth of the educational curriculum and the interests of the faculty ensure a comprehensive approach to this objective, and the economics department holds the business school's finance department in such high regard that it frequently recom-mends that interested students take finance courses to complement their economics coursework.

FSU's classics department is in top form when it focuses on the texts of the Western tradition in Greek and Latin. This department also offers courses in archaeology, and many students are attracted to the educational opportunities for foreign travel offered by several archaeological projects — and therefore are ex-posed to the more traditional elements of the department as well. Classics students have taken part in digs and surveys in a number of countries, including Italy, Greece, Cyprus, England, Israel, and Ukraine. While many students are attracted to classics for the classical archaeology degree, they may also major in Latin, Greek, or classics. The classics degree can be taken with concentrations in classical civi-lizations, ancient history, Greek, or Latin. There is also a joint major in classics and religion, and the department is involved in cooperative ventures with humanities and comparative and world literature. Some of the classes offered through the classics department are increasingly rare on campuses, and it is refreshing to find them listed in the catalogue of a large state university. These include "Greek Prose Writers," "Greek Drama," "Greek Poetry," "Greek Philosophical Writings," "Litera-ture of the Republic," "Literature of the Augustan Age," and "The Roman Historians and Cicero."

Other departments are in worse shape. One such is sociology, which is divided among demographers and ideologues. The demographers in the department are technically oriented, whereas the other group is highly politicized, placing heavy emphasis on race relations, ethnicity, gender roles, and deviancy.

Political Atmosphere: Wining and Dining

The president of FSU since 1994, Talbot "Sandy" D'Alemberte, is a former dean of the FSU College of Law and past president of both the American Bar Association and the American Judicature Society. Although D'Alemberte is politically liberal, he is "not a meddler," an FSU professor says. "Most of his day-to-day operations pertain to fundraising and representing the university. FSU is a mega-university that has so many dimensions — it would be difficult to mold it from the top down."

The exception to this governance comes in the area of faculty hiring and promotions. The FSU administration is seeking to improve its image by hiring bigger names: professors who are frequently cited and at the top of their fields, and those who are published in academically hot journals. The tenure process, however, has reportedly not fallen victim to the affirmative action or politicization rampant at so many other big state universities.

There is one other facet of life at FSU that has survived onslaughts from the crusaders of political correctness: the school's sports teams are still known as the Seminoles, despite a movement to rid teams across the country of mascots deemed to be racist or offensive to certain groups. FSU's teams are represented by Chief Osceola and his horse, Renegade, and the chief dresses as a stereotypical "Indian," complete with war paint and feathered headdress. The fact that the nickname and mascot appear immune to all assaults is due less to a principled stand against political correctness than to stubborn fan support. Nonetheless, the administration has been forced to defend the symbol, arguing that Chief Osceola actually advances the cause of multiculturalism. "Florida State's historic identification with the heroic Seminole Tribe of Florida is a proud tradition," D'Alemberte wrote in *USA Today*. "Chief Osceola, astride his Appaloosa when he plants a flaming spear on the 50-yard line, ignites a furious enthusiasm and loyalty in thousands of football fans, but also salutes a people who have proven that perseverance with integrity prevails."

The administration has also shown that it will buck academic trends to support the study of free enterprise — at least when the price is right. Again, this decision seems based more on pragmatism than on philosophy, as the question only came up when entrepreneur and philanthropist Devoe Moore offered the university $5 million for the study of "public choice" issues (public choice is a branch of economics that is friendly to the free market). The state matched the gift, bringing the total to $10 million. The money will be used to establish the Devoe Moore Center for the Study of Critical Issues in Economic Policy and Government, which will study the effects of bureaucracy and regulation on the economy. While the administration was more than glad to accept the money, some liberal faculty members were opposed to the gift, calling it a "bribe" and an effort "to dictate the curriculum."

Student Life: Animal House?

Reportedly, a sizable minority of the FSU student body is unhappy with the university's new title as *Rolling Stone*'s top party school. One professor did allow that some students "seem more interested in the weekend than the weekday." However, another faculty member pointed out that, at around 150,000 residents, Tallahassee is not a large city and thus the FSU party life, which is centered primarily at the more than forty-five Greek organizations on campus, is overrated and appears proportionately larger than it actually is. Indeed, fewer than 20 percent of both male and female students join a fraternity, and on-campus activities often occur at the Oglesby Union, rather tamely appointed with various lounges, a bowling alley, a movie theater, a coffee house, restaurants, and a travel agency.

According to public relation materials from the Tallahassee city government,

FSU's hometown is more of a quiet, balmy Southern town than the equivalent of an open bar. "The community prizes its canopy roads, moss-draped oaks and springtime profusion of dogwoods, azaleas and wisteria," Tallahassee says of itself. "Tallahassee has the mild, moist climate characteristic of the Gulf States, and experiences a sub-tropical summer similar to the rest of Florida. However, in contrast to the Florida peninsula itself, the panhandle, of which Tallahassee is a part, experiences four seasons." Tallahassee says it is a part of the " 'other Florida,' with its rolling hills, canopy roads, mild climate and Southern hospitality."

Student residents choose from several dormitories, but assignments are made on a first-come, first-served basis. Options include coed, all-male, or all-female halls. In addition, students may indicate in the application process how many hours of the day they wish to have visitors of the opposite sex.

Some residences are dedicated to special interests, though none is as politicized as those found at some other institutions. One hall has a floor reserved for women studying the sciences, math, or engineering. Another dorm is home to a program for students "interested in developing leadership skills." One dorm is set aside for transfer students in their first year at FSU, and another has "a wellness and physical fitness emphasis," according to university publications.

Florida State loves its football team. Since beginning Atlantic Coast Conference play in 1992, FSU has lost only one conference game (to the University of Virginia) — an accomplishment that pales in comparison to its constant high ranking in national polls. Seminole players are fixtures in the NFL draft's early rounds. There are, of course, other sports at FSU — in all, eight men's teams and nine for women. The school's emphasis on athletics, and football in particular, is shown by recent construction projects. The Bobby E. Leach Center, a $12.9 million student recreation facility, opened in 1991 and houses a gymnasium, spas, racquetball and squash courts, weight and fitness rooms, an indoor track, and other recreational spaces. But that expense looks like pocket change compared to the incredible $90 million spent to renovate the football team's home, Doak Campbell Stadium. The funds were appropriated by the state legislature with help from some FSU alumni serving there. Far from being embarrassed by the huge price tag, the FSU administration, in a May 1997 press release, said, without blushing, that the money "serves as a powerful testament to the political maturity of FSU alumni in the state legislature."

Apart from athletic facilities, the university also recently added a new Media Center and the Heritage Tower. The latter commemorates the university's admittance of male students, and authors William Styron, Kurt Vonnegut Jr., and Joseph Heller (not FSU grads, but World War II veterans who wrote about the war in rather different manners) were also invited to campus to celebrate the presence of veterans in the initial groups of male students.

While there are many student groups on campus, one bears mentioning as most unusual: the FSU Flying High Circus. Started in the late 1940s, the circus has evolved into a professional-quality endeavor, featuring fabulous tricks like triple somersaults on the flying trapeze, a seven-man pyramid on the high wire, and double back somersaults off a sky pole. The circus is entirely self-supporting, using no student activity fees and offering no athletic scholarships or tuition waivers, but it thrives nonetheless.

For something more down to earth, try the College Republicans and the Institute for Conservative Studies (ICS). Recently, ICS brought such conservative speakers as Alan Keyes, Dinesh D'Souza, and Ralph Reed to FSU. In addition, a new chapter of Eagle Forum recently started up on campus, and the conservative/libertarian paper, the *Independent Perspective,* publishes approximately every two months.

There are, of course, leftist groups on campus, including the Florida State University Lesbian Gay Bisexual Student Union, the Black Student Union, and the College Democrats. But compared to smaller schools, these organizations are very unorganized and rather small. The official FSU College Democrats club only attracts about twenty members on average — out of a campus population of thirty thousand. The plain truth is that most students are apathetic when it comes to political concerns.

The other primary campus activity — according to *Rolling Stone* at least — is partying. But there is also the call of the surf to attend to, as well as nonpolitical student organizations like the martial arts clubs (the Aikido Club and the Cuong Nhu Oriental Martial Arts Bamboo Dojo), Seminole "spirit" groups (the Marching Chiefs Drumline and the Lady Spirithunters), and recreational activities (like the Fishing Society and Scuba Club).

FRANCISCAN UNIVERSITY OF STEUBENVILLE

Office of Admissions
Steubenville, OH 43952
(800) 783-6220
www.franuniv.edu

Total enrollment: 1,927
Undergraduates: 1,521
SAT Ranges (Verbal/Math):
Financial aid: 80%

Applicants: N/A
Accepted: N/A
Enrolled: N/A
Application deadline: June 30
Financial aid application deadline: Jan. 31
Tuition: $11,590
Core curriculum: No

Your Faith Will Make You Whole?

Franciscan University of Steubenville distinguishes itself from other institutions by its unapologetic embrace of Catholic orthodoxy. This commitment gives the university its identity; a student planning to attend Franciscan should expect nothing else.

The university was not always this way: it spent the first years of its existence searching (as it were) for the faith that now marks it. Founded in 1946 by the Franciscan Friars of the Third Order Regular, the university was for its first several decades a relatively undistinguished regional college with an eye for neither national prominence nor strong, traditional Catholicism. Its campus was also marked in those days by problems of morality, including drug and alcohol use.

Then, in 1974, came a new president, the dynamic Fr. Michael Scanlan. At the heart of his dynamism was the belief that Catholic higher education had to grow out of vibrant Catholic faith. Today, Franciscan is well known and loved by traditionalists who look to it as a bastion of orthodox theological study and evangelical outreach. Its press has grown dramatically, and it also has a TV presence via Mother Angelica's global Catholic network, EWTN. Orthodox Catholics look to Franciscan for intellectual leadership because of the work of Father Scanlan, and the school he reformed has become one of the most energetic centers of Catholic higher education in the nation.

This evolution has brought with it an ongoing debate over what type of core curriculum a university such as Franciscan should have, and whether it should return to a more traditional liberal arts base in an effort to better fulfill its new mission in the forefront of Catholic higher education. In addition, the campus suffers what one professor calls "an identity crisis that revolves around the problem of moving beyond being a local Catholic college." That is, how far should the university go in positioning itself as a national Catholic university that is capable of delivering the intellectual weight and scholarly accomplishment necessary for such an ambitious mission? A professor notes that "Fr. Scanlan turned the university around, but now the question is whether or not what he accomplished pastorally can be done academically."

The turnaround in Franciscan's devotional life is beyond doubt. The most dominant form of spirituality at Franciscan is the Charismatic Renewal, which is known for such phenomena as speaking in tongues. There is also a significant group that would consider itself more "traditionalist" than charismatic. At times tension flares up between these two groups, and some people report that they are uncomfortable with the dramatic style of charismatic spirituality. But in general the community at Franciscan is bound by a common faith in the teachings of the church.

The efforts to match spiritual renewal in the intellectual sphere have brought more mixed results, and some instructors believe the college is too lenient with its faculty. They wish the administration would take a more aggressive line in promoting and defending the academic, intellectual side of the university community while simultaneously reining in some of the more professionalized elements. There is also the ongoing question of whether the university is hiring truly distinguished scholars, or just those who are theologically orthodox. It remains to be seen just where Franciscan's theological traditionalism will lead.

Academic Life: Not by Bread Alone

Like many other institutions of higher learning, Franciscan University jettisoned its core curriculum in the upheaval of the 1960s. But even then (as now), Franciscan offered bachelor's degrees in many professional fields, unlike, say, the University of Dallas or other schools that tout a strong core common to all undergraduate majors. The professional programs, including education, nursing, engineering, mental health and human services, social work, business administration, and computer science, are an integral part of the history of Franciscan, and they played a major role in the university long before the arrival of Father Scanlan.

There is now a debate on campus regarding what if any changes should be made to the rather soft remnants of the former core. As it stands now, Franciscan general education requirements account for 48 semester hours out of the minimum of 124 needed to graduate. Included are 6 hours in theology, 15 in the humanities, 6 in both natural and social sciences, and 15 in communications, which includes, oddly, mathematics and statistics. The core is, in the words of one professor, "really a set of distribution requirements. There used to be a core that included a lot of theology, philosophy, and Western civilization, but . . . what we have now may not be adequate for a liberal arts college."

The issue of what the core curriculum should look like came to a head in 1996, when several humanities faculty attempted to instill a stronger, broader requirement that would have strengthened the offerings in their fields. "We tried to push for a very moderate tightening of the curriculum, but even that was defeated. So nothing was ever done," says one faculty member. "We would have liked something like the old core, or our current honors curriculum, but there is almost no support for doing that, and it is a real problem because students don't learn a common language to speak." Other professors concur. "Students outside the humanities and social sciences are not getting a strong liberal arts education here," says one.

According to faculty, students can get out of Franciscan University having taken only one English class. A Western civilization requirement was eliminated in the early 1970s; however, the class is still offered and most students do take it. There is a non-Western civilization requirement, spurred by the fact that "the Catholic Church is a universal institution, and we need to know about the whole world," according to a professor who, while longing for a reinstatement of the Western civilization requirement, does not oppose the non-Western class.

The defeat of the effort to rebuild a core demonstrates that many faculty members find the current curriculum sufficient. A large split has developed — and widened — between the faculty who teach in the professional departments and those who teach in the more traditional liberal arts and sciences. That students in professional programs are not subject to the core requirements has meant that the student body in general does not share a common language of thoughts and ideas, according to some faculty members. As is often the case, enrollment concerns complicate the discussion: after years of growth, enrollment has lately leveled off at Franciscan, and the professional programs undoubtedly draw students who might not attend a university that, because of a rigorous core curriculum, forces them to put off more utilitarian classes until they enter professional schools following graduation. Without sufficient funds to satisfy both camps, there is little reason to believe that Franciscan will devote large sums of money to strengthening its liberal arts departments and programs even as it maintains and strengthens its professional offerings. The market for students who demand a more utilitarian education is quite strong, and, with its history of offering so many professional degrees, Franciscan doesn't seem poised to implement the core that many of its faculty members would prefer.

Some of Franciscan's programs, however, remain highly regarded. Theology, one of the most popular majors and best-known departments on campus, contains the largest number of well-known, widely published scholars, including Scott Hahn, Mark Miravalle, Regis Martin, and Fr. Anthony Mastroeni. Philosophy is also strong, although it contains only one Thomist, which is a bit odd in a Catholic university. Notable scholars in that department include John White, Pat Lee, and John Crosby. Also strong are history (with Dominic Aquila, Fr. Conrad Harkins, Kimberly Georgedes, and John Carrigg), political science (including Stephen Krason), and biology. Three other professors of note are Douglas Lowry in economics, Ben Alexander in English, and John Korzi in psychology.

Other departments are not as well regarded on campus, according to faculty members from various disciplines. Education is reputedly weak and, in the words of one professor, "saturated with a secular educationalist perspective." Also, math was called "the bottom of the pile" by a professor, and students complain that the engineering department does not have adequate equipment. However, most of the money for a new science facility has been raised.

One of the best programs at Franciscan is the honors program, available for students with a GPA better than 3.0. The program offers excellent classes with small enrollments, as well as majors in "Great Books of Western Civilization" and "Catholic Thought." The majors can be completed in eight semesters and more than satisfy the core requirements, such as they are. The honors program is so popular that enrollment must be limited to forty incoming students per year. Also of particular merit as a major is "Humanities and Catholic Culture," which is based on the work of the great Catholic historian Christopher Dawson. It is run through the history department and has more than fifty majors. An unusual minor may be taken in "Human Life Issues," which examines its subject in an interdisciplinary manner in order to prepare students, in the words of the college catalogue, to "think, speak, and act intelligently in these crucial [pro-life] matters confronting contemporary culture." Finally, the university operates a campus in Gaming, Austria, and sends one hundred students from any major abroad for a semester during their sophomore year. Classes there are held in a renovated fourteenth-century Carthusian monastery and are taught in English by Franciscan University of Steubenville professors.

Political Atmosphere: Overtly Orthodox

There are no badly politicized departments or courses at Franciscan, where the Catholic mission is taken very seriously and the general ethos of the campus is not conducive to ideological approaches to the liberal arts. As one professor says, "There is no organized feminist movement here, and a homosexual movement wouldn't be allowed. Some of the older faculty members have a '60s mentality, but that's not a big factor. Even they don't go for the new nihilism — they're not into deconstruction, for example."

Considering that Franciscan is a Catholic university that prides itself on its orthodoxy, some faculty see a rather large secularizing influence on the part of some of the professional programs that, in the words of one professor, teach in a way that "brings in from the broader culture an outlook that is expressed in their teaching that is drawn from modern, secular philosophical assumptions. These are made by people who don't understand what they're teaching — who don't see that they're contradicting Catholicism."

Some well-respected faculty say that even though they enjoy their jobs, they would wish for a bit more academic rigor, especially where faculty hiring and tenuring are concerned. "There is some unevenness in academic strength and intellectual depth in some areas, so students don't get the breadth and depth they need," notes one professor. "The question is whether or not enough people can bring spirit and mind together to strengthen their own disciplines." Father Scanlan took up this concern in 1996, urging faculty to give greater heed to the intellectual needs of their students.

Other faculty members say the university has become so devoutly religious, it sometimes misses out on the world it purports to study. "It's almost a four-year retreat," says one. "We are so thoroughly fortressed from the world and homogeneous in our faculty that there is little intellectual excitement. We don't engage the world of ideas enough." According to another professor, serious intellectual work happens only in theology and philosophy. "The liberal arts are seen as entertainment," the professor adds. There is, for example, neither a fine arts major nor a music major (although there is a music minor). "There exists here an intellectual provincialism that robs the curriculum of any intellectual integrity," says one professor.

Another scholar states that the hiring and tenure processes are "too automatic. I don't know anyone who didn't get tenure. There is not enough expected in the area of scholarly work, and therefore there is a division in the faculty between people who want only teaching and those who want to require some publishing." This division, of course, is not unique to Franciscan. At many colleges and universities whose prime purpose is undergraduate teaching, faculty must decide — or have dictated to them — just how to balance teaching and research. Too much emphasis on research, as is common at many large institutions, can cause a deterioration in teaching as professors, eager to garner first tenure and, later, raises and promotion to full professor, expend their energies on the area that pays. Franciscan, on the other hand, can be criticized for de-emphasizing research too much — for erring a bit too much on the side of teaching. There seems to be a tendency to rely on piety in place of, rather than in addition to, rigorous standards for hiring and promotion. While this is preferable to conditions found on many campuses, one could wish for a more academically demanding campus where a larger number of the faculty see no conflict between faith and reason, belief and scholarship.

Student Life: Preserving the Faith

The message to students who consider coming to Franciscan, or to their parents, should include (though not be limited to) this statement by one professor: "Many students these days are afraid that if they go to a Catholic college they'll lose their faith. They won't lose their faith if they come here." Lacking a core curriculum to unite them, most students are bound by an unquestionably orthodox Catholicism that permeates all facets of university life, and which makes Franciscan one of the most spiritually active universities in the country. Attendance at Sunday mass is required, and during the week students meet in organized small groups to discuss issues of the Catholic faith.

The students themselves certainly love their school. This affection stems, no doubt, from the fact that they come to Franciscan fully aware of what they're going to find. As one professor says, "The students here come from traditional Catholic families and are easy to teach because they want the Roman Catholic content. Their faith animates their interest in the search for philosophical truth." Thus, faculty are free to teach their subjects minus the static they might receive at other colleges where such orthodoxies are less appreciated.

Several student groups on campus further reflect this attitude. The Baconian Society, named for the thirteenth-century Franciscan philosopher Roger Bacon, who argued that theological studies should encompass science, is Franciscan University's version of Phi Beta Kappa. Free Enterprise, a national organization, offers students interested in the free market a chance to compete against other Ohio colleges (en route to a national competition) in developing programs that foster a better understanding of the workings of the free enterprise system. Human Life Concerns, said to be the largest conservative organization on campus, supports issues that affect the sanctity of human life.

For sports, Franciscan students may choose from intramural sports such as ultimate Frisbee, flag football, volleyball, and basketball. The university also offers club sports in baseball, women's volleyball, and men's and women's soccer. Although club teams compete against those from other colleges and universities, Franciscan does not sponsor intercollegiate sports. University policy supports the benefits of physical and athletic endeavors, but considers "spectatorship" far less important — thus the existence of club teams in lieu of full intercollegiate squads.

GEORGE MASON UNIVERSITY

Office of Admissions
George Mason University
4400 University Drive
Mail Stop 3A4
Fairfax, VA 22030-4444
(703) 993-4468
www.gmu.edu

Total enrollment: 24,368
Undergraduates: 13,831
SAT Ranges (Verbal/Math): V 470-580, M 460-570
Financial aid: 26%
Applicants: 5,445
Accepted: 68%

Enrolled: 51%
Application deadline: Feb. 1
Financial aid application deadline: Mar. 1
Tuition: resident, $4,296; nonresident, $12,240
Core curriculum: No

Branching Out, but Not Up

George Mason University began in 1957 as a branch of the University of Virginia, back when the state's heart resided more in the rural setting of Charlottesville than in what would become the center of the political and technological boom area of northern Virginia. It became an independent school in 1972, and has grown to thirteen thousand undergraduates and eleven thousand graduate students, supported by the enormous growth in Virginia's Washington, D.C., suburbs. In fact, nearly 90 percent of the school's students come from Virginia, though forty-nine states and 108 foreign countries are also represented.

George Mason is similar to other large state universities in a variety of ways, but it has rejected much of the politicization that often dominates such schools. To be sure, some strange courses can be found in the college catalogue, but they represent only a tiny fraction of the curriculum. "Virginia is a relatively conservative state," says one professor. "Even the Democrats who are in the legislature tend to be conservative Democrats."

George Mason, the university's namesake, was the author of the Virginia Declaration of Rights, which served as the foundation for the nation's Bill of Rights, and quite a revolutionary. But the school named after him is not so revolutionary. The liberal arts requirements at the College of the Arts and Sciences are predictably weak: they may be numerous, but are spread thinly and are far from ideal in content or rigor. The university's experimental college program, a small division called the New Century College, is supposed to be a state-of-the-art interdisciplinary college. In reality, it is closer to what college would look like if it were designed exclusively by social workers and psychotherapists.

However, the university has invested much in its fine economics department, which includes Nobel Prize winner James Buchanan. Even the lesser programs at George Mason are a bargain at around $4,300 for in-state students; after all, the university must remain competitive with the many colleges and universities in the Washington metropolitan area. Out-of-state students must decide if the education at George Mason is worth the $12,000 they pay for tuition.

Academic Life: Choose Many from Many

Of George Mason's eleven graduate and undergraduate divisions, the College of Arts and Sciences is the largest and most directly concerned with the liberal arts. This college contains nineteen departments and about 7,500 students, or approximately 60 percent of the undergraduate student body. Students in this college must take two courses in English composition and one course in oral communication. Those seeking a B.A. degree must take courses in, or demonstrate proficiency of, a foreign language to the intermediate level. Depending on the number of courses a student must take to meet the language requirement, the general education requirements can account for slightly more than half the total number of hours required for a B.A. degree — more than at many similar institutions.

The other general education requirements in the College of Arts and Sciences are standard fare at most large universities, and fairly utilitarian in nature. The university makes no attempt to bring students together in a course that would offer readings common to all. Four courses are required in the humanities, but the two courses in literature can be selected from any English courses above the 200 level or any modern and classical language courses above the 300 level. The other humanities requirements are also broad, and include fine arts and philosophy or religious studies. One course is required in analytical reasoning, as are two from among economics, government, geography, and history, and two from the departments of anthropology, psychology, and sociology. Two courses are required in natural sciences; both must include a lab.

Needless to say, these requirements don't guarantee that students will become familiar with the Western heritage while at Mason. But the university has seen fit to mandate not just one but two courses in non-Western cultures. These include anthropology courses on the native cultures, art, politics, history, and religions of most parts of the world. Though this requirement is a bow in the direction of multiculturalism, the titles and descriptions of the courses that fulfill the requirement are fairly straightforward, devoid of the usual language about Western "oppression" and "hegemony."

George Mason has excellent professors whom students should be able to find given the few constrictions on their choice of general education classes. These include Richard Wagner, Charles Rowley, James Bennett, Robert D. Tollison, Walter E. Williams, Karen I. Vaughn, Tyler Cowen, and Nobel Prize winner James M. Buchanan in economics; Daniele Struppa and Robert L. Sachs in math; Peter J. Denning and Kenneth A. DeJong in decision sciences; Robert Ehrlich in physics; and Eric Pankey in English.

Economics is clearly the best department in the College of Arts and Sciences, and at George Mason in general. The department is home to several professors with national reputations, and the Chicago, Public Choice, and Austrian Schools are well represented. Constitutional economics has been the particular contribution of James Buchanan. A number of courses examine the Austrian tradition of Ludwig von Mises and Friedrich von Hayek.

Associated with the university is the James Buchanan Center, named for Nobel laureate James Buchanan, who has taught at the school since 1983, three years before he won the prize. Buchanan has written several well-known books, including *Fiscal Theory and Political Economy, The Calculus of Consent, The Limits of Liberty, Democracy in Deficit, The Power to Tax,* and *The Reason of Rules.* The Buchanan Center incorporates the Center for the Study of Public Choice and the Center for the Study of Market Processes. The Institute for Humane Studies is a postinstructional institute of GMU, which, though academically part of the university, is privately funded. Both the James Buchanan Center and the Institute for Humane Studies will relocate to Arlington, Virginia, in 1999, although the economics department will remain in Fairfax. All three are among the leading centers in the country for free-market economic theory.

The Center for Public Choice, of which Dr. Buchanan is the advisory general director, concerns itself with research into public policy issues, with a special eye toward "public choice" issues. The Institute for Humane Studies describes itself as an organization that "assists undergraduate and graduate students who have a special interest in individual liberty." The Institute offers several programs for both graduate students and undergraduates, including a variety of scholarships. The third part of the Buchanan Center, the Center for the Study of Market Processes, is an educational and research nonprofit organization that generates solutions to organizational and social problems.

Three other departments at George Mason are also noted for their high academic standards and insistence on proper, rigorous scholarship. These are the departments of math, physics, and decision sciences (a department in the School of Business Administration).

George Mason does have two especially politicized departments — women's studies and African-American studies — but their influence seems to be limited to their own fiefdoms. "The women's studies department and the African-American studies department do not have a significant presence . . . as they often do at other politicized universities," a professor says. Neither department offers a major, and, as in the courses under the "diversity" general education requirement, those listed under African-American studies at least appear to be light on the political histrionics commonly found elsewhere. Some courses required for the minor include "The Afro-American Experience in the United States: African Background to 1885," "The Afro-American Experience in the United States: Reconstruction to the Present," and "Minority Group Politics and Policies."

Women's studies appears to be more ideological. According to promotional materials, minors in this department will "examine the ways that racism, sexism, classism, and homophobia operate and disucss [*sic*] strategies for social change." The department goes on to state: "Women's studies faculty members share a commitment to addressing the experiences and contributions of women previously excluded from the traditional curriculum — including women of color, lesbians, working-class women, and poor women."

The most politicized sector of George Mason is a division called the New Century College (NCC), which offers degrees in "integrative studies," "individualized studies," "interdisciplinary studies," and "social work." One professor calls the NCC offerings "an experimental education," and does not intend it as a compliment. The program has little to do with the traditional understanding of the liberal arts as the disciplines that foster what Cardinal Newman called the "philosophical habit of mind." Rather, the NCC, with its rhetoric of "learning communities" and "integrative learning," seems like a brainchild of academics who grew up in the sixties.

The NCC curriculum is divided into three parts. The first year, called Division I, consists of "common courses and integrated learning," according to the catalogue. The four mandatory six-week units are on "interdisciplinary issues in education," "the natural world," "the socially constructed world," and the "relationship between the individual and society." Division II "is constructed of learning communities, each of which combines subjects usually taught in several separate courses into a single course of study." Division III, subtitled "Specialization," is said to be the equivalent of a major in "a traditional degree program." It can include "learning communities, independent study, seminars, mentored research, experiential learning, and traditional courses."

In fact, "experiential learning" is another college requirement, meaning that students must obtain at least twelve credit hours through internships, study abroad, or courses that include lots of field trips and other off-campus work. Some of the choices are:

- "Experiential Learning (Horizons: 2000 — Expanding Awareness/Breaking Gender Barriers)." "Experiential program focusing on gender equity. Incorporates and promotes active, collaborative group learning through creative, insight-oriented exercises; critical-thinking/discussions; group presentations and realistic life planning activities. Students will become aware of beliefs and attitudes, examine the impact of cultural messages, develop an understanding of themselves and others, confront limitations, explore roles and options. Students who complete the course may be eligible to facilitate a similar program for area youth in Grades 5-12 and other community groups."
- "Energy and Environment." "Investigates current sources of energy, various modes of their utilization and environmental effects. It offers an overview of the mechanical, physical, and chemical methodologies of energy use and delves into the biological, environmental and ecological aspects of pollution-generating mechanisms."

According to the NCC, "integrated learning" includes "collaboration, experiential learning, and self-reflection." Rather than focus on classical literature, students are encouraged, at least in part, to focus on their own experiences — in short, their feelings are considered more important than the great texts. This is not particularly rigorous stuff, academically or even physically, since classes meet at irregular times on occasion so students can fit them into their schedules.

Political Atmosphere: Visitors versus Home Team

Alan G. Merten was inaugurated as George Mason's fifth president in April of 1997, but already some on campus are not confident that he will be successful. In the opinion of one professor, Merten is a "fairly weak president" who has made some errors early in his presidency. The professor says appointing the former dean of the College of Arts and Sciences to the NCC helped cause the politicization at the latter, which lacks credibility among many professors because of its lightweight curriculum and ideological bent.

In addition, George Mason has succumbed to the usual politicized hiring processes of larger universities. Departments must have their search efforts for new faculty approved by an "equity office" that enforces affirmative action policies. Departments are expected to advertise in "black publications" and other media directed at the African-American community so as to secure minority professors.

The university administration also welcomes political correctness by hosting several "multicultural" events on campus, including Asian Awareness Week, Black History Month, Hispanic Heritage Month, Martin Luther King Day, and Women's History Month. In order to promote these events, the university has hosted several celebrity speakers, including Harry Belafonte, Julian Bond, Shirley Chisholm, and Susan Rook.

The new administration must have done something to anger liberals, or must have at least been perceived as unfriendly to certain groups prior to taking office. Merten's inauguration was disrupted by a Mason group called Coalition for a Hate-Free Campus and an off-campus group called the D.C. Lesbian Avengers. At an inaugural prayer service in St. Robert Bellarmine Chapel, two self-described lesbians interrupted the service by standing and displaying vests that read "Praying for a Hate Free Campus," while others (wearing T-shirts announcing "We Recruit") handed out pro-homosexual literature.

Recently, there was an effort to create a homosexual center on campus, but the board of visitors rejected this proposal. The board of visitors, in fact, is fairly conservative; several members were appointed by then-governor George Allen, a Republican.

Student Life: Capital Suburb

George Mason is located in Fairfax County, the Washington, D.C., suburb that boasts one of the ten highest per capita incomes in the nation. The campus is about thirty miles from the District, but isn't far from Interstate 66, which ends beside the Lincoln Memorial on the Mall, and is also close to a Metro (subway) stop where one can board an amazingly clean but not particularly cheap train into the nation's capital. Of course, Washington boasts hundreds of things to do, from the free attractions of the Smithsonian and other governmental tours and buildings to the bars of Georgetown to the fine restaurants all over town.

Mason itself boasts outstanding facilities on its 677-acre main campus. Because the university is so young, there is little in the way of classic traditional architecture. Many of the buildings on campus are better inside than out, including the excellent George W. Johnson Center, which houses a library, computer labs, student services, class space for the New Century College, and a four-story open atrium where students can eat or gather. The Center for the Arts includes a 2,000-seat Concert Hall, two smaller theaters, dance studios, and assorted music and fine arts studios. Students have first crack at five hundred free tickets to each Concert Hall performance, some of which have featured internationally known artists like guitarist Christopher Parkening. The Patriot Center seats ten thousand for indoor sports and rock concerts.

Nearly 90 percent of George Mason's student body is from Virginia. This makes for something of a commuter atmosphere on campus, especially considering the number of nontraditional (i.e., older) students who further or complete their educations at Mason. Still, campus life is active and there are more than 180 officially recognized student groups. Most are recreational or otherwise nonpolitical in focus. There are also eighteen fraternities and ten sororities.

Among the political clubs are the College Republicans and two gay, lesbian, and bisexual groups — the Pride Alliance and the Action Committee — which have recently been energized by the rejection of a university-funded campus homosexual center. The Pride Alliance is the more visible of the two. It brings speakers to campus and hosts discussion groups. The Action Committee was founded as a direct result of the board's decision, and is dedicated to activism. It calls itself "an active, grassroots organizing body" and works with recognized campus groups (including student government) and other local and national homosexual organizations, including the group that helped protest at President Merten's inauguration, the D.C. Lesbian Avengers. That group, according to its web page, endeavors to "identify and promote lesbian issues and perspectives while empowering queer women to become experienced organizers who can participate in political rebellion."

There is also a Women's Coalition at George Mason that publishes a feminist journal called *So to Speak,* as well as multicultural groups like the African Student Association, Black Student Alliance, Club Latino, Hispanic Women's Coalition, and the Student Coalition against Racism. Then there are the groups that, if they aren't at the fringe, can certainly see it from where they stand. These include Children of a Dark Eternity, which promotes "alternative religions" like the Church of Satan, the Covenant of the Goddess, and the Pagan Federation; and Thumbs Up for Democracy, which promotes disenfranchised political minorities such as the Black Panthers and the Green Party.

The George Mason Patriots field NCAA Division I teams in a number of sports. The university also has a sports facility open to students that houses basketball and racquetball courts, an indoor 200-meter track, seven tennis courts, and weight rooms. In addition, the university maintains several outdoor athletic fields on the Fairfax campus.

GEORGETOWN UNIVERSITY

Office of Undergraduate Admissions
Georgetown University
Washington, DC 20057-1002
(202) 687-3600
www.georgetown.edu

Total enrollment: 12,630
Undergraduates: 6,340
SAT Ranges (Verbal/Math): V 640-740, M 630-730
Financial aid: 60%
Applicants: 13,708
Accepted: 21%
Enrolled: 47%
Application deadline: Jan. 10
Financial aid application deadline: Feb. 1
Tuition: $21,216
Core curriculum: No

Small-"c"

John Carroll, S.J., the first Roman Catholic bishop in the United States, returned to America from Europe when the Jesuit order was suppressed in 1774. He was a friend of Benjamin Franklin and a supporter of the American War of Independence. Inspired by the Jesuits schools where he had studied and taught, Carroll founded in 1789 the first Catholic university in the new country. The school, though based on Jesuit tradition, was open to all religions, and nearly a fifth of the students in its first decade were Protestant. Jewish students came as early as the 1830s, and it was not until after the Civil War (in which four-fifths of Georgetown alumni who served did so on the losing side) that the university became more strongly Catholic.

Given its early history, perhaps it is not surprising that Georgetown today is not as Catholic as its association with the Jesuits would suggest. The university continues to rely on its Catholic reputation and the liberal arts tradition of its alumni, but it adopts a more secular viewpoint in recruiting students and formulating curriculum. It is interesting that the prospectus sent to high school students mentions Carroll's formal education in Europe, his friendship with Franklin, and how he "endowed the school with the dynamic, Jesuit tradition of education, characterized by Christian humanism and committed to the assumption of responsibility and action," but it never directly states that he was a priest, let alone the country's first bishop.

"Somewhere along the way," says one faculty member, "the decision was made to make Georgetown a 'small-c' catholic institution."

Academic Life: The Suppression of the Jesuits

Georgetown University offers degree programs through five undergraduate schools: Georgetown College, the School of Nursing, the School of Business, the School of Languages and Linguistics, and the Edmund A. Walsh School of Foreign Service. Each school has its own general education and degree requirements.

Georgetown College, home to twenty-eight academic departments, asks students to complete a loose series of distribution requirements. These courses are taken during the student's first two years in the College, and a student may not take more than four courses in his major prior to his junior year. The list includes two semesters of history, social sciences, and natural sciences/mathematics (though students majoring in biology, chemistry, or physics are exempt from the social science requirements). Each student must take two semesters of what the university calls literature courses, which are directed more at improving writing skills than at studying novels and poetry. Georgetown has retained an impressive requirement in philosophy and theology, mandating two courses in each discipline. The university invokes its "commitment to the Jesuit tradition" as grounds for requiring the religion courses. Finally, the university requires all arts and sciences majors to achieve proficiency in a foreign language at the intermediate level.

The minimal history requirement has been debated and revised recently. In the spring of 1997 the university proposed an "expansion" of its mandatory two-semester course in European civilization, which had been required since 1978. Under the proposal, which has all but been accepted as of this writing, the European civilization course will be renamed "Themes in European Civilization I and II" and will be organized around topics chosen by professors rather than attempt to cover the whole of European history. Some suggested topics include "Society and Religion" and "Church, State, and the Rise of Toleration." However, students would not be required to take this two-semester sequence; they can also fulfill the requirement with one of two yearlong sequences: "World History" or "Atlantic History." The departmental chairman, Rev. Jeffrey von Arx, S.J., has said, "These courses will include an aspect of European history that has been underrepresented — that is, the relationship between Europe and other cultures." Although Georgetown has not yet mandated a non-Western or "diversity" requirement, many on campus view the revised history courses as a step in that direction.

Government is considered one of the best departments at Georgetown, boasting several distinguished scholars. It is also one of the most popular departments, with upwards of four hundred majors. Psychology and classics are considered sound. History, philosophy, and economics are said to be moderately left-leaning, though not distractingly so, while English and sociology are well on their way to joining theology as the university's most radically ideological departments. The leaders of the English department "thrive on notoriety," according to one Georgetown professor, while the chairman of sociology "loves to offend traditional morals."

Students at Georgetown have access to a library comprising 2 million volumes, 2 million microfilms, 21,000 periodicals, and 336,000 government documents.

Excellent faculty, according to students, include George Carey and Father James Schall in government; Dan Robinson in psychology; Marius Schwartz and George Visknins in economics; Wayne Davis and Wilfried Ver Eecke in philosophy; and Paul F. Betz, Alvaro F. V. Ribiero, S.J., Joan Holmer, and Jeffrey Shulman in English.

As at other colleges and universities, the newest faculty at Georgetown are among the most radical. "There are sound and substantial courses from very good professors, but many of them are on the verge of retirement," a student says in reference to the English department. Bringing in less traditionally minded professors has had a number of effects. In political science, for instance, instruction has moved away from political theory toward behavioral studies; in psychology there is a greater emphasis on clinical research and the pursuit of grant money.

This trend is of course motivated by the university's desire to keep up with the competition. The same could be said of recent curriculum revisions, as they seem designed to duplicate curricula at other schools rather than to maintain a high level of liberal education. Two of the more recent controversial changes — the history requirement noted above and the revamping of the major author requirement and disciplinary concentration for English majors — were instituted because studies indicated Georgetown was "lagging behind" peer institutions. According to departmental justifications for the history changes, "the faculty studied history requirements at more than thirty other institutions, including Princeton, Harvard, and Wellesley, and found that most institutions offer more options." The English department changes were settled on after "studying the English curriculum at nineteen peer institutions, including Harvard, Cornell, Princeton, Smith and Yale" — schools that are not exactly bulwarks against the onslaught of multiculturalism. The changes in the English department meant, in part, that majors no longer must study Shakespeare or Milton or Chaucer, where prior to 1997 they had to choose two of those three authors.

The latter decision was met with some dismay by students, alumni, and national media. Georgetown alumnus and *Exorcist* author William Peter Blatty (the steps shown in the movie are near the Georgetown campus) withdrew a sizable donation to the university. "Classical Authors Dropped," headlined the *Washington Times* in a story that began, "Forget Shakespeare, Chaucer, and Milton." At worst, the new curriculum, which allows students to choose from three concentrations (literature and literary history; culture and performance; and rhetoric, genre, and form), is more inclusive than traditional curricula. The director of undergraduate studies at Georgetown, who is also an associate professor of English, was quoted in a university press release as saying, "It's not an either/or situation. The canon and cultural studies can and will coexist, and our students will benefit from both." The department offers nine courses in Shakespeare each year — three times the national average for similar universities, and twice as high a percentage of all students. Even some more traditional faculty now admit that the whole controversy was rather overblown.

Curricular revisions aside, the English department does include some very nontraditional courses. One upper-division elective, "Unspeakable Lives: Gay and Lesbian Narratives," bears a description that, we suspect, is not often seen at church-affiliated schools:

> We will examine strategies of representation occasioned by politically suspect sexualities, the "fag," "dyke," or "queer," especially as these intersect with the construction of the latest version if [*sic*] a traditional social category, the sexual monster. Particular attention will be paid to the language of disease and contagion characteristic of the discourse.

Similarly suspect is an English course called "Entertainment and Dystopia: Introduction to Cultural Studies." Described by the professor as "time-demanding" and "ambitious," the course includes a study of radical theorists (Foucault, Lacan, Marx, de Saussure, Sedgwick); "cinematic texts . . . *Blue Velvet, Zelig, Madonna: Truth or Dare, Pretty Woman, Brazil, To Wong Foo, Thanks for Everything, Julie Newmar,* and *Paris is Burning*"; as well as sitcoms, dramas, music videos, popular music, issues of *Vogue, Details,* and "current 'zines." Politicized courses in other departments include "Womanist Theology," "History of the Biosphere," and "Minding Your Manners: Vice and Modern America."

Classes like these perhaps contribute to the sentiment held by some on campus that Georgetown students tend to be intellectually disinterested. According to a 1995 study, Georgetown students spend less time on coursework than their peers at similar institutions. "There are students working thirty hours on the [Capitol] Hill who are still doing great academically," says one professor. "Most of the bright, active students are not academically inclined — they are political junkies." Grade inflation is also a serious problem, as is the general absence of a campus environment conducive to academic and intellectual community. "Georgetown thinks it has improved its national and international reputation," says one professor. "Everything seems relatively rosy. . . . [But] Georgetown's good rankings are deceiving." Undergraduate writing skills are fairly poor, according to students and faculty, and the general education program does not put enough emphasis on written communication. The honors program is not that great, and advising for all undergraduates is considered inadequate by both faculty and students. "Freshmen soon drift away from their advisors," says one professor. The best students report that they find their advisers through an informal selection process.

Yet there is still a verbal — and many would say a demonstrated — commitment to undergraduate teaching at Georgetown. Although tenure decisions are based almost exclusively on the candidate's publications, faculty are expected to put a great deal of energy into their teaching, and even the most basic courses are generally taught by full professors. The faculty courseload is two courses per semester, or a 2/1 schedule if the professor has administrative duties such as advising. Often, two of the four courses taught each year are in the professor's specialized area of research. In such an accommodating climate, it would be difficult for professors not to put some effort into their teaching. Still, many faculty are concerned by what they perceive as an overemphasis on student evaluations of faculty performance. This has helped turn faculty into "song and dance men," complains one professor. In general, though, Georgetown is having a difficult time negotiating its desire to maintain a commitment to teaching while boosting its reputation for solid research. "The administration is always trying to figure out whether they want Georgetown to be Swarthmore or Berkeley," notes one professor.

Political Atmosphere: In Search of "Centered Pluralism"

To its credit, Georgetown has not simply ignored widespread perceptions about its diminished intellectual stature and diluted Catholic vision. Over the past several years the university has conducted studies of its Jesuit identity and intellectual life. The first of these committees issued a report in late 1996 entitled "Centered Pluralism," which grew out of a series of faculty seminars devoted to a discussion of the Jesuit and Catholic identity of Georgetown. The seminars drew about forty-five participants and included exchanges with several distinguished speakers, including political theorist Jean Elshtain of the University of Chicago and philosopher Alasdair MacIntyre of Duke University.

Throughout the report, the authors seem careful to avoid accusations of authoritarianism or dogmatism. The authors stress that "this document is intended as a basis for discussion" rather than a blueprint for change. The middle ground staked out in the report is shown in this excerpt: "We believe the university should deliberately cultivate its religious heritage. We recognize that some ways of reaffirming Georgetown's Jesuit and Catholic identity would be inappropriate for a university with the pluralistic character it now has. We are confident, however, that the Georgetown community can undertake such a project while maintaining or even strengthening the university's openness to people of diverse beliefs and backgrounds and its commitment to academic freedom."

The call, such as it is, is for retaining those elements of the university's tradition that do not offend, that sell, and that are not necessarily unique to Jesuit schools — hardly a road map for a return to a full-blooded Catholic identity. It is difficult to tell from the document what this new Georgetown would look like, or even what exactly a "Jesuit and Catholic heritage" looks like; it is merely implied that the university would profit from more of it. Elements of a Jesuit education are never clearly articulated, except in such vague affirmations as "the cultivation of the whole person" and a commitment to the promotion of "justice . . . care of and service to the poor, and to the education of men and women committed to the service of others." There is no allusion to the rigorous curriculum (the *ratio studiorum*) that once served as a hallmark of Jesuit education, and no mention of Pope John Paul II's recent document on Catholic education. There is, however, a vigorous critique of the free market as it impacts university education. Indeed, the only church document mentioned in "Centered Pluralism" is a 1984 pastoral letter issued by the U.S. bishops entitled "Economic Justice for All." The document cautions the university to "resist allowing academic policy to be driven solely by market forces," but fails to provide another base (such as the Jesuit tradition) upon which the university should rely.

The second committee's report, entitled "Findings of the Committee on Georgetown's Intellectual Life," was released in 1997. The study was undertaken in response to a 1995 institutional research report that found that Georgetown students studied fewer hours, worked longer hours for pay, and partied more than students at comparable schools. Perhaps the school's embarrassment at being ranked the nation's number one party school that same year by *Playboy* magazine also played a part. "Such a depiction of [students'] use of time struck us as potentially powerful confirmation of what many of us already believed based on our own experiences: many of Georgetown's undergraduates lack a seriousness of purpose and an intellectual habit of mind; they do only what they must to maintain their grades," the report states. "And yet, we had only to reflect on the routinely high grades that so many of our students receive to recognize that we, their professors, shared the responsibility for this discrepancy between the high grades of students and the amount of work they report."

The committee assigned blame in three areas: insufficiently challenging courses and faculty, a campus atmosphere that does little to promote intellectual discourse, and poor representation in campus publications and recruiting brochures of the university's commitment to academic excellence. Recommendations included adopting campuswide grade distribution targets, setting up more committees, doing more to guarantee students quiet living space, making teaching more of a factor in tenure decisions, and redesigning campus ceremonies and publications to present a more academic atmosphere. It is too early to tell whether any of these recommendations will be adopted, and what if any effect they will have, but the study was a necessary first step in reviving the academic life of the university.

The university has not had to worry about activism taking time from studies. By most accounts, the Georgetown student body shuns the usual issues on campuses, though a number of students are "Hill watchers" — more interested in the politics of Capitol Hill than in politically correct causes closer to home.

Georgetown has two journals that provide an alternative to the official campus newspaper, the *Hoya*. One is the *Georgetown Independent*, a monthly student newspaper that has no formal affiliation and receives no funding from the university. The other is the *Georgetown Academy*, "Georgetown's Independent Journal of Satire and Opinion." It also has no official attachment, financial or otherwise, to the university. The *Independent* appears more devoted to publicizing current events, both on campus and in the culture at large. Recent issues have focused on Georgetown's reputation as a party school and the restructuring of Georgetown's history requirement. The *Academy* also covers campus political and social life, but is intent on holding Georgetown accountable to its religious foundations as well. It is published about twice a semester and appears to have strong alumni support and involvement. The periodical recently ran afoul of the administration by suggesting that President Leo O'Donovan, a Jesuit priest, should resign because of his open acceptance of an abortion club on campus. The president defended himself on the grounds that abortion is a "free speech" issue, although it was widely suspected that the administration barred the official alumni magazine from including any reference to the abortion group for fear it would alienate university patrons.

There is no formal sensitivity training for students or faculty at Georgetown. The campus has been divided over the need for a speech code, but faculty recently voted down an attempt to impose one.

Georgetown used to have active chapters of the Intercollegiate Studies Institute and the Young America's Foundation, but student activity has faded in recent years and conservative groups have declined accordingly. Conservative students complain that campus speakers are predominantly liberal. Because of its location, Georgetown regularly hosts high-ranking current and former politicians. Recent speakers include Secretary of State Madeleine Albright, President Clinton, Senator Daniel Patrick Moynihan, and Oliver North.

At the Oliver North speech, student protesters hung a banner of Cuban revolutionary Che Guevara. The banner was torn down by the Lecture Fund, which later apologized for its "irrational" decision. However, most of the complaints about campus lectures come when invited speakers pronounce views decidedly at odds with the Catholic tradition Georgetown is supposed to uphold. According to one faculty member, "The students think it's great to bring abortionists to campus," and this has created some tension in recent years, as has the issue of funding groups that are antagonistic to church teaching, such as homosexual or pro-abortion organizations.

Campus Life: What's a Hoya?

Georgetown indisputably has one of the more beautiful college campuses in the country. Perched above the wide Potomac, its Flemish Renaissance–style spires suggest a medieval monastery or fortress. The surrounding area is full of beautiful row houses, fashionable shops, and world-class cultural opportunities. Students seeking dining, shopping, and other pocketbook-draining opportunities will find plenty along Wisconsin and M Streets. One of the best things about living on campus is that one doesn't need to find a place to park in Georgetown — a notoriously difficult proposition. Although the area is safer than most other sections of the District of Columbia, crime is still a problem, so students are advised to use caution when strolling through the surrounding area during the evening hours.

Many students at Georgetown come from well-to-do backgrounds, both in this country and foreign countries. "Most of the students seem to end up working for law firms or New York banks" after they graduate, according to one professor. Housing in Georgetown is phenomenally expensive, and dorm space is tight (as is building space on campus). The university is considering plans for a new on-campus dorm. As a vestige of its Catholic heritage, Georgetown does not have a Greek system. Some faculty and students view this as unfortunate, contending that fraternities and sororities could provide badly needed social and service opportunities for Georgetown students, who largely lack a sense of community. Others say frats would only exacerbate problems of excessive drinking at Georgetown.

More healthy alternatives include the twenty-four intercollegiate sports offered at Georgetown. The school's teams are called Hoyas, and theories on what that means are plentiful. Here's the true story, straight from the university's website: Years ago the school's teams were known as the Stonewalls. Also years ago, Georgetown students had to take Latin and Greek. Using both languages, a student started a cheer — "Hoya Saxa," meaning "What Rocks!" Hoya stuck, Saxa did not. Students not skilled enough to be Hoyas have intramural, instructional, and recreational sports opportunities.

Georgetown hosts its fair share of campus student organizations, many organized around ethnic divisions, but several devoted to religious interests as well. Controversial groups include PRIDE, Georgetown's Lesbian, Gay, and Bisexual Students' Organization, which receives funding from the university despite the Catholic Church's opposition to homosexuality. There are also many students and faculty who are traditional Catholics, and students run a small but enthusiastic pro-life group.

UNIVERSITY OF GEORGIA

Office of Admissions
114 Academic Building
Athens, GA 30602-6033
(706) 542-2112
www.uga.com

Total enrollment: 29,693
Undergraduates: 23,326
SAT Ranges (Verbal/Math): V 560-650, M 550-640
Financial aid: 33%
Applicants: 12,000
Accepted: 59%
Enrolled: 47%
Application deadline: Feb. 1
Financial aid application deadline: Mar. 1
Tuition: $2,930 in-state; $9,860 out-of-state
Core curriculum: No

The Lights Went Out

The University of Georgia was founded in 1785, literally in a log cabin. It grew rapidly after World War II as a result of the GI Bill, and now attracts many in-state students who pay only $2,300 tuition, or even less through the state's Hope Scholarship Program, which offers college tuition to Georgia high schoolers who maintain a respectable GPA.

Georgia has become a large school of average pretensions and achievements. It is the alma mater of twenty-three Georgia governors, and has a sizable library system of 3 million volumes. Its nearly thirty thousand students enjoy nearly four hundred student organizations. The university boasts excellent programs in the sciences; and the law, vet, and journalism schools have had good reputations for many years. Because the state legislature has invested heavily in the school, it is well-off financially, and there are always building projects in progress: in the last few years the school has added a huge art museum, new swimming and other sports facilities, a conference building, and an addition to the law school.

The rest of the university's story is far more ambiguous. A viper's nest of deception, self-promotion, and constant infighting has made the political atmosphere nearly intolerable for faculty with a traditional cast of mind. The school has swallowed whole the multicultural pill, and the catalogue is heavy with courses that border on the absurd. In the process, Georgia has lost much of its Southern character, though this is truer of the faculty than the student body. While the university was perhaps too provincial in the geographic sense twenty-five years ago, it is now too provincial in an ideological sense; that is to say, the orthodoxies of "diversity" are now strictly enforced. Some departments, especially in the humanities and social sciences, seem to be at war with their subjects, good writing, and the liberal arts. Many of the radicalized professors at Georgia hope to remake the world in their own image. But supporters of the traditional liberal arts can be pardoned for wishing they could just restore Georgia to its former self.

Academic Life: Marching through Georgia

As is the case with most large universities (and many small ones as well), Georgia's mandatory body of study is less a core curriculum than a set of distribution requirements. Students must fulfill the usual range of courses in each area of study: humanities, social sciences, and so on. Georgia does not require the study of Western civilization per se, although all students must demonstrate their knowledge of the history of the United States and Georgia either by examination or by passing a course in American history; they usually opt for the latter. They must also know something about the constitutions of the United States and Georgia and must either pass an examination on those subjects or take Political Science 101 or its honors equivalent. Through these Regents' requirements, as the history and constitutional checkoffs are known, Georgia graduates will gain at least minimal knowledge of the history and political theory of the United States and Georgia, although they may remain ignorant of the grand sweep of Western culture.

Indeed, in fulfilling A.B. requirements, students may avoid all contact with Western culture simply by taking substitute courses in literature, history, religion, philosophy, and the fine arts. These alternatives include "Cultural Diversity in American Art," "Native American Religions," "Multicultural Literature in America," and "Multicultural Perspectives on Women in the U.S."

Other requirements vary from laudable to lamentable. On the good side is the foreign language requirement (four courses for A.B. candidates and three for B.S. candidates). Certain requirements for the A.B. degree are also decent: a course in fine arts, one in philosophy or religion, and another in either category; two math and four science courses (including at least one two-course sequence); and four courses in social sciences. These course requirements would be much better if there was some structure to them.

While Georgia won't force its students to take a set of foundational courses, it has no problems demanding of them a cultural diversity course and an environmental literacy course (whatever that is). The approved areas from which a cultural diversity course may be selected are African-American, Native American, Hispanic American, or Asian-American studies. Some of these courses include:

- African American Studies (AAM)/English 315, "Introductory Black Psychology." This course covers the "study of African Americans by African American psychologists. Deconstruction of traditional thought, behavior, and development as well as reconstruction of the same on contemporary terms, testing of nuances and varieties of multicultural and indigenous models. Topics include the designs and projected future of the Black Psychology Movement."
- Speech Communication (SPC) 128, "Cultural Diversity in Communication." The catalogue says this class is taken "to develop an understanding of public and interpersonal communication processes that promote one's sense of identification with an ethnic group," and "to increase awareness of different verbal, nonverbal, and relational communication styles among North American ethnic groups." Among the requirements for this course is "analysis of culture and communication in a popular film," which counts as 25 percent of the student's grade. For a unit on how communications rituals build group identity, students read an article entitled "Fraternities and Rape on Campus."
- Speech Communication (SPC) 428, "Intercultural Communication." The course description says students will study "everyday racism," "gender as culture," "increasing cross-cultural sensitivity," and "language and (gendered) ethnicity." Sample themes for term projects (kindly provided on the department's web pages) include "ethnic prejudice in voting patterns," "meal-time communication," "communication in health care," and "self disclosure across cultures."

Many faculty at Georgia would support something better, or, if forced to compromise, settle for something at least less silly. There are indeed some excellent faculty, including these who were named by colleagues and students: James Kilgo, James Kibler, and Hugh Kenner in English; Bernard Dauenhauer in philosophy; Noel Fallows in Spanish; Tom Ganschow, Thomas Whigham, Kirk Willis, Emory Thomas, William Holmes, John Inscoe, and Ronald Rader in history; Charles Hudson and David Hally in anthropology; Richard Leseur in classics; and Dwight Lee and Dick Timberlake in economics. Strong departments at Georgia include virtually all sciences, all agriculture programs, forestry, environmental studies, economics, political science, art history, and psychology, which is the largest major on campus.

Political Atmosphere: Different Rules

The university administration, supported by the state's dominant media, talks about the rise in SAT scores, the recruitment of an ever more productive faculty, the expansion of facilities, and so on. These things are all true: Georgia is now the tenth most populous state in the nation, and with this phenomenal growth, particularly in the Atlanta area, has come an increase in the tax base and education level of the state. More money is now available for higher education, and the legislature is made up of men and women favorably disposed to strengthening the state's colleges and universities.

In addition to these material advances, the administration has decided it must chase the winds of change. Not too many years ago the influence of the handful of politicized faculty at Georgia was sufficiently muted to rule out their controlling any departments, let alone creating new ones in support of ideology. But within just a few years, the university has changed dramatically from what students and parents knew in decades past.

The university's initial commitment to multiculturalism came under the administration of Charles Knapp, who resigned as Georgia's president in 1997 (succeeded by Michael Adams) in order to help run a liberal foundation in Washington, D.C. The required multicultural course mentioned above was begun during his administration, as was the takeover (or creation) of what are today the most politicized departments: women's studies, African-American studies, history, philosophy, Romance languages, and environmental studies. There are outstanding teachers in most of these departments, but the programs as a whole are in the grips of radicals for whom education is a synonym for indoctrination.

Georgia's College of Education is another multicultural disaster. The college has adopted a "Multicultural Mission Statement" that includes sentences like these: "Multicultural education is a field of inquiry devoted to research and development of educational policies and practices that (1) recognize, accept, and affirm differences and similarities among peoples; and (2) challenge oppression and structural and procedural inequities that exist in society, generally, and in local educational settings, specifically. These inequalities arise from social, historical, economic, and political structures that influence and are influenced by culture, race, ethnicity, age, gender, educational and socioeconomic status, sexual orientation, world view, and community."

The College of Education also sponsors faculty and staff development seminars to further its goals of expanding the multicultural curriculum. Recently conducted was a seminar entitled "Exploring Expectations in a Diverse Classroom: Self-Fulfilling Prophecies Revisited," in which "members of the audience [were] asked to participate in role play to demonstrate how self-fulfilling prophecies and labeling affect expectations and interactions." Another seminar was entitled "Beyond the Lone Ranger and Tonto: An Introduction to Native American Cultures," in which a professor led "a discussion intended to explore myths and stereotypes about America's forgotten minority, Native Americans" and "to explore the impact of our nation's history on America's indigenous people."

Many other courses in various departments are also overtly politicized. Among these are a bushel of courses offered by the women's studies department, a field of study that pioneered the concept of advocacy as scholarship. Indeed, the department's web pages support this view of women's studies as mere political activism when it quotes two women's studies students. Says one: "The WS Program at UGA is an opportunity for many southern women to come to learn feminist points of view.

For many women it is a first opportunity to see themselves at the center of attention, it is a program that's all about us. We thank the Goddess for a place that our voices can be heard." Notes the other: "At its simplest, women's studies is the study of women, but I like to think of it as feminist studies — the study of how feminist perspectives might transform human thought, activity and well-being. Women's studies classes at their best teach you how to 're-think' or 'think in multiple ways.' "

Women's studies also hosted a lecture series in the spring of 1997 that included the following topics: "Lesbian and Gay Families with Children: Research, Law and Policy," "Dr. Mary Edwards Walker: The Most Famous American Cross-Dresser," "Can I Get Witness? Womanism and the Black Church," and "Public Policy and Epistemologies of Race, Class and Gender: Affirmative Action."

One of the most radical groups on campus, the Lesbian, Gay, Bisexual Student Union at Georgia (LGBSUG), is officially recognized by the university. It "works with administration, faculty, and other student organizations to ensure that the concerns of lesbian, gay, bisexual, and transgendered students are represented." Recent meetings held by the LGBSUG at its offices in the Tate Student Center on the university's campus were described as follows: "The Sex Meeting — We'll discuss gay sexual practices," "The Transgender Meeting — Issues relating to transgendered persons, with guest speakers," and a "Gay Tour of the Web — Exploring gay topics and sites on the Internet."

Politicization at Georgia also extends to hiring and tenure decisions, as is indicated by several recent incidents in departments in the humanities and social sciences. A professor whose students charged her with verbally abusing them in class, showing them pornographic movies, and being largely unavailable for office-hour consultations was nevertheless given tenure in her first try. In the same department, the wife of a professor making a six-figure salary received her Ph.D. from his colleagues and was then given a job in that same department — all of which was written into his contract before he took his job, according to sources on campus. In another case, the husband of a female faculty member was offered a tenure-track position (which was never advertised nationally) in the name of diversity, although the husband and wife are both white. She threatened to leave for what in fact was a non-tenure-track job, a move no one would make. This was recognized as a ploy to get her husband a job, and everyone knew it, but everyone played along as though the woman were serious. The bluff succeeded. "It's like a bizarre mating ritual among animals," says one professor.

Recently, two young, promising, and accomplished scholar-teachers won university-wide teaching awards while holding temporary appointments in one of Georgia's humanities departments. They were the only department members to receive such awards during those years, and yet neither man was considered seriously for tenure-track positions in his field. One was by that time the author of two books and the editor of another, and yet his personal politics were not what the department wanted. As a result, both men left Georgia at the end of their terms, and students were deprived of the opportunity to be taught by two of the finest young teachers on campus.

Georgia discussed implementing a speech code some years ago, but there was a hue and cry against it and nothing was done. As at many institutions, peer pressure and the threat of social ostracism work to hamper free speech on campus. It's enough to make professors look over their shoulders. One professor says he "routinely" censors himself as he teaches. Another professor of traditionalist leanings tells of students who came to him with word that his colleagues had tried to talk them out of taking his courses. One of the colleagues actually told one former student that the student didn't need to read Plato, Aristotle, "and all that" to understand philosophy.

Student Life: When in Athens . . .

According to the university viewbook, 85 percent of students are from Georgia, and the Hope Scholarship Program, which uses lottery money to pay the tuition of in-state students who maintain a GPA of at least 3.0, has prompted many very fine students who might have left the state in years past to stay closer to home and save a bundle. A professor at Davidson College in North Carolina, just the type of school some of these students may have attended before, says Davidson has felt the impact of the Hope Scholarship Program in the form of fewer Georgia students making the trek northward to Davidson each year. The remaining 15 percent of Georgia students represent every state in the country and more than one hundred foreign lands. And for the student interested in just about any element of science, agriculture, art, music, journalism, and some other studies, the University of Georgia — even at out-of-state tuition levels — offers quite a deal. There are still students who clearly don't belong at the university level, but many are capable and glad to have the opportunity to obtain what, depending on their major, can be a very good education at very little expense.

Although the student body at Georgia now tops 30,000 (up from just 23,000 in 1980), there are dorm rooms for only 6,500 students. Thus, most students move off campus by their junior year. The Greek houses, on historic Milledge Avenue, provide a social setting for many members of the student body, including those who don't pledge.

Another social center is the football stadium, which, standing at the center of the campus, is next to impossible to ignore on a Saturday when the Bulldogs play at home. Less known but equally impressive is the fact that the university regularly hosts the NCAA Tennis Championships at its excellent facilities. New athletic facilities insure that a student's interests can be covered, no matter what the sport.

The student body at Georgia can enjoy one of the best college towns in the South. Although Athens has felt the impact of massive growth in Atlanta, some fifty-five miles to the southwest — with its housing market now going full bore, the woods and fields that surround Athens are quickly giving way to subdivisions and shopping centers — it has even more to offer now than it once did, and is more cosmopolitan than ever before.

In recent years Athens has acquired more good restaurants and cafes. There are also excellent places with long roots in Athens, and whether students want to try one of the newer restaurants, munch burgers and dogs at the Varsity, or eat some of the best Southern cooking in the state at Wilson's Soul Food, they will find what they want in Athens. There are many bars and pizza-type places to boot, of course, as well as several coffee houses serving up the latest java. All this in a charming (and thriving) downtown adjacent to the beautiful antebellum part of campus.

GEORGIA INSTITUTE OF TECHNOLOGY

Office of Admissions
Atlanta, GA 30332-0320
(404) 894-4154
www.gatech.edu

Total enrollment: 13,086
Undergraduates: 9,594
SAT Ranges (Verbal/Math): V 550-680, M 700-760
Financial aid: 45%
Applicants: 7,676
Accepted: 61%
Enrolled: 39%
Application deadline: Feb. 1
Financial aid application deadline: Mar. 1
Tuition: resident, $2,370; nonresident, $7,110
Core curriculum: No

Calculated Excellence

The Georgia Institute of Technology is rarely called that. Rather, it is best known as Georgia Tech, and is often referred to in the same breath as one of the finest technical universities in the land. It opened its doors in 1888.

An emphasis on hard science (taught in difficult, demanding courses) has kept the Atlanta school mostly free from the ravages of politicization. Students and faculty are content to work on the most challenging technological issues of the day without wasting energy on various ideological movements. Little room exists in the curriculum or calendar for such things, although one of the newest divisions of the university, the Ivan Allen College of Management, Policy, and International Affairs, has begun to address the liberal arts aspects that had long been dim at Georgia Tech. So far, though, the liberal arts division has left most of the multiculturalism for its fellow state school, the University of Georgia.

Tech students spend long hours at study, and their work pays off in a well-respected degree and a fine education. Obviously, the school is not for students interested primarily in the liberal arts, and it's not for those with less-than-stellar SAT scores (the freshman class of fall 1997 averaged 1305). But those with the interests and aptitudes can find few places that will serve them better than Georgia Tech. The best students can even spend half of the academic year working for companies across the country in their field of study. Graduates swear by the institute, and the technology in use today has been much improved by it. If further enhancements can be made to the liberal arts division of the college without the courses becoming overly politicized, Georgia Tech will remain a technological power for some time to come.

Academic Life: In the Name of Science

Georgia Tech exists to educate engineers and scientists, and its curricular requirements reflect this mission. While the university's humanities and social science requirements are weak, they are not neglected. All students are required to pass eighteen hours of coursework in the humanities and an equal number of hours in the social sciences. And, as at other colleges in Georgia, students must pass either examinations or courses in the history of the United States and Georgia. Most students do so via introductory-level courses in political science and U.S. history, ensuring that virtually all students study American history and politics during their years at Georgia Tech. However, there is no Western civilization requirement per se.

Georgia Tech offers many different degrees in specific technical and scientific fields, and compared with the offerings in these areas at most other nontechnical universities, the choices are vast. The institute is divided into five colleges: Architecture; Computing; Sciences; Engineering; and the Ivan Allen College of Management, Policy, and International Affairs (named for a former Atlanta mayor). Combined, the colleges offer thirty-one B.S. degrees. Many of the programs are regarded among the best in the nation.

The College of Architecture, established in 1908, is well respected in professional circles. It offers undergraduate degrees in architecture, building construction, and industrial design, as well as graduate degrees.

The College of Computing, founded in 1990, grew out of the earlier School of

Information Science. Today students selecting a major in this college make good use of highly specialized facilities packed with the very latest computer equipment and run by some of the best computer scientists in the business. The college is located in a 40,000-square-foot facility built in 1989 to the standards required for this burgeoning field of study.

The College of Sciences holds six schools: biology, chemistry and biochemistry, earth and atmospheric sciences, mathematics, physics and psychology, as well as the non-degree-granting departments of health and performance sciences. In all of these fields, students will find some of the top experts churning out research and working in well-equipped laboratories. Two of the university's best professors — George Cain and Carl Spruill — teach mathematics in this college, and math, along with chemistry, is considered the best in a list of good departments.

The Ivan Allen College represents a recent attempt by Georgia Tech to strengthen its offerings in the nontechnical fields. Founded in 1990, it is billed as "a unique configuration of schools and departments that links the study of management, social sciences, and humanities, as well as Georgia Tech's three ROTC departments." In a school with Georgia Tech's history and strengths in engineering and the sciences, it makes sense to broach the humanities and social sciences from the perspective of these strengths. It has been established that no one goes to Georgia Tech to study Chaucer, so studying the humanities and social sciences as they relate to and are influenced by those areas for which the institution is traditionally known allows students and faculty to take advantage of those strengths even as they expand their understanding of our highly technical society. According to university literature, the programs in the Ivan Allen College "link the humanities and social sciences to the world of technology and science and . . . broaden the range of majors available to Tech students."

For example, students may major in the School of History, Technology, and Society, which, "unlike standard liberal arts degrees . . . requires broad-based training including course work in mathematics, science, and engineering, that is consistent with the overall mission of Georgia Tech as a technological university," according to the catalogue. Classes offered in that department include the "History of American Business," "Engineers in American Life," "History of Electrical Sciences and Technology," and "The Development of Industrial Cities," as well as more traditional historical studies.

Regardless of their majors, Georgia Tech students take their humanities and social science courses through the Ivan Allen College. The college catalogue reveals what is mostly a solid core of courses not unlike those found at many other American universities. But, like many other schools, Georgia Tech has stooped to include some courses that reflect the academic trends of the day in its liberal arts curriculum. Even though these courses make up only a small percentage of Georgia Tech's humanities and social science offerings, which themselves make up only a fraction of its overall curriculum, they constitute the only significant presence of political correctness on the Georgia Tech campus. They are more difficult to find than at most places, and certainly aren't bragged about in university literature, as is sometimes the case. But they are there.

Of course, Georgia Tech is best known for its College of Engineering, and it is here that one finds some of the best and largest programs on campus. The programs in mechanical engineering and in electrical and computer engineering are among the best on campus. There are eight degree-granting schools in this college, and one can study just about any field of engineering with very fine faculty in excellent facilities. Graduates of Georgia Tech's engineering programs command high salaries from the companies that recruit on campus (and around 550 such companies did so in one recent year). Classes are very demanding and clearly not for every student, even bright and motivated ones. But for those with an aptitude for technical thought and the discipline to study hard, Georgia Tech offers an extremely attractive degree.

Another excellent program is the Cooperative Plan, implemented in 1912 for students desiring to combine "practical experience with technical theory," as the catalogue states. Approximately one-third of the undergraduate student body, or more than three thousand students, take the Cooperative Plan, which lasts five years rather than the traditional four. Students are chosen in a competitive process based on high grades and evidence of self-discipline, then work in hundreds of industries around the country for one semester each year and take classes on campus during the other semester. Thus, students are given excellent opportunities to gain both career-strengthening job experiences and financial aid. According to the university, "the plan provides, to a substantial degree, the experience most companies require of their employees before promoting them to positions of responsibility." This opportunity is just another way Georgia Tech provides great chunks of the education students will need for life in their chosen careers.

Incoming students give the university a lot to work with, however. The 1994 freshman class had the highest average SAT scores (1,233) of any freshman class at an American public university, and the same class ranked first in the number of National Merit scholars. More than one thousand foreign students representing ninety countries come to Georgia Tech — a sure sign that its quality is recognized far and wide. And although the percentage of applicants accepted was, at 61 percent, slightly greater than in-state rival University of Georgia's 59 percent, Georgia Tech clearly ranks in the upper echelon of universities, public or private.

Even before students begin regular classes, they receive a model introduction to campus academic life. Within the last decade Georgia Tech has instituted a rigorous summer program for black and Hispanic freshmen. The five-week program had existed prior to that as a remedial program, and its success was mixed at best. "We were starting off with the idea that the kids were dumb," a university administrator told columnist William Raspberry. "We didn't say that, of course, but the program was set up on a deficit model. We were going to fix what was wrong with these minority kids." This model proved inaccurate, however, and before long the teachers in the program started their sessions with "the idea that these youngsters were unusually bright, that we had very high expectations of them," the administrator said. The students responded well, with those who took the so-called Challenge course performing better than nonminority students once regular classes began — in fact, the percentage of minority students with 4.0 GPAs in their first semester at Georgia Tech was twice that for white students. The success of the program brought the university deserved national attention, and today Georgia Tech holds a two-week version of the program for all incoming students — further proof that bright students, when challenged with academic rigor rather than patronized by well-intentioned bureaucrats, can excel in their chosen field.

Political Atmosphere: Buried in a Book

Except for the rather pale hand of multiculturalism on the Ivan Allen College curriculum, the political scene at Georgia Tech is muted, especially for such a large and prominent university. "I don't see much of it, although I do hear that there are some people in the humanities who are pretty bad," says one professor. "It does exist."

Likewise, the administration does push diversity, mainly through structures devoted to recruiting minority faculty and students. "But it's generally pretty tame stuff," the professor says. "The administration practices affirmative action, but in a fairly benign way." Another professor says that in practice, this version of affirmative action means that "if we get one thousand applications for positions in a year, and if there are any blacks or women in the stack, their applications will get looked at."

Georgia Tech does have a "director of diversity," but the serious study that goes on there and the fields in which it is concentrated make moot the multicultural points other places get hung up on. "The hard sciences and engineering are a lot more honest about academics," says a professor. "It's a more serious business here than at many places. Most of my colleagues are ultra-liberal on social issues, but academically we all get along fine. We have very rigorous academics here, and there just isn't the room for nonsense you might get elsewhere." This nonsense includes speech codes and sensitivity training, but such things at present are rare or nonexistent at Georgia Tech, and none is on the horizon.

The most obvious reason the hard sciences and engineering are mostly immune to the ideologies sprouting across so much of the nation is the unassailable need for rigor and truth in the teaching and research carried out by faculty and students in these fields. Who would have thought the day would come when the scientists are the ones relied upon to maintain a humane discourse?

Student Life: Making Much of Time

Students at Georgia Tech spend much of their time preparing for the demanding course schedule necessitated by the rigors of a technical or scientific education. Yet they may also partake of the opportunities afforded by the school's huge athletic programs, the best known of which are basketball and football. Georgia Tech is a member of the Atlantic Coast Conference and competes with other schools that invest enormous sums of money in their sports programs. Even with the high level of competition, Georgia Tech athletes rank among the top twelve NCAA programs in football player graduation rates, and in the top twenty-five programs in overall student-athlete graduation.

Other sports also receive due attention at Tech, which benefited greatly from the 1996 Olympic Games being held in Atlanta. Construction for the Games resulted in a new Olympic-size pool, new dormitories, and other amenities long desired by the Georgia Tech community. For professional sports fans, the city offers the Atlanta Braves, Hawks, and Falcons.

With about 9,600 undergraduates and about 3,700 graduate students, Tech is bound to have clubs to suit most interests. Among the 170 extracurricular activities are publications, a student-run FM radio station, and other low-key sorts of clubs, like a walking and running club and an environmental awareness group. There are, of course, many academic organizations. The Georgia Tech Library and Information Center has more technical reports than many places have books — approximately 2 million. There are also 2.7 million books, 170,000 maps, 700,000 government documents, and a complete collection of U.S. patents. The Georgia Tech Center for the Arts offers relief from numbers and diagrams with several theaters and galleries. The center has hosted the 1992 vice presidential debate; a roundtable discussion with former secretaries of defense; and performers like Itzhak Perlman, Marcel Marceau, Branford Marsalis, and the Canadian Brass.

The city of Atlanta provides the greatest diversion to Georgia Tech students. Atlanta's symphony is now on a par with the best in the land, and the number of other cultural opportunities should satisfy even the most discriminating student. The university reports that more than one thousand students undertake some form of community service. Atlanta is home to nineteen Fortune 500 corporations as well as countless high-tech industries, and boasts one of the largest convention sites in the country. In fact, many professional gatherings are on topics that relate directly to the important fields of study at Georgia Tech.

The university is located in downtown Atlanta, adjacent to "The Connector," the confluence of Interstates 75 and 85 that run through the city. What the campus lacks in aesthetic appeal, it makes up for in the ease with which its students can reach virtually every part of town. Atlanta's subway stops not far from the campus, and students with cars can reach Georgia's mountains in two hours, or the state's coast in five.

GROVE CITY COLLEGE

Office of Admissions
100 Campus Drive
Grove City, PA 16127-2104
(412) 458-2000
www.gcc.edu

Total enrollment: 2,284
Undergraduates: 2,262
SAT Ranges (Verbal/Math): avg. 1254, ACT avg. 27
Financial aid: 55%
Applicants: 2,570
Accepted: 48%
Enrolled: 51%
Application deadline: Feb. 15
Financial aid application deadline: Apr. 15
Tuition: $6,576
Core curriculum: Yes

PC, as in "Presbyterian Church"

Grove City College made national news some twenty years ago when it refused to allow the Department of Housing, Education, and Welfare to, in effect, take control of its administration and policy-making decisions. After litigation that went all the way to the Supreme Court of the United States, the college decided to refuse federal funds of any kind, and today it is one of only a few institutions of higher learning (the other notable school being Hillsdale College) that is genuinely free of federal money (including student grants and loans) and hence federal control.

In keeping itself free from meddling bureaucracies, Grove City's educational philosophy can be implemented fully and honestly. At the heart of this philosophy is the desire to offer its students the best liberal education it can muster.

Founded in 1876 and still closely affiliated with the Presbyterian Church (U.S.A.), Grove City has consistently upheld both high ideals and high standards for its faculty and students. It requires that its faculty be practicing Christians and that its students attend chapel functions a minimum of sixteen times each semester. It is not embarrassed by the Western heritage, and requires an excellent six-semester sequence in traditional humanities. "In brief, Grove City College aims to be a Christian college of liberal arts and sciences," the college states. "It seeks to help its students to grow as persons, to achieve an integrated overview of reality, and master at least one major discipline of knowledge. . . . Grove City College is not narrowly denominational. The college simply aims to give today's youth the best in the liberal arts and sciences in a wholesome Christian environment." In a day when public affiliation with a church and ardent defense of tradition can cause the eyes of the literati to roll back in their heads, Grove City has taken a courageous stand for the pursuit of truth, and has done so with academic distinction.

Academic Life: A Humane Alternative

Grove City requires of its students one class on Western culture each semester for their first three years, and doesn't try to hide the fact that the classes will concern themselves with Christianity, Western culture, and the American heritage. "While many points of view are examined, and comparisons made to other civilizations, the college continues to unapologetically advocate preservation of America's religious, political, and economic heritage of individual freedom and responsibility," the catalogue description concludes. These courses are the best evidence of the educational philosophy at Grove City. "Rejecting relativism and secularism, [the college] fosters intellectual, moral, spiritual and social development consistent with a Christian commitment to truth, morality and freedom," the catalogue states. "Rather than political, ideological or philosophical agendas, objective truth continues as the goal of liberal learning." This type of clear-sighted and principled language is rare in college catalogues, so we'll quote some more: "At the core of the curriculum, particularly in the humanities, contemporary perspectives are not emphasized to the neglect of books and thinkers and ideas in the West proved across the ages to be of value in the quest for knowledge. Intellectual inquiry remains open to the questions religion raises and receptive to the answers Christianity offers."

At Grove City students are introduced to the enduring classics rather than the trendiest fads. This commitment to genuine quality at the expense of the ephemeral marks Grove City as a place in which neither teacher nor pupil need be embarrassed by their beliefs, a place where no one is "beyond" Christianity or the realm of what is true and beautiful. In the humanities core, students study seminal works of literature, art, philosophy, and more, from the ancient Hebrews through the classical world, the Middle Ages and Renaissance, and on to modern times.

These classes constitute a significant commitment on the part of the college to ensure that every student, no matter what his major, will receive a broad liberal education before graduating. And the fact that it is carried out over a three-year period means that students have a common set of readings for most of their college career — something that is radically different from the intellectually incoherent and fractured environment found on most American campuses. "It is a recognition that some prescription on the part of the university is needed," a professor says. "One needs to be an educated person, and you do so by coming in close contact with some of the best that has been thought and written. It works very well."

Other general requirements at Grove City are more properly described as distribution requirements: all students must take two courses in social sciences/international studies, two in quantitative and logical reasoning, and two laboratory courses in natural sciences. Students seeking a B.A. degree must demonstrate second-year proficiency in a foreign language, and that is the only general requirement not made of all students (although some distribution requirements may be fulfilled with courses that also count toward a major). Students must also demonstrate writing competency either by scoring high on their SAT II (Writing Test) or by enrolling in a tutorial geared to that purpose.

Despite its small size (about 2,300 students), Grove City offers a large selection of majors — not as many as a large state or private university, naturally, but with a wide enough range that most interests are served. The most popular fields are in the liberal arts and the sciences, but majors are also available in both electrical and mechanical engineering, many fields of education, and several areas within the broad rubric of business administration. Preprofessional programs (which also require the general education classes) have extremely high success rates when it comes to sending graduates on to further study. One weakness is the absence of a major in classical languages and civilization, although students may take New Testament Greek through the department of religion and philosophy. Also, no majors are offered in art and art history, nor in theater and drama. An unusual major, reflective of the college's history and purpose, is a combined program in Christian thought (religion) and communications.

Not only is the range of courses broad, their content is exemplary. Many essays in this guide list courses that range from the narrowly ideological to the laughably mindless. Grove City, however, offers no such courses. Instead, its courses are conceived of and taught as they ought to be:

- "Literary Criticism and Theory." "A detailed examination of the major literary critics and theories of Western civilization. Part I is devoted to key figures of the Classical tradition; Part II uses basic tenets of that tradition to critique the 'new wave' of critical theory."
- "Poetry." "This course explores a wide range of traditional and contemporary poetry; gives insight into ways poets use imagery, rhyme, meter, persona and sound qualities to create meaning in poetry; provides experience with prosody and with problems in translation; and offers in-depth experience with the work of selected poets." This class requires students to read the poets themselves rather than the literary theorists who deconstruct them.
- "British History to 1781." "A general survey of British history with special emphasis on the development of the common law, the parliament, and the British constitution."

While most professors at Grove City share this commitment to the liberal arts, some even exceed that standard. According to faculty, these include John Dixon in English, Marvin Folkertsma in political science, John Sparks in business administration, Jeff Herbener and Dirk Mateer in economics, William Anderson in sociology, and Paul Schaefer in religion. As noted in the course listings above, the excellent English department has "a faculty dedicated to actually studying the intent of the writers and the background out of which they wrote," according to a professor in another department. Also strong are business; economics, which emphasizes free-market theories represented by Austrian and Public Choice schools of thought; and political science, which offers its students internships in state and national offices.

Political Atmosphere: Having None of It

Given Grove City's love of Western tradition, Christianity, and traditional morality, it comes as little surprise when a professor says, "We have no politicized departments whatsoever." While at some colleges this boast might be seen as an effort at damage control, at Grove City it is believable. Professors are recruited not only for their academic gifts, but for the way in which their teaching and personal philosophies fit with the stated purpose of the school. "There are no pockets of opposition," says another professor. "There are many fine faculty out there with good Ph.D.s. We let them know we're committed to Christian values and we check their references. We don't get bamboozled. There has been no erosion of commitment to the college's core commitments."

Finding people who match the college's requirements and philosophy and "are not tainted by political correctness" is getting more difficult, says another faculty member. "It's especially difficult in literature and theology. We check references very thoroughly. We say right up front that we're evangelical and are committed to personal and economic liberty."

Perhaps the most valuable aspect of Grove City's ideology-free environment is the freedom it gives to both faculty and students. "Because we have a clear statement of purpose and a mission, we attract like-minded people and we're able to concentrate on the intellectual development of our students," says a professor. "People who come here to teach can actually do what they're most interested in."

Many small schools have taken the popular media's bait and tried to raise their standing in the ubiquitous (and largely meaningless) commercial magazine rankings by hiring and promoting faculty who put publishing first and teaching second. Grove City is above all that, for it has been wise enough to recognize that the true purpose of a liberal arts college is to teach the next generation to search for truth and to live responsible lives in the light of what reason and revelation have made known. Grove City's "position is that if you produce useful research it's a plus, and that's fine as long as it's not about minutia," says a professor. "This is not a publish or perish atmosphere, but one geared toward the conveyance of knowledge from one generation to the next. Quite a few of us publish, but basically this is not a publishing place." Publishing does figure in such things as pay and assessment, but it is not the central mission of those who teach first and publish second.

"This is a teaching college, but we do encourage publishing if you have something to say," says one professor. However, given the culture at most large graduate schools today, it is not always easy to convince new Ph.D.s that they can be secure in putting teaching (or any other matter in life) before publishing. "You must deal with this matter when fresh Ph.D.s come on board," one professor says. "They come out of the publishing culture. The majority of people we've hired in the last three or four years are from other colleges, so they already have ten or fifteen years of experience. And they're not left alone here — we evaluate them."

Tenure — often the carrot waggling at the end of the publishing stick — is not an issue at Grove City: no one gets it, ever. Every single employee is hired on a year-to-year contractual basis. While one might assume that this would result in a high turnover rate among faculty, just the opposite is true. "The college has a very low attrition rate among the faculty," says one professor. "We don't dismiss someone for transient reasons. If I ceased to teach they would first try to rehabilitate me, but they wouldn't put up with me indefinitely. There is a great deal of trust here. You don't worry about it if you do a good job." The unusual arrangement was undertaken to prevent the type of abuses of tenure that have of late made news — a professor who stopped writing lectures years ago, or who regards his students as impediments, or who is absent more often than not. At Grove City the absence of tenure acts as a natural braking mechanism for those who would turn the campus into a place of indoctrination.

In another rare practice, Grove City does not accept government aid of any kind. "Grove City College operates on a balanced budget, refuses all federal aid, and remains virtually debt-free, thereby proving that higher education can operate responsibly by providing an affordable, first-rate education without government funding or mandates," the college viewbook states. According to a faculty member, "Our independence means that the state and federal governments don't have to look beyond our own rationales and reasoning. They don't have to do anything about our needs, and the speed of change on campus and the content of it can be self-determined. Also, we can pay attention to other academic groups and other private accrediting agencies." Even without government money, the cost of tuition *and* room and board at Grove City is just more than half the national average for four-year private schools — an amazing $11,000. That's much less than the tuition alone at many inferior schools. Included in the cost are new laptop computers and printers that students keep upon completing their degrees.

No wonder so many people want to get in. Grove City received 2,300 applications for the five hundred openings in the freshman class that began school in the fall of 1996 — proof that many students are still interested in quality liberal arts educations. Nearly 51 percent of those accepted were enrolled, a very high number.

With all the applicants, Grove City was able to select a freshman class with an average SAT score of 1,240 and an average high school GPA of 3.7, thereby ensuring that excellent students will be sitting in the college's excellent classes.

Student Life: Rules for Living

Grove City's commitment to Christian values is apparent in its student life policies. The college's philosophy reflects concepts of dignity, truth, and honor that are ridiculed elsewhere as hopelessly out-of-date. For example, students are required to live in single-sex campus housing unless they are commuters living with families, and there are no coed dorms. All students must attend chapel or convocations at least sixteen times per semester. Similarly, students are warned that certain types of behavior will result in disciplinary action, perhaps even dismissal. Among these are the use of drugs and alcohol as well as premarital sex, homosexuality, or "any other conduct which violates historic Christian standards."

The college catalogue frankly describes what students will find should they choose to attend: "Students in a free society have the right to choose the college which best suits their needs, interests and lifestyles. Students, having chosen their college, have the responsibility to observe the standards and regulations established by the college they have selected. Members of the Grove City College campus community are expected to observe Christian moral standards, as they have been understood by most of the Christian community historically." As the application and enrollment figures demonstrate, many find this structured environment a highly desirable alternative to the anything-goes attitude found on most campuses today.

The college has also preserved architectural traditions, and its stunning Collegiate Gothic campus includes spires, stained glass, and green malls.

Grove City students compete in eighteen intercollegiate sports at the NCAA Division III level and play on four club teams. The Physical Learning Center contains two swimming pools — one for recreation, one for competition — as well as fitness and weight rooms, an "Intramural Room" with four full-size basketball courts, a dance studio, a bowling alley, and racquetball courts.

With more than one hundred student organizations and activities, the college caters to virtually every interest. Because of the school's religious and intellectual orientation, there are no worries about liberal political or activist groups disrupting the campus. Instead, seventeen religious groups and activities are available, including organizations for Protestants and Catholics. Many performances are offered throughout the school year. There are sixteen honor societies and as many departmental and professional clubs. Eight local sororities and nine local fraternities fill out the social scene on campus; about 40 percent of students join them.

Grove City, Pennsylvania, is a small town of only eight thousand. But should students want to reach a big city, Pittsburgh is only sixty miles to the south.

HAMPDEN-SYDNEY COLLEGE

P.O. Box 667
Hampden-Sydney, VA 23943
(800) 755-0733
www.hsc.edu

Total enrollment: 975
Undergraduates: 975
SAT Ranges (Verbal/Math): V 510-610, M 500-610
Financial aid: 52%
Applicants: 750
Accepted: 89%
Enrolled: 43%
Application deadline: Mar. 1
Financial aid application deadline: Mar. 1
Tuition: $15,373
Core curriculum: No

A Few Good Men

Hampden-Sydney is a rare bird among colleges, even small liberal arts colleges. In a day when single-sex education is under attack, especially when that single sex is male, Hampden-Sydney remains an all-male school. In an age when core curricular requirements are either thrown out entirely or reduced to cafeteria-style distribution requirements, Hampden-Sydney maintains a curriculum that, although not a core per se, gives its men a solid and thorough grounding in the history, literature, and culture of European and American civilizations. Finally, while most liberal arts colleges are trying to gain respect by encouraging their faculty to pursue abstract research agendas, Hampden-Sydney seems to have struck a balance between teaching excellence and a solid reputation for faculty research. "Hampden-Sydney's standards remain steadfast, while society's shift back and forth," says the school's promotional material. "And it has paid off: our students appreciate the stability that comes from our adherence to the ideals and standards of our founders."

Those founders go back quite a ways. The college has been in operation since 1775, and is the tenth-oldest in the country. Its campus in southern Virginia is a National Historic Preservation Zone. The college was one of a group (also including the College of New Jersey, now better known as Princeton University) founded by Scotch-Irish Presbyterians who wanted to duplicate in this new land the ideals of the University of Edinburgh. The founders chose the names of two English martyrs for representative government who had died in the previous century, John Hampden and Algernon Sydney, then got their own local patriots — Patrick Henry and James Madison, among others — to serve on the college's first board of trustees. Students fought in the Revolutionary War and the War between the States (the college kept its doors open through both conflicts).

While men in those days were the only constituency any college served, Hampden-Sydney has lately flirted with members of the opposite sex — that is to say, it has questioned whether to admit them as students. The board voted down a change in 1996, but the faculty favored it by a vast margin, saying that the quality of students would be improved by more competitive admissions. It may yet turn out that female students will come to Hampden-Sydney, ending all-male education. But the college's dedication to its past has served it well, and it is to be hoped that it will continue to do so.

Academic Life: The Best Foundation

Hampden-Sydney does not have an actual core curriculum, but its distribution requirements are more structured than most. The college has a definite idea of what it wants its students to learn, and that alone makes the requirements preferable to many found at other schools. "The college is committed to the development of humane and lettered men and to the belief that a liberal education provides the best foundation not only for a professional career, but for the great intellectual and moral challenges of life," the college catalogue says. The school's respect for its own traditions has been a worthwhile influence as well. "Our curriculum is strong because it hasn't been reinvented every decade," a college publication says.

The finest feature of the standard curriculum consists of two yearlong sequences in history and the humanities. This feature would be even better were both sequences required; however, students choose one or the other. The history sequence, the more popular of the two, emphasizes political and cultural history since the Renaissance. The humanities courses incorporate the art, literature, philosophy, theology, and history of the ancient, medieval, and modern periods. Neither sequence is considered easier than the other, and in both students are exposed to the great thinkers, books, and ideas of Western civilization. At many colleges such a sequence would be under near-constant attack from radical faculty, but at Hampden-Sydney the faculty's "only impulse is to make it more difficult," says a professor.

Hampden-Sydney students must also demonstrate their skill in rhetoric, a term not often heard on campuses these days. Two introductory-level courses are required, after which students must either take a proficiency exam or pass an advanced rhetoric tutorial. In addition, all students must pass either two 200-level courses or one 300-level course in a foreign language.

The remainder of the requirements fall into typical categories. However, Hampden-Sydney doesn't just let students pick and choose as their fancies dictate: the distribution areas each contain only a handful of classes that will fulfill the requirement. For example, four courses are required in the area of natural sciences and mathematics. The catalogue states that two courses must be selected from among Biology 101, Chemistry 110, Astronomy 105 or 106, and Physics 131. One of the courses must include a lab. To round out that category, students must take one of nine different math courses, plus an additional course outside the student's major. A similar situation is found in the social science requirements — two of the three courses must be chosen from about ten offerings. The final distribution category, humanities, demands five courses in addition to the history or humanities sequence. These are fulfilled by taking one of eight courses in philosophical and religious thought; one course in classics, English literature, or classic and modern literature; one course out of six fine arts offerings; and two additional courses outside the student's major.

The classes selected as worthy of the general education requirements aren't the politicized nonsense found elsewhere. The six fine arts courses, of which a student selects two, include introductory courses in music, literature, the visual arts, and theater, as well as a survey of the history of Western art and a class called "Topics in Music History." The catalogue says the history of art courses emphasize "the classical tradition and its transformations first by Christianity, then by the Industrial Revolution and the emergence of modernism." The college does an admirable job of not capitalizing the "isms" in its course descriptions, which is rare enough, but also of insuring that art classes are about art, that music classes are about music, and that course offerings pertain to the broader topic at hand, rather than serving as forums for the condemnation of Western culture. The faculty "take the liberal arts seriously, the Western Tradition seriously," a professor says. "They take the life of mind seriously. The students understand this."

Some of the best professors at Hampden-Sydney include James Pontuso and William Jones in political science, James Arieti and John Brinkley in classics, William Schear in biology, and Kenneth Townsend in economics.

Ever traditional, Hampden-Sydney has not followed the trend toward more and more departments; rather, it concentrates its considerable resources on a list of about thirty standard majors. Without the need to spend money disproportionately on fringe departments, the school has consolidated its strengths. One of the strongest departments on campus is political science. At Hampden-Sydney, the political science department is not dominated by discussions of voting behavior or contemporary legislation. Rather, it sees contemporary political problems in the light of the writings of the great historical Western and American political thinkers. Consider the catalogue description of one course:

- "Introduction to Comparative Government" (which is one of the few courses that satisfies a social science distribution requirement). "An examination and comparison of ancient and modern regimes, including the ancient *polis* and modern liberal democratic and totalitarian regimes. The intention is to contrast ancient and modern political principles and forms, and show the range of alternatives available in modernity."

The same course at many other institutions wouldn't dare include the political philosophy of the ancients as a legitimate line of inquiry, lest the professor be accused of worshiping at the altars of dead white European males. Hampden-Sydney doesn't so much buck current trends as it just plain ignores them. One can only wonder what might happen if enough colleges committed themselves to this sensible line of thinking.

The classics department, though only three people strong, is also considered one of the college's best teaching departments. Chairman John Brinkley is described, favorably, by a colleague in another department as "the last guy who knows everything." From the smallest major we turn to the largest: economics, in which approximately 30 percent of Hampden-Sydney students major. This department is also strong, and has struck a balance between theory and practice. A course is offered in the history of economic thought, reaching back to Plato and Xenophon, and another focuses exclusively on the Austrian School.

The English department is good on its own, but quite good when compared to the politicized departments at other schools. "They don't seem to care about postmodernism or deconstructionism," a professor says. "They teach the canon." While in many undergraduate English departments courses in feminist and ethnic studies outnumber those in the traditional subfields, Hampden-Sydney's department has only two courses — one in Afro-American literature and one called "Women and Literature" — that fit this bill. However, both are offered infrequently, and the latter course, at least according to the catalogue description, emphasizes writers like Jane Austen and Virginia Woolf rather than contemporary radical feminists.

Not all departments are strong, and some have shown a tendency toward political correctness. The history department (described by a professor from another department as doing "a lot of film-showing") has a somewhat revisionist stance on the Civil War. This phenomenon is apparent at other Southern schools, and defies any explanation other than that the professors themselves got their information from politicized graduate schools, perhaps in the North. Hampden-Sydney's history department has adopted an "old-fashioned, 60s style," according to a professor. Whatever the reason, the attitude is curious at a strongly traditional school just miles from Appomattox Court House, located in the state that was the site of nearly two-thirds of all battles fought in the War between the States.

The foreign languages and philosophy departments are both described as "weak," but clearly their shortcomings are not the result of ideology but of lower-quality teaching. Both departments have lost a well-regarded teacher in recent years, which didn't help their problems. One professor gives credit to foreign languages for recognizing its own deficiencies, and for making some efforts to improve.

Political Atmosphere: A Vote for Real Diversity

At the same time Virginia Military Institute (VMI) was losing a lengthy court battle to remain male-only, Hampden-Sydney was undergoing its own crisis regarding enrollment policies. When a decision by the U.S. Supreme Court erased the nation's only public all-male colleges (VMI and The Citadel), that left Hampden-Sydney, Deep Springs College, Wabash College, and Morehouse College as the only remaining nonmilitary colleges that did not admit women. A fellow Virginia college with an equally impressive pedigree, Washington and Lee University, had gone coed in 1985. Hampden-Sydney, in the fall of 1996, came very close to doing the same.

College faculty had voted 43 to 17 in favor of coeducation. According to the *Chronicle of Higher Education*, faculty thought opening admissions would bring better students to campus and make classes more challenging. Hampden-Sydney's applications were dropping, off more than 25 percent to 750 after a high of 1,000 a decade earlier. Because of the low number of applicants, the college admitted nearly 90 percent of applicants — too high a number to consider its admissions at all competitive. However, 85 percent of the students wanted to keep women out, according to a student government survey. Alumni were also in favor of continuing the single-sex policy, though by not so hefty a margin as one might guess — that vote was close.

No vote count was released, but Hampden-Sydney's trustees decided to stick with their 220 years of tradition and remain all-male. Students greeted the news with relief, and while some faculty were disappointed, a college dean who had favored coeducation told the *Chronicle,* "Any disappointment they feel will be very mild compared to the deep commitment that they have to the students they've been teaching for years." To others on the faculty, it was puzzling that the issue was even raised at all; there are plenty of places to get a coeducational college experience, but very few like Hampden-Sydney. "It reminds me of the man who goes into a Chinese restaurant and orders roast beef," classics professor Brinkley told the *Chronicle.*

It is interesting that the vote came about because of concerns about academic standards and quality students, and not because of some misguided concerns about diversity or multiculturalism. Another small, coed college would have done nothing to advance the cause of true diversity, yet would have been a victory for those who assume anything all-male must be evil. The world of academe is more diverse — not less — thanks to Hampden-Sydney's decision.

In fact, the politics prevalent in the world outside of Farmville, Virginia, rarely come into play at Hampden-Sydney. There are no radical student groups and no activist faculty. A senior professor reports that "a few race problems existed several years ago" as part of a debate over whether the college would fund "The Brothers," an African-American student group. The controversy was settled when the group agreed to structure itself as more of a social and leisure group than as a political group. A current list of campus groups does not mention any such organization, nor does any other minority social or advocacy group appear. Any disagreements faculty might have over curriculum is solved in reasonable debate rather than raised voices. "Any drive for black or minority studies is sensible," a professor says. The casual observer might also speculate that the traditionalism of the curriculum and the college's gentlemanly expectations of its students produce well-mannered young men, where civil debate and general good will make agitation unnecessary.

One of the strongest indicators of the character of Hampden-Sydney students is the high place the school's Honor Code holds in their minds. "For us, it means more than simply signing a card as freshmen, pledging not to cheat on work in college," a student writes in the candidate's guide. "Instead, we view it as a law to be followed for the rest of our lives." The Honor Code is enforced by students, not faculty or administration, and the penalties for lying, cheating, stealing, and other infractions (including not reporting Honor Code violations by fellow students) are stiff, usually expulsion or a dishonorable suspension. Students must write on every piece of written work the following pledge: "On my honor I have neither given nor received any aid on this work, nor am I aware of any breach of the Honor Code that I shall not immediately report."

Rather than making Hampden-Sydney's atmosphere unbearable, the Honor Code gives the students a certain amount of freedom, since they expect that their fellow classmates will always act like gentlemen. One professor tells of thirty-seven cents left on a desk in a classroom for several weeks before it was claimed. A picture in the candidate's guide shows piles of letters sitting in front of the closed campus post office window, with the required funds for extra postage sitting next to or on top of each letter, undisturbed. Certainly the expectation that one's peers will always act with honor and goodwill contributes to the congeniality of the campus.

Student Life: Rare Club for Men

Prospective students who are put off by the all-male atmosphere should note that many not-male-only schools (Duke University, the University of North Carolina, North Carolina State, the University of Virginia, the University of Richmond, the College of William and Mary, Washington and Lee University, Randolph-Macon College, and Longwood University, not to mention all-female schools like Hollins College, Sweet Briar College, and Randolph-Macon Women's College) are located within an hour's drive of Hampden-Sydney. Visitation is allowed (with limits) in the dormitories. Not a lot of limits, mind you. "Don't be surprised if there are more women on your hall some weekends than there are guys," a student writes in the candidate's guide. The guide makes a point of including several pictures of Hampden-Sydney students with women at college functions. Later, the student mentions another benefit of being a man among men: "It makes it much easier to decide what to wear in the morning."

If the school sounds sort of like a big fraternity, it is not far from that. Fraternity Circle is home to the college's Greek organizations, and the center of the weekend social scene. "Many weekends, the Circle seems like one big party," according to the candidate's guide. There's certainly not much else to do in Farmville, the small town nearest the college. However, students enjoy the rural atmosphere and establishments, including a restaurant that still lets customers put their meals on a tab. Outdoor activities seem to be the most readily available source of recreation. If Farmville doesn't have what students are looking for, it's less than one hundred miles to Roanoke, Richmond, Charlottesville, Norfolk, and Raleigh-Durham. Washington, D.C., is slightly farther away.

Hampden-Sydney competes in eight intercollegiate sports at the NCAA Division III level as a member of the Old Dominion Athletic Conference. Football games are considered major social events. There are also club sports in fencing, rugby, skeet, volleyball, water polo, and wrestling. About 80 percent of students participate in at least one of the thirteen available intramural sports.

The forty or so student groups are generally quiet and serious in nature. These include a few rare listings, like the Madisonian Society and the Society for the Preservation of Southern Heritage, as well as a debate society, publications, InterVarsity Christian Fellowship, Amnesty International, and Habitat for Humanity.

HARVARD UNIVERSITY

Dean of Admissions and Financial Aid
Harvard and Radcliffe Colleges
Byerly Hall, 8 Garden Street
Cambridge, MA 02138
(617) 495-1551
www.harvard.edu

Total enrollment: 18,250
Undergraduates: 7,050
SAT Ranges (Verbal/Math): V 700-790, M 690-790
Financial aid: 52%
Applicants: 18,180
Accepted: 11%
Enrolled: 78%
Application deadline: Jan. 1 (Dec. 15 preferred)
Financial aid application deadline: Feb. 1
Tuition: $20,865
Core curriculum: No

In Name Only

It has long been an article of belief in American popular culture that Harvard University is the best, most elite, most prestigious school in the country and, along with Oxford and Cambridge Universities in England, one of the best in the world. It might seem churlish to begrudge the university its reputation. Over its 350 years of existence it has acquired the world's largest university library; one of the widest ranges of schools, departments, and programs available at any university; and a gathering of first-rate scholars who, traditionally, were not merely the elite of their professions but of the intellectual world at large. It is also, not coincidentally, the richest university in the world, and it uses its fiscal and intellectual capital to influence the world of ideas and policy from Washington to Tokyo to Moscow.

Harvard still retains many of the best-known scholars and thinkers in the country. And, for all the (often just) criticism leveled against it, even its strongest detractors would gladly admit that it has a glorious past and unequaled resources for what could be a glorious future. The very name Harvard will always carry great weight in cultural and intellectual circles — that fact may never change. What has changed, of course, is the relative quality of many other institutions of higher learning. Strong though it still is, Harvard no longer occupies the absolute top of virtually every field in the way it did for decades. Too many other schools now vie for the world's intellectual resources, and talent and money are now far more diffused than was once the case. This is a situation over which Harvard had virtually no control.

What it could control, but has chosen not to, is its embrace of the new ideological orthodoxies. This fault has changed the complexion of Harvard and has moved it away from its moorings as a center of original research. Ironically, Harvard has lost much originality and now marches in lockstep with the dominant trends of the intellectual world. When a tiny college does this, perhaps in search of notoriety, one can ignore it. But when Harvard does something, that thing suddenly acquires a stamp of intellectual approval. Unfortunately, the school now turns with the wind, rather than charting its own course, as it once did.

This new style of thought does not affect everyone on campus. A fair number of professors remain who, even if they are quite liberal on many issues, nevertheless resent being ordered to think or speak in a particular way on a host of complex issues. But it must also be said that at Harvard, as at so many other universities, the future seems to belong to those who place political self-righteousness before rigor, or who value feeling secure in the faculty lounge over pursuing truth no matter the cost. Thus, although Harvard has always been elitist in the best sense of the word —in demanding excellence unapologetically — it now uses a bastardized notion of elitism to demand conformity in its neopopulist schemes by which it hopes to enforce egalitarianism from the top down. There are real problems at Harvard: the core curriculum is large and undefined; grade inflation has become outrageous; and political correctness is to many there a higher calling than intellectual integrity. Still, there is almost nothing that could topple

Harvard from its traditional place of honor. It is no longer the best university in the nation, but its name will never fade, and may never be superseded.

Academic Life: Decisions, Decisions, Decisions

Harvard has what it refers to as a core curriculum, but this is really more of a distribution requirement than anything approaching a set of readings common to all undergraduate students. Some faculty consider this "core" the university's laughing-stock. "We like to brag 'of course we have a core curriculum. It contains over 350 courses!' " says one faculty member. Says another: "We have a hollow core. You can take whatever you want." And yet another: "Our core . . . exists for the convenience of the faculty, who can't decide on what an education is. Harvard provides absolutely no guarantee that a student will emerge with a broad liberal education."

The only course required of all students is expository writing. No course or courses common to all students require a broad range of reading, or involve history, the humanities, or basic science. "Most students don't like it — they're pretty firmly against it," says a professor. "We have bright kids, but many aren't well read, or at least not as much as they should be. Many don't seek out challenges. But they're not guaranteed a solid education, although they can get it. The curriculum is debased, but the old, good stuff is still there."

One of the principal problems faced by Harvard and so many other institutions is that there is no longer a consensus as to what an educated person should know. The canon has been under attack for years, and today entire departments or schools of thought are sagging under the dead weight of ideology. "The task of finding good courses falls upon the student's shoulders, and most don't succeed," says a student. "Many of them graduate very uneducated."

In fact, one of the most common complaints among students is that the structure of the "core" gives them no guidance in obtaining a broad liberal education. With so many choices, nothing stands out as important — especially since the university refuses to say what's important. "The core here is terrible," says one student. "It's perhaps not as lenient as at some other schools, but it is a very absurd system. The point isn't to teach any particular knowledge but instead to teach approaches to knowledge. Usually you get a professor teaching their latest knowledge. Therefore, what you study isn't important — it's the approach that counts. You can get away without learning a scrap of European or U.S. history."

The university does allow a "shopping week," the first week of each semester, during which students may drop and add courses or just visit a variety of classrooms in an effort to locate good professors or teaching fellows. This is a superb opportunity for the student who cares about his education, and, used properly, it can bring some order to the chaotic distribution offerings. Many tainted classes can be scratched off the list and many good ones can be found, thanks to shopping week.

Asked why the curriculum at Harvard is so disordered, one faculty member says many faculty are driven by ideology, but many are just "mediocre academic liberals who till their narrow fields. So it's just ignorance and also some laziness." Students are largely left to their own devices. "They have a tremendous choice of courses with virtually no guidance. There's no rhyme or reason, because we can't agree on what knowledge is," a professor says. "It's absurd. It's like a hospital in which the doctors can't decide on what is health. If you call up professors at Harvard and say 'what's an educated person?,' most would be tongue-tied."

Not only can Harvard not decide what an education is, its upper-level faculty are starting to forget about *educating* as well. Well-known scholars, of which Harvard has a boatload, mainly teach large lecture classes. Teaching fellows (graduate students) are used in most classes. "Under the best circumstances, you can get both: the great scholar who is a great lecturer, and then a good grad student who is a good discussion leader for sections," a student says. Another student says high-quality professors who do teach are "very isolated" because of their commitment to their students and their (by Harvard's standards) political heterodoxy.

Perhaps it is this hands-off attitude that is to blame for the high grades professors have begun ladling out like water. Grade inflation has been in the news at all Ivy League schools recently. It seems that the difficult part of a Harvard education is getting admitted. After that, just about anyone who remains sober half the time and shows up for class can, in most cases, count on a high grade. Yale recently attempted to address this issue, but if Harvard has done anything at all, it isn't showing. A senior professor reports that a full 45 percent of grades are A-minus or better. "Grade inflation is even seen in the sciences now, because they think their students are being disadvantaged," the professor says. "There was some worry last spring [June 1996] that too many people graduated summa cum laude." Another professor says that in the English department, the *average* grade in all undergraduate classes is an A-minus. And, the professor says, "Women's studies has never graduated anyone without at least a magna cum laude. Virtually everyone is a magna across the College."

Some of the best professors at Harvard are well known, and it would be false to imply that no one there teaches his or her own classes, or that no one demands much of his or her students. Faculty and students name these professors as the most outstanding on a star-studded faculty: Robert Barro and Martin Feldstein in economics; Peter Berkowitz, Harvey Mansfield, Stanley Hoffman, Steve Rosen, and Richard Tuck in government; James Hankins, Stephen Thernstrom, Ernest May, Abigail Thernstrom, Thomas Bisson, Ernst Badian, Steven Ozment, and Brendan Dooley in history; Owen Gingerich in history of science; Ruth Wisse in Jewish studies; Peter Rosen of international relations and Roger Porter of American politics; Robert Levin in music; John Sherman in fine arts; Donald Fanger in comparative literature; Thomas Scanlon in philosophy; Jon Levenson in the Divinity School; and Larry Benson and Helen Vendler in the English department. Not to be missed is one of the great courses at Harvard, General Education 105, "The Literature of Social Reflection," taught by

Pulitzer Prize–winning psychiatrist Robert Coles. The most outstanding departments are said to be government, physics, mathematics, biology, and chemistry, and it should also be noted that Harvard's English department is the only one among all the Ivies that requires its majors to take a course in Shakespeare.

On the other side of the street are politicized courses and departments, some of which pioneered the academic obsession with victimhood. African studies, social studies, the Center for Literary and Cultural Studies, English, fine arts, anthropology, Romance languages and literatures, comparative literature, and women's studies (whose website seeks to advance the interests of women by providing links to cyber-porn) are full of politically correct faculty, according to many professors and students.

"Many departments, especially in the humanities, are very politicized," a senior professor says. "There are a number of egregiously bad courses, and the way they teach is also politicized. This is pervasive in the humanities, less true in the social sciences. It is not so true in political science or economics. History is in between the humanities and social sciences."

Social studies draws the ire of another professor. "Social studies is a terrible department because they indoctrinate the best of the students with multicultural-ism," the professor says. "They're drawn to multiculturalism by a grab-bag of social theory, Adam Smith, Hume, and Weber, but then they bring out the feminists and the multiculturalists." The department didn't fool at least one student. "I found the Social Studies department especially left-leaning," the student said. "The fundamental premise of the department — the 'social studies method' of approaching social phe-nomena — seems derived ultimately from Marx. That is, the major historical events (the French Revolution, the rise of capitalism) are assumed to arise out of economical and social conditions. The independent role of ideas and philosophy in shaping history is underestimated." Political and social theory are introduced at the sopho-more level, but the first semester mainly centers on the Continental tradition (Marx, Durkheim, Weber, and Freud), while postmodernists like Foucault, Habermas, and contemporary feminist theorists get the second semester. John Locke and the Amer-ican Founders, for example, do not appear on the syllabus.

The Center for Literary and Cultural Studies is "big on affirmative action" and now runs the institution that schedules most humanities lectures and talks at Harvard, according to a professor. "The speakers on panels are all in lockstep politically," another professor says. No wonder, then, that the humanities — especially English, fine arts, and art history — are considered by some to be almost totally in the hands of multicul-turalists. While "multiculturalism and deconstruction seem to have a stronghold" in the English department, according to one student, the fine arts department has recently replaced a popular survey course on Western art with something entitled "Art and Visual Culture: Introduction to the Historical Study of Art and Architecture." One student calls the new offering "a postmodern course that offers a lecture on subway graffiti and popular visual culture while eschewing the outdated or imperialist idea of a linear tradition of high Western art running from Greece to Europe to America."

The Romance languages, especially French, are also very radical. "You can't just take a regular literature course in them any more," says a student. "There are many joint appointments in French and women's studies."

Despite the push for diversity and multiculturalism in the curriculum — a movement often described by its perpetrators as an attempt at unity and togetherness — students and faculty at Harvard say they have rarely felt more alone or isolated. Where once a spirit of collegiality and friendship existed among faculty themselves as well as between professors and students, there is now a feeling of competition, some say. Now that being a professor can turn into a lucrative job, perhaps at another university, there is less a sense of loyalty to the school and students than a concern for oneself.

"The people here work very hard. It's a very isolating experience and not very sociable at all. It can be a very lonely place," a professor says. "You see people on campus and may stop and talk for fifteen or twenty minutes, but collegiality is always on the run. And it's the same for the students. . . . They have to eat every day so they see each other in the dining halls, but only there."

Political Atmosphere: Moving On

The political atmosphere at Harvard is permeated with the same ideological fervor that has become so widespread in American higher education. There are some differences, however, most of which stem from Harvard's will to maintain its prestigious name, and from the fact that the faculty is so intelligent that whatever it does, it does wholeheartedly, whether that entails acquiescence or rebellion.

Those who rebel against the trends at Harvard, however, do not get far. University disciplinary structures are stacked against them, and, in the opinion of one well-informed source, they even border on the violation of constitutional rights. "There is an utter obsession by Harvard's middle-level administrators, assistant deans especially, with multiculturalism and diversity," the source says. "I do know how it impacts on the fairness of Harvard's internal disciplinary mechanism, the Administrative Board at Harvard College. . . . Students charged with 'politically incorrect' behavior do not have a chance. They are convicted before they are tried. They are abused by the deans and assistant deans, and even by the Harvard University Police Department, which is under the direction of Harvard's Office of the General Counsel. There are no rational fact-finding procedures when such a student stands accused, because they don't want to learn the truth; they want to make an example and demonstrate that Harvard will not tolerate politically incorrect behavior. There is a frightening level of utter fanaticism among these administrators." Much of this behavior occurs behind closed doors; this is rationalized under some guise of protection for the person whose case is being heard, but the truth is, the proceedings often could not stand the light of day, the source says.

Political correctness only goes so far among students, owing to their intellectual abilities, says a professor. Faculty, however, also very bright but very liberal, have bought into the "statist idea that the state is the arbiter for social improvement," the professor says. Liberal faculty control all faculty committees, including those involved in hiring and tenure decisions. Another professor says that what keeps Harvard from totally rolling over on its multicultural side is worries about the school's good name. "What acts as a check is the desire to maintain Harvard's prestige. So, as for tenured hirings, they're still quite tough." While Harvard is home to the biggest-name African-American scholars, including Henry Louis Gates, Jr., William Julius Wilson, and Cornel West, the school has not been able to attract large numbers of black professors because of the tight job market; in fact, the number of black professors is about the same as it was thirty years ago. Harvard has hired many more women, mostly in the humanities.

Harvard is notoriously stingy at giving tenure to anyone coming up through the ranks of its professoriate, preferring instead to use its prestige to take faculty from other schools after they earn their scholarly reputations. This attitude is extended to virtually all young scholars, including those who have earned their Ph.D. at Harvard itself — this at a place that is notoriously inbred. It's a bit like a farmer who only harvests what others have sown rather than planting the fields himself. Most teaching falls to assistant professors who are fully aware that they will not be given tenure. "The assistant professors can teach what they want to, and they usually teach their next article because they're so professionally oriented," a professor says. "So, they have a good time here, but they know they have to move on."

It's hard enough for a politically moderate professor to obtain tenure at Harvard, let alone someone on the conservative side. It is in fact rare that a conservative would be hired to begin with, according to one professor. Of a professor up for tenure in one of Harvard's most respected departments, a student says: "I think it would be amazing if he got tenure because he is one of those professors who is both an amazing scholar and a great teacher." Says a longtime Harvard professor: "It is hard to document the denial of tenure on political grounds, but it happens all the time."

Conservative students at Harvard have no jobs to fear for, but their beliefs bring other consequences, both socially and academically. "Conservative students who speak up are treated as pariahs," says a student who graduated with honors. The student estimates that around 20 percent of students are Republicans, a small enough percentage to make conservatives feel isolated. "Being unpopular is the price you pay for speaking up," the student says. "I haven't been penalized for my political views per se, but for being unwilling to use deconstructionist types of theory in papers. It will really hurt your grades if you don't use the usual feminist platitudes in your papers."

The upside to being a conservative student at Harvard, according to a senior professor, is that you may get a better education. "They don't lap up what's in front of them," the professor says. "It is better for conservatives to go to a liberal university, because the most valuable thing to be learned in a democracy is to learn to stand up to public opinion."

Public opinion is imposed though speech codes and sensitivity training, another sign that the nontraditional elements are in control at Harvard. Undergraduates are subject to gender-neutral language directives and "mandatory sensitivity sessions which would be a joke were they not such a serious intrusion," says a source. "The program is run by fanatics. It is quite upsetting." This comes at a time when schools and courts have begun to question seriously the propriety and sometimes the constitutionality of speech codes; however, the source says, "The faculty, at the urging or at least with the acquiescence of the dean, actually adopted a set of sexual harassment guidelines that seriously impinge on speech at the Law School." The Derek Bok Teaching Center is the base for sensitivity training, and all residential units at Harvard have "affirmative action and sex tutors," a professor says. "The job of the latter is to help heterosexuals 'discover' they're homosexuals, and to help women who've had sex realize they've been 'raped.' " Freshmen face sessions on race and sexual orientation, according to one student. "There are also mandatory safe sex educational sessions featuring instructions on the expert use of condoms (on bananas), dental dams, rubber gloves, and other devices," the student says.

Student Life: Go Play in the Yard

Freshmen live and dine at Harvard Yard, a quadrangle of buildings whose name is often used as a term of opprobrium. Upperclassmen live in one of Harvard's famed houses. These residential and dining units give the student body a smaller unit of identity than would be possible in undifferentiated dorms, and this style of housing is one Harvard tradition that seems safe. There are twelve residential houses, all coed, each of which contains a library, various university personnel, and some recreational facilities. Students seem to enjoy the arrangement, and the university has no Greek system.

Radcliffe College, once known as one of the nation's premier undergraduate women's colleges, is now essentially indistinguishable from Harvard College, under whose auspices it operates de facto if not de jure. In this it has followed the lot of most other women's colleges, such as Barnard and Newcomb, in that all classes are now coeducational, as are the housing units of these once-grand women's institutions.

Some of the more famous student organizations include the *Crimson* (the College's student newspaper), the Hasty Pudding Club, the *Lampoon,* and the Glee Club. Harvard surely has more student organizations than just about any other school, and a student can find a niche no matter what his interests. In fact, one of the hallmarks of student life at Harvard is the unusually high degree of involvement in extracurricular activities. With A's and B's virtually guaranteed thanks to grade inflation, many students place as much emphasis on their activities as they do on their academic work.

Harvard does have an alternative, mainstream conservative newspaper called the *Salient*. This paper is mainline Republican in its editorial policies, and "it's respected by at least some of the student body," says a student. However, the more conservative paper *Peninsula* runs counter to too many of the community's sacred positions, especially with its strong Christian right, pro-life stance. "It's abhorred," says a student. "You can't read it in public without getting ugly stares."

Harvard's football team hasn't won a national championship since 1919, but it and other varsity-level teams still attract the attention of the student body year in and year out. The school fields forty-one of them, which it claims is more than any other college in the nation. Harvard has excellent facilities for recreational sports such as tennis, squash, and the like. There are numerous intramural teams, most of which are formed around the residential houses. The university's literature says that about two-thirds of the student body participates at some level in sporting activity.

Among the more active political groups at Harvard is the Asian-American Association, which, with 200 members, is the College's largest culturally defined student group. The Black Students Association has about 175 members. There are numerous other special-interest groups on campus whose memberships define themselves by some sort of minority status, be it race, ethnicity, or sexual orientation.

Cambridge offers many cultural incentives, from pizza to excellent restaurants, and its bookstores are numerous and of exceptionally high quality. Harvard Square is a quirky, pseudobohemian hangout for all manner of people, where on ready display are almost continual chess matches, the serious student or scholar relaxing with a book, and the affected posing of intellectual wanna-bes. It's a great place to watch people. On the larger scale, Boston is one of the nation's last truly livable large cities, with a vibrant downtown of beautiful architecture and countless stores and shops. And the close proximity of other Boston universities, most notably next-door neighbor MIT, makes for a large number of college types all over the area. Certainly, the number of speakers, plays, and other events catering to the interests of students is hard to match elsewhere, and students can take advantage of endless opportunities in virtually every field of study or interest.

So, Harvard students enjoy their school years, secure in the knowledge that their upcoming degree will harm none of them in their pursuit of just about any career. The quality and number of contacts available to the Harvard student are unparalleled. The university does have much to offer, and those who would seriously consider attending Harvard should not be dissuaded by the sheer number of politicized courses and professors. As many professors and students told this guide, despite the trendiness that has affected the campus, the school is now and will remain one of the very few truly influential universities in America. Excellent facilities and an aggressive and intelligent student body make for an exciting experience for anyone who attends Harvard. Given that leaders of so many fields have graduated from it, readers of this guide might do the nation a favor by making their influence felt there.

HAVERFORD COLLEGE

Office of Admissions
370 Lancaster Avenue
Haverford, PA 19041-1392
(610) 896-1350
www.haverford.edu

Total enrollment: 1,147
Undergraduates: 1,147
SAT Ranges (Verbal/Math): V 630-730, M 630-720
Financial aid: 43%
Applicants: 2,769
Accepted: 34%
Enrolled: 32%
Application deadline: Early decision, Nov. 15; regular, Jan. 15
Financial aid application deadline: Jan. 31
Tuition: $21,534
Core curriculum: No

Fords along the Main Line

Haverford College is a small, elite institution occupying some two hundred prime acres along the Main Line, one of the plushest areas of suburban Philadelphia. Founded by Quakers from New York and Philadelphia in 1833, it is the oldest Quaker-founded college in the land.

With only 1,100 students — all of whom are undergraduates — Haverford is able to pay close attention to its students and to insure their immersion in the college's culture. Students at the school call themselves "Fords."

Haverford was an all-male institution until 1980, and it continues to have close ties with neighboring Bryn Mawr College, an all-female institution about a mile down the road. Students at the two schools frequently cross-register in order to fill in the gaps in their curricula by making use of the other college's strengths. Students at Haverford may also take classes at Swarthmore and the University of Pennsylvania.

Academic Life: What Do You Do with All That Leeway?

Haverford has no core curriculum. Students must instead take at least three courses from three different areas: humanities, social sciences, and the natural sciences. They must also fulfill a "social justice" requirement and demonstrate competence in a foreign language. There is both good and bad in this arrangement. The Haverford curriculum leaves something to be desired because it gives students too much leeway in choosing which classes are important — a choice few underclassmen are informed enough to make. And the "social justice" requirement is a clearly political move that seeks to substitute ideology for knowledge. On the other hand, in an age when many schools have relegated language study to only those students actually majoring in that language, Haverford's insistence that all students study a foreign tongue is evidence of some commitment to the traditional liberal arts curriculum of generations past.

Another positive aspect of the Haverford curriculum is the absence of pre-professional majors, such as business or education, that have so diluted the curricula at institutions nationwide. Haverford obviously believes that its students should be taught rather than trained. "Haverford is a lot like the University of Chicago," says a recent alumnus. "It attracts genuinely intellectual students but not merely pre-career types." This alumnus continues, "It's institutionally superior to many of today's colleges, but compared to the curriculum it offered in the 1950s, it's quite weak." Says a current student: "Haverford has a broad liberal arts requirement, and I took many classes outside my particular field of interest. It most certainly imparted a broad liberal arts background to my education."

There is no Western civilization requirement, and students may easily fulfill the humanities and social science requirements with classes on other topics. Good classes are available, however, for the student willing to seek them. "My professors in the humanities are all talented and dedicated," says a student.

Haverford students benefit tremendously from the college's association with Bryn Mawr College. They may make the fifteen-minute walk or take the bus that runs between the two campuses. All students at either college may take classes on both campuses and may even major in a program not available at their home school. This allows Haverford students to take advantage of Bryn Mawr's nationally known programs in classical civilization, languages, and archaeology, as well as its excellent art history department. About 90 percent of Haverford students take at least one class at Bryn Mawr, and most take more, according to college literature. This same literature notes: "You may take any course at Bryn Mawr, even if the same course is offered here — perhaps the time is a better fit to your schedule or you like the professor's sense of humor better." No special permission is needed, and students at both schools have the same chance of getting into any class offered on either campus. Credit transfers are automatic and require no special requests. Says a student: "A lot of men are afraid to take a class at Bryn Mawr, because it's not our campus and we know it. You don't go there alone because there are some really militant types there. Of course, there are some very nice women who go there too. You tend to keep to your own while you're there." A student says that the close association with Bryn Mawr is "definitely a reason to go to Haverford." Students speak of Haverford and Bryn Mawr as the bi-college community; when Swarthmore is thrown in, it becomes the tri-college community.

Students may also take classes at Swarthmore and Penn. Only about 10 percent do so at Swarthmore, however, which is less convenient than Bryn Mawr even though a shuttle takes students there. And even fewer go to Penn, which isn't terribly convenient and lies in a high-crime neighborhood in West Philadelphia.

Classes at Haverford tend to be quite small: the average class size is fifteen students, and 40 percent of classes have ten students or fewer. The student-to-faculty ratio is only eleven-to-one, and an astounding 75 percent of faculty live on campus. "It can be a little island of civility," says a graduate. All of this is in keeping with the school's Quaker roots as well as the excellent real estate it occupies, which makes the campus feel safe and inviting.

While all of the humanities and social science departments at Haverford offer courses that are certainly worthwhile, some areas of campus life have become very politicized. One student took a political science course, "Structures of Power," in which he learned that capitalism lies at the root of most of the evils of the modern world, and that women and minorities are always subjugated. "I really had to fight to get my point across," says this student, who also offers a strategy for success in the politicized classroom. "If I soft-shoed it and was lightly oppositional, and constructed my argument carefully, I could bring the class along with me. Then the professor had to really work to get everyone back in her camp. But if I'd just hit them with a full-force argument, I would have been attacked."

Asked about the degree of freedom of speech that exists on campus, a student says: "There are people who will agree with me one on one. But broadly speaking, it's funny how often people will not speak about politics at Haverford. It's not a particularly galvanized political campus. More people are liberals, and a lot are that way because of the faculty. I really think that's the type of person they're looking for in admissions. It helps you get in during your interview. It's the kind of place liberal folks would tend to come."

Students say the political science, sociology, and English departments can be quite politicized, as can peace studies, feminist and gender studies, and intercultural studies.

Among the good professors are Paul Jefferson and Linda Gerstein in history, C. Stephan Finley and Kim Benston in English, and Vernon Dixon and Richard Ball in economics.

The sciences are very good at Haverford, and students mention biology and chemistry as particularly strong. "About 95 percent of students who make it into the pre-med program get into the medical school of their choice," says a senior. Bryn Mawr is also strong in the sciences.

Political Atmosphere: Conservative Liberalism

As noted above, only 1,100 or so students attend Haverford. Yet the number of organizations devoted to multiculturalism is as large as what one would expect in a much larger institution. For example, there is BGALA (Bisexual, Gay, and Lesbian Alliance) Lounge, which, according to campus literature, "provides a safe space and a support network for queer studies on campus. In addition, students of *all* sexual orientations are welcome at our meetings. We strive to activate and educate the Haverford community about Gay, Lesbian, and Bisexual issues. We also want to throw lots of great parties."

Then there's the Multicultural Center, a "resource and support center for people interested in multicultural issues." According to campus literature, this office is "responsible for sensitizing the Haverford community to the concerns of people of color." Recent speakers brought to campus by this office include George Stallings, founder of the African-American Catholic Church, a small Afrocentric breakaway group from the Roman Catholic Church, and labor organizer Cesar Chavez.

One shouldn't overlook the Women's Center, which "hopes to reach out to both men and women. . . . The center sponsors speakers, events, symposiums, and the like on campus." There are also numerous organizations for students of every ethnic group. The Black Student League strives to "provide a comfort zone where black students can be totally comfortable with their black identity in this predominantly white institution." Among the student groups are Women of Color, the Feminist Alliance ("We raise consciousness about women's issues and take action against inequality at Haverford and outside"), and the Progressive Labor Party, described in college literature as: "An international revolutionary communist organization. We are dedicated to fighting against racism, sexism and nationalism and to fight for communism on the Haverford campus."

An alumnus remembers Haverford fondly, although he adds: "It's always 1968 there. 'We gotta go plant trees in Nicaragua' was the attitude of many. But I enjoyed it — at least they're not yuppies."

From the makeup of the faculty, the course offerings, and the general tone of the campus (confirmed by students and alumni), it seems highly unlikely that tradition-minded scholars have much luck obtaining teaching posts at Haverford. Unfortunately, this policy reduces the options available to students, who must often settle for one voice rather than many. Yet a student notes that "This is a quiet, do-your-own-thing campus, and that's part of the Quaker tradition. You don't condemn anyone," and that the political atmosphere "isn't electrified the way it is on many campuses." Students practice what one student calls "a conservative liberalism, if that makes sense." That is, while many students, and most faculty, are left-of-center politically, the campus itself is not rife with political conflict, and politics is not the favorite topic of conversation at the coffee bar or in the classroom.

Student Life: No Problem with Boredom

Haverford students get to enjoy a picturesque campus located in a highly desirable neighborhood of suburban Philadelphia. Campus life is a bit different from that found at many campuses both because of the small size of the college and the very close relationship it has with Bryn Mawr College. As noted above, over 90 percent of Haverford students enroll for at least one class at Bryn Mawr, and they may eat at any of that college's dining halls and even live in its dorms. Back at Haverford, 95 percent of students live on campus — one of the highest rates anywhere — where most have their own room because 70 percent of the housing is arranged as suites of singles. Nearly two-thirds of freshmen also benefit from this, which certainly fosters a sense of community at Haverford. About 25 percent of the student body lives in Haverford College Apartments, which allow "upperclasspeople" to live on campus yet forgo the meal plan.

The Haverford and Bryn Mawr student bodies are served by the *Bi-College News,* as well as a literary magazine titled *Musomania,* also a bi-college publication. *Common Sense,* an alternative student newspaper for the tri-college community, offers a very different and independent editorial and news-gathering voice. *Third Side of the Coin* is a humor magazine, and the *Tri-College Guide* is a weekly events publication that also includes Swarthmore.

Students may also participate in any number of extracurricular activities, including the Debate Society, which teams students from Haverford and Bryn Mawr for intercollegiate contests up and down the East Coast. The Zymurgy Club studies "the fine art of homebrew" in the tri-college community and allows students to gather to "enjoy the taste and history of beer and its construction." Looney Tunes is a coed a cappella group of the bi-college community, and the Oxford Blues is Haverford's only all-female a cappella group. As a college with Quaker origins, Haverford sponsors the Quaker Action and Activities Committee (QuAAC), which maintains a Quaker influence on the nonsectarian campus. Other religious organizations include the Jewish Student Union; Christian Fellowship, which is associated with the InterVarsity Christian Fellowship; and Catholic Campus Ministries, which ministers to the Haverford and Bryn Mawr communities.

The Republican Club at Haverford has some twenty-five members and is very active, according to a member. Eighth Dimension, a volunteer group that coordinates students' activities in the community, "does a great job," says a student. Fords against Boredom is "a cool club organizing trips into the city [Philadelphia] to see the Phillies or attend a monster truck rally, which is a kick," says a senior.

Sports are very popular, as some 85 percent of the student body is involved in athletic programs, and fully 40 percent plays on Haverford's intercollegiate teams. Student-organized teams play ice hockey, volleyball, and basketball, among many other sports. Intercollegiate competition is available in soccer, track, cricket, and squash, along with most traditional sports (but not football). There are eleven varsity teams for both men and women.

Academic and social life is deeply influenced by the Honor System, described by the college as "not a list of rules, it is a philosophy of conduct through honesty, integrity and understanding." Finals at Haverford have been unproctored since 1898, and all academic work is expected to reflect the student's best efforts. There are no resident advisers in the dorms because students are expected to work out any difficulties on their own. The Honor Council of sixteen students, four from each class, "fosters discussion and awareness of the Honor Code, and helps to resolve questions and issues concerning the Code throughout the year."

Haverford lies only eleven miles from Center City Philadelphia, which may be reached easily via train. Philadelphia offers numerous restaurants, nightclubs, and other attractions for the work-weary student. The Philadelphia Museum of Art is the largest of many cultural institutions available, and historic sights dating from the founding of the nation are within easy reach. The New Jersey and Delaware beaches are an easy drive away, as are ski resorts in the Poconos. Closer to home, Haverford, Bryn Mawr, and neighboring towns along the Main Line offer a large assortment of restaurants and other centers of shopping and entertainment.

HILLSDALE COLLEGE

Director of Admissions
33 East College Street
Hillsdale, MI 49242
(517) 437-7341 ext. 327
www.hillsdale.edu

Total enrollment: 1,220
Undergraduates: 1,200
SAT Ranges (Verbal/Math): V 570-690, M 520-660
Financial aid: 80%
Applicants: 1,042
Accepted: 75%
Enrolled: 45%
Application deadline: Rolling admissions
Financial aid application deadline: Mar. 15
Tuition: $12,840
Core curriculum: Yes

Taxes Aren't Legal Tender

If you are reading this guidebook straight through, you are by now familiar with several possible story lines. Basically, there are the once-great schools now in decline; there are the schools that were never great but now have enough money to pretend to be; and there are the ones that don't really have either their past or their present going for them. There are, of course, quite a few exceptions, and we're happy to report that Hillsdale College is one of them.

Hillsdale is unique in two notable ways. First, it is well known for refusing any and all federal money, including federally insured student loans. Ironically, the college is richer today than it was when it accepted federal money. This independence enables Hillsdale to remain free of federal affirmative action programs and the political atmosphere created by such government-sanctioned schemes. (In fact, Hillsdale beat the government to the nondiscrimination punch by about a century.) Second, Hillsdale, unlike most colleges, has actually improved its core curriculum recently and did so in a thoughtful, well-considered way, taking into account the traditions that should (but rarely do nowadays) accompany any school that considers itself a liberal arts institution.

As a small (about 1,150 students) school located in the Michigan countryside, Hillsdale probably had an easier time getting away with both of these things than a larger school on either coast would have. Be that as it may, both fly in the face of the prevailing winds of today's academic world: the determined pursuit of large federal grants, a willingness to allow the ideology of multiculturalism to radically undermine scholarly rigor and social norms, and a core curriculum so loose it more resembles satellite television than a liberal arts education. Hillsdale is now better than it was just a few years ago, and a few decades ago, and that — considering the competition — is more than distinction enough. Given its consistent high scores in the *U.S. News and World Report* rankings, as well as numerous awards, Hillsdale is getting the national recognition and attention it richly deserves.

Academic Life: The Good Kind of Reform

Many schools are in the process of reforming their curricula, but what that usually means is adding "multicultural" courses, loosening graduation requirements, or, frequently, both. Hillsdale, too, has reformed its curriculum recently, but has done so without committing either of these sins.

A professor who helped with the revamping process says the college had three goals in its curricular revision. First, it wanted to give its students a shared intellectual experience by eliminating the popular cafeteria approach and reducing the number of classes that compose the core. Second, the school wanted all students exposed to the foundational disciplines of the liberal arts. And third, it wanted, so far as was possible, to integrate the content and development of the core classes. "Overall, I'm very much satisfied with what we've done," says the professor. Hillsdale students must now study Western history, literature, philosophy, fine arts, science, and languages. "It's still not as much of a core as it was seventy-five years ago, but we are definitely moving in that direction," another professor says.

It is hard to ask for much more — not without expecting to be disappointed, at least. Every student must now take yearlong sequences in Western history and in Western literature. Beginning in the fall of 1997, all nonscience majors must take a yearlong, team-taught science sequence covering topics in biology, chemistry, and physics. Students must already take mathematics, philosophy or religion, a foreign language, and an upper-level course in Western literature. The fine arts departments have begun developing an interdisciplinary, yearlong sequence, paralleling the new science offering, for eventual inclusion in Hillsdale's core. "Though we're still fine-tuning things," says a professor, "I think our students now can get as inclusive and as thorough a grounding in the liberal arts here as they could at virtually any campus."

For example, professors who teach the Western civilization sequence have weekly staff meetings "to instruct each other," says a professor. Not only do faculty teaching the same course consult with one another, but faculty teaching parallel courses do so as well. The history department faculty teaching Western civilization also meet weekly with their colleagues who teach American history to share plans and information and to discuss the most effective means for teaching.

"Students leave feeling they've been given a well-rounded education," notes one pleased professor. It helps that the students are doing their parts. The classics department was reconstituted ten years ago and last year had 76 (out of 340 freshmen) students in Latin 101. A third classics professor will be hired soon to meet the demand. This is quite a change from just a few years ago, when classics "was teaching Latin to four or five students and Greek to virtually none," says a professor. Now, classics is "having to turn people away from Latin, is filling its Greek language classes, and has just reworked its curriculum so as to offer several courses cross-listed with history, religion, philosophy, and Christian studies," the professor says. "I'm not sure just how they're managing it, but any program that has to turn people away from studying a 'dead' language has got to be doing something extraordinary."

Hillsdale has had the most trouble finding a way to combine instruction in writing with literature. Students are arriving on campus without much instruction in writing, faculty say. But again, the school has refused to fall in step with what other places are doing and is not afraid to study the matter until finding a satisfactory solution. "We've discussed writing-across-the-curriculum approaches but, given their results at other campuses, have made no move to implement one," a professor says. "At present, we try to divide the effort simply by encouraging instructors in introductory-level classes to assign a good deal of written work and to devote as much time as possible to comments on syntax and style; virtually all of us do."

There are a number of outstanding professors at Hillsdale, including John

Willson, Tom Conner, and Robert Eden in history; Mickey Craig and Alexander Shtromas in political science; Donald Asselin, Thomas Burke, James Stephens, and Michael Bauman in philosophy and religion; Michael Jordan, John Reist, John Sommerville, David Whalen, and Daniel Sundahl in English; Richard Ebeling and Gary Wolfram in economics; and Mark Kalthoff in history and philosophy and religion. Political science, history, and economics are thought to be Hillsdale's strongest departments, along with two interdisciplinary programs: the American Studies program (made up of faculty from English, history, and political science) and the Political Economy program (made up of faculty from history, political science, and economics).

Classroom offerings are complemented by the largest lecture series in American higher education, an incredible accomplishment for a small school. The series, known as the Center for Constructive Alternatives (CCA), hosts "four week-long seminars on a variety of topics from Shakespeare to biotechnology" each year. Students may enroll for academic credit. One CCA each year is cosponsored by the Ludwig von Mises Lecture Series (named for the famed Austrian economist) and focuses on free-market issues for economists, businessmen, and students. Though Hillsdale is conservative in its politics, it does not shy away from inviting guests from both sides of the political rainbow: past speakers have included Jesse Jackson, Eleanor Clift, Stanley Fish, Gary Hart, George McGovern, Patricia Schroeder, and William Sloan Coffin, as well as Ronald Reagan, Dan Quayle, William F. Buckley Jr., Jack Kemp, George Bush, Lynne Cheney, and Jeane Kirkpatrick. They also brought in Leonard Nimoy and Roger Ebert.

Other excellent programs take Hillsdale's philosophy to both on- and off-campus audiences. The Shavano Institute for National Leadership is the school's off-campus lecture division. In the past twelve years, the institute has sponsored nearly one hundred programs for nearly ten thousand business and community leaders around the country. A free monthly newsletter, *Imprimis*, published by the college in defense of the free market and Western values, goes to nearly three-quarters of a million subscribers each month and defends the free market and Western values. The college's education department is closely connected to Hillsdale Academy, a private school for kindergartners through eighth graders that opened in 1990. And the Family Business Institute works with small businesses to find effective solutions to problems peculiar to their enterprises.

Political Atmosphere: In the Old Sense of the Word

The platitudes of the new multiculturalists ring hollow when compared with the policies of inclusion Hillsdale has practiced for years. When it opened its doors in 1844 as a Freewill Baptist school, Hillsdale was the first college in the nation to have a policy of nondiscrimination written into its charter. It admitted women, blacks, and other minorities on a par with white males for two decades before the Civil War.

During World War I Hillsdale refused to segregate its ROTC units, and won a battle with the federal government over the matter. In the 1970s, when the government finally got around to ordering equal opportunity, Hillsdale had had enough of Washington telling it how to do what it was already doing, and refused to sign federal compliance forms. Since the school did not accept federal aid, it did not have to be controlled by a faceless bureaucracy.

All of Hillsdale's funding comes from private sources and tuition, and it is today known nationally as the college that bucks national educational trends in favor of genuine liberal learning. It has succeeded splendidly in this undertaking. Whatever dollars the college may have missed out on, it has earned back through its reputation for tenacious independence in the face of enormous pressure to conform to the banal orthodoxies of the moment. Hillsdale's faculty and students in fact seem to draw strength from their independence and to relish a good fight with the powers that be.

Instead of wilting under budgetary pressures, Hillsdale has expanded its faculty, and its reputation has made the school a prized appointment for those who value the tradition of liberal learning. Which is good, since those are, for the most part, the only people Hillsdale will hire. "Hillsdale takes more care with new hires than does any institution with which I've been associated," says one professor.

Hillsdale does not seek, hire, or promote people simply because they are friendly to the ideas behind much of what the college stands for. They must also be excellent in their given fields of study. However, Hillsdale also seeks to gauge the candidate's agreement with the university's way of thinking by sending along some issues of *Imprimis* and asking for the candidate's reaction. "It is not unusual for some people to reject us then," a professor says. While several faculty members stress that there is no litmus test for faculty hires, they also are adamant in their insistence that all new faculty hires be dedicated to and in agreement with the educational philosophy of the college. Says one professor: "We work very hard on insuring that we get the very best faculty. Our young faculty are overwhelmingly conservative. We try not to hire those who would subvert the ideals of the college." Says another faculty member: "We're an 'open church' and not a 'conservative school' per se. You really can't call an Austrian School economist a conservative."

Although the faculty at Hillsdale is without a doubt more conservative than that found at most academic institutions, the teachers don't make it a point to teach only specifically conservative beliefs, says another faculty member. "Most of us are simply convinced that most of what goes on under the headings of multiculturalism, postmodernism, and whatnot, is simply bad scholarship and false to the texts and figures that we take to define the Western intellectual heritage," this professor says. "It's for this reason, not because we're primarily concerned with ideological purity, that we're likely to hold the line as regards innovations in the curriculum." Another faculty member explains: "Coke doesn't hire a Pepsi-praiser for its sales rep positions."

Faculty claim that despite the number of nonscholarly grad programs in the country, the Hillsdale professoriate is better now than it was twenty years ago, and that many programs have been strengthened. In the early 1990s Hillsdale committed to increasing the faculty by 25 percent with no increase in the size of the student body. With help from endowed chairs, the school is now two-thirds of the way to its goal, and when the faculty expansion is complete Hillsdale will have a student-faculty ratio of eleven-to-one. The increase in the size of the faculty has allowed the college to offer a better range of excellent courses within each major.

There are no trendy or chic courses in Hillsdale's catalogue. Even its English department, in which one could expect to see classes on gender, race, and sexuality, contains only solid offerings in the history of literature. The history of the West is championed at Hillsdale, in part, because, as one professor puts it, "No other culture created a sanctity of individualism the way the West did. So, in learning about the West, a student has a great grounding in the study of freedom." Another professor says his students read works by thinkers he admires as well as by those with whom he has large disagreements. But, he says, "you can't know something is wrong until you learn about it. So, it's not bad to have some liberals on the faculty, some diversity and tolerance and sensitivity in the older sense of those words."

Hillsdale professors publish, but they don't have to. They are expected to teach. "No amount of publication counterbalances an inadequate teaching record," a professor says. Nonetheless, the faculty at this small school have published several hundred articles and several dozen books in the last two years. This is due in part to the expansion of the faculty, which allowed professors to lighten their teaching loads. But, as one professor says, "There's enough academic interaction and excitement among the faculty now that people are publishing things no matter what the College's requirements." And Hillsdale professors don't confine themselves to stuffy (or trendy) academic journals; they write for popular outlets as well.

Despite the expanded faculty, teaching loads (usually four classes a semester) are still heavy. Professors don't complain loudly, but one professor admits that he wouldn't mind seeing his family more often, especially during the busy times that accompany the end of each semester.

Sometimes the conservative reputation of Hillsdale hurts those professors seeking to publish. "It's harder getting published from here than from other places," one professor says. This fact, however, reflects the bias, even bigotry, of those now in charge of the so-called mainstream academic journals more than it does the quality of work turned out by Hillsdale's faculty, and is no doubt one of the reasons Hillsdale recognizes the importance of publishing in nonacademic or nontraditional venues when assessing a candidate for hire, tenure, or promotion.

Although some faculty members are labeled "liberal" by some of their colleagues, relativistic multiculturalism has not invaded Hillsdale's campus. Sticking with solid works that have stood the test of time seems the best way to keep out the third-rate books and ideas taught on many campuses today. As one professor puts it, "Multiculturalism has practically zero inroads at Hillsdale." This professor argues that the refusal of federal monies has allowed the school to retain its philosophical independence.

Of course, there are a handful of liberal professors, mostly in the foreign language departments. "In the modern languages the faculty are Clintonites, but their job is to teach a foreign language, not political philosophy," a professor says. "So, a student in an informal discussion can hear a left-wing opinion, but that's good, because [it means that] there is no political litmus test in hiring." Another professor concurs: "The liberal left are in foreign languages, but even there they are good professors."

All told, things are well at Hillsdale. Considering the state of many other institutions, things might even be said to be ideal. While other schools are cutting back programs, staff, and funding, Hillsdale has tripled its endowment, expanded its faculty, given its faculty considerable annual raises in pay, and doubled the size of its library and computer facilities. In return it has attracted a student body several notches above that hosted in the past. "The most striking thing about Hillsdale is that the students today are much better and more serious about getting a serious liberal arts education" than they were years ago, a professor says. The high school grade point average of incoming freshmen is up nearly a full point (out of four), and their average scores on standardized tests are up nearly a standard deviation.

Campus Life: Into the Woods

Students at Hillsdale are a "self-selecting" bunch, says one professor. For one thing, a student attending Hillsdale shouldn't have his heart set on living in a big city. The college, located in the rural hills of southern Michigan, is safe "because we're out in the woods," a professor says. "And these days that's not a small thing — you can go to the dining hall and find the hallway filled with personal possessions, and the same is true of the dorms."

Some of the better student groups on campus include InterVarsity Christian Fellowship, with almost three hundred members (more than a quarter of the student body); Praxis, a club for political science, economics, and political economy majors; the College Republican and Libertarian clubs, which host debates and sponsor speakers; and honorary societies for history and political science. However, "even serious students like to be entertained," says a professor. "So we do have some suitcase weekends, but this is less a suitcase college now than it used to be. Yet that's a matter of personal taste. We don't hear any complaining because they're too busy academically."

There is a large Greek presence on campus, with five fraternities and four sororities that some 50 percent of the student body joins. No alcohol is allowed in these organizations, and no midweek parties are allowed on campus. Weekend parties must be registered. Dorms are single-sex with visiting hours.

Hillsdale offers varsity sports at the NCAA Division II level in track, football, baseball, basketball, volleyball, and women's swimming. There are eight intercollegiate and ten intramural sports for both men and women. A new sports venue provides students with excellent facilities for observing and taking part in sports.

COLLEGE OF THE HOLY CROSS

Admissions Office
College of the Holy Cross
One College Street
Worcester, MA 01610-2395
(800) 442-2421
www.holycross.edu

Total enrollment: 2,730
Undergraduates: 2,730
SAT Ranges (Verbal/Math): V 570-650, M 550-650
Financial aid: 56%
Applicants: 4,183
Accepted: 50%
Enrolled: 35%
Application deadline: Jan. 15
Financial aid application deadline: Feb. 1
Tuition: $20,700
Core curriculum: No

Tolerance before Tradition

The College of the Holy Cross, located in the heart of Massachusetts (fifty miles from Boston), is the oldest Catholic college in New England, founded in 1843 by Bishop Joseph Fenwick, S.J., of Boston and administered by the Jesuits. The college began as an all-male school but became coeducational in the 1970s, and its nearly 2,700-member student body is now equally divided between men and women. The school remains a small liberal arts undergraduate institution that offers solid degrees in the sciences, arts, and humanities.

287

Despite its past — or maybe partially because of it — Holy Cross has begun to move away from both its roots in Catholic theology and its liberal arts heritage. Multiculturalism can be blamed for much of this, but Holy Cross's multiculturalism seems at least partially based on the Jesuit tradition, which for centuries has studied and written about diverse cultures. At their best, the Jesuits were really the first multiculturalists, respecting and cherishing the cultures in which they worked. However, some forces at Holy Cross have gone further down the road to politicization, embracing liberation theology, a social interpretation of the gospel that borrows heavily from Marxism. Recent theological comments from the church hierarchy in Rome, while acknowledging the strong element of social justice in liberation theology, have questioned both the theological and political wisdom of liberation theology.

Holy Cross describes its mission as "education for social justice" and states that its goal is to teach students about their responsibility to "the world's poor and powerless." This emphasis on social justice seems to have displaced the idea of the liberal arts education as a grounding in knowledge for its own sake, although recruiting materials still call attention to the school's liberal arts tradition. Instead, the mission statement iterates and reiterates the teaching of tolerance; according to the statement, Holy Cross students and faculty are to "be open to new ideas," to show "respect for the views of others," to "acknowledge and respect differences," to "be sensitive to one another," to "serve others," and to "seek justice within and beyond the Holy Cross community."

This rhetoric sounds at times more like a mission statement for social workers than a charter for a liberal arts institution. A letter to prospective students speaks highly of the Bishop Healy Multicultural Awareness organization, which "works to provide a forum for discussing the problems of racism and ethnocentricity," as well as other student organizations like the Black Student Union, the Women's Forum, Asian Students for International Awareness, and the Latin American Student Organization. All these, the letter states, "ensure that we, as a community, discuss issues of oppression, racism, sexism, and stereotyping. At Holy Cross, these organizations are extremely active and deeply valued for their contributions to the College's mission of challenging people to confront the most important social issues of our time."

Lost, it seems, is the school's founding mission: the guarantee of a fine, traditional liberal arts education, which educates students to choose the good, and to form their intellectual and moral virtues. It was the great Catholic theologian Cardinal Newman, after all, who wrote in *The Idea of the University* that the first and only mission of education is knowledge for its own sake, not for political or other purposes. Holy Cross has replaced this with a simplistic program of tolerance and social justice. However, the ideological tone of the mission statement does not adequately characterize the college as a whole, including several academic departments that do maintain the basic elements of a traditional education in the arts and sciences. It is still possible to get a very good liberal arts education at Holy Cross.

Academic Life: A Changing World

The curriculum at Holy Cross is traditional in content, if not always in emphasis. "Holy Cross retains more of a traditional liberal arts curriculum, I am surprised to say, than even Williams College," one professor notes. There is no core curriculum at Holy Cross, but students are required to complete distribution requirements in six areas, including one course in arts and literature, one in religious and philosophical studies (very low for a church-related school), one in historical studies, and one in cross-cultural studies, plus two social science courses and two more in natural and mathematical sciences, at least one of which must be a natural science. All students are provided with a faculty adviser who assists them with curriculum planning and course selection.

Holy Cross offers A.B. degrees in eighteen majors, each of which requires completion of at least thirty-two semester courses within eight semesters of full-time study. Courses within the major account for ten to fourteen of those classes. In addition, all students must demonstrate competence in a classical or modern foreign language. This language requirement may also fulfilled by proficiency in American Sign Language.

The college says changes in and additions to the curriculum are designed to "meet the needs of a changing world." These changes include "an increased focus on interdisciplinary studies and multicultural educational experiences based in our Center for Interdisciplinary and Special Studies." The center, according to the college catalogue, offers several interdisciplinary concentrations, including African-American studies, peace and conflict studies, and women's studies. The center describes itself as a "catalyst for innovation and experimentation in the curriculum."

The experimental nature of the center's programs means that requirements are not confined to the classroom. Students are able to participate in special off-campus programs which "link learning and living" by working with "community-based internships and service opportunities" and student-designed curricula that can include independent research. One off-campus option is the Washington Semester Program, in which juniors and some seniors spend a semester studying and working in Washington, D.C. Holy Cross professors have a high regard for this program. "The director of the Washington semester program is very conscientious and makes a serious effort to put students in something other than Xeroxing," one faculty member says. Students, depending upon their individual interests, have worked at the White House, in Congress, or in nongovernmental agencies such as the American Enterprise Institute. Supreme Court Justice Clarence Thomas (a Holy Cross alumnus and currently a college trustee) meets with students in this program and encourages them in their public policy endeavors.

Students also move off campus for the Study Abroad Program, open to students with a 3.0 grade point average or better. Language proficiency is required of those who would take courses in a language other than English, and the committee that reviews all applications for study abroad looks favorably upon candidates who have already taken courses related to the intended destination's history and culture. A similar program, called the Semester Away Program, is offered through the Center for Interdisciplinary and Special Studies. In that program students submit proposals for academic work at other institutions. Some have attended the Sea Semester Program, cosponsored by Boston University and the Woods Hole Oceanographic Institute. "An exciting new option in the Semester Away Program allows students to study at an historically black college or university," the catalogue notes.

Holy Cross even offers students a way to take a year off from college entirely. The Venture Consortium is a joint project of eight New England colleges and universities (including Bates, Brown, Connecticut College, Hobart and William Smith Colleges, Swarthmore, Vassar, and Wesleyan University) that provides "alternative work and study opportunities" that "emphasize social responsibility and involvement and forge links between higher education and the community at large." The Venture Consortium includes an "Urban Education Semester" that awards a full semester of academic credit for working in New York's East Harlem public schools in an "experimental study of inner-city education."

Juniors and seniors may apply for the College Honors Program. Limited to twenty-five students in each graduating class, this program requires two seminars on topics outside the student's major, interdisciplinary discussions, and independent research. The research is presented orally to the entire college at the end of a student's senior year.

Research is aided by three major on-campus libraries: the Dinand Library, the O'Callahan Science Library, and the Fenwick Music Library. The facade of the Dinand Library is in a beautiful classical style, with eight large Roman columns at the entrance; inside, this Romanesque style is preserved on the main floor, but additional rooms are modern, with metal bookshelves and small cubicles for study.

Outstanding professors at Holy Cross are found in the humanities, and include Donald R. Brand, David L. Schaefer, and Denise Schaeffer in political science; Joseph P. Lawrence in philosophy; Thomas M. C. Lawler in English; William A. Green and Noel D. Cary in history; and Ann G. Batchelder, Thomas R. Martin, and Blaise J. Nagy in the classics department.

The classics department, widely regarded as Holy Cross's finest, is one of the largest undergraduate classics departments in the country. The curriculum focuses on the Greek and Roman sources of Western culture and includes courses in politics, philosophy, religion, archaeology, mythology, and literature.

The history department has not abandoned Western history, as have so many of its counterparts at other universities. Holy Cross offers a breadth of courses that range from the history of ancient Greece and the Roman Republic to that of medieval Europe and the United States. However, some courses in the department are reportedly taught from the perspectives of multiculturalism, feminism, and socialism.

The political science department offers classes in four subfields: political philosophy, American government, comparative politics, and international relations. The department has resisted behavioralism and retains a more traditional, philosophic, and constitutional approach to the study of politics. A sign of the strength of this department are two new hires: Steve Teles, a welfare policy expert, and Ward Thomas, whose specialty is in ethics and international relations.

The biology and chemistry departments are also said to be excellent at Holy Cross, and graduates from these programs have a high admittance rate into graduate and medical school.

As at the much better known Notre Dame University, religious studies at Holy Cross is considered one of the most politicized departments on campus. The college catalogue says that Holy Cross is a Jesuit school and that most of its students are from a Catholic background. However, "the department believes it is necessary to provide [students] with an opportunity to know and understand this tradition as well as to situate it in the larger context of other religious traditions and in the broader cultural context in which [students] live. Students from any tradition must come to terms with the fact of pluralism — both religious and cultural." A religious studies major, therefore, must take a total of ten classes, including one from each of four "concentrations" (world religions, the Bible, theology, and ethics), plus two more in the student's selected concentration. It is puzzling that a student at a religious school could graduate with a major in religious studies having taken only one course on the Bible. Courses include "Women and the Bible," which focuses on "the feminist interpretation of Scripture." The college catalogue says "particular attention is paid to character portrayal within the patriarchal family structure, as well as to the characteristics of those females who emerge as exceptions to patriarchy." Also a part of the intermediate courses in the Bible concentration is "Early Christian Communities," wherein is examined the way early Christian communities contended with "the role of women, the poor, 'outsiders,' and the resolution of conflict" in order to "determine what may be said about the social function of the New Testament writings."

The politicization of the religious studies department is surpassed at Holy Cross only by the sociology department, which describes its mission as providing "a critical assessment of the modern world and a familiarity with the latest issues in social theory and research." Courses offered by this department include "Structures of Social Inequality" and "Health Care and Society," the latter of which examines "academic medical empires and medical education, health care profiteers, the death industry, and governmental policy." Also offered is "The Sociology of Men," which can only be taken with the permission of the instructor — often a sign that the instructor prefers to handpick students sympathetic to the views being taught. These views, according to the catalogue, include "men's antifemininity, homophobia, inexpressiveness, success-orientation, relations with family, and grandparenting."

Political Atmosphere: A Bridge Too Far

In the fall of 1995 the president of Holy Cross, Gerard Reedy, S.J., overturned an action by the student government in order to side with the Black Students' Union (BSU). Various publications, including the *New York Times,* covered the event, in which Reedy permitted the BSU to retain a clause in its charter mandating that only students "of African descent" could hold leadership positions in the organization. The student government had rejected the clause on the grounds that none of the other seventy-plus organizations excluded students based on race.

"What they were asking to do was invade our last safe space," the president of the BSU told the *Times.* Almost all of the sixty-eight black students (less than 3 percent of the student body) on campus at the time had been boycotting classes for a week, and complained that the school was not doing enough to recruit black students, especially male nonathletes. Father Reedy was quoted as saying, "You have to have black leadership. We rely on the Black Students' Union as a bridge. There is a need to have black kids oriented by kids who are also in the minority and who can say, 'It's okay here.' "

Father Reedy's actions are especially ironic since Associate Supreme Court Justice Thomas (class of 1971) was one of the first officers of the Holy Cross BSU. As a judge, Thomas has been an outspoken critic of preferential treatment based upon so-called group rights. One professor noted that the administration's vision of education "places personal experiences and feelings over academic standards." Another professor, however, says that the administration, "while liberal, is absorbed in traditional administrative functions, such as fundraising."

Despite provisions for a "safe space" for one group, there are no such protections for self-selecting groups like fraternities and sororities, which are not permitted at Holy Cross. The college says such groups are "antithetical to the College's traditions of openness and friendship between all members of this community" because of the "social separation that such organizations encourage." The assertion that fraternities and sororities somehow destroy "openness and friendship" is curious — especially when the assistant dean of students has called residential life at Holy Cross an "acceptance and celebration of diversity."

Holy Cross has a homosexual rights organization known as Allies, which "is dedicated to creating a humane campus environment for all persons regardless of sexual orientation." Allies hopes, through "education," to "make the environment of Holy Cross safer and more supportive for gay, lesbian, and bisexual students." The group suggests that members wear an "Allies button," an upside-down red triangle, which designates the wearer as "a 'safe' person to talk with," presumably about homosexual issues. The group is also involved in something it calls "National Coming Out Day festivities." In addition, Allies hosted a student/faculty luncheon prior to attending a Dignity Mass in Boston. Dignity is a national gay and lesbian "Catholic" organization, which is not officially recognized by the church because of its opposition to church teaching on homosexuality.

There are, of course, voices on campus that speak in support of orthodox Catholicism and traditional values. Speakers on campus reflect a true diversity of opinion; for example, the speakers in one semester in 1997 included neoconservative James Q. Wilson, an authority on criminal justice issues and professor of management at UCLA; Cornel West, professor of religion and Afro-American studies at Harvard; Serrin M. Foster, executive director of Feminists for Life of America; and Barney Frank, the gay U.S. congressman from Massachusetts.

Student Life: Worcester Sauce

Worcester is a college town, with more than ten colleges, universities, and academic societies in the area, including Assumption College and Clark University. More than thirty-six thousand students reside in and around Worcester, the second-largest city in New England with a population of 170,000. The Holy Cross campus is spread out in a wooded area in several groupings of buildings (quads) set upon a hill overlooking the city. The campus is not isolated, however — a large elevated freeway passes by the football and baseball stadiums and the campus is within walking distance of Worcester neighborhoods. Most students live in the nine residence halls on campus, and with no fraternities or sororities, college materials say "The social life of the college is a mix of formal occasions, informal gatherings, all-campus parties, and just hanging out." Boston is less than fifty miles away, and New York City is a three-hour drive.

The college's promotional materials don't mention what has been a major extracurricular activity: drinking. Students at Holy Cross have the reputation of drinking too much — "study hard, party hard" is the unofficial motto. In any case, there have been several efforts at Holy Cross (including seminars and informal counseling) to persuade students to become more interested in an intellectual way of life, and to illustrate to them the relationship between intellectual and moral virtues. Many students do volunteer their time for service work. "Because of the emphasis on social justice at Holy Cross, you will find a far higher number of students involved in things like soup kitchens," says a professor. "There are more opportunities for that sort of thing here. But many of the students who participate in these activities are not necessarily ideologues. Many of them are simply being compassionate." The Office of College Chaplains supports nineteen student-run programs that work within the Diocese of Worcester; sponsors service trips to Appalachia, Maine, Mexico, and Northern Ireland; and, of course, celebrates several Masses on campus each day, although student attendance at Mass is not mandated.

Holy Cross is one of the smallest schools in the country to support a Division I athletics program, but the 2,600-student college's Crusaders have some success against much larger foes. The school offers twelve sports for men and eleven for women, and Lake Quinsigamond, home to the men's and women's crew squads, is considered one of the world's finest sites for competitive rowing. With more than thirty intramural sports and several club teams, the college calculates that at least 90 percent of the student body is involved in sports at some level.

Student organizations include two of a traditionalist nature. The *Fenwick Review,* an unofficial student publication, carries commentaries on political correctness on campus, articles on local and national cultural and political events, as well as (often successful) attempts at satire and humor. There is also a chapter of an organization known as Students for Life.

Left-of-center groups include the officially recognized homosexual support group Allies, the feminist Women's Forum, and two multicultural groups, the BSU and the Latin American Student Organization. Another liberal group, this one in keeping with the liberation theology emphasis at Holy Cross, is the Interdisciplinary Peace Studies Group, considered by the college to be a "co-curricular" rather than an "extra-curricular" group.

UNIVERSITY OF ILLINOIS AT URBANA-CHAMPAIGN

#10 Henry Administration Building
506 South Wright Street
Urbana-Champaign, IL 61801
(217) 333-0302
www.uiuc.edu

Total enrollment: 36,160
Undergraduates: 26,740
SAT Ranges (Verbal/Math): V 560-660, M 590-690
Financial aid: 50%
Applicants: 17,250
Accepted: 70%
Enrolled: 49%
Application deadline: Jan. 1
Financial aid application deadline: Mar. 15
Tuition: in-state, $4,554; out-of-state, $11,370
Core curriculum: No

Popping the Champaign

The University of Illinois is distinguished from other mammoth state universities by the quality of several of its departments and its library, the third-largest academic library in the nation. Research possibilities in all departments are enhanced by this 14-million-item collection.

In fact, Illinois itself is like an enormous collection of disparate parts, and anonymity is almost guaranteed for the twenty-seven thousand undergraduate and ten thousand graduate students on campus. While it's true that a student can find just about anything he's hoping to study here, it's also likely that it will be taught in a large class, possibly by a teaching assistant. Only juniors and seniors are guaranteed smaller classes and interaction with a real, live professor. Similarly, the traditional liberal arts are lost in the multiple options for fulfilling the distribution requirements, but good classes can also be found.

The university's tuition is a steal for in-state residents, and more than 93 percent of the student body comes from Illinois. Illinois residents who know what they want from their education could do much worse.

Academic Life: The Snowflake in a Blizzard

Degrees from Illinois do not require a core curriculum. Instead, there are distribution requirements. For students in the College of Liberal Arts and Sciences, these requirements are very general: ten courses, equally divided between "Area I" (the humanities and social sciences) and "Area II" (hard science and math). The university requires two courses in English composition and up to four semesters of a foreign language, though the language requirement can be circumvented with four years of high school study. All students must also take a course in quantitative reasoning, in which they might study mathematics, computer science, statistics, or formal logic. Majors involve between forty and sixty credit hours, twenty-one of which must come from advanced courses.

All students must take one course in non-Western culture. This can be fulfilled with something like a course in Third World geography, described by one student as something of a joke, academically speaking. Admirably, there is also a Western cultures requirement, and many good courses that meet it. A number of more tangential choices are also available, including "Sex and Gender in Classical Antiquity," "Introduction to Contemporary Dance," "Women and Gender in Premodern Europe," and "Viking Mythology."

"It's a smorgasbord," one professor says of the distribution requirements. Some on campus say a core curriculum is highly unlikely, and would not be a guaranteed success at Illinois anyway. "There are so many courses offered and ways to go, that a core is seen as peripheral and, given today's university, perhaps it should be peripheral," another professor says. "The students just pick and choose."

For elective credit the university has approved several courses offered by religious foundations in the Urbana-Champaign area. Students can take up to ten semester hours of credit from these private foundations.

Illinois has had an ROTC program since it opened in 1868, and today the Army, Navy, and Air Force all have programs there. A special honors program for the best one hundred students pairs a cadet with a professor in his field of study, offering an excellent opportunity for the student to get to know the professor professionally and personally. This kind of program is especially valuable at large state universities where interaction between students and faculty is much less frequent than at small colleges.

Within Illinois' massive faculty are some excellent professors, like Lee Alston, Salim Rashid, Larry Neal, and Fred Gottheil in economics; Robert Weissberg in political science; David Bordua (emeritus) in sociology; William Bryan in finance; J. Fred Giertz in government; Timothy Van Laar in art and design; and Keith Hitchens and John Pruett in history.

The strongest fields are engineering and most other science programs, economics and other business programs, history, journalism, labor and industrial relations, and the College of Agriculture. All departments are improved by the university's library, which is the third-largest academic library in the United States (after Harvard and Yale) and the fifth-largest in the Western Hemisphere. The library system, including thirty-eight departmental libraries scattered across campus as well as a main library, owns more than 8 million bound volumes, 14 million items in all.

Both the economics department and the labor and industrial relations programs are friendly to free-market theory. "The journalism department is great, with small classes and much personal attention," according to a student. Engineering and science departments are of excellent quality, and also nonideological. According to another student, "Religion has a strong Roman Catholic element. There are no horror stories there."

The most politicized department at Illinois is English, but history, where the newer professors focus almost exclusively on social history, is close behind, according to professors and students. The oft-politicized areas of sociology and women's studies are pretty much what you'd expect. And the College of Education is driven more by ideology than by traditional teaching, people on campus say.

The English department offers a scholarship endowed by journalist Robert Novak, an Illinois alumnus. The scholarship recognizes the recipient's excellence in previous work and promise as a writer or journalist. It is an award that merits the attention of serious English majors and aspiring journalists.

Another sign of politicization — and a more telling one — can be found in some of the courses offered by the department. "Race, Gender, and Revolution in Modern American Poetry" focuses on "women poets, minority poets, and writers on the political left" during the first half of the twentieth century. According to the course description, these writers "created whole literary subcultures [and] also entered into dramatic debates with more conservative writers, so that a kind of poetic war took place between feminism and misogyny, between a new African-American vision and a resurgent racism, between poets committed to radical change and those determined to preserve traditional power relations." The catalogue claims that this "cultural life" has since been "forgotten or repressed" in favor of "only the handful of white male poets who were honored in the modern poetry canon." The class reads some "canonical poets" like Eliot, Frost, Williams, and Pound, but emphasizes "the noncanonical poets who are now available again for reading and reflection — Langston Hughes, Edwin Rolfe, Genevieve Taggard, Gertrude Stein, [and] Sterling Brown."

Another English course, "Seminar in Sixteenth-Century Literature: The Body in the Renaissance: Gender, Health, and Deviance in Literary, Medical and Cultural Texts," looks at "recent scholarship on the body — in the wake of Foucault and Laqueur." According to the course description, "Topics will include the humoral body, the erotic body, the mortal body, the one-sex/two-sex controversy, illness (including madness), sexualities, childbirth and lactation, death and dying." Questions confronted during this class include: "What does it mean to historicize the body? What sort of dynamic interactions between cultural texts can be postulated and analyzed? At what sites and in what ways does the body acquire gender, sexuality, class, race? How are these attributes connected to health and deviance?"

Because of courses like this, both in English and elsewhere, a recent graduate found it necessary to be cautious when choosing classes. "In sociology and political science I dropped a bunch of classes during the first week of the term and signed up for others," the graduate says. "I could see that I wasn't going to get a fair shake because of politics. And I once had a sociology [teaching assistant] who really went off on Reagan and Thatcher on the first day of class."

With this in mind, faculty advising becomes essential. However, the Illinois faculty as a whole no longer does formal advising — that is handled by designated academic advisers. These advisers are, by and large, fair and objective in helping students meet graduation requirements, but some departments' advisers are blatantly political. In one social science department, the adviser is "an outright communist who makes no bones about it," according to a professor. "All majors must go through him during their freshman and sophomore years, and he can really mislead people." Another professor says this person's office walls are covered with socialist labor posters and that his bulletin board is filled with political announcements. "This comes across as official university policy, but it isn't," the second professor says. "The university keeps a blind eye to abuses on the left and is horrified if the right does anything 'bad.' "

Political Atmosphere: More Talk, Less Action

Illinois is not a radical campus, and though political correctness is often discussed, it has not become etched-in-stone policy. The university's mostly homegrown student body comes from a mostly conservative state.

"It's all here, but the size of the university allows students to mostly escape it," a professor says of political correctness. "There are endless numbers of studies about the evil of men, women's advocacy, consciousness raising, and so on."

Faculty are careful, however, not to be perceived as too traditional. "Young faculty must watch their backs all the time because there are stupid people who'll misunderstand what you say," a professor says. "In some fields this drives white males into mindlessly technical research in an effort to mask their true beliefs. So, women write about oppression, and white men write mathematical essays. That way, the administration knows they're safe."

This problem has caused Illinois to lose some of its brightest teachers. "The best are leaving or have withdrawn," a professor says. "Others will move on. The university makes life miserable for smart people, and your very smart people are leaving. . . . It's the best people we're losing because they can't stand it any longer."

Illinois exacerbates the problem with affirmative action hiring practices. "There is obviously a dual track for tenure considerations," a professor says. "It's a lot easier for women and minorities than for white men. And it's clear that the default option is that women and minorities are assumed to get tenure when they're hired."

The university has not introduced a formal speech code, though it attempted to do so in the early 1990s. "The [Faculty] Senate, however, in a flash of good sense, voted it down," a graduate says. Though the vote speaks well of the majority of the faculty, the informal speech code regarding politically correct thought has much the same effect as a formal code would have; that is, not everyone on campus feels free to speak his mind.

Especially not at freshman orientation. "We had pro-homosexual propaganda thrown at us," a recent graduate says. "We had to do role playing in which we took the part of a homosexual." In addition, Illinois, like many other universities, also offers a special orientation session for minority students.

Student Life: A Room of One's Own — Maybe

Illinois is large enough to accommodate students' interests, no matter how unique. This element of student life can be a major selling point for students looking to enjoy a small circle of friends in an anonymous setting. With many highly qualified professors on campus, not to mention first-class research facilities, the inquisitive student can certainly find his niche.

The downside of a large, anonymous state university is that it is just that: large and anonymous. Classes at Illinois can be enormous, and many are taught by teaching assistants. "In the first two years when you're trying to get liberal arts classes you have very little interaction with professors," a student says. "I've been in class with eight hundred other students." In most cases, students must wait until they're juniors to take smaller classes taught by senior professors.

Such a large place does, however, offer many student organizations — more than seven hundred are registered. One of these, the Student Government Association, recently lobbied the Illinois legislature — and won, by a 55-1 vote — for a voting seat on the university's board of trustees. (The university, incidentally, opposed the student vote, saying that such a huge enterprise should only be run by the experienced.) Another group, the Illini Union Board, is "an opportunity to run bookstores, hand out lecture money, book music shows, and more," a student says. "It's a wonderful thing to become involved in."

Other student groups worth noting are the various engineering societies, professional fraternities organized by discipline, and religious groups catering to every believer. The Greek system is vibrant and a "big force on campus," according to students.

Illinois College Republicans are also flourishing, according to a recent graduate. A conservative alternative newspaper, the *Orange and Blue Observer,* continues to grow, although it received a hostile reception when it debuted: An English professor, writing in the primary student newspaper, the *Daily Illini,* said the *Observer* was written by "Nazis." The *Daily Illini* attacked the *Observer* eighteen times in the latter's first semester of existence, but the *Observer* only increased in popularity.

Political student organizations also include pro-homosexual groups and multiculturalists. Such groups aren't hard to find on such a large campus, yet they don't dominate the environment. One group, the Cannabis Reform Coalition, has held a "Hash Wednesday" event every year since 1974. The group gathers on the university's main quad to support legalized marijuana and, according to an alumnus who advises the group (as quoted in the *Daily Illini*), hopes to educate the campus on the "medical, environmental, industrial, and economic aspects that would improve if cannabis production and usage were legalized." One student dresses as George Washington, alleged by the group to be the United States's most famous hemp farmer. Some students don't agree with the group. "Hash Wednesday is a crock because it started as a political movement and has turned into another reason to smoke," one student told the newspaper. "Not one of these people has done anything for the movement, like writing to their legislature."

Campus speakers tend to be liberal rather than conservative or libertarian, but there are notable exceptions. Robert Novak speaks every year, and recent visitors have included Richard Pipes, Linda Chavez, Ed Meese, and Jack Kemp. A former student recalls a debate on the Supreme Court's *Roe v. Wade* decision with Phyllis Schlafly and a proponent of that case; a speaker on the 1989 massacre in Tiananmen Square; as well as speakers like Sister Souljah, Angela Davis, and a medical doctor from Chicago who claimed the AIDS virus was injected into black children by Jewish doctors. Funding for speakers is said to be fairly distributed to those who ask for it.

About one-third of the student body lives in university dorms. There are twenty-two residence halls on campus, some new and others in need of repair. The university offers both single-sex and coed dorms. As more than 93 percent of students are from the state of Illinois, many live at home and commute to campus. Students have free use of buses on campus and in the Champaign-Urbana area.

The area around the university is known as Campustown and is home to many student hangouts: coffeehouses, bars, and restaurants. Chicago, St. Louis, and Indianapolis are all within three hours of campus. Cultural events on campus include theater, opera, and music performances. However, in a decidedly nonscientific survey taken by the *Daily Illini*, thirty-two of the eighty-two students polled said the thing they would remember most about the past academic year was — and we quote — "drunkenness." "Friendships" was second with fourteen votes, but the winner outpolled athletics, academics, graduation and the future, significant others, and "growing up/adulthood" combined.

Illinois is a Big Ten school, and its intercollegiate athletics are a Big Deal. Its football and basketball teams are the most well known nationally, but the university has seventeen teams. The intramural program has nearly seventeen thousand participants, and the university's Division of Campus Recreation runs thirty-two tennis courts, thirty-four playing fields, the Intramural-Physical Education Building (with racquet sports courts, a pool, and gym), as well as an ice arena and two eighteen-hole golf courses.

JAMES MADISON UNIVERSITY

Office of Admissions
James Madison University
Harrisonburg, VA 22807
(540) 568-6147
www.jmu.edu

Total enrollment: 13,714
Undergraduates: 12,551
SAT Ranges (Verbal/Math): V 550-640, M 550-640
Financial aid: 35%
Applicants: 12,570
Accepted: 56%
Enrolled: 36%
Application deadline: Early action, Dec. 1; regular, Jan. 15
Financial aid application deadline: Feb. 15

Tuition: in-state, $4,148; out-of-state, $8,816
Core curriculum: No

A Growth Experience

Thomas Jefferson has the University of Virginia. George Washington has Washington and Lee. And another Founding Father — the drafter of the Constitution and the nation's fourth president — is memorialized in Harrisonburg, Virginia.

Harrisonburg, a small town tucked in between the Blue Ridge and Allegheny Mountains, is home to James Madison University (JMU). Once a women's "industrial" school, JMU is now a major (coed) public university. After years of rapid growth, it is now recognized as one of the top regional universities in the South.

Undergraduates at JMU cite a number of things when asked why they like being there; among them are the friendliness of the student body, the beauty of the Shenandoah Valley, and the many outdoor activities available nearby. Indeed, a ski resort lies just ten miles from campus; hiking trails and campgrounds also abound.

Both inside and outside the university's classrooms, politics plays less of a role than at many other institutions of higher learning. Student and faculty radicals are few at JMU, and most of the students are conservative in outlook and culture. There is considerable wealth at JMU, but one does not have to be wealthy to attend: tuition is quite low (in-staters pay around $4,000, out-of-staters just over twice that).

James Madison is growing. It has boosted its student enrollment, launched new fund-raising drives, and begun constructing new buildings. It's an institution determined to live up to the greatness of its namesake.

Academic Life: Clusters of Learning

Academic departments at JMU fall into one of five schools: the College of Arts and Letters, the College of Business, the College of Education and Psychology, the College of Integrated Science and Technology, and the College of Science and Mathematics. Students may choose from among forty-five majors.

A bachelor's degree requires 120 credit hours at JMU; a bachelor of fine arts or a bachelor of music, slightly more. In addition, students have to master a foreign language at an intermediate level, take a philosophy course of their choosing, and complete the requirements for their major, as well as the general education requirements.

JMU introduced new general education requirements in 1997. Previously, students had to fulfill what were known as liberal studies requirements, a series of eleven areas in which they had to take a course or two. The new requirements are slightly more complicated and drew many complaints from faculty and students — from faculty because they were not adequately consulted about the changes, from students because the requirements were too rigid and didn't allow enough "flexibility."

Under the new requirements, students take forty to forty-three hours of coursework designed to ensure that they acquire skills and knowledge that will help them later in life. Students take courses in each of five "clusters": "Skills for the 21st Century," "Ideas and Expressive Forms in the Human Community," "The Natural World," "Social and Cultural Processes," and "Individuals in the Human Community." Within each cluster, students choose one of several "packages," which are an established set of courses across several fields. For example, within the "Ideas and Expressive Forms" cluster, students might choose Package C, the "Greek Experience," which requires three courses: one in the foundations of Western philosophy, one in Greek epic poetry, and one in Greek culture in the fifth century B.C. Those three classes complete the requirements for that cluster.

This unique general education program mixes elements of a core curriculum and distribution requirements. Students are given some latitude to choose areas that interest them, but once they have chosen, the courses they must take are specific. Unfortunately, leaving the choices to students means that some will not receive as well rounded an education as they would with a strong core curriculum. Examining all the clusters and packages, one JMU student club researched and found that it was possible to graduate without taking an American history course.

On the positive side, students do get to examine topics in depth across disciplines and are not forced to pick courses from thick catalogues in order to meet vague distribution requirements. In addition, several of the packages emphasize knowledge of Western civilization, and few include the sort of politicized courses obsessing on race, class, and gender that are commonly found at many universities today. For the student who chooses wisely, the general education curriculum could be a boon.

JMU has an honors program. Entering freshmen who graduated in the top 15 percent of their high school class and scored better than 1,200 on the SAT are eligible to apply for the 125 spots in this program. By offering small, special classes and independent study, the honors program seeks to cultivate critical thinking and creative expression.

An unusual option available at JMU is a minor in "music industry," which is designed to provide students whose specialties are in other disciplines a chance to explore career opportunities in the entertainment business. The program is one of only a few such in the country.

One famous Shakespeare touring troupe — Shenandoah Shakespeare Express — is based at the university. Founded and run by JMU English professor Ralph Cohen, the company reinterprets Shakespeare's plays and performs them in two hours, substantially less time than required for traditional Shakespearean performances. Actors sing Elizabethan songs in the text to the tunes of modern songs. In *A Midsummer Night's Dream*, for instance, actors put the Bard's words to the tune of "Strangers in the Night" and the theme from the TV show *Gilligan's Island*. Cohen says such adaptations are precisely what Shakespeare would have wanted: his works were meant to be entertaining and full of topical references. Though the actors in the group were all JMU students when the company formed in 1988, today all are professionals.

James Madison's College of Business has a strong reputation among students and faculty. The college offers degrees in international business, hospitality and tourism management, accounting, economics, finance, computer information systems, and marketing. Business is one of the most popular majors at JMU.

High marks are also given to the psychology department, which offers both bachelor of arts and bachelor of science degrees. In addition, the department offers a five-year program that leads to both a bachelor of science and a master's degree in psychology. The university also runs the Human Development Center, which offers clinical services to the Harrisonburg community and gives students hands-on training.

The university boasts a large, first-rate music program for those interested in becoming music teachers, industry professionals, performers, or composers. The School of Music gives its students a solid background in the theoretical, historical, and stylistic aspects of music, and sponsors a variety of concerts and recitals throughout the year. Though not connected to the School of Music, the JMU marching band is excellent and has won several national awards.

Outstanding professors at JMU include: Robert Geary in English, Elizabeth Neatrour in Russian language and literature, Mark Usry in business, Stephen Bowers in political science, Lee Congdon in history, and David Kreutzer in economics.

James Madison lacks the highly politicized academic departments that are found in many of the country's so-called leading universities. Students report that, for the most part, professors stick to the subject matter and do not use classrooms as their bully pulpits. However, some political biases do occasionally penetrate some courses. "If you're politically minded, you can tell they're sometimes leaning one way," says one sophomore. "Generally, the professors are pretty open, but it's tough to get into much discussion and get your point across in a class of 40 people."

Students say the politics that does creep into the classroom is often in the social sciences and humanities: history, political science, English, economics, sociology. Both liberal and conservative faculty can be found in these fields. "It's pretty even as far as the number of conservatives versus liberals," one student says.

James Madison does offer a minor in women's studies, a field that at other universities tends to be highly politicized, emphasizing victimization and advocating political activism. JMU minors take two introductory women's studies courses and then select four more approved courses from such fields as sociology, history, English, and economics.

Political Atmosphere: Communications Breakdown

In recent years JMU president Ronald Carrier's administration has been noted for its repeated clashes with faculty members who protest that they are not consulted sufficiently before the administration makes decisions. In 1995, after Carrier announced his plan to eliminate the major in physics and fire the university's ten physics professors, members of the faculty voted that they had no confidence in Carrier's leadership. Six months later, after a group of professors sued him over the plan, Carrier changed his mind, and no physics faculty were let go.

Carrier faced another lawsuit in 1996 after he went against university policy and reduced the sanction of two students found guilty of cheating. A faculty and student honor board had suspended the students for a semester, as university policy dictated, but Carrier reduced the suspensions. A university spokesman said it was "more important to the president to be fair to the students than to follow procedures," according to the *Chronicle of Higher Education*. The lawsuit, filed by a member of the university's honor court, did not succeed.

The tension between the faculty and administration has even reached a personal level. Some professors called for Carrier's ouster after he received a subpoena to testify in a murder trial involving a prostitute and her pimp. The prostitute testified that the pimp, who had been murdered, had named Carrier as one of several men who would be her future customers. In the trial, a store owner testified that Carrier had rented an X-rated videotape ten years earlier. Carrier denied ever renting such a tape or knowing the prostitute or pimp. Despite the allegations, Carrier retains the support of JMU's Board of Visitors and many of the students, according to the *Chronicle*.

The university runs a Center for Multicultural Student Services, which is responsible for "assessing the needs of multiethnic student populations at JMU and coordinating programs and services to meet those needs." JMU says it is dedicated to "a supportive environment for minority students, faculty, and staff." The university's student body is around 7 percent black and 13 percent minority overall.

Administrators have said they would like to increase the percentage of minority students at JMU but that, lamentably, they receive too many applications from whites. "It's a real struggle to try and promote the notion of diversity," said Linwood Rose, JMU's executive vice president. "We have an applicant pool that is more homogeneous than we would like to have."

Enrollment at JMU has risen substantially in recent years, and administrators have embarked on an aggressive fund-raising drive and are expanding many of the university's facilities. With an eye toward improving health and information sciences, JMU has particularly been developing the College of Integrated Science and Technology.

Some students complain that the availability of classes has not kept pace with the number of students, and as a result, it has been increasingly difficult to enroll in classes required to graduate.

Student Life: Safe and Friendly

JMU's 472-acre campus in Harrisonburg is located in Virginia's beautiful and historic Shenandoah Valley. The Blue Ridge Mountains lie to the east and the Allegheny Mountains to the west. Although a small town (population thirty-three thousand), it's the center of commerce and travel for the surrounding area. Three other institutions of higher education are also located in or near Harrisonburg: Eastern Mennonite University and Seminary, Bridgewater College, and Blue Ridge Community College. Besides education and tourism, the area is known for its poultry industry. Harrisonburg is about a two-hour drive from Washington, Richmond, and Roanoke, and it's just off an interstate highway.

The crime rate in Harrisonburg is also low; the town was rated the second-safest college town in the country by a 1994 book, *Crime at College: The Student Guide to Personal Safety.* Only Cedar Falls, Iowa, was deemed safer.

JMU has many different clubs and activities in which students can participate. The student newspaper, the *Breeze,* is published twice weekly. An impressive number of religious groups are available, including gospel choirs, prayer groups, and organizations for all different kinds of denominations. There's even a break-dancing club, designed to practice and promote the dancing craze of the mid-1980s.

The most prominent groups on campus are the student government association and the College Republicans, which claim to have more members than any other political group at the university. They sponsor forums and debates on current political issues.

Other vocal groups include Harmony, the gay and lesbian association; Earth, a liberal environmental organization; and the Young Democratic Socialists of America, which describes itself as a "feminist, anti-racist, democratic, Socialist organization." Its issues include "fighting the militaristic and homophobic ROTC on campus" and "taking on the racist INS [Immigration and Naturalization Service]." The organization's web page includes photos of Karl Marx.

The Socialists got into trouble recently when several members went into a local clothing store and surreptitiously (and illegally) stuffed propaganda into the pockets of all the pairs of Guess? jeans. In their defense, the Socialists claimed that Guess? uses exploitive labor practices.

Though these liberal groups may sound popular, students say their memberships are small and incestuous. Overall, the student body at JMU is conservative.

The JMU student government has an active multicultural committee that plans activities designed to "raise awareness" of minority women on campus. In a November 1997 panel that sought to address racial diversity, some feminist activists complained that the panel failed to address women's concerns.

Around 20 percent of JMU students belong to fraternities or sororities, but the Greeks do not dominate the social scene. Much more common than frat parties are smaller get-togethers in students' rooms, or jaunts off campus to a bar. Students report no excessive pressure to drink at parties and plenty to do that does not involve alcohol.

One popular hangout is JM's Bar & Grill, which was named one of *Playboy* magazine's "Top 100 College Bars in America" in 1997. Students say its popularity is due to its location close to campus. "It's a good place to blow off steam after a hard week's work," said one senior.

JMU fields teams in twenty-seven intercollegiate sports. In addition, the school sponsors approximately forty intramural sports as well as sports clubs.

JOHNS HOPKINS UNIVERSITY

Office of Admissions
Director of Admissions
The Johns Hopkins University
140 Garland Hall
Thirty-fourth and Charles Streets
Baltimore, MD 21218
(301) 338-8171

Total enrollment: 5,024
Undergraduates: 3,658
SAT Ranges (Verbal/Math): V 620-720, M 670-740
Financial aid: 60%
Applicants: 8,456
Accepted: 40%
Enrolled: 28%
Application deadline: early decision, Nov. 15; regular decision, Jan. 1
Financial aid application deadline: Feb. 1
Tuition: $21,700
Core curriculum: No

Research Opportunities

Johns Hopkins was founded in 1876 as a research institution modeled on nineteenth-century continental European universities, which emphasized research and scholarship at the advanced level. According to a current college catalogue, Johns Hopkins still considers itself loyal to its founding vision as "a graduate university with an associated preparatory college, a place where knowledge would be created and assembled, as well as taught."

Although they outnumber graduate students by over two to one (roughly 3,400 to 1,400), undergraduates may continue to feel like something of an afterthought at Hopkins, where the emphasis is still largely on graduate research and faculty scholarship. As one cynical graduate student puts it: "Undergrads bring in revenue."

Still, the university's traditional strengths in research and scholarship can work to an undergraduate's advantage. As the university proclaims in its undergraduate handbook, the faculty's "involvement as leaders in their professional fields cannot help but benefit their students." And unlike most universities, where such claims usually translate into distant faculty who are uninterested in undergraduate life, this is often not the case at Hopkins. As one student notes, "One of the best things about Hopkins is the opportunity for research. It is very easy to get started on top-notch projects. My ex-roommate, a mechanical engineer, walked down to the med school one day and started doing robotics research the next day. A year later, the person he was working for left and he took over the project — as an undergraduate."

Academic Life: Distribution Blues

Johns Hopkins is comprised of eight degree-granting divisions: Arts and Sciences, Engineering, Medicine, Hygiene and Public Health, Nursing, the Peabody Conservatory of Music, the School of Advanced International Studies, and the School of Continuing Studies. In addition to requirements for their major, students in Arts and Sciences must complete a fairly broad and unstructured set of distribution requirements. All students must take four writing-intensive courses. In addition, humanities and social science majors must take a total of thirty credits in natural sciences (N), mathematics or other quantitative studies (Q), humanities (H), social or behavioral sciences (S), and engineering (E), excluding the category for their major (H or S). At least twelve of these credits should be in the N, Q, or E categories, in any combination.

This loose set of requirements could hardly be considered a core curriculum; indeed, an undergraduate majoring in history could conceivably fulfill them by taking twelve credits in engineering and graduate without any courses in mathematics or the natural sciences. Students interested in pursuing a liberal arts education will thus have to structure their own program by carefully surveying the courses that satisfy the distribution requirements and selecting those that appear to correspond to the traditional categories of a core curriculum, such as "Science in the Western Tradition: The Rise of Modern Science" or "Introduction to Greek Philosophy."

Some solid programs still exist in the humanities and social sciences, although many disciplines have become increasingly politicized. Political science is considered strong, and the department administers an excellent program in international studies. Advanced students in this program may be able to avail themselves of Hopkins's Paul H. Nitze School of Advanced Studies (SAIS) for a semester. Located in downtown Washington, D.C., the SAIS campus is primarily for graduate study and emphasizes foreign languages, international law, and diplomacy. Courses in international relations are also offered through Johns Hopkins's campus in Bologna, Italy.

History, it is said, still retains some good faculty. However, the English department is awash in the latest theoretical trends; in the current listing of faculty interests, over a third cite "critical theory" among their specializations.

Science and engineering are strong disciplines at Hopkins. "There are lots of premed and science students," notes one undergraduate. The university has an innovative FlexMed program for entering medical students that offers flexible options regarding admission so that students can pursue "one-of-a-kind, individual learning experiences" such as research, study abroad, or service work between their undergraduate and advanced medical studies. The university's program in Biomedical Engineering (BME) also has an excellent reputation.

The highly politicized areas of study at Hopkins are the recently established Program in Comparative American Cultures and the Institute for Global Studies in Culture, Power, and History, which offers a minor in Multicultural and Regional Studies. The Humanities Center, which administers an Honors Program in Humanistic Studies, also appears to be in the grip of current ideological trends. While the Humanities Center announces that "the coordinated study of Western civilization through its literature, art, philosophy, and history has been one of the oldest continuing concerns at Hopkins," the center's primary concerns are "comparative literature, intellectual history, and feminist theory," and it offers such "advanced" undergraduate courses as "Trauma and Feminism: The Case of Multiple Personalities."

Advising at Hopkins is thought to be fair, and although faculty are frequently preoccupied with research endeavors, many make themselves available to their students. Graduate students, according to one student, are not routinely used to teach undergraduates, perhaps because their emphasis is on research and scholarship. Bright students may find themselves sharing courses with graduate students at the upper level, and within the humanities qualified students can participate in honors programs in comparative literature and intellectual or cultural history.

Because of its prime location in the greater D.C. area, Hopkins students have ready access to world-class research and curricular opportunities. Students can easily avail themselves of the resources at the Library of Congress, the Folger Shakespeare Library, and numerous other area libraries. Closer to home, the Hopkins library facilities are described as "excellent" by one student, who also praises their electronic resources. "The library was just recently renovated," notes another, "and if they don't have something you need, they will get it for you through interlibrary loan."

The average Hopkins student is extremely intelligent and hardworking. One student points out that "some students here have a chip on their shoulder because they're not at an Ivy League school." Whether they compare themselves to Ivy Leaguers or not, it's clear that most Hopkins students spend more time at the library than at the local bar.

Political Atmosphere: Special, and Not So Special, Interests

The political climate at Hopkins appears to be in constant flux, with a lingering core of traditional faculty being rapidly replaced by more liberal and activist professors, and a moderate undergraduate student body existing alongside a contingent of radical graduate students. According to one student, "The undergraduates tend to be much more conservative than the graduate students." And in general, notes another, "politics do not enter the vocabulary of many of the students. They are too busy studying."

Most members of the administration appear to have little interest in undergraduate liberal education. One professor refers to senior administrators as "faceless bureaucrats," and laments that the two presidents preceding the current officeholder, President William R. Brody, "had no serious educational interests." Brody, by contrast, has moved his family on campus, and some have interpreted this as a sign that he is serious about his leadership of the university. "He may even have a philosophy of education," says one hopeful faculty member.

Increasingly, faculty members at Hopkins are becoming warriors in the ideological battles gripping American higher education, especially in the humanities, where the qualification of strong scholarship all too frequently translates into the hiring of professors engaged in politicized study. Older faculty members lament the loss of collegiality among the faculty, and complain that there is very little conversation across the disciplines, let alone among members of the same department. Speaking of the gradual demise of the Hopkins Faculty Club, one professor notes that it once "played an academic role. . . . You learned things. You got new ideas. You got perspectives on what you were doing. That's not true anymore, and that's a loss. We don't really have a community anymore." Another adds that "things that are associated with the university as an entity have lost their appeal. The Hopkins spirit is not a real entity. It doesn't exist anymore," according to an article in the *Chronicle of Higher Education.*

The reasons for this decline of collegiality are numerous: Younger faculty are more interested in pursuing their own scholarship than in exchanging ideas with other professors, and often view faculty gatherings as elitist and unproductive. As one professor notes, newer faculty "are pressed for publishing rather than perishing, and they don't want to be distracted from their pursuit of professional advancement." A junior member of the English department echoes this cynical and utilitarian sentiment: "What one cares most about is being evaluated on one's work. . . . It's much harder for women and minority faculty members to come into a university and be socially incorporated than to be professionally incorporated. . . . You shouldn't require that someone be socially graceful in addition to being very good in their field." Such attitudes have only further devastated an already flagging social and intellectual environment at Hopkins.

As at similar institutions of higher learning, tenure at Hopkins appears to be dictated primarily by publications and research potential rather than teaching ability. And, along with a growing number of universities in our litigious society, Hopkins has found itself embroiled in legal battles over tenure disputes in recent years. A couple of years ago the university was sued by two members of the medical faculty, husband and wife Samuel Ritter and Rebecca Snider. Drs. Ritter and Snider were recruited by Hopkins and left their tenured posts at Cornell and Duke, respectively, with the understanding that they would be granted tenure. Dr. Ritter was denied tenure after both the dean of the school and the school's promotions committee recommended him for it. The couple was awarded $822,844 by a Maryland circuit court, but lost in appeals court, according to the *Chronicle of Higher Education*. The case points up the ad hoc manner in which tenure proceedings are frequently conducted in higher education.

Hopkins hosts numerous special-interest groups, including the Diverse Sexuality and Gender Alliance and Students for Environmental Action, as well as chapters of College Democrats and College Republicans. Regarding campus politics, one student remarks that "the most politically sensitive issues have been with the gay and lesbian community and the black students organization." The campus student weekly, the *News-Letter*, is considered politically balanced, although it ran afoul of student groups a few years ago after printing a political cartoon considered derogatory to Chinese people.

In general, most of the media attention Hopkins gets is incidental to the political atmosphere of the institution, in contrast to other universities where controversies usually arise out of the radical campus climate. The shooting death of a student by a member of the campus Republican group a few years ago, as well as the tenure dispute of Dr. Ritter, could have happened on any university campus and do not denote any particular political excesses of the students or administration at Hopkins. Indeed, if anything, the undergraduate student body is moderate to conservative, and perhaps one of the few advantages to the lack of a cohesive undergraduate environment is the comparative political apathy of Hopkins students. Learning is thus much easier in a climate relatively free from the activism and multicultural "sensitivity" so prevalent on other college campuses.

Student Life: I'd Rather Be Studying

Homewood, the main campus of Johns Hopkins, is located on 140 acres in a residential area of Baltimore, on the former estate of Charles Carroll Jr., son of the signer of the Declaration of Independence. One student likens the campus to "a little postage stamp." Another comments that "the campus is small — one could walk across it in ten minutes. It is also very pretty — especially in the spring." The east side of campus is what one student calls a "student ghetto," while to the west is a white working-class neighborhood bordered by a park and wooded area. In addition to the wealth of cultural opportunities available down the freeway in Washington, D.C., the Baltimore area offers several nearby attractions. The impressive Baltimore Art Museum is on the edge of the campus. Other prime cultural venues include the Walters Art Gallery and the Peabody Conservatory of Music.

Hopkins requires freshmen and sophomores to live in residence halls. The university also owns a number of apartments, homes, and row houses, which it makes available to upperclassmen, and students desiring nonuniversity housing can usually find reasonably priced rentals in the neighboring area. Campus safety is a perennial issue, with crimes ranging from petty theft to rape. The university has established several safety measures to reduce the risk of crime, such as an evening escort service to places like the library and a shuttle to convey students to off-campus locations.

Decades of emphasis on research and scholarship have not aided Hopkins in the establishment of a sense of community among students and faculty. "There's not much undergraduate or graduate social life," laments one student. When asked to characterize the social climate of the university, another student remarks, "Hopkins, summed up in a nutshell, is a place where students spend most of their time studying. Studying has a higher priority than anything else — social life generally takes a back seat." There is a Greek system at the university — one sorority and two fraternities — though it "is not emphasized," according to one student, and "only a small percentage of the population" are members.

More than ninety social, cultural, religious, athletic, and related student groups exist at Johns Hopkins. Religious groups range from the Hopkins InterVarsity Christian Fellowship to the Zen Meditation Society. "Cultural clubs organize events often," according to one student. The university is home to scores of ethnic and cultural associations, ranging from the Association of Thai Students to the European Students Union. There are also numerous activity clubs, for everything from chess to bicycling.

Athletics have not traditionally been a focus of extracurricular life, though one student says "sports are gaining ground across the board." Lacrosse is big, and the university is home to the Lacrosse Hall of Fame. Until recently men's lacrosse was the university's only Division I sport, but it will soon be joined by women's lacrosse. Men's and women's swimming and men's fencing are also traditionally strong, and field hockey, water polo, and men's soccer have grown in recent years as well. But as with most nonacademic concerns at Hopkins, student interest in athletics remains relatively low. "As an athlete," notes one student, "one complaint I have always had is the lack of interest of the Hopkins community in athletic events. Only a small percentage of the population attends events — they would rather spend it in the library. It's a shame since many of our teams are doing well."

KENYON COLLEGE

Dean of Admissions
Ransom Hall
Kenyon College
Gambier, OH 43022-9623
(800) 848-2468 (toll free)
www.kenyon.edu

Total enrollment: 1,536
Undergraduates: 1,536
SAT Ranges (Verbal/Math): V 620-710, M 580-670
Financial aid: 39%
Applicants: 2,314
Accepted: 70%
Enrolled: 27%
Application deadline: Feb. 15
Financial aid application deadline: Feb. 15
Tuition: $26,840 (comprehensive)
Core curriculum: No

Half of College Is Ninety Percent Mental

There had to be something inspired in the founding of Kenyon College. Philander Chase, the first Episcopal bishop of Ohio, envisioned not just a college, but a college in the European traditions of curriculum and architecture — and this was in 1824, when Ohio was not that far from the new nation's frontier. But Chase collected donations from English lords (including a Lord Kenyon and a Lord Gambier, for whom Chase named the village next to the college) and built Gothic-style buildings and a program of classical education. Among the early graduates were Edwin Stanton, U.S. secretary of war during the Civil War, and President Rutherford Hayes.

While it might have seemed impossible in 1824 that a classic college could grow among the uncut woods of Ohio, it is not at all likely that such a college would be able to survive today with its commitment to traditional education intact. But more recent graduates — poets James Wright and Robert Lowell, novelist E. L. Doctorow, and Olaf Palme, the late Swedish prime minister, to name some — received much the same quality of education as did their older fellow alums. And a curricular review was recently begun that will probably make the educational program even better.

Not only is the education good, but the atmosphere on the neo-Gothic, lovely campus is seemingly as peaceful as the countryside surrounding it. Students and faculty are dedicated to reasoned debate, meaning that whatever other improbabilities arise in the coming years, it is likely that Kenyon will beat the odds once more. It has certainly done it before.

Academic Life: Upon Further Review

Kenyon's general education plan requires that students take at least two semesters of courses in each of the college's four divisions: humanities, fine arts, natural sciences, and social sciences. No courses are required by name, so just about any course qualifies. But caveats have been designed to encourage interdisciplinary thought: in each semester, a student's courses must come from at least two different divisions, and of the sixteen units (thirty-two semesters) required for graduation, no more than seven (fourteen semesters) can come from any single division. As such, no department can demand more than seven units of majors (though the seven may include courses in another division), meaning that students will spend the majority of their time in courses not only outside their majors, but outside the division in which their majors fall.

What this means, of course, is that students are not required to take a course in Western civilization, and that students hold their curricular plan, for the most part, in their own hands. There is no foreign language requirement, nor are there history or laboratory science requirements. Kenyon's notion of the liberal arts, therefore, focuses more on students becoming "well rounded" or "broadly educated" than on a specific conception of a "tradition," or body of knowledge that should be common to all students. A recent Kenyon graduate says that, as a result of the college's structure, "There wasn't any coordination, no backbone tying courses together." The college prospectus mentions this freedom approvingly, quoting a senior English major: "Just about every semester I've taken a class that's had nothing to do with my major: a year of Mayan hieroglyphics, an advanced seminar in Matisse and Picasso, the history of Russia, a drama class on character analysis, the anthropology of sports and games."

Kenyon does have a concentration called the Integrated Program in the Humane Studies (IPHS), like a miniature great books program but without the standing of a major. One faculty member calls this program the college's "closest equivalent to a general ed requirement." Instruction in the IPHS consists of small seminars and individual tutorials with a minimum of lecture. At its core is a reading program of classic texts from several disciplines, organized on the theme of the "human predicament." As opposed to true great books programs, which last for all four years at places like St. John's College and Thomas Aquinas College, Kenyon's IPHS involves four semesters of work — two during the freshman year, one during the second year, and a senior seminar. The program is popular and highly regarded; each year sixty to seventy students in the incoming class of around four hundred choose the IPHS.

Despite the absence at Kenyon of a true core curriculum, faculty say the college is dedicated to a rigorous, traditional liberal arts program. Just how far the college is willing to go in that direction will become apparent in the outcome of a curricular review begun in 1997 under the leadership of college president Robert Oden. The collegewide review is the first since 1978, and everything is on the table. The process is expected to take at least two years and will examine what should and should not constitute a general education at a liberal arts college. Kenyon's lack of a core curriculum and Western civilization requirement is "clearly . . . going to be brought up," says a faculty member committed to the traditional humanities. "This is the moment in the college's history when everyone will be weighing in on his view" of what the curriculum should be, the professor says. It is comforting that the president's view is a traditional one: Oden, a scholar of ancient religion and formerly a professor at Dartmouth College, has been perceived during his tenure as a champion of "the serious liberal arts," according to a professor.

Thankfully, the discussion will not be conducted in a highly politicized atmosphere, nor will the participants forget their manners should there be disagreement. It is likely that the conversation will be conducted in an "atmosphere of little rancor," according to the college's newspaper, the *Kenyon Observer.* Civilized community conversation about ideas is one of Kenyon's prized virtues, and perhaps the preeminent aspect Kenyon advertises about itself.

The curricular review will not merely answer the larger questions about the composition of education, but will specifically state new requirements. On the agenda will be the natural sciences distribution requirement, which drew scorn from an *Observer* columnist just before the review process began. "The natural sciences requirement at Kenyon is a joke," the columnist wrote. "I will leave Kenyon in May having learned more about science in a philosophy class than I learned fulfilling my natural sciences requirement." The student's integrated view of philosophy and science, of course, is a testament to the current educational quality at Kenyon.

The curricular review will also include discussions on the degree to which new theories and criticisms have altered how the humanities are taught at Kenyon, as well as the effects of the quickly paced growth in information technology. Other issues that will be addressed include possible grade inflation — "a national concern," one faculty member says — along with new faculty recruitment and a greater emphasis on the performing arts.

Kenyon is proud of its reputation for teaching, and justifiably so. Outstanding professors include Fred Baumann, Harry Clor, Kirk Emmert, and Pamela K. Jensen in political science; William Ezra McCulloh in classics; Jennifer Clarvoe, Adele Davidson, Perry Lentz, Sergei Lobanov-Rostovsky, Timothy Shutt, and Judy Rae Smith in English; John Jursinic and Hideo Tomita in modern languages; Reed Browning, Ellen Furlough, and Roy Wortman in history; Rosemary Marusak in chemistry; Joel Richeimer in philosophy; John Macionis in sociology; Royal Rhodes in religion; and David Harrington and Kathy Krynski in economics.

The strongest departments include political science, English, classics, economics, and choral music. Philosophy and the sciences are good and getting better, according to faculty in other departments.

The political science department is highly regarded for its teachers and its uncompromising commitment to the traditional liberal arts. Compared to its counterparts at many colleges, the department places a strong emphasis on political theory and philosophy. A number of faculty are theorists in the tradition of Leo Strauss, who earlier in this century sought to answer questions of politics by studying their philosophical roots in classical antiquity. Whereas the study of politics at many colleges deals with the mechanics of elections and quantitative methods, Kenyon's political science department tries to "show students that some of the issues of political statesmanship really have a bearing on politics," a professor says. The department's introductory course, a yearlong seminar entitled "The Quest for Justice," studies classic sources like Plato, the Bible, Aquinas, Hobbes, and Machiavelli.

The English department has traditionally been one of Kenyon's most prominent programs, and remains the most popular major on campus. The department initially gained fame in midcentury under the leadership of the Southern poet and literary critic John Crowe Ransom. Robert Lowell left Harvard to study with Ransom, graduating from Kenyon in 1940. The department is known nationally for its literary journal, the *Kenyon Review*, which recently celebrated its fiftieth anniversary.

In both its public relations and recruitment materials, Kenyon highlights the department's distinguished literary history. However, the New Criticism espoused by Ransom (who actually coined that phrase) has all but disappeared from the department. Although there is still a wide range of viewpoints, recent hirings have tended toward postmodernism and there has been a trend toward critical theory and non-Western literature. For example, the department offers courses such as "Studies in Popular Literature and Culture" and "Wild Justice: Revenge, Repressions, and the Origins of Criminality." But courses like these are few, and one can still find an excellent selection of traditional courses in the department.

The English department's biggest problem is its small size in comparison to the number of students, meaning that, as one recent English graduate says, "Sometimes people are relegated to courses they're not particularly interested in," or they have trouble fulfilling requirements. The department's greatest strength, however, continues to be the excellence of its teachers and the dedication of its students. The recent graduate tells of a power outage one morning that shut off students' alarm clocks all over campus. While most classes got late starts that day, every student showed up on time for a class taught by English professor Perry Lentz. And, the student says, "He's not the only one who's thought of [so] highly."

Kenyon's history department is cited by those on campus as the college's most politicized. Its traditional emphasis on intellectual history has recently faded in favor of a more revisionist and multicultural approach that can be, according to one professor, "downright anti-Western." The department's offerings include many courses devoted to ethnic categories (African-American history and Native American history) or ideological categories ("Women in Search of Utopia" and "Explorations in the History of Radical Movements in the United States"). This variety has not hurt the selection in American history courses, but the department's catalogue shows a paucity of European history courses. According to faculty and students, the department's hiring policies show a clear preference for ethnic and ideological specialists. But, one faculty member says, while "there are a good number of liberal faculty members" in history and elsewhere at Kenyon, "no department is entirely on the left."

The anthropology-sociology department's perspective is shown in courses like "Deviance" and "Gender in Cross-Cultural Perspective." Students in this department may also select concentrations in African-American studies and American studies, which generally have a radical political focus. Although the department is considered highly politicized, Professor John Macionis has, in the words of another professor, "a kind of Tocquevillean approach to sociology." Macionis is also the author of a textbook used by roughly half of all students in the country in introductory sociology courses.

There is a women's studies program which offers a concentration but not a major. The program is "relatively tame" and "feminist-leaning," says one professor, "but not out to change the curriculum." Politicization is also apparent in the biology department, of all places, and one professor says some courses there are "more feminist ideology" than science. A few years ago it looked like the campus and curriculum were coming apart at the gender gap, but, according to another professor, things calmed down quickly. "There hasn't, as we'd feared, been an escalation," the professor says.

Political Atmosphere: Debatable

Kenyon's strong commitment to argument and debate has helped it avoid the polarizing effects of multicultural and diversity issues seen at other institutions. Though the discussions have been animated, they have not strayed into stridency and divisiveness, professors say. "Kenyon has been pretty good, even at its worst times," one professor says.

These discussions most occupied the college in the late 1980s, when a new provost arrived with an agenda full of ethnic and gender issues. Faculty, including many of those listed above, held on to their traditional conception of the liberal arts and fought to keep open the channels of free expression. The controversial administrator did not stay long, and while it took a while for the college to recover, "the environment right now is extremely healthy," a professor says.

Still, questions of multiculturalism persist at Kenyon. The college does have a multicultural center, and the prospectus highlights specific "Academic Awards for African-American and Latino students." There is a "Racial Awareness Program" for freshmen. But the primary effects of multiculturalism are more hidden, some say.

"There's a subtle censorial atmosphere that stifles people sometimes" with regard to issues of gender and race, not merely students of "moderate to conservative persuasions [but] even liberal students," a professor says. The professor also notes a "certain doctrine and dogma" that seeks to "minimize the heritage of Classical Greece and Rome, and Europe."

But most on campus maintain that the political atmosphere does not damage the students or the college. "Let me put it this way," a professor says. "It could be a lot worse." Furthermore, the multicultural debate at Kenyon appears to be largely abstract, since Kenyon, located in rural Ohio, has had very few minority students. (The prospectus notes that a "strong effort to increase racial diversity" has raised the number of minority students to 12 percent of the student body.) In the early 1990s the small number of minority students and faculty precluded many multicultural tensions, but, according to a recent graduate, that small number is now "somewhat of an embarrassment" to the college. Debate on the issue of racial representation tends to be all or nothing, the graduate says. "On occasion an issue will become hot and the campus will rally around it."

The administration's change in attitude on its minority enrollment has resulted in more minority students, but the college has done a good job of avoiding the segregation characteristic of other colleges. And while there are still very few minority professors at Kenyon, the administration has refused to bend its standards to meet hiring quotas. During the spring of 1997 the board of trustees denied reappointment (in effect, tenure) to two African-American professors, lowering the number of black professors at Kenyon from four to two (out of nearly 150 faculty). The decisions sparked comment from African-American student organizations, who called on the administration to increase diversity among Kenyon faculty. At the end of the spring term the affected faculty were in grievance proceedings, but the college has stood by its decision. "The president and provost are very strong in support of faculty standards fairly applied," says a faculty member.

In fact, both President Oden and Provost Kate Will receive high acclaim from many quarters. Oden is "a spark of light," says one professor. "He believes in genuine diversity, to include intellectual diversity." Under Oden and Will, the college has also become richer, nearly doubling its endowment in less than five years to $70 million, up from $37 million in 1993-94.

The college's stance on other political issues is less encouraging, but still is an improvement on that of many other schools. One professor says the college does not invite conservative speakers to campus, and especially not black conservatives: "It would be a cold day in hell if Thomas Sowell or Shelby Steele were invited by the Faculty Lectureships committee," the professor says. The political science department, however, has a grant from the Bradley Foundation to bring its own speakers to campus. There are several homosexual groups on campus — including a theater group and a group that calls itself "Queer Action" — and they host a "Coming Out Weekend" each year. A rather mild speech code is also on the books, largely concerning ethnic slurs. Speech code grievances are handled by a committee composed of faculty and staff.

Student Life: The Run of the Village

Gambier, Ohio, is considered the smallest college town in America — its 650 citizens are badly outnumbered by the 1,500 Kenyon students. The location, between Columbus and Cleveland, is rural and quiet. The college itself stands on eight hundred hilltop acres, and its Collegiate Gothic buildings are stunning. The original building, Old Kenyon, now a residential hall, was completed in 1826 and is thought to be the oldest Collegiate Gothic structure in the nation. The campus's Church of the Holy Spirit was built in 1869, and Pierce Hall contains a large student dining room with oak tables and stained-glass scenes from classic works of literature. A former student praises Kenyon for its scrupulous commitment to preserving the campus's architectural integrity as it expands its physical plant. One of the best ways to enjoy the area's scenery is the Kokosing Gap Trail, an old railroad bed that runs adjacent to the campus and follows the Kokosing River through the forests and farmland.

Freshmen live in residence halls near the center of student activities, Gund Commons. After their first year, students enter a housing lottery, either individually or in groups of ten or less. Upperclassmen can choose to live in fraternities or "other group-living societies," according to the prospectus.

Given the distance from urban concentrations (to wit: the prospectus is reduced to listing the fast-food establishments in nearby Mount Vernon, population fifteen thousand), students need to pay a hefty activities fee in order to fund the more than 130 student organizations. The choices include clubs in the areas of music, science, service, ethnic groups, academics (including one of the nation's oldest Phi Beta Kappa chapters), and other special-interest organizations. One graduate recalls helping to organize a chess club "so we could get our money." There are not many groups dedicated to political causes, but a faculty member says the students' political consciousness most often "manifest[s] itself in relation to the environment."

Kenyon also fields twenty-two sports, and has won two national titles in women's tennis and been ranked number one in men's soccer. Those achievements pale in comparison to what the prospectus properly calls "college athletics' most dominant dynasty": the eighteen consecutive national titles in NCAA Division III won by the men's swimming and diving team, and the fourteen consecutive won by the women's squad. There are also club sports and intramurals.

Though Kenyon is a very traditional campus, it is not a particularly religious campus. The college was founded under the auspices of the Episcopal Church, but the connection is now tenuous at best. There is an ecumenical Board of College Ministries, including Roman Catholic and Jewish chaplains. Episcopal students are welcomed by the local parish, which is nearly as old as the college itself. Student religious groups include Hillel, Christian Fellowship, Fellowship of Christian Athletes, Unitarian-Universalists, the Zen Meditation Group, and a Newman Club — that's *Cardinal* Newman, not Kenyon alumnus Paul Newman.

Kenyon has something of an image as a party school, but others on campus say such reports are overblown. Fraternities are more often in the campus news for their complaints about living space than for out-of-control parties.

LEHIGH UNIVERSITY

Office of Admissions
Director of Admissions
Lehigh University
Bethlehem, PA 18015
(215) 758-3100
www.lehigh.edu

Total enrollment: 6,316
Undergraduates: 4,483
SAT Ranges (Verbal/Math): V 550-644, M 587-679
Financial aid: 59%
Applicants: 7,777
Accepted: 54%
Enrolled: 28%
Application deadline: Jan. 15
Financial aid application deadline: Feb. 1
Tuition: $22,300
Core curriculum: No

The Art of Engineering

Lehigh began in 1865 as an all-male engineering school. It remained all-male until, in the final years of the 1960s, a group of students known as the Committee of Undergraduates for Responsible Education issued thirty-one demands to the administration. The twelfth of these was the inclusion of women, and in the fall of 1971 Lehigh admitted its first female undergraduates. Males still make up almost two-thirds of the undergraduate enrollment, and the admission of women, and their minority status within the student body, has become a politicized issue for many Lehigh faculty and students who advocate a progressivist vision for the traditionally conservative university. The director of Lehigh's women's center told the *Lehigh Bulletin* in 1997: "We've only had coeducation for twenty-five years. . . . Lehigh is still somewhat of a conservative university. But we've come a long way. I think it's getting better."

The student body in question numbers about 4,500 undergraduates, with an additional 1,500 graduate students. One faculty members says the university is "a nice size . . . big enough to strive for excellence in a number of areas, but small enough for a personal atmosphere." Lehigh students are historically very happy with their educational experience at the university, although the recent focus on the liberal arts has left some alumni fearful that Lehigh's traditional strength in engineering and applied sciences may consequently suffer. However, more than 55 percent of alumni make gifts to the school, giving Lehigh the third-highest rate of alumni giving in the nation among major private universities.

Across the country, the sciences have come through the multicultural wars as unadulterated as could be expected, especially compared to the havoc that has been wrought on the humanities. In tune with this, Lehigh's traditional programs remain strong and intact, though the percentage of students taking them has shrunk. The fact that the university's alumni have shown some opposition to the emergence of the humanities at Lehigh probably says more of their commitment to the school they knew than it does of their displeasure with the way these disciplines are being taught. It remains to be seen whether Lehigh is adding a new area to its tradition or changing its identity, but it can be said with certainty that what the school has done for so long, it continues to do well.

Academic Life: An Engineering Solution

A little less than half of Lehigh's undergraduates enroll in the College of Arts and Sciences; an additional third are in Engineering and Applied Sciences, with the remainder in the College of Business and Economics (with a few students in a dual Arts-Engineering program). The College of Engineering and Applied Sciences remains the largest graduate program. Regardless of their affiliations, both faculty and students at Lehigh are serious about academics. "Lehigh has traditionally been an engineering school, and although engineering is less emphasized than in the past, the seriousness that is required of students in such a rigorous discipline spills over into other academic areas," says one professor. And students can't afford to be lazy: requirements for honors graduates are quite stringent and impressive. According to a science professor, "Both chemistry and biology emphasize research for their students, requiring lab research for departmental honors."

Strong departments, according to faculty and students, include the sciences and engineering. Also recommended is urban studies. Noteworthy faculty in the chemistry department include Kamil Klier and John Larsen, both editors of professional journals, and Ned Heindel, recent past president of the American Chemical Society. Biology professor Michael Behe is the author of a highly acclaimed book, *Darwin's Black Box*, which critiques certain aspects of Darwinian theory.

Rather than fulfill a core curriculum, Lehigh undergraduates must satisfy a set of distribution requirements. Students in the College of Arts and Sciences must gain three credit hours in mathematical sciences and eight each in sciences (including at least one lab course), social sciences, and the humanities. The other two colleges have fewer requirements outside the chosen field of study. Business and Economics requires only twelve credit hours in nonbusiness topics (six in composition and literature and six in calculus), along with a "business and economics core" of up to forty-five hours. Students in Engineering and Applied Sciences have a basic requirement of two English courses and one introductory economics course, plus an additional twenty-four credit hours to be chosen from virtually any nonscience field.

As with most such distribution requirements, the traditional categorical breakdown in the College of Arts and Sciences does not ensure that students will get a thorough grounding in the liberal arts, since they may opt for an eclectic "cafeteria-style" range of courses. "Within those categories," notes one faculty, "the student is free to choose among a broad range of courses." In addition to the distribution requirements, each student must take one "College Seminar," a one-credit course entitled "Choices and Decisions," and two courses in English composition, all during the first year. Like many composition programs at liberal arts schools, the focus, according to one faculty member, has recently changed from a literature-based study of genres (fiction, drama, or poetry, for example) to a more ideologically charged writing course based on readings from various politically correct sources. In general, notes one faculty member, there are a fair number of "diversity"-based courses, and multiculturalism is "approved of at the highest level" of the administration. But another faculty member notes that even though "some faculty are interested in multicultural activities . . . in general, they do not foist them upon the rest of us."

There is no foreign language requirement, though students majoring in certain fields (such as history and English) are encouraged to study a second language. Lehigh describes its "College Seminar" course with impressive language, boasting that "this unique course allows students to study a subject of personal academic interest with an established faculty member who is an expert in the field. Seminars are usually limited to twenty students and encourage close interpersonal relationships with faculty and peers, heightened intellectual engagement, and freedom to explore and discuss ideas as they arise." In recent years many well-known universities have established such seminars in response to freshman complaints of large, impersonal courses in which a well-known professor presides from a distant lectern and most work is handled by graduate teaching assistants. But, as is also the case at other institutions, the courses at Lehigh can lack serious intellectual content. In fact, in the opinion of one Lehigh professor, the required college seminar means only that "students are forced to take an easy course." Recent seminars have included such heavyweight topics as "In Search of Big Foot," although, to be fair, more serious subjects such as "The Death of Western Civilization" have also been taught.

The university recently added one credit to each class, making a normal course worth four credits rather than just three. This rather puzzling move has annoyed some faculty, who note that, logically, the additional credit should have resulted in a course requiring more work. However, coursework has generally remained the same. In effect, says one professor, the decision was made to lighten the load of both faculty and students.

Faculty advising is said to be "reasonably well-constructed," although the problem, according to one professor, is not so much inadequate advising as the lack of adequate choices for students who want nonideological courses. Humanities departments, for example, get mixed reviews from faculty and students. Philosophy is said to be politicized, while the verdict is still out on disciplines like history. Of the seventeen English department faculty, eleven list specialties in critical theory or multicultural literature (such as women's literature or gay and lesbian studies). These interests manifest themselves in nontraditional course descriptions, like that for a less-than-generous survey of Restoration and early eighteenth-century literature in which literature is no more than a reflection of a homogenous and oppressive entity called "culture": "The course will pay special attention to the changing roles women occupy in the cultural imagination. . . . We will investigate the construction of the 'domestic' space to which, increasingly, eighteenth-century culture attempts to limit women and women's aspirations."

There is also a course offered through the English department entitled "Language, Gender, and Power," which illustrates the tendency of radical feminist discourse to turn inward upon itself: "Examination of issues that have been traditionally brought up in feminist discourse on language, such as grammatical gender choices in the lexicon, assignments of male/female characterization to emergent figures in texts, female writing styles, etc. We will also examine discourse about the redefinition of Women's Studies as Gender Studies and its effects regarding 'centrality of women' vs. 'male appropriation' in gender discourse."

History offerings are largely void of such politicized language; indeed, one course still employs the politically incorrect title "The Barbarian West." To a large degree, the courses offered reflect Lehigh's traditional emphasis on the mechanical sciences, with particularly strong listings in urban and technological history. Courses such as "The Machine in America," "History of Japanese Industrialization Since 1800," "Technology and World History," "Engineering in the Modern World," and "History of American Industrial Technology" abound, and aspiring architectural or urban historians will appreciate such specialized offerings as a full course in the "Evolution of Long-Span Bridge Building." An impressive number of courses are also available in classical Western civilization, such as "Roman Law" and the "Golden Age of Greek Democracy," and to its credit, Lehigh has a major in, and department of, classical studies.

Even though students are generally considered serious and intelligent, one faculty member says that, thankfully, they are not deeply engaged in the current radicalized intellectual climate of higher education. "The nicest thing about Lehigh," notes the teacher, "is that the students are largely anti-intellectual." However, one professor has noted a significant drop in the academic performance of students in the past several years. In a set of quizzes this professor has administered over the past decade, the top third of the curve has vanished. The professor attributes this to a variety of factors, including a lowering of the average capabilities of incoming college freshmen and a general collapse of social discipline among students. Having said this, the professor also notes that Lehigh is not unique in this regard, and that generally the standards are tougher there than at other schools. Graduates report having an easier time in graduate school than their fellows who came from other undergraduate programs.

Political Atmosphere: Liberal by Default

Lehigh students are largely characterized, both by themselves and by faculty, as politically neutral, or even moderately conservative. However, the average Lehigh student will likely be exposed to the university's increasingly political agenda. This is because, as one professor laments, by the time most students reach Lehigh and other, similar Eastern institutions, they have already been indoctrinated into multicultural ideology during their high school years. "To be a Northeastern, upper middle class person in this age of permissiveness is to be a liberal whether you know it or not," says the professor. Such permissiveness rears its head in programs like Lehigh's Sexual Health Peer Education Program, where a group of well-trained student volunteers "explain the uses of various kinds of contraception" to students "in a fun, relaxed atmosphere." In a bulletin sent to all incoming freshmen, one of the peer educators is shown wearing a T-shirt bearing the message "Everything you ever wanted to know about SEX but were afraid to ask." She is holding one of her educational props, a "Wheel of Fortune" with various slots for "AIDS," "GENITAL WARTS," "LUST," and "TRUE LOVE." How many students, we wonder, ask to buy a vowel?

Other agendas originate with the university administration. All dorm monitors, called "Gryphons," have to go through sensitivity training. There used to be a system of faculty oversight of dorm living, but unfortunately, the professor continues, "faculty have generally lost touch with undergraduate living arrangements," leaving the intellectual and social climate of dorm life largely at the mercy of the Gryphons.

Students cite the Progressive Student Alliance and the lesbian and gay club, LesBiGay Alliance, as the most influential political groups on campus. The college also has a twice-weekly newspaper, the *Brown and White,* as well as a publication called *Outposts,* which is dedicated to "gender issues." College Republicans at Lehigh are neither active nor particularly conservative. Other conservative and libertarian groups, such as Young Americans for Freedom and the Lehigh Objectivist Club, have surfaced at various times over the past several years but have not been able to sustain support and interest on campus. Although both sides of the political spectrum are represented in public lectures, the university sponsors its fair share of politically correct forums, including a recent celebration entitled "Women's Empowerment Week," which included lectures with titles that would have to struggle to be more clichéd: "Say No to Victimization/Say Yes to Empowerment" and "Strengthening Our Inner Selves — A Celebration!" By contrast, American Enterprise Institute fellow and author Dinesh D'Souza and *Weekly Standard* publisher Irving Kristol have spoken on campus in recent years, and David Blakenhorn, founder and president of the Institute for American Values, delivered a talk on "Fatherless America" as part of the Lehigh Chaplain's Forum.

One is permitted to dissent on Lehigh's campus, according to the school's catalogue and its explanation of the "Policy on Dissent." The policy supports free inquiry and expression, and threatens disciplinary action for those whose "coercive activities" are designed to repress "legitimate dissent," calling such actions a "threat to the openness of the academic community."

Some dissent has come from the alumni of the school. Since taking on the mission of transforming the university into a liberal arts institution, Lehigh's president, Peter Likins, has attempted to steer the school away from its traditional strengths in engineering and to focus energy and resources in the College of Arts and Sciences. So legitimate discussion is probably warranted on whether the school should have relied on its traditional, nonliberal arts foundation or attempted to become more things to more people. On several occasions Likins has locked horns with alumni, many of whom majored in engineering and the sciences and resent the increased emphasis on the arts. As if the future direction of the university weren't a big enough question, the president raised a smaller one as well when, a couple of years ago, he announced that the Lehigh Engineer would no longer be the school's athletic mascot. Alumni went ballistic, and the plan was temporarily shelved. But the president hired a New York public relations firm, and for a princely sum the re-christening of the mascot as the "Mountain Hawk" slid through.

Campus Life: Larger Town of Bethlehem

Founded by well-heeled Episcopalians, Lehigh is located in the old steel town of Bethlehem, Pennsylvania. The university encompasses more than 1,600 acres spread over three connected campuses, including a wooded mountaintop added when the university bought the land formerly inhabited by a Bethlehem Steel research center. This area, on the northern slope of South Mountain, serves as the main academic campus. Half of the campus is preserved as open space. The buildings and grounds are kept in perfect order; indeed, as one faculty member boasts, "We've been spending money like water when it comes to physical facilities." The Lehigh library system is one of the best money can buy. Two libraries, the historic Linderman Library and the newer Fairchild-Martindale Library and Computing Center, hold more than 1 million volumes and more than twenty-four thousand rare books, including an original edition of Audubon's *Birds of America* and three copies of the first edition of Darwin's *Origin of Species.*

On-campus housing is guaranteed for freshmen, sophomores, and first-semester transfer students. Lehigh has a thriving Greek system, with twenty-eight fraternities and seven sororities. The Greek community comprises roughly 45 percent of undergraduates, and official campus literature boasts that "the university has one of the strongest Greek systems in the nation." The administration seems largely supportive of Greek life on campus, and it does provide valuable accommodation, leadership, and social opportunities for undergraduates. But one faculty member notes that "the only major problem is the tradition of drinking associated with the fraternity system." The professor says the problem has been lessened somewhat by new state laws. In general, though, the Greek system makes a positive contribution to campus and community life at Lehigh: in 1996, for instance, one fraternity collected a whopping 3,772 pounds of food for the South Bethlehem Neighborhood Center.

Lehigh has a thriving intercollegiate sports system, with twenty-three NCAA Division I teams. The university is a founding member of the Patriot League, and competes against such schools as Army, Navy, Bucknell, and Colgate. Roughly 80 percent of undergraduates participate in some thirty intramural sports.

Unlike many universities that have distanced themselves from ROTC in recent years, Lehigh is proud of its decorated association with the Army Reserve Officers' Training Corps. Lehigh's ROTC program, established in 1919, is one of the oldest in the country, and the head of the nationwide Army ROTC program, Major General James "Mike" Lyle, is a Lehigh alumnus.

Lehigh's tuition is more than $22,000; with room, board, books, and miscellaneous costs, total expenses for the 1997-98 academic year hover close to $30,000. This high price tag, however, is offset by the generous $34 million the university provides annually in financial aid. In the 1995-96 academic year, the average financial aid package was $17,640. The university also has an interesting program called President's Scholarships. These twelve-month tuition scholarships are awarded to graduating Lehigh seniors with a grade point average of 3.5 or better, who then spend their initial postgraduate year completing either a second bachelor's degree or a master's degree at Lehigh. This is an attractive option for Lehigh graduates who are unsure about graduate school or want to pursue additional interests. As one student noted in *LEHIGHlife!*, "It's better than regular financial aid because it's not based on need, but on academic merit. It makes studying more worthwhile." Of course, as the university president notes, it has the added benefit of adding to Lehigh's graduate student enrollment.

LOUISIANA STATE UNIVERSITY

110 Thomas Boyd Hall
Baton Rouge, LA 70803-2802
(504) 388-1175
www.lsu.edu

Total enrollment: 26,850
Undergraduates: 21,420
ACT Ranges: 20-23.5
Financial aid: 32%
Applicants: 7,690
Accepted: 81%
Enrolled: 62%
Application deadline: Rolling admissions, Jun. 1
Financial aid application deadline: End of fall semester
Tuition: resident, $2,711; nonresident, $6,311
Core curriculum: No

Louisiana's Purchase

Louisiana State University (LSU) began its first courses less than a decade before the Civil War, and today is rather typical of large state universities — especially in its pursuit of research grants and a larger student body. LSU is among the top 2 percent of American colleges and universities in terms of research activities and grants, according to the Carnegie Foundation. Its operations are an important part of the Louisiana economy, bringing in more than $60 million of out-of-state money each year.

Several departments at LSU have very distinguished pasts: the late poet laureate Robert Penn Warren was once a member of the English department, and renowned philosopher Eric Voegelin taught political science. However, the university's educational efforts for undergraduates are compromised by a less-than-stringent set of admissions standards, the lack of a directed course of study for all students, and something of a party-school atmosphere that values big-time athletics perhaps too highly.

What LSU does have is several fine departments, good graduate research opportunities, and a very fine press and literary quarterly. And unlike many institutions, its curriculum is mostly traditional in content; the politicization found at other places has not yet arrived with any force. The administration is led by folks who are traditional in matters of education and not given to endorsing radical ideologies. Enrollment continues to grow, and recent faculty hires do not reflect the radicalism espoused by many new graduates of doctoral programs. The overall program at LSU hovers around average, but it does avoid some of the traps that have snared its fellow universities.

Academic Life: Floating Downstream

The general education requirements at LSU lead to little or no common reading among the student body. Like most universities, LSU has adopted a set of distribution requirements that students fulfill by choosing courses from various departments. These requirements are "spread and scattered," in the words of one professor, in the broad categories of English composition, analytical reasoning, arts, humanities, natural sciences, and social sciences. Three courses must be taken in the humanities and natural sciences, one in arts, and two in the remaining categories, according to the university catalogue. Students can escape some of the math and composition requirements with good standardized test scores.

The university does not require a Western civilization course, and the wide selection of courses that may be used to meet the general education requirements makes it easy for a student to substitute a variety of courses for the study of Western history, art, literature, or philosophy. At LSU, as at most large state universities, the quality of the courses depends largely on the quality of the professors who teach them. Fortunately, many introductory courses are taught by accomplished senior faculty. While it is certainly possible to skate through LSU "unscathed by learning," as one professor puts it, it is also possible to study with some truly excellent and dedicated teachers.

Many classes at LSU exist merely to remedy incoming students' deficiencies in math and writing. The Louisiana public education system has traditionally performed below national averages, and for many years any student with a high school diploma from this system was guaranteed admission to LSU. In the past several years the university has tightened its entrance requirements, employing a sliding scale that considers both the applicant's high school GPA and his SAT or ACT scores and requiring that the student has taken a fair number of academic courses prior to applying. Admissions are certainly more selective because of this, but many students still must take remedial classes upon arriving in Baton Rouge.

The best professors at LSU include Ellis Sandoz, James Stoner Jr., Cecil Eubanks, and Eugene Wittkopf in political science; John R. May in English and religious studies; and James Olney, Dave Smith, Robert McMahon, and Kevin Cope in English. The strongest departments at LSU are political science, history, English, economics, geography, anthropology, philosophy, and religion. The College of Engineering is also quite good.

Among the departments, the one with perhaps the proudest history is English, once home to Robert Penn Warren, Cleanth Brooks, and other prominent men of letters. Its faculty are responsible for publishing the *Southern Review,* one of the region's top literary quarterlies.

The department of political science also claims a rich history and is today one of the strongest departments on campus. It counts among its former members Eric Voegelin, Walter Berns, and Willmoore Kendall. "Political science is very good," says a professor in another department. "It's relatively small but nicely balanced between conservatives and liberals, both philosophers and quantitative [scholars], which means any battles aren't between merely liberals and conservatives."

Of the economics department a faculty member says: "Economics is quite good. There are no Marxists — it's a main line department. The majority of economists are identifiably pro–free market, but there are no members of the Austrian school." The history department also draws favorable comments from faculty. "It is not so much conservative as apolitical," a professor says. "They're good scholars and teachers."

Also contributing to the academic life of the school is the LSU Press, the preeminent scholarly house in the South and one of the best in the nation. It is particularly well known for its distinguished titles in Southern history and literature, as well as political philosophy. In the past several years it has not published as many works of traditional scholarship as it once did, but it seems far less susceptible to works of ideology than most other university presses.

LSU also houses the Eric Voegelin Institute for American Renaissance Studies. Voegelin taught at LSU from 1942 to 1958, and the current director of the institute, Ellis Sandoz, studied with Voegelin in Munich. "The mission of the Institute is to explore through research, conferences (seminars and short courses), and publications the American Renaissance now underway in the world, with emphasis upon Eric Voegelin's thought and political philosophy more generally, constitutionalism, individual liberty, and free market economics," according to college literature. The institute does not offer courses, but the university considers it a close ally of its political science department; both the director and assistant director hold joint appointments in that department. Each year the institute sponsors a variety of lectures in political theory, philosophy, history, English, and related disciplines.

The university also hosts the United States Civil War Center, which operates an extremely popular website with countless links to other centers of related interest and facilitates scholars and amateurs in their research on American history from the antebellum period through the Reconstruction. It also hosts conferences; recent topics include "The Legacy of Robert Penn Warren" and "Civil War Perspectives: An Interdisciplinary Conference."

The continued existence of such a center owes much to the fact that Louisiana is a traditional state — even by Southern standards — and its people are generally unwilling to support the revisionist and multiculturalist thinking tolerated at other universities, including some in the Deep South. Likewise, the student body is quite conservative and not receptive to the more demagogic forms of classroom politics. LSU's chancellor, William Jenkins, has also done a fine job of reserving classrooms for learning rather than ideology, and has done much to further the cause of education throughout the state.

Nevertheless, the ideologized nature of most of the better graduate and professional schools has made it difficult for LSU, like other schools, to avoid hiring and promoting a handful of radical faculty. Such faculty at LSU are most noticeable in the women's studies department, a highly politicized entity founded on the pretext of political advocacy. And though English is listed here as one of the strongest departments, its several excellent teachers are undercut by an increasing number of radical colleagues. Across the board, however, LSU remains far less politicized than the average university of today. "The PCers are fairly low-profile here," a professor says.

Except for a few noteworthy exceptions, LSU's curriculum has not been affected by multiculturalism the way those at so many other schools have. The most nontraditional courses can be found in English, the department that brought LSU so much acclaim in the past. The department offers a class on "Vampire Literature," in which students study, among other things, ghoulish "male and female vampires (heterosexual and homosexual), alien vampires, and succubi and incubi," according to the catalogue. A course billed as an introduction to women's literature is dedicated to the analysis of both "historically significant texts created by and about women" and " 'woman-centered texts' created by men — for example, excerpts from 'literary texts' such as . . . DeFoe's *Moll Flanders* as well as 'film texts' such as [Spike Lee's] *She's Gotta Have It*." Several politicized courses are also offered on ethnic literature, including "Blackwomen [sic (in original)] and the Body Politic." The title is said to indicate "a once doubled identity now unified"; the course description says students will look into "popular discourses (Hill-Thomas), literary discourse (novels), and cultural discourses (ritual female circumcision)."

Political Atmosphere: Old Boys

As shown by its curriculum, LSU has avoided the politicization that has beset many other colleges, though political correctness has made inroads even in the university's most prized departments. Compared with other large state universities, LSU remains a conservative to moderate place. There is no speech code, and the university makes little if any effort to subject incoming students to sensitivity training.

At a time when the newest faculty on a campus are often the most radical, one professor says that, on average, younger faculty at LSU are at least as conservative as the veteran faculty. "LSU has avoided undue politicization," says another professor. "I think it will stay that way under our new chancellor . . . and a conservative Republican governor, Mike Foster."

Conservative speakers invited to campus are well received but outnumbered by liberal invitees by seven or eight to one, according to a professor. "A trickle, shall we say, of conservatism gets through," the professor says.

Even though a majority of the faculty is liberal, students are almost never penalized for holding an opposing view. As a whole, the LSU campus is very tolerant of diverse opinions. The editors of LSU's student newspaper, the *Daily Reveille*, though rarely conservative themselves, publish the writings of conservative student columnists. Despite the lack of institutional funding, alternative papers spring up from time to time.

Though there is little radicalism on campus, a more homegrown type of politics has been detrimental to the university, according to a professor. Louisiana political graft is legendary, and some of that behavior has appeared in the university system. "The main problem here is in a different vein than at many schools," the professor says. "Ideology is not too strong, but the good-ole'-boy politics is very strong." Although LSU lies in the same federal circuit that rendered the decision against affirmative action policies at state institutions in Texas, the university has ignored the decision and still distributes some scholarships on the basis of race. "They ignore it because, they argue, they have a consent decree," the professor says.

One professor suggests that because the student body mostly disdains intellectualism, the university has been spared some of the excesses of modern ideologies. "Students tend to be pretty conservative but with little concept of what that means," the professor says. "They're anti-intellectual by and large. There's no culture of learning at LSU." Says another: "We're a good party school [but] there's not heavy drug use here. We have good athletics." Another professor agrees that the biggest problem facing LSU is "the party school image" under which academically serious members of the university community must labor. "LSU is very much a football, fraternity, and boozing school," the professor says.

Student Life: It's the Heat *and* the Humidity

The oldest buildings on the LSU campus are Italianate structures near the banks of the Mississippi River, surrounded by live oaks and magnolias. The entire land-grant campus covers 2,000 acres, though the principal buildings occupy about 650 acres; however, not all of this area is built up in classic style. For example, the eighteen dorms at LSU have "architectural styles ranging from a Renaissance style typical of the older core of the campus to modern high-rise buildings," according to university literature. The varied dorms offer varied comforts: despite Baton Rouge's heat and humidity, the residents of Annie Boyd, Evangeline, Highland, Jackson, Lejeune, and Taylor halls must go without air-conditioning. The university also maintains on-campus apartments inhabited by several hundred students.

In all, only about one-fifth of the student body of twenty-three thousand undergraduates and five thousand graduate students lives on campus. About 15 percent of both men and women join Greek organizations, which also provide a reliable source for campus social life.

Southern traditions, fading throughout the region, are alive at LSU, and old-fashioned manners still count for something there. Baton Rouge is the state capital and contains a fair number of eateries, shopping areas, and other diversions. New Orleans is about an hour away, and the beaches of the Gulf Coast are only a little east of the Crescent City. Winters are brief and easy to take by Northern standards; summers are long and languid.

As is the case with most large state universities, LSU offers a student group for just about every interest and taste. Many social service, religious, political, and honorary groups exist at LSU. Among them: Baptist Student Union, Chi Alpha Christian Fellowship, Chinese Student Association, College Democrats and College Republicans, Pre-Law Society, Fencing Club, and the Engineering Student Council.

Athletics are the biggest social draw at LSU, and football is the king of sports. Over the past ten years the football team has drawn an average of over seventy thousand fans for home games. Basketball is also followed very closely, as is baseball. The women's track team is a perennial power that has won ten consecutive national outdoor championships.

UNIVERSITY OF MASSACHUSETTS AT AMHERST

Admissions Center
Amherst, MA 01003
(413) 545-0222
www.umass.edu

Total enrollment: 34,000
Undergraduates: 18,340
SAT Ranges (Verbal/Math): V 510-610, M 510-620
Financial aid: 58%
Applicants: 18,006
Accepted: 73%
Enrolled: 28%
Application deadline: Feb. 1
Financial aid application deadline: Mar. 1
Tuition: in-state, $2,004; out-of-state, $8,952
Core curriculum: No

No Mas

Without its deeply politicized curriculum and accommodationist administration, the University of Massachusetts at Amherst would be indistinguishable from most large state universities. As it is, few places have invested so much in ideological faculty and courses, and even fewer have acceded so quickly to the sometimes violent protests of radical students.

Many faculty at UMass report that life at the 24,000-student university is growing increasingly politicized. The 18,000 undergraduates follow no core curriculum, but make do with a standard set of distribution requirements that demands two multicultural courses but none in Western culture. Except for those in the sciences, most programs are politicized, some very much so.

Students planning to attend UMass will have to search diligently for professors and courses that will provide them with a genuine liberal arts education. In an institution of this size, that goal may still be achieved, but one wonders whether future historians of higher education in America won't single out UMass as a striking demonstration of late twentieth-century ideological excess.

Academic Life: UMiss

Like many big state universities, the University of Massachusetts requires that students fulfill a set of distribution requirements rather than a traditional core curriculum.

Among the general education requirements are six courses chosen from the areas of literature, historical studies, arts/liberal arts, social sciences, and behavioral sciences. Students must also take courses in the sciences, mathematics, and analytical reasoning. All freshmen must take "College Writing," offered in seminars of two dozen students, as well as another writing course. In all of these areas UMass is on a par with most other institutions of its type.

There is no Western civilization requirement at UMass, although students must take two courses in multicultural studies. The two-course "diversity" requirement can be satisfied with courses from a variety of departments, including everything from the obviously politicized "Inequality and Oppression" to subjects that seem to have only a tangential relationship to diversity, such as "Culture through Film." "Despite the ideological courses, it is still possible, at present, for an informed student to fulfill this requirement with serious courses," a professor says. "Of course, as elsewhere, there are those who would like to 'tighten up' this requirement to prevent students from escaping the 'oppression studies' type of course. But, to date, I do not believe this has come to pass." For example, there are solid courses in Chinese history that count toward the requirement.

Students looking for bona fide courses might seek out these professors: Herbert Gintis, Robert Costrell, and Dale Ballou in economics; Daphne Patai in Spanish and Portuguese; John Palmer in biology; Jeffrey Sedgewick and Jessica Korn in political science; Paul Hollander in sociology; Paul Mariani and Vincent DiMarco in English; and R. Dean Ware and William Johnston in history.

The best departments at UMass are in the sciences, particularly polymer science and engineering. Political science is also strong.

Beyond these departments, there are many ideologically driven professors, and the university operates under a system that is imperfect at best. A good education at UMass sometimes hinges on the luck of the draw. "The student feels very confused," says another professor. "It all depends on whom he takes. We have some good teachers, and some very bad ones."

Among the most politicized departments are anthropology, English, women's studies, and Afro-American studies. "Identity studies are all politically correct," says a professor, but adds that Judaic studies is still "very good." Another professor mentions a women's studies professor who said, "in print, that racism and genocide are the core of American society." But the real test of politicization, says a professor, is "whether or not a program seeks to produce converts. If it does, it's a bad program."

The most politicized curriculum on campus belongs to the Social Thought and Political Economy Program (STPEC), organized in 1973. The university describes it as "an interdisciplinary undergraduate program in social and behavioral sciences." A professor, however, calls it "a Marxist bailiwick." No comparable program on campus promotes a traditional view of the same subjects.

STPEC is not an academic department; rather, it draws faculty on a part-time basis from humanities and social sciences departments. "The program also encourages its students to involve themselves in practice as well as theory by enrolling in internships" and by "playing a role in university and community affairs," according to university literature. "The exploration of the intersection of theory and practice is at the heart of STPEC's curriculum." In STPEC, those two items invariably intersect on the left side of the political spectrum. In fact, the title of the program's annual alumni newsletter is *Left Justified*.

Afro-American studies majors can pick up a second major in STPEC with no extra work. "There are many courses which can be used to simultaneously fulfill both Afro-American Studies and STPEC requirements," the catalogue states. "Any course which will fulfill a requirement in each major may be counted towards both. There is no limit to the number of classes that can be double counted. You will find it easier to double count courses if your concentration in Afro-American Studies is either social science of [sic] history."

One source familiar with STPEC's record says the program "engages in a range of activities inappropriate to an academic program." According to this source, STPEC "does not restrict itself to teaching politics, but openly endorses a particular political viewpoint. It encourages its students to take part in political activity in support of the program's left-of-center stance. Most damaging to the university, STPEC invites both its faculty and its students to take an active role in inciting campus protests and building occupations." All this comes at state expense; even if only private funds were used, however, the intellectual value and philosophical consistency of the program would still be minimal, according to some on campus.

Political Atmosphere: UMess

The administration at UMass is perhaps the most politicized of any state school in the country. Its positions are supported by a remarkable number of radical professors and a vocal minority of politically correct students. What sets apart the UMass administration from others is its willingness — some even say eagerness — to cooperate with the most radical factions on campus.

This is best illustrated by the administration's response to a recent series of acts by radical students — building takeovers, the physical intimidation of students, the theft of student newspapers, and even the physical beating of some students. In every incident the administration either sided openly with the radical students, caved in to their demands, or turned a blind eye to the actions of these privileged few.

Two incidents stand out as particularly egregious. In the wake of the reaction to the 1992 acquittal of the policemen charged with the beating of Rodney King, student radicals, supported by allies in the administration, launched attacks on two campus buildings. First, the students took over the offices of the *Daily Collegian*, the student newspaper, apparently because of the paper's alleged mishandling of minority issues. The students broke a stereo and a plate glass window, then ripped up files, photographs, and documents belonging to the paper.

Next, the mob moved to Whitmore Hall, home of the administration, where they took over the building. Students demanded that ten minority faculty members be hired prior to the following semester; the estimated cost to the university was $350,000. Then-Chancellor Richard O'Brien several times expressed his sympathy and understanding at the students' outrage, and even praised them for their "courage and selflessness" in taking over Whitmore. O'Brien's only counteroffer, as it were, was a request that UMass be given three years rather than just a few months to meet the hiring demand.

The highly politicized STPEC was directly involved in these affairs. Writing in *Left Justified,* STPEC director Sara Lennox stated: "This spring many STPEC students and staff were active in events on campus after the Los Angeles rebellion, including the occupation of Whitmore that resulted in an administration promise to hire ten more minority faculty over the next three years."

According to a source who has studied this affair closely, "Professor Lennox's praise of STPEC activists confirms the impression given by STPEC literature, that both faculty and student members of the program are at least as much involved in affecting the governance of the campus — turning the university in a leftward direction — as they are in scholarship." As one source says, "The university derives no benefit from such protests. While the majority of professors carry on praiseworthy research and teaching, and most students are engaged in learning, a minority of activists is increasingly responsible for determining a radical atmosphere on campus and, by extension, for creating an unfavorable public perception of the university."

Another takeover, this one in 1994, traumatized the staff of the UMass Undergraduate Admissions Center. Fifty to seventy-five students raided the building and occupied it until 3 A.M. the following day in order to protest a coming rise in tuition. The students only surrendered the building when the new chancellor, David K. Scott, assured them that tuition would not increase.

Following this, Arlene Cash, director of admissions, wrote a letter to the *Daily Collegian* describing the terror felt by those workers subjected to the violent actions of the students. The letter was also signed by thirty Admissions Center employees. "Taking a building is, by definition, an act of violence on staff members," Cash wrote. "When we learned that students were planning to take over the Undergraduate Admissions Center, we didn't imagine how threatening the experience would be. . . . Most of us with locks on our doors were quick enough to lock ourselves into our offices, where we waited to see what would happen next. Those of us who were unable to lock ourselves into protected space faced students who forced us out of our chairs, who went through our drawers and our mail, who handled pictures of our children and other personal possessions, who took photographs of us without our permission. Students took over the phones and restricted our calls." Students, shortly after their arrival, began chanting anti-tuition-hike slogans and stomping their feet. Their protests literally rattled the building, and Cash wrote that the shaking was "so violent that pictures fell from walls and an overhead light fixture crashed from the ceiling."

The violence was clearly directed at the university employees as well as incorporeal tuition costs. "Students tried to roust us from the safety of our offices. The door banging started, the repetitive pounding of anger misplaced against us," Cash wrote. "When that drew no result, huge slamming blows and kicks, screams telling us to 'go home.' Students came to take over a building, but some of them would not rest until they had taken over the people inside as well."

In March 1997, two hundred students occupied the Goodell Administration Building. This was the last straw for Massachusetts state representative Dennis Murphy and seventy of his colleagues, who wrote in outrage to Chancellor Scott and convened a hearing on the matter. In that hearing Scott said that he "would do things differently now." Unsatisfied with Scott's response, Murphy and his colleagues took the matter directly to UMass president William Bulger. Shortly thereafter, the university agreed for the first time to uphold a tough policy against appeasing demonstrators.

Recently, the UMass administration began requiring — with the consent of the faculty union — that faculty members record on their year-end self-evaluation forms how they "made significant contributions to multiculturalism" in their classrooms. These forms have become an important element in tenure and pay-raise decisions, according to a faculty member. "The criteria have always been teaching, service, research, and then fill-in-the-blank," the professor says. "It is absurd that someone in Shakespearean studies should be at a professional disadvantage." The faculty union allowed the form even after its own survey found that 77 percent of the faculty didn't want it — "everyone who was against it was branded a racist," a professor says. Even a resolution by the Faculty Senate opposing the form went unheeded. "The faculty union is extraordinarily politically correct and is in no way representative of the faculty as a whole," says another professor. "This question represents a disregard for principle."

The hiring and tenure process at UMass obviously favors ideologized teachers. "I'm an anomaly here," says one humanities professor nationally noted for more traditional forms of scholarship. "Most people who have read my work would be surprised to know I'm from UMass." This professor says he is marginalized by his younger colleagues, and that "the retired people, those professors I respected, are gone and glad they got out." Another professor says it is getting more difficult to find good professors on the campus. "In the next seven to eight years the best professors will have retired," this professor says. "And retiring professors aren't being replaced within their fields." A professor estimates that 90 percent of faculty get tenure, and that the main reason someone might not has to do with personality conflicts rather than scholarship.

To find and hire minority and female faculty, UMass uses a Special Opportunity Fund (SOF), established in 1985, "to increase diversity and redress imbalances of ethnic origin, race and gender in the faculty ranks," according to a memo written by Provost Patricia Crosson. To date, 88 percent of the money spent from the fund has been used to hire minorities, with the remaining 12 percent going to hire white, female faculty.

Of course, the legality of such a fund is suspect; with this in mind, the university has drawn up "Guidelines for the Special Opportunity Fund." This document notes that if in advertising a position the university were to state specifically that the SOF money would be used for the position, it would most likely have committed an illegal act. Instead, the guidelines advise deception. "Care should be taken not to write letters or make statements which are tantamount to [this] kind of advertising," the guidelines state. "It would, for instance, be quite inappropriate to write to an individual and say 'We are considering you as a candidate for a position which is available only to women and minorities.'" All written communication regarding positions funded by the SOF must be authorized by a high-ranking university administrator "in order to avoid misunderstandings," the guidelines say. "Ways will have to be found to explore delicately the interest of an individual in moving, then to explore the appointment internally in the way indicated below, and then to make an offer directly to the individual in appropriate cases," the document states. "One might then say 'The department of X has a strong interest in the possibility of your joining the department. We believe that your record of scholarly achievement would be a valuable addition to us.'"

The administration tried to introduce a speech code in 1995, but it was criticized on campus and in a *New York Times* column by Anthony Lewis. "The administration vigorously defended the proposed code, but in the face of such opposition never pushed ahead with it," a professor says.

Student Life: Wants Met

UMass students enjoy life in a pretty college town located in the scenic Pioneer Valley of western Massachusetts. They also reside in the largest dormitory system in the nation: forty-two dorms that house eleven thousand students. All students must live on campus for their first two years of school.

The UMass residence system reflects the politicization of the school it serves. The system offers Special Interest Residential Programs (SIRPs), which "enable [students] to live with smaller groups of students who share [their] interests and concerns," according to the university. Among the choices are arts communities, language houses, and "ethnic and cultural affinity housing," including special rooms for blacks, Asians, and Native Americans. Also listed is the "2 in 20" program, which "provides a supportive community living experience for gay, lesbian, bisexual, and transgender students and their heterosexual allies." According to UMass literature, "Residents are committed to working together to end homophobia and heterosexism." The name "2 in 20" is taken from the dubious assertion that 10 percent of the general population is homosexual. According to a recent article in the *Chronicle of Higher Education,* one student calls the "2 in 20" floor a "gay fantasy world." According to the *Chronicle,* "On a walk down the hall, [one] would know that the doors featuring sultry photographs of Sharon Stone and Madonna had been decorated by women, and that the door with pictures of shirtless male models belongs to a man." In 1997 about twenty-five students lived on the floor.

The university offers all of the usual attractions one would expect at a large state school, including numerous club and intramural sports, excellent athletic facilities, and many student organizations. Among the latter are musical organizations, fraternities and sororities, honor societies, performing arts groups, political organizations, and religious groups.

UMass competes in the Division I Atlantic Ten Conference in all major sports. Its basketball team recently became nationally known under former coach John Calipari, but the university had to forfeit its Final Four finish in one NCAA national tournament because of off-court actions that violated association rules.

MASSACHUSETTS INSTITUTE OF TECHNOLOGY

Office of Admissions
Room 3-108
77 Massachusetts Avenue
Cambridge, MA 02139-4307
(617) 253-4791
web.mit.edu

Total enrollment: 9,950
Undergraduates: 4,430
SAT Ranges (Verbal/Math): V 680-770, M 680-750
Financial aid: 59%
Applicants: 7,836
Accepted: 24%
Enrolled: 55%
Application deadline: Jan. 1
Financial aid application deadline: Jan. 17
Tuition: $24,050
Core curriculum: Yes

Gravity's Rainbow

In a garden at the Massachusetts Institute of Technology (MIT) grows a tree said to be a distant relative of the one that dropped the apple that provided Sir Isaac Newton with the correlative for gravity. Regardless of the truth of that tree's lineage or Newton's mode of innovative thought, MIT itself is directly descended from the great scientists and thinkers of the past; the things discovered there today will change our future.

MIT is the nation's premier institution for the study of engineering, science, and computer science, and its faculty includes ten Nobel laureates and eight recipients of the so-called MacArthur "genius" grants. The institute's renown does not extend to the humanities and social science programs in which only 6 percent of the five thousand undergraduates enroll. However, the institute has of late made serious efforts to bring its humanities departments closer to the standard set by its scientists, and has had some success.

Still, not many students choose MIT for a liberal arts education. The emphasis there is definitely on scientific research, and faculty double as the leading inventors and innovators in their fields. Students, likewise, are driven and highly intelligent —

MIT application materials talk about holding on to SAT scores "until you've seen those 800s." Graduates, in addition to procuring a fine education, are instantly credible and respected upon mention of their alma mater, which is one of the finest compliments a school can receive.

Academic Life: Earth, Wind, and Fire

MIT is divided into five schools: Engineering, Science, Humanities and Social Sciences, Architecture and Planning, and Management. Nearly two-thirds of undergraduates major in engineering, and one-quarter enroll in the sciences, leaving only 450 or so students to be divided between the other three schools.

All students, however, are subject to MIT's harrowing basic curriculum, the General Institute Requirements. In their first semester students are advised to take Calculus I, Physics I, Chemistry, and one course in the humanities/arts/social sciences (HASS). Most students also participate in an optional freshman seminar. The course list for the spring term includes Calculus II, Physics II, Biology, another HASS course, and an optional undergraduate seminar. About half of the students receive advanced placement for one or more of the science requirements, and can thus move on to a course in their prospective major or an elective.

MIT no longer has a foreign language requirement, but students do need to accumulate eight "physical fitness points": two points are allotted for a quarter-length class, four points for playing on an intercollegiate team. However, all students must prove their ability to swim — despite the fact that after they graduate from MIT they will likely be able to make an emergency boat out of baling twine and water.

All told, the General Institute Requirements amount to six science courses, eight HASS courses, two electives in science and technology, and a laboratory requirement. About 15 percent of students are involved in special programs with modified core course lists. These programs, entitled "Concourse," "Experimental Study Group," and "Integrated Study Program," stress "individual initiative and close student-faculty relationships." Professors interviewed for this guide recommended the "Concourse" program, a yearlong, highly structured group of courses that, according to the huge institute catalogue, explores "both the unity and the conflict of technical, scientific, and humanistic viewpoints and ideas." According to the catalogue, "The objective, possible only because of the unique combination of assets offered by MIT, is not only to achieve competence in the separate disciplines but also to examine the mutual relevance of freshman-year calculus, physics, chemistry, biology, and humanities."

Because of their heavy interest in science, some students undervalue the humanities and social sciences forced upon them by the MIT curriculum. Writing in the journal *Counterpoint*, MIT student Min-Hank Ho notes that "by lumping humanities with the other requirements, it becomes just another chore that needs to be completed before graduation." He reports that many MIT students take their HASS courses on a pass-fail basis just "to get them out of the way." Unlike in the rigid science requirements, students are allowed to choose which HASS courses they will take — although some complain that their choices are essentially taken away because of scheduling conflicts. Others select the most science-oriented courses, such as "Microeconomics" or similarly analytical courses, in order to fulfill the requirement. While some on campus suggest that the HASS course list should be adapted to fit students' taste, a better suggestion might be to institute a humanities core that is as well thought out as the science core seems to be.

The humanities courses at MIT remain generally free of politicization, and science courses are all but immune to such intrusions. (Obviously, it's difficult to teach "Feminist Physics" or "The Calculus of Oppression.") To fulfill the HASS requirement, students will find many courses on Western civilization, but a few non-traditional selections as well. There is a class called "Gender and Science" and another called "Riots, Strikes, and Conspiracies in American History." But, as one student says, "No one department at MIT is particularly politicized. A handful of courses deal with social issues such as homosexuality and gender relations, and multicultural classes do exist, but none are required or particularly biased." As a general rule, the curriculum is "certainly unpoliticized," according to one professor, who notes that linguist Noam Chomsky is a "colorful exception." Chomsky, probably the best-known humanities professor at MIT, has written numerous books on linguistics, mass media, and foreign policy, and is somewhat notorious for spinning a number of controversial conspiracy theories.

MIT students can enroll in courses at nearby Harvard University and Wellesley College, but for the most part they find all they need at MIT, where the list of Nobel laureates is longer than the list of good faculty at other schools. Strong departments at MIT are what one would expect from a blue-ribbon technological institute: mechanical engineering, electrical engineering, computer science, and physics. Surprisingly, about one-quarter of undergraduates come to MIT to major in premed.

The Sloan School of Management also has an outstanding reputation. Though most of its programs are directed toward graduate study and research, the school does offer a B.S. degree in management science, which is heavy on the use of mathematical, statistical, and computer technology in its approach to the topic.

While MIT has a world-class reputation for scientific research, the school has brought its reputation to bear on efforts to strengthen its humanities and social sciences programs as well. More undergraduates — though still not a lot — are coming to MIT for liberal arts disciplines; programs in economics, political science, philosophy, linguistics, and biology are also considered excellent. The research emphasis of the rest of the school seems to have manifested itself in the humanities departments as avant-garde creativity. Among the distinguished faculty members in the arts, humanities, and social sciences are several with interests in such areas as media arts, creative writing, architecture, and linguistics. Professor Tod Machover, for instance, is the creator of computerized hyperinstruments; Nicholas Negroponte is founder of *Wired* magazine; and MacArthur fellow Evelyn Fox Keller is the author of *Reflections on Gender and Science.*

Faculty are generally very pleased with their jobs at MIT, where they get to pursue their own research, work with some of the best in their field, and teach bright, motivated students. Although tenure decisions are based almost exclusively on research, most faculty take their teaching seriously. According to one professor, "Senior faculty often teach introductory courses."

Political Atmosphere: Better Things to Do

The stereotype of MIT students is that of extremely serious, hardworking "computer geeks" who study excessively and rarely take time off to enjoy their college years. While this characterization certainly did not come about out of thin air ("the dorm lights burn late here," notes one professor), in truth, students' academic motivation is fueled as much by the rigorous nature of the school's curriculum as it is by personal disposition. Indeed, many in the MIT community have questioned the wisdom of the institute's frequently excessive workload. According to one professor, some faculty have made efforts to "relax" the academic program, but "students resist" because they want the challenge and want their degrees to be valuable.

However, there were enough complaints from students, deans, housemasters, and athletic coaches about the workload that in the spring semester of 1997, the chair of the faculty issued a statement calling on faculty to be more realistic and fair in making assignments and formulating exams.

According to that statement, it is not unheard of for professors "to schedule classes on Saturday mornings," hold "evening quizzes or exams without either canceling a class or a problem set during the same week," or extend assignments into reading week, exam week, or January term. Frequently, it is the professor's travel or research schedule that forces changes to the class calendar. The institute's Faculty Policy Committee has drafted guidelines that specify reasonable requirements, grades, and other aspects of the academic calendar, and the institute is trying to enforce these rules. Even if the rules were applied to the letter, an MIT education would still be extremely challenging and demanding.

The academic work leaves little time for much politicking, and students and faculty alike report that MIT is not a strongly politicized campus. One professor notes that "the kind of students attracted to MIT are usually not politically inclined." According to one student, "An atmosphere of political apathy among most MIT students prevails."

However, MIT has not been immune from debates about affirmative action and quotas. There has been pressure on MIT to increase minority enrollment (even though one-third of the student body is Asian-American) and to diversify the faculty.

In one very public gesture, a mechanical engineering professor fasted and camped outside the president's office every Wednesday to protest the underrepresentation of "faculty of color." He was joined at one point by one hundred students, and, according to *The Multicultural Student's Guide to Colleges,* "the president of MIT has instructed heads of departments to look for more minority faculty members, and his office will provide financial help for the search."

The institute usually makes a public reaffirmation of its dedication to equal opportunity and affirmative action at some point during Black History Month, a student says. Most recently, MIT president Charles M. Vest did so in a public address on the legacy of Martin Luther King Jr. "Whatever its imperfection," said the president, "affirmative action has improved access and opportunity for women and minorities in America." He cited numerous statistics illustrating MIT's progress toward a more diverse faculty, but said, "Clearly, we have far more work to do."

Although he argued that diversity would continue to make MIT a better institution, Vest also seemed prepared to sacrifice quality in academics for the sake of political correctness. "In the end, we must pursue these policies in spite of their cost and regardless of their benefits," Vest said. "We must pursue them because they are right and just."

The president, who generally has good rapport with faculty, has disturbed some professors with the mandated diversity plan and the possible negative impact it may have on standards at MIT. On the whole, though, the faculty at MIT are too busy to "get involved in administrative squabbles," according to one professor.

There has been a movement on campus to ban the institute's ROTC program on the grounds that military policy on homosexuality violates the school's nondiscrimination statement. This has not caused concern on campus, either by those opposed to or in favor of such a move. "ROTC has been a topic of discussion in the campus media for quite a while," notes a student, but so far no formal actions have been taken to remove the campus chapter.

The daily paper at MIT is the *Tech,* but there is also something called the "Alternative News Collective" that publishes a progressive biweekly newspaper, the *Thistle.* The *Tech* also "tends to be PC," according to one professor, "but no one really reads it." Another campus paper, *Counterpoint,* is published jointly ten times a year by MIT and Wellesley and calls itself a "Journal of Rational Discourse and Campus Life." Recent issues have included stories on MIT's dining situation and the inadequacies of campus child care at Wellesley. Although the journal has a reputation for being conservative, recent issues show little signs of a distinctively conservative viewpoint.

Campus lectures at MIT usually have a distinctively scientific tenor to them. Several recent discussions addressed intersections of science, technology, and culture: "The Impact of Computers on Children's Lives," "Do We Need NASA?" "A Discussion of the Ethical and Scientific Implications of Cloning," "On the Question of Stupidity," and "Technologies of Freedom? Emerging Media in Modern Culture." A panel discussion, cosponsored by the Program in Science, Technology and Society and the Program in Women's Studies, addressed recent challenges to feminism and included such speakers as feminist Katha Pollitt, columnist for the *Nation.* Other speakers of note have included Coretta Scott King, Lani Guinier, and Salman Rushdie. A lecture by Charles Murray, noted libertarian and author of the controversial book *The Bell Curve,* was protested by a small group.

The majority of lectures, however, appear to cater to a much more specialized audience: "Hot Electrons in Quantum Cascade Lasers," "Interactions between Manganese and Freshwater Algae," "Centrifuge Modeling of Immiscible Flow Processes," and "Estimating Attractor Dimension for a Simple Permixed Flame Propagation Model."

It's not hard to see how the stereotypes about MIT students got started.

Campus Life: No Tea Party

MIT is located on a 150-acre campus in Cambridge, across the Charles River from Boston. The area might have one of the highest concentrations of students in the nation: Harvard, Wellesley, Radcliffe College, Boston University, Boston College, and Brandeis University are all nearby. All these schools are within easy reach of the Boston Museum of Fine Arts, Gardner Museum, the New England Conservatory of Music, the Boston Symphony Orchestra, the Boston Pops, and the Boston Ballet Company.

Because of its prime New England location, the MIT campus is also an excellent port of embarkation for scenic and historic day and weekend trips to places like Cape Cod or the villages of Lexington and Concord.

However, getting around by car in the Boston area is nothing but a hassle; "automotive anarchy" prevails, says one student. MIT students largely rely on their feet or their bicycles for local travel. But lock your bikes: they are stolen from bike racks with some regularity. Increasing petty crime also extends to labs and residences, from which computers and memory chips are sometimes lifted.

Roughly two-thirds of MIT students choose to live in campus dormitories, where they can choose from numerous single-sex or mixed-sex residences. The remaining students live in the twenty-five fraternities or six sororities, or off campus. Housing is guaranteed for all four years (a real plus given the Boston market) and mixes all classes (freshman through senior). The school's push for diversity has resulted in the presence of a "Women's Independent Living Group" and a black campus residence called by its inhabitants (in what might, from another source, be considered racist terms) "Chocolate City."

Men still outnumber women at MIT (about 60 percent to 40 percent of the student body), but the institution intends to make incoming classes "equitable in gender," according to a student. One professor says female students are not only as bright and motivated as their male peers, but also have "the same nerdish demeanor" — not considered a bad thing at MIT.

Though MIT students are preoccupied with their academic performance, this does not preclude their involvement in extracurricular activities. In fact, many students find time for music, theater, athletics, and various other extracurriculars.

"MIT is a busy place," notes one faculty. "Students like to get involved in a lot of activities." The institute has more than two hundred student organizations on campus, including many research-specific societies, some divided along ethnic and gender lines (American Indian Science and Engineering Society, Society of Women Engineers, etc.). More than sixty intramural and club sports programs are offered, as are more than a dozen musical and theater groups, including the Guild of Bellringers and the Gilbert and Sullivan Players. One professor says student musical performances are "extremely professional" and observes that there is a "serious avocational interest" on the part of students when it comes to fine arts pursuits. Political groups range from the subdued College Republicans to the more active Radicals for Capitalism/Objectivist Lyceum. According to one undergraduate, the College Republicans Club hasn't even asked for university funding in recent years due to its inactivity.

There are numerous student religious groups, representing everything from Campus Crusade for Christ to the Pagan Student Group. One recent addition is MITAAH (MIT Atheists, Agnostics, and Humanists), which proclaims itself "the only Freethought group at a leading scientific institution." A founding member, writing in *Counterpoint,* bemoaned what she considered to be the fact that "Christianity underlies the accepted world view of the majority of MIT students," and sought an alternative to "world views based on blind faith and superstition to the exclusion of skepticism, reasoning, and analytical skills."

MIAMI UNIVERSITY

Office of Admission
Campus Avenue Building
Oxford, OH 45056
(513) 529-2531
www.muohio.edu

Total enrollment: 16,000
Undergraduates: 14,100

SAT Ranges (Verbal/Math): V 510-620, M 510-630
Financial aid: 48%
Applicants: 10,560
Accepted: 58%
Enrolled: 28%
Application deadline: Mar. 1
Financial aid application deadline: Feb. 15
Tuition: $5,406 in-state; $6,100 out-of-state
Core curriculum: No

There First

Miami University is in Ohio, not Florida. Students like to point out that their school was founded before Florida was even a state. Miami University was actually begun by a bill signed by President James Madison in 1809, but classes didn't begin until 1824 as the result of delays due to the War of 1812. By the time classes began, the United States had in fact purchased Florida from the Spanish, but there was no University of Miami there.

Miami offered a classical education to its early students, like President Benjamin Harrison. Times have changed though, and while good courses and programs are still offered (especially in history and politics), the curriculum in general is very politicized. Although many options are available to meet the requirements of Miami's highly complex set of general education mandates, students must also take a few multicultural courses.

If a student is careful and sticks with the better programs, the education offered at Miami can be quite good. The school is even more attractive for Ohio residents, who get an excellent deal on tuition.

Academic Life: Plan B

Of the seven colleges and schools within Miami University, two of them — the College of Arts and Sciences and the School of Interdisciplinary Studies (known as the Western College Program) — offer programs for students interested in a liberal arts education. However, all students at the university are subject to the school's distribution requirements, known as the Miami Plan for Liberal Education.

The Miami Plan consists of two sets of requirements: "Foundation" and "Focus." The Foundation requirements involve twelve courses in the standard distribution areas — English composition (two courses); fine arts and humanities (three courses); social science and world cultures (three courses); natural science (three courses, including one lab); and mathematics, formal reasoning, and technology (one course).

Among the twelve courses must be two specially designated classes, one to satisfy a requirement called "historical perspective" and another to meet the multicultural "non-dominant perspective" requirement — a course that, according to the catalogue, "presents a perspective different from the dominant cultural heritage of the United States." The nondominant perspective courses are largely politicized, which is hardly surprising. The surprise is that about two-thirds of these courses also appear on the list of historical perspective designees; these cross-listed courses make up about 40 percent of that list. Some of the courses listed twice include "Introduction to Black World Studies," "Africa in History," "African Americans in Sports," "Social Systems," "The Diverse Worlds of Music," and "Creativity and Culture."

The Focus portion of the Miami Plan involves a three-course sequence in a particular topic outside the student's major. The groups of courses, from which there are more than one hundred to choose, often contain more than three courses. This allows the student a little freedom, but also extinguishes whatever claim Miami may have had to a core-style curriculum. The Focus requirement concludes with a "capstone experience," one senior-year course that can be chosen — again from a very long list — either from within or outside the student's major.

Of the long list of Focus sequences, not many would appeal to a student searching for the genuine liberal learning upon which Miami was founded. The classics department offers a literature sequence that is very good, and there are a few courses in ethics, politics, science, and naval science (yes, this is the Miami in Ohio) that do not appear to be politicized.

Most of the sequences, however, suffer from the same ideologies that afflict the distribution requirements. Some titles give away the biases: "Cultural Studies and Public Life," "People and Power in the Americas," "Popular Culture," and "Earth, Ecology, and Human Culture." There is even a sequence in "European Cinema," a topic that may be worth a single course but hardly warrants three (outside of a film school).

The capstone experience is supposed to act as "a sharing of ideas, synthesis, and critical informed reflection as significant precursors to action, and each includes student initiative in defining and investigating problems or projects," according to the catalogue.

"Half of the capstone class is flashy — it sounds good — but there is definitely some substance to it," a student says. "Capstone courses require students to focus on a specific subject, rather than take a broad view or interdisciplinary approach. . . . The classes are smaller and more comprehensive." The courses usually involve a lot of out-of-class research and, frequently, a twenty-five-page paper.

In addition to the large number of courses required in the Miami Plan, students in the College of Arts and Sciences face additional general education courses called "The College Requirement." For students seeking a B.A., this includes courses in humanities (three courses), social sciences and world cultures (three courses), natural sciences (three courses plus a lab), formal reasoning (one course), and a foreign language (through the fourth-semester level). Students earning a B.S. need only complete the language requirement, but have more courses in their major; other majors exempt students from some of the courses in their field of study.

If it sounds like some categories are repeats from the Miami Plan, they are — and the university confuses the issue even more by allowing some courses, but not all, to count in both sets of requirements. Students say they are flabbergasted by the official graphs, charts, and figures used to illustrate how and where the two plans overlap. And it is abundantly clear why the university has academic advisers living in student dorms. If that's not enough help, the university will provide a computer printout of the courses a student still needs to graduate.

The Western College Program of interdisciplinary studies is less confusing but even more politicized. This curriculum yields a bachelor of philosophy degree and involves a semi-defined set of requirements for freshmen and sophomores. The mandatory interdisciplinary studies are combined with the electives to meet the Miami Plan requirements. Teaching at this college is done in "learning communities" — seminar groups with about twenty students. Students create their own areas of focus; some have drawn up programs related to business, premedicine, and pre-law, while others choose broad-based humanities programs, such as European culture and politics.

Students throughout the university may join the University Honors Program, either as freshmen (by application or invitation) or as returning students (by application). Participants complete two freshman seminars, a yearlong freshman colloquium, six hours of advanced seminars, and a year of directed independent studies.

The best professors at Miami include Ryan J. Barilleaux, Augustus Jones Jr., and Warren Mason in political science; John A. Dutra and Michelle P. Wilhelm in classics; Edwin Yamauchi, Jay W. Baird, Michael O'Brien, and Andrew Caytan in history; and Marilyn E. Throne in English.

Students and professors say the best departments at the university are political science and history. Political science offers three degree tracks: political science, diplomacy and foreign affairs, and public administration. The history department contains several excellent faculty members, and coursework is stellar. Solid courses include "American South to 1877" and "The Roman Republic."

Another worthwhile program is the John E. Dolibois European Center in Luxembourg, where students take classes for credit while living with a local family. In addition, Miami has agreements with several foreign universities, allowing its students to study at the Federal University of Paran in Brazil, the Kansai University of Foreign Studies in Japan, the University of Glasgow, or the Vienna University of Economics and Business Administration. Miami ranks fourth nationally in the number of students studying abroad, according to recruiting material.

Miami's mission statement speaks of the university's will "to preserve, add to, evaluate, and transmit the accumulated knowledge of the centuries" and "to promote good education, virtue, religion, and morality." And while a traditional education is not that hard to find at Miami, the Western College Program is not a good place to look for it. "The [program] is a den of political correctness and dilettantism," a professor says. A student says the program is "segregated academically and socially from the rest of the campus." The basic curriculum required of all students in the program includes two semesters of a course called "Social Systems," whose description claims that "views that articulate and challenge dominant values and life styles stimulate students to analyze both arguments of others and their own beliefs."

Some departments in the College of Arts and Sciences are a little fuzzy around the edges.

About a quarter of the philosophy department specializes in feminist theory. One of these professors describes her work as a search "to 'triangulate' Continental, pragmatist and feminist philosophy on the particular issues of epistemology and the role of the body in philosophy." Another is developing "a psychoanalytic model of ideology which elucidates the formation of sexual subjects." Some professors in the other 75 percent of the department don't focus on traditional philosophic subjects either. One course, "Confronting Death," includes an examination of suicide and euthanasia in literature and films. There is also a course on environmental philosophy.

The black world studies department offers an ideological program on the issues of class and race. Courses include "Feminism and the Diaspora: U.S. Women of Color," in which students "read works by and about women of gender, ethnicity, class, sexuality, and other differences," according to the department catalogue.

English is the largest department at Miami, with sixty tenure-line faculty on the university's main campus. "[It] has been thoroughly radicalized," says a professor in another department. "Literature, for example, is giving way to multicultural studies, and composition has turned into free writing." In the words of a student, "The English department sacrifices writing, thinking, and great literature to politics." But another student says that while the department is heavily ideological, "they haven't thrown out all of the good classes." A large number of courses, however, deal in gender and race categories, while others ("Alternative Traditions in Film," for example) are also far removed from traditional literature.

Faculty from several departments teach courses cross-listed in the women's studies department, which offers a minor. These include a religion course called "Christianity and the Role of Women" and a family studies course titled "Couple Relationships: Diversity and Change." The department also offers its own courses, including "The Role of Women in a Transforming Society." Students in that class "position themselves as creators of knowledge about women's experiences and as members of self-critical communities of activists who are transforming society and women's positions in that society," the catalogue states.

The religion department devotes only about one-quarter of its courses to Judeo-Christian topics. The rest represent just about everything else, including the indigenous religions of Mexico, Guatemala, African tribes, and China, as well as

Taoism, Shintoism, the Shin sect, and Buddhism. There is also a course in existentialism.

Political Atmosphere: One Word Is Worth a Thousand Pictures

Miami University was named after the Miami Indian tribe. However, in 1997 the Miami tribe, now of Oklahoma, withdrew its support for the school's longtime athletic nickname, the Redskins. The school's board of trustees unanimously agreed, and the university's teams are now the RedHawks. (The school did retain, however, the logo bearing an Indian warrior with a feathered headdress.)

One faculty member told the *Miami Student* that he was glad to get rid of the nickname. "I have never felt comfortable with any human being described as a Redskin," the professor said. Students interviewed by the newspaper had other opinions. "I find it interesting that after all these years of the positive use of the Redskin name that it is suddenly so offensive," one student said. "I feel the university caved in to politically correct terms," said another. One student believes that the motivation for the change came more from politically correct faculty than the Miami tribe, citing a University Senate initiative early in 1996. But most students don't really care. "I think it's cool as long as we get to flap our arms around and shriek like the killer birds of prey we have become," said one ironical wag.

This minor controversy came to a university that has a reputation of being rather conservative. That reputation, however, may be somewhat dated. "Poorly informed people have an image of Miami as being conservative, but it is country-club Republican rather than truly conservative," a student says. "Students are economically conservative, but socially apathetic."

It seems, though, that the administration has a multicultural streak. There has been an effort at Miami to keep an eye on diversity during admission decisions, and as a result the number of minorities in the freshman class has increased by 62 percent in the last three years. According to the university, 8 percent of a recent freshman class were minority students — about the same composition as the current student body. The university has said it would like that number to reach 10 percent by 1998.

To enhance recruiting efforts, Miami maintains an office of minority affairs that offers academic assistance to minority students and seeks to "educate Miamians on diversity issues." Office staff work with groups like the American Indian Awareness/Action Group, the Hispano American Association, and the Black Student Action Association.

Another group, the Black Action Movement, formed recently after a minority student received a series of harassing calls on an answering machine. The group used the unfortunate incident to, according to one student, "storm the Residential Life Building" and demand, among other things, an expanded multicultural center. Shortly thereafter, two hundred students rallied in support of the demand. The university responded with a twenty-three-page memo, promising, essentially, the entire store: a "President's Council on Multicultural Affairs," an institutional plan for diversity, a reexamination of support services for minority students, and accelerated planning for the expansion of the multicultural center.

"Things have quieted down since [then] regarding the perceived race problems on campus," a student says. "I think that everything kind of got blown out of proportion. The university seems to be bending over backwards to make this a place for everybody."

Meanwhile, multicultural attempts continue on another front: the curriculum. In 1996 the dean of the College of Arts and Sciences, along with a group of faculty, proposed an additional multicultural course for freshmen. The proposal was defeated by a broad coalition of faculty because, according to a professor, "the requirement was too much like indoctrination; it was not sufficiently academic in nature; and the Division of Student Affairs was to be involved in the program." Reportedly, the dean is still looking for ways to install the new class.

Most faculty are also opposed to the indoctrination inherent in another program, the freshman orientation sponsored by the university's residential life office. "The Emerging Differences Workshop gets freshmen together to hash out ethnic angst," a student says. "Students are subjected to the entire panoply of racism, gender inequities, and homosexual rights." The Division of Student Life, to which the residential life office reports, is described by one person on campus as "the rotten borough of Miami which is populated by professional multiculturalists."

Student Life: No Day at the Beach

The fourteen thousand undergraduates at Miami, along with nearly two thousand graduate students, come close to doubling the size of Oxford, Ohio. The university has done its part to see that its students tread lightly: a permit is required before a student can keep a car on campus, and students are encouraged to walk or ride bicycles. Some say the policy lends the campus a European flavor. There is also an in-town bus service, as well as arranged bus trips to Cincinnati (thirty-five miles to the south) most weekends and rides to Cleveland, Chicago, and Pittsburgh at vacation time. Since 90 percent of the students come from the eastern Midwest (Ohio, Indiana, Illinois, Michigan, and Wisconsin), many don't have that far to travel.

Oxford has several rows of small shops, bars, and restaurants that students frequent. "We call Miami 'the bubble' because we are so insulated from the outside world," a student says. "Oxford is not very big, and things to do are not abounding. Most people do a lot of drinking on the weekends."

Fraternities rule the social scene. About one-third of the students join a Greek organization, many of which have lovely chapter houses on campus. There are social fraternities and sororities, as well as academic and service chapters. Students who are not partying in bars or fraternities frequently host small get-togethers in student houses.

Only freshmen are required to live in university residence halls. Each hall has its own academic adviser, a necessity in figuring out the arcana of the Miami Plan and the College Requirement. There are many traditional, single-sex dormitories, but the university has also established "special-interest halls" that cater to the passions of like-minded students. These include an international living hall, a health and fitness hall, and a hall for women in the physical sciences, among others. Most upperclassmen live in fraternities or rent places in town.

Miami has a new athletic center, completed in 1994 at a price tag of $22 million. This very fine facility includes a weight room with a spiral staircase that ascends to an open atrium where other workout machines are available. The center also has a fifteen-person spa, a fifty-meter pool, a suspended jogging track, and a forty-foot climbing wall.

Students compete in twenty-five intramural sports. Teams usually represent a dorm floor or fraternity. One unusual intramural event is broomball, played on ice, like hockey, but without skates and with brooms instead of sticks.

The university brings some popular rock bands to campus, as well as nationally known classical artists. Recently Miami hosted the Indigo Girls, the Allman Brothers, Gladys Knight, the Canadian Brass, the New York City Opera National Company, and Yo Yo Ma.

About the only active conservative group on campus is the College Republicans, which is active in local, state, and national politics. The group, tongue in cheek, sponsors a "Republican Awareness Week," as well as a more serious birthday party for Ronald Reagan and an annual trip to Capitol Hill. The group may soon have some political allies: a campus chapter of the Christian Coalition is said to be in the planning stages.

The most active liberal group is the Miami University Gay Bisexual Lesbian Alliance (MUGBLA), which has a university-funded office in the student center. The group's web page says that it seeks to increase the visibility of homosexuals on campus and to "promote issues of diversity on campus." Many members of MUGBLA also join more militant groups like the Lesbian Avengers. MUGBLA did persuade the university to include sexual orientation in its official statement on "respect for human diversity." It also sponsors campus activities, lectures, and a float in the homecoming parade. Its web page (on the university's server) can be used to reach the websites of many national homosexual groups.

But just as conservative activism is minimal at Miami, so is activity on the other side of the spectrum. Very few groups ever gain the members or the clout to make much of a political dent on what is generally considered a quiet, fairly studious campus.

UNIVERSITY OF MICHIGAN

Office of Admissions
1220 Student Activities Building
Ann Arbor, MI 48109-1316
(734) 764-7433
www.umich.edu

Total enrollment: 36,530
Undergraduates: 23,590
SAT Ranges (Verbal/Math): V 550-660, M 590-700
Financial aid: 52%
Applicants: 19,720
Accepted: 68%
Enrolled: 40%
Application deadline: Feb. 1
Financial aid application deadline: Feb. 1
Tuition: $6,000 in-state; $18,800 out-of-state
Core curriculum: No

The Mother of All State Universities

The University of Michigan was the first truly huge institution of higher learning in this country. "The mother of all state universities," the school may not be the oldest state school in the nation, but it had grown to be a very large school already in the late nineteenth century. Here is an astounding statistic: today one in every thousand Americans is an alumnus or alumna of the University of Michigan. During the nineteenth century, while other state schools were small colleges catering to the social elite of their states, Michigan, financially well-off, was spending millions of dollars to provide a huge variety of programs to thousands of students and to allow its large faculty to carry out research and writing in scores of fields.

The effects of this legacy continue today. For example, the school has the largest papyrus collection in the Western Hemisphere; one of the largest university libraries (at 7 million volumes) in the world, containing huge special collections in Asian history, Slavic studies, and the social sciences; the second-largest college football stadium on the planet (a few seats shy of the University of Tennessee's); no fewer than nineteen schools and colleges; a chair in Armenian history; and scholars specializing in everything from Assyrian studies to nuclear engineering. Michigan doesn't just have a scholar who studies China, it has a bunch of them, plus a Center for Chinese Studies, plus a huge collection in the library on the subject, and so on.

Michigan can be overwhelming for eighteen-year-old freshmen. A huge bus system ferries students around campus, especially between Central campus, the oldest and most populated part of the school, adjacent to downtown Ann Arbor, and North Campus, a newer, aesthetically impoverished collection of buildings constructed on the hillsides across the Huron River from the rest of the city. A student can get lost in the curriculum, and easily be distracted by multicultural classes posing as core requirements. Yet the school has such a rich collection of people and resources that students can find a group of friends who will share their beliefs and concerns, regardless of what they are. The student body contains a small but highly vocal cadre of professional students who seem to spend all of their time agitating for politically correct changes. Most students, though, hail from middle-class homes where achievement is defined in ways other than arrest records or the cultivation of an ersatz moral superiority.

Unfortunately, free speech on campus is an iffy proposition at best, and the administration does exert a strong politicizing influence. Undergraduates, not worried about keeping their jobs or fellowships, have an easier time than faculty and graduate students, but the pressures are felt by all. Students in search of a serious education can find one, and part of that will come from the way they are forced to defend their beliefs against the orthodoxies prevalent on campus.

Academic Life: Go Your Own Way

The University of Michigan has no core curriculum as such. Like most other large universities (and, indeed, liberal arts colleges as well), it has distribution requirements that are very broadly construed, allowing students to choose within a designated area of study. This hurts those students who are most vulnerable to being misled by the politicized and the trivial. There are many worthwhile courses at Michigan, and many dedicated professors who genuinely love to teach. But finding these people in such a giant multiversity, as it were, is not always easy, and students should begin their search when they arrive on campus.

Students seeking to earn an A.B. or B.S. degree must complete a minimum of 120 credits with a cumulative GPA of 2.0 or better. The difference between the two degrees lies in the fact that B.S. candidates must complete 60 credits of approved courses in the physical and natural sciences and mathematics. All students must take two English composition courses and a course in quantitative reasoning, and learn a foreign language to the fourth-semester level. They must also take 30 credits from outside their field of concentration, distributed in the categories of natural sciences, social sciences, humanities, mathematical and symbolic analysis, and creative expression.

These requisites, while far from a demanding core, merit applause for maintaining the foreign language requirement as well as demanding courses in the sciences and mathematics. They would be even more laudable had not administrators several years ago added what they termed a "race and ethnicity requirement," known on campus as the "diversity" requirement. Stipulated in lieu of any mandated study of Western civilization, this requirement can be fulfilled by a number of courses that contain the requisite discussions of "(1) the meaning of race, ethnicity, and racism; (2) racial and ethnic intolerance and resulting inequality as it occurs in the United States or elsewhere; (3) comparisons of discrimination based on race, ethnicity, religion, social class, or gender," according to the university catalogue.

Concentrations (what majors are called at Michigan) consume anywhere from 24 to 48 credits outside the general requirements, and Michigan offers them by the boatload. Undergraduate concentrations are offered from many of the university's eighteen schools and colleges, and graduation requirements vary with the college and degree program. Thus, Michigan offers a major for just about everyone: from engineers and historians to artists and kinesiologists. Most students choose to concentrate in a discipline within the largest single unit on campus, the College of Literature, Science, and the Arts (LS&A). Here one finds a huge array of departments and programs, from the excellent to the absurd.

Students in LS&A may choose to work toward an A.B., B.S., bachelor of general studies, or a special degree called bachelor of science in chemistry. The first two degrees are typical of those earned by most students at most colleges and universities across the country. The general studies degree "encourages students to take responsibility for structuring their own multidisciplinary academic programs within guidelines emphasizing upper-level courses elected in three or more departments." It is, in effect, an interdisciplinary program that a mature and informed student could use to great benefit, but which a less developed person could turn into a meaningless hodgepodge.

For the A.B. or B.S. degree, students may choose one of three tracks — Pattern I, with a typical course distribution system; Pattern II, which offers a more structured approach; and Pattern III, with allows students to "work out an individual plan that reflects exposure to a variety of methodologies and approaches to intellectual experience." While students meeting Pattern I requirements do not need an academic adviser's approval for the distribution coursework, those electing and meeting the requirements for Patterns II and III need an adviser's written approval, a step that seems well taken given the unstructured means by which one advances even through the more structured curricula at Michigan.

In each plan, a good education can be had by those who want it and are willing to seek it out. The sheer quantity of courses can work against the struggling undergraduate, however; a student can just as easily as not spend all four years taking politicized courses from activist faculty members.

A trusted adviser, therefore, is always the best way for the new student to learn to navigate the quirkiness of Michigan's curriculum — and the fact that students need to do this only points up the university's failure to determine what is and what is not important to a true education.

Michigan's devotion to research often comes at the expense of teaching. The use of low-paid teaching assistants is intended to relieve professors of their undergraduate teaching burdens. In a system that rewards publication and ignores good teaching, it is the undergraduate (who pays a lot but does not supply the money upon which the university relies) who loses out. While Michigan employs scores of world-class scholars, few of them are contractually obligated to teach freshmen or sophomores. Some do so anyway, it should be noted, and do so very well. But they are a minority within the profession, and younger professors who spend a great deal of time preparing for class will be looked down upon by their research-obsessed senior colleagues. As one professor said to a graduate student, "You're an excellent teacher. Too bad it won't do anything at all to help you get a job."

Among the outstanding professors at Michigan are Ralph G. Williams, William Ingram, Ejner Jensen, John Knott, Robert Lewis, Robert Weisbuch, and James Winn in English; H. Don Cameron, Glernn Knudsvig, Ludwig Koenen, and Charles Witke in classics and great books; Marvin B. Becker, Thomas N. Tentler, Diane O. Hughes, Thomas Green, Mills Thorton, John Fine, and Michael MacDonald in history; Piotr Michalowski in Near Eastern Studies; Kenneth Lieberthal and Arlene Saxonhouse in political science; Steven Everson and Stephen Darwall in philosophy; and Joseph Adelson and Chris Peterson in the psychology department. Michigan boasts more excellent departments than some colleges and universities have departments period. These include political science, history, classical archaeology, classical civilization, classical languages and literatures, anthropology, chemistry, physics, all engineering concentrations, Chinese language and literature, Greek language and literature, Latin language and literature, Medieval and Renaissance Collegium, philosophy, psychology, economics, business administration, mathematics, music, Near Eastern studies, neuroscience, sociology, and art history.

The flip side of that coin is that Michigan has more politicized departments than some colleges and universities have total departments. The administration has been unwilling to stand against the small minority of students who are smug, professional activists. The new president, a former law school dean and First Amendment scholar, gave his blessing to the university's infamous speech code — a code that was struck down in federal court shortly after its promulgation (hardly an encouragement to the careers of those who would dissent).

There are faculty who don't like these developments on campus. As one professor said when told about a change in the curriculum of a well-known course, "I deplore these changes, but most of my colleagues think they're just great." Says another: "Many of these changes are being pushed by people who have never read the material they campaign against." Nevertheless, these more traditional scholars are no longer in the majority in Ann Arbor, and many who retire will almost certainly be replaced by their philosophical opponents bearing newly minted Ph.D.s.

Many of the courses that may be used to fulfill the "race and ethnicity" requirement, for example, derive from politicized, advocacy-oriented disciplines that rely upon both administrative approval and radicalized faculty to survive financially and socially. One wonders just how well some of these programs would do without a hostage audience needing to check off a requirement. For example, how many would take Women's Studies 483, "Women in Prison: Gender and Crime among Blacks and Latinos," if the university did not include it in the general requirements list? "Interviews will be scheduled with women at the prison which will be the basis for a final paper," the course description says.

Among the most politicized departments are the usual suspects: women's studies, Afro-American and African studies, American culture, education, social work, cultural anthropology, and comparative literature. There is also a gaggle of institutes and research centers such as the Institute for Research on Women and Genders, which, along with the women's studies department, recently sponsored a "theme semester" called "Genders, Bodies, Borders." The program literature explains that " 'Genders' is a term which suggests cultural constructions of manhood and womanhood while 'bodies' is suggestive of the biological and physical. The last term, 'borders,' refers to national boundaries and other geographic and topographic distances as well as the fluidity and interaction of the socially constructed aspects of gender and the 'real.' "

The substitution of the study of popular culture for what was once known as high culture is behind the growth of American culture programs nationwide. At Michigan, one may choose "Themes in American Culture: Nature and America: From Wilderness to Winnebagos — Changing Ideas about the Natural World." But students should beware, for among their assignments will be examining "their own assumptions about what is natural by visiting woods, a park, a farm, and a shopping mall in or near Ann Arbor."

As is the case in English departments across the country, Michigan's offers esoterica for every taste (as well as some outstanding courses). Many different instructors, mostly graduate students, teach English 239, "What Is Literature?" One finds a broad range of approaches to teaching this class, including this from the fall of 1997: "*The Classics and Trash* is the title under which somebody recently examined 'tradition' and 'taboo' in 'high' and 'popular' literatures. What do all these categories mean? . . . Indeed, what roles do such things as essays and final exams written by students — and the grades and college degrees they then receive — contribute to the picture?" Now there's a good question.

Political Atmosphere: Multiplicity

The extent to which Michigan has endorsed the multicultural and diversity mentality is obvious enough from the university catalogue. Michigan has money to burn, and it does: all of these developments came at the expense of a more substantive curriculum, and any new department or program that is funded takes money that will not be spent on more legitimate offerings.

Some examples of Michigan's monetary priorities include the many offices set up to aid minorities and other special-interest groups. There is the Office of Minority Services, which maintains a full-time staff. This service is basically duplicated by Trotter House, which also exists to serve the minority community at Michigan and also has full-time employees, as well as live-in student staff members. Michigan annually awards $5,000 Johnson Diversity Awards to faculty members who make an "outstanding commitment to the development of a more culturally and ethnically diverse campus community." The president of Michigan also has at his disposal the New Century Fund for Diversity, which, according to promotional literature, "provides support for projects conducted by faculty, staff or students that will advance diversity and multiculturalism on the Ann Arbor campus, especially activities that will advance the goals of the Michigan Agenda for Women and the Michigan Mandate."

Michigan's Lesbian Gay Bisexual Programs Office (LGBPO) recently celebrated its twenty-fifth anniversary with a bash that included, among other things, "a Law School colloquium on the legal and social issues facing lesbian, gay, bisexual, and transgender youth; presentations by local historians and Michigan alumni; an open house; a reception; and Club Fabulous dance party." There are four staff members in the office, which publishes a newsletter that mentions the annual homosexual Valentine's Day "Kiss-In." Literary submissions are also sought; under the heading "Gay Men: Nonfiction Erotic," an author "wants to hear from you if you've ever had gay sex with a fraternity brother. As a pledge, were you ever compelled to perform homoerotic acts with fellow pledges while others watched? Did gay sex figure prominently in any of your fraternity's hazing rituals?" Also available from the LGBPO is a local publication called *OUTspoken,* which in a recent issue denounced "the radical Christian right-wing" and "arch-homophobe Senator Jesse Helms," and ran a feature article on "the Christian nation fallacy."

Then there is the Center for the Education of Women, a unit of Michigan "devoted to service, research, and advocacy" that was established in 1964. The center "sponsors a year-round calendar of programs and events, and a full range of services, including counseling, internships, scholarships, and library services," and offers more than thirty scholarships. It works closely with the Institute for Research on Women and Gender and the Michigan Initiative for Women's Health.

In the case of centers like this, the point is not that their services aren't worthwhile, or that they are all run by ideologues. But one has to wonder at the wisdom of spending so much money on such services while underclassmen suffer through classes of up to four hundred students, other departments trim budgets, and needy students go without scholarships.

Then there are the legal bills the school faced in defending a speech code that was found to be indefensible. Michigan in fact was one of the pioneers in introducing speech codes designed to punish anyone who spoke up against the reigning orthodoxies. "It was obviously an attempt not to prevent harassment of minorities or women but to intimidate anyone who might want to voice his opposition to the administration's policies," says a former student who was on campus when the speech code was introduced in 1990. "Everyone knew you could get into a lot of trouble by saying what you thought."

The speech code was challenged in court and thrown out. "The speech rule is in limbo now," says one student. "It's implicitly enforced and all students get a handout warning them about harassment." Recalls a former student: "Students in my department received notices that among the actions for which we could be charged with sexual harassment was 'failure to take feminist scholarship seriously.' Of course, we all knew that that meant 'keep your damn mouth shut.'"

The cost of failing to do that is seen in two infamous cases involving Michigan's department of sociology. The first occurred in 1988 when Professor Reynolds Farley was forced out of teaching a course on race when he was unjustly accused of racism. Farley had included in the curriculum writings of W. E. B. Du Bois and others which included the word "n — — ," and was accused of other acts deemed "insensitive" by some of his radical students. In 1993 this type of nonsense struck again when Professor David Goldberg was accused of racially and sexually harassing his students, as well as with being professionally unqualified to teach his courses. It was obvious from the beginning that the charges were false, yet the administration failed to come to Goldberg's defense, just as it had let Farley be sacrificed to his enemies five years before. Goldberg's sin? As a nationally known expert on sociological statistics, he questioned the degree of accuracy of some studies' conclusions that women on average make less per hour than men, and that SAT scores and the approval ratings for bank loans for whites were higher than for blacks. Goldberg did not question that problems were evident, but simply showed how the figures could be manipulated for political reasons.

"There's a sort of 'ethnic cleansing' of inquiry going on at this university, in which the minority is purging the majority," a faculty member told a newspaper regarding the Goldberg incident. Another professor says that very little remains at Michigan that is not controlled by the radicals. "That's why there is no argument over controversial issues — it's a completely vanquished battlefield."

Student Life: A Pack of Wolverines

Attending a school like Michigan can be an invigorating experience. The intellectual challenges are real and numerous, and the student body is made up mostly of energetic, driven people who do not intend to be left behind. It's a given that the students will be very bright, and professors at Michigan (the ones that teach) say such students are a delight — they take their work more seriously, tend to be more socially mature, and are willing to work very hard to achieve their goals. Michigan is perhaps alone in its ability to offer such a huge array of concentrations, research opportunities, and athletic prowess, all in a quintessential college town an authentic cosmopolitan flair and East Coast–type intellectual environment.

Ann Arbor is a very pedestrian-oriented town, full of excellent restaurants, bookstores, bars, and all manner of shopping. Every student will come to love the original Borders Book Store, which was founded by the Borders brothers in 1974 and became the model for the mega-bookstore chain. It isn't easy to lose weight in Ann Arbor, what with the combination of long winters and such eateries as Zingermann's delicatessen, Sevah, and Grazi serving up excellent fare year-round. Ann Arbor is well served by a bus system that is unusually punctual, and although Detroit is less than an hour away, there is little reason to make the trek with so many conveniences and diversions in your own backyard.

Michigan's campus offers an eclectic selection of architecture. The most famous building on campus, Angell Hall, houses several arts and sciences departments and is the central focus of that college. The Law Quadrangle, a beautiful group of buildings, includes the massive reading room of the law library. This room is open to undergraduates as well as law students, and is a favorite place for serious study. Other notable buildings include the Michigan Union, an oak-paneled gem with many offices for student organizations, a billiards room, and a very large eating area with numerous fast-food joints. It also houses an arcade and the university bookstore. Unfortunately, postwar planners, enthralled by the utilitarianism then sweeping the nation's architecture schools, designed and built several extraordinarily ugly buildings on campus in the early 1950s, prime among which is Mason Hall; 1970s' architecture contributed the Modern Languages Building. Both of these eyesores do their best to ruin the otherwise attractive Mall that runs between the Hatcher Graduate Library and the Rackham School of Graduate Studies.

No report on Michigan would be complete without a mention of athletics. A perennial powerhouse in many sports, Michigan holds many Big Ten records and has filled its massive football stadium with over 100,000 fans for every home game for more than two decades. There are, in addition, many intramural and club sports, and the facilities are excellent for almost every activity. This athletic strength gives the large and diverse academic community a rallying point and provides a great diversion for students, faculty, alumni, and fans across the nation.

MICHIGAN STATE UNIVERSITY

Office of Admissions and Scholarships
Michigan State University
250 Administration Building
East Lansing, MI 48824-0590
(517) 355-1855
www.msu.edu

Total enrollment: 42,603
Undergraduates: 33,308
SAT Ranges (Verbal/Math): V 480-600, M 490-620
Financial aid: 76%
Applicants: 20,520
Accepted: 81%
Enrolled: 41%
Application deadline: Rolling admissions
Financial aid application deadline: Jan. 1
Tuition: in-state, $4,822-5,302; out-of-state, $11,887-12,300
Core curriculum: No

Taming the Behemoth

Michigan State University (MSU) was founded in 1855 as a research university focusing on farm science. Though the school still has a decidedly pastoral way about it — more than half of its 5,240-acre campus is devoted to experimental farms and natural areas — it has now grown to fourteen colleges and thirty-two thousand undergraduate students.

The late conservative scholar Russell Kirk, who attended MSU as an undergraduate before World War II, once characterized the place as "Behemoth University." Kirk's term was thoroughly pejorative: like a massive beast — the biblical Behemoth — MSU symbolized to Kirk the abandonment of liberal learning for a utilitarian educational philosophy.

But even Russell Kirk might be surprised by some of the more positive developments at MSU. Size has not brought MSU all the problems that beset other enormous state schools. Its students have not become heavily politicized — especially compared to those at MSU's rival, the University of Michigan — and, though most departments show signs of being caught up in ideology, the university has several excellent programs, including the James Madison College (JMC) for the study of public policy. This college within a university has a national reputation for teaching public policy skills and maintains an excellent curriculum in the liberal arts. The president of the university served in the Bush administration and has not pursued the national rankings and politically correct programs that have preoccupied many of his counterparts.

The presence on campus of JMC provides an enormously valuable counterpoint to the tendencies alluded to in Kirk's image of "Behemoth University." If more state universities emulated the JMC model, the cause of higher education in America would be served, because JMC demonstrates that the liberal arts tradition can still flourish within — and positively influence — the modern mega-university.

Academic Life: Find the College Inside the University

There is no core curriculum at Michigan State; rather, the basic undergraduate program requires only a set of distribution requirements. These include competency in either statistics or calculus and a writing requirement that can be met with writing courses per se or with courses that require a good deal of writing, such as certain English or philosophy classes.

The third and largest mandate — a total of seven courses — is the integrative studies requirement, which includes work in the arts and humanities; physical and biological sciences; and social, behavioral, and economic sciences.

Because of the small number of requirements and the unfocused way in which they may be fulfilled, the university certainly overstates its hopes for their effects when it says:

> The [integrative studies] program . . . provides students with a sense of the interrelatedness of knowledge, especially the intersection of liberal learning with the professional, technical, and specialized knowledge of the major. The program enables students to understand, analyze, synthesize, and use data and to compare historical and contemporary social, cultural, economic, political, and environmental phenomena in the United States and the world. . . . [It] encourages the development of analytical skills and the use of a variety of methods of inquiry, including scientific, artistic, and literary approaches as well as the latest information technologies. The program fosters the student's sense of responsibility as an effective citizen of a diverse yet interdependent world.

Two courses are required in the arts and humanities, one of which is "United States and the World," a survey of national culture "presented in international and comparative context" that includes "influences from native Americans, Europeans, Africans, and Asians." The second course is chosen by the student from a list including both Western and non-Western topics. The student also chooses two courses in the social, behavioral, and economic sciences, and two in biological and physical sciences — one in each discipline, one of which must have a lab. One "transcollegiate" course, usually taken after one or more of the other integrative studies courses, can be chosen from a list that ranges from the sublime to the ridiculous. These courses, interdisciplinary in nature, are designed to "underscore the fact that the solutions to complex human problems require the knowledge and methods of more than one discipline." The thirteen choices listed in the catalogue include "Science, Technology, and Values," "The Impact of the Automobile," "Feminist Perspectives on Women in Culture and Society," "The Black African Diaspora and World Civilization," and a course on acoustics.

Multicultural courses are available in the non–hard science integrative studies categories, so students need not search long to fulfill the final component of the distribution requirements: that two of the courses be designated as "diversity" courses. Some courses, including some of those above, are noted as either "N" for national diversity, "I" for international diversity, or "D" for multicultural diversity. Students need an "N" and an "I," or they can exchange either one for a "D."

Three of MSU's fourteen colleges are more relevant than the others to further studies in liberal arts. The College of Arts and Letters includes most of the traditional liberal arts disciplines as well as nontraditional programs like American studies, women's studies, and the Consortium for Inter-institutional Collaboration in African and Latin American Studies. The College of Social Science boasts very good departments of economics and politics, as well as some less distinguished ones.

But the finest educational opportunity at MSU is clearly JMC, the only MSU school limited to undergraduate students. As a liberal arts college within a major public university, JMC is practically in a category of its own. Its mission statement states its purpose as providing "liberal education in public affairs for undergraduates." Its residential setting nurtures a collegium of scholars among students, faculty, and staff and results in an intimate and challenging environment in which to learn.

JMC offers concentrations in international relations, political economy, political theory and constitutional democracy, and social relations. Five Rhodes scholars, six Truman scholars, four Marshall scholars, and six Fulbright scholars are listed among its graduates. Established in 1967 as a school of public affairs, it now enrolls about one thousand students. Consequently, JMC classes are smaller than the average MSU class (between twenty-five and forty students per class), and student participation is expected and frequently evaluated.

In addition to fulfilling the university requirements, JMC offers students at least fifty-one credits (usually seventeen classes) within the college — about half of all the coursework required for a degree. Students take a specialized, yearlong version of the university writing courses, wherein the readings focus on the individual in American society and culture. According to the JMC catalogue, the writing courses examine "the themes of individuality, identity, and community in American life. They focus on the individual in society, the search for selfhood, or identity, and the social circumstances in which decisions and identities are shaped. They also study community, its nature and purposes, its advantages and disadvantages, and the tensions between, as well as possibilities for, individuality and community." In both semesters of the writing program, students read and write on themes in American history.

JMC students can also substitute a two-semester sequence of courses called "Introduction to the Study of Public Affairs" for the university's social science requirements. The two classes cover the economic, political, and social aspects of American society, and readings include a diversity of texts from the fields of economics, history, political science, and sociology. In addition, JMC students must take two semesters of introductory economics.

The final JMC requirement is field experience: students must spend at least one semester as interns with public policy organizations, such as businesses, legislative offices, nonprofit organizations, or governmental agencies. Interns often work in Washington, D.C., for groups of all political stripes, including the Heritage Foundation, American Enterprise Institute, Democratic National Committee, and Carnegie Endowment for International Peace.

Some of the best teachers in JMC are William B. Allen, Louis D. Hunt, Eric S. Petrie, Constance Hunt, and Richard M. Zinman. Other fine professors at MSU include Werner Dannhauser, James Granato, Jerry Weinberger, and Michael Bratton in political science; Peter J. Schmidt, Richard Baillie, Jeffrey Woolridge, and Paul S. Segerstrom in economics; Dan Ilgen in psychology; and Mike Mazzo in finance.

The more radical professors and teachers can be found in women's studies, one of the most politicized departments at MSU. One professor says the department keeps a low profile on campus. Certain classes, though, are high-profile ideology-wise. Some examples from the catalogue:

- ■ "Introduction to Contemporary Feminist Theory." "Contemporary feminist theories of patriarchy, oppression, liberation, sexuality, and the meaning of 'woman.' Influences of liberalism, Marxism, Freud. Intersections of sex, race, class, and ethnicity. Theories by women of color."
- ■ "Women's Studies Senior Seminar: The Impact of Assimilation on U.S. Women's Lives." "This capstone course will focus on the question, 'In what ways have U.S. women accepted or resisted prevailing cultural norms on gender?' We will grapple with that question by examining the coercive impact of cultural assimilation during the early 20th century and since the emergence of second wave feminism (1968 to the present). We will take into account the influence of such cultural ideals as the 'angel in the house'; the 'New Woman'; the 'Super Mom'; etc., racist stereotypes as well as self-defined constructions."

MSU's English department has a reputation for being hospitable to deconstructionist and feminist theories. Among the offerings in a recent catalogue is the following:

■ "Film and Society." "In this course we shall deal with images of gays and lesbians in film, as well as with gay and lesbian filmmakers. We shall also take a look at Queer Theory, one of the newest trends in film theory."

Or take this excerpt from an exuberant and lengthy course description:

■ "Introduction to Popular Culture." "On February 8, 1995, Edward Albee was asked to recommend a good Broadway play. He said there were none that season. On the following evening John Simon in answer to a similar query announced that no good films had been produced in the preceding year. If every vice is the excess of a virtue, these two eminent visitors to our campus carried in their baggage an excess of good taste. Plato said that the acceptable horse or the acceptable man existed only in the mind of God. What men got to see were imperfect representations. And, as for the arts, he would ban all of them — fine and popular — from his ideal Republic. His student, Aristotle, like all good students, challenged what his teacher said and found it wanting. Hip student that he was, Aristotle reasoned that the fact that this earth supplies us with no perfect horse or perfect man or perfect play does not relieve us of our obligation to study and analyze, to classify and criticize whatever it is we do have to work with. A world full of imperfect students still has room for plenty of 'A' students because we can create useful standards by which to measure less than perfect human beings. After all, popular culture is the culture that the majority has voted for. That makes it neither good nor bad; it just makes it popular. Different mobs at different times have voted for William Shakespeare and Count Basie as well as for bearbaiting, Married With Children, and Rush Limbaugh. Far from meaning 'Anything Goes,' the study of popular culture imposes on its practitioners the obligation to study what drives the public to elevate some of its experiences into crazes, fads, manias, trends, and to consign others stillborn to oblivion. It studies why people insist that Paul McCartney is dead and that Elvis Presley is alive."

Political Atmosphere: Conservative Credentials

The administration of Michigan State University is traditional compared to those of the majority of state universities. For example, President M. Peter McPherson was a member of the Bush administration, and Vice President Charles Greenleaf was one of nine hundred citizens whose FBI files were examined with questionable legality by members of the Clinton administration. McPherson has defended traditional values by taking a controversial stand against extending benefits to gay and lesbian partners of MSU employees. In addition, he made national news with his "tuition guarantee" program that mandates that MSU tuition will not rise faster than inflation.

To this end, the president has placed controls on physical plant maintenance costs and has limited the expansion of the faculty.

"The university is in social rest," a professor says. "This is a blue-collar town, and most students are working their way through school. There isn't time for protests." One student explains the lack of political activism on campus: "MSU is a lot more quiet politically than other schools. MSU was originally founded as an agricultural school, and I think there is something to that. A lot of the students here come from the Western and rural parts of the State, which tend to be more conservative than the Eastern side of the State. Those students usually go to U of M [Univ. of Michigan], which is very liberal."

The most political activity seen on campus in the past year has been the Latino student organization's effort to make MSU "grape free." There is a concern among Hispanic students that Latino agricultural employees are oppressed. One student says, "The Hispanic students have been demonstrating against grape consumption . . . and they have also encouraged other students to join in solidarity by fasting on certain days."

The biggest scandal at MSU in recent years wasn't political, but party-related. In the fall of 1997, evening party-going MSU students went out of control on Gunson Street in East Lansing. The small crowd grew larger as passing students joined in setting several couches on fire in the street. As the crowd grew, chaos erupted, climaxing with public nudity, including topless female students running out in front of local cameramen. When the MSU and East Lansing police arrived, students began to smash the windows and sides of the patrol vehicles with beer bottles. There were several arrests and numerous tickets handed out to students.

Students insist on calling the event the Gunson party, but the local and national media referred to it as the Gunson riots. It achieved its greatest notoriety on the national television show *Real TV.* One student reports: "Now some local vendors are selling tee-shirts that say 'Michigan State' on the front, and on the back there is a burning couch with the slogan 'There may have been alcohol involved.'"

Since the Gunson riots, police have stepped up patrols. Students complain that police simply stop them while walking on campus and demand that they open their bags and/or submit to sobriety tests. Underage students who are carrying beer or fail the test are given MIP tickets (minor in possession). These tickets start at $135, and can result in the loss of a driver's license for up to six months (even if driving is not involved in the infraction). One student complains: "The police are really harassing students. If you are walking with a backpack at night, even if you are coming from the library, there is a very good chance you will get stopped by police because they think you are concealing beer."

Despite the problems with the riots, one student reports that "MSU has a carefree atmosphere. During the day, it's amazing how many people are just hanging out on campus, talking with each other, even strangers. The students are very friendly and open with each other. Since I have been here, I have never heard or seen a fight between students."

Student Life: Classes Optional

According to faculty, the biggest problem they face is student apathy. One professor says "30 percent of students don't come to class on a regular basis. The problem with the students at MSU is not one of intellect, but of motivation."

Apathy is not a problem when it comes to athletics, especially when a contest against the University of Michigan Wolverines is concerned. MSU has fourteen intercollegiate teams for men and eleven for women, and boasts that it has the largest intramural program in the world: more than 2,300 teams involved in more than two dozen sports. The sports facilities are immense. For example, the football stadium holds seventy-two thousand and the basketball arena seats more than fifteen thousand. MSU also has an ice hockey venue, an eighteen-hole golf course, and a baseball field, among other facilities. For quieter athletic pursuits, there are hiking trails and bike paths.

Other campus structures are also built to the scale of a large state university. The MSU libraries house more than 4 million volumes, plus an additional quarter-million rare books in a special collection. The Wharton Center for Performing Arts contains two theaters: the Great Hall and Festival Stage, which can hold 2,500 audience members, and a smaller theater with 600 seats. The Kellogg Hotel and Conference Center, named for the Kelloggs of cereal fame in nearby Battle Creek, hosts more than 400,000 guests each year at more than a thousand conferences and meetings. The center also allows MSU hotel and restaurant science majors a chance to practice.

MSU is also home to the Kresge Art Museum, which contains more than five thousand works of art, as well as classrooms and art studios.

Though the political atmosphere at MSU is extremely quiet, there is at least one flourishing student political organization, the College Republicans (MSU president McPherson was once the head of the campus CR chapter). One student points out: "The College Republicans [at MSU] have a much larger membership, and are much better organized, than the College Democrats. The Capitol is only 15 minutes away, and the College Republicans have great access to legislators. There are more requests for interns than the College Republicans can fill, so students can pick among the best positions available — they don't have to grovel." One leader in the College Republicans explains: "Our meetings are usually at 5:30, and the congressmen in Lansing usually finish for the day at around 5:00. So we have had several senators and representatives stop in on their way home to give us a 15 or 20 minute lecture, and then take some questions. It has really worked out great."

East Lansing is a haven for student-socialites with a plethora of bars, restaurants, and fraternity parties. Unique to East Lansing are the bars, including the always-packed and smoky Silver Dollar and The Riv, a favorite of fraternity brothers (in terms of employment — the majority of employees at the Riv are MSU frat boys).

Sparty's (which plays off the MSU nickname, the Spartans) is one of the most popular nightclubs in town.

One bonus for students at MSU is the extensive and relatively inexpensive transportation system. In addition to the university bus system, city buses conveniently go to local malls and other shopping and entertainment districts. One student reports: "It is very easy to get around on campus, and to all the hot spots in East Lansing. Even if you don't have a car, for 25 cents, you can get to wherever you want to go on the public buses."

MIDDLEBURY COLLEGE

Admissions Office
The Emma Willard House
Middlebury, VT 05753-6002
(802) 388-3711
www.middlebury.edu

Total enrollment: 2,120
Undergraduates: 2,120
SAT Ranges (Verbal/Math): V 660-730, M 650-710
Financial aid: 40%
Applicants: 4,600
Accepted: 27%
Enrolled: 41%
Application deadline: Dec. 15
Financial aid application deadline: Dec. 31
Tuition: $30,475 (comprehensive fee)
Core curriculum: No

Been through the Wars

Middlebury College was for years a good liberal arts college in the New England tradition, but it suffered under a reputation as a rich kids' paradise, complete with its own ski area and mountainous surroundings worthy of a resort. The professors were known to be dedicated, but the student body seemed more interested in personal pleasure than in the life of the mind. Notes one professor: "Our main debit is our reputation of being a club. Middlebury's primary challenge is to emphasize the importance of intellectual work."

Over the past several years Middlebury has labored mightily to meet this challenge, and has had a good deal of success. Today the student who matriculates at Middlebury will find a rigorous curriculum taught by some extremely gifted and dedicated professors in a setting that is the quintessence of New England.

This move into the world of top-notch colleges was not accomplished without a few philosophical battles — not all of which were won unanimously, or finally. Still, the supporters of traditional education who have held out against radicalizing forces have every right to feel proud of the result. Even though it is forced to compete with reputable schools in its own region of the country, Middlebury has done an admirable job in preserving a sense of the importance of the liberal arts. While no small number of faculty members would be happy to see the college become more ideological, they are, for now, balanced and counteracted by scholars who have won what today amounts to a rare victory in academia.

Academic Life: Finding the Teachers

Middlebury has no core curriculum, instead allowing its students to choose courses from seven out of eight distribution areas: literature, arts, philosophical and religious studies, historical studies, physical and life sciences, social analysis, foreign language, and deductive reasoning and analytical processes. Though this setup is hardly a shining example of the liberal arts tradition, Middlebury makes up for the looseness of its requirements with fine teaching. Of course, it is also possible to fulfill the distribution requirement with politicized options. But, as one professor says, "With careful choosing and good advice, a student can obtain an excellent broad, liberal arts education."

In addition to the seven classes that make up this requirement, students must also complete a three-course "cultures and civilizations" mandate. As is the case for the distribution courses, the students make the choices here, though they must come up with one class on the United States, one on Europe, and one on "a part of the world other than the U.S. or Europe."

"We have some pretty loose and undemanding cultural literacy requirements," says one professor, who along with other faculty is working on a proposal for a required humanities core. Faculty interviewed for this guide were divided as to whether Middlebury needs a core, not because they weren't committed to the liberal arts, but because some saw the present curriculum as strong enough to accomplish the goals of such an education.

Middlebury also requires two intensive writing seminars for all students. The first must be taken during the student's first semester on campus, and the second falls prior to the end of the sophomore year. The first-year seminar is taught via a thematic, interdisciplinary method, and the instructor chooses the theme and reading list. Each student's instructor for that seminar becomes his adviser for his first year at Middlebury.

Though many of the writing seminars are very well taught, some focus on topics more likely to be found in a radicalized graduate program than in the first semester of college enrollment, in a required set of courses. Instead of classic texts or disciplined scholarship, the first-year seminars have included subjects that likely could not find a place in most of the college's departments. Recently, these more intellectually tangential courses included "Transforming the Earth: The Ecology of Global Change," "Women and Mathematics," a seminar on community volunteerism, and "Queerly Figured in History."

The catalogue description for the latter course reads, in part: "Some figures having the most impact on individuals' thinking in European-based cultures — on the neural pathways encoding how we perceive and the associations we make — were queerly deviant from their society's dominant erotic norms. . . . We shall study their articulations through our own performances to enact their/our 'artistic revolutions.' "

Middlebury's majors — forty-three of them, including five area studies in the international major — involve ten to sixteen courses, making them of slightly more than average bulk. Students can opt for an unusual major known as the "Independent Scholar," in which, according to college literature, "outstanding students with clear educational goals that cannot be fulfilled within the framework of normal departmental requirements may plan their own curricular programs with the assistance of a faculty advisor."

Several special programs are designed to prepare students for professional careers, yet Middlebury offers only the B.A. degree — no B.S. degrees, and no bachelor's degrees in education or other nonacademic subjects. A pre-med course list exists, but not as a major. Other preprofessional programs are cobbled together for students with, say, business or nursing interests, but the same degree requirements that apply to other students also apply to those choosing these paths.

Middlebury operates on a semester schedule, but offers a Winter Term each January. During that month students elect a single, intensive program of study that involves an independent project overseen by a member of the faculty.

Among the best professors at Middlebury are Bob Prigo and Rich Wolfson in physics; Murray Dry and Paul Nelson in political science; Kristen Powell in art history; Robert Hill, Robert Pack, David Price, and Marion Wells in English; John Bertolini in English and drama; and James Ralph and Travis Jacobs in history.

As for the most recommended departments at Middlebury, faculty rate these as the best: history, political science, English and American literature, described as "very strong." Physics, economics, classics, theater, and foreign languages are respectable. More than one-third of the student body majors in the social sciences and history, fully ten percentage points ahead of the average for similar institutions.

Middlebury's English department is best known for its association with the Bread Loaf Writers Conference, a summer program in literature and creative writing it hosts each year. The best Middlebury undergraduates are permitted to enroll in Bread Loaf courses in the summer between their junior and senior years. The conference brings well-known writers to Vermont (and a few other locations) to teach courses and work with individual students. It is an excellent opportunity for students to become acquainted with the world of professional writers, editors, literary agents, and publication.

Even without Bread Loaf the department is strong. "They have as fine an undergraduate creative writing program as you'll find anywhere," a professor says. "It is insisted that all writers be grounded deeply in the Western tradition. English literature here is also very strong." Middlebury is among only a handful of top colleges to still require a Shakespeare class of its English majors, who must also take several period courses and pass a comprehensive senior exam. The Program in Literary Studies has a required reading list drawn from the masterworks of eleven national literatures.

Bread Loaf is not the only summer program for which the college is known. Its summer language schools, founded in 1915, offer students from Middlebury and elsewhere the chance to immerse themselves in one of the eight languages offered each year. Each participant must promise not to speak English during the entire session, and the credits earned can be applied to a Middlebury degree. Even during the regular school year, a large group of students study foreign languages, among other things, at Middlebury: nearly 12 percent of the student body majors in foreign languages and literatures, a rate almost four times the national average.

Some professors caution, however, that Middlebury's reputation for foreign language studies — the program best known outside the campus — is overblown. "The summer programs [in foreign languages] are great, but that's a whole new faculty," one says. Says another: "The irony is that the reputation of the college is built on the language instruction. But language instruction here per se is not that good. Most of their best students are French majors. They're just not good teachers."

Nonetheless, students may put their language skills to work through the Middlebury Schools Abroad program, which offers study in one of several European cities. In addition to the language students, Middlebury's international relations majors also make good use of this program, as well as other college-approved programs in the Far East and Latin America. Closer to home, Middlebury offers semesters in Washington, D.C., or at the Williams College–Mystic Seaport Program in American Maritime Studies, where students delve into coastal history, literature, culture, and oceanography.

Middlebury is also heavily involved in the Center for Northern Studies, located about an hour away in Wolcott, Vermont. Students majoring in geography, environmental studies, or biology and who hear the call of the wild north may spend a semester or a year in residency there. The program involves many field trips in the nearby woods and bogs, as well as a month of field study in northern regions such as Newfoundland, Alaska, or the Scottish Isles.

Environmental studies attract about 5 percent of students, a large number for that field, and Middlebury is noted nationwide for its environmental programs. But, like the college's other acclaimed program, language studies, it's not all it's cracked up to be, according to some on campus. "The administration is promoting this department very hard, and it will be the biggest department very soon," a professor says. "They get the big dollars, and they get a bunch of kids who after four years wonder, 'what did I do?' There's still a battle here over it, because enough of the hard scientists are opposed to it."

Students preferring wood paneling to the actual woods use the Geonomics Institute at Middlebury, described in college literature as "a dynamic international organization of business executives, policy makers, lawyers, bankers, and regional specialists." At the institute, leaders in government, business, and academe hold symposia on economic, political, and social problems — and undergraduates are invited. Recently the institute considered ways to create private-sector economies in the former Soviet Union, East Asia, and Latin America in cooperation with the West.

Despite its strengths, Middlebury has several politicized programs. Chief among these is women's studies, which one professor describes as "very weak with almost no majors, and everyone is afraid to debate it." The program does not have a lot of respect on campus, and the administration is not afraid to stand up to it; according to another professor, a radical member of the department was recently approved for reappointment, but the president of the college overrode the decision and fired her.

"There have been efforts to politicize the curriculum, but these efforts for the most part have been successfully resisted," says a professor. "Often, the most politicized courses, a relatively small number, are recognized as such by the students and do not attract large enrollments; usually it's a case of preaching to the choir."

Political Atmosphere: Weathering the Multicultural Storm

Middlebury is a rarity in higher education today in that multiculturalist talk seems to be waning rather than gathering strength. "There's a fair amount of talk about multiculturalism and diversity [but] not as much as there used to be," a professor says. Several years ago the college endured a skirmish over the curriculum, but because several faculty stood up for the principles of liberal learning, the most politically correct proposals were defeated. For example, the required reading list for English majors disappeared temporarily several years ago, but has since been brought back.

It seems that Middlebury has pursued a more reasoned version of diversity than that found at some of its competitors. "Multiculturalism is such an elusive term," says another professor. "Nathan Glazer has recently argued that we are all multiculturalists now, and his assessment probably defines campus life at Middlebury. We value diversity here. There is no question that the trend at Middlebury is to cultivate a greater awareness of traditions outside of the U.S. and western Europe."

Middlebury has also toned down an early 1990s version of a speech code described by one faculty member as "absolutely atrocious." The original code was employed briefly on campus before the faculty voted in a more sensible version. However, one professor who refused to comply with the rules of the original code was not offered a position the following year; he was, though, reinstated shortly after the new code was adopted, a faculty member reports. "Things are better now," a professor says. "We've turned the corner, partly because of the organizations that have taken [the cause of free speech] up." The current policy contains enough qualifications and protections that "it does not seem to be too powerful a censoring force," another faculty members says. "Of course, how much self-censoring it produces is difficult to say."

The college tends to look for more politicized candidates when filling an opening on the faculty, but the appointment of ideologues is often blocked by individual departments. "It's a political battle every time they go through a search," says one professor. "But some of us are determined to hire a real scholar instead of an ideologue. . . . The gratification is that the students know it."

According to professors, the college puts a great deal of stock in a professor's publishing record, but also considers his teaching abilities when making tenure decisions. "Excellent teaching is an absolute at Middlebury," says a professor. "Substantial publishing is required for tenure. In general now, a candidate for tenure needs to have a book published or under contract with a reputable press." College president John McCardell Jr. has been known to intervene and deny tenure to professors with insufficient publications, professors say.

For their part, students abide by the honor system as a condition of matriculation. Under that system all quizzes, tests, and finals are unproctored. At the conclusion of each, students must write and sign the following statement: "I have neither given nor received unauthorized aid on this examination." The student-managed Judicial Council hears allegations of code violations, and penalties can be as severe as indefinite suspension from the college.

Student Life: Sharing a "Common System"

Faculty at Middlebury tend to become involved in the lives of their students. The college recently instituted a "common system" (similar to the college system at Yale University), in which students and faculty are assigned to communities (not actual residential communities in this case) to share cultural and "fellowship" experiences beyond the normal rampages of a typical college student weekend and "night off." The common system replaced the Greek system of fraternities and sororities and, according to a faculty member, "offers students social options beyond weekend drinking bouts." This is especially important because of Middlebury's rural setting, giving students a structural kind of living that makes the formation of friends easier than the typical "cliquishness" of Greek life. This system is still developing in terms of its residential possibilities, but on the whole it seems to be an excellent way for students and faculty to relate to one another as adults, as one professor puts it. In turn, it is highly successful in attracting the best and most mature people, thus determining what will most likely be an excellent program in the future as well.

Middlebury, Vermont, is a very small, isolated town of eight thousand people. It is two and a half hours from Montreal, four from Boston and Hartford, and around five from New York City. Because of this, the manner in which students and faculty interact is even more important than at urban campuses — there really is no other game in town. A faculty member says that relationship is "always predicated on the belief that the faculty and students can approach each other as adults." The campus hosts, according to the college viewbook, "four hundred films, one hundred twenty-five video presentations, one hundred professional or student concert and dance performances, twenty theatrical productions, twenty readings of fiction or poetry, ten gallery exhibitions, ninety dances and parties, and five hundred club meetings" each year.

The student body of about 2,000 will increase to around 2,350 over the next several years if college projections are correct. Middlebury intends to hire additional professors to keep up with the increase in enrollment, and plans call for the student-teacher ratio to remain around its current level, approximately eleven-to-one. The new faculty positions are earmarked for what are already the college's most popular and well-known programs, including literature, language study, international studies, and environmental studies. With the increase in the student body will come major construction projects, including a new science center, a new dining hall, new dorms, and an expansion of Starr Library (already home to about 1 million items).

The landscape around Middlebury is a gorgeous valley, situated between the Adirondacks to the west and the Green Mountains to the east; naturally, many students pursue outdoor activities in their free time. But the college also offers numerous student organizations, the best of which are reported to be the International Students Organization, the Political Forum, the Thomas Fellowship, the Christian Fellowship, and the Newman Club. Like most colleges of any size, Middlebury also has the usual gamut of radical student groups, but these are not considered disruptive to the community.

Both students and faculty look forward to Winter Carnival, a three-day event with ski trips, parties, concerts, and ice shows. No one need travel very far to ski: Middlebury is not only close to, but *owns* the 800-acre Snow Bowl ski area near the Bread Loaf campus. Snow Bowl is the largest college-owned ski facility in the nation.

Of course, both alpine and Nordic skiing figure in Middlebury's intercollegiate sports programs, as does ice hockey, a sport in which the school has won three consecutive NCAA Division III national titles. More common (i.e., warm-weather) sports are also offered, including baseball, basketball, cross-country, field hockey, football, golf, tennis, squash, and soccer. Club teams compete in crew, cricket, cycling, martial arts, rugby, softball, and other sports.

UNIVERSITY OF MINNESOTA–TWIN CITIES

Office of Admissions
Director of Admissions
University of Minnesota
Minneapolis, MN 55455
(612) 625-2008
www1.umn.edu/tc/

Total enrollment: 37,615
Undergraduates: 23,240
SAT Ranges (Verbal/Math): V 480-580, M 520-600
Financial aid: N/A
Applicants: 13,270
Accepted: 62%
Enrolled: 53%
Application deadline: Rolling admissions
Financial aid application deadline: Feb. 15
Tuition: $4,268 in-state; $11,315 out-of-state
Core curriculum: No

Progressives on the Prairies

Founded in 1851, the University of Minnesota–Twin Cities is situated on more than two thousand acres and is one of the largest campuses in the country, with an undergraduate enrollment topping twenty-four thousand and a total student body of close to thirty-eight thousand. Because of its size, the U of M can be an anonymous and overwhelming place. This is a particular danger for students with a more traditional cast of mind, for they will find themselves surrounded by scores of politicized faculty, courses, programs, and student organizations.

Known as the "Land of Ten Thousand Lakes," Minnesota has a strong regional flavor, popularized by Garrison Keillor's radio program *A Prairie Home Companion*. But these days students at the University of Minnesota are more apt to encounter radical activists than staunchly conservative Lutheran farmers. Because of the powerful influence of this progressive state university, the St. Paul/Minneapolis area has been rechristened "Land of Ten Thousand Liberals" by some conservative wags.

"The U of M is one of the most politically correct campuses in the nation," notes one professor, who continues: "It has relentlessly and aggressively pushed the entire 'PC' agenda: affirmative action, multiculturalism, radical feminist studies, separate minority facilities, and so forth." Unlike many institutions, the university does not try to mask its radical agenda and ideological predilections. In a recent bulletin for the College of Liberal Arts, for instance, the only photo advertising the college's humanities programs is that of a young female student eagerly taking notes while another young woman (either a junior faculty member, graduate teaching assistant, or fellow student) fills the chalkboard with trendy theory jargon like "re/presentation."

Academic Life: Uniformly Diverse

Students enrolling in the College of Liberal Arts (CLA) can choose from a wide range of majors — everything from traditional disciplines such as English, philosophy, and history to more obscure and/or recently established programs like Chicano Studies, Cultural Studies and Comparative Literature, and Scandinavian Languages and Finnish. In addition, students can apply for a "Bachelor of Individualized Studies" degree (BIS), in which they design their own major and submit it for the approval of two or more faculty advisers. Most programs at Minnesota are on the quarter system, and a typical course carries four or five credits.

The university has revised its general education requirements for liberal arts students in recent years, and some confusion has resulted, as students enrolled under the former requirements pursue their education alongside those attempting to fulfill the new ones. Liberal arts students are now required to take three courses each in arts and humanities, history and social sciences, and physical and biological sciences, as well as one course in mathematical thinking. There are also writing and foreign language requirements.

This "Diversified Core Curriculum," as it is rather oxymoronically labeled by the university, can be fulfilled by taking courses so disparate and tangential to a traditional liberal education that they can hardly be designated a "core" of liberal studies. In addition to division courses, students must complete courses in a variety of "Designated Themes of Liberal Education." The descriptive justification for these themes is dominated by ideology: "Cultural Diversity" ("understanding of the roles gender, ethnicity, and race play in structuring the human experience"); "International Perspectives" ("in which you are part of a rapidly changing global environment dominated by the internationalization of most human endeavors"); "Environment" ("interdependence of the biophysical systems of the natural environment and human social and cultural systems"); and "Citizenship and Public Ethics" ("your present and future civic relationships and your obligations to the community").

According to one professor, "In the past five years the familiar General Education program has been scrapped and students are now required to take six of their ten required general education courses in a multicultural/minority context." The former curriculum had been no better, requiring a course in U.S. cultural pluralism (focusing on "issues of social and cultural diversity, with special emphasis on issues of race and ethnicity") as well as a world studies requirement (focusing on Asian, African, Latin American, and American Indian cultures). In neither the former nor revised general education requirements is a survey course in Western civilization or U.S. history mandated.

The result of this shift to multicultural general education requirements has been a rapid politicization and intellectual dilution of the curriculum. In order to obtain high enrollment for introductory courses, many departments are now offering obscure, tangential, or politically motivated courses to undergraduates in lieu of the traditional general surveys that once gave students a thorough grounding in the liberal arts. "There are probably 50-60 courses which fulfill the 'cultural diversity' requirement," notes one student. And one professor relates that "the former program has become devastated as departments compete for students. Instead of a standard Introduction to American Lit, for example, students will take such courses as Literature of American Minorities, Introduction to Women's Literature, The Harlem Renaissance, and so forth, since this satisfies the multicultural/minority requirement." There has been virtually no discussion of general education requirements since the multicultural emphasis was introduced, and traditionalist faculty lament the destructive impact it is having on undergraduate education at the U of M. "What is particularly galling is that there has been no reexamination of the appalling consequences. . . . The system is in place and is likely to remain so."

Unfortunately, much of the U of M curriculum has been eroded by the domination of ideological agendas, according to conservative students and faculty. "This is especially true of the College of Liberal Arts," notes one professor. "However, it is a mistake to generalize about the university as a whole because large sections of it — the hard sciences, the medical school — are relatively free of these developments." Indeed, students and faculty alike praise the chemical engineering and materials science programs, which also enjoy top national rankings. Most science departments are highly regarded, with the biochemistry and microbiology programs being described as "outstanding" by one professor. Economics has a strong reputation, but students should be prepared for enormous class sizes. Journalism and political science are also recommended. The Law School is considered far to the left.

Literary studies at Minnesota are particularly disappointing. English is characterized as "a disaster" by one professor, despite the existence of a few remaining excellent teachers. The English department does offer many courses with traditional titles and reading lists, and all majors are still required to take a survey of English literature and a course in Shakespeare. But undergraduate survey courses satisfy only the "Literature" category of the general education requirements, while courses like "Gender and the English Language" or "Literature of American Minorities" also satisfy the "Cultural Diversity" requirement, so nonmajors are very likely to take the latter. Undergraduates could take a course in "Figures in Anglophone Literature: Ken Saro-Wiwa," for which the description reads:

> We will read some of Saro-Wiwa's writing, and will discuss his experiment with "broken English" in "Sozaboy," but this will not be a purely literary course. I welcome students from a variety of disciplines, and I want to explore the whole of Saro-Wiwa's "case", including such questions as: the role of the various human rights organizations that were finally unable to stop his execution; cultural survival for small ethnic groups like the Ogoni; failure of the post-colonial state in Nigeria, including Saro-Wiwa's depiction of the Nigerian civil war; the effect of the post-colonial "nation" on marginal groups; the place of multinationals like Shell in the destruction of the Ogoni and their environment; the effectiveness of Saro-Wiwa's tactics of resistance; the politics of international responses to his execution.

Yet, while students could take this course on an arguably obscure Anglophone writer, not one course devoted exclusively to the works of Geoffrey Chaucer or John Milton was listed in the spring 1997 course offerings.

Comparative literature, French, and the Department of Discourse and Society are all dominated by advocates of "cutting-edge" theory ("the latest fads from Paris") and a multicultural agenda. Indeed, Cultural Studies and Comparative Literature, grouped into a single department, is perhaps the department most driven by leftist ideological assumptions. Students majoring in this program must take introductory courses in "Rhetoric, Power, Desire" and "Knowledge, Persuasion, and Power," as well as "advanced" courses selected from such categories as "Social Construction of the Subject," in which students will analyze "gender, sexuality, race and class as discursive constructions productive of human subjectivity and cultural difference." Indeed, it is not difficult to find courses in these radicalized departments that are largely void of intellectual content. "Sexualities — from Perversity to Diversity" and "Gay Men and Homophobia in American Culture" are but two of the recent offerings in Cultural Studies and Comparative Literature; the course description for the former reads as follows: "Contemporary constructions of Western sexuality (heterosexuality, homosexuality, lesbianism, romance, pornography, erotic domination, and lynching), institutions that constitute or compel them, and moral discourses. Materials include fiction, personal narratives, manuals, ads, journalism, and scholarship and theory from several disciplines."

As far as class size is concerned, one student notes that his language classes were small, with from fifteen to twenty students on average. Other introductory classes had upwards of two hundred students, but were broken into smaller "recitation" groups led by graduate students. Honors students often take upper-level courses in their major department along with graduate students. Despite its considerable size, advising at the university seems to be adequate for most students, and with a little effort undergraduates find their professors approachable. Under the U of M adviser system, students must see their advisers every quarter, and can also take advantage of walk-in advising through their major department. "Professors are pretty accessible, especially with e-mail," notes one undergraduate.

Despite its emphasis on research, the university still retains many faculty who are committed to their teaching. One professor notes: "There are many outstanding professors, both as teachers and scholars and occasionally both." For students seeking a more rigorous educational experience, the honors program in the CLA is highly recommended. "Any student who can get in, should," notes one professor. "Class sizes are small, and the instructors mainly excellent."

Ultimately, undergraduates at Minnesota will continue to get the short end of the stick, as resources and energy are predominantly focused on research and graduate and professional education rather than teaching or the liberal arts. As one professor laments, "Despite the usual ceremonial statements about dedication to teaching, the university has little interest in undergraduate education. It defines itself as 'research oriented,' which inevitably means concentration on graduate study and research."

Political Atmosphere: Woe unto You

According to insiders, the administration at the University of Minnesota–Twin Cities is primarily concerned with pursuing politically correct policies and garnering favorable public attention. "The main priorities for the past decade," according to one professor, "have been to satisfy the demands of women and minorities, to hire as many as can reasonably be done given the constraints of minimum qualifications, and to attract as much favorable publicity for itself as possible." Tenure appears to be based largely on publications, research, and political factors rather than excellence in teaching. "Of course there are teaching awards," quips one professor, "but that is mere window dressing." Another faculty member notes: "I have good reason to believe that search committees are highly politicized. The pressure is constantly on to hire more women and minorities."

Tensions between faculty and the Minnesota Board of Regents have been particularly high in recent years, as the regents sought to implement a new set of policies regarding tenure. According to the *Chronicle of Higher Education*, the controversy initially began in the spring of 1996, when the regents unveiled their ideas regarding tenure, which included provisions for cutting the base salaries for tenured professors with poor performance records and the ability to fire tenured professors "if their programs were eliminated or restructured and the university was unable to retrain or reassign them."

In the fall of 1996 faculty organizers garnered enough support to hold a referendum on forming a collective-bargaining unit, but professors voted 692 to 666 against the union in February 1997. After plenty of ill will on both sides, faculty politicking, and mediation by Governor Arne Carlson, the tenure dispute ended in the spring of 1997 when the regents backed down on their stringent tenure code. The experience was an exhausting, if ultimately heady, one for faculty opponents of the code, many of whom put into play the radical organizing and protesting tactics usually reserved for their student disciples. After the Faculty Senate approved the revised tenure code, professors sang an adapted version of an antiwar ballad they dubbed the "Tenure Song," according to the *Chronicle*.

In the midst of the tenure dispute, then University of Minnesota president Nils Hasselmo announced that he would step down to return to his faculty position. The university has thus recently ushered in a new president and dean of the CLA, and although their public statements have been "the usual boilerplate about excellence in teaching and research," the verdict is still out on their actual leadership and vision for the university.

There is no formal speech code at the U of M, but, as one professor notes, "woe unto any student who strays from the straight and narrow in speech or writing." There have been some well-publicized incidents of discriminatory behavior, notably an attempt a few years ago to prevent the student Republican group from distributing materials critical of President Clinton and the Democratic administration during Freshman Week. "There was a public outcry and the university had to back down," notes one professor. According to one student, the university is continually trying to put through formal "sensitivity training" in freshman orientation.

There are numerous political clubs at Minnesota, most of them liberal. Recognized groups include the Association of Gay, Lesbian, Bisexual, and Transgender Student Organizations and Their Friends; Minnesota College Republicans; Minnesota Public Interest Research Group; Student Organization for Animal Rights (SOAR); and Students against Fee Excess. The campus Republican Club is fairly active and visible. In the fall of 1996 several members of the group demanded the removal of a poster of Planned Parenthood founder Margaret Sanger from the main library, arguing that she was a racist who had spoken at Ku Klux Klan rallies. They also were critical of birth control literature distributed from the campus student center, which encouraged students to "Be Like Margaret Sanger." A *Chronicle of Higher Education* story noted that campus feminists dismissed the Republican Club members' demands, arguing that the group members "are against birth control altogether."

As one faculty member notes, "The campus paper is way over on the left and it is very influential." Speakers on campus are also predominantly liberal, and, according to students and faculty, conservative speakers are rare and have been shouted down in campus appearances.

Student Life: Cold Landscape, Warm Heart

The Twin Cities campus is actually two campuses, one in Minneapolis where most liberal arts students take courses, and one about three miles away in St. Paul for students studying agriculture, biology, human ecology, natural resources, and veterinary medicine programs. The "East Bank" area of the Minneapolis campus is the most attractive, boasting the university's original buildings and traditional architecture. One student describes it as a "pretty campus" and praises its proximity to the Twin Cities as its most viable social feature.

Indeed, in recent years the St. Paul/Minneapolis area has earned national recognition as a highly "livable" area, a peculiarly Midwestern blend of cosmopolitan vitality and historic charm. Those of a more artsy bent have found the local music and theater scene to have much to offer, while the Minneapolis Institute of Art, Walker Art Center, and Minnesota Museum of Art serve up more traditional cultural fare. As one professor notes, "The Twin Cities of Minneapolis/St. Paul are a treasure house of cultural resources: theater, music, museums, and so forth — and all easily accessible."

There are numerous extracurricular clubs on campus, centered around everything from ballroom dancing to fencing, chess, juggling, tae kwon do, paintball, and cycling. About three-quarters of the students hail from Minnesota, and despite the wide range of minority and ethnic groups on college campuses these days, the university has to be one of the few in the country with a Norwegian student organization.

On a campus so large, it would be unusual if athletics were not conducted on a grand scale as well. The Minnesota Golden Gophers field Big Ten teams in ten women's and eleven men's varsity sports. The football team plays in the vast Hubert H. Humphrey Metrodome, sharing that venue with the Minnesota Vikings and Twins.

If you're looking for a location that offers year-round fun in the sun, the University of Minnesota–Twin Cities may not be for you. Although plenty of outdoor activities are available to students, such as rollerblading, sailing, and cycling, the cities' northern clime makes ice skating and cross-country skiing the activities of choice during much of the year. "The winters are brutal and very long," notes one professor. Still, opportunities abound for dipping into cafes or bookstores for a hot drink, studying, or socializing in the neighboring commercial districts, such as the "Dinkytown" area on the campus's northwest edge.

In general, the intellectual landscape of undergraduate education at the U of M has been so thoroughly politicized, and traditional liberal studies have become — in the university's *lingua franca* — so "marginalized," that it is a formidable prospect for entering undergraduates to piece together a true liberal education, at least from the general education offerings. As one professor notes, "When 'Destruction of the

Brazilian Rain Forest' will satisfy the science requirement, why take a tough course like biology?" Still, the sheer size of the school ensures that, at least for the short term, some good professors, courses, and programs remain. The key to accessing them is determination and resourcefulness. "It is easy for a determined student to find out who has won awards for excellence in teaching, which courses actually teach something, which professors really care about their students."

MOREHOUSE COLLEGE

Office of Admissions
830 Westview Drive, SW
Atlanta, GA 30314-3773
(404) 215-2632
(800) 851-1254
www.morehouse.edu/

Total enrollment: 2,855
Undergraduates: 2,855
SAT Ranges (Verbal/Math): V 460-580, M 456-584
Financial aid: 77%
Applicants: 3,714
Accepted: 45%
Enrolled: 19%
Application deadline: Feb. 15
Financial aid application deadline: Apr. 1
Tuition: $7,430
Core curriculum: No

The Morehouse Man

While Washington, D.C., may be the nation's capital, Atlanta, Georgia, is widely regarded as the capital of black America, and with good reason. Not only is the city famous as the "cradle of the civil rights movement," and as a dynamic center for international trade, but it has proven to be a major arena for the development of black leadership in business, academia, and government.

As the nation's "only historically black, all-male, four-year liberal arts college," Morehouse College has been a major contributing factor to Atlanta's success. Founded in Augusta, Georgia, in 1867 as the Augusta Institute in order to "prepare black men for ministry and teaching," the college was moved to Atlanta in 1879 and in 1913 became Morehouse College.

Morehouse's alumni roster reads like a list of the most famous and successful black men of this century. Foremost of these, of course, is Dr. Martin Luther King Jr., whose memory is prominently honored on campus by the Martin Luther King Jr. International Chapel. But the alumni roster also numbers former secretary of Health and Human Services Louis Sullivan, filmmaker Spike Lee, actor Samuel Jackson, *Jet* magazine associate publisher Robert Johnson, and former Atlanta mayor Maynard Jackson, all of whom (despite their differences) share in the near-mythic identity of the "Morehouse Man" and the attendant "Morehouse Mystique." Accordingly, unlike at many small liberal arts colleges, a sense of pride and decorum pervades the atmosphere at Morehouse, where many young men wear coats and ties to class and where one professor from the North confessed, "When I first arrived, I was called 'sir' so often I thought it was part of my name."

Perhaps Morehouse's climate of respect is due to the fact that — again, unlike other colleges that have wandered from their roots, and whose identities are in continual evolution — it embraces a keen sense of its history, in both religious and secular arenas. Though the college is independent of any religious body, it maintains close ties to the historically black churches, and there's a quality to the campus rhetoric, in official publications and campus landmark inscriptions, that can be described as nothing less than inspirational. Furthermore, the very campus encompasses the highest point of Atlanta, where the Battle of Atlanta was fought during the Civil War, and underneath Graves Hall, at the hill's summit, black Confederate soldiers are buried.

That black Confederates are buried in the heart of the campus is an unintentional but resonant irony for those who maintain that the placidly traditional face of the institution covers a significant degree of internal turmoil. One professor who has since left Morehouse noted that the college has been in a "kind of malaise," coasting on the reputation of its illustrious graduates and stuck in the era of Benjamin Mays, the famous educator and legendary president of the school during the forties, who greatly influenced Dr. King. Progress, however, did not keep pace with time. "My assessment," this same professor stated regarding the Morehouse of ten or twenty years ago, "was that there was a great discrepancy between what Mays had created and what one would want [of a college now]."

Some critics have charged the college with "academic incest" in hiring Morehouse Men to chair departments and programs. Others have complained that the administration has maintained an official "climate of secrecy" regarding decisions that concern both faculty and students. Even during those years, however, "the benefits [of a Morehouse education] far outweighed the problems," one parent held.

"The whole symbolic notion of the 'Morehouse Man' was still in place," inspiring young black men to confidence and academic attainment, even when other areas at the college needed work — in 1994, for example, Nima Warfield became the college's first Rhodes scholar. And since the 1995 appointment of Dr. Walter E. Massey as president, Morehouse has begun a process of self-evaluation and modernization and, in the words of the *Brief History of Morehouse*, "embraced the challenge of preparing for the 21st century and the goal of becoming one of the nation's best liberal arts colleges."

Academic Life: Growing into the Crown

In keeping with the decorous campus demeanor, where signs at the entrances of buildings request that "Gentlemen: Please remove your hats," one distinction of Morehouse's curriculum is that it is, comparatively speaking, highly structured. While the core curriculum of most colleges consists merely of loose distribution requirements that give students considerable latitude in choosing courses, Morehouse requires a series of specific courses. In addition to the requisite English composition course, students must complete two prescribed courses in world literature, which set Western classics and genres alongside African-American classics and works of other cultures.

A similar approach obtains with regard to the history requirements: students must take the required "World History: Topical Approaches" sequence, in which, according to the college catalogue, "One-third attention [is] given to the United States, including the African-American experience; one-third attention given to Europe; one-third attention given to Africa." Such a seemingly balanced approach has not always been popular. A faculty member who has taught the courses complained of the sequence as little more than a "pastiche of Western civilization and African civilization" that was "poorly thought-out. . . . What it turned out to be was a course where one would go in and teach his or her expertise." The caliber of the material has also received criticism. Regarding the sequence, the same faculty member said he'd heard students remark that "they'd had more interesting classes in high school."

Finally, with respect to the mandated courses, all students must take the "Biological Science" for nonmajors course, while biology majors must take the two-semester "General Biology" sequence. Similarly, students must take the introductory "Physical Science" course from the physics department, which emphasizes, in addition to basic principles of physics, "the interplay between technology and science, and the influence of technology in the world community." In addition, the catalogue course entry notes that "the approach is primarily conceptual, and physics is presented as a historical and humanistic development of the human intellect." Such a course description bears witness to a couple of the phenomena with which Albert Massey, himself a well-known physicist, has been credited in his tenure as president:

an increased emphasis on real-life application of pure science to the business world, and a recognition of the interdisciplinary nature of study.

In mathematics, students have to elect two out of four possible courses in order to fulfill a sequence requirement; there is a track for nonscience majors as well as one geared toward business and engineering.

In language, Morehouse men must advance to and complete six hours at the intermediate level of a modern foreign language, which choices include French, Spanish, German, Japanese, Russian, and — given the college's strong connections to African scholars and disciplines — Swahili. There is no classics department, a rather large gap for a liberal arts institution, nor are any classical languages available. The most extensive departments are of course French and Spanish, both of which offer electives in French and Spanish "Diaspora" literature alongside the full complement of traditional readings.

Another core curricular area in which students have some latitude in course choices is humanities, where they must take three courses out of a list of eleven. For some reason the list is heavily weighted toward music courses, with only two offerings of "Introduction to Religion" and "Introduction to Philosophy." In social science, students must choose two out of seventeen courses, which include the popular "Men in Society" in sociology, taught by Larry Crawford, and psychology professor Timothy Moore's "Psychology of the African-American Experience," which is one of the "favorite social science requirements."

While neither a traditionalist academic nor a leftist radical would be happy with Morehouse's approach (the aforementioned "radical" professor registered dissatisfaction about how "conservative" and "pretty religious" the college is), the strength of Morehouse's core is its coherence and the very fact that it is a common experience to which all students subscribe. The other core requirements seem to have as their end the formation of students into ideal "Morehouse Men" — there is even an "Oral Communication Effectiveness" requirement, which focuses on business or public speaking, activities in which these future leaders are expected to excel.

The college is sensitive to student learning or opportunity deficits, and has, for example, "since 1939 . . . sponsored a Reading Program for freshmen and upperclassmen who need and/or desire to improve their reading skills and abilities in college level reading." Extensive tutoring is also available in the Frederick Douglass Commons, a large and quiet study center at the middle of the dormitory quadrangle.

There is a physical education requirement, in addition, but the final and most characteristic feature of the core is that students earn at least twenty-four units of "Crown Forum" during their matriculation. Crown Forum is basically chapel, though its focus appears to be inspirational and empowering rather than directly theological. A "college-wide" assembly, Crown Forum meets eight times a year, which means that a student must log a full three years of attendance in order to fulfill the requirement. Its title derives from a statement by theologian and Morehouse alumnus Howard Thurman that has become part of the Morehouse mythos, and which reads, "A crown is placed over our heads that for the rest of our lives we are trying to grow tall enough to wear." One student confesses, however, that "Some students feel it's a waste of time" — there is a certain cynicism in some quarters about the college's ever-present "Morehouse mystique" rhetoric.

Outstanding professors at Morehouse include: Alton Hornsby Jr. and Marcellus C. Barksdale in history; Harold Braithwaite, Timothy Moore, Duane Jackson, and Madge Willis in psychology; Aaron Parker in religion and philosophy; Aakhut Em Bak in physics; Emmanuel O. Onifade in accounting; Melvin Rahming in English; and Larry Crawford in sociology.

Among the strongest departments are psychology, religion ("but not Philosophy," a self-confessed radical claims — the two disciplines are grouped together but are considered separate departments), history, sociology ("on the verge of being strong," according to one professor), and business administration.

As far as specifically academic politicization goes, the main concern at Morehouse in the past has been the desire for a more African American–centered curriculum, but it wasn't until President Massey arrived that the college instituted an African-American studies major. Most courses, however, had been already specifically geared to the needs of an African-American student population: "I teach my courses from an African-centered perspective — period," one professor proudly claims, and this seems to be the case with most members of the faculty. The same professor also complains of the philosophy department, of its tendency to be "old school," and that "there isn't any philosophy that comes out of the African tradition."

One distinctive way in which some Morehouse faculty attempt to make their courses "African-centered" is to mandate community service hours as part of course requirements. In one course fifteen hours of community service were stipulated for the semester, roughly equaling one hour per week, in addition to other assignments. While traditionalists might complain that such requirements only pad a syllabus, one professor maintains that the practice helps to fulfill the college's mission: "I came to Morehouse because the mission statement says to build leaders for the community."

The "community," at Morehouse, is not far away — although the campuses of Morehouse and the other Atlanta University Center colleges are manicured and safe, this is not the case in general with the West End neighborhood in which they are located. "Some of the worst drug trade and highest incarceration rates [in Atlanta] are in the area around the Atlanta University Center," the same professor says. Such a requirement makes coursework "real," he explains, because the students then "have to go out and . . . put what they know about black folks into action." Now the practice has "become normative among about one-third of the faculty," and is a growing phenomenon. It is still somewhat controversial, though, and appears to predominate in departments such as sociology and psychology that naturally lend themselves to social activism.

Beyond the given that an "African-centered" slant to the curriculum more or less exists throughout the departments, Morehouse otherwise appears to have much less political and theoretical strife than other liberal arts institutions. Whereas at most colleges the English department is the site of great political high jinks, arcane critical theory, or touchy-feely therapeutics, Morehouse's English offerings largely consist of service courses. The one course that has even the faintest hint of trendiness, a post-colonial literature course entitled "The West Indian Novel," is taught by the highly respected professor Melvin Rahming, who is universally acclaimed for being challenging, hard, and fair — "a phenomenal teacher; a wise man," remarks one of his colleagues. One student says he knows "a lot of Seniors" who, if they could get into Dr. Rahming's class, would "rather take a C as opposed to taking another course and getting an A."

The reason for the relatively apolitical academic atmosphere at Morehouse is unclear: a former faculty member says there is simply "not that kind of debate," but rather there has tended in the past to be "a lot of pressure [on the faculty] to conform and be quiet." There apparently are old-style radicals at Morehouse — not everyone is wildly enamored of the free market. However (and especially since Albert Massey has become president), Morehouse has strengthened its already excellent corporate connections, and its curriculum emphasizes the global nature of business.

As would seem proper to the nation's only all-male, historically black college, a sense of community spirit pervades all programs, but a couple are particularly notable. Since 1990 Morehouse has been home to the Morehouse Research Institute, whose stated objectives are, according to the college's website, to "increase the availability of scholarly work on issues concerning the status of African-American men and boys, and increase the visibility of researchers . . . who work on solutions to problems that threaten not only the vitality of the black community, but also the social and economic health of the nation." As well, under the aegis of the history department, Morehouse is home to the noted and historic *Journal of Negro History*.

Political Atmosphere: Paradoxical

The political atmosphere at Morehouse is paradoxical. Since the college is historically black and male, one might be inclined to regard the campus's political character as left of center. Indeed, as one professor states, there is "almost a proliferation of student organizations focused on the African and black community," but this seems to be a testament to bonds of faith, blood, and loyalty rather than a commitment to ideology. Rather, outside the classroom, the general conclusion of many faculty is that Morehouse men tend to be "so conservative" — "Kids aspire to be bourgeois," the same former faculty member notes.

Gender relations are one area in which Morehouse has been characterized as conservative, and gender has been a hot topic of conversation in the last couple of years. "Morehouse men [have] needed to rethink gender," one professor stresses — there's been "a kind of male identity that smacked of the worst form of patriarchy."

The problem has manifested itself particularly with regard to female faculty members, who have traditionally "felt a little bit uncomfortable" in the midst of this all-male environment. "You don't find many women in prominent positions," one faculty member said of the college in the pre-Massey era, and the general atmosphere led to the creation of an organization called Black Men against Sexism to draw attention to the issue.

Furthermore, the issue of gender is brought even closer to hand because, as part of the Atlanta University Center, Morehouse allows cross-registration, which brings women into the classroom, especially those from nearby sister school Spelman College. A couple of Morehouse men interviewed even echo the sentiments of one student regarding his psychology class: "A lot of students at Spelman . . . come in and bring a lot to the table." Some students, therefore, see a movement toward coeducation as inevitable: "The all-male institution is going to be challenged." Still, faculty response to the prospect consists largely of amusement. "Not unless Sherman marches through Georgia again," quips one. "The alums would probably have a 'conniption fit' if anybody even spoke about it becoming co-ed," seconds another, although he admits the possibility that "in ten years the mentality would be quite different."

Other problems concerning Morehouse's political atmosphere revolve around what many see as the administration's stony refusal to debate controversial issues facing the community. "Morehouse [has] had a horrendous problem with the school newspaper," one professor states, and once even "put it out of business" when it raised some questions the administration didn't want to answer. "The paper was not allowed to publish, under the pretext that a faculty advisor could not be found," he says. Much later, after a savvy faculty member agreed to step in as adviser, the paper went on to "win top prize in two categories at a regional convention." Most dismaying to one professor was the general apathy most students displayed toward the event — the majority "didn't miss the absence of a newspaper," and it "didn't occur to students to raise the issue of due process."

Morehouse does require sensitivity training, and there has been some nebulous controversy on campus concerning homosexual students. One year, it was a matter of comment when "a couple of the guys went out dressed as women" to Freaknik, a black music festival that is held in Atlanta annually. "I know a couple of students on campus who are obviously gay and flamboyant," admits one student, but "on campus they should behave and dress as men." There are also rumblings concerning an incident in which a gay student sexually harassed a fellow (straight) student, but "the heterosexual guy was punished," the same student complains. Another student, however, mentions that while there was "some upheaval" when "a homosexual organization tried to rally support," "there's a large range of acceptance at Morehouse as long as you don't go overboard into the extreme."

We mentioned above that some have charged Morehouse with a tendency toward nepotism in the hiring of faculty and administration, a problem that reached its crest, by all popular accounts, during the administration of Dr. Leroy Keith, Morehouse president from 1987 to 1994. Since Massey's arrival in 1995, however, the college is reported to be putting a premium on hiring talented young scholars who are involved in original research, although the focus remains upon teaching: President Massey himself teaches a class. Everyone, as well, agrees that Morehouse's campaign of modernizing and improving itself would not have occurred without the inspirational example set by Dr. Johnnetta Cole, former president of Spelman College, who led Spelman through a capital campaign and a major program of modernization during the late '80s and the '90s. What Cole was doing was "light years ahead of what Southern black colleges were thinking of at the time," admits one professor, and "Morehouse felt embarrassed." The hiring of Massey, a nationally known figure as well as a Morehouse alumnus, and the burgeoning efforts to modernize are predicated on the "perception that we can do better," one faculty member notes.

Student Life: Brotherhood

"What happens in the classroom is important," student Kozmo Miller of Atlanta is quoted as saying in the college's promotional bulletin, "but it's mostly what happens outside the classroom. . . . Back at the dorms, when there's no one else around but your Morehouse brothers. It's about trust and support, respect and lifelong friendships. You really have to live it to understand it."

Accordingly, the college has a rich campus life, and a multitude of student organizations that serve as the ground for cultivating the close ties and loyalties for which the college is known. Many of these focus on areas of particular and historical interest to black students: there are chapters on campus of both the NAACP and the Southern Christian Leadership Conference, as well as the National Student Support Council for Africa. A surprising number of clubs are available for students from various states, such as the D.C. Metropolitan Club and the Pacific Northwest Club, and many preprofessional and business organizations.

In the realm of religion are the Fellowship of Christian Athletes, a gospel choir, and the Morehouse Gospel Theatre Ensemble, but two Muslim student organizations also exist on campus, one under the aegis of the controversial Nation of Islam. While Christianity is a strong cultural presence at Morehouse, its effects are gentle and diffuse. And, as Muslims are making some strongly evangelistic efforts at Morehouse and in the Atlanta University Center as a whole, playing upon black desires to find in Islam a unified heritage, Muslim influence will likely increase. During the fall of 1997, for example, a sign in the student post office questioned students:

> Did you know that
> nearly all those West and North Africans
> enslaved in the U.S. who could read and write,

spoke, read, and wrote
in Arabic?
Why not follow their example?

In the fall of 1997 the Morehouse College Republicans joined the College Democrats group on the campus political scene. When the founder decided to start the club, he got "a lot of sneers here and there," but went ahead anyway, as "one professor said, 'Do it!' " There are a lot of Republicans around Morehouse, he claims, and "every week I'm getting more inquiries." The Morehouse ethic of brotherhood predominates, and there is apparently a lot of good-natured debate — "Democrats come to our meetings!"

There are two student-run publications on campus: the *Torch*, which is the school yearbook, and the *Maroon Tiger*, the student newspaper. There are intramural sports, in addition to varsity teams in football, basketball, tennis, cross-country, and track and field, which are part of the Southern Intercollegiate Athletic Conference and the NCAA Division II.

The most controversial area of student life concerns the fraternities. There is a strong fraternity tradition at black colleges, most famously illustrated in Morehouse alum Spike Lee's film *School Daze*, but it is the *School Daze* image of the fraternity that Morehouse would like to get away from. Currently "there's only one chartered fraternity," according to a student who entered the college in the early '90s, took some time off due to finances, and later returned, and who thinks the social atmosphere of the college has changed negatively in the meantime.

As of fall 1997, the charters of two of the most famous black fraternities, Kappa Alpha Psi and Alpha Phi Alpha, are suspended. Nationally, several black fraternities have been plagued with legal problems as a result of hazing, but the reason for the Morehouse suspensions is not commonly known, another testament to the college's zealous PR. "It's so hush-hush," the same student says. It is presumed that the suspensions were due to hazing, since "black fraternities aren't really big on drinking." Whatever problems might have occurred as a result of the fraternities' existence, it was they who popularized the "classic image of the Morehouse man — bowties, sport coats, etc.," as well as provided the college's most ritualized social scene.

Since around 1993, however, and especially since the fraternities' absence, this student has seen a turn in the campus demeanor toward more of a Northeastern mode influenced by hip-hop music. "The talk and attitude is very urban now . . . [they're all] hip-hop heads from . . . New York, Philadelphia, and D.C." Now, the bowtie types are "not as visible as they once were." The same student complains: "The guys now don't know what it's like to work real hard during the week and know that on the weekend there's going to be a step show," and also comments, "If there were some way that [the fraternities] could be cleaned up and monitored, I'd personally like to see them return," a sentiment echoed by many Morehouse men.

A final note regarding student life at Morehouse concerns the expense of attending the institution; a number of students interviewed spoke of having dropped out at various times in order to raise money to attend, even though Morehouse has generous funding available. The cost for tuition, room, and board approached $15,230 in 1996-97, cheaper than many comparable liberal arts colleges but impossibly expensive for many. The difficulties students have in attending seem only to increase the loyalty that Morehouse men have for the college.

MOUNT HOLYOKE COLLEGE

Office of Admissions
Director of Admissions
Mount Holyoke College
College Street
South Hadley, MA 01075-1424
(413) 538-2000
www.mtholyoke.edu

Total enrollment: 2,001
Undergraduates: 2,001
SAT Ranges (Verbal/Math): V 576-683, M 561-677
Financial aid: 70%
Applicants: 2,030
Accepted: 65%
Enrolled: 36%
Application deadline: Jan. 15
Financial aid application deadline: Jan. 15
Tuition: $22,200
Core curriculum: No

Holy Cow

In its promotional literature, Mount Holyoke College adamantly defends the institution of the liberal arts college and eloquently promotes the lofty goals of a liberal education. "The liberal arts college defends the right of all to seek knowledge for its own sake, without immediate regard to its utility, and affirms also that the world would suffer without the leaven of those who engage in this pursuit," says one passage.

It is difficult to square this elevated and inspiring language with the increasingly politicized academics at the nation's oldest continuing institution of higher education for women. Although Mount Holyoke still speaks of liberal learning, much of the traditional content of the curriculum has been set aside to make way for issues of race, class, and gender. Both socially and academically, Mount Holyoke is leaning further and further away from traditional liberal arts, and seems intent on training women more to be political activists than freethinking "individuals committed to humane values, capable of rejecting oversimplification of ideology or method, and liberated from narrow definitions of themselves, of others, and of human problems in general," as the college statement of principles claims. And a recent disruption by some students seeking to alter the curriculum and residential structure of the college may have ended the collegiality on which the school has long prided itself.

Academic Life: Talking the Talk

Mount Holyoke's set of distribution requirements appears to span the breadth of the liberal arts disciplines: three courses in the humanities, two in science and mathematics (including at least one lab course), and two in social sciences. Students must also take a foreign language through the intermediate level, take two semesters of a new foreign language, or take a literature course taught in a foreign language.

The college lacks any formal requirement in Western thought or culture, but has a "multicultural perspectives" mandate: one course, chosen by the student, which covers an aspect of the culture of "Africa, Asia, Latin America, the Middle East, and the non-white peoples of North America," according to the college catalogue. The list of courses that fulfill this requirement is long, and includes "Ethnographic Film," "Political Economy of Racism," and "Race, Class, Culture, and Gender in the Classroom."

The catalogue's "Academic Overview" section mentions that "recent core curricular reforms include a course in quantitative reasoning and a year-long course examining Western heritages." But these are only drops in the deep bucket of choices satisfying the distribution requirements, and their resemblance to traditional courses in statistics or Western civilization is slim at best. In "Case Studies in Quantitative Reasoning," which could count as one of the two science and math requirements, students use "basic concepts in statistics and calculus" to study three situations: "witchcraft in seventeenth-century New England; education, occupation, salary, gender, race, and ethnicity in the United States; [and] global population and resources." "Pasts and Presences in the West" (the yearlong interdisciplinary course "in Western heritages") "approaches Western heritages as a series of problems and values to be analyzed and reinterpreted, not as a sequence of ideas and institutions to be surveyed," according to the course description. Although this course had the potential to be a balanced examination of the Western tradition, the "cultural-theory" language of the course description (i.e., "studies each topic as both product and producer of contexts") and the title's intentional distance from traditional understandings of Western heritage (without the "s") suggest otherwise.

Mount Holyoke also seems interested in transforming its traditional liberal arts curriculum into an innovative one in which disciplines such as history and literature are suddenly made interesting or relevant by incorporating a cutting-edge, technological approach. The history department recently introduced a multimedia course, "Computing Applications in History and the Humanities," in which students create "a multilayered study" of Mary Wollstonecraft Shelley's *Frankenstein* using computer software. The course combines faculty lectures and group projects utilizing multimedia equipment, and is billed as having both intellectual and practical value, providing "a concrete lesson in how a liberal arts education can be applied to the work world." At the same time, elsewhere in the catalogue, the college states: "In an age of unprecedented technical competence, the word 'training' is often used interchangeably with 'education.' But the power to form sound opinions and make critical judgments can never be supplied by training alone — and it is precisely these abilities that are crucial to individual self-fulfillment and responsible citizenship."

Traditionally, the focus at Mount Holyoke has not been only on the cultivation of the life of the mind, but on educating young women to reform society. That emphasis continues today. "There is a strong sense of social mission," says one professor, who indicates that students there pursue education not only for self-fulfillment but "for the good of the world." In this sense, the professor adds, Mount Holyoke continues to be "the opposite of a party school . . . there is a place for personal, academic, and social seriousness here."

Mount Holyoke is still considered the most scientific of women's colleges, and historically has been the top producer of female doctors. "Mount Holyoke has served as the standard for other institutions" in being attentive to women in the sciences, one faculty member says. Biology and chemistry are considered strong programs, and the college recently implemented a new, interdisciplinary offering entitled "Unity of Science," a two-semester, team-taught course designed for both scientific and nonscientific students. Students and faculty alike praise the course for its ability to explore the sciences in a rigorous yet unthreatening way. "We want to make science understandable, but we're not willing to let go of real science content or intellectual rigor to reach students," a professor says. The course has been of benefit not only to the one-quarter of Mount Holyoke students majoring in the sciences, but to students from all disciplines, offering a model for integrating liberal learning.

Although Mount Holyoke frequently invokes the spirit of a classical liberal education in its promotional literature, much of the curriculum is politicized. Course titles that begin "Women and . . ." are common. The list of economics courses leans heavily on discussions of racism, sexism, the environment, and "radical political economy." "Labor Economics," for example, focuses on "marriage, fertility, the labor supply of married women, and housework." The politics department offers courses like "The Politics of Patriarchy," which examines "sexism and other oppressions manifested in various sociopolitical arenas." That department also teaches a course called "Invitation to Feminist Theory."

By contrast, the English department (the most popular major at Mount Holyoke) still maintains several solid courses despite the increasing encroachment of feminist theory and multicultural literature. In its promotional literature, the department encourages its majors to select courses "in classical and modern languages and literature, art history, philosophy, religion, and history" that will complement their English studies. Individualized reading programs are also encouraged; the department offers as an example "a core of such works as Homer's *Iliad* and *Odyssey;* Vergil's *Aeneid;* Ovid's *Metamorphoses;* Dante's *Divine Comedy;* Cervantes' *Don Quixote;* and such books of the Bible as Genesis, Psalms, Job, Isaiah, the Gospels, Paul's letters to the Corinthians, and Revelations [sic]." The benefit to the student, according to the department, is that "she will find such works an independent source of enlightenment and pleasure, as well as a great help to her in reading their successors and heirs in English and American literature."

Notable Mount Holyoke professors include Richard Moran in sociology; Joseph Ellis in history; and Anthony Lake, a professor of international relations who was nominated by President Clinton to head the Central Intelligence Agency.

Mount Holyoke classes are usually small — about fifteen per class, according to one student whose largest class was an introductory biology course with about eighty students. The strongest students can participate in a first-year tutorial in which they work in groups of two or three with a faculty member on a research or reading project. There are numerous opportunities for independent research with faculty in both the humanities and the sciences, though these chances come along more often in the latter. Science majors present a research project in a science fair at the end of their senior year.

The college's Junior Year Abroad program is very popular, and many students opt to spend either a semester or a year studying overseas. Mount Holyoke is also a member of the Twelve College Exchange Program, which allows its students to take classes at other member schools (including Amherst, Bowdoin, Connecticut College, Dartmouth, Smith, Trinity, Vassar, Wellesley, Wesleyan, Wheaton [Mass.], and Williams).

Mount Holyoke also offers a "January Term," during which students participate in some form of internship or self-study. This program has earned a reputation for being academically lightweight — "more fun than serious," one student says. "The formal academic aspect of it has faded," says a professor, who adds that because most faculty are preoccupied with administrative duties (hiring, for example) during that time of year, "they don't have time to teach January term."

Political Atmosphere: Roll Over, Mary Lyon

Mount Holyoke ranked second in a recent *Mother Jones* magazine survey of the nation's most activist campuses. "A lot of the students see themselves in leadership roles," a professor says. "There is a long tradition of political involvement here." Students accept the fact that their peers are politically active, but recent events have made it clear that some are uncomfortable with the way in which the political atmosphere of the college is dominated by radicals.

In the spring of 1997 a group of students conducted a sit-in at Mary Lyon Hall to draw attention to a variety of grievances focusing around diversity and financial issues. The protesters had occupied the hall for more than twenty-four hours before Mount Holyoke president Joanne Creighton issued a letter responding to their complaints. The response was an almost complete capitulation: The students got almost everything they asked for, including the immediate allocation of one house for the Asian/Asian-American community and one for the lesbian/bisexual/transgendered community. They even got a concession that the space allocated to these groups would "not include any basement space or basement rooms." The administration also agreed to the creation of an Asian-American studies program; the hiring of at least one tenure-track Asian or Asian-American professor within that program; and the hiring of four permanent chaplains "of varied backgrounds . . . that are able to meet the needs of a spiritually diverse community," according to the *College Street Journal,* a university publication.

The concessions came after the president first told the group that Mount Holyoke would merely investigate or consider the demands for curricular changes and "cultural space," the term for the special housing requested by the protesters. These positions were "clarified" in a matter of hours, and the protesters got what they wanted. The only demand not met was for the ability to pay college bills with a credit card; the college turned that one down on the grounds that it would cost the school $100,000 a year in bank servicing fees.

Initially, all twenty-three students involved in the takeover were suspended from the institution. On appeal, however, the penalties were reduced to "social probation" for one year, meaning that the students could be suspended if they violate the college's "Social Honor Code" within a year of the incident. "I don't think we did anything wrong, so I agree with the lessening of the penalty," one of the protest leaders told the student newspaper, the *Mount Holyoke News.* "I think we were abiding by the honor code." The honor code states, incidentally, that "demonstration of opinion will not take forms that are coercive or seriously disruptive."

President Creighton didn't think the takeover was *prima facie* wrong, either. In a statement, she struck an accommodating tone, noting that "additional ways need to be found for students to have their voices expressed and heard" and predicting that "we will emerge from all of this as a stronger Mount Holyoke, committed to building a community that will be a model for other institutions to follow — after all, that is our legacy."

Yet the entire incident left many students disenchanted with the behavior of their peers. Some disagreed with the protesters' demands, and others abhorred their methods. "A splintered, stratified student body appears among the wreckage of the storm of takeovers, protests, demands, and press conferences," an editorial in the *News* stated. "The melodrama of the past week was inescapable," the editorial continued. "But perhaps even more damaging were the subplots that developed. The closest of friends and roommates became divided over the controversies in which the campus was embroiled. People had angry messages left on dorm whiteboards and e-mail. In general the level of personal interaction on campus was compromised."

The writer says respect and honor — two things for which Mount Holyoke likes to be known — were "painfully absent" in a meeting at the conclusion of the standoff. She describes the protesting students as immature young women unwilling to conduct themselves with civility in public; at the meeting, she writes, "people shouted questions out of turn, interrupted students and administrators, and presumptuously leapt onto the stage and grabbed the microphone so their 'voice could be heard.'"

Even in normal, nonsiege conditions, the most active student groups on campus are the Lesbian/Bisexual Alliance and African/Latina/Native American Sisters in Action. There are small chapters of College Republicans and Collegians for Life, as well as a number of Christian organizations, but the majority of student political groups are liberal. One student recalls a recent lesbian "kiss-in" on campus. And one recent fall, more than three hundred students and faculty gathered under a rainbow arch to "protest homophobia and support lesbian, bisexual, and gay rights," according to a college publication. The crowd also visited the grave of college founder Mary Lyon to decorate it with flowers and rainbow ribbons.

Poor Ms. Lyon seems to get it from all sides. A Founder's Day celebration "featured expanded festivities to hail Mary," the college communications office reported, rather irreverently. Events included a solemn procession to Lyon's grave, complete with candlelight and singing, but also a student-directed play "in which Lyon rose from the dead to protest the possibility that [the college] might go coed," according to the communications office. The play was titled *Mary Is Back for Twentieth-Century Tea and She's Pissed!*

Student Life: Whatever Shall We Do?

Social life at Mount Holyoke does not revolve around partying and dating, but rather focuses on community activities, strong friendships, and dormitory living — which was part of the reason the above-related student takeover of a campus building and the ensuing hard feelings were so disruptive. The majority of students live on campus; dorms are mixed by class; and each dorm has its own kitchen where students typically eat breakfast and lunch with fellow residents. "Most of my social life is in the dorm," says one student, adding that there is a late-night snack in the dining hall each evening.

But the college is uneasy with its rather ho-hum residential nature. "The college is worried about its 'frumpy reputation,'" according to one professor. The definitely un-happening magazine *Town and Country* recently rated Mount Holyoke students' quality of life as the best in a survey.

There is definitely a country-club quality to some of the choices available to students. Mount Holyoke has one of the finest equestrian facilities anywhere in the country — not just in academia — and students may board horses for $425 per month. The college has a Donald Ross–designed golf course as well. The popular intercollegiate and club athletic offerings are considered typically upperclass pursuits — tennis, squash, field hockey, lacrosse, water polo, rugby, croquet, and fencing among them. (Of course, volleyball, basketball, and other common sports are also represented.)

The arts are also popular extracurriculars at Mount Holyoke. More than two hundred students participate in some form of vocal performance, including Concert Choir and several a cappella groups. The college also hosts numerous alternative music performances; under a section entitled "Cultural Opportunities," the catalogue notes that Arrested Development, Toad the Wet Sprocket, and the Smithereens have visited campus recently. Well-known classical performers, like the Tokyo String Quartet, perform at Mount Holyoke too.

The remaining slate of clubs and activities is unusual, possibly unique. Perhaps no other campus offers a Boffing Club, interested in mock sword fighting, and a Lapidary/Silversmith Club listed alongside the Chronic Fatigue Immune Deficiency Syndrome support group and the Helping Overcome Problematic Eating group. Then there is the Lunar Howling Society, which gathers monthly to howl at the moon. "I love wolves, it's a great stress release, and we have a great time," says a member.

Some are concerned that Mount Holyoke women often seem far removed from real-world concerns. A recent discussion of "Racism and Other Forms of Discrimination" held on campus provides some basis for those concerns. As reported in the *Mount Holyoke News,* one professor at the meeting lamented the absence of "cultural space" on campus for all racial and cultural groups. "This campus has very few safe containers for anger," she complained. Another noted that "cultural space allows for a place where people who feel targeted can get together and vent." As examples of being "targeted," a student at the meeting told how uncomfortable she had once felt being the only white person in a restaurant. "Several women talked about feeling marginalized because they were wealthy," according to the *News*. "It bothers me that people assume I wouldn't know what it's like not to have money," confided one troubled student. In light of such statements, it is difficult not to view the typical Mount Holyoke student as a bored, overprivileged young female who turns to "victim politics" for a sense of validation.

Tuition, room, and board for the 1996-97 academic year was almost $30,000, although the college promises to fund the demonstrated financial need of all admitted students, and admission policies are need-blind for 90 to 95 percent of admissions decisions.

NEW YORK UNIVERSITY

Office of Undergraduate Admissions
22 Washington Square North
New York, NY 10011-9191
(212) 998-4515
www.nyu.edu

Total enrollment: 36,060
Undergraduates: 17,060
SAT Ranges (Verbal/Math): V 600-690, M 590-690
Financial aid: 73%
Applicants: 18,990
Accepted: 44%
Enrolled: 32%
Application deadline: Jan. 15
Financial aid application deadline: Jan. 15
Tuition: $22,586
Core curriculum: No

Hip to Be (Washington) Square

New York University (NYU) was founded in 1831 as a traditional liberal arts institution, but with courses in the practical sciences and arts, such as business, law, and medicine. The first president of its board of trustees was Albert Gallatin, once an adviser to President Thomas Jefferson. Gallatin's goal was a university that provided "a rational and practical education for all."

New York City is an excellent place to attempt such an effort — the "all" Gallatin mentions can definitely be found there. NYU is located on Washington Square, in the middle of Greenwich Village, which might be the most likely site in the world to find just about anything one seeks.

Unfortunately for NYU, a little too much of the Village has entered the college. The 17,060 undergraduates there must negotiate the politicized curriculum with the same caution they need to pass safely through the city's streets. "A major influence of the political correctness on the university campus comes from being in the city," a professor says. Moreover, undergraduate classes are often large, and not always well taught.

It must be said, however, that the city has also benefited the university. Opportunities for internships and exchange programs for faculty and students that simply could not be offered in a smaller setting are available at NYU. The university makes good use of its $1 billion endowment to make the best of life in New York City. But the challenge now is to keep the bad stuff at bay.

Academic Life: A Gallatin Attempt

There are thirteen divisions of NYU, ranging from the schools of medicine, dentistry, and law to schools of business and social work. The most important colleges for the student interested in the liberal arts are the College of the Arts and Sciences and the Gallatin School of Individualized Study.

The College of the Arts and Sciences is the largest of the undergraduate colleges. The curriculum is expansive, and the choices on the general education list (known as the Morse Academic Plan after Samuel Morse, the inventor of the telegraph and once a faculty member at NYU) are many. The Morse Plan is a set of distribution requirements, though it was once intended to be a core curriculum taught only by full-time faculty in small seminars that debated the classics of Western literature. Unfortunately, NYU did not create the necessary faculty slots and the program sprawled; many courses are now taught by junior faculty or teaching assistants, and sections originally planned for twenty-five students are now as large as two hundred.

The Morse Plan includes four components: Foundations of Contemporary Culture, Foundations of Scientific Inquiry, Expository Writing, and Foreign Languages.

The first of these, Foundations of Contemporary Culture, comprises a four-course sequence usually completed during the student's first two years at NYU. The four courses are called "Conversations of the West," "World Cultures," "Societies and the Social Sciences," and "Expressive Culture." All courses are interdisciplinary, and are ordered so as to expose students to intercultural similarities and differences.

The Foundations of Scientific Inquiry requirement is also a sequence: three courses called "Quantitative Reasoning," "Natural Science I (An Introduction to the Physical Universe)," and "Natural Science II (Our Place in the Biological Realm)." These courses are taught using solid quantitative and analytical methods.

The final requirements demand one year of expository writing classes and the equivalent of two years of foreign language study.

Morse requirements are usually completed in the first two years of study — before a student moves on to the more specialized courses required for a major. On paper, the courses form at least an approximation of a traditional core curriculum, but the reality is that they are often taught by professors more intent on their own research than on undergraduate teaching, faculty say. "The undergraduate courses are large and anonymous," one professor says. "The undergraduate curriculum does not meet the standards of higher education," says another.

An alternative for students looking for smaller classes and a different setup is the Gallatin School of Individualized Study. The school describes itself as "an innovative college that encourages individual exploration." Most notably, the Gallatin School offers students the opportunity to study the great books, or the seminal works of the Western tradition. One professor characterized the Gallatin School as a "splendid program that emphasizes the great books with a small setting."

The requirements of the Gallatin School are broader than those at a prototypical great books program, such as that found at schools like Thomas Aquinas College. Students need thirty-two credit hours in liberal arts courses in the humanities, social sciences, mathematics or science, and expository writing. The courses can come from virtually any college of the university and are not required by name, only by category. Once this "core" requirement in the liberal arts is completed, Gallatin students declare a concentration, the bounds and requirements of which are not even loosely defined. Consequently, students are able to declare almost anything as a concentration, including women's studies, environmental studies, performing arts, pre-law, or any other field that interests them.

The Gallatin School also requires participation in a "First-Year Seminar." These seminars are limited to about twenty students and involve discussions on the fundamental questions of liberal education. There is a rhetoric requirement (two expository writing courses, limited to fifteen students per section), and all seniors face a "Senior Colloquium," an oral examination conducted by three professors covering specific texts related to the student's concentration. The exam not only tests students' knowledge of their field, but also explores "ways of integrating their academic, professional, and personal experiences with the great books they have been reading and the ideas they have been examining in their Gallatin courses," according to the university catalogue.

The best courses at the Gallatin School are "Interdisciplinary Seminars," which cover great works by classical authors like Shakespeare, Plato, Homer, and Nietzsche, as well as modern works by Toni Morrison and Elie Wiesel. However, the school also teaches a few more dubious courses, such as "African Queens and Harlem Slaves" and "Gender and Resistance, Race, and Rebellion." And the trend in the school is toward greater politicization. "What has happened to the Gallatin School is a great tragedy," says one professor. "They are exploring crazy, post-modern studies. If they had notable professors . . . that would be one thing. But the professors are not very good at what they do."

A student says that, overall, NYU's program lacks both intellectual urgency and the proper focus. "Intellectually, the program is very soft. It is as if there is nothing to learn, but there is emoting to be done," the student says. "The recurrent question is 'how do we feel' about this or that. Students aren't studying literature, as much as they are studying themselves."

Exceptions to this observation are the classes taught by these fine professors: Carol Iannone and Herbert London in the Gallatin division; Israel Kirzner and Mario Rizzo in economics; Paul Vitz in psychology; Norman Cantor in history; James

Tuttleton, Dennis Donoghue, and Anthony Low in English; Russell Hardin and Steven J. Brams in politics; Larissa Von Fonte in classics; Evelyn Birge Vitz and Seth Benardete in medieval and Renaissance studies; and Wolf V. Heydebrand in sociology.

One of the best departments at NYU is economics, where Ludwig von Mises, one of the fathers of the Austrian School, once taught. Today's department is home to both free-market proponents and welfare-state types, but these distinctions are virtually invisible in the classrooms, where the department is unified on methodology. Teachers tend to ignore public policy questions and ideological debates in order to concentrate on the deeper questions of economics: What is science, and what is the contribution of economics?

Two other good departments are psychology and medieval and Renaissance studies, both of which have avoided the encroachment of politicized courses.

NYU has an enormous library that is of benefit to all departments. The Elmer Holmes Bobst Library, one of the largest open-stack research libraries in the nation, stands twelve stories high and occupies an entire city block. Its collection of 2.5 million volumes includes, according to the university, strengths in "American and English literature and history, economics, education, science, music, United Nations documents, Near Eastern and Ibero-American languages and literatures, and Judaica and Hebraica." The library also has a special collection in labor history.

Among the most politicized departments at NYU is French, said by one student to have been "captured by a certain sect of literati that is enamored with feminist and deconstructionist theories." The classes that examine nineteenth- and twentieth-century French thought are the most politicized.

The Africana studies department, according to the catalogue, covers "black consciousness, black feminism, and questions of class and gender dynamics within black communities." The department offers two concentrations within the major: Pan-African history and thought and black urban studies. Students in the Pan-African concentration study feminism and communism from an African-American perspective, and examine literary and political movements like "the Harlem Renaissance, the Negritude movement, black consciousness, black feminism, and black intellectual leaders such as W. E. B. Du Bois, Zora Neale Hurston, C. L. R. James, Malcolm X, Angela Davis, Leopold Senghor, and Kwame Nkrumah," according to the catalogue. Students in black urban studies look at, among other things, "music and sports industries, mass media, the police, and public schools."

Some of the politicized courses in the Africana studies department include "Race, Power, and the Postindustrial City" and "20th-Century Black Feminist Thought and Practice in the U.S.," which, according to the catalogue, "examines various forms of social/sexual policing, larger social narratives about black women's sexuality, black women and urban poverty debates, class politics within feminism(s) and gender, and class tensions within black social protest movements." There are seminars in "Pan-Africanism" that vary from semester to semester, with topics that include "African unity, black rebellion, colonialism and racism, the black diaspora and culture, and relationships between Pan-Africanism and movements such as nationalism, Marxism, and Afrocentricity," according to the catalogue.

The comparative literature department spells out its ideology in the university catalogue: "What also makes this study of literature comparative is that it examines texts not ordinarily seen as literary for their uses of language and traces the effects of such literature on cultural representations of gender, race, and class." A look at the course list shows that the department is not exaggerating.

Political Atmosphere: The Village People

The president of NYU, L. Jay Oliva, is like many modern university presidents in that he concerns himself more with fund-raising than with academics, according to professors. The president and his administration have not taken a hard line against political correctness, nor have they gone out of their way to encourage it. However, according to one professor, "The administration would be hospitable to innovations in the curriculum, especially those that would attract new students."

The NYU administration has encouraged the departments of the university to hire more minority professors and has set goals for affirmative action hires, according to professors. Like other universities, NYU has had difficulty retaining black professors; because of the scarcity of black academicians in a time of affirmative action hiring pushes, other schools have offered NYU professors more money to change jobs, a professor says. Women have also been historically underrepresented on the NYU faculty, but the administration has not pushed departments to hire on the basis of sex. "Women faculty would rather hire excellent colleagues than just people of the same sex," one professor says.

The university's surroundings — Greenwich Village — augment the generally liberal atmosphere on campus. "The diversity here is as wide as the rainbow, and there are protests all the time," says one student. "The problem is when you are walking around NYU you can't tell what is a student protest, and what comes from the Village." Campus activists post scores of advertisements for rallies and events held both on and off campus. "The protests are usually pretty large," a student says. "At a minimum, you will see about twenty students holding placards or screaming out some slogans." One hot topic is animal rights, and students have demonstrated for it on campus and in Washington Square. A march to a Manhattan furrier was organized to protest fur coats.

Homosexual activism is common, and, reportedly, a sizable sector of the student body is homosexual. The university funds an Office of Lesbian, Gay, Bisexual, and Transgender Students, which supports the many officially recognized student homosexual organizations, including Queer Union; the AIDS Awareness Club; Out-Artists; Lesbians, Gays, Bisexuals and Transgenders in Public Service; Lesbian, Gay and Bisexual Association of Business Students; Lesbian, Gay, and Bisexual People in Medicine; and Bisexual, Lesbian and Gay Law Students.

The Office of Student Life also hosts the Office of African-American, Latino, and Asian-American Student Services, which provides minority students with academic and professional services, including counseling. The office works to increase the number of minority students who graduate from NYU and to help these students find employment after college. Along with the university's Office of Career Services, the multicultural office holds an annual "Job Fair for Students of Color," which gives minority students exposure to recruiters from various firms.

Student Life: Bright Lights, Big City

NYU students face both the advantages and disadvantages of life in one of the world's most fascinating cities. The possibilities for entertainment, eating, and shopping are unlimited; traveling by subway or taxi, students can catch Broadway musicals and plays, watch a taping of David Letterman's show at the Ed Sullivan Theater, or tour the United Nations, the Statue of Liberty, the Empire State Building, the World Trade Center, and hundreds of other places. Many students spend their free time in bookstores, including Strand Books, one of the largest in the city and specialists in out-of-print and used books; Gotham Book Mart, good for literature and philosophy titles; and Patelson's House of Music, noted for its selection of musical scores and books on literature.

The most obvious drawback of life in New York is crime. Greenwich Village is the scene of a lot of drug trafficking, but the area around NYU is considered safer than the neighborhoods around Columbia University, for example. "Crime in general is improving in the city," an NYU professor says. "Of course, you have to be very careful at, say, two in the morning — which, ironically, is when students are usually out on the town." There are usually police officers in Washington Square, and the university grounds are said to be comparatively safe.

Students live in residence halls or in off-campus apartments, though the latter can be very expensive. About 60 percent of the student body lives on campus. Although the administration inquires each year about interest in theme houses, so far the only housing with a designated issue are "health conscious" floors whose residents oppose alcohol and drug abuse.

There are fifteen active fraternities and four sororities at NYU, but only seven frats have residential houses. Because of the innumerable options in the city, Greek life is not the focus of NYU social life, except perhaps for fraternity members. "Sure, students will go to fraternity parties, but they don't live and die for them," a student says. "There are plenty other places to party."

Student groups include ethnic organizations, several publications, performance groups, and social clubs like the Society for Creative Anachronism and the Outdoors

Club. There are a few religious organizations, like the Baptist Student Union, several Jewish groups, a gospel choir, and a couple of Christian organizations. Overall, the list of official student organizations is fairly short considering the size of the university, but this is likely another result of NYU's location in a city with so many other things to do.

NYU athletes compete in twenty intercollegiate sports, with the university's most recent success being a national Division III championship won by the women's basketball team. Historically, NYU can boast of its win over Manhattan College in the first-ever intercollegiate lacrosse game, played in 1877 in Central Park. Also, the model for the stiff-arming figure atop the Heisman Trophy is former NYU star Ed Smith, who posed for the statue in 1935. The university has eighteen club sports and several intramural choices as well. Recreation facilities on campus include tennis, squash, and racquetball courts; fitness rooms; and a track.

STATE UNIVERSITY OF NEW YORK AT BINGHAMTON

Office of Admissions
Assistant Vice President for Enrollment Services and Management
State University of New York at Binghamton
Vestal Parkway East
Binghamton, NY 13901
(607) 777-2171
www.binghamton.edu

Total enrollment: 12,000
Undergraduates: 9,349
SAT Ranges (Verbal/Math): V 550-650, M 570-670
Financial aid: 60%
Applicants: 15,660
Accepted: 42%
Enrolled: 28%
Application deadline: Feb. 15
Financial aid application deadline: Mar. 1
Tuition: in-state, $3,400; out-of-state, $8,300
Core curriculum: No

What's Past Is Past

In recent times the State University of New York at Binghamton (SUNY-Binghamton) has been hailed as a "public Ivy," the most prestigious state university in New York and one of the nation's leading liberal arts institutions. But that was then, and this is now: although it still enjoys a strong national reputation, and does retain a number of good professors and programs, Binghamton is gradually shedding the rigorous liberal arts tradition that once distinguished it from the other universities in the state system.

The school began as a branch of Syracuse University in 1946, but was incorporated into the state university system four years later as Harpur College, renamed for local colonial patriot Robert Harpur. Harpur College was led by a cadre of East Coast intellectuals eager to implement an innovative liberal arts curriculum. Its first dean envisioned an Ivy League–caliber liberal arts institution modeled on such small, prestigious colleges as Swarthmore College (as it was then, of course). High-ranking professors from Princeton were brought in, among them noted Augustinian scholar Bernard Huppe and Aldo Bernardo, a distinguished expert on Petrarch. The faculty were charged with implementing a rigorous cycle of required undergraduate courses, with a broad-based liberal arts curriculum that stressed language and the tutorial system of teaching, a curriculum and method that according to one of the original faculty were "second to none for that period." Students worked their way through a three-year series of courses on the nature of language, the history of ideas, the natural and social sciences, foreign languages, and the fine arts.

But within twenty years the program began to unravel amid a general spirit of student dissatisfaction with what they viewed as faculty dogmatism and curricular constraints. Today the noble plan on which the college was founded continues to crumble; in fact, Binghamton seems to be running, not walking, from its past. Sadly, one won't find Binghamton boasting about its prestigious intellectual heritage in the current university promotional literature. Although the university still considers itself a premier liberal arts institution, the attack on the solid core of studies that once distinguished Binghamton as an innovative, intellectually rigorous school has intensified in recent years, and, according to more traditional faculty and students there, it seems only a matter of time before the radical ideologues finally win the day. State budget cuts and radical graduate student and faculty activists all threaten to undermine the years of good work accomplished by many of this century's finest scholars. As one wistful faculty member observes, the fine reputation Binghamton now enjoys is based on "what it once was" rather than what it currently aspires to be.

Academic Life: Out with the Old

The Harpur College of Arts and Sciences at SUNY-Binghamton is the academic home for 70 percent of the university's nearly ten thousand undergraduates. There students pursue majors in the humanities, sciences, and social sciences. The remaining Binghamton students are divided among four other schools: the Decker School of Nursing, the School of Management, the School of Education and Human Development, and the Thomas J. Watson School of Engineering and Applied Science. Within Harpur College, a limited number of distribution requirements must be met by all liberal arts students. These include two courses each in the humanities, science and mathematics, and social sciences, and four additional liberal arts courses from divisions outside the student's major. There is also an all-college writing requirement.

Binghamton has gone the way of many other institutions in requiring various sorts of multicultural-style classes, and numerous varieties of "diversity" courses have been voted in and out of the curriculum since the early '90s. Beginning in the 1996-97 academic year, undergraduates are required to take two courses in "comparative cultures" as part of a new initiative entitled "Creating a Global Vision: Pluralism in the United States and Global Interdependencies." Another requirement for a two-semester course in oppression and inequality (see "Political Atmosphere" below) was recently struck down by the College Council.

Binghamton also offers several programs and degrees in minority studies. While there are currently no women's studies or Asian and Asian-American studies majors, students may opt for a concentration in these areas (or a minor in the case of women's studies); majors are, however, offered in Latin American and Caribbean studies and in Africana studies. These programs are, as one might expect, slanted to reflect a single political viewpoint. An offended Jewish student complains that the head of the Africana studies department compares Zionism to apartheid. Women's studies courses also tend to be highly radicalized. One student related an incident in which a male student disagreed with the perspective of the professor and argued that "we only study left-wing professors" in the class. The professor's response to this student dissident? Calling the campus police on him.

The university is also home to the Fernand Braudel Center for the Study of Economics, Historical Systems, and Civilizations, established several years ago to study Marxist thought. Though one student characterizes the economics department as "mainstream," some course offerings tend to stray far to the left: one freshman-level course offered to undergraduates is Econ 129, "Radical Political Economy," in which students study "mainstream thought and capitalist structure from [a] radical perspective," including the "nature and function of private property, class exploitation, and economic crises" from the standpoint of reformist and revolutionary ideology. The sociology program, considered "highly politicized" by one professor, also receives low marks from conservative students. "It's really just consciousness-raising," notes one.

Several excellent faculty and programs do exist at SUNY-Binghamton, in spite of the pall that ideological multiculturalism has cast over the campus in recent years. Many faculty, regardless of their political affiliation, are able to teach courses without bias. Students give high praise to history professor W. Warren Wager, philosophy professor John Arthur, Judaic studies professor Alan Arkush, and classics professor Saul Levin, to mention just a few. Students and faculty alike praise the biology program for its professionalism.

In addition to the more traditional humanities and social science majors, Binghamton also offers some innovative study options and degree programs that are in keeping with the traditional liberal arts ideals upon which the university was founded. One such program is "Philosophy, Politics, and Law," a course of studies offered to both liberal arts and pre-law students. Administered through the philosophy department, the program is premised on the idea that a study of law should be part of a general liberal education, since law "leads far beyond the narrow confines of legal cases to perennial questions of law's origins, operation, and justification." For this major, students take a broad span of required courses in philosophy, political science, and history.

The "Languages across the Curriculum," or "LxC" program, was developed with one eye "toward the global village of tomorrow." The wording of that description may make one skeptical, but the program itself is worthwhile and well conceived: it involves students reading from foreign language textbooks and secondary material in selected nonlanguage courses. The premise is that students who are proficient in a foreign language should be using that language throughout their curriculum of studies. The ambitious long-term goal of the program, as expressed in university literature, "is to bring about a situation where students can use any foreign language they know in any class at any level anywhere in the University curriculum." To facilitate movement toward this goal, the university trains a corps of language resource specialists whose job is to help students assimilate foreign language materials into their courses of studies. The university also has a medieval studies major, in which all students are required, among other things, to take either two courses in medieval Latin or one in a medieval vernacular language. Additionally, Binghamton offers several interdisciplinary courses in which students can major, minor, or earn certificates.

Although some of its liberal arts programs are solid and admirable, Binghamton's love affair with the experimental and the politically correct is increasingly at odds with its foundation of liberal arts studies. Perhaps because students, parents, and employers in today's competitive job market seem more impressed with the utilitarian than with meaningful statements about the value of a liberal education, Binghamton has begun stressing aspects of the school that would impress these constituencies, such as low tuition (the 1996 *Money Guide* ranked it the seventh-best buy in the nation) and an emergent reputation for research (a recent national study ranked it third in the nation among public universities of its size). In this environment, it is difficult to say how much longer Binghamton can preserve its stated commitment to undergraduate teaching and a true liberal arts curriculum.

Political Atmosphere: Inequality and Oppression

In the spring of 1997 a brewing controversy over a proposal to require two politically charged courses on race and gender came to a head. The courses, "The Social Construction of Inequality" and "The Nature of Oppression," had the support and sponsorship of a number of faculty, including an anthropology professor who saw them as "an opportunity to address diversity in an in-depth way." More savvy students and faculty, however, saw the proposal as yet one more attempt by the doyens of multiculturalism to indoctrinate all Binghamton students into the ideology of power and oppression. A bitter feud erupted between promoters and detractors of the proposed "diversity requirement," resulting in protest marches, sit-ins, a student takeover of the administration building, and the exchange of pleasantries between conservative and liberal factions in campus publications. Writing in the conservative *Binghamton Review*, political philosophy major John Carney warned, "Force me to bow down and study 'The Nature of Oppression' and I will reach for my long bow."

Fortunately, no arrows flew. Student and faculty representatives on the College Council voted 21-16 to drop the proposed courses. While many students were elated, the proponents of the courses on oppression and inequality had sour words for the victors. "With this vote," the Graduate Students Organization president complained dramatically in the mainstream campus paper *Pipe Dream*, "the right wing has consolidated its hold on this campus, and the neo-fascist takeover is complete." Despite the vote, the "oppression" studies requirement, at this writing, continues to be debated, and one professor laments that the process will inevitably be of a highly charged nature. "The whole thing," the professor says, "will be flawed by political issues that should never be a part of the discussion."

Politics of this sort are introduced to incoming Binghamton students in a two-day summer orientation session. A concurrent seminar is held for their parents. Some students have complained recently about the "sensitivity training" introduced by university staffers during the orientation, saying it amounts to little more than multicultural indoctrination. The corny titles of some games do little to hide the activities' real agenda. For example, students are asked to play "Wheel of Oppression," in which they break into small groups and talk about the roots and evils of oppression. They also play "Cultural Pursuit," a game modeled on Trivial Pursuit but with categories like "Experience being stereotyped," "Is white, male middle or upper class," or "Has a friend or relative who is gay, lesbian or bisexual." One student dismissively refers to the whole experience as "Kindergarten 101" and advises opting out of it if at all possible.

Some balance is provided by the conservative campus newspaper, the *Binghamton Review*, which acts as a thoughtful alternative to *Pipe Dream* and monitors radical happenings on campus. However, the *Review* is not welcome in some quarters. It survives even though the student assembly voted to cut its funding a few years ago because of "offensive cartoons"; since then, the *Review* no longer solicits or accepts funds from the university. Staff members face a chronic problem of the newspapers being stolen from campus distribution points. And during the 1997 academic year a furor erupted when the interim director of women's studies allegedly sent an ultimatum, written on official university stationery, to the campus bookstore: either stop advertising in the *Review* or face a boycott from the women's studies department. The bookstore yielded to the threat and withdrew its advertising from the conservative paper. After some sleuthing, *Review* staffers discovered the existence of the letter, and an official investigation of the incident is currently under way.

The majority of speakers brought to campus have political agendas to promote. Binghamton has hosted Leonard Jeffries, Louis Farrakhan, Bob Abrams, and Ralph Nader. But conservatives have also appeared on campus, though usually without any financial support from the university. Jeremy Rabkin, Erik von Kuehnelt-Leddihn, and National Association of Scholars member and professor of Austrian economics Barry Smith have all spoken on campus as well.

Campus Life: Across the River

SUNY-Binghamton is nestled on more than 600 wooded acres near the Susquehanna River, bordered at the southern tip by a 117-acre nature preserve. Students envisioning ivy-covered spires or bell towers rising in the distance as they approach the university will be disappointed — all buildings postdate 1958 and are for the most part typical examples of soulless modern architecture. The housing environment, however, is designed to take advantage of the beautiful natural surroundings — none of the campus residences stands higher than three stories. Undergraduates are required to live on campus for their first year, and can choose from among three residential colleges (Hinman, Newing, or College-in-the-Woods) or the community of Dickinson (apartment-type housing). Residents may also select one of several special-interest living situations. All are reputedly academic-based, though the current options include everything from foreign language interests and African or Asian culture to environmental awareness and fitness.

SUNY-Binghamton's Colonials, the university's sports teams, proudly wear the school's green and white colors in a variety of intercollegiate athletics. Men's basketball is coached by Dick Baldwin, the nation's all-time winningest college basketball coach. The women's tennis team has recorded, at this writing, thirteen consecutive winning seasons. For those with more modest athletic activity in mind, there is a wealth of student-organized or intramural sports, including crew, cycling, equestrian, Frisbee, lacrosse, rugby, snowboarding, and karate clubs. The university also sponsors "co-rec" touch football, played on the lawns outside the residence halls. This popular pastime involves six-player teams (three men and three women); one of the women must play quarterback.

The university recently opened a 4,000-square-foot exercise facility called Fit-

Space, which offers air-conditioned workout and aerobics rooms to students for a modest fee. The university also completed construction of a million-dollar track and soccer complex, and has articulated a commitment to the continued support and expansion of the college athletic program. As one athletic brochure proudly states: "The athletics program is growing rapidly and enjoys strong student and administrative support. Watch for Binghamton University and its student-athletes to move more and more into the national spotlight." With state government slashing the New York university system budget, however, this upbeat pledge of support could signal a future educational liability, with sports expansion threatening to divert resources from other important programs.

In addition to athletics, some 130 student organizations operate on campus, including some rather vocal political groups like the Gay People's Union, the Black Student Union, the Democratic Socialists of America, and others. These groups reportedly have a large influence on Binghamton's student government group, the Student Association.

The campus is not actually located in Binghamton, but across the Susquehanna River in the small town of Vestal. Binghamton, though, is home to two professional sports teams (the Binghamton Rangers hockey team and the Binghamton Mets baseball team), as well as a professional opera company, symphony and pops orchestras, theaters, and shopping malls. The downtown Arena is a popular music venue, as is the excellent Anderson Center for the Arts on campus, which also hosts plays, recitals, and other performances.

UNIVERSITY OF NORTH CAROLINA AT CHAPEL HILL

CB 2200 Jackson Hall
Chapel Hill, NC 27599
(919) 966-3621
www.unc.edu

Total enrollment: 24,440
Undergraduates: 15,640
SAT Ranges (Verbal/Math): V 560-670, M 560-660
Financial aid: 40%

Applicants: 15,800
Accepted: 37%
Enrolled: 56%
Application deadline: Jan. 15
Financial aid application deadline: Mar. 1
Tuition: in-state, $2,225; out-of-state, $11,210
Core curriculum: No

Bleeding Carolina Blue

The University of North Carolina (UNC) has long been one of the country's better state universities, and it remains so today. The politics seen at peer institutions play only a small part in this university's daily life, and the school rightfully maintains a sense of pride rooted in its prestigious past and bright future. Professors want to teach there — its educational program is solid; the campus is beautiful; and the intellectual community, both in Chapel Hill and the famous Research Triangle, is vibrant, supportive, and challenging.

There have been reports that the university has begun to favor research over its traditional excellence in teaching. Of course, the nature of university teaching throughout the country has tended toward a professionalization of knowledge. For now, though, there remain in Chapel Hill scores of excellent teachers, and if a student can use his own discretion rather than the haphazard advising system, he can find them.

As a state university, UNC is not the most selective institute around, and despite its prestige, there are students who would rather party than pursue excellence. This does rob UNC of some of its potential to be a community where thought is more highly valued. However, for its atmosphere and the vast resources it offers, UNC will remain near the top of a list of institutions of its kind.

Academic Life: Perspectives

UNC once required students to spend their first two years studying the best-known literary and philosophical works of the Western tradition, as well as the history of the West. Those days are gone: the university has settled for a set of distribution requirements. The old core curriculum died in 1981 when traditional faculty were outvoted by those who considered the value of various "perspectives" to outweigh the substance offered by the core.

Today, students must fulfill basic requirements in English composition (two courses), foreign languages, and mathematics. Other requirements are called "perspectives": thus, the requirement for a literature and a fine arts class is called the

"Aesthetic Perspective." There are also requirements of two science courses ("Natural Sciences Perspective"); one course in philosophy, religion, or political science ("Philosophical Perspective"); and two courses from two different social science departments — the "Social Sciences Perspective."

"The question in my mind about the requirements is that there are ways of getting around it with very little 'perspective' being gained," says a faculty member. "Students see it a little bit like pieces of a puzzle they're putting together. They don't always see the whole puzzle." "Teachers find they wind up with, say, seniors taking a 'perspective' in order to 'taste' philosophy, for example," says another professor. "But they lack the vocabulary of philosophy majors who may be in the same class, making a number of academic levels to teach to."

There is also a "Western Historical/Non-Western Perspective," consisting of two courses. This unwieldy name encompasses one course on a pre-1700 Western history topic and a second course on either a Western or a non-Western historical theme. These may be satisfied in several departments: classics, history, religion, anthropology, and economics. The first course must be chosen from a list of twenty-three, including ones with titles like "Women of Byzantium" and "Women and Marriage in Medieval and Renaissance Europe." While these two courses may be legitimate in and of themselves, their narrow topics are more suited to graduate research than to a broad liberal education.

A third requirement was instituted in 1994. The "Cultural Diversity Requirement" mandates that students choose one course that gives them "the opportunity to gain a better understanding of cultural diversity," according to the university catalogue. Among the courses that may fulfill this requirement: "Race, Poverty, and Politics," "Black Women in America," "Folk and Popular Music in Latin America," and "Leisure in a Diverse Society."

However, the long list of excellent professors at UNC means that hundreds of very good courses are there for the taking. Professors to find include: Judith Farquhar in anthropology; Stella (Beth) Grabowski in art; Jean DeSaix, Alan Feduccia, William Kier, and Patricia Pukkila in biology; James Jorgenson in chemistry; Kenneth Reckford, Sarah Mack, George Houston, and Cecil Wooten in classics; Beverly Long and Paul Ferguson in communication studies; Michael McFee in creative writing; Barbara Day in education; Michael Salemi in economics; Doris Betts, Kimball King, Richard Rust, George Lensing, Frank Wilson, Trudier Harris, Christopher Armitage, Weldon Thornton, Tom Stumpf, Joy Kasson, Reid Barbour, Robert Kirkpatrick, James Seay, Theodore Leinbaugh, and Lee Green in English; Risa Palm in geography; Roger Lotchin, Joil Schwartz, Jackie Hall, Jay Smith, Judith Bennett, Willis Brooks, William Barney, Miles Fletcher, Peter Coclanis, and John Kasson in history; Jim Shumaker in journalism; Sue Ellen Goodman in mathematics; Michael Zenge, James Ketch, and Thomas Warburton in music; Richard Smyth in philosophy; Laurie McNeil and Larry Rowan in physics and astronomy; Jeff Obler, Joel Schwartz, Jurg Steiner, and Michael Lienesch in political science; Richard King in psychology;

Ruel Tyson, David Halperin, and Peter Kaufman in religious studies; and John Shelton Reed in sociology.

UNC has an equally impressive list of exceptional departments, including English, biology, history, chemistry, journalism, economics, political science, business, sociology, classics, religious studies, French, German, and philosophy.

The English department is noted for its attention to teaching, its traditional curriculum, and its freshman composition program. Though the university does not offer a graduate program in creative writing, English does offer a minor in that field that is as good as many graduate programs in the country. The classics department and the program in journalism and mass communication also are among the best in the nation. The art history department's strength is teaching, supported by the university's art collection.

UNC's honors program offers seniors in all departments the opportunity to conduct independent research in their fields, ending in a sixty-to-eighty-page paper that must be defended before a faculty panel. "Many of these results have been impressive," says a professor. "A senior honors student will have lived through the equivalent of many M.A. theses."

Despite all its good programs, UNC has its share of politicized alternatives. "A big university is like a city," one professor says. "You have all sorts of upper class as well as slum areas." But UNC has fared better than most large research universities in this regard. "Most professors have a liberal ideology and don't hide it, but I don't think it interferes with education," a student says. "Old-fashioned liberalism — the sort that values tolerance, even of conservatives — is the dominant ethos," says a professor.

That would make the communications studies department an exception at UNC. Many consider it the most politicized program on campus because of the Marxist slant it offers on its subject matter. Professors there "like to talk a lot about the masses being exploited by corporations and media conglomerates," a student says. The department is well regarded nationally and a popular choice among students, but "it's too trendy and showy," a professor says. "They have potentially valuable courses, for example political rhetoric, and it has potential. But a simple lecture would give the information needed."

UNC's department of women's studies, which, like similar programs at other schools, has its roots in politics, offers both a major and a minor. Its courses are "premised on the belief that women are unjustly treated in society," according to a student. The cultural studies department has several courses that overlap with women's studies, and is similarly politicized, according to a faculty member.

The history department has a number of politicized courses, but these are not always apparent from its catalogue. "Even in courses that appear harmless, like European history, professors find ways to inject personal political biases into class," a student says. One former student tells of a U.S. history course in which the professor attributed George Bush's victory in a 1992 class straw poll to the fact that many in the class were freshmen, and therefore more conservative than students who had been through several years of UNC.

Many UNC students must deal with less-than-great teaching during their first two years, when they are likely to be stuck in classes led by teaching assistants (TAs). While some TAs (especially those in freshman composition) do commendable jobs, others are not up to university standards, some students say. According to a longtime faculty member, teaching has declined over the last two or three decades because of the emphasis the university places on faculty research. "This used to be one of the premier undergraduate colleges in the South," the professor says. "My department is now anemic compared to what it used to be regarding undergraduate teaching. And that's true of other departments across campus that have attempted to become research departments." Research is the primary criterion for tenure decisions, the professor adds. "You have to be terribly inept to be turned down for bad teaching."

The university has taken steps recently to correct the slide in teaching. A Center for Teaching and Learning offers help to professors and TAs. Both alumni and several departments sponsor teaching awards that include money, and the university has started some short-term chairs that are filled solely on the basis of teaching excellence.

Many on campus hope the administration will soon give the same attention to the university's academic advising system, now considered, according to a student, "practically incoherent."

"Students here just don't put a lot of faith in their advisors," the student says. "Most of us never see them — I haven't seen mine in two years. . . . Most students I talk to have complaints about their advisors." A professor says students at UNC have a great will to succeed, and since their assigned advisers aren't helping, they seek advice from older students and spend quite a bit of time making connections that could help them once they graduate. "A bright kid can get good training with good people," the professor says. "But the average people tend to get lost in the crowd." Honors students and athletes, two groups most likely to seek academic advising, get the best assistance, another professor notes.

However, students don't always make the most of their opportunities for advising. "Students will tell you their advisors only give them 10 minutes and rubber-stamp stuff," a professor says. "Advisors will tell you they hold office hours regularly, and nobody comes to see them until panic pre-registration. Both reports are correct."

Political Atmosphere: Very Varied

UNC is far more liberal than the state of North Carolina, and the university has welcomed many aspects of the modern multiculturalist and diversity agendas. Still, it is nowhere near as politically correct as neighboring Duke University, and is less politicized than today's average large state research institution. One student says the most visible multicultural events are along the lines of "awareness" weeks or months for gays and lesbians, Asian-Americans, women's history, and African-American history.

"Black-white relations are the continuing dilemma, for both understandable historical reasons and less understandable political ones," says one professor. The political reasons mentioned by the professor include a recent battle over whether the university should build a $7 million black cultural facility at the center of the campus. (The university ultimately decided to construct the building, and fund-raising is under way.) "Though the conflict ended several years ago," a student says, "there is still a lot of self-segregation at UNC." Others say tensions have eased considerably since the debate over the cultural center concluded.

The university maintains a separate orientation program for black freshmen, who arrive on campus a few days earlier than their classmates. "The most obvious effect of the separate orientation is that they've formed friendships before the general arrival of students, and they've been convinced by those in charge of orientation that white people here will be against them," a student says.

The student newspaper, the *Daily Tar Heel,* has been criticized for its lack of attention to diversity issues and, according to one student, "for failing to portray blacks in a favorable enough light."

The alternative student newspaper, the *Carolina Review,* has been subject to vandalism. In the spring of 1996 hundreds of copies of the *Review* were stolen from distribution stands, and although there was evidence that the thieves were fraternity brothers of the student body president, UNC authorities declined to press charges under the student judicial code. Additionally, the *Review* lost its funding for "proce-dural reasons" just after it published a controversial critique of this student body president. After a Supreme Court decision forced the University of Virginia to fund student projects regardless of religious or political views, the *Review* and other student enterprises at UNC received money from the university. However, according to one person who writes for the *Review,* "it is kept on a short leash by the student congress." Another group, Common Sense, which brings conservative speakers to campus, has had its funding slashed several times in the last year despite following through on its promises to bring in such speakers as black conservatives Armstrong Williams and Walter Williams.

UNC has no formal speech code, though one was talked about after a conser-vative student magazine published what one professor described as "an allegedly anti-Semitic — in fact, just stupid — cartoon." The professor says: "There is a lot said here about sensitivity, but it has not gone so far as a formalized speech code or sensitivity training for freshmen of the sort I read about elsewhere."

Faculty and the administration do exert some control over politics in the classroom through hiring practices and tenure evaluations. "You couldn't get a job here, even if you're great in your field, if you're not politically correct," a professor says. Another professor says some departments will not accept traditional scholars, but if one should be hired, factors other than politics (i.e., research and teaching) are more important when it comes to keeping one's job. Another professor believes the situation in Chapel Hill to be a bit better: "In the range of my experience, at UNC a candidate's personal political position is not taken into account in hiring or tenure. It is possible for a scholar favoring a more traditionalist approach to make the short list."

Student Life: The Triangle's Lovely Corner

Chapel Hill is one of America's most idyllic college towns. It is small and quaint in the best sense of those words. The university campus is extraordinarily pretty. Most of the architecture in the old part of campus, which abuts downtown, is traditional to the area and evokes a feeling of the Old South. Many original brick and marble buildings are still to be found in this area of campus, including Old East, the oldest state university building in America, constructed in 1793. The campus, with lots of open spaces and an arboretum, is conducive to strolling or reading.

Living in Chapel Hill is one of the primary delights of attending UNC. The town has the usual number of bars and eating joints as well as some very good restaurants. Durham, home of Duke University, is only minutes away, but other than attending a Durham Bulls' game (minor league baseball), UNC students see little reason to drive over to the "City of Medicine," as Durham bills itself. When students do leave town, they tend to head for the Outer Banks or the mountains, both of which can be reached in three hours or so.

The university is a bargain for in-state students — tuition was only $2,225 for the 1997 academic year. Five out of six students come from North Carolina. The university does its part to keep the money coming from the state legislature, with an active news bureau; a faculty speakers program; public service projects through the schools of medicine, public health, and education; as well as institutes for school principals, elected officials, and other public servants.

There are hundreds of student organizations on campus, including club sports, InterVarsity Christian Fellowship, the student government and courts, and the Campus Y, which, according to one professor, used to be the YMCA — "Some person's objections to the 'C' part took 'Christian' out of the equation." Other opportunities for student involvement include *Cellar Door*, an undergraduate literary magazine, and the Catholic Campus Ministry.

Students choose from three different groups of housing complexes, which vary in amenities and distance from classes. A bus system carries students to and from the dorm rooms on the south side of campus. While returning students as well as freshmen are guaranteed housing, over half of the junior and senior classes opt to live off campus, a trend found at virtually every state university. About 18 percent of the student body joins the Greek organizations, which have for years played a large role in the social life of UNC and most other Southern schools.

The research facilities at Chapel Hill are top-notch and include a library system of over 4 million volumes, one of the largest in the South. The city forms one angle — with Durham (and Duke) and Raleigh (and North Carolina State) forming the other two — of the fabled Research Triangle, the combined resources of which are difficult to surpass. A tremendous amount of primary research in nearly every field is carried out within the Triangle.

UNC fields varsity teams in the most common women's and men's intercollegiate sports. A member of the stellar Atlantic Coast Conference, the Tar Heels have long been annual contenders in men's basketball and have, more recently, become nationally ranked in football as well. The women's soccer team continues to be one of the most successful teams of any kind, in any sport, in the nation. Still, Chapel Hill is basketball country, and the games against much-hated Duke and North Carolina State are always well attended. The program was brought to national prominence by Coach Dean Smith, who retired in 1997 as not only the winningest Division I coach of all time, but also as, arguably, the most respected sports figure in the country's recent history.

NORTHWESTERN UNIVERSITY

Office of Undergraduate Admission
1801 Hinman Avenue
P.O. Box 3060
Evanston, IL 60204-3060
www.nwu.edu

Total enrollment: 11,600 (Evanston campus)
Undergraduates: 7,630
SAT Ranges (Verbal/Math): V 620-710, M 630-720
Financial aid: 60%
Applicants: 13,862
Accepted: 37%
Enrolled: 39%
Application deadline: Jan. 1
Financial aid application deadline: Jan. 1
Tuition: $22,392
Core curriculum: Yes

Making the Ivy Grow

If Northwestern University had its druthers, it would be an Ivy League school. Many consider the Illinois institution to be one of the non-Ivy Ivies, but that's not good enough for Northwestern. The university just isn't comfortable being a good liberal arts school with excellent programs in journalism and other media fields. Instead, Northwestern has planted at least one foot firmly on the multicultural bandwagon. Administrators may think this politicization makes Northwestern more Ivy-like, but it has certainly not done much for its quality of education.

Northwestern is still considered moderately conservative, but in the past several years the administration, faculty, and student body have shown diminished interest in traditional education and increasing support for an ideological agenda, both at the curricular and social level. Free speech has been an issue recently, whether it involves violence against a professor who published an odious book denying that the Holocaust happened, a campus lecture by a black supremacist, a homosexual "kiss-in," or a trumped-up charge of sexual harassment. In some cases the administration has done a better job than some of its counterparts in protecting freedom of expression. Unfortunately, the university's uneven performance in this area may be of little comfort to many on campus.

If the administration can maintain some integrity in the face of PC demands, students seeking a solid liberal arts education may be able to navigate their way through four years at Northwestern University. For motivated undergraduates, opportunities abound for individualized research and internships, and in this respect a Northwestern education can serve as a fitting preparation for those intending to pursue advanced degrees after graduation.

Academic Life: Reserving a Soapbox

Approximately 7,600 students from all fifty states and forty-five foreign countries make up Northwestern's undergraduate population. These students matriculate into one of six undergraduate schools: the College of Arts and Sciences, the School of Education and Social Policy, the McCormick School of Engineering and Applied Science, the Medill School of Journalism, the School of Music, and the School of Speech. The core curricula vary based on the school, and each major has its own requirements as well.

The Medill School of Journalism, with about six hundred undergraduates, has one of the most acclaimed journalism programs in the country, having graduated forty Pulitzer Prize winners. The School of Speech houses a nationally recognized program in radio/television/film, although students should be prepared to encounter the progressivist views that often accompany such disciplines. Also recommended are some of Northwestern's preprofessional, policy-oriented programs, including one in organizational studies. Students report some good faculty in political science, psychology, and anthropology. Political science and history are said by one professor to possess "a range of voices." Religious studies is considered fairly liberal, while interdisciplinary centers such as World Systems Studies and the Center for International Comparative Studies are quite radical, often hosting left-wing speakers. One undergraduate cautions students to "stay away from sociology" because of its politicized character. There are a number of first-rate scholars at Northwestern, such as adjunct history professor and Pulitzer Prize–winning writer Garry Wills.

For those interested in the liberal arts, the College of Arts and Sciences requires two courses in each of six areas: natural sciences, formal studies (encompassing everything from calculus to logic), social and behavioral science, historical studies, values, and literature/fine arts. The study of Western civilization is not required; however, there is a "Western Civilization" option under which students can work off their values and literature/arts requirements with courses in classics or European thought. To its credit, Northwestern has not gone the way of many liberal arts universities in mandating a "diversity" or "multicultural" requirement for undergraduates, though distribution requirements can be fulfilled by taking courses in women's studies and African-American studies.

In addition to the distribution requirements, which can be covered without taking particularly rigorous classes, all freshmen must take two seminars offered in a variety of subjects. The pedagogical method for these courses (discussion-based, with enrollment limited to fifteen) is a sound one, especially when freshmen often find themselves lost in jam-packed introductory courses. But the subject matter varies widely, and one wonders why students are asked to choose from among an eclectic list of courses at this stage of their educations while at the same time no attempt is made to ensure that they are exposed to even a few of the classic texts of Western thought.

This is not to suggest that there are no worthwhile freshman seminars offered at Northwestern; indeed, the list for the spring quarter of the 1996-97 school year included courses entitled "Satiric Comedy," "The Death of Socrates and the Rise of Political Philosophy," and "The Cruel War Is Raging: Narratives of the American Civil War," where students would be exposed to many great works. Even in one course entitled "The Literature of Deviance," students are still reading Shakespeare and Melville, among others. And one freshman praised the writing-intensive element of the seminars, noting that "it gives you the personal attention you need to become a better writer." But there are also freshman seminars such as "Alternative Healing," "Reproductive Technology," and "Mafia, Shtarkers and Tong: Gangsters and Ethnicity in Fiction and Film," many of which seem intellectually vapid and politically driven.

While the university's literature says all students receive "a solid foundation in the liberal arts," the experience of some students and faculty suggests that the reality is less impressive. "The courses are much easier than I thought they would be," notes one freshman. The luxury of small freshman seminars is offset by high student enrollment in most freshman and sophomore courses. One student says classes often have eighty-five to one hundred students, and class size begins to taper off only in the junior year. There are several enormous undergraduate courses in which student performance is evaluated almost exclusively by multiple-choice exams. The formal advising system is weak: a student and his adviser meet once a semester to discuss scheduling, but seldom meet again. Despite these relative disadvantages, students are serious and hardworking; indeed, the library is one of the most popular student hangouts.

According to one faculty member, two things diminish the quality of education at Northwestern. One is the fact that faculty in certain departments only want particular views taught; students thus get a limited exposure to the full range of attitudes toward a particular study or discipline. The views excluded are, not surprisingly, usually traditional. The second academic deficiency at Northwestern is what the professor calls a "reserved soap box policy," in which certain faculty appointments are earmarked for left-wing scholars in order to maintain the radical hegemony on campus. In one recent illustration of this, a prominent Northwestern law professor, a libertarian, was offered a position elsewhere. Northwestern made an attractive offer to keep the professor by adding his wife (an eminently qualified law professor at another university, and also a libertarian) to the faculty. Student groups protested that if this came to pass, there would be too many libertarians in the law faculty, and the Northwestern administration did not rehire the husband or hire the wife.

Political Atmosphere: Unequal Protection

Students and faculty agree that the Northwestern student body seems more focused on academics than activism and is largely apathetic at both ends of the political spectrum. However, there has been student activism at Northwestern in recent years related not only to political issues, but also to curricular and social matters. In April of 1995 Asian-American students engaged in a hunger strike in an attempt to force the university to add an Asian-American studies department (even though an Asian studies program already existed). The university administration did not accede to the demand in so many words, but has since made a public commitment to expanding the number of courses in that area.

In addition to Asian studies, the university has programs in African-American studies, women's studies, and Latin American and Caribbean studies. There is currently no gay and lesbian studies department. Traditionalists on campus, however, fear that the administration will eventually capitulate to radical student demands to expand existing "diversity" programs, or to start new ones. Such piecemeal programming, laments one professor, threatens to divert even more university resources away from the traditional liberal arts disciplines.

Students and faculty who cannot endorse the regnant ideologies at Northwestern are worried about their freedom to speak freely in academic settings. Professors are cautioned, in rather nebulous terms, against using "verbal behavior that creates a hostile or intimidating environment" in the classroom. In a recent poll at Northwestern, half of those surveyed believed faculty should not be free to say what they want in class. One senior administration official is on record as saying, "We wouldn't be a university without academic freedom, but that doesn't mean you can say anything you want."

Whatever encroachments are made on freedoms at Northwestern will likely be published in the *Northwestern Chronicle,* the campus alternative paper, whose staff reports valuable information about the political and educational climate at the school (along with some biting humor from time to time). The paper receives no financial support from the university, nor does it seek it. A 1995 attempt by the governing councils of two dorms to curtail the *Chronicle's* distribution was struck down by the university's appellate system. Recent issues of the *Chronicle* have highlighted controversial campus events, including a "Kiss-In" organized in April of 1997 by gay and lesbian students. At this event, guest speaker Rick Garcia, director of the Illinois Federation for Human Rights, announced: "We come here today to celebrate who we are, who we love, and how we love." Participating students, who hailed the Kiss-In for its "throw-it-in-your-face" tactics, eventually staged a demonstration during which they shouted slogans at prospective students and parents.

The *Chronicle* was also responsible for clearing the record of a professor falsely accused. An anthropology professor was charged in the late 1980s with sexual harassment, but a university investigation found him innocent of the charge. However, the Women's Coalition successfully lobbied the university to keep a record of the unfounded charge in the professor's permanent file — where it remained for six years until the *Chronicle* reported the injustice.

Other students focus on injustices far from the Chicago area; they have adopted Burma as a favorite cause, much as they adopted South Africa prior to the ending of apartheid in that country. While conditions in Burma are certainly cause for concern (as were those in South Africa), it is fairly obvious that a herd mentality governs which causes students choose to support at any given time. And while many students are sincere in their concern, the activities they undertake to further the cause range from serious to silly. In 1997 Northwestern's Free Burma Coalition held a hunger strike to boycott the use of Pepsi products on campus, since Pepsi had active franchise operations in Burma. After Pepsi decided to pull out of Burma, legislation was introduced by Northwestern's Associated Student Government (ASG) that would "implement a selective purchasing policy for the organization."

At Northwestern, some views can be expressed while others cannot be so freely offered. One professor notes a double standard regarding expression of radical political views: there is a recognized campus International Socialist Organization, yet any student or faculty member who wishes to argue the merits of fascism, for example, "would be shouted down." Both ideologies are repugnant and have caused the deaths of millions, yet only one is condemned in Western intellectual circles. The administration and the students, according to this faculty member, draw no distinction between recognizing one's right to speak freely and endorsing that person's ideas.

Northwestern has had its fair share of radical views expressed within recent years, both by existing faculty and invited speakers. Electrical engineering professor Arthur Butz had his car firebombed after publishing a book that, despite survivors and documented facts, denied the Holocaust. According to faculty and students, Butz has frequently been offered early retirement, which he steadfastly refuses. Northwestern president Henry S. Bienen was forced to make public statements distancing the university from Professor Butz's views after understandably irate students and faculty discovered Butz was using his university-sponsored web page to promote his mendacious, revisionist thesis.

Of course, Northwestern should not be (and is not) paying for the marketing of an obviously bogus piece of scholarship. But that doesn't mean it won't pay for something equally hateful. In February of 1997 the black student group For Members Only brought Khalid Muhammad to speak as part of Black History Month. Muhammad, whose many public statements advocating violence against whites are not fit to recount here, delivered an on-campus speech entitled "Destroying White Minds among Black Students: Exposing Falsehood and Embracing Truth," and his appearance was funded by student fees. Many student groups protested because of Muhammad's hateful views of Catholics, Jews, and homosexuals; however, the administration did not disavow Muhammad's ideology as it had Butz's.

Northwestern's ASG holds the purse strings for most student-sponsored campus speaking events. For Members Only receives the second-largest amount of funding from the ASG — upwards of $50,000, which goes to events like the Khalid Muhammad speech. Speakers approved by the ASG for the 1997-98 academic year include Louis Farrakhan and O. J. Simpson attorney Johnnie Cochran. Conservative students can join the campus Conservative Council, which has been active in bringing its own speakers to campus, including Dan Quayle, William F. Buckley Jr., and Alan Keyes. The Quayle and Buckley talks were two of the university's most well-attended events in their respective years, and were financially supported by the ASG. Funding was denied, however, for a recent attempt by the council to bring Charlton Heston to speak on campus. The ASG argued that because Heston is an alumnus of Northwestern, he did not require a student-funded honorarium. Most conservative speakers are met with low-scale protests by the International Socialists Organization, characterized by one undergraduate as "a bunch of radical graduate students." Other speakers — and there are many — are much less controversial, and include former Senator Paul Simon, former presidential candidate Ross Perot, and U.S. poet laureate Robert Pinsky. One student suggests taking advantage of campus lectures at nearby Loyola University, where the political climate is far less radical.

Campus Life: Open to Debate

Located on the shores of Lake Michigan in Evanston, Illinois, Northwestern is only twelve miles from downtown Chicago. Everything one hears about Chicago's harsh climate is confirmed by Northwestern students, who complain about severe winters and strong winds on campus. They also complain — oddly, given Chicago's proximity — about the lack of readily accessible social and cultural opportunities. According to one freshman, "Evanston is kind of boring," and even though Chicago is within striking distance, many students "are pretty land-locked" and do not make frequent trips into the city.

According to recent housing figures, approximately 4,100 students live in residence halls; 1,000 live in fraternities or sororities, with the remaining 2,500 commuting or living off campus. Single-sex living arrangements are an option. One student recommends staying away from North Campus, where most of the fraternities are located, because of the high noise level. Much of the campus's social life revolves around the Greek system, of which more than one-third of Northwestern's undergraduates are members. Many of the Greek events involve a good bit of alcohol. This has resulted in numerous complaints, but some of the fraternities have tried to make amends: at the end of the 1996-97 school year, eleven frats hosted a campuswide alcohol-free party, the first party of its kind to be held on such a large scale.

Both resident assistants and campus police at Northwestern take part in sensitivity training, and one student notes that "student coalitions on race relations frequently publicly endorse the institution of 'voluntary' sensitivity training for professors," although no such training currently exists. Northwestern has an extensive freshman orientation, however. The entire week before classes begin is considered "New Student Week." According to students, there is a heavy "diversity" component to freshman orientation; as one student relates, "Each orientation group, comprised of ten to fifteen students, is forced to discuss multicultural and diversity issues, led by an upperclassmen." Another student describes a similar experience: at the end of her orientation, students attended a Sunday morning convocation where speaker Barbara Jordan addressed multicultural issues. "After the talk, students broke up into small groups to meet with a designated peer advisor and discuss issues raised by the talk," the student says.

Northwestern is home to over 160 student organizations, running the usual gamut from Campus Crusade for Christ to the Gay and Lesbian University Alliance. The university certainly has a busy and diverse activities calendar, sponsoring everything from Asian American Heritage Month to a host of events celebrating Earth Week. There are also active theater and musical groups, including an orchestra for nonmusic majors. Students may participate in competitive organizations such as Northwestern's highly rated debate team. In 1997 Northwestern, whose debate team has won eight National Debate Tournament titles, became the first school ever to win titles in both that tournament and the national Cross Examination Debate Association.

But by many accounts, athletics dominate the extracurricular scene at Northwestern. In 1995, after years of mediocre or worse performances, Northwestern's football team proved to be a legitimate Big Ten team by going to the Rose Bowl. The men's golf team recently won an NCAA title with much less fanfare.

UNIVERSITY OF NOTRE DAME

Office of Admissions
Notre Dame, IN 46556
(219) 631-7505
www.nd.edu

Total enrollment: 10,280
Undergraduates: 7,860
SAT Ranges (Verbal/Math): V 600-690, M 620-710
Financial aid: 44%
Applicants: 9,450
Accepted: 39%
Enrolled: 51%
Application deadline: Jan. 6
Financial aid application deadline: Feb. 15
Tuition: $20,000
Core curriculum: Yes

Identity Crisis beneath the Dome

The University of Notre Dame has long been the most visible and prominent Roman Catholic university in the United States. Well known for its football program, in which athletes capable of reading and commenting on complex texts nevertheless take on and usually defeat the best teams in the country, the university has also made possible an excellent education to the broad Catholic middle class whose children were often excluded, either by bigotry or financial lack, from the most elite universities. The WASPs had their Ivies, and the Catholics had Notre Dame. Although the university for years has had an excellent law school and many professional and graduate divisions, its primary strength throughout most of its existence has been the high caliber of its undergraduate curriculum.

In years past students could rest assured of both the authentic Catholic identity of the school and the personalized attention of the excellent teaching faculty.

But this was before a meeting in 1967 of Catholic colleges and universities held at Notre Dame's retreat in Land O' Lakes, Wisconsin, during which it was decided that the Catholic identity of these schools was a liability in a secular age. As the Land O' Lakes statement puts it: "To perform its teaching and research functions effectively, the Catholic university must have a true autonomy and academic freedom in the face of authority of whatever kind, lay or clerical, external to the academic community itself." This is a rather Protestant reading of the Catholic tradition in higher education, and its consequences are everywhere visible at Notre Dame today.

Today, many at Notre Dame want the school to be what one faculty member calls "the Great Research University." There can be no doubt that in striving to achieve this goal, the school has lost or weakened many of its historically unique traditions. Of course, this process is problematic for a university whose purpose had been defined not by acceptance of worldly trends but by a willingness to change the world. There is evidence that some scholars and administrators at Notre Dame believe the secularization of the university has gone too far, and that its Catholic identity needs to be protected and cultivated. While the outcome of this identity crisis remains uncertain, it is still possible to carve out a challenging — and Catholic — liberal arts education under the shadow of the Golden Dome.

Academic Life: Orthodoxy under Siege

Freshmen at Notre Dame must enroll in a yearlong studies program that used to be called the Freshman Year of Studies but is now referred to as the College of First Year Studies. (The word "freshman," it seems, is considered sexist language.) Freshmen do not choose a major but must instead enroll in the College, which has its own faculty and dean, and is one of only four of its kind in the United States. A total of ten courses are required, five per semester. They include a freshman seminar, as well as grammar and composition — classes one student calls "pretty remedial. You have TAs [teaching assistants] who are not first-rate." Students must also complete distribution requirements that include two courses each in theology and philosophy.

Following their freshman year, students enroll in one of four colleges (Arts and Letters, Business Administration, Engineering, and Science), according to their majors. Business Administration and Engineering are the largest colleges. One excellent choice is the Program of Liberal Studies, known around campus as the "Great Books" major, which is administered through the College of Arts and Letters and features seminars conducted in the Socratic dialogue method. Tutorial courses augment these seminars, and students read closely and write extensively about the books covered. This program offers what at one time would have been the standard liberal arts education at most of the country's colleges — an education that has for the most part been replaced by a smorgasbord approach to learning. By choosing it, students ensure that they will be educated for life rather than merely trained for a particular job.

Overall, the core at Notre Dame is not as strong as it could be. A faculty member says: "The core course reflects faculty compromises and is not exclusively devoted to the reading of great books. Now even *this* core course is under attack." Another professor notes: "It's possible to do a pretty good job in general by picking and choosing your courses, but the offerings are quite uneven." Certainly, it is possible to find some very good professors. Remarks one of them: "A qualification [to criticism of the university] is that Notre Dame still hires a core of substantial scholars. Because of its tradition and the high quality of the applicant pool in all areas you can find solid people."

The degree of politicization within the curriculum is less at Notre Dame than at the major research universities, but is significantly more than one might expect from what is arguably this nation's flagship Catholic university. As one professor says, "Like any mantra, multiculturalist education is not an experience but an experiment. And like any experiment, the money is deposited where you have the most need to keep up certain appearances." This teacher continues: "Diversity makes people very prickly. It entails performance anxiety. We take our pulse too often. We ask ourselves every day, 'How diverse are we today?' "

The most politicized department is arguably theology. As one professor says, theology at Notre Dame "is awful. The president always rushes to their aid and says things that are completely incompatible with the teachings of the Holy Father." This faculty member notes that the Catholic document *Ex corde ecclesiae* ("from the heart of the Church") is meant as a governing guideline for Catholic universities and colleges and calls on them to remember whence they came and by whose authority (namely, the Holy See's) they call themselves Catholic. And yet, says this faculty member, "They really don't know what that means any more. Their ecclesiology is so fragmented they don't get it. And once their ecclesiology fell apart, the theology department was transformed. Bishops are seen as external to the campus — they won't allow any external influence." A longtime professor notes that the department's problems are "probably not too well known among the alumni. A lot of people in their fifties and sixties probably don't know what's going on. They see a good life in the dorms and think it's OK."

"Being an orthodox Catholic is a real liability — it will disqualify you from the theology department," one professor notes. "Being a lukewarm, dull Roman Catholic isn't a liability. But if you're conspicuously orthodox, even if you're hired anywhere in the university, you're never going to be groomed for a leadership position on campus." A student remembers that a professor in one theology course lectured on ancient creation myths and questioned the veracity of the Old Testament. This student defended the Bible, although "the professor's position was that she was innocent until proven guilty, and the burden of proof was on anyone who defended the Bible."

Also politicized is the English department. Religion is not generally broached in the hiring of English faculty, but, as one professor notes, "They'll ask [prospective hires] about T. S. Eliot and get them to play their cards."

Aside from theology, however, the most overtly politicized unit is the Gender Studies Program. Certainly an unexpected feature of this program's home page on the web, which is accessible directly from Notre Dame's home page, is that it offers access to a "Gay and Lesbian Links" page, from which one may jump directly to purveyors of Internet cyber-porn. Thus a web user can go from the home page of the nation's premier Catholic university to pornography with about five clicks of a mouse.

Offered through the Gender Studies Program is a required introductory class in which are examined, among other things, the "history and theory of sexuality and queer theory." Also offered is "Gender, Sexuality and Power in Medieval Europe," entry to which requires permission from the instructor. The course description reads, in part: "What has gender to do with sexuality and how can we think about their entanglements in terms of a history of power? How do shifting borders between what counts as masculine and what counts as feminine produce other kinds of bodies in medieval societies: bodies that don't matter? Using original sources and material remains produced from the 3rd to the 15th centuries C.E. together with current feminist and queer theory, students will think about the work of gendered embodiment and the production of bodies that don't matter."

The push for professional education may pose the biggest danger to Notre Dame. "The careerist drive is the greatest threat," says a longtime professor. "The drive for excellence is the engine of secularization. We hire faculty who we see as qualified not because they add to the Catholicity of the school but because they help in our quest for greatness."

Of course, Notre Dame still boasts many outstanding professors, including Denis Moran, John Matthias, James Dougherty, and Thomas Werge in English; Ralph McInerny and Alvin Plantinga in philosophy; Marvin O'Connell, George Marsden, James Turner, and Jay Dolan in history; Charles Rice in the Law School; and Walter Nicgorski in government. Besides the Program of Liberal Studies (whose professors include Frederick J. Crosson, Walter Nicgorski, and Mary Katherine Tillman), Notre Dame is home to excellent departments of philosophy, history, and government. However, many undergrads will find themselves being taught by teaching assistants. "Most of my colleagues wouldn't be here without their graduate students," says one professor. "Those students are necessary for the operation of the university — they're the heart of the place, because they do so much teaching."

Political Atmosphere: A Growing Moral Vacuum

In considering the various problems troubling Notre Dame at the moment, one professor says the greatest concern for many traditionalist faculty members is the moral values promoted on campus. "There is almost no discussion open or private of values here," the professor says. "The idea is 'don't bring up values or we won't get along,' and therefore we can't discuss it." Notes a student: "The defining ethic is that we all need to do a lot of social service and be nice to everyone."

A significant change in the faculty has occurred in the years since the Land O' Lakes conference removed Notre Dame from the direct control of the order of Holy Cross priests who founded and, theoretically at least, still run the school. Every year since, the percentage of faculty who are Catholic has declined; today it is about 65 percent. However, only 29 percent of new faculty hires over the last several years have been Catholic. The rate dips to 25 percent when the most Catholic division of the university, the Law School, is factored out. Says a professor: "Those who are hired say they're never asked about their religion, that it just never came up, that they could have been at an interview for a position at Berkeley. And when you consider that 26 percent of the U.S. is Catholic, that's not much effort on Notre Dame's part." Given Notre Dame's close identity with the Catholic Church and the image it markets to the public and alumni, the numbers are surprising. "Catholic parents assume a Catholicity among the faculty which just isn't here," says a faculty member. Agrees another: "Many people are willing to believe it's more orthodox than it is, that it's more the servant of the Church than it is."

In short, the political atmosphere at Notre Dame is less Catholic than it used to be because the university has imitated the secular model of elite Eastern schools. The campus has become imbued with an array of ideologies that have rushed in to fill the void left by the retreat of the church's influence on campus life. There is an occasional administrative intervention on behalf of the traditions upon which the school was founded, but "an overtly conservative academic would prove more offensive to peers and have a more difficult time than an overtly liberal academic," says a professor. A senior professor adds: "I would advise any young faculty member who comes here to keep quiet about any religious beliefs. Don't make your faith a matter of general knowledge, because it's much, much harder to be hired if you're an orthodox Catholic. There isn't much debate on this any more — it's been this way for twenty years."

More evidence of the degree to which the school is embarrassed by its Catholicity came a few years ago when the administration canceled an anti-abortion conference on the pretext that they weren't given sufficient warning about the conference's content. In fact, say the conference's supporters (as reported by the *Chronicle of Higher Education*), the administration caved in because they "became worried when they learned that the conference would criticize the university for not supporting anti-abortion activities." In 1992 Notre Dame awarded Senator Daniel

Patrick Moynihan, who is unwaveringly pro-abortion, with its oldest and most prestigious award for American Catholics, the Laetare Medal. More recently the school has allowed the independent gay and lesbian journal *Intersection* to be made available on campus. A student notes that the debate on this issue "is getting a lot more shrill. And the administration is trying to stay neutral. They are allowing speakers from Dignity [a pro-homosexual group] to come to campus and speak." Unlike most other universities, however, Notre Dame denies homosexual groups university funding and meeting space.

The school is at a crossroads, according to a senior professor. "Notre Dame is salvageable, but it could be lost [to the Catholic tradition]. It's possible that in a generation it could be like Georgetown." Says another professor: "Any politicization of the university is dangerous, because you create a vacuum and open the door for ideologies." Apparently many Notre Dame alumni are not aware of the condition of the campus. One professor with many decades of experience on campus notes: "The alumni need to see that Notre Dame is a cultural treasure and not merely an institution. I haven't met a single parent all year because they don't come to talk to the teachers — they only hear about dollars from the administration. But no university can go on for long by just selling football tickets."

Student Life: Prayers Can't Hurt

Student life at Notre Dame has much to commend it, because the student body is more conservative than the faculty. People can always be found at the Grotto, a replica of the shrine of Our Lady of Lourdes. Masses are held several times daily in the basilica, and most dorms have their own chapels with daily mass. As a former student says, "They're a well-scrubbed student body. Most are from professional families and most are headed for the professions. There's not a lot of counter-cultural stuff there."

There are no coed dorms, and a priest or a nun lives in every dorm. These rules, which would appear draconian on most college campuses, have long been a part of life at Notre Dame. Former president Fr. Theodore Hesburgh, who governed the university for some twenty years, is said to have remarked that Notre Dame would have coed dorms only over his dead body.

While some students agitate for coed dorms and the general loosening of social policies at the school, others tell stories that indicate that the enforcement of these regulations is not particularly tight. "A lot of the political correctness on campus is not only in the curriculum, but in student life," a student notes. This person was "suckered into being a hall counselor, and we had to watch a Spike Lee movie and hold a discussion on diversity." As for the rules restricting visitation in the dorms, one student claims they are not hard to break. "There is an awful lot of drinking in dorms, even though booze is officially forbidden," the student says.

About 60 percent voted Republican in mock student body elections in 1992, while the faculty voted Democratic by a three-to-one margin. The faculty also voted Democratic in 1996.

There is a pro-life movement on campus that is now active again. A few years ago the movement's leader pressured a reluctant administration into speaking up publicly in favor of life. As one former student said, "They just sort of went to the administration and said, 'why aren't you more openly pro-life?' That got them moving on the issue."

Other student groups include ROTC, several chorales (including a liturgical choir), Habitat for Humanity, an undergraduate investment club, and Humor Artists, a comedy troupe.

Naturally, athletics at Notre Dame revolve around football, but other sports have also been quite successful, including baseball and women's soccer. But, unless a high school senior is a highly regarded football player in search of a spot on an NFL team, other criteria will determine whether he should attend Notre Dame. Much of it has to do with the maturity of the student in question. Says one professor: "A reasonably well informed 18-year-old who has access to one good professor and is told to select his classes with care will be OK." This faculty member continues: "There are a lot of good groups with kids who get together and pray, read, or just hang."

OBERLIN COLLEGE

Office of Admissions
Dean of Admissions
Carnegie Building
Oberlin, OH 44074
(216) 775-8411; (800) 622-OBIE
www.oberlin.edu

Total enrollment: 2,963
Undergraduates: 2,907
SAT Ranges (Verbal/Math): V 610-720, M 590-690
Financial aid: 54%
Applicants: 4,795
Accepted: 53%
Enrolled: 30%
Application deadline: Jan. 15

Financial aid application deadline: Feb. 15
Tuition: $22,282
Core curriculum: No

Missionary Zeal

Oberlin College was founded in 1833 by two missionaries to train teachers and missionaries for excursions into the still-wild West. Just four years later, Oberlin became the first college in the country to admit women, and one of the first to admit African-Americans.

Though the school is now entirely secular, the zeal of the early mission workers lives on — albeit in different ways. Political correctness is the religion today, and at Oberlin it's not so much debated as instilled. In fact, the widespread acceptance of modern ideologies makes the place rather calm in its overall political activity, although students and faculty with traditional beliefs certainly feel otherwise.

The academic program can be rigorous, despite a recent curriculum revision. "It makes you a great contestant on *Jeopardy*," a recent graduate says. Carefully selecting the best of Oberlin's classes makes all the difference, regardless of the radical ideas that preoccupy much of the campus. Certainly, politics is a major force on campus, but a force mostly unopposed causes few ripples.

Academic Life: The Open Field

Oberlin College abolished its core curriculum in the early 1970s, a time when such steps were not uncommon among highly rated schools. Until the early 1980s there were no required courses: students merely had to choose a major and collect a certain number of credit hours in any manner they wished. But in the 1986-87 school year Oberlin began to restore "bits and pieces of requirements," according to one professor.

Today there is little support on campus for a return to a traditional core curriculum. Distribution requirements are general, mandating 112 hours of credit for graduation, with at least nine credits in each of the college's three divisions: Arts and Humanities, Social and Behavorial Sciences, and Natural Sciences and Mathematics. The selected courses must represent at least two departments within each division. "Beyond this minimal expectation the college encourages its students to explore the growing scope and substance of human knowledge by taking additional courses outside the area of their primary interests," the catalogue states.

Oberlin does have a writing requirement and a "quantitative proficiency" requirement, both of which may be satisfied with high scores on standardized tests or by designated courses. The writing courses must come from two different departments, and choices include "Traditional African Cosmology" in the department of African-American studies and "Sexually Transmitted Diseases" in the biology department, among others. Quantitative proficiency requirements are similarly interdisciplinary — courses in American history and politics (for example, "American Inequalities") will suffice, along with other more substantive options, such as an art course entitled "The Technology of Ancient Architecture."

There is also a "cultural diversity" requirement, which, despite the radical attitudes of many Oberlin faculty, was not introduced without "mild controversy," according to a humanities professor. The requirement is ostensibly designed to expose "students to several minority cultures," in the words of the professor, but because of lobbying by foreign language departments, the study of a language other than English can also count toward the nine credits required in this area. Because of the latitude permitted in fulfilling the cultural diversity quota, the requirement is "neither onerous for students or really clear in what it's accomplishing," says the humanities professor. The college catalogue does claim that "in mandating education in cultural diversity, the requirement is not intended to promote the subordination of the Western tradition to other traditions." Still, the course of study at the college doesn't enforce the promotion of a deeper understanding of Western culture, either.

All students must take at least three Winter Term classes while at Oberlin. This four-week January session is designed to "affor[d] students an opportunity to devise and pursue programs of independent study or research," the catalogue states; independent study, it says, is intended to "encourage and enable students to discover the value of self-education." During Winter Term, students can select a course offered by the college or create their own. The possibilities can be worthwhile, and usually are as taxing as the student wishes to make them. One student analyzed her extensive childhood diaries and wrote an analytical paper on what she had learned. The same student, during another Winter Term, obtained half of her credit for working at the local historical society and the other half for putting together a schedule of physical exercise, which previously had not been a priority for her. Professors have some guidance over independent studies, but there has been controversy on campus over the latitude permitted by some professors in interpreting the requirements.

While many colleges allow some form of independent study, few have a program that is entirely student-run. Oberlin's "Experimental College" (EXCO) is just that, offering short courses taught by either faculty or students. These courses count in small bits toward the hours needed for graduation, and while they don't replace regular classes, students do use EXCO offerings "to pad our schedule a little bit," one student says. In the past, courses have included "Football Appreciation" (taught on Sunday afternoons by members of the football team) and "Essential Films of the 80s" (featuring *Ferris Bueller's Day Off*, among others). Other courses are activity-based, such as knitting and self-defense. "My roommate took a class on *Days of Our Lives*," a student says. While the media classes are designed to stimulate critical discussion, most are not taken very seriously.

These professors teach more traditional courses, and do so very well: Robert Longsworth in English; Jeff Witmer in mathematics; David Benzing, Yolanda Cruz, and Roger Laushman in biology; Norman Craig and Martin Ackermann in chemistry; and Robert Warner in the physics department. The natural sciences, especially biology, chemistry, physics, and neuroscience/biopsychology, are considered very strong, as are the departments of mathematics, philosophy, politics, religion, and classics.

One of Oberlin's best-known programs is the Conservatory of Music, separate from the College of Arts and Sciences, which encompasses all other disciplines. The conservatory, which shares the college campus and enrolls more than 550 students, was founded in 1865 as a private music school and became part of the college two years later. Oberlin says it is "the only institution in the country to combine a leading liberal arts college and a world-renowned conservatory on one campus." Many Arts and Sciences students take courses at the conservatory, and double majors are possible if the student can gain separate admission to both entities (conservatory admission is very competitive). The conservatory is one of the best in the nation, and its undergraduate program is a match for some graduate programs. Its 188 Steinway pianos constitute the largest collection under one roof outside the Steinway factory. There are three major performance halls, including Finney Chapel, named for the nineteenth-century revivalist whose support was critical to Oberlin's early years.

The natural science departments' stature on campus is compared by one professor to that of the conservatory's. "I think natural science at Oberlin is a little-known jewel — it has a crucial function in maintaining [Oberlin's] academic caliber, and does attract some of the best students," the professor says. "It's comparable to having the Conservatory of Music, one quality of uniqueness which is inarguable." Probably the strongest of the several strong sciences at Oberlin is chemistry, according to a professor from another department. "It's worked very hard to build and maintain a coherent identity," the professor says. "I've heard rich testimonials from students about how valuable this experience is. The department is, without question, crackerjack." Two chemistry professors, Norman Craig and Martin Ackermann, have won the Catalyst Award of the American Chemical Society. Craig is a former Oberlin student, and both are noted for making strenuous efforts to involve students in their research, both during the summer and throughout the year.

Biology is known for several superlative teachers, including David Benzing and Yolanda Cruz. Physics is also highly regarded; its strengths lie in its teaching rather than its professors' reputation for research outside the Oberlin community. The physics department has been successful in serving both its most advanced majors and students taking a course to fill out their distribution requirements.

There is considerable politicization among the humanities departments, but philosophy and classics have escaped much of it. Religion is also quite strong, according to those on campus. Art history, though more radical, is known for its strenuous academic requirements.

In other humanities departments students will find varying degrees of politicization. In general the social sciences are Oberlin's weakest area from a traditional point of view. English and history are in close to the same predicament, their faculties representing the full spectrum of radical positions. English is the largest major on campus, claiming one out of every five members of the average graduating class. In the Oberlin catalogue, English department course descriptions are terse and sober, but, nevertheless, the titles give some indication of their teachers' leanings: for example, "Post-Colonial Criticism" and "American Fiction and Sexual Difference." Even apart from the subject matter, many courses are politicized by the emphasis on criticism rather than the great books themselves. Even standard survey courses have given in to this. For example, the catalogue description for "British Romantic Literature" states that the course will highlight "canon, genre, and interpretation based on aspects of gender."

In history, the same tendency toward theory prevails. In one course titled "The Body as Historical Subject," students "explore the use of the body both as a site of symbolic representation and as a site for the construction of experience, gender, and sexuality," through readings that include libertine French philosopher Michel Foucault. "Roots of Feminist Analysis" and "History of Latinas in the United States" were recently offered during a year in which "American Intellectual History" and "Machiavelli and the Renaissance" were not. While the catalogue does list traditional survey offerings in American and European history, a professor in another department says no history professors are specialists in European history. When the European history position came open not long ago, the department hired a specialist in South Asian history, the professor says.

Oberlin's women's studies program is, according to a professor from another department, internally divided into various feminist camps, and its pedagogy "is a matter of deep dispute among warring factions in the students and faculty." This professor says disputes within the department have become distractions for the college community, and for that and other reasons the program has yet to gain standing as an official department. African-American studies, on the other hand, is a department and has a very "clear sense of self-identity," the professor says. Oberlin does not have a gay and lesbian studies program, but a handful of humanities courses pay significant attention to homosexuality. Asian students have recently begun to lobby for more courses on Asian history and culture, and on the Asian experience in America.

Political Atmosphere: Going Underground

Traditional and conservative students and faculty can have a tough time at Oberlin. One professor says segments of the Oberlin community are "ideological and aggressive." Another person familiar with the campus estimates that as many as one-fifth of the students are "unbelievably intolerant" of traditional beliefs. The pockets of political conservatives and evangelical Christians on campus, including the Oberlin Christian Fellowship and Ecumenical Christians at Oberlin, use the hostility to their beliefs as a source of self-strengthening and challenge, a student says. Some Christian faculty have placed fish symbols on their doors, perhaps unconsciously using the sign as early Christians did: in the face of persecution.

"The whole public atmosphere is pretty much confined to the left," a professor says. "In the rhetoric that is constantly used at this place, in questions of sexual orientation and racial divides, there is a real balkanization that has taken place in recent years." This, the professor says, is over and above the mere leftism of the past.

The most prominent radical group at Oberlin is the gay community. "I don't think any accurate depiction would avoid the fact that the gay presence is strong and vocal," one professor says. Another calls the college "a haven" for gay, lesbian, and bisexual students. All agree that the groups are politically shrewd: Oberlin's homosexual community schedules its "Gay Pride" festival to coincide with a program for incoming students. This has "caused a good deal of Administrative consternation," a professor says, but the events have occurred during the same week for several years running. The Drag Ball held every spring is easily the most popular social event on campus. About 1,600 of the college's 2,800 students attend, and recently they have been joined by college president Nancy Schrom Dye. Even students who begin college opposed to these activities often give in to social pressures and eventually attend, a recent graduate says. This person recalls that a friend of hers who was "Republican and very religious" refused to go to the Drag Ball his freshman year but changed his mind as a sophomore and went.

Other sexual issues attract Oberlin's attention. Since homosexual couples may live together in college residence halls, the administration has been pressured — unsuccessfully — to allow heterosexual couples the same privilege. Some residence halls have coed bathrooms. A student sadomasochism club is reportedly in formation, although it has not received official sanction from Oberlin's administration. One bizarre incident occurred in 1997, when, as part of a student's composition recital at the conservatory, two masked students entered the recital hall and one began performing fellatio on the other. Though this was considered extreme even by Oberlin standards, the administration took no disciplinary action and said only that the display fell under the license of artistic expression normally granted performers.

Oberlin has also debated "program houses," student residences dedicated to common interests or ethnic backgrounds. The college has four houses whose residents are interested in a particular foreign language, as well as an Asia House, Afrikan Heritage House, the Women's Collective, Hebrew House, and Third World House, each of which offers events for residents and sponsors programs for the community at large. Lately the program houses have objected to being located in an isolated section of the campus and have asked to be placed elsewhere so as to become better integrated into the campus community.

Despite the predominance and acceptance of radical policies and groups, one professor says the college's nihilistic image is more hype than substance. While it's true that the multicultural issues "tend to stimulate a good deal of conversation," and that Oberlin tends to "harbor" and value its reputation for politicization, the professor says that, lately, students have been "much less politically interested or perceptive" than in the past. "The number of relatively passive students and faculty members has grown in the last decade." While the dominant voices on campus may be given to sensational rhetoric, there does exist a sort of underground comprised of a variety of opinions and ideas, the professor says. A recent graduate says she was pleasantly "surprised at the number of conservative students" and glad to find that she and they did not feel "like they were hunted down." Within the college's more moderate elements, this graduate says, "you can find people like you, even if you might not be in the majority, or of the opinion Oberlin's known for." She found, however, that in general, "people are very open minded as long as you have the right opinion."

Still, it is more practical to keep quiet and not offend the more powerful campus radicals. Oberlin's campus judicial proceedings are said to be secretive and particularly vicious when dealing with sexual harassment charges. The college has a sexual offense officer who "operates totally in an atmosphere of confidentiality," one faculty member notes. As a result, there are "relatively few formal proceedings" of a high-profile sort, and the hushed hearings tend to contribute to a subtle paranoia in the college community, the professor says. The college has an elaborate sexual offense policy that spells out "what are regarded as linguistic misbehaviors to faculty, students, and employees," a professor says. Once someone is accused, there is an "elaborate grievance process — almost grotesquely elaborate," particularly in the application of parliamentary procedure, the professor says. "Plagiarism is nothing in comparison with that."

Student Life: . . . and the Wisdom to Know the Difference

Many things are not permitted at Oberlin, but smoking marijuana "is, if not countenanced, then at least tacitly permitted," says a graduate. And, unlike ideological transgressions, recreational drug use does not normally result in campus judicial proceedings, "unless it's a big problem," the graduate says. "It does give Oberlin the reputation for being a little bit of a 'druggie' school."

According to the student newspaper, the *Oberlin Review*, some students feel comfortable enough around drugs to advertise their use. In 1997 an anonymous group of students sent out flyers announcing "Trip Saturday," intended, in the words of the *Review*, to "create a community atmosphere and to explore the options created by use of psychedelics throughout the country." The campus was not sure what to make of this, but the administration was: it responded not with statements on the moral or ethical implications of illicit drug use, but with advice from the counseling center on "how to deal with a 'bad trip,' " the *Review* reported. Several students were quoted anonymously in the article, with one admitting that "it's known I sell psychedelic drugs" and another saying it is "really, really, easy" to obtain drugs at Oberlin.

The town of Oberlin is dry, although some liquor licenses have been issued to various establishments, including the Oberlin College Inn. In addition to harder drug use, some "people drink a lot of beer," according to one student.

As for the *Review*, it also feels free to flout societal taboos, making liberal use of the "f-word" in articles on subjects as mundane as a women's lacrosse tournament.

At the other end of the scale are events such as a recent protest of the "United States blockade of humanitarian aid to Cuba," an event involving "people from all over the country seeking social justice in foreign policy" and incorporating a drive to collect "school supplies for the children of Cuba." One of the allied Oberlin groups participating in the event was an organization that calls itself the Coalition against Apartheid and White Supremacy and involved the support of Oberlin's Office of Chaplains.

Student organizations include the Lesbian, Gay and Bisexual Union; College Democrats; Oberlin Christian Fellowship; Students for Free Tibet; and Oberlin Zionists. There are also several "theme residences" at Oberlin, including Spanish, Russian, French, German, "Afrikan Heritage," and Third World varieties.

Oberlin, a town of eight thousand, is thirty-five miles southwest of Cleveland. Its tree-lined streets boast some of the most unique residential architecture in Ohio, including charming clapboard houses. Among the many cultural perks of life at Oberlin are good bookstores (the Co-op and Miranda Books) and great coffee shops (the Feve; the Java Zone, where faculty and staff hang out; and the more elegant Main Street Mercantile Store and Tea Room, known locally as the MERC). Another architectural gem in the downtown area is the Apollo movie theater, an art deco building that features current films (as opposed to the more vintage and artistic film series shown on campus). Admission at the Apollo is only three dollars — two dollars on Tuesday and Thursday nights.

UNIVERSITY OF PENNSYLVANIA

Dean of Admissions
University of Pennsylvania
1 College Hall
Philadelphia, PA 19014-6376
(215) 898-7507
www.upenn.edu

Total enrollment: 22,150
Undergraduates: 9,450
SAT Ranges (Verbal/Math): V 620-710, M 640-730
Financial aid: 46%
Applicants: 16,651
Accepted: 29%
Enrolled: 48%
Application deadline: Jan. 1
Financial aid application deadline: Feb. 15
Tuition: $23,254
Core curriculum: No

Philadelphia "Freedom"

The University of Pennsylvania was founded in 1740 as a charity school for Philadelphia children. In 1750 American patriot Benjamin Franklin merged the Public Academy of Philadelphia with this charity school and named the new institution the College, Academy and Charitable School of Philadelphia. Due to its early founding, Penn claims to be "the nation's first university [but not the first college], the nation's first medical school, its first collegiate business school, the first journalism program, [and] the first university teaching hospital."

As an Ivy League school with an impressive founding, Penn has had a lot going for it. But increasingly the version of freedom celebrated by this Philadelphia institution is one based not on tradition but on the new multiculturalism, which dictates freedom for some and straitjackets for others. In the hands of recent administrations, the university's motto — "*Leges Sine Moribus Vanae* (Laws without morals are useless)" — has been stretched, twisted, and occasionally even contradicted.

Along with an aggressive ideological regime has come, predictably, an abdication of the principles of liberal education. Penn is rapidly abandoning these traditions, and the next century can't arrive soon enough to satisfy the president, whose 21st Century Program will have students even more engaged in job training and service projects than the extensive degree to which they presently are on campus. Penn's attempt to redefine the meaning of freedom — the "liberal" in "liberal arts" — has made it one of the more controversial Ivy League schools, and may well come to haunt it in the twenty-first century.

Academic Life: Undergraduates, Underdogs

Penn has nothing even remotely resembling a core curriculum, even going so far as to refer in its catalogue to classes in "The General Requirement" as "electives." Students enrolled in one of four undergraduate schools (the School of Nursing, the School of Engineering and Applied Sciences, the Wharton School, and the School of Arts and Sciences) must take ten General Requirement courses distributed among six "sectors." The university makes little effort to direct the students along any particular path, and even states in the course catalogue that "it is also recognized that the plenitude of University courses is in itself bewildering; informed choice is only possible if the number of General Requirement alternatives is reasonably contained."

Philly's own Rocky may not have been as big an underdog as are students forced to discover a solid liberal arts education at Penn. Their choices are contained only by the sectors, which include society, history and tradition, arts and letters, formal reasoning and analysis, the living world, and the physical world. Students must take six courses from the first three sectors and four from the last three, and substitutions are permitted. The problem is that the sector with the shortest list of possible courses, formal reasoning and analysis, contains seventeen courses in six departments. The longest list, arts and letters, permits ninety-six courses in any of twenty-four departments. Lists contain a mixture of Western and non-Western topics, in traditional and nontraditional fields, ranging from "Discrimination: Racial and Sexual Conflict" and "Sociology of Popular Culture" to "Comparative Western European Politics" and "Epic Tradition." Students are told to take what interests them, with a little help from their advisers. The number of courses offered in the General Requirement makes it quite possible to avoid all of the texts and issues that once constituted a traditional liberal arts education, a student says.

With the right choices, the General Requirement can be used to select an extraordinary education. In a highly politicized academic environment such as Penn, a loose curriculum is a better alternative than a required partisan multicultural curriculum. In the early 1990s, the university proposed the adoption of a "Diversity Requirement" in the School of Arts and Sciences. After vigorous opposition from the faculty, the proposal was defeated.

Undergraduates must also complete a minimal foreign language requirement by demonstrating proficiency in one of the fifty-seven languages offered, either by taking classes or by passing a test. A writing requirement was added to the general requirements in 1993, which also can be satisfied by taking one writing course, a class with an attached writing lab, or two classes affiliated with the Writing across the University Program. Some courses that count in the latter category include "Past, Present, and Future of Africans in America: A Critical Look," "Weird and Eccentric: Unusual Individuals in the History of the Philadelphia Area," "Student Movements and the Political Process," and "Star Wars: The Cosmology."

The general requirements apply to all Penn undergrads who select one of the more than fifty majors under the School of Arts and Sciences. The other three schools have their own general requirements, each more focused on the area of the school's specialization. The Wharton School, considered by many the nation's top graduate business school, also offers prestigious undergraduate degrees in business fields. According to publicity materials, Wharton is ranked "first nationally in finance, real estate, entrepreneurship, finance, insurance/risk management." Its departments of accounting, marketing, nonprofit management, quantitative studies, business ethics, and global management are considered among the top five in the country. The School of Nursing is the only Ivy League school to offer bachelor's, master's, and doctoral degrees in nursing, and is regarded as one of the three best nursing schools in the country.

Penn students who want to get out of Philadelphia for a time can choose from a wide range of semester-, year-, and summer-abroad programs that reach seventy-seven countries on all six inhabited continents. In 1994-95, nearly a thousand Penn students (about 56 percent of them undergraduates) took advantage of Penn programs for credit abroad.

In addition to its 9,500 undergraduates, Penn enrolls more than 8,500 graduate students in twelve graduate and professional schools. Besides the Wharton School and the nursing school, the School of Arts and Sciences, the Law School, and the School of Medicine are thought to be among the top ten nationwide. Penn is home to the only veterinary school in Pennsylvania, one of only two private vet schools in the country. The university also is home to the Annenberg School for Communication, the School of Dental Medicine, the School of Engineering and Applied Science, the Graduate School of Education, the Graduate School of Fine Arts, and the School of Social Work.

Several good professors are available to undergraduates at Penn. In English there are Al Filreis and John Richetti. In history Alan Charles Kors, Marc Trachtenberg, Walter McDougall, Ann Moyer, Arthur Waldron, and Thomas Childers are outstanding. In philosophy there are Gary Hatfield, Lisa Downing, James Ross, and Zoltan Domotor. In history and sociology of science Mark Adams and Margaret C. Jacob are considered excellent.

The best departments on campus are the ones least touched by ideological fever. Psychology is said by a professor to be "rigorous, and deeply grounded in both biological science and in humanistic study." Mathematics, physics, and other sciences are also highly regarded. "The hard sciences are good in terms of academics," a student says. Despite these comments, most conservative members of the Penn community are silent when asked to name exceptional departments at Penn.

Quite a few departments are dominated by a politicized atmosphere, however. "Most departments in the School of Arts and Sciences are hostile to traditional political views," says a student. "One student reported getting a paper back that said, 'Maybe you would have gotten a better grade if you had not learned how to write from *The Red and Blue*' [the conservative newspaper on campus]."

English is one of the most politicized departments at Penn; one professor calls the curriculum there "politicized, self-indulgent, and intolerant," while a student says the department's take on literary criticism resides "on the cutting edge of wackiness." A recent graduate calls the department a "haven for Neo-Marxists." One professor, Nina Auerbach, has written a book entitled *Our Vampires, Our Selves,* which is based on the thesis "that vampirism springs not only from paranoia, xenophobia, or immortal longings, but from generosity and shared enthusiasm."

Political Atmosphere: Can Anyone Here Play This Game?

Penn has suffered from recent university administrations committed to surfing on the multicultural wave now sweeping over the academy. The current president, Judith Rodin, a Penn alumna, took office in 1994. Rodin came to Penn from Yale University, where she served as the dean of the Graduate School of Arts and Sciences and as provost. Rodin's Yale years had their share of controversy. In fact, many Yale students and alumni blame her for the loss of Lee Bass's $20 million grant for the establishment of Western civilization studies. When Rodin was provost at Yale, a committee set up to determine the implementation of the Bass grant recommended to Yale's president that some of the money be used to hire four new junior professors to teach Western civilization. Rodin strongly advised against this, even though a well-known professor who was instrumental in securing the gift said the new hires had been expected and should be made. The president sided with Rodin, and the $20 million was returned to Bass, a move that led to the loss over nearly $100 million in donations from other disgusted Yale alumni.

It is possible that Rodin has learned her lesson. "[She] is very savvy when it comes to public relations," a student says. "Over the past year she has tried very hard to do away with Penn's image of ideological policing and intellectual intolerance." In fact, Rodin has stated publicly that she wants a diversity not only of race but of opinion, including both conservative and liberal ideas, and has called the guarantee of "free expression, reasoned discourse, and the diversity of ideas" a necessary function of the university.

There is no doubt that damage has been done to Penn's reputation, damage that began during the tenure of Sheldon Hackney, who left Penn briefly to serve as director of the National Endowment for the Humanities under President Clinton. Students at Penn came to call Hackney "the Pope of Political Correctness," and two incidents among many that occurred during his term as president help explain why.

In 1993 a guest conservative columnist for a university-recognized student publication, the *Daily Pennsylvanian*, wrote an editorial critical of the university's hate-speech code, admissions policies that favored minorities, and over-the-top multiculturalism. A group of black students accused the writer of racial harassment, but the charge was dropped by the administration when the journalist pointed out an official university policy that expressly forbade investigation of students for opinions published in school papers. In retaliation for the dismissal of charges, a group calling itself "The Black Community" stole an entire pressrun of the newspaper. Even after the students proudly confessed to vandalism, Hackney refused to discipline them. "After the event, the number of reported newspaper thefts on campuses quadrupled," says an alumnus. "There was no question that Hackney's unwillingness to punish the students was a green light to copycat cases of newspaper thefts around the country. The message at Penn was clear: if an article insults you, feel free to steal and destroy the paper."

Then there was the so-called water buffalo incident. In January of 1993 a group of female African-American students were chanting and making other noises outside a dormitory where several students were studying and sleeping. It was around midnight, and the students in the dorm, disturbed by the noise, gathered at the windows to shout at the women to be quiet. Eventually police were called. Based on the complaints of the students outside, the police interrogated dormitory resident Eden Jacobowitz, who admitted to shouting "Shut up, you water buffalo." The Judicial Inquiry Office of the university charged Jacobowitz with racial harassment under the hate-speech code. A publicity storm ensued, and the unfavorable publicity caused the board of trustees to order the speech code scrapped. Hackney is back at Penn as a full professor of history.

Student Life: The Broad Street Bullies

Located in West Philadelphia, Penn's campus is an oasis of prosperity in an area wracked by urban decay. The wealthy university is sandwiched between run-down buildings (slums, really) and a major expressway. In order to improve the surrounding areas, the university runs a program called the West Philadelphia Improvement Corps, where Penn students "incorporate real-world research into their academic studies" by providing classes and educational opportunities to community residents and public-school students. University promotional materials say "the president works to maintain good relations between Penn and its neighbors in West Philadelphia with the support of the university's multi-faceted academic and volunteer service activities. Hundreds of Penn students currently volunteer in West Philadelphia. Moreover, the University offers approximately 50 courses that involve its students and faculty in academic work with the community." Penn has more than three hundred volunteer and community service programs in which six thousand students, faculty, and staff participate.

Despite these depressed surroundings, Penn is the first Ivy League university to complete a $1 billion fund-raising campaign in five years. It has the twelfth-largest, and the fastest-growing, endowment of any university in the country, but its endowment per student remains one of the lowest of the major universities. Nevertheless, it is still expensive to go to Penn, where the undergraduate tuition is $23,254 a year and room and board fees are approximately $7,000. Still, the university in one recent year received more than fifteen thousand applications for admission and accepted 29 percent of the applicants. The university notes that 36 percent of the most recent incoming freshman class was from ethnic minorities — a credit to the multiculturalist objectives of the administration. What the university will not publish are the dropout rates of its minority student population.

The 262-acre campus includes attractions such as Houston Hall, the nation's first student union; the University of Pennsylvania Museum (established in 1887, its one-million-item collection includes artifacts from Egypt, Mesopotamia, Africa, Asia, Polynesia, and the Americas, and it is considered one of the finest university archaeology and anthropology museums in the country); and Franklin Field, the oldest collegiate football field still in use and the country's first double-decked college stadium. Victorian buildings are intermingled with modern structures on the campus. Locust Walk, once a city street but now open only to nonmotorized traffic, is perhaps the most beautiful part of the campus. "During the day, Locust Walk hosts an on-going ballet of people, coming in and out of class," says an alumnus.

While virtually all underclassmen live in West Philadelphia, many upperclassmen and graduate students live across the Schuylkill River in Center City, the heart of Philadelphia. One benefit of living away from campus is comparative safety. In 1996 a Penn student was shot on campus. This was the last straw for students tired of panhandlers on campus (around the intersections of Thirty-eighth and Spruce and Thirty-sixth and Chestnut) as well as residents of West Philly who run red lights, roll through stop signs, and throw trash on the ground. Public drunkenness has reportedly been a problem, and graffiti can be found on the buildings of local businesses. The administration has now allowed campus security personnel to carry semiautomatic weapons. Other students have requested "a police officer on every corner" and a "big wall around campus." One recent alumnus characterized the Penn campus as "extremely unsafe."

The administration did recently install floodlights on top of three high-rise dormitories on campus, but has done or can do little about the surrounding streets. Next to campus, for example, cheese steaks and alcohol are available twenty-four hours a day at a place called Billy Bob's, and fights break out on a regular basis near where the student was shot. "When it comes to safety, the Rodin administration has a very fuzzy definition of what is 'on campus,'" a student says.

Students enjoy the ever-popular South Street (which holds bars, restaurants, stores, coffeehouses, and booksellers) and can visit Philadelphia's rich array of museums and historic sites. Undergraduates who crave a party but wish to avoid the dangers of the streets can usually find something going on at one of the several fraternities or sororities on campus.

Several conservative groups are active on campus, especially the *Red and Blue* magazine. There is also an active chapter of the College Republicans.

One of the most politicized student groups on campus is the Lesbian, Gay, Bisexual Center (LGBC), an official university office.

The administration sponsors the highly politicized Penn Women's Center, which provides advising, advocacy, counseling, and referrals regarding contraceptives and abortion. The organization networks with a number of feminist student groups, including Women for Equal Opportunity at the University of Pennsylvania; Penn Women's Alliance; Sister, Sister, a black women's group for students, staff, and faculty; *Voyage Out* (a publication of the Women's Alliance); Women United for Change; and Multicultural Women at Penn.

Under the Hackney administration, the Women's Center was the focus of several politically correct campus outrages. Under President Rodin the Center's radicalism has not subsided. One of the groups sponsored by the Center is White Women against Racism, a group of "white women struggling with our own racism and speaking out against racism on the Penn campus and in the larger community." At one meeting of the group, the center's director, Eli DiLapi, ejected a student from the group, telling her that her presence was inappropriate. The student was black. The incident made the PC headlines, but Penn refused to reprimand the Center's director. One Penn professor described the White Women fiasco as "one of those moments when you can't tell the difference between parody and the real thing." A year later Rodin increased the Center's budget and staff and moved the offices into one of the most prized locations on campus — an evicted fraternity on Locust Walk.

Penn runs a very active sports program at both the varsity and intramural level. Its baseball, basketball, and football teams were Ivy League champions in 1996.

PEPPERDINE UNIVERSITY

Seaver College
Office of Admission
24255 Pacific Coast Highway
Malibu, CA 90263-4392
(310) 456-4392
www.pepperdine.edu

Total enrollment: 7,802
Undergraduates: 2,820
SAT Ranges (Verbal/Math): V 570-660, M 580-670
Financial aid: 75%
Applicants: 4,776
Accepted: 56%
Enrolled: 30%
Application deadline: Jan. 15
Financial aid application deadline: Feb. 15
Tuition: $21,000
Core curriculum: Yes

Western Arts Supply

The beautiful surroundings of Pepperdine University — in the foothills of the Santa Monica Mountains, overlooking the beach — should not be taken to imply that the university is interested in sun and surf to the exclusion of studies. In fact, the university offers a very strong liberal arts curriculum in a traditional atmosphere. The sun and the beach are extras.

Pepperdine was founded in 1937 by businessman George Pepperdine, who had made his fortune as the owner of the Western Auto Supply Company. Pepperdine, a member of the Church of Christ, wanted a university that would "help young men and women prepare themselves for a life of usefulness in this competitive world and to help them build a foundation of Christian character and faith which will survive the storms of life." The university's mission statement and policies still hold that this development of Christian character is central to the institution's work.

The university's undergraduate program remains strongly dedicated to the liberal arts, and all students take a core of classes devoted to Western history and humanities. There are few, if any, politicized courses in the entire undergraduate curriculum. When compared to outstanding liberal arts institutions like Hillsdale College or the University of Dallas, however, Pepperdine just can't boast the same density of outstanding faculty. To some extent, therefore, Pepperdine promises a little more than it delivers when it comes to a traditional education. At the same time, it must be said that Pepperdine rests firmly on its Christian foundations, which serve as the impetus for its academic search for truth. The university's mission statement says that "spiritual commitment, tolerating no excuse for mediocrity, demands the highest standards of academic excellence." With that standard to live up to, Pepperdine is headed in the right direction.

Academic Life: Dream Seaver

Pepperdine University comprises five colleges: Seaver College for undergraduates, the School of Law, the School of Business and Management, the Graduate School of Education and Psychology, and the School of Public Policy, which enrolled its first class in the fall of 1997. Seaver College, the public policy school, and the law school are housed exclusively in the Malibu campus; the other two schools are administratively based elsewhere and offer courses throughout the Los Angeles/Orange County/San Fernando Valley area.

Seaver College of Letters, Arts, and Sciences is home to Pepperdine's 2,800 undergraduates. Each student, regardless of major, must complete a series of requirements known as the General Education Program. Most students meet these requirements in their freshman and sophomore years, prior to the specialized courses that constitute a major.

The program involves a combination of required course sequences and a few courses students select from very short lists, making it a very close approximation of a traditional core curriculum. A two-course sequence is required in English composition, both of which are to be taken during the freshman year. A three-course sequence in religion includes "The History and Religion of Israel," "The History and Religion of Early Christianity," and "Religion and Culture." Another sequence fulfills the "Western Heritage" requirement; its three courses take an interdisciplinary look at the history, literature, religion, philosophy, and art of Western civilization.

In the category of "American Heritage," students must select two of these three offerings: "Economic Principles," "The United States of America," and "American Political Process." Students must also choose one of two courses in the area of behavioral science. Pepperdine requires competency in a foreign language through the third semester, as well as courses in mathematics, speech and rhetoric, laboratory science, and physical education. All freshmen participate in a seminar whose content includes an introduction to college life, discussions on the value of higher education, and the use of critical thinking skills.

Pepperdine does require one course in "Non-Western Heritage," but the seventeen choices consist primarily of solid historical surveys (such as "Pre-Columbian Civilizations of North America," "East Asian Cultural History," and "Chinese Thought and Society Since A.D. 1000") rather than politicized courses. And since students are also required to study Western culture, they have a point of reference from which to understand non-Western cultures — something many curricula do not provide as part of "diversity" mandates.

Pepperdine's extensive general education requirements are fairly popular with the students, though some say they don't appreciate the courses until after a few years of college. "Some of the time you feel like, 'Why am I in this class?' but a lot of times you come back to the material in a few years and are able to see the value," says one senior.

Some core requirements can be replaced by a "Great Books Colloquium," available to the best students who apply prior to their freshman years. The program usually involves one course per semester for two years, and is devoted to the study of the masterpieces of Western civilization. "The purpose of the colloquium is to engage students in close, critical reading and small group discussions of selected works from the time of the ancient Greeks to the modern day," the catalogue states. "The courses are conducted almost wholly by discussion under the leadership of a qualified professor dedicated to fostering open, shared, and rigorous inquiry." Courses involve a considerable amount of reading, but the writing assignments are similar to those found in other freshman courses.

Just as the general education requirements are traditional, so are most departments at Pepperdine. The humanities are for the most part free of the trendy politicization found at so many other schools, and the more professional departments are also dedicated to excellent teaching.

The business administration division, one of these professional departments, offers B.S. degrees in accounting, business administration, and international business. The department connects its courses with the university's core curriculum via the philosophy of John Stuart Mill, paraphrased in the course catalogue: "Persons are persons before they are businesspersons, and if they are educated to become capable and sensible persons, they will make themselves capable and sensible businesspersons." The quality of teaching in the department is said to be well above average.

Similar excellence is found in the sports medicine department, a popular major at Pepperdine. Majors take several science courses in a variety of disciplines, providing them "with a foundation in the role of science in exercise and health promotion," according to the catalogue.

Pepperdine offers year-round study-abroad programs in Australia, England, Germany, Italy, and Japan, as well as summer programs in Argentina, France, Israel, Russia, Scotland, and Spain. There are also two summer area tours — one to Asia, another to the Mediterranean. Students who participate in these popular programs are taught by Pepperdine professors, and the credits they earn often apply to the general education requirements. Students who study abroad — and about half of the students do — usually do so in their sophomore or junior years.

International issues can also be studied on campus; the university has an interdisciplinary major in international studies. Students examine "social, economic, political, management, communication, and cultural facets of a multinational environment," the catalogue states. There are six specializations in the international studies major: Asian, economics, European, international/intercultural communication, international management, and political studies. Of course, students in this program are strongly urged to study abroad, usually during their sophomore year.

Political Atmosphere: Stable

Pepperdine's administration is rather traditional in its political views. It has shown little interest in the current radical trends in academe, and President David Davenport has said repeatedly in the press and in university literature that he wants the university to instill in students a respect for Christian values through the study of traditional liberal arts. Davenport's leadership made possible the School of Public Policy, one of the few such schools on the West Coast. The school emphasizes a free-market, limited government approach to social problems. For example, it has on its faculty Jack Kemp, former U.S. secretary of Housing and Urban Development and the 1996 Republican vice presidential candidate. Kemp began teaching at Pepperdine in 1996, but beginning in 1998 he will visit campus twice a year to lecture and lead discussions.

Political activism among students is minimal at Pepperdine. The most popular political groups are hardly radical: the College Democrats and College Republicans. Some speakers that come to Pepperdine would most certainly not be welcomed elsewhere. Recently the cofounder of the National Association for Research and Therapy of Homosexuality told a student convocation that homosexuality is based on envy and is a psychological disorder that can be cured. There was hardly a protest, though debate over the claim continued on campus for several days. "I wanted to see civility, conviction, and compassion," an assistant dean told the *Graphic*, the school's student newspaper. "I think we did fine. The lecture brought out perspectives that aren't usually addressed in public."

Student Life: Making Waves

One graduation requirement at Pepperdine is not academic, but it is also not optional. A card reader records students' ID cards as they enter and leave convocations held each Monday morning, and all undergraduates must average at least fourteen convocations (or smaller makeup sessions) per semester or they will not be permitted to graduate. Convocations usually consist of a speaker or forum; topics include religion, politics, science, and other fields. Some students complain about the convocation requirement and some of the specific speakers, but others enjoy the experience and say it helps build community among students and faculty alike. The attendance policy is strict: students get less attendance credit if they arrive up to five minutes late, and none if they get there more than five minutes late or leave early.

Attendance at religious services, though encouraged, is not required. "They don't try to force it on you, but it's there if you're interested," one student says. The university is not affiliated with any church, and its administrators, regents, and faculty represent many religious backgrounds. About one in five students belongs to the

Church of Christ, under whose auspices the school was founded, and a majority of the school's regents must be Church of Christ members. The university is committed to its religious foundations, and the catalogue and other university publications prominently feature a combination confession of faith and university mission statement.

Part of that statement asserts that "the student, as a person of infinite dignity, is the heart of the educational enterprise" and that "the quality of student life is a valid concern of the university." Pepperdine's student life policies expect "that all students will adhere to biblical teaching regarding moral and ethical practices." To that end, Pepperdine prohibits dishonesty in all forms, the use of drugs, threatening language, sexual harassment, "participation in any student organizations not approved by the university," and "sexual relations inconsistent with traditional Christian values or sexually compromising acts on campus or at university-sponsored events."

Given the emphasis on religion and morality, it is no surprise that Pepperdine students tend to be a self-selecting group. They typically choose to attend because they like the religious atmosphere and the collegial quality that Pepperdine offers. The student body is generally conservative. About half the students are from California, and the rest are from all over the country. The school also has international students — sixty foreign countries are represented. The student body is nearly 60 percent female, and, overall, 75 percent receives some amount of financial aid.

Malibu, overlooking the coast only forty-five minutes northwest of downtown Los Angeles, might not be the first place one would expect to find an unpoliticized, Christian liberal arts college. The presence of the big city is apparent, and students often visit L.A.'s museums, sports events, and other attractions. Malibu itself has few social spots, especially late at night — though it does have a beautiful beach where students surf, in-line skate, or just relax. Santa Monica, thirty minutes away, has more restaurants, bars, movie theaters, and the like, and students often head there for entertainment. Farther away, one finds the Sierra Nevada just a few hours off; San Diego and the Mexican border are about two hours to the south.

Unless they are twenty-one years old, freshmen and sophomores are required to live on campus, or with their parents if they live nearby. Housing is not guaranteed for upperclassmen, and most move off campus, though some stay in university-owned apartment complexes. About 25 percent of men are in fraternities and about 35 percent of women are in sororities, but students say the Greek system is not a dominant presence on campus.

Community service is very popular with students, as is illustrated by the fact that in recent years the total hours of volunteer work by students rose from ten thousand to nearly twenty-nine thousand per year. Students lead and manage several outreach programs, and the Pepperdine Volunteer Center provides training and referrals.

The university has seven varsity teams for men and seven for women, all known as the Waves. Pepperdine's water sports (particularly swimming and diving) have an excellent reputation; in fact, the water polo team won the 1997 NCAA title. Basketball games are very popular, and the men's golf team won the NCAA tournament in 1997. Men's volleyball is also strong, having won four national titles in the last twenty years. Club sports, including those one expects near a beach, such as surfing, sailing, and in-line hockey, are available, as are recreational and intramural activities.

POMONA COLLEGE

Office of Admissions
333 North College Way
Claremont, CA 91711-6312
(909) 621-8134
www.pomona.edu

Total enrollment: 1,549
Undergraduates: 1,549
SAT Ranges (Verbal/Math): V 680-750, M 680-750
Financial aid: 55%
Applicants: 3,892
Accepted: 33%
Enrolled: 34%
Application deadline: Early decision, Nov. 15; regular, Jan. 1
Financial aid application deadline: Feb. 1
Tuition: $20,500
Core curriculum: No

New England, California Style

In 1887 the founders of Pomona College set out to establish "a college of the New England type" in a southern California setting, thirty-five miles east of Los Angeles. By all measures they succeeded. Today Pomona is very much a New England–style liberal arts college: it's small (1,549 students, all undergraduates), it's intimate, and it's regarded as excellent by the usual cadre of rankers and raters who take it upon themselves to determine such things.

Furthermore, Pomona belongs to the consortium of Claremont Colleges, a group of five undergraduate schools and one graduate school that share buildings, libraries, dining halls, and some classes. This allows students to take advantage of the offerings of a larger university while maintaining the advantages of a small liberal arts college. Pomona is often regarded as the top school of the Claremont Colleges, much as, say, Amherst is viewed as the shining star of a similar consortium of schools in Massachusetts.

But in attempting to imitate its New England colleagues, Pomona has also taken on some of the more familiar problems found at many leading liberal arts colleges. Despite its small size, the school has established several politicized ethnic and gender studies departments. It has abolished a core curriculum, replaced it with ten vaguely worded "learning objectives," and then washed its hands of the responsibility for providing academic guidance. The administration routinely succumbs to political pressure applied by ideological students and faculty, who are in the majority at the college. There still exist many courses on traditional subjects at Pomona, but a fair share are also dedicated to the latest intellectual fads, and especially to the unholy trinity of race, class, and gender.

It's hard to criticize such an elite institution. After all, Pomona students are bright — the median SAT score is 1,420. And the school's endowment has grown dramatically, as has the number of applications. But these statistics won't guarantee that a genuine liberal arts education will be still available at Pomona — if current trends continue unabated.

Academic Life: Interesting — and Relevant

In the 1920s Pomona College president James Blaisdell returned from a trip to England and convinced faculty and trustees that instead of growing into a large university, the college should model itself on the pattern of Oxford and Cambridge. In other words, it should build several small, independent colleges that work together and share facilities.

Pomona is the oldest and largest of the Claremont Colleges. Since its founding it has offered a comprehensive curriculum in the liberal arts and sciences. In the forty years since Blaisdell returned from England with his plan, four undergraduate colleges and one graduate college have joined the group. In 1925 Claremont Graduate School joined the consortium. In 1926 Scripps College, a women's college focusing on the humanities, became a member. Claremont McKenna College, which emphasized political science and economics, was added in 1947. In 1955 a school specializing in the physical sciences and engineering, Harvey Mudd College, joined the consortium. The final consortium member, Pitzer College, was founded in 1963 to emphasize the behavioral and social sciences.

Each of the six colleges operates independently. Each has its own campus, administration, academic specialties, and educational goals. The colleges have a combined enrollment of 5,600 — 4,500 of whom are undergraduates.

Today Pomona students more or less reflect the ethnic diversity of California, although just 40 percent of students come from the state. The current freshman class is 4 percent black, 21 percent Asian, 10 percent Hispanic, 3 percent multiracial, and 11 percent of other non-Caucasian descent. Minorities at Pomona aren't relegated to the margins of student life, either — Asians particularly take an active role in campus life. In fact, three of the top four student government officers in 1997-98 were of Asian descent.

The advantage to attending a small liberal arts college rather than a large university is that, generally, students have closer relationships with faculty members. Pomona is no exception. Class sizes are small, with only about a dozen or so having more than fifty students.

But beyond small class sizes, students say, professors take a genuine interest in the well-being of their students. One student we interviewed, for example, told of a professor who knew of the student's interest in Asian economies. The professor worked with the student to secure travel grants that enabled the student to travel to Hong Kong for the summer and study these economies firsthand. "He went the extra distance and took an interest in me after class," the student said. "I'd say that's really the norm."

To graduate with a bachelor's degree from Pomona, a student must complete thirty-two courses. The school offers forty-one majors, ranging from the hard sciences to the social sciences and the humanities. If nothing within the established curriculum catches your fancy, you can design your own major (or "concentration," as the college calls them) with the help of a faculty member.

In 1994 Pomona scrapped its distribution requirements and implemented general education requirements, which are popularly known as PAC courses (perception, analysis, and communication). Literature from the college states that the purpose of the Pomona curriculum is to "equip students to live resiliently in a changing world." Students must take at least one course in each of ten areas. At other colleges, requirements spell out specific fields of courses that must be taken. At Pomona, though, the curriculum places a premium on acquiring academic skills that faculty and administrators claim will aid students in later life.

The ten categories prepare students to:

1. Read literature critically.
2. Use and understand the scientific method.
3. Use and understand formal reasoning.
4. Understand and analyze data.
5. Analyze creative art critically.
6. Perform or produce creative art.
7. Explore and understand human behavior.

8. Explore and understand a historical culture.
9. Compare and contrast contemporary cultures.
10. Think critically about values and rationality.

There are no core courses at Pomona. Says the college's bulletin: "No specific course or department — with the exception of Critical Inquiry — is prescribed for graduation. Pomona students are responsible for their own education. The College believes that the classes students choose for themselves are more likely to be interesting, relevant, and worthwhile in the long run than a specific list of required courses." In other words, the college lets students choose the courses that seem the most "interesting" and "relevant" within a large framework of loose requirements. Given this lack of structure, an undergraduate could get through Pomona without ever studying Western civilization or reading Shakespeare.

The one course Pomona students must complete is called "Critical Inquiry," a seminar taken during the first semester of a student's freshman year. The purpose of the class is to examine a subject in depth, learning critical and analytical abilities and honing writing and speaking skills along the way.

It really cannot be considered a core class, since the topics addressed in each section vary widely from year to year, as do the professors who teach them. Some topics are in traditional subjects, such as "Homer" and "The Roman Empire and Its Discontents." One course covered "Black Women and the Arts." And some classes, while focusing on subjects in depth, center on rather dubious topics, such as "The Nature of Chess Players." The syllabus of this course reveals that class requirements included watching the movie *Searching for Bobby Fischer* and then visiting a chess club and writing a 500-word article "describing the experience." Toward the end of the semester, students were required to "play several games of computer chess using at least 3 different chess programs" and then to "record your impressions as you play these games, paying particular attention to how you felt as the computer was playing you."

Other "Critical Inquiry" courses are more political, if equally dubious. For instance, there's the course titled "Mothers, Fathers, Sisters, Brothers: Gender Roles, Family, and Society." Sample readings listed on the syllabus included tracts on "Homophobia, Homosexuality, and Heterosexual Marriage" and something titled "Man Child: A Black Lesbian Feminist's Response."

Because students must sign up for "Critical Inquiry" classes the summer before they arrive at Pomona, they do so without guidance from faculty members or other students. Some wind up dissatisfied with their "Critical Inquiry" sections because of this lack of guidance, and some don't get into their first-choice classes.

In addition to "Critical Inquiry," students must take one course deemed "writing intensive" and another considered "speaking intensive." Students must also demonstrate proficiency in a foreign language by taking three semesters of a language. This requirement can also be met by scoring a 650 on a language achievement test or earning a "4" or "5" on an advanced placement test.

During their senior year, Pomona students must complete what is known as a "senior exercise," which is usually a thesis but could be some other academic activity that demonstrates a deep understanding of a particular subject. They work independently on their senior exercises, under the guidance of a faculty adviser.

Pomona's science departments are highly regarded, and graduates of the college's premedical school sequence boast an excellent rate of acceptance to medical school. Economics is also highly regarded, as is English. Students say there are strong teachers in nearly every department at Pomona.

Particular professors who have been recognized for their teaching abilities include Fred Grieman (chemistry), Jerry Irish (religious studies), David Menefee-Libey (politics), Daniel O'Leary (chemistry), and Monique Saigal (French).

Despite its small size, Pomona has a surprising number of politicized faculty. While exhibiting some of the strengths of its Northeastern counterparts, Pomona has also mimicked those institutions' excesses — particularly their emphasis on ethnic identity politics. Typically, courses in politicized departments stress exploitation, victimization, colonialism, and other dour themes that reflect professors' leftist political bents.

Take, for example, media studies. Its stated purpose, according to college literature, is to "provide students with a comprehensive understanding of visual and media literacies." What that translates to in actual terms is courses based on the school of "cultural criticism" — a Marxist-inspired analysis of contemporary culture cluttered with academic jargon.

Students in Media Studies 51, "Principles of Visual Literacy," had to complete an assignment on how the media contribute to our desire to be "cool." They analyzed the cover and content of magazines such as *Glamour, Esquire*, and *Seventeen*, and also explored the subtexts in the hit TV sitcom *Friends*. In discussing an episode in which one main character leaves his Asian girlfriend for another (Caucasian) woman, a student wrote: "The love triangle . . . resembles closely the 'Madame Butterfly' schema: The white male imperialist who travels to the Orient to get a 'taste of the other' — the 'exotic,' quiet Asian female — but finally rejects her and settles down with the security and comfort of the Caucasian female."

The courses offered in Pomona's literature department read like a shopping list of professors' political interests. There are "The Female Body as Icon," "Marxist Literary Theory," "Consuming Fashions: Class and Gender in Europe Since the Eighteenth Century," and "The Roots of the AIDS Crisis."

Political Atmosphere: A Department of One's Own

One of the most recent campus controversies that Pomona president Peter W. Stanley and his administration had to face was the demand in 1997 for the establishment of an Asian-American studies department at Pomona. Pomona already offered a major in Asian studies and had a well-developed Asian-American Resource Center. But activists demanded the creation of an Asian-American studies department. Opponents of the new department asked where the creation of ethnic-based departments would end — why not an Italian-American studies department or a Nepalese-American studies department?

After considerable campus debate, the administration acceded to the demands of the political activists and created a full-fledged Asian-American studies department in the fall of 1997. Supporters say the department is the first of its kind at a small liberal arts college.

That is just one of several examples of the administration caving in to the pressures applied by political activists. In January of 1996 President Stanley appointed a committee to study whether Pomona's "free-speech wall," a 200-foot-long flood wall in the middle of campus that has traditionally been set aside for student graffiti, should be torn down. Stanley claimed he wasn't opposed to free speech, but he was concerned with the inflammatory views some students were expressing — someone had written "Kill O.J." in the fall of 1995. Occasional messages scrawled on the wall have also been deemed offensive by blacks, lesbians, and gays. The wall stands as of this writing, but some still want it to come tumbling down.

A few years back, in 1993, about one hundred students, demanding more hiring of minority faculty members, staged a sit-in at Pomona's administration building, closing it down for two days. The protesters emerged victorious after the administration agreed to step up the hiring of minority professors and include more student input in the hiring process.

In an effort to appease campus gays, lesbians, and bisexuals, President Stanley has demonstrated a willingness to offend those who support the U.S. military and the traditional family. Under his leadership, he boasted to the *Chronicle of Higher Education* in 1994, the college has banned the ROTC and established a health benefits plan for homosexual partners of Pomona employees.

In 1994 Pomona's board of trustees voted to join just a handful of other colleges and universities and sell all of its tobacco stocks for moral reasons. "The harmful effects of tobacco were so many and so serious that it was not appropriate for the college to own this type of stock," one board member told the *Chronicle* in 1997.

Student Life: Laid-Back on the Left Coast

Although college brochures tout the interaction among the Claremont Colleges, Pomona students often stay on their own campus since they believe they have the best resources. While they do have access to dining halls and events on the other campuses, Pomona students say it's far more common for students from other colleges to set foot on Pomona's campus than vice versa.

Pomona students generally involve themselves in extracurricular activities.

Some organizations draw members from all Claremont Colleges, while membership of others is restricted exclusively to Pomona students.

Numerous student organizations are dedicated to ethnic politics, some of which put out their own publications: *Harmony,* a "multicultural newspaper"; *Las Voices Unidas,* a Latino student newspaper; *Pacific Winds,* an Asian/Pacific Islander newspaper; and *The Re-View,* a feminist newspaper. Other active groups include the Five-College Women's Coalition; the Lesbian, Gay and Bisexual Students Union; the Minority Student Action Program; the Women's Union; and a group calling itself Racial Awareness and Cultural Experience (RACE). A fledgling College Republicans chapter at the Claremont schools has recently been formed.

Pomona's seven fraternities do not dominate the college's social scene. None is nationally recognized, and four are coed. There are no sororities. The fraternities sometimes hold parties, but more common are smaller get-togethers in residence halls or at someone's off-campus house.

Politically, most students lean to the left. "It's very politically correct here," says one senior. "Students tend to be much more liberal than conservative." Perhaps California's laid-back lifestyle has the greatest impact on student behavior, because few students are radically liberal or staunchly conservative. The vast majority seem to be moderately liberal, students say. Claremont McKenna College has more of a reputation for harboring conservative students.

With downtown Los Angeles just thirty-five miles away — and accessible by a rail system with a stop one block from campus — some students arrive at college expecting to travel to California's largest city on a regular basis. Not so, upperclassmen say. "That's a big misperception," says one. "It's not right in our backdoor." Some do make the trip, however, venturing to L.A.'s clubs, museums, restaurants, and theme parks.

Ninety-five percent of students live on campus in one of Pomona's twelve residence halls. In addition to traditional dorms, Pomona also offers housing in its Oldenborg Center for Modern Languages and International Relations. There students interested in foreign languages live together, converse in foreign tongues, and hold cultural events.

Pomona combines with Pitzer College to field nineteen varsity athletic teams, which compete in Division III. The school mascot is the sage hen, a bird native to desert regions of the southwestern United States. The school's main sports rivals are Occidental College and Claremont McKenna.

There is also a strong interest in intramural athletics. Each year approximately nine hundred students compete in eighteen sports, including beach volleyball and inner-tube water polo, along with the more conventional sports such as basketball and softball.

For those wanting to nurture their spiritual side, the Claremont Colleges share three full-time chaplains, representing the Jewish, Roman Catholic, and Protestant faiths. The chaplains hold weekly worship services for those three faiths; other religious organizations also meet in their facilities.

PRINCETON UNIVERSITY

Admission Office
P.O. Box 430
Princeton University
Princeton, NJ 08544-0430
(609) 258-3060
www.princeton.edu

Total enrollment: 6,340
Undergraduates: 4,593
SAT Ranges (Verbal/Math): V 670-770, M 680-770
Financial aid: 43%
Applicants: 13,400
Accepted: 13%
Enrolled: 66%
Application deadline: Jan. 2
Financial aid application deadline: Feb. 1
Tuition: $22,920
Core curriculum: No

Princeton's Ransom

In its 250 years of history, Princeton University has made a number of wise decisions, not the least of which was moving in 1756 from Newark, now seedy and crime-infested, to the lovely town of Princeton. Over the decades and centuries, the university acquired a substantial endowment and gained in stature.

Unfortunately, many of Princeton's advances are now coming undone. True, its name is still among the most prestigious in the country, and some of its professors are at the top of their fields. But the curriculum is increasingly bedeviled by politicized courses. The university's Office of Student Life, which exercises a large — some would say draconian — amount of control over the campus, is one of the most radical in the nation. This office has forced students to listen to nonacademic propaganda against their will and operates a fund used to pay for students' abortions. In response to these developments — all of them counter to Princeton's heritage as a liberal arts university — there has been a significant backlash on the part of students and alumni. A number of traditional student organizations now exist that seek to provide alternatives to the ritualistic politics of campus radicals. So far, these groups have not had as much effect as they would like.

Everyone knows what Princeton has been. The question now is, what will it become?

Academic Life: Poisoned Ivy?

Like most of the other Ivies, Princeton has settled on a broad distribution requirement instead of a core curriculum. And, as an Ivy, Princeton is permitted to call its distribution categories by fancy-sounding names while less prestigious schools have to content themselves with such generic terms as "math" or "social sciences." Aside from a proficiency in one foreign language and completion of an intensive writing requirement, one course is also required from each of seven groups: "Epistemology and Cognition," "Ethical Thought and Moral Values," "Historical Analysis," "Literature and the Arts," "Quantitative Reasoning," "Social Analysis," and "Science and Technology." The course fulfilling the last requirement must include a lab.

The teaching method in the quantitative reasoning and science courses is objective and mathematical. However, the courses in the other five requirements tend to reflect the ideologies of the faculty that teach them. Much of the distribution requirement can be met with only highly politicized courses, and the ideas taught in these courses will not be tempered with any information on the great minds of Western civilization. In the area of epistemology and cognition, a course called "Race, Class, and Intelligence in America" will suffice. The historical analysis requirement can be completed with the anthropology department's "Cross Cultural Texts," a history offering called "The Sunbelt in Modern America," a religion department course on "Sexuality and American Religious History," or a women's studies course on "Sex and Sexuality."

The literature and the arts options include "Jazz in American Society," "The American Cinema," and "Erotic Tradition in Chinese Literature." Social analysis courses are laden with race and gender emphases; "Law and the Politics of Race," "The Anthropology of Gender," and "Inequality: Class, Race, and Gender" all meet the requirement. In short, the distribution requirement does not ensure that Princeton undergraduates will receive a grounding in the great texts of the Western tradition.

Among the most respected academic traditions at Princeton are the two junior papers required of each liberal arts major and a senior thesis that must be written by most every undergraduate. (Science departments usually require some sort of research project from juniors.) Students work with a faculty member of their choice to complete the two junior papers, which average about thirty pages each. According to one student, the junior papers can be a valuable part of the Princeton experience: "The different departments have vastly different requirements for independent work such as the junior paper. For example, a creative writing major can write an original play for his thesis; an engineer may build a vacuum cleaner in lieu of a thesis; and an anthropology major may write a 100-page paper on the yam-currency of the New

Guinea Trobrianders. But despite these wildly divergent forms of study, I have found that the academic integrity of the system stands firm."

The senior thesis is a yearlong project that can become a source of great anxiety and frustration. For many students, though, the completion of the thesis is the most rewarding part of their academic work at Princeton. Others take the assignments in stride. "Junior papers are not hard in terms of length, but they are a little bit of extra work that you didn't need to do in the first place," one student says. "Humanities students are used to writing a lot anyway. The junior and senior papers don't faze you."

The honor code, adopted in 1893, is another respected, time-honored Princeton tradition that still receives almost universal student support. Students must sign the code as a condition of admission. Under the terms of the code, they must write on each examination paper: "I pledge my honor that I have not violated the honor code during this examination." The code seems to work: exams are not proctored, yet cheating is extremely rare, students and faculty say. Violations are the province of the undergraduate Honor Committee, which recommends penalties to the university president. Punishment can include one to three years of suspension.

Some people on campus say none of the university's departments is excellent from top to bottom, although there are many good professors. One student, however, says the history department is among the "finest in the world." The department includes several very good professors, including Peter Lake; Civil War specialist James M. McPherson; Peter R. Brown, an expert in late antiquity; and William C. Jordan, author of a best-selling series for children on the Middle Ages.

Excellent professors in other departments include Robert George, Paul E. Sigmund, and Steven F. Cohen in politics; John DiIulio, a scholar of criminology, Henry S. Bienen, and George W. Downs, all in both politics and the Woodrow Wilson School of Public and International Affairs; Burton Malkiel, Alan S. Blinder, and Harvey S. Rosen in economics; Martha Himmelfarb in religion; Richard P. Martin in classics; Saul A. Kripke in philosophy; and Robert Hollander, a Dante expert in the comparative literature department who also teaches Italian in the Romance languages department. The Creative Writing program boasts two of America's leading novelists, Toni Morrison and Joyce Carol Oates.

Princeton has no mandatory classes on diversity. However, the university issues a pamphlet to undergraduates entitled "Race, Ethnicity, and Cross-Cultural Encounter" that provides a list of recommended multicultural courses. But even though ideologized classes are not required, they are difficult to avoid, especially in the humanities. And, just as many departments are improved by the presence of several good faculty, a similar number are made less palatable by radical faculty. The Woodrow Wilson School, for example, is home to feminist and former congresswoman Patricia Schroeder.

The English department has more than a few radical professors, including Elaine Showalter, a feminist literary critic. In fact, the English department offers one of the university's more politicized course lists. But one student believes it is possible to steer a course around the most ideological offerings: "My experiences so far in the English department have been very good. There *is* a strong emphasis on feminist interpretation, and one professor I had read long tracts about how to deconstruct *Huckleberry Finn* and other works. But most of the English classes I've taken have included great reading lists."

Of course, Princeton is home to several major research institutes, including the renowned Institute for Advanced Study, which has supported not only the work of world-class physicists like Albert Einstein, but also that of scholars in the humanities and social sciences. The presence of these distinguished "think tanks" enriches an already heady learning environment.

Political Atmosphere: The Various Meanings of Mandatory

Though the politicization of Princeton's courses is extensive, more notorious is the university's Office of Student Life. Religious and conservative students have become increasingly vocal in their criticism of the dean of student life, who some consider to be among the most aggressive radical activists in higher education today.

The dean's office is responsible for all aspects of undergraduate student life. Thus, any bias against traditional students has a direct effect on their lives, and the effects of this office are unavoidable, according to some familiar with Princeton. This influence is not a positive one in many cases. "There seems to be a strong push on campus to stigmatize students with strong traditional convictions about behavior and character," an alumnus told the Council of Princeton University Community (CPUC). "And, more disturbing, such a push seems to be supported by the university as an institution."

The Office of Student Life includes, among other things, Health Services, which not only refers students for abortions but also provides contraceptives, offers the controversial "morning-after pill," and will pay for abortions out of a special fund controlled by the dean's office. One Texas organization that provides abortion malpractice litigation support has even advertised in the *Daily Princetonian* to let students know that if they are injured during an abortion paid for by the university, they might have grounds for a lawsuit.

Health Services also runs the Sexual Harassment/Assault Advising, Resources, and Education (SHARE) Program. SHARE puts out a booklet called *The Source: A Resource Guide for the Lesbian, Gay, Bisexual and Transgendered Community and Friends,* and also sponsors a peer education program entitled "Sex on a Saturday Night," which incoming freshmen are required to attend. After seeing graphic depictions of sexual practices and a condom-use demonstration, one student tried to walk out of this required meeting and was physically barred from leaving by one of the Office of Student Life's residential advisers.

Another department, the Office of Religious Life, "has engaged in much politically driven activity," according to a student. The office was a sponsor of Gay Pride '96 week, which included a "Rock and Roll Queer Bar" and a "Coming Out to God" dance. At the same time, some legitimate student religious organizations, such as the Princeton Evangelical Fellowship and the Christian Choir Kindred Spirit, receive little to no support from the Office of Religious Life — and in some cases get only active opposition.

The Office of Student Life also includes the powerful, well-funded Lesbian, Gay, Bisexual Alliance (LGBA), and the Women's Center, said to be openly hostile to pro-life women.

Several students in the spring of 1996 petitioned university president Harold Shapiro and the CPUC — a committee composed of administrators, faculty, students, and alumni, which, according to university policy, has "the authority to consider and investigate any question of university policy or governance" — to look into intimidating actions on the part of Dean Montero's office. For starters, there were the peer-group sessions moderated by the LGBA and SHARE. The students also alleged that they were discriminated against because of their religious and political beliefs when they applied for positions as residential advisers.

Another component of the complaint involved a peer educator conference, a one-day program held by the Office of Student Life for upperclassmen serving as peer educators. The conference included a session entitled "Overcoming Resistance to Peer Education," in which administrators identified specific student organizations as "resistance groups." This list included religious and conservative groups — Campus Crusade for Christ, for example.

Among those attending the meeting was the founder of the Coalition of Princeton Students for Tolerance (CPST), undergraduate Alex Fulks. (The CPST is composed of members of several student organizations, including the College Republicans, the Chesterton Society, the conservative undergraduate publication called the *Sentinel,* and Princeton Pro-Life.) According to Fulks, "They were telling peer educators that anyone who disagreed with them was obviously wrong and that they should be discredited. They taught peer educators to mock these organizations and try to make them look irrational. The session degenerated into name calling, which was encouraged by the administration. They even referred to students in the CPST as fascists."

Fulks, who was interested in becoming a peer counselor, had received permission to attend the event, but several administrators later attempted to disinvite him. At the conference, three employees of the Office of Student Life bluntly asked him to leave — even though a notice published prior to the event had stated that attendance was mandatory for those "interested in becoming peer educators next year." Fulks said later that organizers of the conference had made him feel isolated from other students, and even attempted to dissuade peer educators from answering his questions or speaking to him.

A few weeks after the conference Fulks was charged by the Residential College Disciplinary Board with two "breaches of university guidelines." And in a private meeting that he was not allowed to attend, Fulks was found guilty of the charges and reprimanded.

Naturally, nothing came of the students' complaint — the administration simply ignored the charges. Montero publicly invited students to come and speak with her, but did not set up a committee to look into the charges. The students claimed Montero had no business adjudicating a complaint that concerned her, but no unbiased third party was ever put into the mix.

Traditional faculty also face discrimination at Princeton, most notably during tenure decisions. Politics professor Robert George was nearly denied tenure despite an impressive academic background that includes law and philosophy degrees from Oxford and Harvard, a fellowship at the U.S. Supreme Court, and several academic publications. Politics professor Graham Walker was denied tenure by his department because of his personal convictions — and some that were merely imputed to him. An internal memo was discovered that stated there were "too many Catholics" in the politics department. Walker did graduate from Notre Dame but is not Catholic, contrary to the assumptions of a number of his former colleagues. In protest of the tenure vote and the fact that its outcome turned primarily on political and religious grounds, the chairman of the department refused to hire new professors for a year.

Student Life: The Care and Feeding of Tigers

Princeton's main campus is perhaps the most beautiful among the Ivy League schools. Its six hundred acres are dominated by stone Collegiate Gothic buildings. Large, tarnished bronze statues of tigers (the symbol of the university) are found across campus. The city of Princeton, lovely in its own right, has many fine restaurants as well as the historic Nassau Inn. The city is almost completely free of crime.

The university's 4,600 undergraduates and 1,800 graduate students are the beneficiaries of the university's massive endowment — the largest per capita endowment of any college or university in the country. This money has bought some of the country's best facilities for housing, athletics, research, and social life. Among Princeton's finest assets is the Firestone Library, which was one of the largest libraries in the world even before its recent expansion. The university's art center and museum have just been completely renovated, and a new molecular biology building ranks among the nation's top undergraduate research facilities in that field. Computer facilities at Princeton are abundant and easily accessible to students.

Much of the social life at Princeton is centered on the eating clubs housed in the beautiful mansions of Prospect Street. Admission to the clubs is highly competitive; several use a "bicker process" to select their members. "The bicker process is similar to a fraternity rush," a student says. "The various eating clubs throw parties, and occasionally they will host bands to play for their guests. . . . Once you have decided which club you would like to belong to, you put your name on a list. However, not everyone gets in. Admission to an eating club is by invitation only, and a lot depends on who you know." Groups of friends have been known to split up when some are chosen above others. Even acceptance into the nonselective clubs is not guaranteed, as remaining membership slots are given out via lottery. One student notes: "People may not realize that all eating clubs do not include the 'bicker' process. I myself joined a 'non-bicker' club with several of my friends, where by signing-in early we assured that we would all be in the same club. Our club has brought lots of big bands this year and it's a lot of fun."

Athletics at Princeton is strongly supported by the administration; one student says the admissions policy is designed to favor "the perfect athlete-student." Besides the sixteen men's and fifteen women's intercollegiate teams, the university sponsors forty-five intramural teams. There are a number of athletic clubs as well. Again, the facilities are excellent. They include a superior aquatics center, a golf course, an ice rink, an Olympic-level water course for crew and sailing races, a 6,500-seat gymnasium, and a 45,000-seat football stadium that is packed for games against rivals Yale and Harvard.

Many student organizations suffer from the politicization encouraged by Princeton's Office of Student Life. The several conservative groups spend much of their time opposing that office's policies. There are two outstanding conservative student publications on campus (the *Princeton Tory* and the *Sentinel*), as well as the CPST and Women for the Right to Be Informed, a pro-life group concerned with abortion-related injuries. There is also a group called Princeton Pro-Life, which is not as vocal as it had been previously. Two reading groups, the Chesterton Society and the Jacques Maritain Society, often bring speakers to the campus. Many religious services are available both on and off campus.

The university's Women's Center, another branch of the Office of Student Life, operates programs for female students. These include career and professional training. The center also seeks to fulfill the "religion and spirituality" needs of women; its contacts include Dignity, a dissident "Catholic" organization of practicing homosexuals, and the New Jersey Lesbian and Gay Havurah, a Jewish homosexual group.

Besides these groups, the eating clubs, and some fraternities, there are very few organizations with significant memberships. There is a small performing arts theater on campus for college productions, and the university does sponsor film festivals. Otherwise the university does not get visits from major performers, as some of the large city universities do. Should students wish to get away, Trenton, the state capital, is fifteen minutes away, and New York City is a little more than an hour away by train.

REED COLLEGE

Office of Admissions
Portland, OR 97202
(800) 547-4750
web.reed.edu

Total enrollment: 1,338
Undergraduates: 1,316
SAT Ranges (Verbal/Math): V 640-730, M 600-690
Financial aid: 50%
Applicants: 2,100
Accepted: 76%
Enrolled: 23%
Application deadline: Feb. 1
Financial aid application deadline: Feb. 1
Tuition: $22,180
Core curriculum: Yes

Majoring in Academe

Reed College, founded in 1907, requires its students to read some of the great texts of Western civilization, which is more than can be said for other institutions, even many small liberal arts colleges. But while the best colleges in the country ask their students to read so that they will become truly and liberally educated, Reed seems more interested in providing students with raw material that can later be consumed in the fires of the ideological furnace.

Moreover, Reed College, despite the vaunted individualism of its students, seems to encourage them to acquire knowledge with the goal of one day getting into graduate school, picking up an advanced degree, and finding a job somewhere in academe, teaching the hot topics that future Reed students will then study. If Reed has a characteristic fault, it is that there is too much learning for learning's sake, and not enough for the sake of truth.

Though Reed students enter their educations through the right doors, they can end up sidetracked by passing fads. A Reed education virtually assures a student acceptance in graduate school, which is indeed a great privilege. But the more urgent question is whether Reed can assure its students a profound understanding of the ideas and principles that have shaped our civilization.

Academic Life: But What Does It Profit a Man . . .

One could argue that Reed College is a mirror of the intellectual world of academe in that it simultaneously insists that its students work very hard at acquiring a classical education even as they subject that education to radical critique. As one professor says, "We read the Greeks because it just so happens that they wrote about how to think about complex issues in a way that doesn't presume too much foreknowledge." The point of education at Reed is not, this faculty member continues, "to introduce people to the roots of Western culture, but to get them to think about the most important human questions with the best writers."

Reed's philosophy of education demands of students a genuine commitment of time and effort in order to graduate. All students must take Humanities 110, which requires that they read carefully, write about, and discuss many of the most important primary sources of the Western tradition. Thus, Reed requires of its students a familiarity of the West much stronger than that found at many colleges and universities with larger reputations.

The two-semester humanities course consists of reading, writing about, and commenting on the Greek and Roman classics, and ends with a reading of St. Augustine's *Confessions*. It is taught by what one professor termed the "conference method," in which lectures are followed by smaller weekly conferences limited to sixteen students per section. About twenty faculty members teach the course, taking turns lecturing. "We rotate all of the lectures, and they are meant to be taken very critically," says a faculty member who teaches the course. "They are a critical engagement with the texts and with each other."

Humanities 110 was instituted in 1943 and has remained the foundation of a Reed education ever since. After taking the course, students are encouraged — though not required — to take one of three other humanities courses. Two of these cover Renaissance and modern Europe, and a third, instituted in 1995, covers classical Chinese civilization. The latter should not be seen as a move away from rigorous studies, since it does not fit the typical multiculturalist mold of substituting Western-inspired radical works for the foreign culture supposedly being studied. Rather, it was conceived, says one professor, as a means of "dealing with a non-Western humanities subject with rigor. We decided to do a classical, and then an Early Modern, Chinese course. It's important that things be done really well. We don't jump on band wagons, and some students are disappointed because they're trendier [than the faculty]."

The humanities courses, one professor says, "gives everyone a common language." He continues: "From the faculty's perspective, teaching the humanities courses is great, because we all go to each other's lectures, and everyone updates their lectures yearly." Nothing makes an academic sweat like having to perform in front of his colleagues, and these public performances certainly help to quell any faculty apathy that might arise.

And yet, as one professor notes, it is quite possible, in the atmosphere created by Reed's offbeat culture, for faculty to deliver lectures on the Greeks or Romans that are themselves a bit off center. "Because most faculty come from literary backgrounds and are themselves trendy, we have a fair share of rather wacky lectures," the professor notes. And yet, there still remains in the required humanities course a balance, for, as a faculty member says, "No narrow specialty group can control it, and this exerts a conservative control. The lunatics are largely compensated for by conservative faculty."

The college also has distribution requirements of a full year of literature, philosophy, or "the arts"; two credits in history, social sciences, or psychology; two courses in the natural sciences; and two courses from either mathematics and formal logic or foreign language. However, the connection between the courses that could be used to satisfy the distribution requirements — not to mention those that count as electives — and the serious study of the Western canon varies from close to barely even perceptible. By studying the course catalogue at Reed, one surmises that many classes in the humanities and social sciences are geared to an exploration of methodology and theory rather than a close reading of primary sources. Such courses include:

- Classics 314, "Gender and Sexuality in the Classical World," in which students will study "how male and female are constructed, how literature and literary criticism participate in this process, the possibility of resistance to gender codes, and the role of cosmetics and cross-dressing."

In the history department, one finds courses dealing with "Peasants and the State in China," "East Asian Business History," and "Gender and History," as well as many more traditional offerings such as "American Revolution and Constitution," in which "the Revolution will not be treated as a military event." The English department's offerings are replete with courses top-heavy with theoretical and methodological approaches, including:

- English 338, "The Unspeakable Embodied in Nineteenth-Century American Literature," which "explores the interplay between these two meanings of the unspeakable (both verbal and non-verbal) in texts that call attention to the ways in which figures of the body — portraits, sculpture, tattooed or veiled bodies — bear the signs of what cannot be named."
- English 363, "Studies in Shakespeare: Elizabethan/Jacobean Drama and the New Historicism," in which "plays by Christopher Marlowe, Thomas Kyd, [and] Ben Jonson . . . will be studied, especially with respect to questions of class and gender."
- English 384, "Poetry and History: The American Grain in the Late 18th/Early 19th Centuries," in which "we will look at ante-bellum constructions of an American poetic tradition" and read those that "raise questions about the poets' assumptions about readership, race, class, and gender."

However, one searches the Reed catalogue in vain for courses covering the European Middle Ages, the Renaissance, the Reformation, or — surprisingly for a college located in Oregon and founded by money from the estate of pioneer Simeon Reed — the American West.

Despite the examples given above, English and classics are not among the departments listed by faculty as Reed's weakest. Those departments include Spanish, German, economics, sociology, and anthropology. There are several strong departments on campus, including the sciences, especially chemistry, physics, mathematics, and biology (probably the best department on campus). Also well regarded are art history and philosophy. Philosophy ranks number one in the country in majors who go on to graduate school. Outstanding teachers can be found at Reed, including Peter Steinberger in political science, Lisa Steinman in English, C. D. C. Reeve in philosophy, Peter Parshall in art history, Walter Englert in classics, and Robert Kaplan in biology.

In all classes, professors assign grades to students, but the college does not actually tell a student his grades unless he requests them. An exception to this rule is made if a student scores below a C in any class; the student is then told of his grade and meets with his professor. The college does this, it explains, because "Reed College encourages students to measure academic achievement by self-assessment of their grasp of course material and intellectual growth. . . . The college does not wish to divide students by labels of achievement. While a conventional letter grade for each course is recorded for every student, the registrar's office does not routinely distribute grades to students, providing work continues at satisfactory (C or higher) levels."

This philosophy is one of the most important pillars supporting what is known around campus as the "Reed ethos." In other ways, however, Reed requires that its students bare their minds, if not their souls. All students must pass a junior qualifying examination before moving on to their senior years. In this exam, administered by the major division and/or department in which the student will work, weaknesses are identified and students who are not yet ready to work independently on their senior theses (also required of all students) are encouraged to either bone up or choose another major. The senior thesis itself is a "sustained investigation of a carefully defined problem — experimental, critical, or creative — chosen from the major field and considered as one part of an overall senior-year program," according to the college catalogue. Finally, before graduating students must sit for a comprehensive two-hour oral review given by the major division or department. Focusing mostly on the senior's thesis, "the committee of examiners will include faculty from the student's own department and division, a second division, and, on occasion, professionals from outside the college." As noted above, Reed requires a great deal of work from its students, and a degree is by no means an assured result from matriculating at this little school in Portland.

Political Atmosphere: A Farm Team for Graduate Schools

The student body and faculty at Reed College tend to be left of center in their politics and social attitudes even as they defend a strong core curriculum and work ethic. There is at least a minimal degree of tolerance for those who depart from the norm. As one professor who has taught at Reed for decades notes, "There has been something of a distancing of the faculty from students of the opposite sex. There has been a chilling effect on frankness and openness on campus — people are less willing to speak their minds these days."

The process of politicization has become more entrenched as older professors retire and are replaced by younger radicals. One professor notes: "A big disappointment is how poorly we've capitalized on the buyers' market for professors. We have tenured mediocre people when we could have gotten better." According to another professor, "Tenured radicals are really very dull people because they think they know the answers to all the biggest questions. Here just ten people is 10 percent of the faculty, so it's easy for them to change things even if they're not the majority."

Recently, some faculty have been unhappy about what seems to be a toning down of the intellectualism on campus in an effort to avoid losing students. "Reed looks more like any other college now," says a disappointed teacher. This relaxation of standards, which is by no means peculiar to Reed, occurred because college marketers decided that the image of a school where students read even more than they are assigned, study late into the night, and argue great books with their peers over dinner does not sell to the great American middle class.

Yet the type of community that results when colleges are run like businesses can be undesirable from the standpoint of those who champion quality education. A Reed professor notes that some 20 faculty members, out of 100 total, are adjuncts, i.e., temporaries or part-timers. Yet, he notes, "They have a huge effect. They can all vote, and they were all politicized, so they have a big influence on our students." Those professors cannot contribute long-term to the Reed ethos because they will move along soon. Without the continuity derived from a stable academic community, the college (and students) will suffer.

But teaching is still taken very seriously at Reed, and the imbalance between teaching and research that plagues so many colleges and universities has not taken hold. "The single most important criterion is teaching, and we are evaluated by students and by faculty. No matter how many books one has written, no tenure is awarded without good teaching," says one professor. "Most faculty do publish, but they're also very good teachers."

Much pride is taken at Reed because it was named the "most intellectual college in the country" in a recent book on higher education. Whether or not one agrees with this claim, it is certainly true that many Reedies, as they are known locally, see their undergraduate education as a primer for graduate school and a career in academe. Reed proudly trumpets statistics showing that over the past several years it ranks second in the nation among all institutions of higher learning in the production of future Ph.D.s, and third in the percentage of science/engineering graduates who go on to earn Ph.D.s. Overall, in percentage of graduates who go on to take doctorates, Reed ranks second in the nation behind the California Institute of Technology. The graduate, medical, and professional schools most frequently attended by Reed graduates include Harvard, Yale, Stanford, and the University of California-Berkeley. The thirty Rhodes scholars produced by Reed since 1915 is equaled by only one other liberal arts college.

This impressive record is both a result of and a defining factor in the Reed ethos, which, as we have seen, seeks to maintain very high academic standards while exposing students to the very latest methods of research in every field. And while it is certainly an achievement of which everyone in the Reed community can be proud, it goes a long way toward explaining why so many of the courses at Reed are reflective of the dominant trends in the academy, whatever they may be. More than most colleges and universities, Reed is a farm team for the better graduate schools. Its graduates, in turn, excel in their fields because the stuff of the graduate department is what they were fed as undergraduates. This gives them a leg up on their colleagues from most other institutions.

Student Life: A Group of "Individuals"

Alongside the rigorous courses at Reed exists a very strong and quite trendy culture that is all but required of anyone who would matriculate there. As one professor says, "The '60s Berkeley look is very big here, but we work them very hard." Ironically, today this look is not so much countercultural as it is mainstream.

Be that as it may, life at Reed is intensely academic and a bit different from similarly sized schools across the nation. Most notable is the total absence of a Greek system: there are no fraternities or sororities at Reed. There are numerous student organizations, however, ranging from arts groups like Coffeehouse, during which "students participate in an open-mike forum, while lolly-gaggers and slack-jawed gapers watch on and injest [sic] their mixtures of coffee and half-and-half (quantities are limited)," according to college literature, to Christian Fellowship and Chaverim, a Jewish student organization, to groups that cater to more avant-garde interests. Among the latter are environmental groups, Pagan Circle, Queer Alliance, and the Safer Sex Society, which proudly "provides you Reedies with condoms, dental dams, personal lubricant, and safer sex literature. For free! We're the nice people who give you condoms!" Reed is also home to the Women's Center (a "safe, queer-friendly, women-only space"); the Reason, Egoism, and Liberty Forum (a libertarian group); the Beer Collective; and the Fetish Student Union, which hosts a "Fetish and Bondage Ball," wherein one may explore personal fetishes, "whether you fancy household appliances, deep sea mammals, Velveeta fondue, or just the classic leather and 'cuffs.

Things we believe contribute to a successful ball include a whipping room, jello pit, various take-home inflatables, prizes for OutRageUs dress, and lots-O-latex."

About 60 percent of Reed's 1,300 students live on campus, a rather low number for a small liberal arts college. Housing is said to be a problem, since not enough dorms exist to take care of all who would like to live in them. Some of the dorms are quite nice, while others are aging and spartan. Freshmen are "encouraged" to live on campus for their first two semesters, and they alone are guaranteed campus housing. A lottery determines which students get dorm rooms in subsequent years. The Residence Life Office also allows students to create "theme houses" in the different residences on campus. These seem to be real losers: most recently one dorm designated itself the "Pagan House" and determined to "focus on earth-based spirituality and Neo-Pagan practice, including but not limited to healthful eating and life choices (quiet dorm, no smoking), seasonal celebrations, gardening, cooking and a greater understanding and appreciation of [sic] non-Judeo/Christian heritage of Europe [sic] and similar indigenous peoples." Correct grammar and human sacrifice are, we assume, optional.

But even the residents of the Pagan House and those students visiting the whipping room are not without honor, apparently. The Honor Principle at Reed dates from the college's founding and is taken very seriously. Students are not required to sign a code, but everyone in the community is expected to abide by the principle, which states, among other things, that "we declare our commitment to responsible and honorable conduct in academic and community affairs." The Community Constitution, which applies to all students, faculty, and staff, adds that "we further declare that dishonesty, intimidation, harassment, exploitation, and the use or threat of force are incompatible with the preservation of this freedom." A student judicial board enforces the principle among students. The Honor Principle allows faculty to leave tests unmonitored, which is certainly laudatory. Yet its sweeping definition of harassment could leave the door open for the prosecution of those whose sensitivity level is deemed unfit.

Portland offers not only scenic beauty but an increasingly sophisticated cultural life. Residents say the number of good restaurants increases yearly, and outstanding bookstores such as Powell's offer Reed students almost unlimited titles. When they're not reading, students can take advantage of the numerous diversions found in this exciting city.

RHODES COLLEGE

Office of Admissions
2000 North Parkway
Memphis, TN 38112
(800) 844-5969
(901) 726-3700
www.rhodes.edu

Total enrollment: 1,430
Undergraduates: 1,420
SAT Ranges (Verbal/Math): V 590-690, M 590-680
Financial aid: 75%
Applicants: 2,210
Accepted: 75%
Enrolled: 23%
Application deadline: Feb. 1
Financial aid application deadline: Feb. 1
Tuition: $16,392
Core curriculum: Yes

What's in a Name?

Rhodes College is a fascinating and perhaps unique institution in modern America. It has been associated with the Presbyterian church since 1855, although it traces its roots to earlier in that century when it was known as the Masonic University of Tennessee. Since then it has borne many names, both at its original campus in Clarksville, Tennessee, and at its current home in Memphis, where it relocated in 1925 and came to be called Southwestern. The college was known by that name until 1984, when it boldly renamed itself for former president Peyton N. Rhodes. At the time of the college's rechristening, forty other institutions had the word "Southwestern" in their names; the school changed its name to distinguish itself from the rest, and to signify a very serious commitment to become one of the best elite liberal arts colleges in the country.

Changing its name was just one of the many gutsy actions Rhodes has taken in the past fifteen years. Despite the prevailing winds of ideological conformity and imitation that have buffeted the academy, Rhodes has remained firmly rooted in tradition. For example, the college has stuck with a campus plan that calls for beautiful neo-Gothic buildings rather than the more contemporary (and less expensive) institutional buildings now in favor on college campuses. The result is not only a truly lovely campus, but one where the surroundings elevate the mind. The integrity of the college is also evident in its commitment to the Presbyterian Church (U.S.A.), a relationship the college has deliberately sought to strengthen — not in order to become a narrow-sighted school of religious indoctrination, but as a way of keeping itself in touch with the ancient traditions uniting faith and reason, and with the philosophical foundations of the liberal arts.

Rhodes College describes itself with the following terms: "coeducational," "metropolitan," "private," "small," "well rounded," "beautiful," "church-related," "genuine and excellent," and "liberal arts college." Along with these attributes, the college displays a worthy and even noble commitment to genuine liberal learning and an optimistic belief that its future lies along the way that today is less trodden. But while Rhodes has bravely set off down this road, dangers in its path will have to be addressed if it is to hold the course and avoid the politicization that has beset so many institutions.

Academic Life: Traditional Campus, Traditional University

As we've just noted, two things in particular stand out about Rhodes: the first is its beautiful Gothic campus, and the second is Rhodes's commitment to strengthening its long-standing relationship to the Presbyterian Church (U.S.A.).

A word about the buildings. The college states that it "maintains a campus that is second to none in its design, function, and beauty. Students benefit because elegant architecture inspires, broadens the mind, expands the consciousness to beauty and harmony, and reminds the community of the history and breadth of learning." This commitment to architectural integrity, the college notes, is not an end in itself, but is undertaken "because such a campus shapes the quality of education and provides students a constant vision of excellence." In a day in which the beautiful part of any older college campus is almost always the section built before World War II, after which the cold utilitarianism of modern design spawned buildings that seemed abstract and inhuman, Rhodes's accomplishment deserves high praise.

Equally impressive is Rhodes's conscious decision to refuse mere sycophancy in its ties with the Presbyterian church. The college's "Statement of Christian Commitment and Church Relationship" notes: "Too many colleges today, lacking a clear identity and direction, have become imitative. The prestige image they follow is often a secular pattern since most of the well-established private institutions in this county are secular in outlook. For church-related institutions the problem is especially serious because imitation draws them away from their own distinctive purposes."

This is an impressive and succinct statement of one of the most pressing problems facing higher education today. Although many colleges and universities lack money, more than anything else they lack the confidence to maintain — or, in most cases, reclaim — their dedication to the pursuit of truth. The Rhodes "Statement" reaffirms the college's belief that reason and revelation are allies, not enemies: "Rhodes has chosen to go in the other direction, and in these disturbed and crucial times, restates its distinctive and extraordinary function as a church-related institution."

Yet this commitment to an overtly Christian mission does not impede Rhodes's insistence on critical thought in dialogue with a world it hopes to change. Rhodes is not a cloistered, reclusive school in which students and faculty are forced into intellectual cells or made to read pious literature in lieu of confronting the most important works of the Western intellectual tradition. As the college itself states: "Rhodes' commitment to the church and to the Lord of the church does *not* mean that it is a doctrinaire institution requiring intellectual adherence to creedal religion. It does *not* mean that Rhodes excludes persons from its student body, faculty, administration, or governing bodies who may hold other views. The College does *not* exclude people, ban books, or avoid ideas" (emphasis in original). The statement later notes, however, that Rhodes is committed to maintaining Christian governance and leadership by appointing to positions of power people with Christian beliefs that are in line with those upon which the college is founded, and thus "a large majority of trustees and administrators, as well as faculty, [are] Christians." Rhodes is not afraid of ideas and books but sees a liberal education as the best way of using one's talents in the service of God and country.

This church-college relationship provides the guiding vision of the college, the means of defining what it stands for and what it hopes to accomplish. But Rhodes should not be confused with more sectarian colleges in the South; in practice, this commitment to Christian education is more oriented toward preserving the classical liberal arts curriculum than it is of creating a bastion of puritanism. "Rhodes is a church-related institution, but it isn't all that closely related to the church. It isn't a chapel," notes one professor. "Anyone would feel at home here." Notes another: "Obviously, a Protestant from the Southeast would feel more at home here than some others might, but it is open to everyone."

As befits the college's mission, the curriculum at Rhodes is designed to expose students to the Bible and to the Western tradition of which Christianity is the formative part. The college requires students to take two years' worth of Bible classes, and offers a variety of courses in Bible and religion that "reflect on the Judeo-Christian heritage, the life and teachings of Jesus Christ, and the implications of these for the whole of life," according to college literature. Freshmen must choose between two core curricula: "The Search for Values in the Light of Western History and Religion" and "Life: Then and Now." Each program involves twelve credit hours earned over a two-year period. Either choice requires a great deal of reading in primary sources, as well as extensive discussions and writing assignments.

"Search," as it is commonly called, has been taught at Rhodes for nearly fifty years. The current college catalogue quotes from an early description of the program: "Our . . . Christian background is traced and analyzed, and the pageant of [Western] Civilization is viewed from its beginning to present time." It is, "in both content and method . . . essentially a dialogue between the biblical faith and western culture." Students read the Hebrew Bible while simultaneously studying Mesopotamian civilization, and they study the Gospels as they learn about Greco-Roman culture and history. In the second year students continue this intellectual adventure by reading primary sources from one of four disciplines: religious studies, history, philosophy, or literature.

The other option, the so-called "Life" program, is more concentrated in the Hebrew-Christian tradition per se, and to that end students electing this means of fulfilling the college's humanities requirement study the Bible in detail during their first year, while during their second year they "may choose among a variety of ways to approach an understanding of the meaning of faith, belief in God, religion, knowledge of the ultimate, ethical responsibility." The three subdisciplines offered are "Studies in the History of Religion," "Philosophical and Theological Studies," and "Studies in Ethics." Students are free to choose from any of these areas in fulfilling the third and fourth courses in the Life program. Most of the courses in the Life sequence are offered through the religious studies department, although a few are offered by philosophy.

The honors program, open to seniors who maintain a 3.5 GPA, allows participants to engage in intensive, independent work. It is seen by the college as an excellent introduction to graduate study because it is of a "scholarly and creative nature." Thus, the best students can work closely with a professor on a specialized topic of interest even as they complete a broad liberal arts education. All majors require a senior seminar "which both reviews and integrates important areas within the discipline." This seminar may carry from two to six hours of credit and may be one or two semesters long. And, in a policy that illustrates the college's belief that a student's formal educational experience should occur within a definite framework — during the student's years on campus — attendance at commencement exercises is required in order to receive a degree.

Rhodes is home to many well-regarded teachers, including Ben Bolch in economics and business; Kenny Morrell in foreign languages (classics); Dan Cullen and Steve Wirl in political science; Cynthia Marshall, Brian Shaffer, and Debra Pittman in English; Carolyn Jaslow in biology; and Brad Pendley in chemistry. And good professors tend to create good departments: the programs mentioned by faculty as the best on campus include foreign languages, political science, English, biology, and chemistry, as well as physics.

Political Atmosphere: Holding the World Close, Holding the Worldly at Bay

At Rhodes, most faculty share the administration's vision of the college as a preserver of genuine learning, willing to stand up to the trends that have perverted the educational mission of so many other institutions. As one professor says, "Even the left-wingers here are good teachers." And yet, there is inevitably a small cadre of faculty who would push the college toward a more mainstream position if they had their way. "In the aggregate, we have a moderate, collegial faculty," another professor notes. "But there is a high-strung, left-wing part of the faculty who would change things if they could. But they don't have the administration's ear, so they're civil and quiet, whereas at so many other places, the administration goes along with the radicals, and the mushy middle gives in."

Another professor says that "politically-correct junior faculty don't last long enough to gain tenure. They must read and subscribe to the mission statement of the school." This professor also notes that college president James Daughdrill has "stood up to people who would change the nature of the college" and has refused to recognize groups "that advocate sex outside of marriage" by turning down a request to install condom machines in the dorm and by refusing to be swayed by "militant homosexuals." Rhodes College, like Franciscan University of Steubenville, is a shining example of what a determined president with a confident, secure vision can accomplish. Because of Daughdrill's resolute determination to preserve the liberal and traditional nature of education at Rhodes, students who matriculate there will find a superb school where ordered liberty is sought, attained, and preserved. Notes one longtime faculty member who came to Rhodes after a long career at a major research institution: "Informally, there is a high degree of civility required here. We have very civil faculty meetings. But none of this would occur absent an administration to hold back the radicals."

While one need not question any particular professor's dedication and erudition, the fact that some members of the faculty are favorably disposed toward the more extreme versions of multiculturalism points out the importance of a president endeavoring to minimalize such influences. However, in one recent instance the president's wishes were overridden by a faculty vote when Rhodes turned down an offer of accreditation by the American Academy for Liberal Education. This academy accredits schools based on their commitment to a solid core curriculum and the liberal arts. Of the five schools (at this writing) who have sought academy approval, Rhodes is the only one where faculty have opposed the move. Other accredited schools include the University of Dallas and Thomas Aquinas College. One faculty member told the *Chronicle of Higher Education* that the faculty opposed the academy's accreditation (by a better than three-to-one margin) because of "the risk (of) being associated with a small group of schools that are ideologically backward." The professor continued: "We don't want to be identified as an institution that is no longer open-minded, tolerant, and progressive." The faculty vote on the matter, taken in the spring of 1997, is a discouraging sign, for experience illustrates that once the idea of a solid core of liberal arts classes is rejected, it is almost never again fully adopted.

Rhodes does have an Office of Multicultural Affairs, which seeks to aid minority students. The fourth-largest student group on campus (138 students out of about 1,400) is the Gay Straight Alliance, which maintains a website accessible from Rhodes's own web pages. Even though a disclaimer notes that Rhodes neither sponsors nor recognizes the organization, the website provides a link to sex-related pages elsewhere on the Internet.

The faculty, however, is better policed than the web pages. Among the departments at Rhodes, the most politicized faculties are found in history, sociology, and anthropology. The history department, says one professor, places "far too much emphasis on other cultures and on social history. Their stress is in the wrong areas." History is also among the weaker departments, and for basically those same reasons — although another professor says it is "a bit better" than it used to be. An Interdisciplinary Studies Program allows students to major in urban studies, which includes many courses from the weaker anthropology department and the much better political science department. And although there is at this writing no women's studies major, one can minor in that field.

Because of Rhodes's commitment to quality, a commitment that is reflected, as we have seen, in everything from its architecture to its relationship with the church, Rhodes has resisted more successfully than most small colleges the drive to emphasize research at the expense of teaching. Scholarship at Rhodes is seen as a means of bringing discipline to teaching. "People are fairly serious when it comes to research," says one professor. "But it's organized around the principle that your teaching will suffer if you do little but research for publication. Rather, the research supports the teaching here. . . . The administration is keenly aware that it will never be a research institution. Our bread and butter is in presenting ourselves as a teaching institution." Says another professor: "The administration concentrates on instruction first and research next. You do what you can in publishing, but you shouldn't become obsessed with it." And yet another faculty member sums up the college's commitment to teaching in these words: "Teaching is far and away the single most important criterion here. Rhodes has a strong commitment to excellence that would rival Princeton or Harvard. But this commitment is expressed in excellent teaching."

Campus Life: Urban Bliss

Rhodes College reflects the city in which it is located, and, in turn, Memphis values the college. Memphis, a river town, has a certain carefree quality to it that makes it "a beautiful place to work," in the words of one Rhodes professor who grew up far from the area. "Our urban setting is distinctive because we're in the middle of a very vibrant, extraordinary city," the professor notes. "Memphis has no pretensions, but it has aspirations and knows its problems. It is truly a unique and distinctive area — the Mississippi Delta, the blues, rock — it's a wonderful place." This urban setting is also trumpeted by the college itself, because it is seen as giving the school an urbanity and sophistication it might otherwise lack. Such an environment is not conducive to a cloistered life, and it helps Rhodes's students remain engaged with the surrounding world.

The percentage of students who enroll at Rhodes once accepted is less than 23 percent, which is rather low for a college of Rhodes's credentials, and about the same as that of Emory University. This figure shows that a fair number of those who apply to Rhodes make it their second choice and see it as a "safe" application for admission. Yet this low number should not dissuade anyone from coming to Rhodes, nor should it be thought that, once on campus, those who do come show themselves to be anything other than first-rate. The college's own statistics show that nearly a quarter of its students scored over 700 on the verbal portion of the SAT, with nearly half over 600. Further, more than 60 percent graduated in the top tenth of their high school class, and 11 percent were first or second in their class. Just under 70 percent of students come to Rhodes from out of state, and their religious affiliation is nearly evenly split among Presbyterians, Catholics, Methodists, Baptists, and other religious groups.

More than half (55 percent) of Rhodes scholars (pun intended) are women. About 65 percent of the student body participates in intramural sports, and 21 percent is involved in Rhodes's eight men's and eight women's intercollegiate sports teams. The Greek scene is thriving and active: over half of both male and female students join fraternities or sororities. After the Greek system, which includes some 740 students, the most popular organization on campus is the Kinney volunteer program, in which some 350 students volunteer with various groups in the community.

Rhodes graduates have a very high success rate in applying to graduate and professional schools. The school reports that 100 percent of grads seeking admission to law or business schools were accepted, and that 85 percent of those applying for medical school were successful. Overall, 93 percent of applicants to graduate schools are accepted. Despite the high quality of the science departments, only 49 B.S. degrees were awarded in 1997, compared to 262 B.A. degrees. Rhodes boasts a Phi Beta Kappa chapter, as well as Omicron Delta Kappa and Mortar Board societies, both organizations that recognize leadership and character.

RICE UNIVERSITY

6100 Main Street
Houston, TX 77005-1892
(713) 527-4036
(800) 527-OWLS
www.rice.edu

Total enrollment: 4,285
Undergraduates: 2,714
SAT Ranges (Verbal/Math): V 650-760, M 680-770
Financial aid: 85%
Applicants: 6,375
Accepted: 27%
Enrolled: 40%
Application deadline: Jan. 2
Financial aid application deadline: Feb. 15
Tuition: $13,900
Core curriculum: No

A Serious Player

Unlike many of the schools covered in this guide, Rice University cannot draw upon a centuries-old institutional tradition of excellence to bolster its reputation. Its founder, Massachusetts-born William Marsh Rice, made a fortune in Houston before deciding to found an institute for higher education. He actually traveled the globe studying universities so that he could draw upon the finest models for his school. He was particularly taken with Princeton and Oxford Universities, and they inspired the foundation of Rice Institute in 1912. Ironically, Rice was founded a dozen years after its founder was murdered by scoundrels who tried to forge his will and thus steal his fortune. From the beginning, Rice was organized as a small institution of the highest quality where students would live in residential colleges and where faculty-student relations would be warm and intense. Only six years later, in 1918, the school awarded its first Ph.D.

Rice is, then, a twentieth-century university that has worked very hard to establish itself as a serious player in the academic world. Today it employs a highly qualified faculty and attracts many of the best students from Texas, the Southwest, and, increasingly, the entire nation.

Long known principally for its engineering and science programs, Rice is expanding its offerings in the humanities so that it can compete with the best universities in the nation. President Malcolm Gillis is committed to strengthening the school's offerings in the humanities across the board, a promise fulfilled in part by the construction of a new humanities building. Gillis has big plans for his school: "Our aim is to become, without question, the pre-eminent private university between the eastern seaboard and San Francisco Bay," he told a campus publication. A professor echoes these sentiments. Asked what makes Rice a great place to teach, he said: "Great students make good teachers." Moreover, the students, according to this professor, have "outstanding intelligence. Many are National Merit Scholars, and admission is highly selective."

This rapid growth was made possible by money, and lots of it. Rice has an endowment of nearly $3 billion and a student body of only four thousand. It can therefore afford to construct splendid (even award-winning) new buildings, purchase the best lab equipment, and hire superb faculty, many of whom could write their own tickets in the academic world. The endowment also allows Rice to keep tuition unusually low for a first-class university. Whereas peer institutions regularly charge upwards of $20,000 a year for tuition alone, Rice charges under $14,000. And the school guarantees to meet the demonstrated financial needs of every student it admits — a practice increasingly rare in today's cost-conscious academic world.

Academic Life: Theoretical and Applied

Each student must enroll in one of six schools, each of which contains numerous departments. The schools are architecture, engineering, humanities, music, natural sciences, and social sciences. Students declare their choice on (if not before) Majors Day in the spring, at which time representatives from all departments and pre-professional offices assemble to assist in the decision-making process. Students can choose what Rice calls "traditional majors" in numerous departments, as well as double or even triple majors — a choice encouraged by the university. Also available are area majors, which allow students to develop an interdisciplinary major not satisfactorily covered in traditional areas. Rice awards only the B.A. and B.S. degrees to its undergraduates, a praiseworthy policy that excludes several weak or overly professionalized degree programs common at most universities (such as the B.S. in education or business). Rice students, therefore, are educated rather than trained, and are prepared to enter any walk of life. As one professor says, "Rice emphasizes a broad liberal arts program."

Although there is no core curriculum, all students must take at least twelve semester hours in each of three groups of disciplines: Group I, the humanities; Group II, the social sciences; and Group III, the natural sciences/engineering. It is not uncommon for Rice students to double-major in disciplines that fall into different academic groups. Music, architecture, and cognitive sciences majors must meet unique requirements.

Rice requires what might be called a structured set of distribution require-ments. There is no way to escape the broad set of disciplines represented by Groups I-III, even though there is no common reading per se. In this sense Rice requires more of its students than most universities and colleges, large or small.

Outstanding professors include Robert Curl and Richard Smalley in chemistry (they shared the Nobel Prize in chemistry in 1996); Werner Kelber in classics; Albert Van Helden, Michael Maas, John Boles, Katherine Fischer Drew, Ira Gruber, and Thomas Haskell in history; Donald Morrison in philosophy; Gilbert Cuthbertson and Earl Black in political science; and Ewa Thompson in German and Slavic Studies.

Some of the strongest departments include chemistry in particular and the sciences in general, all engineering departments, history, mathematics, classics, me-dieval studies, political science, music, and architecture.

A student comments: "Computational and applied mathematics is the best. It has a very good national reputation, and there isn't much of politics in the class-room." Says another: "Bioengineering has top faculty and students."

Among the more politicized departments and programs, anthropology, Study of Women and Gender, English, and linguistics stand out. Says a student: "The English department is very left wing, as are linguistics and anthropology. As to which is worse, it's a toss-up."

The number of overtly politicized courses at Rice has grown in recent years, as it has at most institutions in the United States. Students cannot be assured they will not face a professor who is perfectly willing to offer ideology rather than liberal learning, and freshmen should find a reliable adviser whose word can be trusted in order to navigate through each department's offerings. Advice from mature peers can also be very useful in this search. Still, the degree of politicization at Rice is substan-tially less than that found at institutions of comparable academic quality, and even at many lesser institutions. Here again is visible the legacy of Rice's engineering and scientific excellence, since both areas are far less politicized than the humanities and social sciences.

A few clearly politicized courses can be spotted in the Rice catalogue.

- English 498, "Studies in Literary Criticism: The Queer." Among the books to be read: *Passions between Women, Another Kind of Love, Epistemology of the Closet, Apparitional Lesbianism, Lesbian Postmodern, Fear of a Queer Planet, Bodies That Matter, Forms of Desire, Sodometries,* and *Surpassing the Love of Men.*
- History 425, "Colonial/Post Colonial Discourse." "The constitution of col-onized peoples as subjects of knowledge by their colonizers is known as colonial discourse; the reactions of the colonized, post-colonial discourse. The first half of the course will analyze the theories of colonial and post-colonial discourse. . . ."
- Study of Women and Gender 336/Anthropology 308, "History as a Cultural

Myth." "Ideas of history and attitudes toward the past as culturally conditioned phenomena. Emphasizes history as statement of cultural values as well as conceptualizations of cause, change, time, and reality."

- Study of Women and Gender 407/English 481, "Introduction to Feminist Literary Theory." "[We] will turn our attention to recent work that engages the pressing concerns of feminist theory in the 1990s, work that investigates the shape of gendered subordination and strategies for feminist agency in the contexts both of cultural diversity and of particular women's negotiation of race, class, sexuality, and national identifications (among others)."

Political Atmosphere: Generation Gap?

Rice has a better record on this score than most comparable universities. This is no doubt due in part to the central role engineering, science, and mathematics played in its origins as Rice Institute — disciplines that are traditionally more conservative than the humanities. Many faculty members are liberal, but the number of radicals is lower than average. The administration has, over the past several years, allowed for the establishment of an official Office of Multicultural Affairs, which now celebrates Diversity Week. Among student groups are found the usual assortment devoted to race, ethnicity, homosexuality, as well as traditional concerns, but their role is rather small, and the vast majority of students are simply too busy with their rigorous coursework to concern themselves with such things.

Rice's president, Malcolm Gillis, is on record as favoring affirmative action. In a recent interview he said: "No university is working harder than we are to try to compensate for the adverse effects of the Hopwood decision," which effectively put an end to the practice of affirmative action by universities and colleges in Texas. It would be wrong to assume that multicultural and diversity slogans are shouted from every rooftop on the Rice campus, but given the politicized climate of academia today, there always exists the potential for such matters to explode onto the scene at just about any school.

There is no speech code at Rice, and the amount of sensitivity training to which students are exposed is minimal.

Close examination of the faculty rosters reveals the unsurprising fact that many newer faculty members are concerned with scholarly topics that range far from what their predecessors often examined. As a first-class university, Rice recruits faculty from the best graduate schools in the country, and, as this guide reveals, it is precisely these universities at which one finds the most egregious forms of political correctness and ideological scholarship. This may indicate that Rice, like so many other schools, will be more politicized in the decades to come. Again, most new faculty at Rice are not fire-breathing radicals, but many in the humanities are significantly more concerned with questions involving the unholy trinity of race, class, and gender that have made studies in the humanities a much more problematic affair than was the case only a few years ago. Students should know that the course they take on Chaucer, for example, will be concerned not only with his works per se, but will spend more time on questions of gender than one might expect from such a traditional-sounding subject. Other seemingly mainstream subjects may also receive such treatment at the hands of scholars trained to approach great works as "cultural artifacts" rather than as the highest expressions of the human spirit.

Student Life: Desperately Seeking Housing

Upon arriving at this groomed campus, where Spanish moss drapes languidly from the massive live oaks that cover the grounds, students report to their residential college, to which they will be connected for all four of their years at Rice. Each of the eight coed colleges houses some 225 students, and each has its own dining hall, commons rooms, intramural teams, and personality. A faculty member, called a master, is assigned to each house and lives in an adjacent house. His job is to lead the students into new intellectual and cultural adventures and to support the self-governing mission of each college. The residential college system is one of the most unique features of student life at Rice, and it is fair to say that all other elements of life there flow from this arrangement.

One problem of residential life is a lack of college housing that forces students to participate in a dreaded lottery every year. Even freshmen are not guaranteed on-campus housing, although the school assures applicants that "every effort" is made to place them there. Given the uniqueness and worthiness of the residential college system, it is a shame that only 65 percent of undergraduates can live on campus. The 35 percent who must move off campus say that living is cheaper and quieter in their nearby houses and apartments, but that they miss the camaraderie of on-campus living. The university recognizes this problem, however, and hopes to build a ninth residential college. Dean Currie, the vice president of Finance and Administration, told the student newspaper (the *Rice Thresher*) recently that "There's one thing standing between us and a ninth college — an enormous amount of money."

All students must subscribe to the school's honor code, first promulgated in 1916. Many examinations are not proctored, and students self-schedule many of their finals.

There are numerous student organizations to choose from, although Greeks are not among them. William Rice did not like nondemocratic societies, so fraternities have never existed at Rice. Students name the Rice Republicans as the most conservative student group on campus, and the Rice Democrats, Rice for Choice, and SA, or Student Association, as the most liberal. Among the groups worth examining are the Rice Players, a theater group made up of students, faculty, and staff that presents at least four productions per year, and, among religious organizations, the Baptist Student Union, Catholic Student Association, the Hillel Society, Chabad, and Inter-Varsity Christian Fellowship.

Other student organizations span a very wide range of interests, especially for such a small school. A few that sound particularly interesting are the Aegean Club, which introduces members not already familiar with Greek culture to topics concerning Greece; the fencing club; the Marching Owl Band (MOB), which invites all students, with or without musical talent, to participate in its halftime antics; and the Owen Wister Literary Society. Of special note is the George R. Brown Forensics Society, a nationally recognized interscholastic debate team usually ranked among the top ten in the nation.

Students may also participate in a variety of academic honor societies, including many engineering and scientific organizations not found on every campus. Phi Beta Kappa has been at Rice since 1929, making it the second-oldest chapter in Texas, according to a professor.

Twenty club sports are available, including men's and women's rugby, a shooting club, men's and women's soccer, volleyball, and cricket. Some 40 percent of undergraduates participate (alongside graduate students and faculty) in intramural sports. No fewer than 290 teams compete in eleven sports between the walls at Rice. In varsity athletics, the Owls field teams in all of the usual sports in the Western Athletic Conference, NCAA Division I-A. The '97 Owls baseball team made it all the way to the College World Series in Omaha and ended its season ranked seventh in the nation, the best showing ever. Also strong in recent years are both men's and women's indoor track and field. Teams in other sports fare less well most of the time, but Rice athletes are not academic pushovers and must be able to compete in the classroom as well as on the field.

Rice has a handsome campus about three miles from downtown Houston. The architecture is Mediterranean, and the campus is well landscaped and beautiful. Adjacent to campus is the huge Texas Medical Center, as is the Houston Zoo and Hermann Park. Houston itself is the fourth-largest city in the nation and the second-busiest seaport. It contains all of the amenities of a major metropolis, although students will need a car to get around this sprawling Sun Belt city. Lying along the Gulf Coast, it is flat, hot, and humid. This does mean, however, that students can get outdoors year-round, and the beaches as well as the hill country of Texas are within an easy drive. As is true throughout the Deep South, everything is air-conditioned — usually to bone-chilling but refreshing temperatures.

UNIVERSITY OF RICHMOND

Office of Admissions
University of Richmond
28 Westhampton Way
Richmond, VA 23173
(804) 289-8640
www.richmond.edu

Total enrollment: 3,500
Undergraduates: 2,850
SAT Ranges (Verbal/Math): V 590-670, M 600-680
Financial aid: 66%
Applicants: 5,410
Accepted: 50%
Enrolled: 30%
Application deadline: Feb. 1
Financial aid application deadline: Feb. 25
Tuition: $17,570
Core curriculum: No

UR Here

The University of Richmond (UR) is a private, nonsectarian university in Richmond, Virginia, that has taken great strides in the last decade or so toward becoming a selective, top-notch regional university with a focus on the liberal arts. Average SAT scores for entering freshmen have risen two hundred points in the last ten years, and the university's endowment has swelled from $250 million to $654 million in the same period.

The basic curriculum consists of little more than a set of distribution requirements. A humanities course is required of all students — though only half the authors studied are from the Western tradition. Perhaps this is symbolic of Richmond's condition at this time: in its push for recognition, it has made more than a few concessions to the trendiest ideas in academia. While the university administration has sought such laudable goals as a more diverse student body and a more international focus, it has not pursued them without politicizing the curriculum, at least to some extent.

Academic Life: A Course in Human Events

Richmond's 2,900 undergraduate students take classes in one of three schools: the School of Arts and Sciences, the E. Claiborne Robins School of Business, or the Jepson School of Leadership Studies. Freshmen are automatically enrolled in the School of Arts and Sciences, and then apply to the other schools during their sophomore years, should they so choose.

All undergraduates must fulfill general education requirements during their freshman and sophomore years. The common core curriculum consists of one class: "Exploring Human Experience." This yearlong course, which must be taken as a freshman, features texts from a number of cultures and historical periods, and is taught by professors from various departments. Half the texts are Western, while the other half originate elsewhere in the world. The course involves readings, discussions, and frequent writing assignments with the purpose of incorporating "students into a community of learners from the very start of their collegiate careers," according to the university catalogue. "I really liked that class because you basically sit around and talk about history, philosophy, religion or whatever using different books," one student says.

Richmond also has general requirements in expository writing (though this can be passed with good advanced placement or achievement test scores) and in a foreign language, where students must either take classes through the second year or test out of the requirement. In addition, all students must take two physical education classes: one called "Dimensions of Wellness," which exposes them to "selected health, fitness, and wellness concepts," and one activity course of their choosing.

The final part of the general education requirements is what Richmond calls "fields of study." These are really distribution requirements in the areas most often covered by such requirements: historical studies, literary studies, natural sciences, social analysis, symbolic reasoning, and the visual and performing arts. Students choose one course (or two, in the case of natural sciences) from the lists.

Students working toward a bachelor of music degree, oddly, are exempt from the general requirements (except for the core course). Not so oddly, bachelor of science candidates add an additional calculus requirement.

The university's school of business, the choice of about 350 juniors and seniors, offers degrees in business administration and accounting. Business administration majors can pursue concentrations in more specialized areas such as international business, finance, and marketing.

While the business school mirrors that found on any number of campuses, the Jepson School of Leadership Studies is one of only a few such schools in the country. Relatively new (founded in 1989), the school's place in a liberal arts school such as Richmond is still the subject of some debate. About eighty students enroll in the Jepson School, which offers a B.A. in the interdisciplinary major of leadership studies. The school's goal is to "prepare [students] to meet the challenges of life and to develop their leadership abilities." The major involves twelve classes on topics such as critical thinking, ethics, group leadership, and conflict resolution. Students are also required to perform community service, intern at a local business or nonprofit agency, and complete a senior project.

In recent years the university has tried to take on more of an international character, and has thus increased its offerings for studying abroad. It sponsors a number of summer programs all over the globe, and students are encouraged to study overseas in university programs or in programs administered by other universities.

Biology students can spend a semester on the North Carolina coast in a program Richmond runs in cooperation with Duke University's marine laboratory. The program provides hands-on learning about coastal ecosystems and marine life. In addition, the university maintains a special research fund for undergraduates with research interests. The grants can cover the expense of material, equipment, or travel involved in a research project that is supervised by a faculty member. Such projects usually count for academic credit.

As befits a university in the once-besieged capital of the Confederacy, Richmond has a department of military science — although majoring in this field involves an after-graduation commitment to the U.S. Army and service in the campus Army ROTC. The program involves seven courses on topics including military history, military leadership, and advanced military science.

The best departments at Richmond, according to some on campus, are English and religion. The English department has remained traditional, and does not stress race, class, ethnicity, and gender as the predominant factors in its interpretation of works of literature. Richmond's religion department also has a reputation for being grounded in tradition. Although the number of religion majors is low compared to other departments, religion has several fine courses, including "The Bible and Western Culture" and "Religion and Moral Decisions."

According to people on campus, Richmond's best professors include Louis Schwartz (Renaissance literature) and Terryl Givens (Romantic literature) in English, Joe Ben Hoyle in accounting, Samuel Abrash in chemistry, and Albert Dawson and Laila Dawson of the Spanish department.

For better or for worse, Richmond claims its women's studies honors program sets it apart from other universities. Along with the main women's studies department, it is certainly the most politicized entity on campus. Known as WILL — Women Involved in Living and Learning — the selective program accepts only thirty female freshmen per year. Men are not allowed. The four-year program seeks to "increase the self-esteem, self-confidence, and self-awareness of women as well as an awareness and acceptance of women different from themselves."

Seen by traditionalists on campus as a group of radical feminists, WILL students complete a minor in the politicized women's studies department. The WILL program also features an internship, which allows students to "take their tools of critical thinking and gender analysis" learned in the women's studies classes and "put them into practice in the outside world." Recent speakers include Naomi Wolf and Susan Faludi.

The women's studies major involves a core course called "Introduction to Women's Studies," which exposes students to issues regarding "gender socialization, education, work, marriage, motherhood, sexuality, violence against women," and "new opportunities for growth and change," according to the catalogue. In looking at these issues, the course promises to pay special attention to "race, social class, and age."

Both the major and the minor require courses from at least three different departments, though all focus on women's issues. Students say the choices are mostly politicized, and that the interdisciplinary approach is used to spread the politics of women's studies to other areas of the curriculum. Examples include a biology course, "Special Topic: Women and Science"; a psychology class, "Human Diversity"; and a sociology department offering, "Sociology of Sex and Gender."

Political Atmosphere: Help Wanted

The University of Richmond administration has made great strides in the last several years to put itself on the map as a high-ranking university: *U.S. News and World Report* named Richmond the top regional university in the South from 1995 to 1997.

The author of this rise in recognition, university president Richard Morrill, announced in the fall of 1997 that he would resign following the 1997-98 academic year. Morrill holds a doctoral degree in religion and had previously served as president of Centre College, where he established a reputation as an excellent fund-raiser.

His replacement, according to the university's presidential search committee, will also be asked to raise money. In addition to "a distinguished record of academic and educational achievement and a commitment to excellence in liberal and professional education," committee guidelines say that the new president should have "experience in and eagerness for all forms of fund raising and a demonstrated ability to relate to large donors, to obtain major gifts, and to lead intensive fund-raising campaigns."

Another important trait of the successful candidate: he or she will have "respect for the university's religious heritage and should embrace the university's unique culture, including its central commitments to diversity, to internationalization, to interdisciplinary studies, to the development of the whole person, and to a strong sense of community."

Diversity, too, has been a goal of outgoing president Morrill. According to some students, the university has been eager to enroll more minority students, especially in light of a perceived lack of minorities at the school. "It's something the administration is very aware of and very concerned with," says one student. A running joke around campus has it that the only diversity at Richmond can be found in the kinds of cars students drive: Mercedes, Jaguars, or BMWs.

To aid in recruitment and retention of minority students, the university's Office of Multicultural Affairs actively sponsors many programs especially for members of minority groups. Some say these programs exacerbate racial tensions on campus by segregating students on the basis on skin color. For example, the aforementioned office holds something called the "University Pre-Orientation Program" for "entering first-year students of color." This special program introduces minority students to the university over the summer so that they can make "a smooth transition from high school to the University setting," though white students are not offered such assistance.

Morrill's administration has also pushed to internationalize the curriculum and increase the enrollment of international students. The Office of International Education sponsors courses, lectures, and seminars by international scholars, and visiting international students often help American students learn about their home cultures. Many courses in the arts and sciences reflect an international focus.

Student Life: If All the Girls Lived across the Sea . . .

The University of Richmond began in 1830 as Richmond College, which was founded by Virginia Baptists as a college of liberal arts and sciences for men. Originally the university was located near the center of Richmond, but after World War I it moved to its current 350-acre suburban location. From Richmond, one drives through what seems to be a forest. Then the road opens up and there sits the university, with fifty major buildings in Collegiate Gothic style, plenty of lawns, and a lake. This secluded location, and the fact that 93 percent of undergraduates live on campus, some students say, fosters a spirit of community not found on many other campuses.

The name Richmond College still applies to the all-male residential college on one side of the lake. Westhampton College, all-female, was founded in 1914 and stands on the other side of the water. The two residential colleges have separate dormitories, student governments, and administrations. The university says in its course catalogue that keeping the colleges single-sex creates more opportunities for all students. For example, women are guaranteed leadership positions in student government at Westhampton College because it is all-female.

University of Richmond students have a reputation of being smart and rich. The small size of the colleges and the amenities provided by the administration add to the sense of community, but also to this reputation. "They really pamper us here," says one student. A grossly unconfirmed rumor going around the student body says that a few years ago someone donated $10 million to be used exclusively for desserts in dining halls. Some swear it must be true, judging by the quality of the after-dinner delectables.

The separate-sex residential college system — one of only a few of its kind in the country — has led to gripes over the last few years from some students, particularly men who claim the women are given preferential treatment by the administration. (The women's dorms are nicer, some men say.) But other students dismiss these complaints as attempts by men to live closer to the opposite sex.

Overall, though, students are very satisfied with life at UR. A January 1997 poll found that 97 percent of freshmen said they were "satisfied" or "very satisfied" with the quality of their experience at the university.

About 60 percent of the student body belongs to one of Richmond's ten fraternities and eight sororities. Greek organizations do not have separate houses, but do throw frequent parties in a row of buildings separate from the dormitories. These parties are popular, especially among underclassmen.

The residential colleges themselves provide a basis of social and educational activity, as each brings in speakers and lecturers on a regular basis. Recent speakers include James Baker, Tom Clancy, Mikhail Gorbachev, Dr. Ruth Westheimer, and General Norman Schwarzkopf, who is a member of the university's board of trustees.

Each college looks forward each year to a few traditional events of its own. Each fall, for instance, Westhampton holds Proclamation Night; seniors wear gowns and freshmen wear white. The freshmen sign the university's honor code and write letters to themselves describing their feelings about being in the university. At the same time, the seniors open the letters they wrote to themselves when they were freshmen. Richmond College has similar traditions.

Although the campus is idyllic, students often venture into the city of Richmond, which has more than 200,000 people, a very high murder rate, and numerous attractions. Virginia's state capital is rich in history, with more than thirty museums and other historic sites that commemorate the city's colonial and Civil War history, including colonial plantations and the White House of the Confederacy. It has an Edgar Allan Poe museum and one of the finest publicly supported art museums in the country. Richmond claims its own symphony, ballet, and opera; it also offers minor-league baseball, ice hockey, and an annual NASCAR race. Along with students from Virginia Commonwealth University, the Medical College of Virginia, and other area schools, Richmond students frequent the bars and restaurants in an area of town known as Shockoe Bottom.

The city is ninety minutes south of Washington, D.C., while the natural attractions of the Blue Ridge Mountains are also ninety minutes away. The overbuilt seaside town of Virginia Beach is two hours to the east, depending on traffic.

Like many urban areas on the Interstate 95 corridor, the city of Richmond has problems with drug trafficking. That plague visited the university campus in April 1997, when three students were indicted for leading a campus marijuana ring said to involve more than forty students. Some students not indicted but suspected of involvement were disciplined by the school. According to the university's annual student surveys, attitudes toward drug use have become more permissive in recent years. In 1989, 22 percent of incoming male students and 13 percent of incoming female students thought pot should be legalized. In the 1995 survey, however, those percentages had doubled to 40 percent and 30 percent, respectively.

Although now nonsectarian, the university does maintain some of its religious connections. The university chaplain is a senior official in the administration who reports directly to the president and is in charge of "encouraging men and women from diverse backgrounds" to develop and explore their faith. The chaplaincy's $1.5 million endowment is used for programs of a spiritual, though ecumenical, nature. The university is home to a number of student religious groups.

Richmond fields eleven men's and ten women's intercollegiate sports teams, and is one of the smallest schools in the country whose teams all compete at the NCAA Division I level. The teams are known as the Spiders, a name that came about early in the school's history when its athletes were described as "all arms and legs." More than two-thirds of UR students compete in intramural sports.

RUTGERS UNIVERSITY

Office of Admissions
Assistant Vice President for University Undergraduate Admissions
Rutgers — The State University of New Jersey: Rutgers College
P.O. Box 2101
New Brunswick, NJ 08903-2101
(732) 445-3770
www.rutgers.com

Total enrollment: 47,810
Undergraduates: 35,060
SAT Ranges (Verbal/Math): V 500-620, M 520-640
Financial aid: 46%
Applicants: 22,050
Accepted: 66%
Enrolled: 39%
Application deadline: Dec. 15
Financial aid application deadline: Mar. 1
Tuition: in-state, $4,262; out-of-state, $8,676
Core curriculum: No

Law School?

Rutgers — The State University of New Jersey has many characteristics of an Eastern state university, including a sprawling campus in an urban environment and a tendency among students toward anonymity. "Diversity" is not just a cliché (though it's that, too, of course), for the campus is home to individuals from a variety of social and ethnic backgrounds and to a faculty and student body with wide-ranging interests. One faculty member describes the atmosphere at Rutgers as "intellectual permissiveness," which can work to the advantage of motivated students, including those who want a strong liberal arts education.

According to faculty and students, Rutgers has suffered in recent years from an intrusive and inept administration that is more interested in self-aggrandizement than in the interests of students and faculty. As a result, the Rutgers faculty and administration have an adversarial relationship that has resulted in some faculty resignations and more than a few lawsuits.

Faculty and students agree, however, that despite the frequently inhospitable political climate, Rutgers students can obtain a good undergraduate education. There are numerous fine professors and many solid courses from which to choose. The areas around Rutgers's several campuses are considered by many to be, odd as it may sound, "cultural meccas," and, according to one professor, "there are few places you can get access to really good faculty for such a cheap price." The key to success at Rutgers, according to another professor, is to be an "informed consumer."

Rutgers is "not a place for the weak-minded," cautions a faculty member; another notes that "it is not a school to be unlucky at," and warns students to be prepared for heavy consequences if they express "unfashionable opinions." Rutgers is "also a place where you can disappear and be as lonely and alienated as possible," comments one student. However, there are myriad challenging courses and professors, and strong support for undergraduate research. Students must thus weigh the pockets of excellent faculty, courses, and programs — and the low tuition — against the heavy bureaucratization and radical student politics, and decide whether they are motivated and resilient enough to make the most out of a Rutgers education.

Academic Life: Jersey Barriers

Since 1945 Rutgers has been the official state university of New Jersey and has evolved into a mammoth institution, enrolling roughly forty-eight thousand students on campuses in Newark, Camden, and New Brunswick. Each campus has liberal arts programs in addition to more specialized areas of study. Camden houses the School of Business, for instance, while the College of Nursing and the School of Management are located in Newark. At the New Brunswick campus is Cook College for agricultural studies, as well as the College of Engineering, the College of Pharmacy, another School of Business, and the Mason Gross School of the Arts. This essay will focus almost exclusively on the New Brunswick campus because of its liberal arts emphasis, and particularly on Rutgers College, which is located there.

The New Brunswick campus, the largest and oldest in the Rutgers system, comprises more than 2,800 acres and caters predominantly to liberal arts students. The campus is divided among four liberal arts colleges: Douglass, Livingston, Rutgers, and University. Each has its own distinct identity and focus, but share many of the same resources. University College is for "nontraditional" students, those typically older students who are pursuing educational opportunities part-time while holding a job or raising a family. Livingston was founded almost thirty years ago "to foster an understanding of an involvement with complex social issues" and is considered the most progressive of the liberal arts colleges; its motto is Strength through Diversity. Douglass College was founded in 1918 as the New Jersey College for Women, and is currently the largest women's college in the United States, enrolling nearly three thousand undergraduate women. Douglass women are considered intellectually strong, and the dean of the college, Barbara Shaler, is a trained classicist who receives high marks from students for her professional and personable demeanor.

The largest of the liberal arts colleges, Rutgers College, enrolls nearly nine thousand undergraduates. It is also the oldest and most distinguished of the New Brunswick liberal arts colleges. Chartered in 1766 as Queen's College by Benjamin Franklin's son William to train Dutch Reformed ministers (in a building that was once a tavern, no less), its name was changed in 1825 to Rutgers College in honor of Revolutionary War veteran Colonel Henry Rutgers. The college has long since shed any vestige of its Dutch Reformed heritage, although it still makes a verbal commitment to "maintaining its long-standing tradition as a liberal arts institution."

Rutgers College does not have a core of courses that all students must take; rather, students are asked to satisfy a series of distribution requirements, or "general education requirements," that the college has deemed essential to a liberal arts education. As the college's literature explains: "General education is . . . the common denominator of the liberal arts experience. It is knowledge that, in the late twentieth century, continues to provide students with the possibilities for common educated discourse, and that continues to prepare them for citizenship and for leadership in a democratic and pluralistic society."

Unfortunately, there is little to distinguish the Rutgers general education curriculum from that of the many other so-called liberal arts colleges that have weakened curriculum and standards in the name of "diversity." All students must take an expository writing course and one additional writing-intensive course; they can bypass the former with high advanced placement test scores. One math course is required (again, students may place out of it), along with an additional course chosen from among other mathematical disciplines such as computer sciences, statistics, and logic. Students must take two courses in the natural sciences and two courses in both social sciences and the humanities. There is no foreign language requirement, although Rutgers "recommends that its students establish proficiency in a foreign language."

Rutgers makes no requirements involving European history, literature, art, or music, but all students must take one course "about the non-Western world." Within the social science and humanities requirements, students can find excellent courses in history, classics, philosophy, and other traditional offerings; however, they can also bypass these altogether by choosing from courses in Africana studies, Puerto Rican and Hispanic Caribbean studies, women's studies, African languages and literatures, or Chinese. An emphasis on diversity might be partly defensible considering Rutgers's high minority student population (more than 35 percent), but to have no formal requirement in the humanistic areas of Western thought that have formed the foundation of a traditional liberal arts education comes close to intellectual fraudulence (not to mention false advertising).

According to one professor, three efforts in the last ten years have been undertaken to reform the general curriculum at Rutgers; after much "politicking" among faculty, the result is characterized by one faculty member as the "Chinese menu" approach (one from column A, one from column B . . .).

In its promotional literature, Rutgers proudly points to frequent undergraduate involvement in both self-designed and faculty research. This advertising is true: in a recent student survey, the university reports, more than 40 percent of graduating students said they had the opportunity to participate in a faculty-sponsored research project. As one student notes, these research projects "teach you how to work with a single professor over an extended period of time on an individual project," an experience that can help prepare students for graduate school and professional research projects.

In addition to more traditional disciplines, students at Rutgers can major in such emerging fields (or pseudofields) as Africana and Afro-American studies, Puerto Rican studies, or women's studies, and can choose from a dizzying number of multicultural courses. Rutgers is a hospitable environment for anything promoting the modern notion of diversity: the university was recently chosen by the African Studies Association (ASA) to be its official home for African research for the next several years. The student newspaper, the *Daily Targum*, highlighted the event with the headline "RU Embraces Africana Studies" and quoted elated Rutgers faculty, one of whom said the ASA's presence "will be very helpful for putting Rutgers on the map."

Despite its frequent obeisance to the gods of multiculturalism, Rutgers has not forsaken all allegiance to traditional education. There are still many good professors and courses to be found both within and outside of the mainstream programs. When asked to name the finest departments, faculty, and courses, students and faculty are hard-pressed to narrow their preferences, so generally enthusiastic are they about the quality of academics at Rutgers. There are good faculty in medieval and modern philosophy, and Rutgers offers an undergraduate medieval studies major. The English department is characterized by one student as a "repository for people who don't know what else to do," although it boasts some good faculty as well, including Richard Poirier, editor of the Library of America (a series of classic American authors). Classics, history, political science, and archaeology are all thought to have pockets of excellence. The biological sciences, especially microbiology, are world class. Disciplines that typically have a radical slant today, such as sociology and anthropology, still retain some excellent faculty, including one sociology professor who does research on "critical perspectives on family issues" and has argued the importance of fathers in family relationships. Although the majority of professors are described as liberal, there are also a considerable number of traditionalists, and ideology doesn't seem to be an overly significant player at the curricular level. Undergraduates seeking to major in traditional liberal arts disciplines will generally not be disappointed with Rutgers.

Class size varies at Rutgers, although with the variety of traditional and newer majors offered, some departments instruct as few as a dozen students in upper-level undergraduate courses. Introductory courses naturally tend to have a larger enrollment, but the large number of students who enroll in traditional courses is a testament to both the solid advising system at Rutgers and the good instincts of the student body. A lower-level Greek civilization course, for instance, can attract upwards of seventy students.

Faculty and students alike give high marks to the Rutgers College Honors Program, the benefits of which include, in the words of one faculty member, "excellent advising, small classes with very bright students, and an environment where intellectual ambition is encouraged."

Political Atmosphere: See You in Court

According to one professor, Rutgers University is probably the largest academic litigating body in the country, with around eighty lawsuits pending against the university at any given time. The Rutgers administration is said to be "heavily bureaucratized," and operates in an "adversarial and custodial" manner, according to one professor. Like those at similar institutions, Rutgers administrators are handsomely paid and possess a great deal of power. According to one source, many administrators are "out of touch with the needs of the students" and are often so lacking in intellectual sophistication that "they couldn't even be students at Rutgers." Thus, their job often amounts to "enforcing low expectations for the university," and faculty consequently feel demoralized. "Our administrators don't know what a faculty looks like," says one dejected professor.

Rutgers faculty have suffered in recent years from New Jersey governor Christine Whitman's budget cuts and the lack of a faculty contract. Low faculty morale has led to what one professor describes as the "I'm here, I'm doing my time, I'm getting out" syndrome. In the spring of 1997 the *Daily Targum* published a series on "The

Downsizing of Academia," which reported widespread faculty unrest and a distressing loss of top-drawer faculty. According to the article, the number of Rutgers faculty has fallen from 2,640 in 1985 to its current level of about 2,400; enrollment over that period, however, has remained fairly consistent. Professor of Communications Stanley Deetz was quoted as saying he was leaving for the University of Colorado because "it is such a mess here. . . . The administration is so bad here, and Gov. Whitman's cuts just add to the complications."

The administration seems to be universally reviled by faculty, and the disciplinary code is said by a faculty member to be "Byzantine and unfairly administered." While the actual written regulations concerning such matters as sexual harassment and academic freedom are quite good, they are enforced indiscriminately. Treatment of sexual harassment allegations, for instance, is described as "capricious": one professor may be unduly interfered with because his course material is considered offensive by a female student, while another who has actually performed an overt act of harassment goes uncharged. Recently, Rutgers president Francis Lawrence recommended the dismissal of William K. Powers, a professor of anthropology, because of pending sexual harassment charges by university students. According to the *Daily Targum,* Professor Powers claims that "the trouble began when a female graduate student filed false sexual harassment charges against both him and his wife," the latter an anthropology professor at Seton Hall. Since the charges were lodged, several students have organized the Student Coalition against Powers' Expulsion.

There also appears to be race-related tension on campus. In 1995 President Lawrence came under fire for a public remark that implied the genetic inferiority of minorities. Although he apologized for the statement, which he claimed was misinterpreted and taken out of context, student activists called for his resignation. In one widely reported protest, a group of students swarmed onto the court in the middle of a Rutgers basketball game in order to express their displeasure.

While Lawrence got in trouble for opening his mouth in that case, some members of the Rutgers community say the administration's silence has allowed other ethnic tensions to simmer unaddressed. There are many Jewish students at Rutgers, as well as a sizable contingent of Jewish faculty. In recent years the Jewish population has suffered from an "anti-Semitic undertone" and an "inhospitable atmosphere," according to one professor. Racial tensions are also said to exist between Jewish and minority students.

As for the students of the New Brunswick campus, they have plenty of opportunities for radical activities. Livingston College, for instance, was host to Earthstock 97, a northeastern student environmental conference cosponsored by Free the Planet!, the New Jersey Public Interest Research Group, and the Sierra Student Coalition. The event, organized "to cultivate a new generation of political activists," according to a campus newspaper report, featured 1985 Nobel Peace Prize winner Helen Caldicott and Sierra Club president Adam Werbach as keynote speakers.

Meanwhile, Douglass College held its sixteenth annual Women's Conference in the spring of 1997, focusing on "topics such as reproductive health, body images and food, and women of color." The conference was attended by, among others, more than one hundred high school students who had been accepted into Douglass, and it seemed to some to be little more than a thinly disguised attempt to promote the virtues of lesbianism to young women. In one "sexual diversity workshop," headed by the copresident of the Bisexual Gay Lesbians Alliance of Rutgers University (Bi-GLARU), "students discussed being queer on a college campus and how heterosexism is related to sexism," according to the *Daily Targum*.

There are currently no conservative newspaper nor active conservative student groups at Rutgers. Chapters of the Intercollegiate Studies Institute and the Young Americans Foundation have cropped up at irregular intervals, but have had difficulty sustaining interest because of the heavy study load, not to mention the opposing nature of the student body. Conservative faculty have fared little better: a chapter of the National Association of Scholars never made it off the ground, although there is a Rutgers Committee on Academic Freedom. Conservative speakers come to campus infrequently, while left-wing programs such as the Center for Comparative Study of Civilization have richly funded lecture budgets. President Bill Clinton and actress Susan Sarandon are among the recent speakers the university has publicly touted, although Steve Forbes also came to speak to a political science class.

Student Life: It's Home

More than 90 percent of Rutgers students hail from New Jersey, although the university's viewbook contains facts and tidbits about the state (it has the nation's second-highest per capita income; the steam locomotive, the motion picture, the electric guitar, and the submarine were all invented there; etc.) that are seemingly designed to make New Jersey more appealing to students from other states. The in-state tuition is just over $4,000, which is certainly difficult to pass up for New Jersey students. About 60 percent of Rutgers students live on campus (high, considering how many are from New Jersey, the fifth-smallest state in the land), and housing is guaranteed for the freshman and sophomore years. Off-campus housing is considered expensive, and students should thoroughly research the surrounding area before committing to a living arrangement. About 20 percent of Rutgers undergraduates are members of fraternities or sororities, although all Greek housing is off campus. Safety is also a consideration when finding somewhere to live. Although students can reduce the risk of crime by adopting safe living habits, there is consistent petty theft and the occasional mugging. "New Brunswick is kind of a dicey town," says one student.

However, students at the New Brunswick campus take advantage of the shops, banks, and ethnic restaurants (including a sushi bar) on George Street, as well as the many social and cultural opportunities on College Avenue. Well-heeled students can take the train to New York or Philadelphia to enjoy world-class museums, ballets, and orchestras; popular weekend and summer hangouts include the many seaside resorts on the Jersey Shore.

According to both faculty and students, the "logistics" of New Brunswick pose one of the primary difficulties in navigating Rutgers. The campus is sprawling, and auto congestion is acute. New Jersey is an expensive state (the downside of a high per capita income), so housing can be costly and difficult to find. "Organizing the day is difficult for students," says one professor, who notes that many work to make ends meet, primarily on off-campus jobs. For these and other reasons, Rutgers is sometimes affectionately referred to as "RU Screw" by frustrated students.

Rutgers boasts hundreds of intramural teams and nearly fifty NCAA Division I and III varsity sports (between the three campuses, which field their own teams). High-ranking teams in recent years include the Lady Knights' women's golf team, which took the 1996 Northwest Intercollegiate Championship, as well as women's lacrosse and tennis, men's baseball, and gymnastics, crew, and track. To its credit, Rutgers values high academic performance in its athletes; the 1997 Rutgers Athlete of the Year, for instance, was Hungarian Olympian Balazs Koranyi, a history and political science major with a 3.6 grade point average.

Rutgers is also home to more than four hundred student organizations, including everything from Campus Crusade for Christ to the aforementioned BiGLARU. Its high minority enrollment ensures a wide variety of student organizations divided along racial and ethnic boundaries, many with activist intentions. An increased amount of public space is also set aside for minority students. The Rutgers Asian-American Coalition for Equality (RACE) is an umbrella organization for thirteen smaller Asian and Asian-American groups, and publishes a biweekly paper focusing on Asian-American interests on campus. RACE recently held a "Call for Action" forum devoted to discussing "Japan bashing, gender issues, and the Asian-American lesbian and gay community," according to the *Multicultural Student's Guide*. Rutgers also has a Latino Student Council, representing sixteen different Latino organizations, as well as a Latino Center for Arts and Culture.

A few years ago African-Americans on campus received their own "cultural space" next to the Busch Campus Center. The $1.1 million Paul Robeson Cultural Center is named for one of Rutgers's most famous graduates. (The third African-American to graduate from Rutgers, college football star Robeson gave the 1919 valedictory address before becoming a well-known actor and singer.) The center "provides office space for fourteen student organizations, two conference rooms, a computer room, reading and lounge areas, and a suite for the staff of the center's *Black Voice/Carta Boricua*" paper, according to *Multicultural Student's Guide*. While minority students hail such coalition building and the acquisition of "cultural space," others worry about the further balkanization of the Rutgers student body.

ST. JOHN'S COLLEGE

Annapolis Campus
Director of Admissions
P.O. Box 2800
Annapolis, MD 21404-2800
(800) 727-9238
(410) 263-2371
www.sjca.edu

Santa Fe Campus
Director of Admissions
1160 Camino de la Cruz Blanca
Santa Fe, NM 87501-4599
(505) 982-3691
www.sjca.edu

Total enrollment: Annapolis, 536; Santa Fe, 468
Undergraduates: Annapolis, 455; Santa Fe, 380
SAT Ranges (Verbal/Math): V 650-740, M 550-640
Financial aid: 65%
Applicants: 340
Accepted: 84%
Enrolled: 50%
Application deadline: Mar. 1
Financial aid application deadline: Feb. 15
Tuition: $20,980
Core curriculum: Yes

The Best Teachers There Are

Of all the college publicity materials we've seen while preparing this guide, those handed out by St. John's College may be the most effective. The cover says simply: "The following teachers will return to St. John's next year," and those words are surrounded by some of the greatest names in Western culture, including Homer, Aquinas, Euclid, Ptolemy, Swift, Adam Smith, Melville, Dante, Chaucer, Bach, Schubert, Tolstoy, Yeats, Eliot, and Wallace Stevens. On the inside cover of the booklet is "The St. John's List of Great Books," which shows, by year, exactly what students who attend St. John's will read and hear. It is an impressive list, made even more so by the fact that most college and university viewbooks fill those first pages with lofty (and often fraudulent) rhetoric telling prospective students about the "broad liberal arts education" the school has to offer.

St. John's College is a coeducational, four-year, "Great Books" liberal arts program that has two campuses, one in Annapolis, Maryland, and the other in Santa Fe, New Mexico. The campus in Annapolis was originally called King William's School, and it was founded in 1696, making it the third-oldest college campus in the country. (Francis Scott Key studied there before writing "The Star-Spangled Banner," and it was a venerable institution even then.) The Santa Fe campus was added in 1964.

The total number of students — including both campuses — is around eight hundred. There are no departments, no written final exams, and no research professors. With those three criteria alone, St. John's takes out of play major sources of conflict that bedevil other campuses. A student-faculty ratio of eight-to-one takes care of another concern: huge introductory level courses. The largest classes at St. John's contain about twenty students, but many have just five or six.

There is but one course of study at St. John's: the great books of Western civilization, and everyone reads the same books. They talk about them, and they learn. There are no ideological turf wars, no made-up departments, no standards bent to admit the six-foot-eight swingman with an SAT of around 550, no need for a lucky guess or a road map to find the good courses in dismal majors. This is the straight stuff, a true community of liberal learning. While other schools make students slip through a crack in the wall to get to their intellectual heritage, St. John's provides a broad and stately gate, and invites its students to enter. In an age that is obsessed with "relevance" and "competitiveness," St. John's quietly goes about its business — enabling its students to develop something that is at once timeless and utterly relevant: a critical, reflective mind.

Academic Life: Just One

St. John's says it seeks "to restore the true meaning of a liberal arts education." The college emphasizes reading, discussion, writing, experimentation, mathematical demonstration, translation, and musical analysis in its curriculum. The curriculum is the same for all students, and in each year of their educations students read the same books at the same time as their fellows not only at one campus, but both in Santa Fe and Annapolis.

There are no electives, nor are there distribution menus from which one class will be chosen to represent the full extent of a student's learning in philosophy, literature, the sciences, or music. The St. John's curriculum, known as "The Program," requires readings from original texts that examine the most important questions of the Western philosophic tradition. During their freshman year students read Greek and Latin authors such as Homer, Sophocles, Plato, Aristotle, and Plutarch. During their sophomore year, most readings are from the classical period (more Aristotle and

Plutarch, plus Virgil), but second-year students are also exposed to the writings of medievals such as St. Augustine and St. Thomas Aquinas, as well as moderns such as Machiavelli, Descartes, and Pascal. In the junior year the modern period of philosophic and literary thought is fully engaged, with readings from Spinoza, Locke, Leibniz, Hume, Rousseau, Kant, and Berkeley. The senior year is spent reading several American authors, such as Frederick Douglass, Flannery O'Connor, Lincoln, and Thoreau, as well as nineteenth- and twentieth-century philosophic writers, including Nietzsche, Heidegger, and Marx. Seniors also explore such modern poets as T. S. Eliot, Yeats, and Wallace Stevens. The genius of it comes not from the list itself, but in how the parts harmonize to make the whole: the *Divine Comedy* illuminates the *Four Quartets,* and Palestrina foregrounds the hearing of the *St. Matthew Passion.*

"The academic program at St. John's is a unified, cohesive whole," reads the first sentence inside the college viewbook. The college's catalogue claims that the curriculum represents "the highest achievements in philosophical, historical, and political inquiry, scientific and mathematical thought, and poetic imagination." It continues: "St. John's College is persuaded that a genuine liberal education requires the study of great books — texts of words, symbols, notes and pictures — because they express most originally and often most perfectly the ideas by which contemporary life is knowingly or unknowingly governed."

Students take four courses each year, and the final breakdown includes four years of seminars, three of laboratory sciences, one of music, two each of French and ancient Greek, and four of mathematics.

The "Great Books" seminars are the heart of the curriculum. The seventeen to twenty-one students in each seminar sit in a circle, not to hear a lecture, but to discuss a central question raised by the "tutor" regarding the text they all have read. Students offer answers or solutions to the question, and the conversation can take many turns. In some cases the tutor controls the direction of the discussion, but in others he frequently allows it to progress in new directions if they bear on the central themes of the text. A seminar meets two evenings per week, and each class period covers perhaps eighty pages of reading.

There are but two published rules regarding the seminars: all opinions must be heard and explored, and every opinion must be supported by an argument. The role of the tutor is not to move the students to some "correct" opinion or interpretation, but to make sure of these two things. "Some say the less flamboyant a tutor is the better," a student says. "The tutor is not supposed to be the center of attention. Rather the books and the students are at the center of things."

There is a writing component to the seminars as well. During their first three years, students must write essays on some aspect of the books they have been studying in their seminars (each year at Annapolis and every semester in Santa Fe). Seniors write on an approved topic derived from their overall study of great books, and then must publicly defend their work before a committee in an hour-long oral examination. There is some debate at St. John's over the role of writing. "There are two divisions

— the old school and the new school," says a student. "The old school teachers don't believe in writing. This group understands St. John's to be primarily a conversation school. Moreover, they want the attention put on reading the texts. The younger group is more energetic. They are more into a rigorous approach to the study of science and math." The student adds that both groups are completely dedicated to The Program and differ only in how its objectives are best fulfilled.

Seminars, like any set of conversations, aren't all of equal worth, however. "Some seminars are great, and others are very bad," a student says. "People need to go into the seminar with the right attitude. You have to throw your faith behind The Program, and if you don't, you will be disappointed." And according to one St. John's tutor, an unexpected negative consequence of immersing students in great books is that some develop a "smug familiarity with greatness."

Tutorials in music, mathematics, and language are designed to supplement the seminars. During each year of undergraduate study, students attend one language and one mathematics tutorial three or four times a week. Sophomores take an additional tutorial, in music. St. John's students take Greek for their first two years and French as juniors and seniors. The math classes, in which the field is treated "as a liberal art, not artificially separated from what have come to be called the humanities," dwell on theories, problems, and classical mathematical texts, such as Euclid's *Elements*, Ptolemy's *Almagest*, and Newton's *Principia Mathematica*. As with many St. John's courses, students get out what they put in. "In some cases you walk away from a tutorial feeling that you didn't learn much. But then it's usually your fault," a student says. "The premium is on self-motivation, and it is up to each student to learn the class lesson. The responsibility is with the student, not with the tutor."

In the four years of laboratory classes, to the extent possible given financial, safety, and spatial limitations, students duplicate the experiments of great scientists such as Galileo, Fahrenheit, Kepler, and Galen. It seems that not all great books are printed on paper. For example, students measure the speed of light or perform oil-drop experiments to measure molecules. Experiments range into chemistry, biology (dissections), and genetics (hybrids of plants). Students write reports, which are graded.

St. John's does not provide students with grade reports, but does maintain records of grades for students' graduate school or employment purposes. Final examinations are oral and individual, and tutors meet with each student twice a year to evaluate his or her intellectual progress and performance. Since the grades, especially in seminars, are based on class discussions and other nonmetric criteria, grades are perhaps more subjective than at other institutions. But the system does hold down pressures often felt at those other places. "The grading policy cuts down on the competitive edge in class, and fosters a more mature manner in discussing ideas," a student says. "There is, as a result, not a lot of pretense in the seminars."

Every sophomore faces a little more pressure when it comes time for "sophomore enabling," an unfortunate pop-psychology term for an evaluation that determines whether the student will be allowed to continue at St. John's. A committee considers past performance and written work before making its determination, and weighs the chances of the student being able to eventually write a worthwhile final senior essay. The failure rate is about 7 percent. According to one student: "Those students who fail are given the option to take courses so that they can be reinstalled. Consequently people try to avoid failing. The great majority get by without a problem. One faculty member has said that St. John's applicants need not be the best students in high school, but they need to commit themselves completely to the program. It's kind of like the underdog approach. The tutors at St. John's love to see high-school screw-ups completely transformed by the program."

Once "enabled," as it were, juniors and seniors add to their courseload a nine-week "preceptorial." These are the only classes students can choose in an education at St. John's; they select four from a list of sixteen to twenty, and the college makes the final assignments. Preceptorials focus either on one book or on one subject as covered in several books, and in the past have included Heidegger's *Being and Time*, Joyce's *Ulysses*, Aristotle's *Metaphysics*, and selected novels of Jane Austen.

The entire student body attends formal lectures or concerts on Friday evenings, after which a mini-seminar (a chance for students and faculty to ask questions of the visiting scholars and performers) is held. Recent lecturers have included Martha Nussbaum, James Q. Wilson, Elliot Zuckerman, and Mortimer J. Adler.

According to students and faculty, the most distinguished tutors at the Annapolis campus are Gisela Berns, Laurence Berns, Robert B. Williamson, Stewart Umphrey, and Adam Schulman; the best at Santa Fe include James Cohn, Robert D. Sacks, David Bolotin, and William S. Kerr.

Political Atmosphere: Moot Points

Other things St. John's doesn't have to deal with are speech codes, hiring or student body quotas, and the desire of a misguided administration to teach the latest ideological trends in order to rank high on someone's ill-conceived list. The school chooses its deans from among the faculty, and the deans usually serve limited terms, returning thereafter to their work as tutors.

Consequently, there is great harmony between the administrative and academic functions of the college. And in terms of faculty hiring, St. John's accepts only those interested in the college's mission. "It is a well known fact that St. John's is more interested in having people give themselves over to The Program than having a reputation," a student says. "St. John's faculty want new tutors to be married to The Program, and they hire new tutors based upon their commitment to The Program."

There is, of course, bound to be discussion about what is and is not included in the reading lists — and it can even be argued that one could compose an impressive curriculum just using books that St. John's does not. Since the great books curriculum was adopted in the 1930s, some fifty writers have been dropped from the lists, Dickens and Montesquieu among them. A seven-member committee makes the decisions on what's in and what's out, and St. John's doesn't try to hide the fact that its choices have changed over the last sixty years — that information shows up in school publications, along with well-conceived defenses of a liberal arts education, a great books curriculum, and the teaching methods used by the college.

One college publication even allows that not all seminars are successful. "The progress of the seminar is not particularly smooth; the discussion may sometimes branch off and entangle itself in irrelevant difficulties," says the catalogue. "A seminar may degenerate into rather empty talk, without being able for some time to extricate itself from such a course."

To allay parental concerns about the marketability of plain liberal arts degrees and student concerns about graduate school admissions, St. John's puts out another publication entitled *Graduate Study and Careers after St. John's*. In it the college makes another fine accounting of its methods, and of its products: well-rounded graduates who have the tools for success in any field or further study. The school is thought to be an ideal preparation for law school, and more students than one might imagine go on to medical school despite the rather general science program. The publication says about 20 percent of graduates wind up in business-related fields, while 18.5 percent are involved in teaching. The next-highest groups, all constituting between 5 and 8 percent of graduates, are law, writing and publishing, health professions, and social services.

Reportedly, the faculty and students at Santa Fe are more liberal than at Annapolis. But most students aren't politically active, save perhaps at election time. While there is an officially recognized gay students' group, no group on either campus displays the activism so common at other schools. And while the overall atmosphere is politically and socially liberal, the students are described as more "artsy" than activist. Most of the campus hangouts have a 1960s coffeehouse atmosphere. A certain hostility toward religion is said by some to crop up occasionally in classroom discussions as well as in student publications, such as the *Gadfly*, although the Bible is one of St. John's great books.

Student Life: Tale of Two Cities

Annapolis is a beautiful, historic coastal city of fifty thousand, and most residents are affiliated with the Maryland state government, the U.S. Naval Academy, or the fishing industry. The campus is located in the heart of Annapolis's fine historic district, next to the Maryland State House and the Naval Academy. Santa Fe, of course, has an entirely different atmosphere. The city of sixty-five thousand stands 7,300 feet above sea level, and the campus, located on the outskirts of town, commands a scenic view of the city and the surrounding mountains, including the famous Sangre de Cristo range. The choice for students comes down to which type of brick they prefer: colonial or adobe.

Student activities are coordinated through the Director of Student Activities in Annapolis and the Student Activities Office in Santa Fe. Annapolis is unique in that it affords students the opportunity to engage in sailing and other recreational activities in Chesapeake Bay. Baltimore and Washington, D.C., are both within an hour of campus. Santa Fe has its own scenic and cultural attractions, including the city itself, which is unlike any place in the nation.

Groups and clubs that dominate other colleges and universities are not very popular at St. John's College, principally because The Program satisfies most students' intellectual interests. However, intramural sports are very popular on campus, and many students are involved in them. Along with soccer, basketball, and softball, intramural offerings and other sporting activities include croquet, fencing, fly-fishing, Tai Chi, yoga, and rock climbing. In Santa Fe, the St. John's College Mountain Search and Rescue Team is billed as one of the "best trained and most active groups in the Southwest." This program includes survival skills, backpacking, mountaineering, emergency medical care, and search and rescue techniques. There are no intercollegiate sports, although the college is occasionally confused with Big East basketball power St. John's University.

The only Greeks at St. John's are dead writers, and most campus events are informal (apart from the Friday evening lecture or concert). Some, though, are organized each year. Reality Weekend, the largest such event, comes the weekend before evaluations and could occur only on a well-educated campus that really needs to cut loose. The weekend begins with the performance of a Greek tragedy before lapsing into parties and games. One of the games is "Spartan Mad Ball," which has only one rule: players cannot wear shoes. Otherwise the game is somewhat like rugby with a soccer ball — there are no limits as to how many students can be on the field, and students use all appendages to get the ball across the opponent's goal line. Usually the freshmen and juniors square off against the sophomores and seniors. Another event is the Epicycle Races, based on Ptolemy's model of the universe, with circles circling circles. Teams attached by ropes circle each other while trying to, at best, cross the finish line and, at worst, avoid strangling themselves.

SMITH COLLEGE

Director of Admissions
Smith College
Garrison Hall
Northampton, MA 01063
(413) 585-2500
www.smith.edu

Total enrollment: 2,900
Undergraduates: 2,750
SAT Ranges (Verbal/Math): V 620-720, M 590-670
Financial aid: 56%
Applicants: 3,130
Accepted: 52%
Enrolled: 39%
Application deadline: Early decision, Nov. 15; regular admissions, Feb. 1
Financial aid application deadline: Jan. 15
Tuition: $29,240 (comprehensive)
Core curriculum: No

Keeping Up with the Smithies

From its modest beginning in 1875 with 14 students, Smith College has swelled to a current undergraduate enrollment of 2,700, making it the largest private women's college in the United States. Traditionally, Smith has been known for its strong liberal arts programs and its emphasis on women's issues. The college was founded with a bequest from Sophia Smith, who stated in her will her intent to "furnish for my own sex means and facilities for education equal to those which are afforded now in our colleges to young men." Famous graduates of Smith include poet Sylvia Plath, feminists Gloria Steinem and Betty Friedan, and chef Julia Child. When Smith alumna Barbara Bush became the first lady, Smith students paraded around in T-shirts emblazoned with the words, "There must be a better way to get a Smithie in the White House."

Smith women, or "Smithies" as they are traditionally called, are considered an independent and motivated lot who often combine high academic achievement with a good measure of social activism. One professor characterizes Smith students as "competitive and hard working — they take their studies and prospective careers very seriously."

Some students and faculty, however, suggest that Smith's commitment to the liberal arts — particularly the humanities — has dwindled over the years, with an increased interest and emphasis on the sciences and the addition of majors in such areas as computer science and childhood education. And despite the college's commitment to academic freedom and free speech, students of a more traditional cast of mind may find the feminist perspective — which creeps its way into nearly every course by professorial design, student demand, or both — narrow and stifling.

Academic Life: Advise and Dissent

In keeping with the high level of independence and responsibility attributed to Smith undergraduates, there are no specific course requirements beyond the major. "The college requires almost nothing" in the way of requirements, notes one professor — "just a few guidelines." Not surprisingly, Smith's abandonment of distribution requirements occurred in 1970, at a time when a general relaxation of social and academic standards was taking place in higher education nationwide. Although there has occasionally been talk of instituting more comprehensive general education requirements, the faculty and administration usually only "play around at the margins," notes one professor, by suggesting "skill-oriented requirements" such as a writing-intensive course.

In the past couple of years, however, Smith has exhibited a renewed interest in encouraging a broad liberal arts education. The college guidebook advises students to take courses in seven fields of knowledge: literature, historical studies, social science, natural science, mathematics and analytical philosophy, the arts, and foreign language. In order to graduate with honors, students must now take at least one course in each of these areas to ensure a breadth of knowledge. In addition, all students now have one required writing-intensive course during their freshman year, although the college stresses that "there are *no* further required courses outside the student's field of concentration."

But, because many students want to graduate with honors, they avoid narrowness in their curriculum choices. And students note the advantages to the absence of a core curriculum, such as the option of taking upper-level classes at an early stage in one's studies. "I liked the freedom of being able to take whatever classes interested me," says one. But a recent graduate in mathematics expresses regret that she completed her degree "without taking a single science class."

The commitment to teaching is high among Smith faculty. With a student-faculty ratio of ten-to-one, the college boasts small courses and accessible teachers. One student notes that she has never had a class with more than 25 students. Although they fall victim to the same pressures to publish as at other colleges, "the professors are very, very focused on teaching," says one student. It is not uncommon for professors to invite students over for meals, and most welcome conversations with students in their offices. "I've never had a professor say, 'Oh, I have to get back to my work,'" notes one student of her experience visiting faculty during office hours.

Advising is considered "one way of dealing with the lack of a core curriculum," according to one professor, and a good faculty adviser can help a student devise a solid academic program. "The advisers do a good job of encouraging breadth," says one student. There are no graduate student teaching assistants, and 96 percent of the faculty hold doctoral degrees.

For the most part, Smith students are studious and disciplined. Unlike huge state schools and other colleges where her friends attended, "everybody does their reading for class," notes one student, and the academic environment is described as "pretty competitive." Popular majors include government, psychology, economics, biology, and art. Nearly a quarter of Smith students pursue the sciences. Rigorous interdepartmental majors and minors in medieval studies and ancient studies are also offered at Smith. Medieval studies is described as a "vibrant program" by one professor, while ancient studies has been "undergoing painful changes" and may be absorbed by the classical languages and literatures department.

Recommended faculty at Smith include J. Patrick Coby and Donald Baumer in government and Carol Zaleski in religious studies.

Smith also boasts one of the best college art museums in the country, and one student describes how, in her drawing class, students were given assignments to trace some of the works in the impressive collection. "The studio art facility is right in the Smith art museum — it was a fantastic experience."

In addition to a number of interdepartmental emphases, Smith still offers programs of study in the major liberal arts disciplines: art, classical languages and literatures, economics, history, philosophy, religion and biblical literature. The college also has a major program in Afro-American studies, as well as an interdepartmental major in women's studies. As one might expect, many of the courses inevitably evoke women's issues, and courses with some variation on the title "Women and . . ." are all too common in the curriculum. The women's studies program is unabashedly radical, asserting in its program description that "the women's studies major fosters a feminist, interdisciplinary, cross-cultural and critical understanding of human experience, cultural production and the construction of knowledge." The description further suggests that a women's studies major provides students with a distinctive way of understanding the world and an impetus for action "by transforming the categories through which knowledge is produced and disseminated. The academic field of women's studies is joined to an understanding of the forms of feminist activism around the globe. Research and theory emerge from these everyday realities, and feminist theory, in turn, informs our analysis and political choices."

Smith is a member of a five-college consortium, enabling students to enroll in classes or use facilities at Amherst College, Hampshire College, Mount Holyoke College, and the University of Massachusetts. One student notes that most Smith students take advantage of the five-college system, enrolling in two or three courses at one of the other four schools during their undergraduate career. The majority of Smith students also participate in some kind of Junior Year Abroad (JYA) or exchange program. There are four college-sponsored JYA programs, in Florence, Hamburg, Geneva, and Paris, all of which require at least two years of foreign language. Students without the formal language skills opt to go abroad through the JYA programs of other colleges, and, as one student notes, "Smith will pretty much let you do anything, as long as it's reasonable."

Despite its focus on undergraduate education, Smith does provide research opportunities, particularly through programs such as the Smith Scholars Program, which provides students with credit and research funds for self-designed projects. For nontraditional or mature students, the college generously offers the Ada Comstock Scholars Program to allow women to complete their undergraduate study. About 230 women are enrolled in the program at any given time, and, according to one student, most courses have a couple of Ada Comstock scholars in them. Most students are pleased by this: "It is good to have someone with that kind of maturity and life experiences in class," notes one student, although she suggests that the college administration occasionally questions the structure of the program because they are nervous about giving so much financial assistance to just a few women. The college also offers a small number of graduate programs — including offerings in education, fine arts, and social work — enrolling about 150 graduate students.

Political Atmosphere: All the Isms You Can Imagine

Smith has a firmly established and well-deserved reputation as a liberal campus, particularly when it comes to women's issues. But one recent graduate notes that "the political climate is hard to describe . . . it is not as radical as the impression everyone has of it." Still, one student concedes that nearly every course at Smith, "even something like the History of British Literature, is bound to have a feminist element." Feminist concerns certainly dominate the political landscape at Smith, and the college's active lesbian community is well known. One student notes that there are occasional rifts between the College Republicans and the campus Lesbian/Bisexual Alliance, but that they usually involve only a handful of students.

Recently, Smith inaugurated Ruth Simmons as president, making her the first African-American female to head an elite college. President Simmons is committed to increasing minority enrollment at Smith, though in a *New York Times* interview she argued, "I don't want people to be the object of experimentation. . . . I don't want them to think they're here to be a part of an exotic mix. I always resent feeling that way." So far, Simmons has established a very good rapport with students and faculty: "There was a tremendous positive reaction on campus" to her inauguration, according to one student. The previous president, Mary Mapleston, "was seldom seen on campus, unless she was driving around in her Cadillac," notes a student. President

Simmons, by contrast, keeps open office hours for students to come in and chat and is frequently seen strolling the halls and walkways of campus. "You'd feel comfortable going up and calling her Ruth," beams one student, who adds that she usually gets standing ovations when she addresses groups of students.

Despite the high degree of social autonomy in Smith's living arrangements, campus residence life can be highly politicized. According to a recent report on multiculturalism in higher education, each of Smith's residence houses has a "Managing Diversity Plan," designed to "discourage racism." Under this plan students can be reprimanded for breaking set guidelines on diversity, and "disciplinary action can be taken, such as requiring violators to attend race sensitivity workshops," according to *The Multicultural Student's Guide to Colleges.* One professor says the college's rigid "rubric of diversity" has had the deleterious effect of making it a "more homogeneous place," where the only opinions expressed are those of the left. "Smith would be a better place if there actually was a greater diversity of opinion," laments this professor.

Indeed, Smith College seems thoroughly in thrall to the ideological spirit that has stigmatized every view and opinion as a narrow "ism": heterosexism, classism, and others have become disturbingly common pejorative terms in campus workshops and official statements. One professor notes that Smith is "caught in the throes of PCism." In a document drafted several years ago, entitled "The Smith Design for Institutional Diversity," the college identified "specific manifestations of prejudice," such as *"Ableism," "Classism,"* and *"Heterosexism."* In true feminist theoretical fashion, the college also targeted the dreaded transgression of *"Lookism* — the belief that appearance is an indicator of a person's value; the construction of a standard for beauty/attractiveness, and oppression through stereotypes and generalizations of both those who do not fit that standard and those who do." Smith also sponsors an annual day of workshops in honor of the college's first African-American graduate, Otelia Cromwell. Rather than being dedicated exclusively to race issues, however, the event has turned into a field day for the proponents of the ideology of oppression: "During the workshops, which get decent turnouts, we discuss almost all of the isms you can imagine, heterosexism, racism, ageism, sizeism, you name it," said one student to the editors of *The Multicultural Student's Guide.*

The college administers a lecture series through the five-college system, so prominent speakers rotate between Smith and the other four campuses. Recent speakers at Smith include Toni Morrison, Joycelyn Elders, and Eleanor Holmes Norton. But even big-name lecturers take a back seat to studies: "The question," notes one student, "is always whether or not anyone has time to go to talks." A recent sampling of student meetings and lectures indicates the range of interests and activities represented at Smith, which includes a discussion of St. Teresa of Avila's *Interior Castle* by the Christian spirituality study/discussion group as well as an "Ellen" Coming Out Day Party to celebrate the television character's declaration of lesbianism.

One student admits that "going to Smith as a conservative would be difficult."

Yet despite its liberal political tenor, Smith is "a very civil place," notes one professor, and "free speech is upheld," according to a student. Another professor concurs, noting that "People treat each other well, and the college takes academic freedom very seriously."

Student Life: What You Make of It

The Smith College brick and ivy campus, spanning a modest 125 acres in Northampton, Massachusetts, is small but attractive. The campus includes a beautiful arboretum (Lyman Plant House) and a botanical garden above the scenic banks of Paradise Pond. "The pond freezes over in the winter and students skate on it," notes one student. Northampton is considered a nice college town by most students. "There are two great movie theatres, the Iron Horse Music Hall, which has lots of live music, four or five coffee houses," and numerous shops and eateries, according to a student. UMass, Amherst, and Hampshire are all an easy bus ride away.

Most students live on campus in the Smith housing system, which is composed of 35 houses accommodating from ten to one hundred students each. "The housing system has many benefits and disadvantages," says a student. Most of the houses are attractive and full of history; many date back to the nineteenth century, and it is not uncommon to find a Smithie living in a house once inhabited by her mother or grandmother when she was a student. Each house is equipped with its own kitchen and dining room, its own piano, and its own cook. The atmosphere at meals ranges from casual breakfasts in pajamas to Thursday night candlelit dinners with invited faculty guests. Houses generally have an equal number of women from each year, and students benefit from the mix of lower- and upperclassmen.

Despite these advantages, the housing system "can be kind of overwhelming for people," one woman says. Students are assigned to houses for their freshman year, and one notes that they are expected to live in the house for all four years, although many end up changing. Because students have little to no choice in the housing system, personality conflicts frequently arise. "It's kind of like a sorority without the exclusivity," comments a student. Although some students like the autonomy of the living arrangements, a professor says students live entirely "by themselves, with no adult supervision," which can create problems for those with traditional social mores. And some of the houses are unattractive, such as the 1970s living quarters (affectionately dubbed the "Howard Johnson dorms") on the edge of campus. One resident sums up the living arrangements by suggesting, "It's what you make of it."

The campus social scene is not as quiet as one might think for a women's college. There is no Greek system, yet "there are still parties with kegs of beer," notes one student. With the college's vast female population, there appears to be no lack of college males from nearby UMass, Amherst, and Hampshire inundating the campus on the weekends, and all three colleges are easily accessed by a free all-night bus system. Some women also make a tradition out of taking weekend trips to visit friends at nearby Ivy League schools such as Harvard, Yale, and Dartmouth.

Athletics are an important extracurricular pursuit for many Smith students. The college competes in the NCAA Division III in 14 intercollegiate sports, and also offers numerous club sports, including badminton, croquet, fencing, golf, riding, tae kwon do, rugby, sailing, and synchronized swimming. An ice hockey club was established a few years ago. The fine arts are promoted at Smith, and many students are involved in art, drama, dance, or music at the academic or extracurricular level. Noon concerts are held once a week in the newly renovated Sage Hall for Performing Arts. The Mendenhall Center for the Performing Arts, named for former college president Thomas Mendenhall, houses impressive music, theater, and dance facilities, including a studio theater with movable seats and a television studio. With over ninety student organizations ranging from Amnesty International to the Smith Debating Society, there are ample opportunities for extracurricular activities.

A recent graduate describes her experience at Smith as "unusual" and "peculiar," embodying a uniqueness derived from a combination of its all-female student body, unfettered academic program, energetic political climate, and lingering sense of institutional pride and collegiality. The college's refusal to become coeducational affirms its commitment to women's education. But this brand of distinction may not be for every young woman, especially those who do not embrace the ideology of feminism that has long gripped the campus.

UNIVERSITY OF THE SOUTH

735 University Avenue
Sewanee, TN 37383-1000
(800) 522-2234
www.sewanee.edu

Total enrollment: 1,350
Undergraduates: 1,270
SAT Ranges (Verbal/Math): V 570-660, M 570-660
Financial aid: 41%
Applicants: 1,840
Accepted: 65%
Enrolled: 31%

Application deadline: Feb. 1
Financial aid application deadline: Mar. 1
Tuition: $17,555
Core curriculum: No

Invaded, Again

Sewanee, as the University of the South is widely known, was barely established before it was ruined in the War between the States. Within a decade of the war's end, however, it had risen again, rebuilding not only its finances but its chapel, whose cornerstone had been blown up by Union forces. Help in the school's efforts came from Episcopalian connections in England, and from the universities of Oxford and Cambridge, and Sewanee grew beautiful, intellectual, and strong. In time, it was home to such literary giants of the twentieth century as Andrew Lytle, Allen Tate, Caroline Gordon, and many other writers of note, enhancing its place as a repository of Southern tradition and history.

And though Sewanee remains proud of its past, it has begun to cast bits and pieces of it aside. Yet the further Sewanee goes from its past, the more like other places it will become; without roots, the University of the South becomes just a university — homogeneous, professionalized, and nationalized. Recent events on campus lead one to believe that the school is increasingly embarrassed by its Southernness.

Sewanee is still a very good liberal arts school, and its campus — ten thousand acres on top of the Cumberland Plateau — is still breathtaking. While much may have been lost, much remains. Although many professors are opposed to the changes taking place at Sewanee, the battle with the multiculturalists and relativists at its head may be the one that changes the school even more than the war that once destroyed it.

Academic Life: Reconstruction

Sewanee mandates that students take at least nine required courses, not including up to three more students might need to pass a 300-level course in a foreign language. Two courses, one in each of the student's first two years, must be designated "writing intensive." All told, a student's classes at Sewanee are equally divided among required classes, classes from his major, and electives. The required classes deal with Western civilization and culture, as it is manifested in courses not only in history but also in English, philosophy or religion, and the social sciences. Sewanee even goes so far as to state that "the required history course introduces students to significant developments since classical antiquity. It focuses on the Western tradition, though attention is given to other traditions when and as they affect the experience of Westerners."

All of this amounts to something more than the typical distribution require-ments but less than a true core curriculum. While students must take liberal arts and sciences courses regardless of their major, they do not all take the same classes, nor do they all read the same works of literature, history, philosophy, and so on. Still, "breaking the canon here hasn't occurred," says a professor.

Though still in the acceptable range, Sewanee's list of required courses is weaker now than just a few years ago. Until recently students were required to take both a philosophy class and a religion class, whereas now they can get away with taking one or the other. Only one semester of mathematics is required now, down from two. The same is true in some majors: English majors used to be required to take a full year of Shakespeare, whereas now they must take only one semester. The same major used to require one year on the great works of literature, but that has now been cut in half. There are no majors in the usually politicized fields of women's studies or ethnic studies. There is, however, a major in Third World studies.

The college also offers interdisciplinary majors for students with more special-ized interests, and these can be worked out in a wide variety of areas. Students may also spend semesters off campus studying more specialized fields, such as experi-mental science at Oak Ridge, Tennessee; island ecology at St. Catherines Island, Georgia; or various topics abroad in programs that can last for a semester, a full year, or a summer. Sewanee also offers several joint degree programs with larger schools, including engineering degrees with Georgia Tech and Vanderbilt, among others, and a forestry degree with Duke. Another degree not offered at Sewanee is education: students wishing to obtain teacher certification fulfill the degree requirements for a B.A. or B.S. just as other students must, and then apply for certification from a ten-member Teacher Education Committee. This requirement insures a degree of intellectual rigor rarely found in professionalized schools of education.

Oddly, for a school that places real value on its academic reputation, Sewanee offers students the opportunity to take some courses on a pass-fail basis. To be eligible for pass-fail grading, a student must have a 2.0 GPA, and no required courses desig-nated as a prerequisite for a required course may be taken on a pass-fail system. The grade "Pass" does not affect a student's GPA, but a "Fail" counts as an F.

Faculty and students list these professors as the best on campus: Susan Rid-yard and Brown Patterson in history; Eric Naylor in Spanish; and George Core, Robert Benson, and Wyatt Prunty in English. History, political science, and English are con-sidered the strongest departments at Sewanee.

Although the political science department is strong overall, it does offer several courses dealing with such topics as African political theory and "Women and Politics." There are courses dealing with the Middle East, Asia, Latin America, and Central America and the Caribbean, but no political philosophy courses (except survey courses) on antiquity, the Middle Ages, the Renaissance, the Enlightenment, or the broad modern era.

Political Atmosphere: A History Lesson

To lose something, a school must first have something. Sewanee has a history that, along with its reputation and gorgeous campus, distinguishes it from other schools, especially those not in the American South. It is this past that some at Sewanee would now flee for the ephemeral lures of the present. The current administration at Sewanee concerns itself less with protecting the heritage and mission of this unique school than with raising money, increasing enrollment, and lifting the school in the polls used in the popular media to rank colleges and universities.

The argument that Sewanee needs to do something new and different to get itself noticed loses some of its force when one takes into consideration that this college, whose enrollment is just over 1,200, has produced twenty-two Rhodes scholars and welcomes back as sophomores an astounding 97 percent of its freshmen class.

The center of Sewanee, both physically and spiritually, has long been All Saints' Chapel, a large neo-Gothic church with beautiful stained glass windows, statuary, and a lovely choir in the chancel. Along the nave used to hang the flags of the Southern states whose Episcopal dioceses founded and operate the university. These have had to go, according to the administration, lest someone be offended by their presence. "People thought there was an unreconstructed element in Sewanee that refused to admit that chattel slavery was a tragedy," a professor says. Taking down the flags "was done for outsiders. A central symbol of the school is the chapel itself. The Southern part of the school's identity gives it great wisdom, but the people who were against the flags didn't see it that way. The Southern tradition gives the school a humility that is missing in other parts of the country." This professor continues: "A symbol mediates between the people who read it and what it stands for. It [was] easier to simply take the flags down than to try to explain what they really meant. The question is 'how extensively does the school define itself as a Southern school?' It's very Southern anyway, and when you have something that's seen as racist. . . ."

Along the same lines, the university broke the mace used for years in processionals and at graduation because it bore the Confederate battle flag, another act undertaken to attract the attention of opinion makers. The administration also moved a tattered Confederate battle flag that was encased in glass in the chapel to an obscure spot in the library, then disallowed the distribution of bumper stickers bearing the university's name and the same flag.

The ideology of diversity has also hit Sewanee. "There has been a huge push for diversity on campus, with the addition of full scholarships for minorities and the intentional hiring of female and minority faculty," says a student. "There is also a multicultural center that is funded by the school. The administration has fully embraced these moves and has set them as the number one priority." The degree of sensitivity training for freshmen is greater than one might expect at a church-related school, for it includes a mandatory "Cookies and Condoms" program. There have been no efforts to impose a speech code, however.

Tradition-minded faculty have held out fairly well when it comes to hiring new professors, even though there is tacit administration approval to hire teachers who are somewhat politicized, if not actually raging ideologues. "We get very good applications, and this year the very best people were not ideological," says a professor. Quite a few faculty members, this professor says, would refuse to hire candidates who practice the latest theoretical approaches to the humanities "because they think it wouldn't be good for their students, but not because of their politics."

Sewanee is now somewhere on the fortunate side of the line that divides colleges from universities, one professor explains. "A university is a place where people publish. A college's first order of business is to teach. A university will go the experimental route before a college, because of the new opportunities it affords. But in a college you don't have to write a book every five years, yet you do have the responsibility to prepare a student for a B.A. This is more responsible, and is a built-in restraint on the faculty."

The faculty's dedication is surely one of Sewanee's strengths. According to a professor, students "get a lot more attention here than at many places." The impact of this attention, of course, depends on the student's state of mind. "If by eighteen, you know you want to be a chemist or an M.D., you might do OK to go to Cal. Tech or some such highly specialized school," the professor says. "But 85 percent of undergraduates out there are still very young and still need a liberal arts education. They need to grow up a little bit, and they need to be taught by professors and not graduate students. A small liberal arts college offers a lot to grow morally and ethically. Here they can also absorb the history of the South and the fact that people do make mistakes."

Many on campus remain optimistic about the future. "Despite its problems, Sewanee remains the last bit of heaven on earth," says a student. "One can still obtain a fine education here, as courses in the traditional subjects are still offered. Its close ties with the Episcopal Church also allow for some spiritual development among the student body to supplement learning in the classroom. It is one of the last places that intends to, and sometimes does, educate the whole person, mind, body, and spirit." The number of applicants has been rising by about 10 percent a year, and the quality of students enrolling is heading upward as well. And to its credit, Sewanee is one of the few schools in the country that does not consider financial need when deciding whether to admit a student. "You put all of that together, plus the influx of very good faculty members, and I'm very optimistic," a faculty member says.

Campus Life: The Beautiful Domain

The campus at Sewanee is exceptionally beautiful — a large, landscaped place with huge trees and pleasant yards. It's like a piece of Oxford University was somehow transferred to the hardwood forests of Tennessee. The buildings have traditionally been constructed of native sandstone in Collegiate Gothic design, so there exists at Sewanee a degree of architectural continuity and beauty rare on any college campus today.

Sewanee is very isolated atop Monteagle, a flat-topped mountain in the Cumberland Plateau of southern Tennessee. The school owns some ten thousand acres, called simply "The Domain," and locally one speaks simply of going to "The Mountain," meaning the University of the South. Chattanooga, the closest city, is forty-five miles to the east, and Nashville is ninety miles north.

Sewanee's 1,200 students enjoy a very close community in which most students know one another's faces, and many, one another's names. They also benefit from a low student-faculty ratio and a tradition of close contact with the faculty outside of the classroom. The community of Sewanee is unincorporated and is managed by the university, a fact that allows students to participate in the volunteer fire department and many other community activities.

With no town available for off-campus living, nearly all students live on campus. The spirit of community there is facilitated by dorm life. There are also language houses in which those studying French, German, Russian, or Spanish may live. The true center of campus is All Saints' Chapel, a magnificent structure that, though technically a chapel, would be a sizable church in most towns. Also important to student life is the Bishop's Common, in which are housed a pub, a dining room, a snack bar, a student post office, lounges, meeting and game rooms, and offices for student organizations. The university operates a student-run radio station and a student newspaper, the *Sewanee Purple*. An alternative newspaper, the *Sewanee Legacy*, sees its mission as defending the university's traditions against attack.

The most prestigious student organization is the Order of Gownsmen, to which some 20 percent of the student body belongs. Members may, and in fact do, wear academic gowns to class. They also have special privileges, such as the ability to forgo final examinations for classes in which they have an A average. Many national honor societies, such as Blue Key and Phi Beta Kappa, have chapters at Sewanee. More than 60 percent of the student body joins one of the eleven national fraternities or seven local sororities. Fraternities have their own houses and sororities have rooms in the Women's Center, although members live in dorms with the rest of the student body. Traditionally, all students adhered to a dress code that mandated jackets and ties for men and dresses or skirts for women. Many still follow this code of civility, although in recent years the number of well-dressed students and faculty has declined.

There are well over one hundred clubs and organizations for students to join, an amazing number for such a small school. Included in the long list is the Sewanee Outing Program, the most popular organization. Its members take part in the school's hugely successful canoe team, which has won twenty-two intercollegiate championships, and have access to outdoor equipment, a matter of some importance on a campus surrounded by ten thousand acres on top of a mountain in a rural part of

Tennessee. There is also an equestrian program that offers riding at all levels along miles of trails and thirty acres of pasture.

About 70 percent of the student body participates in an intramural sport. The college also fields nine NCAA Division III sports teams for men and an equal number for women.

The Sewanee Performing Arts Series sponsors six major theater, musical, or dance performances each year. Sewanee also hosts several academic events every year, including the Sewanee Writers' Conference (founded with money from the estate of Tennessee Williams) and the Mediaeval Colloquium, both of which draw nationally known scholars and writers to The Mountain. Those with singing talent may perform in the University Choir, which sings for the services in All Saints' Chapel.

It is predicted that undergraduate enrollment will soon surpass 1,300, and the university has already done studies which claim The Mountain can accommodate 2,000. Two words of caution about the future coherence of the Sewanee community: If the university grows too much more, it seems likely that the closeness and cohesion for which Sewanee has always been known will be diluted, if not lost. Second, some younger faculty members find it necessary to live closer to, or even in, Chattanooga, which is some forty-five miles away. Gone are the days when most faculty wives stayed at home and raised children. Today, many faculty spouses have careers for which they are highly trained, and only Chattanooga offers the economic opportunities they need to further their careers. Clearly, the close student-faculty relationships that have always been part of life at Sewanee cannot continue on the same level if many faculty members must commute fifty or so miles to work.

SPELMAN COLLEGE

350 Spelman Lane, SW
Atlanta, GA 30314-4399
(404) 681-3643
(800) 982-2411 (Office of Admissions and Orientation Services only)
www.spelman.edu

Total enrollment: 1,985
Undergraduates: 1,985
SAT Ranges (Verbal/Math): V 490-590, M 480-560
Financial aid: 87%

Applicants: 3,722
Accepted: 28%
Enrolled: 12%
Application deadline: Early decision, Nov. 15; regular, Feb. 1
Financial aid application deadline: Apr. 1
Tuition: $9,000
Core curriculum: No

Spelman Rising

It is nearly impossible to speak of current developments at Spelman College without mentioning the name of Johnnetta B. Cole, the immensely charismatic and beloved president of Spelman from 1987 to 1997, under whose aegis Spelman advanced from its already respected status as one of the best historically black colleges to become a nationally known academic liberal arts college and research center, as well as an entry point for young black women into the corridors of power. Under Cole's guidance, Spelman successfully conducted a $113 million capital campaign. Not only was the campaign "by far the most successful ever undertaken by a historically black college," according to the *Journal of Blacks in Higher Education,* but it "ranks among the most accomplished campaigns ever mounted by any liberal arts institution." Contributors included not only such high-profile members of the African-American community as Camille and Bill Cosby, who donated a landmark $20 million, and Oprah Winfrey, who logged a $1 million gift, but also foundations and corporations to whom Cole made individual solicitations, at the height of the campaign averaging "two presentations per week," a widely reported figure that has become part of the Spelman mythos.

At present writing, Spelman is pressing even further in fund-raising under new president Dr. Audrey Manley, though its endowment as of June 30, 1997, was $156 million dollars — for black institutions, this is second only to Howard University. Under the banner "Initiatives for the 90's," the college has raised half the money needed for a new science center, as some of the college's most respected departments are currently lodged in cramped quarters.

Yet Cole's influence at Spelman extends far beyond her ability to raise money. An already respected anthropologist, Cole came to Spelman with "a concept of how to modernize a university and make it competitive," says a former Spelman faculty member admiringly. "Her watch was very inspirational." Cole took the lead in helping to raise faculty salaries and to attract new research-focused faculty, in particular more black women. The emphasis on research has yielded positive results: "One of the things Johnnetta Cole has not been recognized for are the notable books written by faculty" under her tenure.

Cole's tenacity has paid off handsomely for Spelman. Now the college's faculty rank 21st in the nation among top liberal arts colleges in *U.S. News and World Report's* 1996 annual rankings, and in the same rankings, the college has improved its simple "regional" status to that of a "national" institution. Perhaps the most prestigious index of the college's rising academic star is the recent bestowal of a Phi Beta Kappa chapter, which has come much more belatedly to Spelman than to neighboring brother school Morehouse, even though Spelman has outpaced Morehouse in many areas for a number of years.

From its tenuous beginnings, Spelman has survived and thrived on both practical hard work and optimism. As was the case for many early black institutions, Spelman was founded by philanthropic whites — two women were commissioned by the American (read Northern) Baptist mission board in 1881 to "study the living conditions 'among the freedmen of the South.'" Barely two years after arriving, Sophia B. Packard and Harriet Giles established a school with a first class of eleven, "mostly ex-slaves," the college *Bulletin* notes, "determined to learn to read the Bible and write well enough to send letters to their families in the North." (With respect to the college's religious origins, Spelman amazingly continues even now to maintain its motto, Our Whole School for Christ, despite high multicultural interest on campus and a growing Muslim student organization.)

Many historically black institutions had similar origins, but Spelman was fortunate at the outset to secure the support of John D. Rockefeller — in fact, the school's name derives from the name of Rockefeller's wife's mother, and several campus buildings bear the names of Rockefeller family members, which can seem something of a WASP-like cultural oddity to an uninformed observer on campus.

The next great advance for the college was in 1929, when Spelman joined the consortium of historically black colleges that make up what is now called the Atlanta University Center (AUC), which also includes Morehouse and provides the "center-wide" Robert W. Woodruff Library. Shared by all the AUC colleges, the library holds over 827,000 volumes and possesses major African-American collections and archival materials, such as the Countee Cullen Memorial Collection, which focuses on the arts, and the Thayer Collection, which contains items associated with Abraham Lincoln, an appropriate holding given Spelman's freedman origins.

Academic Life: Global in Context and Gender-Informed

To the casual observer leafing through the Spelman College *Bulletin*, one of the most striking features, right at the front of the volume, is the college's "Statement of Purpose," and in particular two corollary lists of "institutional goals" and "behaviors" that will help in effecting the Spelman mission. While the "institutional goals" are fairly standard specifics for an academic environment, the "behaviors" extend far beyond academic and career achievement to mandate that a Spelman woman will conform to some rather ambiguous categories, such as "10. Demonstrate self-confidence and self-respect" and "11. Demonstrate pride in her own culture." Such an emphasis on character and spiritual formation places Spelman squarely in the old *in loco parentis* role that most colleges once assumed for students' moral behavior, although in this case the formation is of a pretty clearly liberal, activist variety.

One way Spelman seeks to inculcate its desired "specific behavioral objectives" is through the Assessment of Student Learning and Development Program, which requires that *all* students take a bizarre and dizzying array of tests at almost every level, from freshman to senior year. The practice seems a little intrusive; not only are students required to take the Watson-Glaser Critical Thinking Appraisal *twice*, they also must take the Myers-Briggs (personality) Type Indicator, again clearly showing that Spelman conceives of itself as far more than an academic institution, and truly more of the "family" it purports to be.

Equally structured are the "General Education Requirements." Like most selective colleges, Spelman conceives of its basic requirements in pragmatic or mechanistic terms; one of the purposes of the general education requirements is "to prepare students for the challenges of living in a multicultural, highly technological, and information-based society" with a specific emphasis on "the study of African-American and other cultures and a focus on gender." To achieve the latter, Spelman recently introduced a two-semester sequence of courses, required of all students, entitled "The African Diaspora of the World." ADW, as it is called, is the only set of courses commonly required of students, and is taught from a truly radical perspective: required readings for the course include *Words of Fire: An Anthology of African-American Feminist Thought*, the writings of black lesbian poet Audre Lorde, and works by communist activist Angela Davis. While the first course in the sequence is limited strictly to Africa and the experiences of Africans outside the United States, the second half "deals more with Africans in America," according to one Spelman upperclassman. "The focus is more on slavery, politics, economics, music." The same student reports that the culminating activity in the course is not an essay or an examination, but an oddly termed "ephemeral project," which "has to be some type of presentation," possibly dramatic or poetic, the purpose of which is unclear. Such an attitude is further confirmed by one student's testimony that the "course is not so much tested; it's a dialogue."

There is one other common experience required for Spelman women: attendance at Convocation, which is more or less a required chapel (though its function is inspirational rather than doctrinally religious) serving to build the close community and shared notion of "sisterhood" for which Spelman is famous. In the essay accompanying the notice of Spelman's award as a member of the 1995-96 Templeton Honor Roll for Character-Building Colleges, the program of Convocation included "music, prayer, a speaker or presentation, and an opportunity for questions and answers." In addition, the essay notes that previous speakers have included Children's Defense Fund activist Marian Wright Edelman and First Lady Hillary Clinton.

Otherwise, the general education requirements lack specificity: "computer literacy," math, English composition, and physical education. There is a foreign language requirement; Spanish, French, and Japanese are available at Spelman, but cross-registration is available at other AUC institutions for choices as varied as Arabic (which appears to be rising in popularity, thanks to Muslim evangelism), Chinese, Swahili, German, and Russian. What goes under the heading of a multicultural or non-Western requirement at most colleges is specified as an "International or Women's Studies" elective at Spelman, which offers a pleasantly surprising latitude of choices, from many interesting African electives ("African Politics," "South Africa in Transition") to very traditional art history surveys and studies of French and Spanish literature. Then there are the sorts of distribution requirements that are standard at most colleges: four hours, or one course, in each division of the college, in the areas of fine arts, humanities, social sciences, and natural sciences.

With respect to politicized courses or departments, it is hard to say exactly what *would* constitute academic politicization at Spelman, given that the academic perspective from which faculty teach is almost uniformly left wing and "postcolonial." This is expressed perhaps most succinctly in a college *Bulletin* note that is attached to the signature ADW course: the course is taught, it is said, "within a global context and from perspectives that are both interdisciplinary and gender-informed."

Outstanding professors at Spelman include Charnelle Holloway in art, Pamela Gunter-Smith and Victor Ibeanusi in biology, Judy Gebre-Hiwet and Gloria Wade-Gayles in English, and Beverly Guy-Sheftall in women's studies. Strong departments include biology, chemistry, economics, English, psychology, and comparative women's studies.

Spelman has several notable special programs, and there are a couple of likely reasons why. Given that Spelman is one of only two historically black, all-female colleges, it is keenly aware of having a kind of stewardship role toward its students as black women "redressing the balance" of historical inequities, and toward the African-American community in general — missions the college clearly emphasizes in all of its literature and communications. In addition, and especially since the presidency of Johnnetta Cole, Spelman has established links with corporations and groups outside the AUC network, with the clear intention of forming Spelman women as business and professional leaders in the world at large.

Like its brother school, Morehouse, Spelman is intensely committed to student counseling and preparation, and, if necessary, remediation. The Summer Science Program is specifically geared toward entering Spelman freshmen who have, according to the 1997-98 Spelman *Bulletin*, "indicated an interest in the health professions." Accordingly, freshmen chosen for the program arrive on campus during the summer before the academic year begins for an eight-week program that explores a number of areas in the sciences, from biology, chemistry, and computer science, and includes attention to reading, problem solving, and study skills specific to the sciences. This program appears to be highly regarded by students. Science programs in general are commended by students for their emphasis on research and "real-life" applications.

Morehouse has a similar program, which allows opportunities for making cross-campus friendships in advance of the academic year's beginning.

In addition, a similar Summer Science and Engineering Program for students more interested in engineering and technology-focused science than in pure science or research gives more attention to mathematics and computer science skills.

In a similar vein, for older entering students Spelman offers a service called the Gateway Program, which is specifically geared to women who have been away from school for some time, are "mid-twenties or older" and "financially independent of [their] parents/guardians," and show evidence of having "multiple responsibilities."

Furthermore, the Dow Jones–Spelman College Entrepreneurial Center seeks to enhance opportunities in business for black women, in particular empowering them through resources such as a business library, language courses, and "video and teleconference-style executive courses."

But, for every emphasis Spelman places upon the world of global business and trade, there is an equally balanced emphasis on the maintenance of ties to tradition and an understanding of one's context as a black woman in the societal framework. As such, Spelman is also noted for its Women's Research and Resource Center, which, according to college sources, is "the only women's research center of its kind on a historically-Black college campus," and which focuses not only on pure academics but also on curriculum development and community service.

Perhaps the most impressive of all of Spelman's special programs, however, is the Ethel Waddell Githii Honors Program, which is constituted similarly to other colleges' honors programs for high-achieving students, but which seems to have significantly more structured requirements. All freshmen entering Spelman with a combined SAT of 1,160 are eligible, as well as any freshmen who earn a cumulative GPA of 3.2 for thirty-two credit hours or more. Students who elect the program are required to take "Honors Math" and "Honors Freshman Composition," both of which afford greater independent work than the ordinary course sequences. The *Bulletin* notes that the honors math course requires "independent study papers" in addition to "readings . . . focused on race and gender issues of the 20th century"; the honors composition course requires "a spectrum of writing experiences" as well as "research." Most surprising, however, of the honors program requirements is the "Honors Philosophy Seminar," in which students focus "intensively" and *only* on six selected Platonic dialogues and Descartes's *Meditations on First Philosophy*. The course is a true rarity in these days when students are almost never asked to take philosophy. Finally, the honors program culminates with the student writing and defending a thesis.

Political Atmosphere: Not a Coincidence

As is the case at brother school Morehouse, Spelman College's history and achievements occupy a place of near-mythic reverence in the minds of faculty, students, and alumnae, tending to suffuse just about everything the college does with a kind of inspirational and exalted significance. This tone is especially reflected in the college's publicity materials, which also serve, in both design and copy, to give a good indication of Spelman's common values and conventional wisdom. The cover of one brochure from the office of admissions displays a photo collage of attractive women caught in contemplative poses, surrounding what appears to be an African sculpture, and inside, the copy on the first page reads: "This is not coincidence. You do not receive this publication by chance. You may be graduating in the top tier of your class. You may long for your history, your culture, your roots. You may wonder what you could be if you spent the majority of your waking hours being affirmed. You are being called to Spelman."

Effectively, therefore, the college's promotional materials avail themselves of the rhetorical patterns and cadences of traditional black preaching. Practically speaking, what all this rhetoric translates to is a strong emphasis on the notion of "Sisterhood" (even President Johnnetta Cole referred to herself as the "Sister President"), and an emphasis on service to the community.

The biggest area of political controversy, according to one current student from the Northeast, may well be in the socioeconomic arena. This student lamented widespread competition for Spelman's numerous scholarships and the animosity that tends to exist between scholarship and nonscholarship students. There also might be a kind of "thin line that's drawn" around international students, who tend to stand out on campus.

But another potential agent for change, if not a source of current controversy, is the burgeoning amount of Muslim activity and — there is no other word for it — evangelism on all the AUC campuses. Recently a sign posted in the Manley Center advertised an information session on "The Muslim Woman," stating that it would answer such questions as "Why must you cover your head?" and "Do you consider yourself oppressed?" Muslim students lobbied for a prayer room of their own recently, since "there's no chapel on campus, and they don't have something you can requisition every day"; Muslim women on campus also have to seek special permission to attend services on days when classes are in session. "The overall feeling is that you don't get encouragement from Spelman, but from the student body," states one student involved with the group. (At the same time, it ought to be noted, there are also evangelical Christian groups more or less operating outside the Spelman chaplaincy structure, and billboards in the dorms advertised the resources and contact numbers for groups such as the Arise Christian Fellowship.)

In sum, beyond the standard academic-feminist notion of "the personal as political," Spelman women appear to be pretty apolitical — one college guide quotes a senior as saying, "It has been my experience that Spelman students are not very politically motivated, i.e. not concerned with the ramifications of their actions and beliefs outside the microcosm of Spelman." There certainly are, at this writing, no overtly conservative organizations of an academic or cultural bent, as one might find at other colleges, even at Morehouse, thus rendering the question of college funding moot. Nevertheless, Spelman remains true to its history as the preeminent corridor to power for young black women, and a giver of service back to the community, an admirable goal most eloquently expressed in one of the college's brochures: "If we are successful in our academic endeavors, you will be successful. And if we are successful at touching your heart, you will understand that it is your responsibility to hold the hand of your brother and help them be successful, too."

Student Life: Liberal . . . and Conservative

Spelman's commitment to community service has a strong influence on student life. According to a fact sheet entitled "Spelman Synopsis" delivered by the office of public relations, "Over 45% of our students engage in some form of community service, which resulted in Spelman being designated as a Point of Light," referring to President Bush's famous program that honored major volunteer contributors to their communities. The West End neighborhood where Spelman is located has one of the highest poverty, incarceration, and AIDS-infection rates in the city (though the college itself is sufficiently policed and beautifully manicured). Spelman women feel a particular burden to aid in this regard — another commonly repeated quotation on campus derives from alumna Marian Wright Edelman, famously the founder of the Children's Defense Fund: "Service is the rent you pay for living on this earth."

To put Edelman's dictum into practice, Spelman's Office of Community Service "matches students with volunteer opportunities in the community; coordinates the Bonner Scholars, a group of students committing ten hours a week to service projects; and works with faculty to design academic components to the service program," according to the Spelman entry in the 1995-96 volume for the Templeton Honor Roll for Character-Building Colleges. Although Spelman offers varied service opportunities, Templeton in particular highlighted as an "Exemplary Program" the "Star Team," a project of the drama department that uses drama and oral history to help "young people . . . confront issues, develop critical thinking skills, and resolve problems through analytical methods."

Although only 15 percent of the students actually pledge a sorority, Greek life plays a major part in the social scene, and even in the service life of the college. Traditionally, black sororities such as Delta Sigma Theta and Alpha Kappa Alpha have been at the vanguard of service to the community, much more so than white sororities, a legacy from days of segregation when few recourses to respectability and security were open to black women.

Still, Greek life at Spelman offers more attractions than just community service, and with Morehouse being right across the street, tends to give the campus the air of 1950s-style social courtliness and decorum. Despite the fact that most Spelman women openly identify themselves with leftist politics, one college guide notes that the other items included on a list of "What's Hot" at Spelman included "old-fashioned dating, student government, religion, and music associations." The same college guide noted, in addition, the propensity for Spelman women to be religious (though theologically thoroughly mainline) and socially conservative (drug use and homosexuality are generally frowned upon). Some of these conservative attitudes manifest themselves in campus life in ways practically unheard of at other nonreligious colleges: while the women's dormitories do allow male visitors, they must sign in, and be signed out by 11:30 P.M., "not 11:31 or 11:35," as a notice from the counselor at one particular women's residence emphasized.

Spelman women also tend to dress rather well, and more formally than students on most campuses — even in an all-female environment, dresses, makeup, and carefully arranged hair are the norm, a testament not so much to femininity as to Spelman women's desire to appear polished and professional at all times.

One place in which the seemingly contradictory elements, conservative and liberal, of the Spelman ethos were represented was in the advertisement of the schedule for the 1997 Junior Class Week "Party Like It's 1999," which, in addition to the eponymous celebratory dance, featured "Big Sister/Little Sister Aerobics," a resume-writing forum, and a "Clothing Drive for Battered Women's Shelter and Canned Food Drive for Thanksgiving Baskets."

STANFORD UNIVERSITY

Stanford, CA 94305
(650) 723-2300
www.stanford.edu

Total enrollment: 13,810
Undergraduates: 6,550
SAT Ranges (Verbal/Math): V 670-760, M 660-770
Financial aid: 61%
Applicants: 16,360
Accepted: 16%

Enrolled: 61%
Application deadline: Dec. 15
Financial aid application deadline: Feb. 1
Tuition: $20,490
Core curriculum: No

The Fort Sumter of the Culture Wars

Perhaps one day at Stanford University there will be a monument that says: "The culture wars started here." Many people credit a 1987 antiracism demonstration led by the Reverend Jesse Jackson on the Stanford campus with launching a thousand multicultural ships. The crowd's famous chant of "Hey, hey, ho, ho, Western Culture's got to go!" has echoed since then on many other campuses, and Stanford has remained in many minds the epitome of the modern politically and culturally correct institution.

The students that day were referring to a course called "Western Culture," but even though the Reverend Jackson did remind the crowd that they were a part of this culture, many of the demonstrators wanted to jettison more than just one course. The course was replaced by a disastrous series known as "Culture, Ideas, and Values," which has recently been revised again. The result is a multicultural mishmash that treats the Western tradition like an item in a store window that one passes while walking down the street.

The change in Stanford's reputation and academic fortunes was almost as rapid. Always known as a leader in both the sciences and the liberal arts, the university's undergraduate liberal arts programs are now losing students. It's as if some were scared away by the politicization of the curriculum. According to the *Chronicle of Higher Education,* only 30 percent of Stanford's 1996 entering class wished to study a liberal arts discipline, as opposed to 18 percent interested in engineering, 35 percent who wanted premed, and 38 percent who were interested in the natural sciences.

Today Stanford seems on the verge of becoming, as one professor recently warned, "Stanford Tech." Located in the heart of Silicon Valley, Stanford is certainly in a position to capitalize on the demand for its well-qualified graduates in the technological and engineering fields. However, the fate of the university's liberal arts disciplines is less easy to gauge. Stanford still hosts many fine professors, and it consistently recruits its faculty in all areas from the most prestigious graduate schools. While it is still possible to receive a superior liberal arts education at Stanford, the question is, will there be anyone left to receive that education?

Academic Life: Western Culture Went

Multiculturalism is the new standard in the Stanford curriculum, and it is mandatory for all students. The university's distribution requirements make sure that students will be exposed to feminist scholarship and race-based critiques, while at the same time giving short shrift to the Western tradition.

Over and over, Stanford students seeking to fulfill the nine distribution requirements are forced to choose the lesser evil. Eight of the requirements are satisfied by one course each. These are world cultures; American cultures; mathematical sciences; natural sciences; technology and applied sciences; literature and fine arts; philosophical, social, and religious thought; and social and behavioral sciences. At least one of the eight courses must also be certified as a "gender studies" course.

The world cultures requirements seem to be a mixed bag: many of the courses listed are little more than anti-Western hand-wringing, but others (some in Russian studies or the cultural history of Japan or China) appear to have real intellectual substance. American studies, on the other hand, offers mostly courses on minorities in America, though the definition of "minority" does not extend to groups that are not currently considered aggrieved, like Irish- or German-Americans. Also missing are courses on pivotal eras of American history — westward expansion, for example. Since no one can avoid these requirements, no one at Stanford can avoid politicized courses.

The requirements in social and behavioral sciences; philosophical, social, and religious thought; and literature and fine arts, while not devoid of traditional courses, are also dominated by ideological options. The social sciences list includes anthropology courses like "Ethnographic Film" and "Magic, Witchcraft, and Religion," while the philosophical thought course list consists of a strange mélange of feminist topics, philosophy surveys, and Bible courses. Courses available in literature and fine arts are just as unpredictable. The point is that while some of the courses may offer worthwhile material, few of them are devoted to the traditional core of a liberal arts education: transmitting the fundamental values of the Western heritage.

The remaining distribution requirement is known as "Cultures, Ideas, and Values," or CIV. This is as close to a core offering as Stanford comes; whereas the other distribution requirements can be met with any number of courses, CIV includes only nine choices. These tracks are made up of three courses, each of which is devoted to a theme or discipline. The choices listed in the 1996 university catalogue are "Anthropology," "Great Works," "Europe and the Americas," "English," "German Studies," "History," "Humanities," "Philosophy," and "Structured Liberal Education." In each track students read an epic, part of the Bible, a classical Greek philosopher, an early Christian thinker, an Enlightenment thinker, a Renaissance dramatist, Marx, and Freud. Each of the three courses in a track must also include works discussing race, gender, class, and religion, and at least some works by female and minority writers.

If this program sounds like a nod in the direction of Western culture, it is — but it is little more than that. There has been a great deal of tinkering with the requirements in the last ten years, but the essential features of CIV remain the same. The university has retained quotas on the number of female and minority writers that must be covered, but has to this point refused to name the classic authors — except for Marx and Freud — that it believes are important to a student's liberal education. (This means that Plato or St. Augustine could be avoided in favor of other writers who qualified under the broad categories of "classical Greek philosopher" or "early Christian thinker.")

The result is "a peep-show approach to great texts flickering by," according to a professor who served on the 1995-97 CIV review committee, as quoted in the *Chronicle of Higher Education.* The *Chronicle* also provides evidence that the professor was not exaggerating: in a one-hour class session in the humanities track, the lecturer covered Edmund Burke, Thomas Paine, Jean-Jacques Rousseau, Thomas Jefferson, and Mary Wollstonecraft. It is no surprise that 60 percent of the seniors responding to a 1995 survey said CIV had "little or no value."

The good news is that CIV is on the way out. The bad news is that the structure replacing it will only partially alleviate CIV's weaknesses. Beginning with the 1997-98 school year, part of the freshman class will christen "Introduction to the Humanities," a quarter-length course. (By the fall of 1999, all freshmen will take this course.) The new course will address only four to six major texts, rather than the fifteen to twenty authors found in each quarter of the previous CIV system. The next two courses in the sequence will resemble the old CIV, although the hard quotas on numbers of female and minority writers and gender, class, and race issues ("a weird sort of tokenism," according to a member of the review committee) will no longer exist.

Supporters of the new system argue that it will allow smaller departments to participate, since a three-quarter sequence in one area is no longer an option. Furthermore, they claim that the new course will lessen the "peep-show" problems that plagued CIV. These supporters note that when the quotas are dropped, students will take the material more seriously, since they can no longer complain that they are reading a text only to satisfy a race or gender requirement. Even one student who had for several years been a critic of the old CIV allows that the new requirement has "potential to do some good."

However, many on campus view the new requirement as a defeat. The new course's lack of quotas has provoked consternation amongst faculty in feminist studies, anthropology, English, and other humanities departments. One professor who doesn't agree with the complainants says their exceptions are based on matters of turf and survival, rather than any pedagogical argument: "English would wither on the vine except for the distribution requirements," the professor says. "The same for philosophy and the languages and literatures." Indeed, as about 90 percent of Stanford's incoming classes choose hard sciences or engineering (what one professor calls "voting with their feet"), any reduction in mandatory classes in certain disciplines is sure to threaten if not the survival of, then the continued expansion of, humanities departments that need the distribution requirement to get students into seats.

Some departments have other reasons to fear for their safety. University president Gerhard Casper, upon taking office in 1992, promised to reduce the number of what he called "academic orchids": courses in trendy subjects without much academic integrity. Certainly the president had in mind such courses as "Black Hair as Culture and History," which has been taught for several years in the African and Afro-American studies department, and which became notorious through national media stories on political correctness in the academy. Although traditional faculty say they wish the president were moving more swiftly, they praise Casper for at least having the courage to publicly lament the existence of such courses, which most of Casper's peers would never have the guts to do.

Some Stanford professors named as outstanding by others on campus are John Taylor and Thomas Nechyba in economics; Mark Tunick, David Brady, Roger Noll, John Cogan, Steve Krasner, and Judith Goldstein in Political Science and Public Policy; Norman Naimark in history; Richard Cushman in CIV; Maureen Harkin in English; William Durham in anthropology; Patricia Mueller-Vollmer in Russian; John Bravman in material science; Kathleen Eisenhardt in industrial engineering; Brad Osgood in mathematics; Steven Chu and Douglas Osheroff in physics; George Springer in aeronautics; Eric Roberts in computer science; Michael Bratman in philosophy; and Robert McGinn in Science, Technology, and Society.

While the politics of the humanities departments show up most often in the headlines, the engineering, natural sciences, and applied sciences departments are Stanford's real strengths. This demonstrates more than anything how Stanford has changed over the past several years. Because of the university's proximity to Silicon Valley, the demand for its engineering and computer science graduates and, to a lesser extent, physics and chemistry graduates is acute. "Silicon Valley fights over these people," one student says.

The physics department is strong in both teaching and research opportunities. Two professors who recently won Nobel Prizes in physics have also in recent years won university teaching awards.

The premed program in Stanford's biology department is also excellent, and faculty from the graduate medical school teach some undergraduate courses. About three-quarters of premed upperclassmen also conduct research under the direction of medical school faculty.

While all of Stanford's science departments are strong, the same cannot be said for humanities. The one department that receives high marks all around is economics, which appears to be dominated by quantitative work. Despite (or perhaps because of) the department's emphasis on econometrics and other highly sophisticated mathematical models, economics maintains the highest undergraduate enrollment on campus; the only departments even close are psychology and biology.

Another department credited with excellent undergraduate teaching is political science, which has benefited, along with the departments of economics and public policy, from its affiliation with the Hoover Institution on War, Revolution, and Peace. The Hoover Institution, a privately endowed think tank housed on the Stanford campus, has become increasingly aggressive in recent years in recruiting research fellows, many of whom share joint appointments in the social science departments, thus providing those departments access to prominent specialists.

Apart from these few good departments, though, the humanities picture is rather bleak. "Good teachers are the exception," a student says. "Departments like anthropology, sociology, history, are not top-notch in terms of teaching," a professor says. A student includes English in that list. Not one history course focuses exclusively on, for example, the Civil War (even though the department offers a concentration in U.S. history), though there are courses called "Introduction to African-American History: The Modern Black Freedom Struggle" and "Introduction to Race and Ethnicity in the American Experience." Comparative literature, according to a student, is "horrible." Another student says the languages and literature departments have turned toward wholesale political correctness and deconstructionism. What's more, grade inflation is rampant in most humanities courses, students say.

Stanford offers a host of politicized majors, including urban studies, feminist studies, Latin American studies, African and Afro-American studies, and East Asian studies. Of these, only urban studies had more than ten undergraduate majors enrolled in the 1996-97 school year, and three of these had less than five.

Political Atmosphere: This Side of Diversity

Some have called the politicization of Stanford University the worst in the nation. The late philosopher Allan Bloom wrote in 1989: "Stanford is a trendy place and it responds to trends. Its shameless self-congratulation about this is sufficient to render it ridiculous in the eyes of serious people no matter what their political persuasion." A recent book entitled *The Diversity Myth* delivers a stinging account of Stanford's descent into multiculturalism. The authors, David O. Sacks and Peter A. Thiel, are Stanford alums and founders of the *Stanford Review,* a conservative journal. The book chronicles a horror show of multicultural excesses, hypersensitivity, and intellectual fascism in the course of college events in the ten years prior to its publication.

While Sacks and Thiel allow that President Casper, who inherited much of the mess from his predecessor Donald Kennedy, is doing a better job resisting multiculturalism, they say his policies have, in effect, only slowed its growth at Stanford. Others on campus agree that Casper is an improvement, but continue to hope for more decisive action. As another writer quoted in the book says, Western culture will recover; Stanford may or may not.

The politicization that exists in many Stanford classrooms is carried on outside of class in the form of protests. Stanford students have spent time protesting just about everything: racism, sexism, homophobia, intolerance, human rights abuses abroad, logging, the oil industry, etc. Indeed, the student body vice president elected in 1996 was a young man who made his name protesting against the presence of a Taco Bell in the renovated student union because the restaurant's parent company, PepsiCo, invested in Myanmar, formerly known as Burma. When the election results were announced, he was wearing a black armband to signify his participation in a hunger strike protesting the human rights abuses of the government of Myanmar.

Student protesters, however, are vastly outnumbered by nonactivist students. Only about 12 percent of students even voted in the last student government election. "The media plays up the three to four hundred radicals," a professor says. Things died down a bit after Californians adopted Proposition 187 (regarding social benefits for illegal aliens), one student says. The protest of a visit by Nike CEO Philip Knight involved as many older community members as it did students.

Although most students seem not to take the constant protests very seriously, the administration does — though less now than in the past. "The administration is not activist; it just wants to be left alone," a student says. "They give in to demands to prove that they're not racists [or] homophobes." Not always, though: President Casper's office recently turned down a proposal by the radical group Students for Environmental Action to establish a "Socially Responsible Endowment Fund," which would have been used to support efforts and ventures that environmental activists deemed "responsible." However, the presence of activist student government leaders could make it difficult at times for Casper and Provost Condaleeza Rice (a former Bush administration official and political science professor) to turn away all requests.

Casper has removed some of the politicization from the tenure process, however, by making teaching a more important factor in tenure decisions. Stanford has always had the reputation as a tough place to get tenure, and several professors agree that this is still the case — it's just that factors other than research get more consideration now. "Ten or eleven years ago, undergrad teaching counted for nothing," a professor says. "Today, there's a hurdle — you have to be adequate." Although Stanford still hires ten to fifteen registered Democrats for every one Republican for its faculty, according to a report in the *Washington Times,* the two most controversial tenure decisions in recent years have involved professors working in what are considered politicized fields (cultural anthropology and labor history).

Student housing is perhaps the most radical wing of the administration. Stanford has one of the most intrusive "residential education" systems in the nation. It includes resident fellows (sometimes professors, but usually graduate students) and resident assistants (usually upperclassmen) who are dedicated to conveying a political agenda to their charges. Several students who opposed the multiculturalism they were being handed were scorned publicly by the resident fellows, and in some cases even punished. The punishments came even after Stanford's speech code had been ruled unconstitutional by a federal court. Some campus observers report, though, that the university seems to have become more tolerant of traditional viewpoints recently. There is "less shoving-down-the-throats," one professor says.

Stanford hosts a number of theme houses or dorms, including houses officially dedicated to certain ethnic or racial groups (e.g., blacks, Chicanos, Asians, and Native Americans). In these official houses, the university attempts some degree of integration by requiring that no more than one-half of a house's population be members of the titular ethnic group. A student reports that there are also a few "de facto" theme houses, such as those for gay students and vegetarians.

At the same time, the residential education division has led efforts to shut down fraternity houses. One student reports that the leaders of residential education found the frats "too independent," and that the number of fraternities dropped from twelve to just five in a span of five years.

Student Life: Strike Up the Band

The typical Stanford undergraduate lives on campus for all four years, mostly because rent is so expensive in the Bay Area. Almost all freshmen live on campus, and about 85 percent of upperclassmen stay. This makes the campus rather "insular," as one student puts it. "Social life is all pretty much on campus." Trips to San Francisco are rare, even though the trip from Palo Alto to downtown takes less than forty-five minutes on most days. The university is surrounded by suburbs, which offer some attractions that negate the need to go into the city, but much of this stay-at-home attitude is due to the fact that most students take their coursework seriously.

Stanford enrolls about 6,600 undergraduates and more than 7,200 graduate students. This population is enough to support a long list of student organizations covering virtually every conceivable field of interest. There are more than one hundred official student groups, not including intramural athletics. Though many groups are politically inclined, there are academic clubs, musical groups, ethnic groups, and several religious groups, including True Love Waits, Asian American Christian Fellowship, Campus Crusade for Christ, various Catholic organizations, InterVarsity, Lutheran Campus Ministry, and others. Services are held each week on campus for Jews, Catholics, and Protestants.

Stanford's athletic program has collected nearly 70 national championships in the school's history, including many in typically Californian sports like water polo, golf, tennis, and swimming. The university's students and alumni won 18 medals at the 1996 Summer Olympics.

An interesting footnote to the athletic program is the Stanford marching band, known as the Incomparable Leland Stanford Junior Marching Band. The band found itself suspended twice during the 1997 football season for offensive on-field conduct. The band will not be allowed to play during games against Notre Dame for the next three seasons because of a halftime show in which the alleged entertainment involved, according to the *Chronicle of Higher Education,* "a parody of the Irish potato famine, a mock debate between a Roman Catholic cardinal and the Devil, and a reference to the Irish as 'stinkin' drunks.'" The show went on even though the university, as a rule, reviews copies of the band's programs in advance. Just a few weeks later the band again found itself in hot water because of a decidedly un-Stanford-like spoof of the spotted owl controversy during halftime of a game at the University of Oregon. The band was booed off the field and drew a one-week suspension, even though it claimed in a statement to the *Chronicle* that the crowd was "booing and shouting obscenities" before the show even began, and "probably would have booed our half-time show regardless of its focus." Stanford's acting athletic director vowed that the school would "not be embarrassed again by the band."

SWARTHMORE COLLEGE

500 College Avenue
Swarthmore, PA 19081-1397
(610) 328-8000
www.swarthmore.edu

Total enrollment: 1,370
Undergraduates: 1,370
SAT Ranges (Verbal/Math): V 670-770, M 660-750
Financial aid: 48%
Applicants: 4,270
Accepted: 26%
Enrolled: 34%
Application deadline: Jan. 1
Financial aid application deadline: early Feb.
Tuition: $23,020
Core curriculum: No

Reaching an Understanding

Swarthmore College is one of the most selective and rigorous small liberal arts colleges in the country. It is consistently ranked among the top three such schools in national polls, and statistics show that getting in is a difficult proposition for even very good students. The middle half of freshman SAT scores range from 1,320 to 1,500, and only a third of those who apply are accepted. Once there, students face challenging courses without the "benefit" of grade inflation. Alumni, three of whom have won Nobel Prizes, support the school generously and are thankful for what they received there.

Swarthmore has a whopping endowment of $610 million, and it uses its wealth to keep the student body small (1,370) and the student-to-faculty ratio very low (nine-to-one). The hefty endowment, enhanced recently by a $30 million donation from alumnus Eugene Lang, also allows Swarthmore to admit qualified students regardless of financial need, which heightens the quality of the school and the value of the education it offers.

Though quite a few courses are structured around various ideologies, there is nothing easy about them. One could look for more structure and cohesion in the general education requirements, but Swarthmore decided two decades ago that if all of its classes were good, no education derived from them could be bad.

Academic Life: Good Choices

In a 1967 study of its own curriculum, Swarthmore came out in favor of "a curriculum that leans sharply toward specialized diversity, and away from uniform generality." The college chose to emphasize "encounters with special topics and problems at a comparatively high level of competence, and . . . student programs that reflect individual constellations of diversified interests." This theory, common among modern liberal arts colleges, means that Swarthmore defines a liberal education by the process through which it is gained, rather than by what it includes.

In practice this means there is no core curriculum, and that the minimal distribution requirements are only loosely defined. Swarthmore students must take three courses from each of the college's divisions: natural sciences, social sciences, and humanities. The courses are supposed to be taken in the first two years of study. Two of the courses in each division must be designated "primary distribution courses," or PDCs, which, according to the college catalogue, are limited to 25 students and "place particular emphasis on the mode of inquiry in a particular discipline." The two PDCs in each division must come from different departments.

Apart from those parameters, few restrictions are placed on the way a student may fulfill the general education requirements. "I've run into a few people who seemed a little unfocused," says a student. "But I've found it very good on the whole."

Many of the PDCs are fairly traditional general survey courses, but others are more narrow or ideological in nature. For example, many history PDCs (which meet the social science rather than humanities requirement) concern Europe or the United States, but courses in "Latin America" or "The Formation of the Islamic Middle East" are on equal footing. A recent graduate says, "It's pretty rare that you would get a course that would be a survey of the Western canon." The graduate says many courses emphasize methodology instead of providing an overview of the subject matter. "There tends to be some experimentation with content." One student tells of selecting as a PDC a course on modern Europe, only to find that "it turned into a history of modern gender conflicts and issues, which was really deceiving."

The PDCs cover a variety of time periods, cultures, and current critical theories. But not one such course in the English department, for example, surveys classic Western literature — not even from a revisionist point of view. English instead offers courses like "Cultural Practices and Social Texts" and "Illicit Desires in Literature." There is also a PDC called "Portraits of the Artist," which covers Dante, Salman Rushdie, and others, but also "contains videos by or about African griots, Glenn Gould, Julie Dash, Maya Deren, and Ed Wood Jr.," according to the catalogue. A class entitled "Ways of Seeing" involves popular films and television shows, including *Blade Runner, Seinfeld,* and *The Simpsons.*

"Some of the [English] classes are a little flaky," one student says. "[But] they do teach perfectly standard kinds of things," such as a Shakespeare survey and a Chaucer seminar. However, while those courses could count as the third selection from a division, neither is considered a PDC.

Swarthmore does have a foreign language requirement for all students. It can be met with three years of *high school* language courses, a satisfactory score on a standardized test, or one year of language study at the college level. Students must also take four quarter-length classes in physical education and pass a survival swimming test. And, although politicized courses can count toward the distribution requirements, Swarthmore does not require a multicultural or "diversity" course.

Outstanding professors include Richard Schuldenfrei in philosophy; James Kurth in political science; Rosaria Munson in classics; Maribeth Graybill in art history; and John Boccio, Michael Brown, and Amy Bug in physics. The departments acknowledged as the college's strongest are physics, classics, art history, psychology, and economics. However, one professor cautions against a hierarchical arrangement of departments. "They're all strong," the professor says. "You can't even survive here unless they're strong."

Some departments are also rather strongly politicized. Beyond its PDC offerings, the history department has a tendency to focus on "very, very obscure" time periods and subjects, a student says. Political science is also said to be highly politicized, and does not have "much tolerance for free-market ideas," a student says. Upper-level courses in that department center on theoretical jargon and the common race-class-gender triumvirate. These courses include "Difference, Dominance, and the Struggle for Equality," "Gender, Politics, and Policy," and "Multicultural Politics in the U.S." Though not many upper-level political science courses are offered in European politics, quite a few concern the politics of China, Southeast Asia, and Africa.

The English department's politics are displayed in the titles of upper-level courses — "Lesbian Novels Since World War II," for one. The department also tends to offer courses because students like to take them, one student says. It does require its majors to take courses on periods both before and after 1830, but the student says both sides of the divide are not welcomed equally. "Whenever you get into a class with pre-1830 stuff, people in the class are only in there because of the requirement, and are pretty unenthusiastic," the student says.

Modern languages and literatures includes such radical courses as "Prisons, Madness, and Sexuality: Michel Foucault and European Literature" and " 'Epistemology of the Closet': Literary and Theoretical Constructions of Male Homosexuality." The latter course, according to the catalogue, involves "readings in European and American fiction and contemporary gay theory" and "aims to provide frameworks for a specifically anti-homophobic analysis of literature."

Interdisciplinary special programs, including black studies, women's studies, environmental studies, and the nebulously named "interpretation theory," are not full-fledged departments and do not offer majors, but students can study in these areas in addition to their majors. Courses in black studies and women's studies appear to be on the radical side, while environmental studies' course titles range from scientific to issues-oriented. The concentration in interpretation theory is not aimed at any particular subject matter, but at deconstructing things through a study of language, film, psychology, sexuality, and religion. Special programs such as these are a recent development at Swarthmore, and the college sees them as a sort of tryout for full degree-granting status, a professor says. After five or ten years the programs will be evaluated, at which point they will disappear completely, become true majors, or be subsumed into another department, as was the case with an international relations program that eventually joined the departments of political science and economics. If these programs do become majors, it would represent a further politicization of Swarthmore's curriculum, which to this point has kept its political classes within the confines of traditional departments.

Whatever politics do exist on campus, there is no question that most courses are well taught and are concerned with traditional subjects. Several faculty maintain that the liberal arts departments have kept their essential academic integrity, despite courses like several listed above. "It depends on what you mean by politicized," a professor says. "Professors tend to be liberal-to-progressive, but this does not usually affect the content of courses." There is, however, considerable homogeneity in attitudes and beliefs among the faculty and students, according to some on campus. One graduate says Swarthmore students "tend to be shocked" to find out that someone is "a conservative."

The economics department is said to be open to a variety of views. The department has a free-market emphasis, and is "open to raising a voice for conservative issues," a student says. "They would not only tolerate the expression of those views, they would help you formulate those ideas." Classics is much the same way, according to another student. "It's kind of a small department," the student says. "[But] the reason I found it attractive is that it's particularly immune to individual spur-of-the-moment intellectual trends."

Swarthmore's courses are academically rigorous, regardless of the department in which they are taught. "A lot of our attention here is focused on working with students, [having] the best teaching and research availability," a professor says. Grade inflation does not exist at Swarthmore, and a B-plus is considered a very good grade by most students. "It's still very difficult to do well," one student says. The college bookstore even sells T-shirts that say: "Anywhere Else It Would Have Been an A, Really."

Political Atmosphere: Can't We All Just Get Along?

Like many small liberal arts colleges founded in the nineteenth century, Swarthmore came from Christian roots. Although it has not been officially aligned with a church for nearly a century, this heritage still influences the campus's atmosphere. Swarthmore was founded in 1864 by members of the Religious Society of Friends, the Quakers, as a specifically coeducational institution, something rare at the time. The college catalogue indicates that, though a secular school, it still "seeks to illuminate the lives of its students with the spiritual principles of the Society of Friends."

These principles, in practice, are more ethical than spiritual. The catalogue speaks of "the individual's responsibility for seeking and applying truth, and for testing whatever truth one believes one has found." It notes the Quaker concerns for "hard work, simple living, and generous giving; personal integrity, social justice, and the peaceful settlement of disputes," but immediately adds that "the College does not seek to impose on its students this Quaker view of life, or any other specific set of convictions about the nature of things and the duties of human beings."

The result is a campus predominantly liberal, "but with tolerance for all kinds of views," says a conservative student. "I find it a very comfortable place to be." There is political diversity and, for the most part, factions accord one another proper respect. Another conservative student says she chose Swarthmore over several other competitors because of its "openness to the expression of a number of differing views, including mine." This student speaks highly of Swarthmore's emphasis on a serious examination of one's own values, saying this practice is a direct legacy of the school's Quaker heritage.

Another student thinks the college is sometimes too devoted to consensus at the expense of healthy discord. "I sometimes would have preferred a little more room to remain dissenting," the student says. "There could be more emphasis on the right to disagree."

Another T-shirt available on campus reads: "Anywhere Else It Would Have Been an Issue." For the most part, this phrase is correct: if students can't come to an agreement, they likely don't have the time to become involved in further arguments, let alone more radical political activities. There are controversies at Swarthmore, usually involving multiculturalism and diversity issues, but these don't normally get far. "Most of the controversies are sort of silly," a student says. "They're usually issues about having issues."

One recent example involved the American flag, which some students claimed was representative of imperialism. Further, they argued that political allegiances had no place in an educational community, and asked that the flag not be flown on campus. The group was small but vocal; however, the student body voted to keep the flag.

Other groups are also small but vocal — and radical. There are many debates about race, but the most influential groups on campus include the College Democrats, Civil Liberties, Earthlust, and the Feminist Majority. Gay rights are also discussed frequently, both by campus groups and visiting speakers. A former assistant dean returned to the college in 1997 and spoke about the troubles he and his partner had encountered in their attempts to adopt a girl.

Swarthmore promises to protect freedom of expression, and though a hate-speech code was once proposed, it was not adopted. Tenure decisions are said to be objective, and based on both excellence in teaching and the adequate production of research. Nevertheless, there appears to be a subtle campus undertone regarding "correct" beliefs, even though the college is nominally open to traditional opinions. A student remembers a peer who was counseled not even to write an essay opposing affirmative action, as well as a professor's public pronouncement that students arriving at Swarthmore from Catholic high schools needed to be rid of their "dogmatism." As part of first-year orientation, students participate in a safe-sex workshop that, one student says, is "a bit on the edge."

Still, traditional students say they are generally comfortable at Swarthmore. One student says, however, that Swarthmore is a place where traditional students will "get a lot of skills, but your values and beliefs as a conservative will not be bolstered." Conservative groups do exist on campus (see "Student Life" below), and have cooperated with liberal groups to sponsor debates; recently Wendell Primus and Robert Rector took opposite sides on the topic "Welfare: Safety Net or Web of Dependency." A conservative newspaper, *Common Sense*, receives funding from the college, but some students say the paper is not particularly good.

Student Life: Hangin' at the "Beach"

Swarthmore is located in the western suburbs of Philadelphia, a region dense with outstanding colleges and universities. The campus is certainly one of the most beautiful in the nation, with wide lawns and tree-lined roads and paths that can be stunning when fall colors are at their best. Stately Parrish Hall is the center of the campus, containing not only the administrative offices but also five residence halls and the campus newspaper and radio station. In good weather the lawn in front of this building becomes "Parrish Beach," where Frisbee and other collegiate pastimes are pursued.

Philadelphia and its myriad social, historical, and cultural attractions are only a half hour away by train or car. Swarthmore students thus have easy access to a major city while being able to live in suburban comfort and safety.

Given what's been said about Swarthmore's political atmosphere, it will come as no surprise that many of its student clubs are on the left-hand side of the political spectrum. These include the environmentalist Earthlust and *The L-Word*, a sophisticated, student-edited "Journal of Liberal Thought." But one can also find on campus the College Republicans, who often invite speakers to campus, including recently a representative from Feminists for Life; the Swarthmore Conservative Union; and Swarthmore Students Advocating Life.

Several Christian groups, including evangelical ones, are represented on campus, but there is no Newman Center for Catholic students. Religious and moral issues are plumbed in debate nonetheless, and religious conservatives are not always silent — one student even responded to an atheist's complaint by appealing to logic and the thought of C. S. Lewis, and his editorial was even posted on the Swarthmore *Phoenix*'s website. "There's a religious advisor that some of the churches fund or support" called Caritas, one student mentions, though he warned, "It's very flighty, touchy-feely." Despite the obstacles, conservative students do attend Swarthmore. Says one: "I like the place a lot. I've been very happy there. The teachers are very committed, and the underlying ethic is one I can really respect."

Swarthmore offers varsity competition in twenty-two sports, with most of the competition taking place in the Centennial Conference. Intramural and club teams extend the range of student athletic opportunities.

Swarthmore has recently become the beneficiary of one of its most famous alumni, the late novelist James Michener. Upon his death, Michener named Swarthmore the main beneficiary of his estate (which is estimated to be worth many tens of millions of dollars). Though Michener was neither a scholar nor a literary novelist, his big, sweeping novels about various parts of the world have served to educate, as well as entertain, millions of people about places near and far. Perhaps it is in the quietly educational value of his novels that Michener paid his greatest tribute to the education he received at Swarthmore College.

UNIVERSITY OF TEXAS AT AUSTIN

Admission Center
John Hargis Hall
UT-Austin
Austin, TX 78712
(512) 475-7440
www.utexas.edu

Total enrollment: 47,910
Undergraduates: 35,090
SAT Ranges (Verbal/Math): V 540-650, M 560-600
Financial aid: N/A
Applicants: 14,631
Accepted: 67%
Enrolled: 59%
Application deadline: Mar. 1
Financial aid application deadline: Mar. 31
Tuition: in-state, $2,160; out-of-state, $8,550
Core curriculum: No

As Big as Texas

The enormous University of Texas at Austin is home to nearly forty-eight thousand students and is one of the largest universities in the nation. The advantage of a huge land-grant university in a huge state is that there is certainly something for everyone, and that everyone has ways to avoid what he or she doesn't want to see. A place this large employs excellent faculty — if students can find them. The university has a very good honors program that attracts good students, but has trouble reaching the less gifted, who are known to opt for community college courses to satisfy general education requirements.

The disadvantages of a place like UT-Austin are obvious: there are lots of ways to get lost, and the incoherent distribution requirement system can leave students with a hodgepodge of third-rate experiences.

Courses range from the rigorous to the relaxed, and are taught by full professors or graduate students. It is likely that no two students receive exactly the same quality of education or take the same set of courses. Student life varies for the same reasons.

The university has been in the news lately because of a decision by a federal appeals court (the *Hopwood* decision) that effectively struck down its affirmative

539

action–based enrollment policies. This and other controversies have contributed to a combative campus environment — which can also be avoided if one knows where to hide. But then again, UT-Austin is large enough for that, too.

Academic Life: Multiple Choice

There are 16 graduate and undergraduate colleges and schools at the University of Texas at Austin. Only a select few are exclusively oriented toward graduate study. This leaves undergraduates 11 different colleges in which to pursue degrees. These include the schools of architecture, business, communications, education, engineering, fine arts, natural sciences, nursing, pharmacy, social work, and, finally, the College of the Liberal Arts.

Of these, only the latter is concerned with what is considered a traditional liberal arts education; the rest are more professional in their orientation, and thus will not be discussed at length in this guidebook.

The basic curriculum of the College of the Liberal Arts consists of distribution requirements in four areas: language arts, social sciences, natural sciences, and "general culture," the university's term for the humanities. Language arts requirements consist of two English courses, two courses in what is called the "writing component," and proficiency in the equivalent of four semesters of a foreign language. The social studies requirement is bigger than that found in most distribution-style curricula: UT-Austin requires two courses in government and two in history, plus an additional course from anthropology, economics, geography, linguistics, sociology, or psychology. The natural sciences area also demands a comparatively high number of courses: six must be chosen from the departments of math, astronomy, biology, botany, chemistry, computer science, geology, microbiology, physical science, physics, and zoology. Six semester hours are required in the general culture area, which includes architecture, fine arts, classics, philosophy, and a few scattered alternatives approved each semester and made available through the dean's office. (For example, some alternatives for spring 1998 would be logic, Spanish civilization courses, and these interdisciplinary courses: "African-American Culture," "American Landscape, Art and Photography: Culture of the American West," and "Musical Culture of Turkey and Central Asia.")

None of the courses in these areas is required by name, so the curriculum does not amount to a traditional core. However, the number of distribution requirements is quite high compared with other colleges — too high, according to one professor. "The curriculum has far too many requirements, especially in sciences, but also in American/Texas history and government," the professor says. "The results are farcical courses for the totally uninterested." The teaching efforts of the university are further hampered by the fact that many students there, according to this professor, "shouldn't be in college at all." (Although he adds that one-third of the student body is "as good as any Ivy League school.") A number of students abandon all hope of meeting the distribution requirements and instead take classes at community colleges, where the lowest grade possible is a C. By law, though, the university must accept these credits as if they were taken at UT-Austin.

Because of the size of the university and the number of graduate students in the humanities, many freshman courses are taught by graduate students. This does little to help the quality of teaching or to hold the interest of the better students, the professor says. Introductory-level courses taught by professional faculty are taught adequately, on the average. Teachers are evaluated both by peers and students, and these evaluations are considered at tenure time. "If you choose your courses and instructors well, you can get an education that is equal to any in the United States," a professor claims.

The College of the Liberal Arts offers degree programs in thirty-two fields — most of the regular fields, plus some unusual ones like Australian studies, medieval studies, Mexican-American studies, Middle Eastern studies, Middle Eastern languages and cultures, post-Soviet and East European studies, and rhetoric and composition.

Regardless of a student's major, the university offers a number of exceptional honors programs that usually require a minimum grade point average, a thesis, and participation in designated honors seminars. "These can also be demanding," a professor says. "Not enough students do honors theses, and grade inflation is rampant, but still, for those who seek, the rewards are usually there."

UT-Austin has a freshman honors program open to students with the proper academic prerequisites. Students in this program get to take special honors sections of the general education courses, as well as an additional course called "Liberal Arts Honors," which provides an overview of various disciplines.

A third honors program, called Liberal Arts Honors, involves a series of upper-level interdisciplinary courses in which only select students are able to enroll. For students to receive the Liberal Arts Honors distinction on their diplomas, they must earn a B or better in at least three of these courses and carry an overall GPA of 3.5.

The best faculty at UT-Austin include: Jeffrey Tulis in government; J. Budziszewski in both the government and philosophy departments; Robert Koons, Robert Kane, and Daniel Bonevac in philosophy; Joseph Horn, developer of the Liberal Arts Honors program and a professor in the psychology department; George B. Forgie and Robert M. Crunden in history; Michael Gagarin in classics; and Lino A. Graglia in law.

Good departments include linguistics, classics, psychology, and philosophy. Also noteworthy are the departments of history, government, economics, and anthropology. The classics department is large — twenty-five professors — and encompasses not only the study of literature but also the archaeology, art, history, philosophy, and religion of antiquity.

Among the most politicized departments at the university are African-

American studies, American studies, English, and women's studies — a list that might well fit the profile on almost any campus today.

Among the courses offered by the African-American studies program is "Gender in the African American Community," whose course description states that while the course will focus on gender, "underlying this emphasis on gender within this community is a theoretical stance which understands gender as a social construction which orders power inequalities in human societies in articulation with processes of race and class." The department also teaches "Race and Sport in American Life," which looks at "racial symbolism in sport and seeks to define race and racial stereotypes" and "the history of racialist ideas in the Olympic movement and racial anthropology in Black Africa."

In its promotional materials, the American studies program refers to the "myths of the American dream and rugged individualism," which were "culturally useful" because of the circumstances of economic hardship. The promotional materials go on to say that the curriculum "now focuses increasingly on multicultural issues of race, class, gender, and ethnicity." The curriculum consists of courses such as "A Cultural History of American Photography," "History of Being Cool in America," "Sport, Fitness, and Mass Media," and "Environmental History of North America."

The English department offers a large number of politicized classes, many of which use feminist critiques of literature both well and little known. "Gay and Lesbian Literature and Culture," which is cross-listed in the women's studies department, "offers a context for understanding the recent 'boom' or 'mainstreaming' of literature by and about lesbians and gay men in North America and Britain." Another course, "Feminist Film Theory," involves weekly viewings of Hollywood productions in order to "introduce students to the discipline of women's studies by giving them tools and perspectives for analyzing the representation of gender — 'femininity' and 'masculinity' in film." A seminar for seniors entitled "The Unruly Woman in English Renaissance Literature" focuses on "the dramatic variety in the male renaissance fear of women, and on renaissance writers' reflexive deconstruction and criticism of this misogyny." All the writers studied in the course are male, and, according to the catalogue, whether they know it or not, all "are aware of, and interested in imagining, the special psychology of scapegoating . . . [and] at least try to explore the anxieties and phobias beneath their male characters' scapegoating of women." Students are asked to judge which are the most successful, the catalogue states. "In short, this is a course in the tangled bad conscience of the English Renaissance," the course description says.

Women's studies at UT-Austin, according to its prospectus, "places women and gender at the center of analysis." Courses include "Feminism and Cultural Politics," which covers "the Woman Artist," "Identity Politics," and the "Politics of Sexuality," including the question, "What is the connection between feminism and gay and lesbian studies?" Another course called "Politics of Sexuality and Lesbian Cultures" surveys recent works (including performance art) in order to consider "how sexual politics are conducted in and through culture and representation." Oddly enough, the department also lists a course called "Primate Behavior," which involves laboratory observation of "the social behavior of nonhuman primates."

Political Atmosphere: Decisions, Decisions, Decisions

While the general environment at UT-Austin is not traditional, the campus is large enough that no one person is subject to vast amounts of pressure for political conformity. The same applies to the several areas of the institution headed by conservative leaders and faculty. "The administration line is always basically liberal, though that liberalism is significantly watered down because we are in the South," a student says. "There is an annual call for a diversity course requirement but that has never amounted to anything. When I lived in a dorm my freshman year there were voluntary seminars on [politically correct] topics, but I never knew anyone who went to one."

The two most politically charged recent incidents at the university have both involved race and affirmative action. In March 1996 the U.S. Fifth Circuit Court of Appeals in New Orleans issued what is known as the "Hopwood decision," which held that the UT-Austin law school could not justify admissions policies that gave preferential treatment to minorities. The appeals court ruled in favor of four white applicants who had been rejected by the law school in favor of minority students who were less qualified. This decision effectively ended the entire University of Texas system's policy of affirmative action admissions, and had similar effects on other public colleges in the Fifth Circuit.

UT-Austin did not take the decision quietly. University president Robert Berdahl (who has since gone on to become chancellor of UC-Berkeley) warned that the ruling would mean "the virtual re-segregation of higher education." Bernard Rapoport, chairman of the university system's board of regents, was "distressed" by the ruling and called for an appeal of the decision.

Six months after the Hopwood decision, the same issue was brought up by nationally prominent law professor Lino Graglia. Graglia, speaking at a news conference to announce the formation of Students for Equal Opportunity, a student group for which he is faculty adviser, said "blacks and Mexican-Americans are not academically competitive with whites in selective institutions." Graglia, a constitutional lawyer whose nomination to the federal bench by President Ronald Reagan was unsuccessful because of Graglia's previous statements against forced busing, went on to say: "It is the result primarily of cultural effects. Various studies seem to show, that blacks and Mexican-Americans spend much less time in school. They have a culture that seems not to encourage achievement. Failure is not looked upon with disgrace."

These comments were not well received by the Reverend Jesse Jackson, who came to Texas to lead a rally against Graglia's remarks and the Hopwood decision. Jackson accused Graglia of "espousing a fascist ideology" and said that "people of character across all lines of color should denounce such propaganda." Several Texas state lawmakers called for Graglia to be fired — one even said he did not believe "First Amendment rights are intended to protect professors who subscribe to racist views and are in positions that require them to teach a diverse group of students." Fifty of Graglia's fellow law professors disavowed his remarks in a signed public statement.

That "blacks and Mexican-Americans are not academically competitive with whites in selective institutions" is, of course, the very reason affirmative action policies, like the one struck down in Hopwood, were put in place. *Dallas Morning News* columnist William Murchison wrote that the UT-Austin establishment was already "depressed by a court-ordered cutoff of affirmative action at UT's law school and the consequent drop in minority enrollment" when Graglia made his remarks. Murchison argued that the reaction against Graglia was not a reasoned refutation of his concerns regarding culture and education, but rather a visceral condemnation of the professor stemming from anger over the Hopwood case. Graglia continues to hold his position on the law school faculty.

The new president of UT-Austin, Larry Faulkner, supported affirmative action in his former position as Vice Chancellor of the University of Illinois. He is also known as an excellent fund-raiser with a track record of cutting budgets.

Student Life: The Heart of Texas

Austin was once known as the "City of the Violet Crown" for the ring of low, purple hills that surrounds it. The city has since grown to cover those hills, but the area is still scenic. The Colorado River runs through Austin, and several hydroelectric dams create the Highland Lakes, picturesque spots where university students sometimes go for recreation. Austin (as in "City Limits") is also known for musical performances at its bars, clubs, and nightspots. "The Live Music Capital of the World" (as proclaimed by city government) is host to such musical forms as blues, country and western, jazz, reggae, rock, swing, and Tejano.

Although UT-Austin is far and away the largest university in the region, other academic institutions in the area include Austin Community College, Austin Presbyterian Theological Seminary, Concordia Lutheran College, Episcopal Theological Seminary of the Southwest, Huston-Tillotson College, and St. Edward's University. Their presence enhances the intellectual life of the city (more lectures, debates, bookstores, etc.). It has also led to a growth industry in specialty breweries, including the Bitter End, the Copper Tank, and the Waterloo Brewing Company. Most notably, the famous Celis Brewery, known for its Belgian-style beer, moved to Austin in 1992.

The university itself is built in a Southwestern architectural style, with red-tile roofs and decorative stonework. Statues of famous Texans populate the main university mall.

The sheer size of the campus affects the character of student life, according to a student. "The social life on campus is very spread out," the student says. "I am in a fraternity and the Greek organizations are basically separated from the rest of campus by choice. There are absolutely no organized campuswide social activities that most people go to. Basically, you just find your own niche and ignore the 50,000 other people."

Niches are not hard to find. There are more than 750 registered student organizations at UT-Austin, ranging from conservative to liberal to just plain strange.

The most visible conservative group is the Young Conservatives of Texas. This group is "probably the best known of the conservative groups and they always get a spokesman at any student roundtable," a student says. Other options include the College Republicans at Texas, which publishes a weekly newsletter, and Students for Equal Opportunity, a unique group whose mission is, according to the group, to "stop racist activities at the University." A pro-life group, Lifesavers, sponsors campus debates and contributes time and money to local crisis pregnancy centers.

Left-wing student groups include environmental organizations, feminist groups, gay and lesbian groups, and a huge number of groups dedicated to a particular ethnicity. Among the environmental groups are Earth First!, which has been accused of illegal protests (i.e., trespassing) against loggers and other construction workers, and the Green Party, a campus branch of the political party known for its commitment to environmentalism.

Feminists on campus publish *Twenty-Three Thousand Seven — Campus Women's Issues Forum*, which includes creative writing, news affecting women, and editorial comment on feminist issues. A group called EmPower recently brought Katie Koestner to campus. Koestner, the victim of date rape who appeared on the cover of *Time* magazine in 1991 and whose story was told in a recent HBO movie, has lectured at more than three hundred colleges and universities since 1994.

Along with other groups on campus, Feminist Action is trying to generate university support for a campus women's resource center. The center would provide a library, office and meeting space, as well as a "networking base and center for programming on women's issues." So far their efforts have been unsuccessful.

Other groups serve as advocates for homosexual students. The Lesbian, Bisexual, and Gay Students' Association distributes literature and organizes social events, including a rally on the campus mall on National Coming Out Day. The group encourages homosexuals to "come out and rejoice in themselves, whether straight, bisexual, gay, transsexual, or other." There are also homosexual groups for law students and for the school of political administration.

The UT-Austin chapter of MECHA, a Mexican advocacy group, was successful in changing the university's celebration of Texan Independence Day into a celebration of diversity.

The Longhorn Hellraisers is a student organization dedicated to supporting UT-Austin athletic teams. Their activities consist primarily of attending sporting events in Hellraiser attire and orange and white face-paint. Fraternity members are not permitted to join the Hellraisers — a clause in their student constitution reads: "Males cannot be a member of another social fraternity that is single sex."

While the Hellraisers dress up, the Longhorn Nudists occasionally don't dress at all. This fifty-member group is officially recognized by the university and distributes literature and holds seminars on campus to explain the nudist way of life. The group's Internet home page contains photos of club outings and nude beaches, as well as links to various national and international nudist resources.

Then there is the university chapter of the Texas Hemp Campaign, which supports the legalization of marijuana. The group participates in civil disobedience, distributes leaflets (no pun intended), and maintains that the "hemp/marijuana prohibition is a policy based on ignorance, lies, fear, bigotry, and injustice."

Sports are always in the news in Austin, as thousands cheer on their Longhorns in every major sport, especially football. Other strong teams are fielded in baseball and swimming. For the less talented athlete, club sports and intramurals abound. The school has excellent facilities for virtually every sporting interest.

THOMAS AQUINAS COLLEGE

Office of Admissions
Santa Paula, CA 93060-9980
(805) 525-4417, ext. 359
(800) 634-9797
www.thomasaquinas.edu

Total enrollment: 219
Undergraduates: 219
SAT Ranges (Verbal/Math): V 590-670, M 540-630
Financial aid: 78%
Applicants: 160
Accepted: 62%
Enrolled: 68%
Application deadline: rolling
Financial aid application deadline: Mar. 2 or 30 days after acceptance, whichever is later
Tuition: $14,900
Core curriculum: Yes

Life, and More Abundantly

The 220 students at Thomas Aquinas College don't learn the latest things; instead, they learn the oldest things, and find them to be thoroughly relevant to the concerns of the present. With its "Great Books" program, the Thomas Aquinas curriculum is virtually unparalleled for providing its students with a rigorous liberal arts education. And because the school has a deeply religious character, students quickly discover that faith and knowledge are inextricably related. "Sacred Scripture and the *magisterium* of the Church are understood to be the most important sources of enlightenment," the college states.

The guiding principles of Thomas Aquinas are enumerated in its "founding document," a monograph entitled "A Proposal for the Fulfillment of Catholic Liberal Education." Published two years before the college opened its doors in 1971, the document was drafted by the college's first president, Ronald P. McArthur, and Marcus Berquist, still a tutor at the school. It outlines a powerful vision of Catholic liberal education that has been realized almost without alteration at Thomas Aquinas for over twenty-five years. According to the document, a Catholic college, "if it is to be faithful to the teaching of Christ, will differ from its secular counterpart in two essential respects. First, it will not define itself by academic freedom, but by the divinely revealed truth, and second, that truth will be the chief object of study as well as the governing principle of the whole institution, giving order and purpose even to the teaching and learning of the secular disciplines."

But the true intellectual and spiritual force behind the college is its patron saint. Considered a *Doctor communis* (universal teacher) by the Catholic Church, St. Thomas Aquinas has served as the bulwark for Catholic philosophical and theological thought for over seven centuries. Nearly all of the college faculty consider themselves Thomists, and the college relies on its patron saint for "help and inspiration" in fulfilling its liberal arts mission. Thomas is not a quaint mascot, but an inspiring guide and teacher. Very few — if any — colleges in the country are founded on such an inspired vision, and even fewer remain so faithful to their founding visions. Of course, a small and demanding school like this is not for everyone, but highly motivated young Catholics should give it serious consideration. This college has received a great deal of well-deserved praise.

Academic Life: *Trivium* Pursuit

All Thomas Aquinas students take the same four-year sequence of courses in the "Great Books," described by the college as "the original works of the best, most influential authors, poets, scientists, mathematicians, philosophers, and theologians of Western civilization." The program is constructed along the medieval divisions of the *trivium* (logic, rhetoric, and grammar) and the *quadrivium* (geometry, astronomy, arithmetic, music). All of these disciplines are interrelated and oriented toward the same intelligible truth. This program of study is both interdisciplinary and cohesive — in short, the very essence of a liberal education.

By any standard, the curriculum is rigorous and impressive. The college catalogue speaks of "the natural order of learning" and states that "the object and the method of education are not arbitrary." The college believes "experience leads to art and art to science"; thus, its curriculum "proceeds through the liberal arts . . . which arise as human constructs by which men seek to give order and expression to the reality they experience."

Thomas Aquinas students follow one well-designed track on their quest for truth. They take two years of Latin, four years of both mathematics and laboratory science, three years of both philosophy and theology, and a year of both music and logic. The centerpiece of the curriculum is a four-year great books seminar commencing with the *Iliad* and *Odyssey* and progressing to *The Waste Land*. "The texts studied within the curriculum are the original writings of the greatest minds in our intellectual tradition," writes President Thomas E. Dillon in the preface to the college's founding document. "They are to be read not primarily for historical or cultural reasons, but because they are the best attempts to understand things in themselves while attending to our common experience."

"It is one of the most carefully thought-out curricula in the country," says one professor. Changes are made very infrequently, and are arrived at only after serious deliberation among faculty.

As might be expected, theology is the queen of all disciplines at Thomas Aquinas. The result, however, is not a Catholic version of an evangelical Bible college. The liberal arts are studied not as obstructions to the truth, but as the way to understanding truth. Faith illuminates this path, and that is the reason for its central position in the Thomas Aquinas curriculum. But, as one professor notes, "truth is attainable in the sciences . . . you can move beyond them to wisdom." Another agrees that "math and science are legitimate ways of approaching reality" and that it is important for believing Christians to "come to grips with science" in a field dominated by skeptics and agnostics.

Thomas Aquinas has no electives and no majors; as one faculty member puts it, "to choose the college is to choose a liberal arts major." According to another, Thomas Aquinas is an excellent choice for the "yeoman student." Nearly 20 percent of the student body was homeschooled, and about a third went to another college before choosing Thomas Aquinas; many applied after becoming dissatisfied with the education they were receiving elsewhere.

Thomas Aquinas does not consider its faculty to be "professors" in the literal sense — people whose job it is to dispense their wisdom on students — but "tutors," men and women who serve to facilitate and guide discussion of the great books. Indeed, the college believes "the true teachers are the great writings in which the tradition lives."

The tutorial method of instruction has been abused at other colleges, where it is sometimes in the hands of faculty who are unprepared for teaching and amounts to little more than a verbal free-for-all. According to students and faculty, this is decidedly not the case at Thomas Aquinas. Tutors are expected to guide the discussion, and most are very adept at knowing when and how to participate. "Even when the tutor is doing the 'hands off' thing, he's guiding you with his questions," a student says. "When the tutor isn't giving you a light, it's a really good mental exercise to have to grasp it for yourself." Because of the relatively open nature of the classroom, there is no guarantee against the occasional tangential comments or bizarre speculations. But, as one student notes, "sometimes something that seems strange can actually be helpful."

Students must prepare for seminars by reading and considering the assigned texts. Reading lists can be extensive in some seminars (the senior great books seminar covers twenty-seven authors) but never include criticisms or literary theory-type texts. "The college discourages the reading of secondary sources and commentaries, which are likely to inhibit a direct and unprejudiced acquaintance with the books they read," according to the catalogue.

The college also underplays the importance of standard indicators of progress in college courses, such as examinations. Instead, it has instituted a pseudo-British form of evaluation called the "Don Rags," a twice-yearly event in which a student meets with all of his tutors and receives a verbal "progress report." "A Don Rag," says the catalogue, "unlike a report card, offers specific advice on what the student can do to advance in the intellectual life." Thomas Aquinas also gives letter grades, but says they are not important.

The curriculum requires quite a bit of writing, and each semester students owe papers on a topic from each course. Thomas Aquinas also requires a senior thesis, which must be defended in a public session.

Although the format at Thomas Aquinas is largely tutorial, students do periodically attend lectures. Every other Friday a formal lecture is given by either an outside speaker or a member of the college faculty; on occasion, there will be a musical performance instead. "Most of the subjects are close to the curriculum," says one tutor. The discussions that ensue after the talk are usually lively and extensive.

Political Atmosphere: Make My Words Your Home

A few years ago Thomas Aquinas ran afoul of its regional accrediting agency, the Western Association of Schools and Colleges (WASC). WASC representatives complained about the "restrictive nature of the curriculum" at Thomas Aquinas and put pressure on the college to make its curriculum and enrollment more "multicultural," in compliance with "Standard 4.B.2" of the WASC documents for higher education, which calls for an "appreciation of diversity" as one of the basic requirements of higher education.

The college defended itself, engaging in determined opposition to WASC's politicized agenda. Writing in the spring 1995 issue of *Policy Review*, college president Dillon stated, "We pursue no 'affirmative action' for persons or texts. We look for the best teachers, the best books, and students willing and able to undertake the life of reason."

After the conflict made the pages of the *Wall Street Journal*, larger institutions such as Stanford and UCLA also voiced their concern over WASC's criteria. Thomas Aquinas was repeatedly characterized as playing David to the WASC's Goliath, and WASC ultimately took the figurative stone to the head and backed down. Indeed, recent WASC reports reflect favorably on the intellectual and social life of the college: "In the best tradition of a residential college, students characterize the college as character building in that it not only teaches you, it changes you. Students value their seriousness in leading a life pleasing to God, which includes adherence to virtue in all matters, practicing respect for others, affirming chastity before marriage, and endorsing differentiation of the sexes which nonetheless affirms both sexes as rational truth seekers." The college has also earned effusive praise from a recently formed accrediting agency, the American Academy for Liberal Education.

The college demonstrates in its strict rules and adherence to Catholic doctrine that the learning it offers affects students' social comportment, as well as their intellectual lives. Thomas Aquinas is largely immune from the controversy and scandal that seem to plague other institutions of higher learning. Once every couple of years, estimates a professor, there is a high-profile violation of the Thomas Aquinas student code, which governs everything from appropriate dress to sexual infractions. In one recent case, a student was dismissed from the college because she wanted to live with her boyfriend off campus, in open violation of the student code of conduct. She attempted to sue the college, but the suit was dropped.

According to students and faculty, what political atmosphere exists on campus is overwhelmingly traditional and is highly informed by Catholic doctrine. "We pray every day in the chapel for an end to abortion," notes one student, and students frequently go off campus to pray the rosary at a nearby abortion clinic. But in general, students are more interested in debating the intellectual arguments of the authors read and discussed in class, and one professor notes that the political temperature is kept purposely low: "We try to keep their minds on the program." Apart from the Legion of Mary chapter and pro-life work of students, activism is generally discouraged for the sake of cultivating the intellectual life of students. "It's not the time of life" for such activities, says a professor.

There is a modest degree of political activity among faculty. "Some of the faculty are more politically involved than others," notes one student. One professor, for instance, circulated a petition in support of Proposition 209 (a California ballot initiative to end affirmative action). Campus speakers generally tend to be intellectually and culturally, if not politically, conservative. Past speakers have included Alan Keyes, noted Straussian Harry Jaffa, the late conservative journalist Malcolm Muggeridge, and Boston College theologian Peter Kreeft.

The hiring process at Thomas Aquinas is also distinctive among premier liberal arts colleges and, according to faculty, is not subject to the ideological constraints that so often attend such decisions at other institutions. Neither is continued employment (there is no such thing as tenure there) dependent on the "publish or perish" mentality that often is at odds with an institution's commitment to teaching. "Thomas Aquinas is very, very focused on quality education," says one professor, who adds that the administration "would discourage publication if it adversely affects your teaching."

Although immune to certain pressures, faculty hiring could be accused of a kind of "inbreeding," insofar as a marked preference exists toward hiring graduates of Thomas Aquinas or similar great books schools, like St. Mary's College of California or St. John's College in Annapolis and Santa Fe. Of the twenty-three tutors listed in the 1995-97 catalogue, for instance, ten received their B.A.s from Thomas Aquinas and an additional six either studied or taught at St. Mary's or St. John's.

The value of this practice, of course, is that the college hires only tutors known to support the program it operates. And selecting faculty from among graduates of its own or similar programs is hardly surprising, given the unique and challenging nature of teaching at Thomas Aquinas. Faculty at the college must exhibit a high degree of unity of purpose and approach; all must be prepared to teach any part of the college curriculum. Once hired, tutors remain at Thomas Aquinas under a virtual "permanent appointment" system that dispenses with the usual process of tenure review. Consequently, great care is taken in the search and interview process for a new faculty member. The college "almost always grants permanent employment" if a faculty member wants to stay, the professor says.

Campus Life: On Being and Essence

Since 1978, Thomas Aquinas has been located on a beautiful site in southern California, between the cities of Santa Paula and Ojai. Rugged mountains rise beside the campus, which is built in a Southwestern/California mission style. "The setting is appropriate" for the intellectual undertaking students are engaged in, says one student.

Because the site was previously undeveloped, all of the buildings are new and some are still temporary. "As funds are raised, buildings go up," explains a professor. The college currently has a commons/dining room building, a classroom building, three permanent dorms (two male and one female), and the St. Bernardine Library, completed in 1995. Plans are under way for a laboratory science building, a chapel, and more dormitories, and the college is in the midst of a campaign to raise funds for these projects. The administration "is aware of what is needed," according to one student, and both students and faculty seem generally pleased with the current facilities and future plans.

The social and extracurricular environment at Thomas Aquinas is vastly different from that at most American colleges. There is no campus newspaper, no student government, and no Greek system. The rules of behavior would inspire students elsewhere to rebellion. Students must live on campus unless they are married or granted special permission — and the college's rules of residence state that since "the purpose of the college is to establish a community of learning, such permission is not usually given." No student may enter a dormitory of the opposite sex, and may only linger on the porch long enough to wait for the person he or she is meeting. Alcohol is prohibited on campus, and students must sign out before leaving campus. "Formal dress," including skirts or dresses for women and slacks and collared shirts for men, is "to be worn throughout the week in the chapel, offices, classrooms, laboratories, dining hall, and library," the rules say. In class, students are to address each other as "Mister" or "Miss," and may not chew gum or consume food or beverages.

One student says that, although "students are not always thrilled to discipline themselves in that regard," most are pleased that a code is in place. One of the nice things about these policies, says one professor, is that "faculty don't have to enforce them"; all violations are under the jurisdiction of student prefects, who are chosen by the faculty with help from student suggestions.

When their schedules allow, students can make the ten-minute trip into Santa Paula or visit the beach in Ventura, twenty minutes away. Opportunities for hiking, fishing, and backpacking abound in the Los Padres National Forest, which borders the campus. Occasional group trips to the Los Angeles area (about an hour's drive) are organized around cultural events such as performances by the Los Angeles Opera or Master Chorale.

Organized athletic and musical opportunities are kept to a minimum because of the college's small size and focus on the intellectual life, yet student-initiated sports and musical groups abound. Volleyball, soccer, basketball, and softball are popular, and there is a superlative choir and *scola* trained in Gregorian chant.

Although there is no compulsory religious observance at Thomas Aquinas, mass is offered three times daily, as are opportunities for Eucharistic Adoration and recitation of the rosary.

According to recent figures, roughly half the graduates of Thomas Aquinas go on to graduate or professional schools. Another 11 percent begin a religious vocation. According to one professor, many of the women get married and begin raising a family. Unlike at many of the nation's colleges, "many students leave with greater faith" than when they arrived, one professor says. Most students come to Thomas Aquinas because they believe the college can satisfy their love of and desire for the truth. They are seldom disappointed with their choice. "I came here because I wanted to learn how to think," one student says. "I wanted to learn the best things — things that are worth knowing in themselves."

THOMAS MORE COLLEGE OF LIBERAL ARTS (NEW HAMPSHIRE)

Six Manchester Street
Merrimack, NH 03054
(603) 880-8308
Fax: (603) 880-9280

Total enrollment: 70
Undergraduates: 70
SAT Ranges: N/A
Financial aid: 80%
Applicants: 34
Accepted: 90%
Enrolled: 90%
Application Deadline: Aug. 30
Financial aid application deadline: rolling
Tuition: Rome semester slightly higher — $8,600
Core Curriculum: Yes

A Living Tradition

Thomas More College (TMC) is the smallest institution examined in this guide. Founded in 1978, it exists to instill in its students a love of the liberal arts. It does this with only a handful of professors, a campus of five buildings, and less than a hundred students. Yet, despite its small size, Thomas More is an extremely demanding institution that offers its students an education of the first order. In many ways it is reminiscent of what the first colleges in America were like: small communities of scholars and pupils who viewed themselves not as consumers of professionalized knowledge, but as individual souls who joined their efforts in the search for truth.

Thomas More's promotional literature describes the college as "a Catholic college founded in 1978 to provide on the undergraduate level a solid education in the liberal arts." The curriculum is both Catholic and catholic: students of all backgrounds and beliefs are welcome. There is something refreshing about this educational philosophy, precisely because it keeps an ancient tradition alive rather than succumbing to a nostalgic and static view of the past.

A TMC professor offers this defense of the liberal arts:

It is no secret that many colleges have veered from their original purposes. They seem content with providing mere training rather than true education, with conveying information rather than cultivating the whole person. Thomas More is different — and not only in size. Our philosophy of education runs counter to many current assumptions. We believe in the necessity of the liberal arts, believe that it is important for everyone to withdraw from the concerns of the world for a short time in order to reenter it with renewed understanding and vigor. A good education does not diminish the challenges of life — it may even increase them — but it makes inevitable sufferings more understandable, more bearable, and even an access to joy.

Academic Life: A Larger Human Destiny

The core curriculum at Thomas More lies at the very heart of its educational enterprise. All students are required to complete a core curriculum known as the Cowan Program of Liberal Arts. Says one professor: "Thomas More's core curriculum provides students with what must be about as broad a liberal arts education as it is possible to provide in four years. Its emphasis on the humanities allows them to come into the cultural heritage that is rightfully theirs. All our students study as much literature, philosophy, and politics as students majoring in those disciplines do in some institutions." According to another professor: "The core curriculum at Thomas More College emphasizes the study of the various cultures contained in Western civilization, beginning with ancient Egypt as background and ending with post-modernity. The advantage of this approach is that each culture can be seen as contemporaneous with modern culture."

The college catalogue states the requirements succinctly: "It is, first, through participation in the core curriculum that students discover themselves, holding opinions in reserve until they absorb the thoughts, ideas, images, and actions of the tradition they study." All students must take a six-hour humanities course every semester for all four of their years at Thomas More. Disciplines covered during this time are philosophy, literature, politics, history, and theology. "Hence the entire student body," the catalogue notes, "in any given semester, is enrolled in the same course, freshmen beginning at whatever part of the cycle is being studied when they enter." For the first two years of study, students enroll in a writing course that requires a paper each week on a topic drawn from the humanities course they are taking at that time. Additionally, all students must take two years of either Latin or Greek, and must also pass a reading examination in a modern foreign language.

A professor says of the core: "It provides the breadth of knowledge needed to locate one's existence in the history of mankind, and secondly as a result of the emphasis on disciplines depth of knowledge is gained. . . . Evidence of the success of the curriculum is provided by the desire of our graduates to go on to graduate school and their success in gaining admission, fellowships, scholarships, and terminal degrees." Proof of the college's standing is demonstrated in the fact that, despite its small size and young age, it is fully accredited by the New England Association of Schools and Colleges.

In the humanities classes students study history by reading primary sources, from Homer to the present day, in the context of the civilizations and cultures in which the authors lived. For example, Humanities IV, "The High Middle Ages: Thomistic Philosophy, Medieval Literature," for six credits, is "A study of the flowering of Christian culture in a transformed Western civilization. A consideration of the code of courtesy inherited from the Middle Ages. A study of the Christian hero. Emphasis on the scholastic philosophic tradition. Authors read include Bonaventure, Thomas Aquinas, Dante, Chaucer."

The reasons for this approach are summed up by a faculty member: "Nowadays, of course, we tend to worry primarily about jobs and economic questions. And while these are necessary concerns, practical affairs ought not determine who we are. At our peril we risk losing the knowledge of what it means to live a truly human life." An alum praises the classes taken at Thomas More: "The curriculum is an intense engagement with the greatest and most influential thinkers in history, unfiltered by textbooks and prejudices."

All full-time sophomores spend the spring semester at the college's campus in Rome, Italy. Students live in a baroque convent in Trastevere, the oldest part of the city, and follow the same humanities and writing workshop cycle as in New Hampshire. "The sophomore semester in Rome encapsulates the whole enterprise at Thomas More," says a professor. As the college states it, "Its hoped-for reward is not the mere addition of a new experience, nor the elevation of Roman culture and life over all others. Rather, for the proper participant, Rome enhances the extraordinary value of the ordinary thing. Things taken for granted — one's life, one's family, country, Church — take on a new luster, acquire a deeper significance, and assume a place in the larger human destiny." The remarkable success of the Rome program is attested by the fact that fully 85 percent of all alumni donate to this program.

Since TMC employs only a handful of professors, we won't offer a list of "outstanding" teachers. All of the faculty at TMC are excellent. The college brings in visiting professors of the highest caliber, including Donald and Louise Cowan, renowned educators who helped to design TMC's core curriculum.

Literature, philosophy, and political science are the three most popular majors at Thomas More. The school recently added a biology major, its first venture into the sciences. The facilities for highly advanced scientific research are lacking, however, and students will not find the latest equipment or numerous faculty and researchers who stay on the cutting edge of their fields. But they will find a highly committed faculty whose science courses complement the excellent liberal arts education offered by the rest of the faculty.

There are no politicized courses at Thomas More. Says a professor: "Thomas

More strives to be 'apolitical.'" The comments of a recent graduate affirm this assertion: "Thomas More provides students a rare and most significant opportunity. Unlike most universities today, academic excellence is encouraged and even demanded. The classroom remains the center of community life where honest discussion and inquiries dominate the arena of liberal learning."

Political Atmosphere: The True Meaning of "Amateur"

Thomas More is traditionalist in its curriculum and in its expectations of student behavior and academic performance. It is Catholic in its sensibilities and curriculum, but it welcomes students from all religious backgrounds, or from no religious background. Because professors approach their courses with full confidence in the compatibility of faith and reason, students who choose Thomas More will not find themselves reading only pious literature for four years because professors are afraid to expose them to the ways of the world. In other words, TMC is not a religious camp to which students retreat in order to escape secular society.

Says a professor: "We believe that for all students the college years are formative, developing in them a spirit of liberality and a habit of soul that will endure throughout life. Those qualities that are the fruits of a good education — understanding, high-mindedness, daring, readiness to sacrifice, vitality, patriotism, humility — may seem useless and ephemeral to some, but they are, paradoxically, the guarantees of success and happiness in life." Says another: "Issues of multiculturalism and diversity have not posed a difficulty at the college either in curricular or social concerns. The college does not seek to promote in either its curriculum or its social climate a narrow view of what Western culture is or a narrow view of the person. In a feature which arises out of its catholicity, the college believes in recruiting students from diverse backgrounds and in allowing the students to realize their own personal gifts and destiny."

The small size of the college works to its advantage here. A professor addresses this trait of small-college life: "Here students are known not only by their professors but by other students. All of them can be confident that they make a difference in the history of the place. What they say and do obviously matters. Perhaps this is why there is so little temptation to desperate activism among them."

Thomas More places great emphasis on teaching, and students who go there can be confident that they will receive close personal attention in every class. As a professor says, "The college seeks to hire radicals in the true sense of the word: those who are concerned with the roots of things. The problem is not that graduate schools are churning out radicals, but that they are not radical enough: Most academics — young and old — tend to be rather thoroughbred bourgeois types. The college seeks to hire real thinkers, real intellectuals, those who are willing to think through things deeply and not attach themselves to passing fads of either the left or right." Says another: "We look for professors who love teaching and who love their discipline, but not as scholars who specialize in the esoteric but as those who see their disciplines as a way of life." Typically, professors at Thomas More teach from six to nine hours per semester and also carry out administrative duties. As for publishing, it takes second place to teaching, but it is important. The second professor explains: "Since our teachers have a love of their discipline it is a normal expectation that they do research and publish their findings. This means that they are expected to keep alive in their disciplines."

Yet another faculty member describes the college's philosophy of teaching in these words: "The college does not seek professionals, but rather amateurs in the true sense of the word: teachers who love teaching, who love their disciplines, who are willing to learn from their work and their students, who are willing to make personal sacrifices for a larger aspiration in life."

Student Life: Forming a Community

With such a small student body in a small town in New Hampshire, the casual observer could be forgiven for assuming that social life at Thomas More would be, well, pretty lackluster. In fact, the observer would be dead wrong. Both faculty and students work very hard to assure that a genuine sense of community is fostered at the college — a sense that begins in the classroom with vigorous discussions and extends to lectures, field trips, dining halls, and other elements of collegial living.

"The students live in community," says a professor. "What this means in terms of social life is that they will be required to live and work with others who are as imperfect as they are — those who suffer from contradictions of spirit and body, from anti-social tendencies, from the spirit of rebellion and passion, from deliberate foolishness." Says another faculty member: "The small size of the college fosters lively conversations in class and even at the dinner table, enhanced by the fact that every student is reading the same book at the same time in the core curriculum and . . . that many faculty dine with the students." This person continues, describing the college as "an institution that has a life of its own, which will extend beyond the lives of its present members. It was not founded to meet immediate needs but to root itself into the depth of human nature." Yet it certainly does meet the immediate needs of many students; for example, about 70 percent of its graduates go on to graduate or professional school.

Another faculty member sums up social life in these words: "There are no partisan groups on campus. Students are encouraged to participate in school sponsored activities and events such as the Friday night lecture series, weekend coffee houses, movie nights, choir, and various student-organized poetry and art groups."

Day-to-day life at Thomas More is occupied with preparation for and attendance in class — tasks not to be taken lightly in an atmosphere in which there is no way to disappear into the faceless crowd. There are no fraternities or sororities and no varsity sports. Intramural sports are left up to the students themselves, who participate either on campus or at a health club next to the college, where memberships are available to students. Facilities there include a pool, weight room, jogging track, and tennis, basketball, volleyball, and racquetball courts.

An important part of community life at Thomas More is the lecture series, which brings noted speakers to campus five or six times a semester. Held on Friday nights, the lectures (and film series) draw the faculty and most students, who are expected to attend. This fact reflects more the ease with which students are kept on campus than any effort to force them to stay around for the weekend. As a professor says, "Thomas More is the opposite of a suitcase college. The residential life is considered crucial. Weekends are for studying, for social events on campus, and for day trips, say, to Boston or Cambridge." Says another: "Students are expected to organize and administer the social life of campus. They do this with interest and verve. As a result the social life is interesting and varied. Friday night lectures and film series organized by the faculty help continue the academic spirit well into the weekend."

Merrimack lies about forty miles north of Boston, so that day trips to that city are a popular way to take advantage of the urban environment. Other popular destinations are the mountains of the surrounding states and of New Hampshire itself, and the seacoast. School-sponsored transportation is available for day trips to Boston, Maine, and historic sights in the area.

According to college material, "Dormitory life is ordered to provide the peace and security necessary for study. . . . Faculty often take meals with the students and sometimes also reside on campus." As a Catholic college, Thomas More offers daily mass, as well as special programs, days of recollection, and occasional retreats.

The student body is more diverse than one might imagine for such a small New England school. Over half of its recent graduating class is from beyond the immediate region, with representatives from Arizona, New York, Pennsylvania, Louisiana, Ontario, and even Australia, as well as New England. Others hail from Minnesota, Maryland, Texas, and Alaska. In fact, it is not uncommon for more students to come from California than from New Hampshire.

A faculty member, speaking of the advantages of coming to Thomas More from large universities, notes that "As a rule, students who transfer here from large universities remark that they have a greater number and variety of friends here than they did at the larger institutions, where they tended actually to become well acquainted with only a few people. Here they know everyone and have discussed, in the classroom itself, the ultimate questions. People remark on the variety of characters who flourish in these studies. There is no typical Thomas More student or alumnus."

Perhaps the single best advertisement for TMC can be found in a comment by one recent alumnus: "Thomas More College is probably the only place where you can read a Shakespeare play, translate Greek, write a paper, wash dishes, chat with a professor, pray, laugh, rake leaves, sing, finish a novel, attend class, and read poetry aloud, all between lunch and dinner."

TUFTS UNIVERSITY

Office of Undergraduate Admissions
Bendetson Hall
Medford, MA 02155-7057
(617) 627-3170
www.tufts.edu

Total enrollment: 8,708
Undergraduates: 4,718
SAT Ranges (Verbal/Math): V 600-690, M 630-700
Financial aid: 39%
Applicants: 12,291
Accepted: 32%
Enrolled: 33%
Application deadline: Jan. 1
Financial aid application deadline: Feb. 1
Tuition: $22,230
Core curriculum: No

Crowded Boston Market

Tufts University was founded by members of the Universalist Church in 1852, but is now a secular school with about 4,500 undergraduates and 4,000 graduate students on its campus five miles from Boston. The school has always had a rather progressive outlook, beating other colleges to several punches throughout its history. To take just one example, Tufts had many students in preprofessional programs years before such schools were fashionable.

Today the university prides itself on its rather large number of interdisciplinary and multicultural programs, as well as its aggressive affirmative action hiring and admissions policies. It has some fine liberal arts programs, but its College of Engineering and other preprofessional programs are still among its strongest. Multiculturalism is seeping into the liberal arts curriculum, and more and more that curriculum is coming to resemble those found at other schools in the United States, not to mention New England and Boston. It remains to be seen whether this likeness will make Tufts just another Boston-area college, lost in the shuffle of better-known and better-endowed Northeast liberal arts colleges.

Academic Life: To Each His Own

Students in the university's College of Liberal Arts must take a relatively large number of general education classes, which are divided into two categories: foundation requirements and distribution requirements. The general education courses are not mandated by name, but by subject matter. "There is no rigid program of courses that must be taken by every student," the catalogue says. "Students are regarded as individuals and each student is encouraged to pursue a course of study appropriate to his or her training, experience, aptitudes, and plans for the future."

The foundation requirements include two semesters of writing, a number of courses in foreign languages and cultures, and an elective course in world civilizations. The writing requirement can be reduced by a number of testing-out procedures, and because of that, one student calls it "weak" and "counter productive." The foreign language and cultures requirement is more substantial: take three semesters in a foreign language (or test out to that level) and then take either a fourth semester in that language, another language to the third-semester level, or three courses dealing with "a single cultural area not native to the student," according to the catalogue. Combinations of language and culture studies can also fulfill the second part of the requirement, but the "single cultural area" rule still applies.

However, many of the cultural studies courses are taught with an ideological bias that slights Western and American culture. The one-course world civilizations requirement is much the same way; some traditional students and faculty refer to it as "anything-but-Western-civ." Previously, these were team-taught, interdisciplinary seminar courses. But they were "roundly despised by the students," according to a professor, and, according to a student, "full of preaching about multiculturalism." The requirement has recently been altered: students now choose from a wider selection of courses offered by the humanities and social science distributive areas. The offerings from both of these divisions, however, are noticeably light on European or American history, philosophy, and literature. "Revolution in Latin America" and "Survey in Armenian Arts," however, could count toward the culture courses in the language requirement.

Tufts's distribution requirements are simpler: two courses in each of five areas, including humanities, arts, social sciences, natural sciences, and mathematical sciences. Students are encouraged to choose two courses that are related to one another — the catalogue suggests "Urban Politics" and "Urban Sociology" as a good way to fulfill the social sciences group — but such interrelationship is not required.

One professor says the administration has discussed requiring introductory courses in both Western civilization and world civilization, but he does not expect much to be done in that direction. "What results will probably not be more coherent," he says. Another professor says the natural science and mathematics requirements can be met without truly hard science. The requirements are "stacked towards taking humanities and social sciences," the professor says. For example, several psychology courses count toward the natural science requirement. The professor says that because of this comfortable approach to the distribution requirement, many students do not get the math or science background necessary for advanced coursework. By the same logic, the efficacy of an advanced history or philosophy course are lessened because the student was not required to take a basic survey course that would have provided the context for further study. Beyond these general requirements, most students work toward a specific major in the liberal arts field (history, classical studies, political science, physics), but there is also the "plan of study" option that is more interdisciplinary. Recent programs accepted as legitimate plans of study have included environmental effects of urbanization, aspects of dance, bilingual education, and nutrition and population in national development.

Outstanding professors at Tufts include George Smith and Hugo Bedau in philosophy; Marcelo Bianconi, Linda Loury, Jeffrey Milyo, and Gilbert Metcalf in economics; Gregory Crane and Dennis Trout in classics; Gerald Gill and George Marcopoulos in history; Eric Todd Quinto in mathematics; and Mingquan Wang, a lecturer in the Chinese department.

The 660-student College of Engineering, separate from the College of Liberal Arts, is very highly regarded by those on campus. A professor in a liberal arts department says he is "impressed with the engineering students — they are among the best students I have had." The College of Engineering and the physics department (in the College of Liberal Arts) jointly offer the well-regarded physics major. According to a professor in another department, physics has "distinguished faculty, and few majors," meaning that students get plenty of access to their fine teachers.

The College of Liberal Arts, with the largest number of departments and 3,700 of Tufts's 4,700 undergraduates, is more varied in the quality of instruction it offers. Economics and philosophy are probably the best departments in terms of commitment to undergraduate teaching. Both departments are small by outside standards, but the majority of professors in both are described by their peers as "fair," "objective," and "balanced." One professor says the graduates of the philosophy program are "impressive." Both departments, as well as religious studies and economics, have succeeded despite a limited number of professors. Another department noted for its solid teaching is biology.

The most popular programs and majors at Tufts are in English, political science, and international relations. However, a professor says, based on conversations with students, that the curricula of English and political science are highly politicized. Course listings in political science include traditional topics in American and international politics, but many focus primarily on current events or a specific subject; there are few courses in social science statistics, econometrics, or other topics with wider applications. The strengths of international relations, meanwhile, can only be measured by "what [students] make of it," a professor says. "[There are] so many ways to fulfill the requirements."

Tufts expends many of its institutional resources in promoting and expanding interdisciplinary studies programs like ethnomusicology, peace and justice studies, world civilizations, and communications and media studies. Some on campus say most of the programs in this classification are overtly political in nature. As one professor puts it, they are "dominated by the literary theory types," which "weakens" the quality of the instruction and curricula.

Political Atmosphere: Preceded by Its Reputation

For the most part, Tufts students don't get involved in campus or national politics. One student active in conservative causes says "there is a small, very loud group of radicals." The rest, according to this student, "are apathetic. They're pro-choice, but don't know why; they're pro-welfare, but don't know why."

But the ones that are involved must be deeply involved. For Tufts has appeared on *Mother Jones* magazine's list of the most politically active campuses, and given that publication's political inclinations, some students must have done something to earn that reputation. Indeed, a professor says he has "a feeling that Tufts is more aggressive in Political Correctness" than most other schools.

Political activism plays a definite role in the intellectual atmosphere, as well as in the hiring process. One professor says Tufts has "a strong form of affirmative action, even to the point of directed faculty searches." Tufts, like many institutions, advertises in university trade publications for a specialist in, say, African-American politics or women in literature, with the unspoken assumption that the successful candidate will represent the particular group mentioned, in this case African-Americans or women. This policy, although technically illegal, is rather common in higher education, and is based on the assumption that only a member of the group in question is qualified to address the issues confronting that group.

A professor says that at Tufts there is "a sense that departments are rewarded or punished for hiring the right or wrong color." Administrators never explicitly define diversity, but the word is used constantly when they discuss their goals. "Prizes are given to students for activity and multicultural stuff," another professor says. "There seems to be a slant in the few initiatives coming out of the administration."

Tufts, like many schools, has endured a controversy over a speech code. The university's original speech code, adopted in 1989, was scrapped in the early 1990s after similar codes at Michigan and Stanford were ruled unconstitutional. In its place the university instituted, very quietly, a vague "bigotry policy." Few students know about the policy, since it appears in neither the course catalogue nor the student handbook. Those interviewed for this guide were not aware of any recent disciplinary actions resulting from the policy, but nothing prevents its use in the future by someone wishing to attack another deemed nonsupportive of his cause.

Political activism has already affected freshman orientation and student government matters. Orientation is "an indoctrination session, with silly skits about date rape and racism," says a student. "It's degrading." In the student senate, some representatives are appointed by designated cultural groups, although a recent move to give those special senators voting powers failed because students thought it unfair. Call it Tufts's version of the Boston Tea Party.

Occasionally, all the available copies of the *Primary Source*, Tufts's independent conservative journal, have been dumped into recycling bins, presumably by those who oppose the paper's positions. A former staff member of the paper says Tufts administrators routinely refuse the *Source*'s interview requests.

Tufts was in the news not long ago for admitting a student named Gina Grant. Grant had been accepted at Harvard, but was denied entrance there when it was discovered that she had lied on her application. More exactly, she had omitted the fact that, as a teenager, she had murdered her parents. But Tufts stepped in and not only accepted Grant as a student, but gave her a large financial grant package and a single room, unheard of for freshmen but in this case somewhat understandable.

Student Life: The Greatest Show on Earth?

Social life at Tufts is not centered on campus, but in nearby Boston. "There's not a big Greek system, not a lot of school spirit," a student says. Freshmen and sophomores, unless they live at home, are required to live on campus, and overall, about 80 percent of undergraduates live in university housing — dormitories, apartments, and special-interest houses. The latter includes language houses, international groups, an African-American house, an environment house, and a "substance-free" house. Eleven fraternities and sororities have chapter houses on campus.

The campus is located in Medford, five miles northwest of Boston, past Cambridge, home to Harvard and the Massachusetts Institute of Technology. Though newer university buildings are constructed in modern architectural styles, much of the hilltop campus is composed of older buildings, and the overall effect is quite traditional.

Tufts offers the usual array of student organizations. College publications list an impressive portfolio of arts-related activities, including drama, art, and music produced and performed by students. There are also many political organizations, including several feminist groups and a Gay, Lesbian, and Bisexual Community group. The campus has religious centers for Catholics, Eastern Orthodox, Protestants, Jews, and Muslims.

Campus speakers represent a variety of philosophies. They have included former president George Bush, historian Arthur Schlesinger, Jr., writer Doris Kearns Goodwin, filmmaker Spike Lee, author Alice Walker, and former surgeon general Joycelyn Elders. Well-known artists like the Boston Camerata, Dave Brubeck, Wynton Marsalis, and Empire Brass have also appeared at Tufts recently.

P. T. Barnum, who donated $50,000 to Tufts in its early years, also gave the school the preserved hide of his most famous elephant, Jumbo, after the pachyderm was hit by a train and killed. The hide was displayed for years in a natural history museum on campus, but was destroyed in a 1975 fire. Jumbo, however, lives on as the namesake for Tufts's athletic teams. The Jumbos compete in thirty-two intercollegiate sports at all three NCAA levels. There are also a number of club sports and intramurals.

TULANE UNIVERSITY

Office of Admissions
210 Gibbon Hall
New Orleans, LA 70118-5680
(504) 865-5731
www.tulane.edu

Total enrollment: 11,250
Undergraduates: 4,800
SAT Ranges (Verbal/Math): V 590-690, M 580-680
Financial aid: 45%
Applicants: 8,510
Accepted: 76%
Enrolled: 21%
Application deadline: Jan. 15
Financial aid application deadline: Jan. 1
Tuition: $22,066
Core curriculum: No

Can't Afford the Trends

For over a century Tulane University has remained one of the South's premier private universities — despite some troubles, financial and otherwise. After a sluggish period in the 1970s during which the university actually spent some of the capital in its endowment, it recovered sufficiently to construct several excellent new buildings during the 1980s and early 1990s and now boasts a new engineering building, new law and business schools, a very large recreation center, and apartment-style dorms for upperclassmen.

Yet today Tulane is again in financial need, and one can question the wisdom of some of the spending decisions of the university president, Eamon Kelley, who has announced his resignation effective after the 1997-98 academic year. A partisan Democrat, Mr. Kelley supported Jesse Jackson's run for the presidency in 1988 and, in 1992, was one of 250 college presidents who signed a statement in support of Bill Clinton. More than most of his predecessors, Kelley has attempted to increase the standing of his school not so much through improved programs or solid scholarship but through the cultivation of fashionable causes and funding from the Ford Foundation and similar outfits dedicated to moving America's schools even further to the left.

Kelley used this money to construct a bureaucratic machine whose leaders spearhead the administration's aggressive pursuit of affirmative action quotas. This is particularly important at this stage of Tulane's history because the past few years have witnessed a precipitous drop in the number of faculty at Tulane's main uptown New Orleans campus. Tulane has just named its new president, Scott Cowen, the former dean of the School of Management at Case Western Reserve. Perhaps Mr. Cowen's background in management will help him confront the school's pressing problems.

Tulane has a past of which it can be proud, but faces a troubled present and uncertain future. Perhaps, ironically, its poverty will turn out to be a friend to those who favor a traditional education over trendy indoctrination. For, since the university lost the ability to pay top salaries to the most intellectually stylish of its faculty, many of the more politicized members of its academic community have been lured away by nouveau riches schools like Emory and Duke. Just as New Orleans herself has kept her charm and architectural beauty in no small part because she has been too poor to replace the venerable buildings of her past with the more ephemeral styles of recent decades, so Tulane itself, ever a part of this city, may weather recent absurdities of academic fashion and emerge stronger for having been behind the times.

Academic Life: The Big Easy

Tulane has no core curriculum, and there will not likely be a sudden push for one — at least not from the scholars dedicated to traditional education. There is a widespread belief that implementing a core at this juncture in the university's history would be quite dangerous: given the number of radical faculty on campus, as well as the leftist leanings of the administration and its huge affirmative action machine, the potential for mistakes is too great to risk revamping the curriculum now.

The current system, which a prominent faculty member calls "totally insane . . . [and] so tied up in a large set of distribution requirements that it is Byzantine," requires, among other things, one Western culture course and at least one course in a non-Western area. The rest of the minimal distribution requirements include three courses in the humanities and fine arts, three in social sciences, and three in sciences and mathematics, but many courses can count toward the requirements. Because of this archaic and confusing system, concerned faculty try to carve out some niche for students interested in rigorous, nonideological courses even if the courses are not required. The university does offer an honors program in which students can construct their own curricula, but it doesn't appear to be particularly rigorous. Under circumstances such as these, all a conscientious professor can do is offer courses that will fill the gaps left by a curriculum that leaves quality to chance.

But, despite the best intentions of some professors, Tulane is not exactly fertile ground for courses with a traditional liberal arts focus. "It's a political minefield to try to introduce new courses," says one professor, citing the heated opposition to any classes that may be deemed "elitist." Thus, when a proposal was made to introduce a great books–type course a few years ago, it was opposed by forces led by a particular faculty member who argued that such a course would, through its challenging nature, attract the best students, and that it is bad to bring the best students together in such an elitist way. The course was never taught. "No deliberate policy gives a student a good education here," a senior faculty member says. And things are unlikely to change, given that the new provost has approvingly described higher education as a cafeteria.

An existing program targeted by the anti-elitists is the ROTC. Some students have turned to ROTC out of necessity as tuition costs continued to rise. While this is not only harmless, but noble in many ways, it seems that at Tulane — as at many of America's college campuses — the controversy that surrounded the ROTC and similar organizations in the '60s and '70s has yet to fade away. Today at Tulane not a few of the men and women who serve their country and earn their tuition through this corps are afraid to wear their uniforms to class for fear of being mocked by the professor. In some classes membership in ROTC has lowered a student's grade. The students affected cannot usually afford to forgo their scholarships and call home for money, and even those who can should certainly not have to quit serving their country in exchange for equal treatment by their professors.

Similar politics are obvious in the sensitivity training to which freshmen especially, and the rest of the student body as well, are subjected. The office of the dean of students, which a nationally known Tulane professor calls "one of the really bad sub-units at the university," launches various politically correct harangues at students. Over the past several years this type of propaganda has become quite widespread, and the results can be seen in what is less a chilling of free speech than a growing cynicism on the part of students and faculty alike. "Students learn to dissemble, to parrot, and to please, but they don't learn how to think," says a professor who has seen enrollment in his classes increase sharply because he continues to offer rigorous, challenging courses that buck the politicizing trends at the university.

Among the most politicized departments is English, which is now "beyond redemption," according to a teacher in another discipline. Sociology is also very radicalized, a development that will surprise few who agree with another scholar who says that left-wing views are "just an assumption of the discipline." The Department of Spanish and Portuguese is ideological, as is communications, which is run by faculty enamored with "cultural studies" — an academic euphemism for cultural relativism. History is holding its own at the moment, although the retirement of several senior faculty members over the last several years has opened the door for closet radicals to emerge from hiding to attack their more moderate and professionally accomplished colleagues on both political and personal grounds.

One of the best departments is philosophy, which has done a remarkably good job of hiring and promoting scholars devoted to their research and students rather than any political position. Among its star members are Rona Burger, John Glenn, and Eric Mack. In history Sam Ramer, George Bernstein, Ken Harl, Wilfred McClay, and Colin McGloughlin are all dedicated teachers. Political science is less politicized than most departments, and Paul Lewis, Bob Robbins, David Clinton, and Gary Remer require their students to read primary sources rather than secondary literature. Michael Kucynski in English is very popular with students for his clear presentation of difficult medieval literature, and Bill Alworth in chemistry is said to be very capable and willing to dedicate a great deal of time to his students. In anthropology Harvey and Victoria Bricker have for years made Tulane a leader in the study of Mesoamerican culture. The university's links to that region (the president's house, a mansion on St. Charles Avenue, was donated by United Fruit) are also reflected in its excellent Latin American Studies Program, which boasts over sixty allied faculty from numerous disciplines and schools. The Murphy Institute of Political Economy offers an undergraduate degree, and the economics department tends to be libertarian. Judy Schaeffer stands out as a dedicated and hardworking teacher in the Murphy Institute.

Political Atmosphere: The Off-Target "Target Search"

Even though in recent years Tulane's enrollment has increased modestly and the number of courses taken has gone up by 20 percent, the faculty has decreased by no fewer than thirty positions, or almost 15 percent. This sounds bad, and it is. The administration compounds the problem because it will rarely fund a new or replacement faculty slot except through what it calls a "target search." This program, run by the Dean for Multicultural Affairs, is dedicated to curing what the administration terms the "racism" at Tulane by giving money (most of it from the Ford Foundation) only for jobs that will go to minority candidates. Given the shortage of faculty in most departments, this means, in practice, that any department will have a hard time filling a vacancy unless it conducts a target search. Otherwise, the dean is unlikely to approve the department's request for funds, and the shortage will continue — much to the detriment of the students, who will have a smaller choice of classes, and the professors themselves, who must continue to offer a selection of courses smaller than what is necessary to attract serious undergraduates to their disciplines.

These target searches are conducted by employing a new version of the "good old boy" network that has been so maligned in recent years. To wit: once the target search is initiated according to the normal methods (advertising in national publications like the *Chronicle of Higher Education*), a word-of-mouth search is launched to discover whether anyone already on the faculty, or in the faculty's network, knows of any minority candidates "in the pipeline," i.e., in the final stages of their graduate career. This word-of-mouth campaign goes well beyond the requirements of the law; its sole purpose is to serve blatantly political ends.

While Tulane is not the most oppressive place in the country, freedom of expression is still embattled there. A well-known professor notes: "Higher education is increasingly about acquiring attitudes and opinions one puts on like a uniform." This demand for conformity weighs heavily on both faculty and students.

Thus, faculty are increasingly reluctant to speak up in opposition to radical theories for fear of being denied tenure, socially ostracized, or even sued. More than one faculty member has looked into purchasing insurance not unlike that acquired by medical doctors for malpractice.

Conservative faculty members have in the recent past been hounded and persecuted on purely political grounds. Some well-known and highly regarded scholars have come ridiculously close to being denied tenure after being attacked by colleagues. Personal jealousies, always present among professionals judged on their output and intellectual capabilities, are often combined with philosophical differences to drive from the profession those who in earlier times would have excelled in their careers. As one professor puts it, "There is still a tolerable degree of intellectual freedom, but you have to be willing to pay the price of social ostracism. You get used to it."

Campus Life: New Orleans, a Second Education

A significant element of Tulane, at least in its proud history, is Sophie Newcomb College for women. Predating Radcliffe and Barnard, which were modeled upon it, Newcomb College was the source of Newcomb Pottery, which today is extremely valuable. Graduates of Newcomb College receive diplomas with the name of their college on it, but in fact both Newcomb, for women, and the Paul Tulane College of Arts and Sciences, for men, share the same curriculum in what is a thoroughly coeducational arrangement.

Students at Tulane hail from all over the nation, with a particularly strong contingent from the Northeast. The uptown campus (the medical school is downtown) is pretty and is situated in a very desirable neighborhood. Living in New Orleans is itself an education, and students who go to Tulane get to experience firsthand one of the most interesting and eclectic cities in the nation. Just across St. Charles Avenue from the campus is the Frederick Law Olmstead–designed Audubon Park, with its public golf course, jogging and walking trails, and lagoons. Across Magazine Street at the opposite end of the park is Audubon Zoo, one of the nation's finest, with exhibits that mimic the animals' home territory. The Mississippi River flows by the zoo just on the other side of a huge levee that keeps New Orleans dry. The St. Charles Avenue streetcar runs up and down that street, providing an easy and enjoyable way for Tulane students to ride downtown to visit the French Quarter. The food and entertainment found everywhere in New Orleans are hard to match, and the beaches of the Gulf Coast are only a few hours away.

Unfortunately, New Orleans is also one of the most violent cities in the nation. Students should not avoid coming to Tulane for fear of crime, but they should be extremely careful once they arrive.

Of course, there are plenty of safe and interesting things to do on campus. Tulane has dozens of student clubs and organizations, ranging from the political (Tulanians against Leftism; Bisexual, Gay and Lesbian Alliance; Celebrate Difference) to the cultural (Tulane Literary Society) to service-oriented and religious groups (Community Action Council of Tulane, Green Club, InterVarsity, and Hillel).

Sports are a major part of everyday life at Tulane. The football team has its loyal supporters, but the men's basketball team claims the devotion of a horde of passionate fans. And many of the women's teams are at the top of their divisions. In addition, there are twenty-seven club sports and dozens of intramural teams.

VANDERBILT UNIVERSITY

Director of Admissions
401 Twenty-fourth Avenue, South
Nashville, TN 37212-9976
(615) 322-2561
www.vanderbilt.edu

Total enrollment: 10,250
Undergraduates: 5,880
SAT Ranges (Verbal/Math): V 600-680, M 610-700
Financial aid: 35%

Applicants: 9,487
Accepted: 60%
Enrolled: 30%
Application deadline: Jan. 15
Financial aid application deadline: Feb. 1
Tuition: $21,930
Core curriculum: No

Less Noble

Vanderbilt University, like Tulane, Duke, and Emory, was for most of its existence a Southern gentlemen's school whose student body and faculty were drawn mostly from its home region. Twenty years after the school opened in 1875, a fire gutted its library and destroyed nearly 80 percent of the 23,500 volumes housed there. The children of Nashville collected coins to pay for a bronze bell in the tower of the building (now called Kirkland Hall) that replaced the razed Main Building. That bell remains there today, inscribed with the dictum "Ring in the Nobler Mode of Life."

For much of its history, Vanderbilt did just that. Perhaps the best-known intellectual movement in the school's history is The Fugitives, a group of agrarian poets and men of letters who taught in Vanderbilt's English department and wrote eloquently about the loss of culture in the New South. That culture remained the principal influence at Vanderbilt long after the bulldozers destroyed much of the Old South, and even today Vanderbilt is more Southern than its private school peers of the region. There is enough of the past left at Vanderbilt to ensure that a student who knows how to find the best professors can still benefit from the remnants of a strong academic program. Vanderbilt's curriculum and teaching (with some glaring exceptions) are at this writing not so far gone as those at comparable schools, where the forces of ideology have made deeper inroads.

It is not likely that Vanderbilt will ever rank among the most politicized institutions in the land, but neither will it return to its best days unless a correction is made in the university's course. Time and time again, faculty say the school is not replacing professors in key areas of study and is instead seeking out trendy scholars to add to its ranks. Vanderbilt is significantly more politicized today than it was only a decade ago, and there is no sign that these trends are slowing down.

Academic Life: A Paper Tiger

Most of Vanderbilt's 5,880 undergraduates work out of the College of Arts and Sciences, and even those who don't (the 2,000 or so enrolled in schools of music, engineering, and education, among other majors) must take a sizable number of courses in the College. It sounds a little bit like a core, at least for those in the College, but that's all it is — a little bit like a core. While the number of required classes and the order in which they must be taken are standards to which the College's students are held, far too many options are available for the curriculum to even approach a common core. "We have distribution requirements, although there are requirements for certain types of courses in certain fields," says a professor. "Some courses are soft at the center."

A past chancellor is quoted in the university catalogue as saying: "The work of the College of Arts and Sciences is fundamental. It is the basis of professional study. No professional school can be self-sufficient. The College in its undergraduate and graduate work must remain the heart of the whole situation, and send its quickening life blood into every fiber and tissue." That was in 1925, but to its credit Vanderbilt has — so far, at least — resisted the moneymaking lure of preprofessional undergraduate programs that prepare students for a job but not necessarily for something greater. Those seeking a B.A. degree in one of the College's twenty-three majors must pass 120 hours of classes, with no more than 6 hours (in most cases) resulting from "approved professional work." All students, including those who major in education (traditionally one of the weaker majors in large state universities and many private schools as well), must essentially double-major in a field in the arts and sciences, and even B.S. students in College majors can count only 16 hours of work outside the College.

A freshman seminar is required before a student can advance to sophomore standing. Limited to no more than 20 students per section, seminars introduce freshmen to scholarly methodologies and problems. Depending on the quality of the professor teaching the seminar, this required class can be a worthwhile experience. After the freshman year, students begin the College's Program in Liberal Education, which entails distribution requirements in writing, mathematics, foreign language, history and culture (both American and international), humanities, natural sciences, and social sciences. And that is where students really start to go their separate ways, despite the fact that they all choose from the same list of courses.

The requirements seem solid at first look, but a large number of classes are taught by teaching assistants (TAs) who are not always well trained, and who, oddly, often have sole responsibility for selecting the books that will be taught in the class. Some professors also have a tendency to use their classes as rallies, teaching strongly political messages packaged in academic garb. "In none of these courses is there a standard reading list," says one professor. "The rawest TA is allowed, within very broad limits, to decide what books he will teach and how he will teach them. No two courses are alike; no two students get the same education. Many of the sections are devoted to political and social propaganda. The result is chaotic at best."

Not only do students in the same classes not read the same books, but Vanderbilt has an unusually complex mechanism by which students with good SAT or advanced placement exam scores can skip certain courses fundamental to a broad liberal arts education, including writing and mathematics. This further undermines the education and intellectual community at Vanderbilt. "I often get senior students who opted out of English 101 and are miserable writers," one professor says. "It is a flawed and weak attempt to give students a broad liberal education. Also, there is no insistence on a foreign language and there are all sorts of ways around it."

Add to this the watering down of traditional material and standards, apparent at Vanderbilt and many other universities, and the result — especially in the liberal arts — is like a thin soup with bits of meat available only to motivated students with a talent for finding the best professors. "The people who are majoring in the natural sciences get stronger material in their majors than do those in the liberal arts," says a professor. "You have to learn certain things to do science, but we've removed all the difficult work for them [in the liberal arts]."

Vanderbilt offers majors in all the traditional fields, and has thus far eschewed the temptation to offer majors such as gender studies or women's studies. However, it does offer interdisciplinary majors in African-American studies and urban studies, as well as minors in environmental studies and women's studies. Given recent decisions by the administration, including the appointment in the English department of a chair of gay and lesbian studies, it seems likely that the number of agenda-driven courses, and perhaps even majors, will grow.

Much of the shortfall in Vanderbilt's academic quality can be blamed on the ascendancy of politically correct ideology at the school. In the English department, for example, not even the South, which for so many years lent Vanderbilt its character, young people, money, and gentility, is safe. "The principal teacher of Southern literature hates the South and chooses his texts to show what's wrong with the South and Southerners," a professor says. "People who teach American literature hate America and show the same in the books they use and the way they teach. The cry of racism is a refrain that runs through much of what is taught."

And this occurs in what is thought to be one of Vanderbilt's strongest non-science programs, English. Although the department is not now the pillar it once was, it still is home to some of the university's best professors, namely, Mark Jarman, Chris Hassel, John Plummer, Emerson Brown, Roy Gottfried, Walter Sullivan, Harold Weatherby, and Leonard Nathanson.

Joel Harrington of the history department is also an excellent teacher, but the history department as a whole, like others on campus, suffers from the same misguided patterns of thought now affecting English. "I know that the man who teaches Southern history thinks of the South as a problem which he must try to repair through his teaching," says a professor. "I think it's pretty much the same story everywhere except in the hard sciences."

Political Atmosphere: I Don't Hate the South — I Don't, I Don't

Vanderbilt came relatively late to the ideological wars, and even now there are sectors at the school where the bullets have not yet begun to fly. Some on campus note that, despite the deteriorating political climate, the majority of students remain unaffected. "During my last two years there were noticeable attempts to become more trendy and offer a politicized curriculum," a recent graduate says. "It very much depended on your department and your course of study. You can have excellent professors in some courses, politically correct ones in others." Vanderbilt students tend to gravitate toward courses that ask them to read timeless books rather than the latest in radical political manifestos. It's a pity more of the former are not offered. The reason: the faculty is considerably more liberal than the students, according to representatives of both groups.

Vanderbilt does subscribe to the notion that multicultural initiatives somehow bring about harmony on campus, though the university embraces the tenets of multiculturalism in a more abstract manner than most places. As one professor said, "We're supposed to all get along and be nice to each other so that no one's feelings will be hurt." University literature on freshman programming has a section entitled "Commitment to Diversity" that states:

> Vanderbilt is a geographically, ethnically, and culturally diverse community composed of people of different ages, sexes, races, socioeconomic backgrounds, sexual orientations, religious beliefs, and physical abilities. In order to prepare our students for the future, we nurture this community and encourage our students to develop an understanding of and appreciation for the differences among individuals. While at Vanderbilt, students will have the opportunity to examine the ways in which racism, sexism, religious intolerance and homophobia act as divisive forces within our democratic society. Students will also have the opportunity to evaluate critically their own beliefs, attitudes, and values in light of their exposure to and contact with persons with different beliefs, attitudes, and values.

This critical evaluation is supposed to be helped along by a speech code, although the one at Vanderbilt is not always enforced. A former TA says he ignored the university's inclusive language directives in his classes and was not admonished. Of course, the reverse is also true: more trendy TAs who use or enforce the speech code even beyond what the university asks are not likely to be reined in either.

A main control mechanism, however, for the so-called critical evaluation expected of all students is the Office of Housing and Residential Education and Student Health. All freshmen must undergo three residential life programs sponsored by this office. In the first they are taught about "health issues such as HIV infection, as well as the use and abuse of drugs and alcohol." A second residential life program discusses dating and sexuality, with a focus on "sexual coercion, acquaintance rape, and sexually-transmitted diseases." And the third, as might be expected, centers on "the value of diversity in the residential community." This final program is clearly an effort to enforce an orthodox view of diversity (i.e., a heterodox view of society), and the irony resulting from such an attempt is certainly not intended.

Many Vanderbilt faculty believe that the South itself is something of an anachronistic backwater, and, overall, it seems that many younger faculty are ashamed of Vanderbilt's Southern, conservative traditions. More than a few would be elated if the school were to become more like Duke University, where multicultural-ism is deeply ensconced.

As at other institutions, recent faculty hires at Vanderbilt favor those who teach intellectual trends rather than the great books. By 1998 the English department will contain just one Shakespeare scholar, down from three only a few years ago. In many cases senior professors who leave Vanderbilt are simply not replaced. Again using English as an example, a Milton scholar who retired in 1997 was not replaced, nor was the department's senior scholar in nineteenth-century American literature. Soon the scholars in Spenser and modern American literature will retire, and will not likely be replaced by anybody nearly so expert in those fields.

One professor recalls asking a younger colleague what kind of literature he enjoyed. Much to the professor's surprise and horror, the man said he didn't read literature of any kind. The senior scholar thought the man had to be kidding, but he was adamant in his statement. He didn't read literature, he said, because he didn't have time to read such stuff, and found it boring anyway. He read theory and cultural studies instead. Both men were English professors.

However, at least one scholar believes that Vanderbilt has a chance to salvage some departments, including English. But concerned alumni and students had better make their demands now. "Those of us retiring now and within the next ten or fifteen years will not live to see the damage that is being done now repaired," says a professor. "The politically correct will not give up the universities, one of their last bastions of power, easily. The wrong people are in control. The universities are not going to heal themselves. They will have to be cleaned up from the outside, but it's terribly difficult to make people outside the academic community believe what goes on within that community."

Campus Life: We Are Not Making This Up

Commodore Cornelius Vanderbilt, the New York railroad and shipping magnate, in-dustrialist and banker, donated $1 million in 1873 to build and endow the university that now bears his name, yet he died shortly thereafter and never visited the school. Nevertheless, students who come to Vanderbilt today benefit from a name recogni-tion that cannot be bought. Over 5,800 undergraduates and 4,200 graduate and pro-fessional students attend the Nashville school. Almost one-third of the undergraduates major in the social sciences and history, a percentage that is double the national average for similar schools. This impressive statistic owes much to another impressive fact: the lack of an undergraduate business major at Vanderbilt.

While for most of the university's past its students were mainly from the South, the 1996 freshman class of more than 1,500 students reflected a two-decade-long trend at Vanderbilt in that only about 600 of them were Southerners. More than 250 freshmen came from the Midwest, with about 200 from both the Middle Atlantic and Southwestern states, and about 100 from both New England and the West. Nearly 90 students were from other nations.

Once in Nashville, freshmen must live on campus unless they can obtain special permission. A set of freshman dorms is set aside for the incoming class, and, overall, about 85 percent of the undergraduate student body resides on campus, a very high percentage for a school of Vanderbilt's size. The Greek system is very large and well established (but not residential, except for up to six officers per chapter), with over half the men and a third of the women as members.

The dorm students at Vanderbilt are allowed to vote on some of the rules for life in each dorm. Decisions left up to the student residents include quiet hours, the hours the dorm will be open to visitation by members of the opposite sex, and the attendance requirements for and frequency of dorm meetings. Vanderbilt also leaves one other issue to the students' young minds: whether the condom machines in certain residence halls will be stocked that year.

Another less-than-thrilling program at Vanderbilt is the Mayfield Living/Learning Lodge Program, in which ten students live together in one of six lodges and spend the year working together on a chosen project. The projects are described by the university as "self-directed, year-long program[s] of educational activities," and while one can easily see that they are indeed "self-directed," finding a college-level "educational" component is a much greater challenge. Projects in the 1996-97 academic year included: "Women of Today and Tomorrow," "Sporting a New Image," "I Believe in Me," "Womanhood as Seen through Diverse Cultures," "Pets and People Partnership," "Less Talk, More Action," and "Social Awareness."

The university also offers the McGill Project, described as "a unique living-learning experience at Vanderbilt." In fact, it sounds a lot like the Mayfield Living/Learning Lodges. This dorm, which one student calls "the most liberal group at school," is premised on the university's belief that "if students who live together focus around an educational purpose, their residential experience will have a more significant meaning." According to the university, McGill is host to "fun, interactive programs [which] have included making slime with a chemistry professor and learning how musical instruments from Africa are used to convey feeling and emotion."

While these residence halls certainly attract the liberal students at Vanderbilt, their atmosphere does not seem typical of the university. The campus and its community are described perhaps more accurately by one professor in this way: "Vanderbilt is a very expensive school which enrolls many rich students. Most of these are interested in getting into good professional schools and in having a good time when they're not working. Like all student bodies, ours breaks down into a number of interest groups, but we are not an intensely intellectual or political community."

Sports are an important element of life at Vanderbilt. The school is a member of the Southeastern Conference (SEC), which is known principally as a football conference. Yet Vanderbilt's best teams tend to be in basketball, and it stands out for its commitment to maintaining its membership in the SEC even as it retains the educational requirements for its players. There are also numerous intramural sports formed by dorms and other groups, including the Greeks. Twenty-three club sports are also available.

Off campus, one can do much worse than Nashville. Home of the Grand Ole Opry and the country music industry, the city also provides a huge assortment of restaurants, bars, and attractions. Nashville, like much of the South, has grown a great deal in recent years, and the job opportunities for graduates who want to remain in the area are now quite impressive. Students looking to get away from the city can drive four hours to the Great Smoky Mountains.

VASSAR COLLEGE

Office of Admissions
Director of Admissions
Vassar College
Box 10
Poughkeepsie, NY 12601
(914) 437-7300
www.vassar.edu

Total enrollment: 2,346
Undergraduates: 2,346
SAT Ranges (Verbal/Math): V 630-710, M 590-660
Financial aid: 60%
Applicants: 4,765
Accepted: 42%
Enrolled: 32%
Application deadline: Early decision, Nov. 15, Jan. 1; regular, Jan. 1
Financial aid application deadline: Jan. 1

Tuition: $21,780
Core curriculum: No

Tea and Activism

Founded in 1861 as a pioneer institution in women's liberal arts education, Vassar was long considered one of the "Seven Sisters" — the elite, all-women institutions of higher learning in the eastern United States. Vassar did not become coeducational until 1969, after turning down an invitation to merge with Yale University. When coeducation arrived, social regulations were relaxed and student voices became more prominent in campus decisions. Today Vassar is proud of its image as a "liberal" liberal arts institution with an individualistic and activist bent.

In its current viewbook, Vassar proclaims its mission of "nurturing in its students certain lifelong habits of mind and timeless values: respect for human dignity and freedom, concern for society as well as for oneself, faith in reason, and commitment to action." "Vassar generates a genuine feeling of freedom of inquiry," notes one content professor. But critics of Vassar's unstructured academic program argue that this freedom is often exercised at the expense of a broad liberal arts background.

Despite its adoption of a cutting-edge pose, Vassar still maintains some holdover traditions from its glory days as an elite women's college. All professors are still referred to as "Mr." and "Ms." rather than "professor" or "doctor," and afternoon tea is still served in Vassar's historic Main building.

Academic Life: The Bold and the Flexible

As the college viewbook proclaims, "The Vassar curriculum has always been characterized by boldness, breadth, and flexibility, and curricular innovation has been constant in the history of the college." In keeping with its atmosphere of individuality, there is no core curriculum at Vassar, although a few distribution requirements are mandated, including a freshman writing course, a course on numeracy (statistics, logic, math, psychology), and a demonstrated proficiency in a foreign language. In addition, all freshmen must select at least one course from among a number of "Freshman Courses," introductory courses with enrollments of fewer than 20 students. It is also "strongly recommended" that students take courses in each of Vassar's four divisions (Arts, Foreign Languages and Literatures, Social Sciences, and Natural Sciences).

Students also can avail themselves of something called the College Course Program, which offers broad, interdisciplinary courses. The language describing this program is vaguely reminiscent of the justification for a liberal education, though Vassar always falls short of championing the liberal arts: "The College Course Program was established to ensure that students can have direct exposure in their years at Vassar to some important expressions of the human spirit in a context that is both multidisciplinary and integrative." Again, however, College Courses are entirely optional, and thankfully so, for offerings range from "The Evolution of Everything" to "Work, Gender and Social Change" and "Literary Theory."

As far as the general offerings are concerned, "the curriculum is strongly multicultural," notes one professor. Strong programs, majors, and departments include history, philosophy, biology, and art. English is considered "excellent in spots," and programs in the Romance languages provide fine opportunities for study abroad. The economics department offers the full range of disciplinary courses, including introductory and advanced courses on Marxian economics along with a couple on neoclassical economics and game theory. Emphasis, however, seems to be on policy-oriented courses such as "The Political Economy of Health Care," "Work in America: Policy Issues in Labor Economics," and "Environmental and Natural Resource Economics." Although students majoring in economics can choose from among a number of courses in economic history and theory, also offered are such ideologically driven courses as "The Economics of Gender," in which students discuss "controversies over sex in the marketplace, specifically in the cases of prostitution, pornography, and surrogate motherhood."

Indeed, the radicalization of Vassar's curriculum spans several disciplines, and many course descriptions are characterized by a narrow examination of a particular issue. In "Religions of the Oppressed and Third World Liberation Movements," for instance, case studies include "the cult of Jonestown (Guyana), the Iranian revolution, South Africa, slave religion, and aspects of feminist theology." One course is devoted exclusively to the works of South African/Jamaican writer Peter Abrahams. The multidisciplinary program in American culture seems unjustifiably skewed toward twentieth-century America, with courses such as "The Practice of American Social Movements" (which examines only movements that began in the 1960s, including "civil rights, Black Power, Brown Berets, Plowshares, feminism, and national liberation movements") and "Reading the Fights: Boxing and American Values."

Interest in the fine arts abounds at Vassar; students wanting to study art can avail themselves of the Frances Lehman Loeb Art Center, which opened its doors in 1993. The center houses an impressive collection of art, including nineteenth- and twentieth-century European and American art, Greek and Roman sculpture, and ceramics. Vassar students are often characterized by their artistic flair; consequently, the college dramatic performances are frequently bold and avant-garde. The college has a proscenium theater as well as the recently completed Hallie Flanagan Davis Powerhouse Theatre. The latter structure could be considered an embodiment of Vassar's experimental philosophy; as the college catalogue states: "Created by the reconstruction of an old powerhouse, the theater is a model of flexibility."

To its credit, Vassar still maintains an emphasis on small class sizes, and most faculty are willing to serve as both professors and mentors to their students. "Except for Art 104 — a classic and famous survey — and a few introductory courses in astronomy, chemistry, and physics, ALL classes are under 40, most are under 20, and most seminars are about ten students," notes one faculty member. "There is a lot of effort to keep classes small, so learning can come from discussion and joint endeavor."

Many faculty live on campus, and students are generally pleased with the level of attention they receive from their professors. One professor notes that "faculty and students work closely together . . . inquiry and accomplishment are more valued than rote memorization and 'following rules.' "

Extracurricular academic opportunities are numerous, and interested students should comb the college catalogue and discuss with faculty and other students the unique internship, research, and study-abroad possibilities. "There are lots of internships from the Ford Foundation available in the summer for humanities students," notes one professor. There are also research opportunities in the sciences under faculty guidance, along with a host of impressive semester or year study programs. Vassar participates in the Twelve College Exchange Program, so students may spend a year or semester at schools like Amherst, Bowdoin, Dartmouth, Wheaton (Mass.), and Williams. Vassar also has a seven-week summer program in Münster, Germany; internships at British primary schools or at the Clifden Community School in scenic Galway, Ireland; and numerous junior-year-abroad programs.

Political Atmosphere: Spectators and Participants

Vassar hosts a variety of political student organizations, ranging from the College Democrats to the Republican/Libertarian Alliance and the Young Socialists Club. There are also a number of special-interest clubs, including the Women's Coalition, the Black Student Union, the Student Activist Union, the South Asian Students Alliance, and Queer Coalition.

Students also serve on a host of college committees, alongside faculty and administration. The college boasts in its promotional literature that when it became coeducational, "students acquired more opportunities for self-government and a greater share in the processes by which college decisions are made." Indeed, a partial listing of joint committees intimates the extent to which mammoth bureaucracies drain valuable time and resources at Vassar and other small institutions: the Master Planning Committee, the Student Curriculum Committee, the Health and Counseling Committee, Financial Aid Committee, Residential Life Advisory Committee, Security Advisory Committee, Buildings and Grounds Advisory Committee, Admissions Committee. Probably formed in no small part to head off student protest of unpopular administrative decisions, the committees frequently seem mired in confusion and inactivity. In a recent student newspaper article (April 25, 1997), students complained that their role was often advisory and thus ineffective, and that their opinions weren't valued by senior committee members. In general, though, relations between students and administrators are very cordial; as one professor notes, "The administration is fair, competent, and hard-working, and thus popular with faculty and students."

Facilities for Asian, black, Latino, and Native American students housed in the Inter Cultural Center are impressive. As has been the case at most colleges and universities, other "marginalized" groups are likewise scrambling to get a piece of the minority pie. Recently some students and alumni indicated support for the establishment of a separate cultural space for Vassar's homosexual community. Writing in the campus newspaper, a '96 graduate argues: "Vassar recognizes other minority cultures, like African-Americans, Asian-Americans and Latinos. They have a cultural center on campus, receive funding for educational, historical and pride purposes. They have become specific disciplines. . . . [Vassar needs to] give the queer community what we have been living without: financial support and full acceptance as a community and culture. . . . My suggestion: a queer center on the Vassar campus."

Vassar does have an alternative newspaper, called the *Vassar Spectator*, which had been considered one of the leading conservative student papers until recently. Subtitled the "Journal of Neglected Ideas," the *Spectator* was once edited by Marc A. Thiessen, press spokesman for Senator Jesse Helms at the Senate Foreign Relations Committee. It received support from such conservative stalwarts as William E. Simon and was featured in *Rolling Stone* magazine for its brashly conservative viewpoint. But the current editorial staff thinks the newspaper's conservative image was "giving the wrong impression and being divisive," according to one student, and it has thus recently abandoned its traditional tenor in favor of a consensus approach.

More than anything else, the *Spectator*'s shift in image may have come about because of fear and intimidation. Nearly ten years ago the paper was "de-authorized," thrown out of its office, and denied the use of school facilities for failing to abide by a student government censorship order. Commenting on the decision of the Vassar Student Association (VSA) to defund and de-authorize the *Spectator*, one administrator remarked, "I think VSA did act responsibly. I have felt for a long time that we have to work against those who will be destructive . . . to the Vassar community." Two years later, in 1990, three editors were charged with "political harassment" and threatened with dismissal for publishing an editorial criticizing the vice president of the student government. A group of students formed the Vassar Coalition for Free Speech and collected more than four hundred signatures on behalf of the beleaguered editors. Charges were dropped two days before the trial, and the clause pertaining to "political speech" was dropped from Vassar's harassment policy.

Indeed, despite its public emphasis on academic freedom, the limits of free speech are continually being redefined at Vassar. In the spring of 1997, for instance, two student editors of the *Vassar Daily*, a small campus newsletter, resigned amidst student outcry over the publication of a controversial satire on ebonics, the vernacular spoken by some black people. While the satire was arguably in poor taste (in addition to demeaning blacks, its language was offensive to women), student reaction was swift and extreme. According to the *Chronicle of Higher Education,* "The student government froze the newsletter's budget until rules for the publication could be reviewed."

The current president, Francis Fergusson, receives mixed reviews generally, but, according to one faculty member, "is outstanding, and has great rapport with colleagues and faculty." Tenure decisions at Vassar have not been without controversy in recent years. According to one professor, "Tenure decisions are rigorous and scrupulously fair, and very exhaustive." Still, publishing and administrative activity seem to be given uneven priority in tenure decisions, considering Vassar's commitment to undergraduate teaching. "A candidate must show evidence of more than competent teaching," notes one professor. "Scholarship counts a great deal, as does service." Indeed, Vassar's tenure review process has been under legal scrutiny ever since a high-profile discrimination suit was filed twelve years ago. Dr. Cynthia Fisher, a biology professor, argued that Vassar denied her tenure because she was a married woman and had taken time away from her profession to raise her children. In 1994 she was awarded over half a million dollars and a tenured position by a federal district court; that decision was overturned in 1995 and upheld on a technicality in a 1997 appeal. Vassar continues to claim that Dr. Fisher's "absence from the field had left a major gap in her knowledge," yet the biologist had more peer-reviewed articles in prestigious journals than her three male, tenured colleagues and had been awarded grants from the National Science Foundation. Commenting on the court's latest ruling, Dr. Fisher told the *Chronicle of Higher Education:* "It's a terrible decision, not just for me, but for all the women who take time off to take care of their families."

In general, "diversity" seems to permeate all aspects of Vassar life, although conservative students would argue that such diversity rarely extends to an inclusion of and tolerance for their views. Indeed, conservatives are conspicuously absent from a sampling of recent high-profile speakers at Vassar, which includes Angela Davis, Hillary Clinton, Meryl Streep, Paul Theroux, and Billy Joel.

Student Life: From A to Zeitgeist

Vassar's campus is classically beautiful, with scores of mature trees and monumental buildings. Its oldest and largest building, Main Hall, boasts a facade designed by James Renwick Jr. and was declared a National Historic Landmark in 1986. Part of Main Hall was renovated and expanded a couple of decades ago to create a mammoth College Center that houses, among other things, computer facilities, a snack bar, a cafe, a post office, a bookshop, a radio station, and the college pub, Matthew's Mug.

Over 95 percent of Vassar students live on campus in one of nine residence halls housing from 130 to 300 students each. There is only one remaining single-sex dormitory, Strong Hall. Among other amenities, each dormitory has a parlor equipped with a Steinway piano for students' use. In 1992 the university began a "Substance

Free Corridor" program to offer students a smoke-, alcohol-, and drug-free environment. About 330 students take advantage of this opportunity, in which strict rules regarding smoking, drinking, and noise levels are enforced.

Vassar students compete at the NCAA Division III level in 24 intercollegiate sports, ranging from lacrosse and field hockey to men's baseball. The college also recently welcomed rowing as a varsity sport, after purchasing a ten-acre site on the Hudson River and constructing a new docking facility and a three-building rowing complex.

The college also makes a number of vocal and theatrical organizations available to students, ranging from the Renaissance Singers and the Serenading Club to Improv and the Ebony Theatre Ensemble. A limited number of nonvarsity athletic clubs are also available, including cycling, ski, sailing, and equestrian clubs.

Perhaps one of the few aspects of the college to remain constant over the years is its secure financial health. During the past couple of decades, the college has exceeded expectations in a number of capital campaigns and managed to build endowments for scholarships, faculty salaries, visiting professorships, and curriculum and building development. The college annually awards $13 million of its own money for need-based scholarships. With tuition alone hovering around $22,000, this is welcome news to students without an easy means of financial support.

In sum, the Vassar zeitgeist seems to be one of unfettered freedom and exploration conducted in an atmosphere of academic permissiveness. As one professor notes, "Risk-taking, independence and difference are cherished here.... Vassar is not for the timid or totally conventional student." Vassar assumes that her students are wise and mature enough to chart their own course, although some would contend that this is a rather sentimental assumption to make regarding most of today's college youth.

VILLANOVA UNIVERSITY

Office of Undergraduate Admission
Austin Hall
Villanova University
800 Lancaster Avenue
Villanova, PA 19085-1672
(800) 338-7927
www.vill.edu

Total enrollment: 9,450
Undergraduates: 6,320
SAT Ranges (Verbal/Math): V 550-650, M 560-650
Financial aid: 49%
Applicants: 9,250
Accepted: 65%
Enrolled: 27%
Application deadline: Jan. 15
Financial aid application deadline: Feb. 15
Tuition: $18,370
Core curriculum: Yes

An August Institution

Villanova was founded in 1842 by the Augustinian Order of the Roman Catholic Church. Today Villanova's beautiful 222-acre campus west of Philadelphia is still run by the order, and many professors and administrators are priests or nuns. About 90 percent of the student body is Catholic, but the university welcomes students of all faiths.

The six thousand undergraduates and four thousand graduate students attend a university that is not only strong academically, but which preserves religious values in its student life policies and daily life. Some professors describe Villanova as an extremely compassionate, caring community that is ideal for students who are well rounded, confident, and serious.

Politicization, including some doses of "liberation theology," has crept into the curriculum recently, but has done little to detract from the excellent core requirements found especially in Villanova's College of Liberal Arts and Sciences, wherein all students still read classic texts by the greatest minds of Western culture. Furthermore, the requirements have expanded recently, rather than shrinking as they have at so many other schools, Catholic universities included.

Academic Life: The Old Masters

All four units of Villanova University — the College of Liberal Arts and Sciences, the College of Commerce and Finance, the College of Engineering, and the College of Nursing — ask students to take at least one course in religion and to meet at least some liberal arts requirements. The College of Liberal Arts and Sciences, the home of most of the university's departments, naturally requires a good deal more in the way of liberal arts courses than the others. The general education requirements there are complex and demanding.

At the center of this college's requirements is the Core Humanities program, well regarded by students and professors alike. Under this requirement, all freshmen must take two semester-long seminars that expose them to great works of literature and develop in them critical thinking and writing skills. During their first semester, students take "Ancient, Medieval, Renaissance Thought." The reading list for the course is selected by professors, but one text from each of several categories must be represented. The categories are: Old Testament (Genesis, Exodus, or Job recommended), New Testament (a Gospel is recommended), classical Greece, St. Augustine, medieval Europe, and Shakespearean drama. Recommended additional readings are one text from classical Rome and one from a non-Western contemporary of the above categories.

In the second semester of the Core Humanities program, students take "Modern Thought: Enlightenment to the Present." In this class professors choose an "Augustinian theme" and assign readings that illuminate that theme. Texts must be chosen from five different time periods (early modern, Enlightenment, romantic, modernist, and contemporary) and must represent at least three different genres. "What is prescriptive in choosing texts is that your choice be guided by the selection of texts which raise and grapple with fundamental and significant questions concerning the human experience from a variety of perspectives including, but not limited to, the spiritual/religious perspective," the university advises faculty teaching the course.

Core Humanities courses are taught by professors in a variety of departments, meaning that each section is slightly different and can be structured to take advantage of the professor's area of expertise. Students are expected to write at least 30 pages per semester. A dean is assigned to ensure that only the best professors are allowed to teach in the core. "The core is one of the major positive aspects of our university," says one humanities professor.

In addition to the Core Humanities seminar, students in the College of Liberal Arts and Sciences must take one ethics course, one fine arts course, two intermediate-level foreign language courses, two history courses, two literature courses, two mathematics or computer science courses, two philosophy courses, two religion courses, three social science courses, and two courses in the natural sciences (with labs).

From among the courses meeting the general education requirements, at least four must be designated "writing intensive." Four others must be designated "writing enriched." Villanova has a diversity requirement, and students must also pick up two courses that focus on ethnic minorities, women, or non-Western civilizations.

While other universities have removed general requirements in order to allow students more electives or more courses within their majors, Villanova is moving in the opposite direction. It has steadily expanded requirements in the last several years to the point that even students studying commerce or finance must take some particular arts and sciences courses. "I've seen a change for the better in the way the core is being handled," says a professor who advises underclassmen.

Top students at Villanova may opt for the university's honors program, a four-year schedule of challenging seminars, independent research, and other activities. Incoming students apply before their freshman year; returning students may apply at any time. Admission is highly selective and is based on SAT scores (minimum of 1,300, with at least a 600 in both the math and verbal sections), high school class rank, and other achievements. Most students in the program take one or two honors classes every semester, and some pursue other majors in addition to an honors major. While the program is rigorous, some students claim it is biased toward liberal ideas and is intolerant of conservative points of view. It encourages students to become involved in political causes, and most of the speakers the program invites to campus are left of center, students say.

Villanova offers a program in Irish studies that may be taken as a concentration in addition to a student's major area of study. The program explores the history and culture of the Irish people from a variety of disciplines, including literature, art, history, and politics. Students are encouraged to study in Ireland through a semester-abroad program or with the Villanova-in-Ireland summer program at University College, Galway. Other students study in six-week overseas summer programs sponsored by the university in Chile, France, Ireland, Italy, Israel, and Spain.

A new program at Villanova combines academics and residential life. Inaugurated in 1997, "The Villanova Experience" is open to 160 freshmen per year. Students live in the same residence hall and represent different fields of interest, but they enroll in the same core classes and attend special lectures and other events with faculty members. In addition, small group seminars address items like study skills, gender roles, and substance use and abuse. The program was one of the recommendations of a university task force looking for ways to curb alcohol abuse among Villanova students.

Students say professors are helpful and approachable and will go out of their way to assist them. The ratio of students to faculty is a low 13:1. Some outstanding teachers include Lowell Gustafson, John Schrems, and Colleen Sheehan in political science; Marc Gallicchio in history; and James Kirschke, Patrick Nolan, Robert Wilkinson, and Charles Cherry in English.

Professors and students say the two best departments are political science and economics. Classes in the former are divided into three subcategories: American government, comparative government and international relations, and political theory and behavior. The economics faculty, which is part of the College of Commerce and Finance, is also regarded as first-rate.

The philosophy department has a very good curriculum for undergraduates, but its graduate programs are fairly politicized. Deconstructionist philosopher Jacques Derrida seems to be a hero: he has spoken on campus several times in recent years by invitation of the department.

One politicized program is peace and justice, which offers a concentration rather than a major. The program claims to offer courses that are "fundamental to and constitutive of a Catholic university," according to the university catalogue. But in fact, many of the classes are simply platforms for political activism, students say. Pacifism, sexism, racism, world hunger, and the arms race are recurrent topics in peace and justice classes. The program is linked closely to the Villanova Feminist Coalition and environmental groups, and students are encouraged to participate in political activism. "The classes aren't very substantial," says a recent graduate of another program. "They're kind of flaky."

Some other departments, particularly English and history, have a mix of traditionally minded professors and others whose teaching places the criticism of a work at least as high as the work itself. The latter tendency is particularly apparent in upper-level courses. The history department, for example, offers "Senior Colloquium: Race, Class, Gender in World History," which "deals with political economies and historical analysis of race, class, and gender," according to the catalogue. "Particular interest will be given to the evolution of the concept and the ways in which they interact with one another over time."

Political Atmosphere: Retaining Traditional Values

Villanova is led by Fr. Edmund J. Dobbin, a Catholic priest of the Augustinian order. Several other administrators at the university, as well as just over one-third of its board of trustees, are also Augustinians.

One professor describes the administration as "politically neutral," which he says is "not a bad thing, because they're amenable to the intelligent presentation of the traditional side of things." To take just one critical example, the administration has been strongly supportive of the school's core curriculum.

"Most of the administrators lean to the left, but they're big enough people to see that these courses on Disney World and other trendy subjects are insubstantial," the professor says. Similarly, administrators encourage instructors to talk about values and morals in their classes. Administrators at other colleges balk at the notion that such talk should be encouraged, or try to thrust their own values down students' throats. Not at Villanova.

Because the university retains a strong religious influence, many of the value-free social experiments in place elsewhere don't fly at Villanova. Because it is a violation of Catholic doctrine, administrators decline to distribute condoms on campus, for instance, despite desperate pleadings from some students to install condom dispensers in dormitory bathrooms.

Keeping the administration in check is a fairly conservative board of directors and a largely traditional alumni base. Alumni, one professor says, "wouldn't take too kindly to what you have at some schools," such as special self-segregating dormitories for ethnic minorities. "That idea might initially pass here with the administration, but I don't think it would become policy," the professor says. "There would be an immediate uproar from the graduates."

Student Life: The Call

Villanova is a Catholic university, and 90 percent of its students are Catholic, so not only are there many opportunities for students to participate in religious observances, there is also traditional governance of student life and residential policies. "Religious life at Villanova does not reach out and grab you, but it is definitely there," a student says.

The Campus Ministry reflects the traditions of Roman Catholic and Augustinian spirituality through many of its programs, which include, according to university literature, "prayer, liturgy, community service, leadership development, and pastoral care." Mass is offered on campus three times daily during the week and six times on Sundays. In addition, many of Villanova's residence halls have ministers — either Augustinian friars or campus ministry staff — who live in the dorms, maintain office hours, and counsel students. The Campus Ministry Office also provides information on nearby churches, temples, and synagogues for students of other faiths.

In keeping with its Catholic tradition, the university does not officially recognize student groups whose positions run counter to church teaching. Thus, no official homosexual or abortion rights groups exist on campus. Students say the principal voices in political dialogue are the College Republicans and the College Democrats. A feminist coalition is also active, as well as a small but vocal organization called the Democratic Socialists of America. The university has a St. Augustine Club, the purpose of which is to promote and preserve academic integrity at the school.

Rules for student life are also traditional, for the most part. Men and women live in separate halls, and the university enforces a visitation policy that is constantly under debate. As of 1997, residence halls are open to members of the opposite sex from 10 A.M. to midnight on weeknights and from 10 A.M. to 2 A.M. on weekends. This policy is spelled out in the university's "Code of Student Conduct," which also states: "Villanova University believes that a genuine and complete expression of love through sex requires a commitment to living and sharing of two persons in marriage. Consequently, overt sexual behavior and/or overnight visitation by a member of the opposite sex in residential facilities represent flagrant violations of the Visitation Policy and the Code of Student Conduct. Such behavior will result in disciplinary probation and revocation of campus residency of all parties involved."

Villanova's student government has been pushing lately for a more open visitation policy, although it is refreshing to see a college administration take a stand in favor of traditional morality. Students have also complained that some dorms are inadequate and in need of renovation. Another point of contention is the fact that the university only guarantees housing for three years, meaning that seniors may have to find off-campus quarters. Despite debate on the issue, both administrators and some students who live off campus say no one has been forced off campus because of limited dorm space.

Villanova's students are typically bright and hardworking, but some say the campus's academic atmosphere could do with some improvement. "Intellectualism is not something I would standardly associate with Villanova," says one professor, who would like to see "more intellectual discussions spontaneously occur." Perhaps with this criticism in mind, the university in 1997 became the first institution in the country to ban Cliffs Notes from the campus bookstore. In a public memorandum, Vice President for Academic Affairs John Johannes requested that the guides be phased out so that students could do "serious critical and original thinking, rather than working with simplistic study aids." The move came about after ninety professors signed an anti–Cliffs Notes petition.

Though its intellectual climate is under debate, the athletic climate at Villanova is strong. The university consistently fields an excellent men's basketball team, which plays exciting games to sold-out crowds in "The Pavilion"; the Wildcats football squad usually makes the NCAA Division I-AA playoffs. The women's cross-country team has won the national championship six out of the last eight years. In addition to the 12 men's and 12 women's varsity sports, Villanova offers a comprehensive intramural sports program in which more than 80 percent of students participate. There are also several interscholastic club sports.

Fraternities and sororities attract about 30 percent of students. Other campus activities include theater productions, music recitals, and art exhibitions. Well-known speakers visit with some regularity; recent celebrity guests include Maya Angelou, Tom Clancy, Katie Couric, and Dick Vitale.

Villanova, 12 miles west of Philadelphia, isn't a prototypical college town, but the presence nearby of Bryn Mawr, Swarthmore, and Haverford Colleges means there are a lot of students in the area. The town does have a variety of shops and restaurants near the university. Trains and buses stop on campus and can take students into Philadelphia in a matter of minutes to sample the historical attractions, professional sporting events, and other social activities.

UNIVERSITY OF VIRGINIA

Office of Admissions
P.O. Box 9017, University Station
Charlottesville, VA 22906
(804) 982-3200
www.virginia.edu

Total enrollment: 18,417
Undergraduates: 12,296
SAT Ranges (Verbal/Math): V 590-690, M 610-710
Financial aid: 29%
Applicants: 17,340
Accepted: 33%
Enrolled: 50%
Application deadline: Dec. 1
Financial aid application deadline: Mar. 1
Tuition: resident, $4,827; nonresident, $15,775
Core curriculum: No

To Dissolve the Bands That Have Connected Them

One cannot think of the University of Virginia without thinking of its founder, Thomas Jefferson, a man who possessed a truly liberal education. That is, until recently. Jefferson's conception of a university at the time of U.Va.'s founding in 1819 differs substantially from what goes on today at the Charlottesville campus he designed and could watch over from Monticello, his mountaintop home.

At Monticello, Jefferson drafted one of the most important documents in American history: the Declaration of Independence. But his university has become increasingly dependent on intellectual trends; not a single required course at U.Va. demands that a student read the Declaration of Independence — not to mention the Magna Carta, Chaucer, Shakespeare, or many other seminal writers and works. Instead, Mr. Jefferson's university has abandoned its former commitment to excellence and has shifted its considerable resources away from the humanities in favor of business and law. At the same time, the better professors are dismayed by the poor quality of the newer faculty and by the widespread disregard for standards in U.Va.'s implementation of affirmative action policies. The English department, once home to writer-in-residence William Faulkner, has been decimated, and all of the humanities and social sciences are underfunded. The law and business schools have new campuses, but as a current professor noted, humanities faculty have gone ten years without a significant raise in pay.

While many students still take their educations seriously, the university is spending more and more of its time on things that really shouldn't be taken so seriously. The gap between the real students and those who just want a degree is widening, and many predict it will continue to do so. "Over the next ten years U.Va. will become a two-tiered institution," a senior professor says. "There will be a very small group who take education seriously, both among students and teachers. Even now there are only a few who will take the time to really teach and nurture a student — there is just too much work for too little pay. At the same time, those considered the elite, who are in line with dominant trends, will win more and more honors." Jefferson once wrote: "But when a long train of abuses and usurpations, pursuing invariably the same object, evinces a design to reduce them under absolute despotism, it is their right, it is their duty, to throw off such government, and to provide new guards for the future security." At U.Va. this revolution has not happened yet.

Of course, it is easy to be hard on U.Va., for the very simple reason that it used to stand at the pinnacle of the liberal arts tradition in America. Though U.Va. has toppled off its pedestal in recent years, it remains an excellent university, where a motivated student can still find a first-rate education.

Academic Life: More Disposed to Suffer

A few years ago an ad hoc committee was formed to study the possibility of reforming U.Va.'s core curriculum. Many faculty members worked on the study, but it turned out to be something of a charade: it was all done to please a donor, and the president of the university today will not speak to any of those faculty members regarding this reform attempt. However, the donor was satisfied that the core was to be reformed; the university got its money, and the administration was able to sustain the status quo.

Despite a deep sense of tradition rooted in the university's founding father and continued by the moderately conservative student body, two-thirds of which comes from Virginia, there is nothing even approaching a core curriculum at U.Va. Neither is there a Western civilization requirement. There is, however, a non-Western requirement. This course may be taken in one of the standard, politicized ways, through courses dealing with victimization, the evils of Western civilization, and so on. But it may also, surprisingly, be fulfilled by taking courses in, say, the Old Testament or the New Testament, since at U.Va. Judaism and Christianity are considered Eastern, rather than Western, religions.

Two writing courses are also required, one of which is in the English department. Teaching assistants teach the writing courses and choose the works covered, which means, in the words of one student, "it's a real grab bag as to the quality of the course." Each student must take a history course — any history course at all. What this adds up to are distribution requirements rather than a core. "There is no core at all, and a student can still come out of this place ignorant of the entire Western heritage," one professor says. Notes a student: "It is possible to get a really good education here. But, if so, it won't come to you — you must go find it. You can also get a politically correct and vapid education."

At the same time, a serious disparity has arisen between the humanities — the traditional heart of the university — and the schools of business and law. It seems that the latter programs have taken up an increasingly larger share of the university's budget pie. The graduate business program and the law school have new facilities, while the arts and sciences faculty at U.Va. have not received a raise in the last ten years. The number of complaints among faculty in the arts and sciences is rising and will continue to do so as the university devotes an increasing share of its resources to professional schools while the humanities and social sciences languish.

Among the university's more politicized departments are the soft sciences such as anthropology, which, says one professor, "is really a dormant field and for a discipline like that to grow, it must pick up a lot of the trendiest nonsense." The most popular course in that department is "Race, Gender, and Medicine," in which students are taught that "until the rise of modern science child birth wasn't painful, but became so only after white men invented science," says a faculty member familiar with the course. There are some excellent professors in sociology (like James Davison Hunter) and psychology, but both departments have "picked up all kinds of junky things," says a professor. But perhaps the greatest tragedy at U.Va. has been the decimation of what was at one time perhaps its best department: English. Although several superb faculty members (including Paul Cantor, E. D. Hirsch, George Garrett, Gordon Brader, and Martin Battestin) still labor for their students and their field, most are being replaced upon retirement by younger people who are more committed to advancing their pet ideologies than to teaching literature. "More and more students who are English majors are among my poorest students," says one longtime faculty member from another department.

Also subpar are the sciences, which are "overwhelmed with pre-med students," according to one professor. Because of this, the faculty get adjunct professors and laboratory technicians to teach the undergraduate courses. There is "not much research interest in the hard sciences, and the teaching there is not good, just proforma," according to a professor familiar with the situation. Another very politicized department is women's studies.

Other professors who should be sought out include James Lark in systems engineering, Robert Wilken and William Wilson in religious studies, Patrick Michaels in environmental science, Jennie Straus Clay and Edward Courtney in classics, Michael Holt and Joe Katt in history, Kenneth Elzinga in economics, and government professor James Ceasar. The strength of individual departments is directly related to the good professors mentioned here. It should be noted that the history department possesses dedicated teachers but is very liberal; still, the department is open enough to permit honest debate. Religious studies and modern languages also contain pockets of strength. The Miller Center for Public Policy, while not formally an undergraduate teaching arm of the university, sponsors conferences and brings in many good speakers, including, recently, Howard Baker, Brent Scowcroft, Lawrence Eagleburger, and Nathaniel Howell.

Political Atmosphere: The Consent of the Governed

U.Va. is less affected than its peer institutions by the ideology of multiculturalism. The traditions of the school, coupled with its homegrown Southern student body, have acted to check the speed with which the campus has become overrun with such ideology. And yet the trends favor the substitution of indoctrination for education, and the rate of change is increasing as the faculty becomes politicized through the attrition of those who earlier insisted on a rigorous curriculum. "The younger faculty are increasingly radical, but there is at the same time a loss of zeal among them because their ideas and tactics are becoming so standard," one professor says. "There is a much higher degree of 'understoodness' to it — they have a ho-hum attitude to damaging other people." Adds another faculty member: "The new faculty hires are mediocre because they've never read anything but secondary literature. Methodology is all they know. They can't take a classical text and make something out of it in the classroom, but instead have their students read a secondary source."

Students, too, complain about what one calls "a generational split" among faculty. Ironically, those younger faculty members who, while in graduate school, argued that no one over thirty should be trusted are now mistrusted by students who expect more than esoteric, intellectual games.

Affirmative action policies are pushed at U.Va. with a degree of passion rare even among today's universities. Notes another professor: "There has been a certain corrupting influence through notions of 'diversity.' It is largely *sub rosa*, not blatant and nasty, but it is more dangerous in the long run because it is subtle." Though sometimes it's as subtle as a pink slip: faculty recall one erstwhile academic who was told by two administrators that, although he was "extremely qualified" for an advertised position, there was "no way" he could be considered for it because he was white and male.

U.Va. seems to illustrate the fact that the attempt to celebrate diversity on many campuses today seems mired in contradictions and ambiguities. For example, the efforts directed at incoming African-American students seem to many on campus to reinforce a sense of separatism that may remain with them for the duration of their time in Charlottesville. "The way the university introduces the black freshmen makes them segregated from everyone else," notes one student. "They tell them who to hang around and what classes to take. This is an abdication of responsibility by the administration."

Students arriving in Charlottesville may also find that free speech may not always be practiced at Jefferson's university. One student notes that many students are "cynical" when it comes to saying what's on their minds. "Sometimes you sit on your opinions in order to get along. You can be a hermit because of fear of speaking up and saying what you think," the student says. Notes a professor: "There is no speech code per se, but if you break a non-written rule, you're dead."

Some people on campus have also noted a hostility toward Christian organizations. The truth of this charge was borne out in June 1995, when religious students at U.Va. were finally awarded university funding for the publication of a Christian newspaper. To get their money, the students fought a five-year court battle that ended in the Supreme Court of the United States. The administration had refused to fund the newspaper, claiming that such an action by a public university would violate the constitutional separation of church and state. Yet the Supreme Court held that such a policy in fact discriminated against religious students by denying them the right to free speech while extending that right to students whose publications the university did choose to support.

Of course, U.Va. will always have its heritage in its favor. "I would give the school a cautionary endorsement," a student says. "I wouldn't discourage someone from coming here because of the tradition and the physical landscape that remind a person every day that the world didn't begin in 1945 or 1968."

Campus Life: The Course of Human Events

Day-to-day life at U.Va. can be delightful. The university itself is beautiful and is set in a tranquil, largely rural setting. Jefferson designed the original buildings along The Lawn, where a handful of fortunate students chosen by lottery — as well as some professors — are allowed to live. The school is not too far from Washington, D.C., Richmond, the beaches, and the mountains, and Charlottesville itself is affordable and attractive. The library at U.Va. is quite large (about 4 million volumes and twenty thousand periodicals).

U.Va. enrolls some 18,000 students, including about 12,000 undergraduates. An impressive 91 percent of incoming freshmen graduate within six years. Approximately 66 percent of its undergraduate student body are in-state residents, and nearly 80 percent ranked in the top ten of their high school classes.

There are numerous student groups at the university, ranging from fraternities and sororities to the more radical groups typical of large state universities. Among the latter is the Lesbian, Gay, and Bisexual Union (LGBU), which meets weekly at the Wesley Center (although such meetings were probably not quite what John and Charles Wesley had mind). On the university's web pages, one can learn about the Black Empowerment Association, whose mission statement proclaims that one of the group's goals is to "minimize the control by outsiders and outside controllable factors and elements in order to ensure the survival and flourishment of the Black Nation/Family." More traditional clubs and organizations include the Monroe Society, Circle K, the Blue Ridge Mountain Rescue Group, University Libertarians, and the Jefferson Literary and Debating Society. There are also groups for almost every academic discipline and ethnic group at the university.

U.Va. offers many sports opportunities for students, both as spectators and as participants, in numerous club and intramural teams. The Cavaliers' men's soccer team, which plays on the spectacular grass of the relatively new Klockner Stadium, has recently been the most dominant in the nation, and, like the school's other men's and women's teams, competes in the always exciting Atlantic Coast Conference. A favorite pastime in Charlottesville is hating and lampooning the university's archrival, Virginia Polytechnic Institute (known around the state as Virginia Tech), and games in any sport between these two bring out a combination of the best and worst in almost all Virginians, but especially in students at the two schools.

WABASH COLLEGE

Admissions Office
P.O. Box 352
Crawfordsville, IN 47933-0352
(800) 718-9746 / (765) 361-6370
www.wabash.edu

Total enrollment: 800
Undergraduates: 800
SAT Ranges (Verbal/Math): V 530-630, M 550-650
Financial aid: 90%
Applicants: 780
Accepted: 78%
Enrolled: 37%
Application deadline: Apr. 1
Financial aid application deadline: Dec. 1
Tuition: $14,825
Core curriculum: No

Vanishing Breed

Wabash College admits only men, has an enrollment of just 800 students, and does not accept federal money — making it an unusual institution in more than one regard. The college was founded in 1832 by Presbyterian ministers who, according to the catalogue, patterned Wabash after "the conservative liberal arts colleges of New England, with their high standards." And today, its high standards continue to lift the small Indiana school above many of the rest; Wabash offers its students fine opportunities for genuine liberal learning in a unique, friendly, and challenging atmosphere.

The only question is: How long will this grand tradition last?

Wabash, it appears, has begun to drift. Its students and alumni are as proud of its past as they are concerned for its future. For many alumni, what has happened on campus lately has diminished the school's stature. If they would go to the college now, they would find themselves at a much-changed school.

The administration has hired some faculty who are not as taken with the school's mission, and these faculty have brought a handful of politicized courses that the traditional Wabash would not have tolerated. It would be going too far to say that the college has scorned its tradition, but some there have staged their own small revolutions. It is a fact, however, that if the faculty were given the final say, Wabash would already be coed.

Academic Life: Cultures and Traditions

The curriculum at Wabash is described in its catalogue as having a high regard for the liberal arts. "We the faculty of Wabash College believe in a liberal arts education," the catalogue states. "We believe that it leads people to freedom, helps them choose worthy goals and shows them the way to an enduring life of the mind."

To that end, Wabash offers only bachelor of arts degrees — no bachelor of science degrees. "Our curriculum is based in the traditional liberal arts," a faculty member says. "There are no departments of sociology or anthropology. Basically there is still strong support for the disciplines that are solid, and the students themselves know they're going to work hard."

Two courses are required by name: a freshman tutorial in which small groups of students examine works chosen by the professor in order to improve their reading, writing, and speaking skills, and a sophomore class taken by all students called "Cultures and Traditions," which one faculty member says adopts "a reasonable approach in which we read real books, not secondary sources." Other requirements include three courses in literature and the fine arts; three in the behavioral sciences (a group that includes economics); three in natural science and mathematics; one additional course in mathematics, natural science, or behavioral sciences; and two courses in history, philosophy, or religion.

The resulting plan is thus a mix of core and distribution requirements. To be sure, this is an improvement over the haphazard approach usually taken by college administrators in assembling curricular requirements, and the fact that Wabash still maintains liberal arts requirements for all students — regardless of major — proves its commitment to a genuine liberal education.

There is no Western civilization requirement at Wabash, though until a few years ago the "Cultures and Traditions" course *was* a Western culture course. Now, however, it includes the arts, philosophies, religions, sciences, and social theory of several other cultures. According to the campus newspaper, the *Bachelor,* the class "aims to show the value of different cultural ideas without emphasizing the noble and ever-present with the less noble, or even giving students the appropriate tools to decide between the two." Some basic works of the Western tradition are read by all students, but there is no Western civilization course. The college makes up for this, somewhat, with its fine classics department, which has four professors — a good number for a small school — and offers both Greek and Latin. "We're very anxious to keep the classics program strong," a professor says.

Given the lack of a Western civilization requirement and the college's commitment to keeping a classics department, it seems there is an intellectual tug-of-war afoot between traditionalists who would protect the curriculum's Western base and those who would take Wabash in a more multiculturalist direction. And in the end, this indecision creates at Wabash a problem found at many other schools: as one student says, "There is no guarantee that the average eighteen-year-old can come here and get the formative experience he needs."

Outstanding professors at Wabash include David Kubiak in classics, William Placher in philosophy and religion, Raymond Williams in religion, Edward McLean in political science, and Daniel Stid in government. Classics, philosophy, and religion are considered the strongest departments.

While most courses at Wabash are taught by faculty committed to liberal learning based on the Western tradition, "there are classes that are more politically tilted than one might like," according to one professor. Singled out on this score are English, theater, and religion. "Religion here is taught as sociology," a student says. "It's an exercise in form over substance." Also, the faculty senate recently approved — by a wide margin — minors in multicultural studies and gender studies. Faculty have also held a series of workshops on "developing multicultural curricula for their specific classes," according to a campus newspaper. In doing this, the college is "opening itself up to certain influences which they should do without," a professor says. As a student says, "The older faculty here who are classical liberals haven't awakened to the fact that these new faculty members don't look to Mill for inspiration; they look to Nietzsche."

Political Atmosphere: Going Gently?

The tensions that exist at Wabash stem from the temptation to conform to both popular culture and popular academics. Wabash was founded in 1832 as a men's college, and today it is one of only four such institutions in the nation. The school is under some pressure to change this status in the name of diversity — which, ironically, would entail the further homogenization of American higher education. One professor says only "about ten faculty members . . . want to see Wabash remain all male." Although the student body voted just a few years ago against going coed, there are in the faculty strong voices to the contrary; Wabash's future as a men's college is far less certain today than at any point in the past.

The college administration has, in the words of one faculty member, "refused to address men's education issues" and is prone to import speakers hostile to single-sex education or to fail to repudiate faculty members who attack the college's educational mission. Among the recent speakers invited to campus was Michael Kimmel, who was paid $4,500 by Wabash to attack the concept of single-sex education as well as traditional male roles in society. Kimmel testified against both The Citadel and Virginia Military Institute when those schools were forced by the courts to become coed. It would seem that the administration was more interested in appeasing those outside the college than catering to its alumni, supporters, or students, all of whom have chosen to encourage or avail themselves of the traditional version of Wabash.

Wabash is not stuck on this track, however; the "diversity" train could still be derailed. To its credit, the college has also funded lectures by proponents of single-sex education. In 1996 the Gender Issues Committee sponsored lectures by Elizabeth Fox-Genovese of Emory University and Wilfred McClay of Tulane University, both of whom spoke in favor of single-sex education for both men and women. Both made the point that the opponents of single-sex colleges would destroy the diversity of higher education in the name of diversity. According to these speakers, single-sex institutions may very well be the best choice for many students, and, at a minimum, everyone should be able to decide for themselves whether these institutions are right for them.

Many on campus would agree. Writing in the *Bachelor,* a student laments the fact that Wabash makes no effort to explain to its students why it remains a college for men. The writer cites an early president of Wabash, the Reverend Joseph Tuttle, who said that one of the goals of education should be to instill "physical manliness" such that the student is "impelled to action in order to fulfill some daring and ever present purpose" and is "moved by a noble purpose to be and do something noble." Should the college fail at this, or fail to appreciate the differences between men and women, the writer says, "it has failed in its mission. . . . At best it becomes a college for boys, at worst, it becomes, simply, a college."

Some on campus say the best things Wabash has to offer are what it already is. "Wabash has a rich and even noble history of serving the Midwest," a student says. "For many years it serviced primarily first-generation students — those who were the first in their families to go to college. But it has been drifting for the past several years." Wabash is best evaluated "on its own merits," says another student. "But if you try to make it into an East Coast school, say a Williams College, it'll always be third rate. If I'd wanted to go to Williams I'd have applied to Williams. I mean, you've got eight hundred men in Crawfordsville, Indiana — you'll never have a Berkeley here." A professor agrees: "It's a question of comparing [Wabash] to other places. There's a problem with intimidation when that comparison is made."

Should Wabash hold out against those who would make it coed, it will still have to guard its liberal arts tradition. There are a few outspoken radicals on campus whose actions hardly reflect the daily life at this still-excellent college, but they are already having an effect on the curriculum. Not long ago a psychology professor invited students in his human sexuality class to a screening of a movie based on the Marquis de Sade's book *120 Days of Sodom*. The movie was produced in 1975 in Italy and has since been banned there and in Great Britain, and has been heavily restricted in France. In it, teenage "slaves" are transported to a country estate where they are sexually abused, tortured, and eventually killed. Graphic scenes of all manner of intercourse and torture are depicted, as is the consumption of human excrement. The film was not required for the class, though the professor (who is also the codirector of the college's counseling center) asked students to attend and bring their friends. Wabash's administration approved of the screening and defended it after it was criticized by students.

The same administration has asked an Indianapolis foundation to fund a multicultural/affirmative action program at Wabash. In the proposal the college said it had been able to hire and keep only a few black professors, and asked for money for an administrative position "filled ideally by an African-American whose responsibility, among others, would be to coordinate multicultural hiring."

Hiring such an administrator would be, according to the proposal, part of a collegewide effort to "make sure that our curriculum includes courses with more multicultural content, and that we have faculty members confident and competent to teach multicultural material." The Wabash administration proposes to use as part of this effort the "Cultures and Traditions" course — now described in publicity materials as an opportunity to "seek to discover how a culture's ideas about humanity, society, God and nature make a difference in the way individuals conduct their lives," in an effort to "obtain a deeper knowledge of the arts and acts that constitute our historical tradition of the modern West." According to the proposal, this would change: "We are fortunate in having our required sophomore course, 'Cultures and Traditions,' in place for so many years, so that we are not now challenged with defending the content of that course. We know that it is one vehicle for exposing all students to multicultural literature. But we need many more courses which are focused on multicultural concerns, or which contain multicultural material. Our freshman tutorial is certainly one possibility for incorporating that material, but we need to encourage the development of more courses in the humanities and social sciences which are focused on multicultural history, literature, arts, politics, economics, and psychology."

Such underhanded actions would allow the administration to add an ideological dimension to the class. The proposal even offers the University of Michigan's strongly multicultural freshman orientation program as a model for Wabash's revamped freshman tutorial. Thus, if these Wabash administrators have their way, ideology will become more prominent at the college, and true diversity of thought will continue to decline.

Student Life: By the Rule

All men at Wabash are governed by a rule of conduct, known as the Gentleman's Rule, that is remarkable for its brevity and simplicity: "The student is expected to conduct himself, at all times, both on and off the campus, as a gentleman and a responsible citizen." The rule is enforced by the office of the dean of students.

Student groups on campus participate in common activities and political endeavors on both the left and right. Some campus groups are the Glee Club, Sphinx Club, the Speech and Debate Team, the Parliamentary Union, the Young Republicans, Moot Court, the Hispanic Society, the Malcolm X Institute, the Spanish Club, and the Student Senate. Two-thirds of the student body joins a Greek organization; there are ten fraternities on campus from which to choose. Students can participate on ten NCAA Division III athletic teams, as well as in two dozen intramural sports and four club sports.

The *Bachelor* is Wabash's oldest student newspaper, and students also benefit from the presence of the *Wabash Commentary,* an alternative student newsmagazine published monthly. Both publications have made efforts to counter the faculty and administrators who would like to depart from the college's traditional curriculum and single-sex status. A literary quarterly, the *Wabash Review,* publishes mostly avant-garde verse.

Crawfordsville, in west-central Indiana, is a town of nearly 15,000 residents. Golf and canoeing are listed in the Wabash viewbook as popular off-campus activities. Students are also within easy driving distance of Indianapolis, Purdue University, Indiana University, and the University of Illinois should they be struck by the need for a city or a larger, coed university environment.

Although the total number of applicants has dipped recently, Wabash enrolls an impressive 44 percent of the students it accepts, a percentage much higher than at many more prestigious schools. Its students, it seems, are interested in excellent scholarship both during and after college: a very high percentage of Wabash men go on to attend graduate and professional schools. The college reports that it ranks sixteenth among all U.S. colleges and universities in the percentage of graduates who go on to earn Ph.D.s. Advanced scholarship by alumni is equally well ranked in the three main categories of study: empirical and life sciences, the humanities, and the social sciences. The college has a strong alumni network nationwide, and their support of the college and fellow graduates is legendary. However, unease over the non-traditional trends on campus has resulted recently in lower alumni donations to the college.

Among the things that have the alumni talking are recent attempts to politicize freshman orientation at Wabash. One session included a "safe sex" show by a comedian, hired by the college, wherein were demonstrated several actions that we won't venture to describe. How this performance fulfilled the Gentleman's Rule is anyone's guess. Many students objected and, shortly thereafter, the dean of students retired.

599

WAKE FOREST UNIVERSITY

Office of Admissions
Box 7305 Reynolda Station
Winston-Salem, NC 27109-7305
(336) 758-5201
www.wfu.edu/

Total enrollment: 5,899
Undergraduates: 3,771
SAT Ranges (Verbal/Math): V 600-690, M 620-700
Financial aid: 29%
Applicants: 6,780
Accepted: 40%
Enrolled: 35%
Application deadline: Jan. 15
Financial aid application deadline: Mar. 15
Tuition: $20,450
Core curriculum: No

The Forest for the Trees

Wake Forest was founded in 1834 by Baptists seeking to mold men's minds and characters for church leadership and other professions. This the school accomplished for well over a century, during which time it grew and became an excellent private university serving the South and the world beyond. But problems developed during the 1960s and 1970s between the school's faculty and administrators, on the one hand, and the North Carolina Baptist Convention, on the other, over trends in the curriculum and conflicting definitions of academic freedom. This clash of wills came to a head in 1986, when the university voted to end its relationship with the convention and become an independent, nonsectarian university that still valued its religious roots even as it chartered its own course academically.

Since then, Wake Forest has become more and more like other large private institutions throughout the country. With its ties to its origins severed, it is adapting itself to the prevailing intellectual and political trends, rather than attracting to itself people interested in a specific set of beliefs, as it once did. Some professors who were at the school before 1986 have become disheartened by it all.

Many good professors remain at Wake Forest, however, and even though the curriculum has grown more ideological, the undergraduate student body of about

3,800 is largely conservative. Wake Forest is still a good school, but it's no longer what it once was: either Baptist or singular.

Academic Life: Out of the Fold

While Wake Forest does not have a core curriculum, it requires a number of arts and science courses from all students. Its distribution requirements are more extensive than the norm and set the stage for a reasonably broad education. "In terms of the [time spent on] the required courses, this remains a very traditional school," a professor says. Even students in the school of business must fulfill the arts and science categories required of everyone else. However, the catalogue contains pages of courses that can count toward the requirements, and this waters down the effectiveness of the general education component. As a professor says, "Students take the most popular courses, and often repeat what they took in high school."

Among the requirements are courses in English and American literature; an upper-level course in a foreign language, humanities, the fine arts, or classics in translation; three courses representing two different sciences (biology, chemistry, physics, or mathematics); three courses from history, religion, or philosophy; and three courses from the social sciences. A Western civilization course is required. The requirements are noteworthy for their number, depth, and attention to Western history and literature, if not for their coherence and structure.

Top professors at Wake include Helga Welsh and David Broyles in politics, Robert Utley in humanities, Charles Lewis in philosophy, James Barefield in history, J. Daniel Hammond and John C. Moorhouse in economics, Mark Leary in psychology, Edward Wilson in the English department, and J. Ned Woodall in anthropology.

The philosophy department has produced several Rhodes scholars. "Philosophy remains a bastion of good, solid, academic tradition and is quite Christian," a professor says. "They're unwilling to go along with faddish multiculturalism. They're not all Christians, but they're respectful of one's beliefs." The classics department is also said to be strong. "They are still quite solid . . . and rigorous," says a professor. "There is no aim to propagandize."

Other excellent programs include politics, economics, biology, chemistry, physics, mathematics, and accounting.

Professors say the most politicized departments are religion, English, psychology, women's studies, history, and speech (which recently hired a specialist in rap music). Politics is considered an academically vital department, but is rather politicized in its outlook. "They brought in a bunch of bright Ph.D.s from the best schools, and they've now ousted the old leftists who were in control," a professor says. "It's backfired on them." History teaching is said to be revisionist, such that Columbus, on his voyage to the New World, was attacked for "killing the Indians," a professor says. "History is particularly uniform and one-dimensional," the professor adds.

Traditional professors also complain that Wake Forest, since dropping its association with the Baptist church, has been bent on catching up with the multiculturalism promoted by neighboring Duke and the University of North Carolina. While Wake Forest still has a long way to go to match Duke, the university is starting a minor in American ethnic studies, which will soon become a major, and feminist theories are becoming more prominent in several departments. "There's a slow movement toward strengthening those kinds of programs and an increasing awareness of them among students," a professor says. To that end, the university has commissioned studies on "how to improve the multicultural atmosphere on campus," a source on campus says. The findings of the studies are expected to be implemented in the next five to ten years.

Political Atmosphere: Sleepers Wake

Wake Forest's divorce from the North Carolina Baptist Convention coincided with a period of huge growth in the number of Ph.D.s graduating from the best-known universities in the land. As an independent school that no longer had to consider a church's wishes in its hiring, Wake Forest, like many other institutions that are no longer connected to the bodies that founded them, could choose any new graduates it could attract. At Wake Forest, as elsewhere, this pattern of hiring brought with it curricular changes and research topics that had not been considered in the past.

"You cannot characterize Wake Forest as a Baptist school now," says a faculty member. Much of what made the university unique has now been made over to resemble the programs and ideologies found at literally hundreds of other schools. The tradition of Wake Forest and the founding mission of the school are now less visible than ever, diluted by the administration and faculty's haste to conform with what they see around them. And, as one professor says, in order to keep up with the newest intellectual trends, the school has "compromised excellence for mediocrity."

The university's aggressive affirmative action program and determination to pursue racial and gender diversity has, ironically, resulted in the ideological homogenization of the faculty. Departments that once contained a broad array of intellectual positions, such as history, English, and religion, are today home to one point of view. In fact, as one professor noted, a young, extremely gifted English professor was not considered for tenure because he was a member of a pro-life group. There is also a movement afoot on campus known as "comparative studies," where topics are not studied in the context of specific disciplines, but for how they relate to similar questions in other cultures.

Wake has begun distributing free IBM laptop computers to incoming freshmen (who get to keep the computer when they graduate). Some professors applaud this, but others say it is just another marketing ploy by the administration, done in lieu of offering a true liberal education. "I suspect that in the future we will go the technology trail and lose our heart to technology," a professor says. Some see both the computer distribution and the multicultural additions as cut from the same cloth: the university wants to be on the cutting edge of all things, and is more concerned with the latest trends than with the greatest when it comes to offering students an education.

Other professors favor the laptops-for-all policy. "It's really exciting here," says one. "We're on the web, and classes are now set up so that a teacher can bring his own PC in and tie in with the students'. . . . [W]e can put a student's papers on the web file so that all students can read each other's papers in a course. Class discussion or questions for an exam can come from student papers, and I've seen it work very well. The students feel like they're more a part of the course. . . . The benefits from this can be exaggerated, but many other colleges send representatives to our campus."

Along with a laptop, arriving freshmen get a day of sensitivity training. The sessions, for which orientation was lengthened by one day, deal mostly with sexual harassment and include a few films and a discussion. "The films are not as bad as they could be," a student says. The university has no official speech code, and while talk of one has emanated from a member of the administration, a professor believes "the faculty wouldn't approve it."

Student Life: Take Your Waking Slow

"We have really excellent students," says a Wake Forest professor, "but there is not a strong intellectual climate on campus. They're very goal oriented, but only a minimum are really intellectually serious about ideas for their own sake. That's the reason why we've failed to cultivate a broad intellectual environment."

Intellectual life does exist in pockets on campus, though, and can be found by students willing to seek it out. Among the student groups noteworthy in this regard are the student-run Philomathesian Society and the Euzelian Society. Both are literary/cultural societies that died out at Wake Forest many years ago but have recently been resurrected by students looking for ways to advance the life of the mind on campus. The Philomathesian Society describes itself as "a semi-social, semi-academic organization that offers a wide range of . . . social and academic activities. The idea is that one's social life need not be devoid of intellectual stimulation in order to be fun." Among the Philomathesians' events is a series of lunchtime lectures by university professors.

The Euzelian Society "seeks to cultivate and enrich the intellectual life of Wake Forest students through a variety of colloquia and social events." It, too, sponsors campus lectures by university faculty members and other guests, as well as road trips to the North Carolina Shakespeare Festival in High Point or the Holocaust Museum in Washington, D.C. The renewal of both societies fills a niche missing for many years on the Wake Forest campus — a gap that remains unbridged on some campuses across the country.

Other campus groups include the Baptist Student Union, a still-living remnant of Wake Forest's historical ties to that church. This group lines up students with service projects, including work in retirement homes, prisons, and soup kitchens. Other religious groups, such as the Presbyterian Student Fellowship and the Wesleyan Foundation, are involved in similar projects.

The university does fund many student organizations, including the College Republicans and the Gay, Lesbian, and Bisexual Issues Awareness Group.

About 45 percent of the student body chooses to join one of the fifteen social fraternities and ten sororities. "The Greeks are very much in charge of social life on campus," a professor says. However, the university administration is not favorably disposed toward the Greeks. "The Greek system is under attack," says one student. "The administration blames the Greeks for alcohol abuse on campus. Since the Greeks all rent university houses, they have little power to fight back." Recently the administration shortened the pledge period and raised the grade point average required to join a Greek organization, and is considering making students wait until their sophomore year to rush.

Freshmen (Wake Forest calls them "first-year students") are required to live in university dorms unless they're from the immediate area. Student housing is guaranteed for eight semesters. There are still a few single-sex residence halls, although most are coed by floor. Some dorms are called "substance free," meaning that the prohibitions on drugs, alcohol, and tobacco that once went for all dorms, now strictly apply to just a few. There are also several theme houses that are geared toward student interests or language study.

Wake Forest athletes compete in the Atlantic Coast Conference, one of the nation's most competitive NCAA Division I conferences. For lesser athletic lights, there are intramural programs and recreational facilities.

Wake Forest has seen a lot of new construction over the past few years, and the university is in good financial standing, it seems. The endowment is around $500 million. "The administration is quite sophisticated at raising and spending money," a professor says. The library, however, could use an addition: its collection of 1.2 million volumes is rather small for an institution that wants to become or be seen as a major research university.

UNIVERSITY OF WASHINGTON

Office of Admissions
Executive Director, Admissions and Records
University of Washington
1400 Northeast Campus Parkway
Seattle, WA 98195
(206) 543-9686
www.washington.edu

Total enrollment: 34,597
Undergraduates: 23,414
SAT Ranges (Verbal/Math): V 500-620, M 520-650
Financial aid: 30%
Applicants: 12,530
Accepted: 65%
Enrolled: 46%
Application deadline: Feb. 1
Financial aid application deadline: Feb. 28
Tuition: in-state, $3,486; out-of-state, $11,508
Core curriculum: No

The Thundering Herd

The University of Washington (UW) is proud of its status as a huge state research university. The university enrolls about thirty-four thousand students, including graduate students, and only Johns Hopkins University receives more federal research dollars each year. In addition to this considerable federal largesse, the university receives significant private funds as well. In the 1995-96 academic year, it ranked second among public universities in private giving, receiving over $154 million in private gifts and grants, including a $22 million gift from Microsoft cofounder Bill Gates.

Despite its research orientation and the vastness of its student body, Washington openly proclaims a strong commitment to teaching. But while the school can be justifiably proud of the achievements of its faculty (which include three Nobel Prizes, a National Book Award, and five MacArthur Fellowships), it has less evidence to support its claim to excellence in undergraduate teaching. Indeed, undergraduate complaints about inadequate advising and limited access to desirable classes are not uncommon. Anonymity can be severe at UW. The university awards upwards of 6,000 bachelor's degrees each year, and does not shy away from the designation "degree mill."

605

Nor has UW missed out on the popular calls for diversity and multiculturalism. Reflecting its home state, the university has a high number of Asian students (more than 20 percent in 1995), yet the administration dedicates considerable university resources toward increasing the number of minority students and faculty. As its general catalogue puts it: "The university recognizes as one of its highest educational priorities the need to increase the number of qualified minorities in certain academic fields and professions to which they have been historically denied access or have been traditionally underrepresented."

The president of UW since 1995 has been Richard McCormick, who, despite his doctorate in history, articulates a rather utilitarian attitude toward higher education. McCormick has been quoted by the *Seattle Times* as describing students as "knowledge workers" and saying that he hopes to find ways to herd even greater masses of students through UW in an effort to "open much wider the doors of higher education in Washington state." He advocates an integration of university and pre-college curricula, standards, requirements, and logistics, "so that students can move through the system smoothly and efficiently"; he also seeks ways to "help and encourage students to progress more expeditiously toward their degrees, in order to make way for their successors."

One might question the value of a degree from an institution that seems to value product above educational process. According to some students, the main priorities of the current administration do not involve traditional educational issues, but center instead on such items as tuition control, minority rights, affirmative action, ethnicity requirements, and domestic partner rights. And through its research work, the university seems equally as interested in generating new knowledge as it is in preserving the traditional aspects of a broad education.

At a place so large and so bent on degree production, one can get lost, either by choice or by chance. Good things can be found at UW, but it's almost too big a place for one to assimilate and search thoroughly in four years — or less, if the president has his way. In the words of one professor, "A student who wants to escape an education can do so just as easily as a student who wants to pursue one."

Academic Life: Lost in a Crowd

Reviewing the mammoth University of Washington course catalogue can be a dizzying experience for many freshmen; gone are the early days in the late 1800s when the fledgling university had only one faculty member who was responsible for a curriculum consisting of "Latin, Greek, English, history, algebra and physiology." Students trying to navigate their way through such a large system would do well to seek out guidance and opportunities early on — but don't expect help to come looking for you. One student had a friend who went through his first two years at "U-Dub" (as UW is nicknamed) without ever talking to his adviser. "No one approaches you and asks, 'Are you interested in doing this?'" notes an undergraduate. "You have to be self-motivated and keep your eyes open for opportunities."

The UW faculty numbers somewhere around 3,500, but even with those forces the administration must deal with repeated complaints from undergraduates who have been unable to secure spots in crowded entry-level courses. Ironically, there can be advantages to large lecture classes if you are aggressive, notes one student. Since the majority of students are there only to get a degree, relatively few seek out the professor during office hours. "The professors appreciate interested students," the student says. "It is a real luxury for undergraduates to get quality time with such renowned professors in their field." Thus a single motivated undergraduate, even at a school of thirty-four thousand students, is often granted good conversations and informal mentoring by first-rate faculty.

Unfortunately, many of those conversations will not occur in the context of ideological neutrality. The University of Washington has many politicized faculty and has also established numerous politically motivated "minority" studies programs. As one student laments, "Pretty much everything that comes across the lectern is from the other side of the ideological spectrum." AfricanAmerican studies and women's studies are notorious for training activists rather than educating people. For example, "Gender Equity in Education," a 400-level women's studies course, expresses foregone conclusions about the nature and source of oppression in contemporary American society. The course introduces students to the "implications of sex-role stereotyping in American education, kindergarten through grade twelve." Topics studied include the "image of women and girls in curriculum materials, socialization and career counseling, teacher behavior, [and] effects of Title IX and affirmative action on present school policy." Finally, the course offers "practical alternatives and skills useful for changing attitudes about sex roles."

To graduate, students must complete a set of general education requirements, including 20 "Areas-of-Knowledge" quarter-length classes in each of three categories: "The Natural World," "Individual and Society," and "Visual, Literary, and Performing Arts." They must also select fifteen additional credits from any courses in these fields, for a total of 75 areas-of-knowledge credits. Students must also get a 2.0 grade point average or better in a third-quarter, first year–level foreign language course or a passing grade in any second year–level foreign language class. A five-credit "Quantitative and Symbolic Reasoning" course is required, although one student says the class has been "watered down" in recent years. Students must also take five credits of composition, as well as ten credits in "writing-intensive" courses.

There is currently no formal diversity or multicultural requirement, although minority student groups have campaigned on behalf of an ethnic studies requirement (ESR) in recent years. The proposed ESR focused on "race awareness." Some faculty proposed an alternative "American Culturalism" requirement, but student groups complained that it was too Eurocentric. As one irate student wrote in a multicultural report, "Students have no say in the proposed requirement. . . . We want the requirement to focus on racism, prejudice, and race relations, but now we'll be focusing on the art of this culture and the history of that culture, while never really discussing issues of racism."

Among the professors to seek out at UW are Paul Heyne in economics, and Tracy McKenzie and James Felak in history.

The best schools, departments, and programs at UW include economics, Jewish studies, the business school, the nursing school, engineering (except for mechanical), fisheries, and the Naval ROTC. Although UW's history department has had a reputation for being "backward and traditional," there is an increasing emphasis on multicultural and environmental history. Excellent professors can be found in American and Eastern European history, and grading standards in the department are still quite stringent.

The English department has been home to such great minds as Hazard Adams (now retiring), but is now overrun by trendy theorists. It is easy to be fooled by the traditional-sounding titles of some UW English courses. You have to read the course descriptions for a more accurate indication of the nature and focus of the course. For example, two courses offered in 1997 — "English Novel: Later 19th Century" and "English Literature: The Age of Victoria" — sound traditional enough, and equally so. But the course descriptions reveal which of the two is governed by aesthetic and literary considerations and which has been hijacked by ideological concerns. In the English novel course, the professor resolutely refuses to circumscribe the literature with trendy theoretical interpretations, stating:

> Although considerable attention will be paid to the social, historical, and philosophical backgrounds against which the novels appeared, no attempt will be made to reduce the novels to "reflections" of a ruling class or learned elite, or to an assemblage of dirty tricks played by white Europeans against the rest of the human race. On the contrary, it will be assumed that, as Kenneth Burke once wrote, the law of the imagination is "when in Rome, do as the Greeks."

One can well imagine the type of literary interpretation this professor is consciously denouncing, for it ironically appears immediately beneath this course description in the paragraph describing the "Age of Victoria" course: "This survey of Victorian literature stresses historical, cultural, and political contexts and the making of Victorian (class, gender, sexual, and national) identities. . . . [We will focus] on such key ideological themes as 'domesticity,' 'femininity/masculinity,' and 'Englishness.'"

Even though the UW administration is busy cultivating the university's reputation as a premier research institution, a number of faculty members are still dedicated not only to their research, but to undergraduate teaching and mentoring as well. Even in such a large faculty, the number of outstanding professors is pathetically small, but by seeking out those dedicated to a traditional liberal arts education, and by steering clear of overtly politicized courses such as those found in women's studies, students can piece together a fairly solid undergraduate education.

Political Atmosphere: Special Rights

Though less politicized than some universities, the University of Washington — perhaps owing to its sheer size — is home to a large number of activist groups. There are a handful of conservative groups, but the majority of organizations on campus pledge allegiance to the left side of the political spectrum. These groups have recently conducted loud protests that didn't really hurt anyone, but have also helped induce the university into offering health insurance benefits and housing privileges to the "domestic partners" of homosexual students — a move that resulted in higher insurance premiums for everyone under the university plan. While one faculty member asserts that the university has never had a serious problem with political correctness, some students and faculty might disagree.

One of the most vocal and active lobbies on campus is the environmental movement. Because of its natural beauty and pristine landscapes, the state of Washington seems perennially embroiled in disputes over logging, endangered species, and other habitat-related concerns. While most students share some moderate environmental stance, several activists repeatedly make headlines with their dramatic demonstrations. In one recent Earth First! protest, demonstrators chained themselves to a billboard to protest legislation that opened forest reserves to logging.

Apart from the environmental groups, there is a broad spectrum of political, social, academic, athletic, and cultural interests represented in the more than three hundred student organizations at UW. Probably the second-largest sector of student groups is composed of highly visible homosexual activists. The university has a Gay, Bisexual, and Lesbian Commission and a graduate homosexual group pleasantly titled BOHGOFS (Bitter Old Hags, Grumpy Old Fags). In 1997 domestic partners began claiming special status as well, and the administration acquiesced. Domestic partners now have student insurance privileges and can live in the university's "family housing." The "domestic partners" of straight students have no such recourse.

Conservative student groups such as the Young Conservatives of Washington and the College Republicans are active, while the *Washington Spectator*, an alternative conservative newspaper, has recently ceased publication. A faculty member notes that a number of years ago a colleague wanted to start a chapter of the National Association of Scholars, "but there wasn't enough faculty interest." Generally, the faculty member says, there is a kind of underground "network" of conservatives, and conservative students tend to discover early on which faculty are kindred spirits. However, harassment of conservative students occurs frequently, according to some students, and there have been some celebrated instances as of late. In recent student elections the Graduate Professional Student Senate sent out an official e-mail message that contained false and negative information about the two conservative candidates; members of the Senate were fined by the election committee. In another incident, one board of control member was suspended from his position and banned from the student government for a couple of days because of public statements he made against the Women's Commission while resigning as their liaison.

Perhaps because of the politicized atmosphere on campus, conservative students tend to focus most of their attention on political rather than intellectual issues. Speakers such as David Horowitz and Dale Foreman (the chairman of the state's Republican Party) have been sponsored by campus conservatives recently, with the help of university funds. There are plans to bring more conservative speakers to campus. As one student says, "There is a rule in the bylaws that for every liberal speaker funded they are required to fund a conservative speaker if applied for."

Campus Life: Seattle's Best

Most University of Washington students commute from Seattle and nearby communities, while only 15 percent of undergraduates live in residence halls. This statistic owes something to the fact that 90 percent of UW students come from the state of Washington. There is also an increasing number of "mature" students; the current average age of undergraduates is 25. Because of the commuter atmosphere, students may find it difficult to foster a sense of community on campus. Many take refuge in fraternities and sororities, which serve as popular social outlets. As one student notes, "The Greek system is forty-one houses strong and is active in raising money and in community service, even though the city and the university are consistently harassing them."

Seattle is a mecca for caffeine junkies: Starbucks Coffee and Seattle's Best are two popular coffee chains, and most UW students are well versed in "lattes," "grandes," and other particulars of java jargon. Seattle is also reputed to be the birthplace of grunge music, so the city and university have their fair share of youth in baggy, flared jeans and innovative forms of body piercing.

For those with more elevated cultural tastes, numerous activities are available at both the university and in downtown Seattle. The university has a 1,200-seat theater in the Meany Hall for the Performing Arts, and the School of Drama also stages productions in three smaller theaters. The Henry Art Gallery is currently undergoing a major renovation and expansion, while the Burke Museum contains exhibits on the cultural and natural heritage of the Pacific Rim. Pike's Place Market, located on the pier in downtown Seattle, is a popular place to buy produce, fresh flowers, and crafts produced by local artists.

But the beautiful state of Washington calls many students away from the city during their free time. With the Cascade Range at their doorstep, UW students tend to be ardent nature lovers. Students enjoy biking, hiking, camping, skiing, and other outdoor activities, and it is a well-kept secret that it doesn't rain in Seattle nearly as much as outsiders are led to believe. The gorgeous Victorian port town of Vancouver, British Columbia, is easily within the realm of weekend possibilities.

The Washington Huskies represent the university in a variety of sports, from football and crew to the less raucous but equally combative golf and track. Both the men's and women's rowing teams are superlative, consistently capturing championship titles. Men's soccer has also captured the spotlight in recent years; in 1996 the Huskies enjoyed the most successful season in the team's twenty-eight-year history. The football team has represented the Pacific-Ten Conference in several Rose Bowls.

WASHINGTON AND LEE UNIVERSITY

Office of Admissions
Lexington, VA 24450
(540) 463-8710
www.wlu.edu

Total enrollment: 2,010
Undergraduates: 1,650
SAT Ranges (Verbal/Math): V 640-720, M 630-710
Financial aid: 27%
Applicants: 3,460
Accepted: 34%
Enrolled: 40%
Application deadline: Jan. 15
Financial aid application deadline: Feb. 15
Tuition: $16,040
Core curriculum: No

The Care and Feeding of Tradition

Tradition is something that requires preservation, but tradition can also preserve the institution that brought it to life. Such is the case at Washington and Lee University (W&L), a liberal arts school whose namesakes are matched only by Thomas Jefferson in the illustrious history and culture of Virginia.

The university was founded in 1749 as Liberty Hall, then saved from financial ruin in 1786 by a gift from George Washington. After more hard times during the Civil War, it was the reputation of Southern general Robert E. Lee that redeemed the school. Although Virginia's revered general was university president for only five years — from the end of the war to his death in 1870 — his brief tenure saw the institutionalizing of some of the cultural and intellectual traditions that to this day give W&L its reputation as a conservative institution. This legacy has kept the school from much harm, and kept its academic program rigorous.

This heritage survives today, though not completely intact. W&L went coed in 1985 after more than 230 years as a men's school. The honor system is still prized, but the speaking tradition — the practice, instituted in Lee's day, of greeting everyone one meets while walking on campus — is dissipated. The next several years will indicate just how much the university is willing to do to preserve its tradition, and how much the traditions can still do for it.

Academic Life: Peer Pressure

On paper, W&L's distribution requirements appear fairly standard, though perhaps more numerous than at some other schools. They include a composition component (usually one course or a proficiency exam), two years of a foreign language, two courses in literature, four courses in the humanities (fine arts, history, philosophy, and religion, with at least two of the areas represented), ten credits in science and math (including a lab), three courses in the social sciences, and five physical education units (plus a swimming proficiency test).

As at many universities, these requirements are too undirected to offer a traditional liberal arts education — even though the list of courses that meet them is somewhat delimited. However, two factors make W&L's requirements better than they might otherwise appear. First, the university offers very few politicized courses. Among the classes that can fulfill the distribution requirements, most are solid, survey-style courses not given over to the ideologies of the day. As one professor puts it, "There are not a lot of garbage courses in the distribution requirements." Another professor notes a "certain integrity to the general education requirements." This is due in part to the second factor: W&L students themselves. Having selected W&L largely because it is a liberal arts institution, they gravitate toward the more serious courses. "There are no tight requirements, but you have to work at finding alternatives" to the canon of Western history, literature, and philosophy, an alumnus says.

The students, however, disappoint at least one professor, who says less than half of them take the European history or American history introductory sequences offered in fulfillment of the general requirements. Neither course is mandated, either by the requirements or by the history department, which considers class standing the only prerequisite for upper-level history courses, and it is difficult to see how students can be prepared for further study in history without these classes. In the end, it is the student who determines whether he will take these solid introductory courses, though the intellectual tenor of W&L does much to induce him to give them a try.

Indeed, W&L tends to be fairly straightforward in its academic mission: it offers majors in most of the traditional disciplines, but there are no identity-style programs, at least not at the level of a full department. (Gender studies is not an official program, but a few courses are taught in this and other trendy subjects across several departments.)

The English department has an excellent reputation for rich courses and fine teaching. "It's not like departments elsewhere," an alumnus says, noting that race and gender studies are not stressed in the department. A professor in another department says the English faculty "take writing seriously, emphasizing teaching students how to write." He notes that English "is not overrun with political correctness, though there is some." Another professor says the English curriculum is "difficult" and "superior." A review of the course catalogue bears out these observations, as only a few politicized courses appear in the listing.

The School of Commerce, which includes economics, accounting, business management, public policy, and politics, has an even more difficult and challenging curriculum than English — it is perhaps the most rigorous division on campus. A professor describes it as "less vocational than most business schools," although he also notes that accounting, due in part to the nature of the discipline itself, tends to be more focused on the day-to-day technical skills required for a career than are other majors in the school. The other four departments in the school do a fine job of blending theory and practice — a rare mixture at most business schools, which tend toward the latter.

The presence of the politics department in the School of Commerce lends a certain sense of the humanities to the other business disciplines, a professor points out. This department has as its goal "educating citizens and providing a liberal arts education," including "an emphasis on the Founding Fathers and a solid foundation in American Political Thought." A colleague concurs, noting that the School of Commerce prepares "students for professional work and graduate school." However, a recent graduate says not all the professors are of the highest quality, and that most of the faculty in economics are "not out-and-out socialists, but they're not free-market-oriented either."

W&L's Journalism School (actually a department within the College of Arts and Sciences) is well regarded by those on campus as well as those who hire reporters. The natural sciences, according to one professor, are "in a renaissance" since the building of a new science center and the accompanying expansion of faculty research projects. The university's premed program has been outstanding in placing its graduates in medical school.

Other departments get mixed reviews from those on campus. The history department's reputation as "a conservative outpost" is "undeserved," according to one professor, since some of the most vocal feminists at W&L are professors in that department. However, it is pleasant to know that at a school named in part for Robert E. Lee, the Southern history and Civil War sections of the department are well taught. Perhaps the most politicized department at W&L is art history, where, according to a recent graduate, most of the professors have "very definite political agendas."

On a more positive note, there are professors here doing good work and excellent teaching who would be good directors of study across different fields of interest. They are: in the politics department, Mark Rush and William Connolly; in history, Jefferson Davis Futch; in math, Robert Johnson; in the English department, Suzanne Keen and Dabney Stuart. And in the Journalism School, the nationally recognized columnist Edwin Yoder also teaches on the Washington and Lee faculty.

Political Atmosphere: General's Orders

The atmosphere at W&L is dominated by the two traditions instituted by General Lee himself more than one hundred years ago: the speaking tradition and the honor system. While the latter is still going strong, the former has begun to fade away.

The speaking tradition holds that everyone — faculty, students, and staff — must acknowledge and greet each other as they walk through the campus. One professor reports that the "speaking tradition is 50 percent intact," and he attributes its partial demise to a growing divide between older, less politicized faculty and their more politicized, younger replacements. Indeed, as at many campuses, W&L has had its share of New Dealers who see traditional education, rather than political or social indoctrination, as their responsibility. A professor says most of these older faculty members have died or retired in recent years. The result, for both W&L and many other institutions, has been increased politicization of the curriculum and campus life. As an alumnus says, "The faculty is liberal, and moving further to the left." At the same time, other professors report that the conservative tendencies of the students and the relative isolation of Lexington provide some motivation for the more overtly politicized faculty to seek positions elsewhere.

While the speaking tradition may be on the wane, campus observers report that the honor system is alive and well. It is entirely student-run: all regulations are written by a student committee, and all honor trials are conducted by a student panel. The "single penalty" provision of the system means that the panel has available only one choice — expulsion — if a student is found guilty of violating the code. Even before students arrive on campus, the honor system has the effect of weeding out those who would prefer not to live under its requirements, a professor says. And those who do attend W&L do so in part because of this rare code.

The result is a system of "socially enforced norms," according to one professor. However, another professor believes compliance is just as often "driven by fear, rather than morality or ethics." Whatever the reasons, the result is "a certain element of peace, tranquillity, and order," a professor says. Campus crime is negligible, and nearly all the cars, doors, and dorms on campus can be left unlocked. A long-standing campus story has it that a ten dollar bill was found on the floor in the library, tacked to a bulletin board near the building's entrance, and left unclaimed for weeks. Although no one interviewed for this guide could confirm the truth of that story, all agreed that it fit the category of "useful myth" in that it provided a standard to which all W&L students are expected to adhere. And in truth, it might very well have happened.

As uncomplicated as this approach to campus discipline might appear, there have been challenges to the student-run system. In the late 1980s and early 1990s W&L instituted the Confidential Review Committee (CRC), which was responsible for enforcing a new, vaguely defined speech code. Free speech advocate Nat Hentoff (who is politically liberal on most issues) called the CRC the "most tyrannical, arbitrary, most fanatically ideological body of its type" in a 1991 speech at W&L's Lee Chapel. Pressure from alumni and trustees, combined with court rulings that held similar codes at Michigan and Stanford to be unconstitutional, forced the administration to disband the CRC a few years later.

More recently, the student-run Intra-Fraternity Council, which regulates the Greek system on campus, has had its powers curbed by a new faculty board that oversees its operations. Many campus conservatives, including most of the editorial staff of the alternative newspaper, the *Washington and Lee Spectator,* view such moves as assaults on conservative students and their institutions, although one professor notes that binge drinking and hazing can hardly qualify as traditional gentlemanly behavior.

The *Spectator* itself was the target of radicals back in 1991, when two female junior professors wrote letters to its advertisers — on university letterhead — threatening a boycott of their businesses and accusing the *Spectator* (which receives no university funding at all) of being "blatantly racist, sexist, and offensively conservative." The *Spectator* demanded an apology from the university for allowing its stationery to be used in this manner, but its request was denied by Dean John Elrod, now the school's president. Both of the professors involved in this incident have since left the university, but no disciplinary action was taken against either for misuse of university resources.

Just as multiculturalism has yet to gain the ascendancy in W&L's curriculum, so too have ideological inserts into campus life been largely ignored by the majority in the university community. The W&L administration recently attempted to create a dorm with an environmentalist theme as well as an all-black fraternity, but both ideas died for lack of student interest. The administration's wishes have prevailed, however, during freshman orientation, where incoming students are given "sex kits" containing the usual paraphernalia and literature about "safe sex."

Though many faculty at W&L are active politically, the vast majority of students are not. There are no campus chapters of either the College Republicans or the Young Democrats/College Democrats, and even the "Lee" in the university's name doesn't mean there are chapters of the Daughters of the Confederacy or the Society for the Preservation of Southern Heritage. There is a small gay and lesbian group, which is disproportionately noisy. But the only political activity for which W&L is noted is the quadrennial mock presidential convention, held every election year for the party out of power, which on most occasions accurately predicts that party's nominee.

Campus Life: O Shenandoah

Although student political life is fairly dormant, social activities, especially those involving Greek organizations, are numerous. "Fraternities drive the place," says one professor. Nearly 80 percent of W&L's male students are fraternity members. W&L only has a small number of sororities, but then again, it has only admitted women since 1985. One of the most famous campus events is the Fancy Dress Ball (dating back to 1908 or 1871, depending on which version of the story one believes), which brings together students, alumni, professors, and dignitaries for an annual party centered around a particular theme, chosen annually.

Social life apart from the fraternities is described by those on campus as "small," "congenial," "collegial," and "intimate."

As far as extracurricular activities are concerned, one thing stands out immediately: W&L seems to be a veritable hive of journalistic activity. In addition to the *Spectator,* mentioned above, are two other newspapers, the *Trident* and the *Ring-tum Phi,* as well as a magazine, the *Southern Collegian,* plus cable television programming and a radio station. Add to all that a chapter of Sigma Delta Chi, otherwise known as the Society of Professional Journalists.

W&L's preoccupation with words and using them well can also be seen in its successful Forensic Team and Debate Society. Other student organizations include the College Libertarians, G&L (the gay, lesbian, and bisexual group), InterVarsity Christian Fellowship, and the Environmental Awareness Committee.

Lexington is a small, picturesque town in the scenic Shenandoah Valley that is dominated by two colleges (the Virginia Military Institute is also located there), with the usual array of fast-food restaurants and shops but few other social attractions. Outdoor activities in the Blue Ridge Mountains are popular, and include winter sports at several nearby resorts. Also popular are trips to Washington, D.C., Richmond, and the many other colleges and universities located in central Virginia.

With a name like Washington and Lee, the university had little choice but to call its sports teams the Generals. The teams compete in twenty sports — seven for women, thirteen for men — at the NCAA Division III level. Over 75 percent of the student body participates in a variety of intramural sports. Club sports include equestrian, field hockey, lacrosse, rugby, soccer, softball, and water polo.

WASHINGTON UNIVERSITY (ST. LOUIS)

Office of Admissions
Campus Box 1089
1 Brookings Drive
St. Louis, MO 63130-4899
(314) 935-6000
http://wustl.edu

Total enrollment: 11,600
Undergraduates: 6,081
SAT Ranges (Verbal/Math): V 610-710, M 640-730
Financial aid: 60%
Applicants: 13,792
Accepted: 56%
Enrolled: 23%
Application deadline: Jan. 15
Financial aid application deadline: Feb. 15
Tuition: $22,422
Core curriculum: No

Which Washington?

Washington University in St. Louis was founded in 1853 by William Greenleaf Eliot to instruct youth in "the principles of morality and reverential regard for truth." The university was originally called Eliot Seminary but was renamed Washington University in 1869, meaning that it took its name prior to the founding of the state university with which it is so often confused. Originally located in downtown St. Louis, the university received an attractive hilltop campus west of the city as part of the planning for the 1904 World's Fair. The university now enrolls roughly 6,000 undergraduates, with about as many in graduate and professional programs, and though many know it as a school not located where its name implies it should be (like Miami of Ohio or Indiana University of Pennsylvania), the scene on campus is not quite so confused; in fact, Washington University does a number of things better than its more aptly named peers.

However, some of the school's best qualities do not apply to undergraduates: Washington University is increasingly known for the quality of its graduate and professional programs. About half of the university's nearly two thousand faculty teach

617

in the highly rated School of Medicine, and the graduate programs of the George Warren Brown School of Social Work recently ranked number one in a *U.S. News and World Report* national survey. Prominent faculty include novelist and literary philosopher William Gass, winner of the National Book Critics Circle Award, and Douglass C. North, winner of the 1993 Nobel Prize for economic science.

In general, Washington University appears to be experiencing something of an identity crisis. No longer content to be an institution valued — as it had been in the past — for its teaching commitment and solid programming in the liberal arts, the university seems eager to assert itself as a high-profile research institution, a place where its professoriate is on the popular cutting edge and yet intimately involved in the lives and studies of undergraduates. But as students and faculty both attest, these goals are frequently at odds with one another, as faculty become increasingly specialized and preoccupied with publishing and less interested in debates about undergraduate curriculum or even in the quality of their teaching. To maintain its standing as an excellent liberal arts institution, Washington University must reverse this trend toward specialization and professionalization and begin to recognize faculty for their serious commitment to their students — not for their ability to publish peer-reviewed articles in all the right journals.

Academic Life: Respectability Where It's Not Often Found

About 3,000, or two-thirds, of Washington University's undergraduates enroll in the College of Arts and Sciences; another 1,000 are in the School of Engineering and Applied Sciences, with the remainder divided among the John M. Olin School of Business, the School of Architecture, and the School of Art. The programs with the best teaching reputations are history and English, and the most highly ranked nationally are biology and German.

There are several general requirements for a B.A. degree from the College of Arts and Sciences, but these do not amount to a traditional core curriculum. Unless students pass advanced placement tests, they are required to take courses in both English composition and quantitative reasoning. The rest of the necessary classes come from a series of distribution requirements that includes three courses each in physical and life sciences, social and behavioral sciences, and literary classics and historical perspectives. Additionally, a student must take three courses in at least two of these categories: language study, art forms, aesthetic and ethical values, and modes of reasoning. In the fall of 1993 the university instituted a diversity requirement, insisting on one course from two of these three categories: minority groups, non-European societies outside the United States, and gender studies. If approved, courses counting toward this multicultural requirement may also serve double duty for other distribution requirements, further diminishing the likelihood that students will graduate with a coherent grasp of the liberal arts tradition.

The cultural diversity requirement did not precipitate much opposition, according to faculty. A general consensus exists among arts and sciences faculty that students should be exposed to a culture outside of their own; however, one faculty member confided that because of a lack of faculty leadership on curriculum issues, some courses were approved as electives when they shouldn't have been, and that there "are too many courses now that can meet the distribution requirements." The problem with the distribution requirements, according to another faculty member, is that they are "not so much politically correct as too narrow."

Because of this confined focus, students can either avoid or miss out on a broad general education. However, good academic advising can help remedy the narrowness inherent in Washington University's general education requirements. One faculty member describes the advising system as "better than most universities," and adds that the dean's office chooses and trains a core of advisers — a fact that would not be comforting at all universities, but is beneficial to the students at Washington University.

Still more help for students is available in the form of FOCUS, a program in which freshmen take a two-semester core seminar on a particular topic as well as a course chosen by FOCUS professors related to that topic. "The objective of FOCUS," states a program description, "is to provide students with a coherent learning experience that still allows time for electives." According to one Arts and Sciences faculty member, the FOCUS program grew out of a "need to synthesize"; that is, a recognition that undergraduates were unable to make meaningful connections between their disparate courses. The subject matter, according to one professor, is not as important as the interrelation of the courses, and the program ensures that a student's curriculum is "not all carved up into different disciplines" but has some sense of interconnectedness. FOCUS themes have included "The Search for Values," "Environmental Science and Policy," and "Childhood, Adolescence, and Society."

Like many of its higher education brethren, the university has programs in fields such as African and Afro-American studies and women's studies, although they are less politicized than similar programs found on many campuses. While at least some faculty within each department try to steer clear of the political radicalism that seems to plague such programs, there are a fair share of multicultural ideologues as well. As the women's studies literature claims, departmental courses "examine not only gender but also race, class, religion, sexual orientation, physical ability, appearance, and other categories relevant to the subordination of women." One course in Marxist feminist theory exposes students not only to the works of Marx, Engels, and Sojourner Truth, but also to the writings of radical Michigan law professor Catherine MacKinnon and "street murals." A philosophy professor teaches a course in feminist philosophy that examines "the sources and nature of patriarchy." It is the only course listed in the philosophy department that requires the "permission of the instructor" as an essential prerequisite, and the instructor is said to use this requirement to weed out men and heterosexual women from the class, which she refers to as an "ovular" rather than a "seminar."

The current chairman of the African and Afro-American studies department, Gerald Early, has come under fire from militant black students for not being thoroughly Afrocentrist. Early, a distinguished scholar and writer, has published several books as well as articles in such journals as *Harper's, Atlantic Monthly, Academic Questions,* and *Civilization,* and is a frequent guest commentator on National Public Radio (NPR). Perhaps the criticism of him from certain quarters is justified: Early has given the department a credibility and academic legitimacy often compromised by ideological tunnel vision at other universities — rarely a popular move in these departments.

Washington University's creative writing program has traditionally been one of the best in the country, boasting at different times such gifted poets as Howard Nemerov and Mona Van Duyn (both poet laureates) and fiction writer Stanley Elkin. The program is still highly ranked, but both Nemerov and Elkin have passed away and students complain that the department lacks the faculty stature it once had. But recently appointed director Carl Phillips, who holds appointments in English and African and Afro-American studies, is optimistic about a recent favorable ranking the university's writing program received: "There can be a new generation of literary prominence at Washington University," he asserts.

The English department is in a state of transition as well, but may hold less cause for optimism. The department seems relatively immune to the emphasis on theory that plagues so many departments at similar institutions; indeed, most of the faculty are dedicated to their teaching and have a deep appreciation for the aesthetic and artistic genius of literature. However, if recent hires are any indication, the future makeup of the department will be vastly different. One trendy eighteenth-century literature professor does work on "eighteenth-century shopping and West Indian Creoles" and has published a book entitled *Fashion as Cultural Discourse: Commodity, Style, and Gender in Eighteenth Century England.*

Political Atmosphere: A Butterfly Garden

The previous chancellor, Bill Danforth, and his wife, Kitty, living in the stately presidential manor on Forsyth Avenue, gave the campus a distinct air of gentility. Danforth, Purina heir and brother of Missouri's former senator John Danforth, had an impressive conservative pedigree, and he and his wife frequently displayed their considerable social graces with students and faculty at campus functions; indeed, the university recently unveiled a butterfly garden in honor of Kitty. As chancellor, Danforth was instrumental in gaining in 1992 the financial support of Anheuser-Busch, which allowed Washington University to host the first debate between presidential candidates Clinton and Bush, and helped to increase the university's sizable endowment.

The new chancellor, Mark S. Wighton, formerly a provost at the Massachusetts Institute of Technology, is an unmarried scientist. Although his administration will definitely have a different social tint to it (a recent article highlighted him eating a frozen custard with a student in one of his collection of Corvettes), it is still unclear what his priorities will be.

Perhaps the old-fashioned graciousness of the Danforths helped keep campus politics to a minimum. Apart from the typical tilt to the left observable at most prestigious liberal arts universities, Washington University usually steers clear of political imbroglios. The most contentious issue in recent years, according to one faculty member, has been tenure decisions. "Some departments are outraged at tenure decisions made by the dean," the professor notes, adding that a lawsuit is pending in relation to one tenure dispute. Although the university prides itself on its strong teaching reputation, strong undergraduate teaching is not sufficient to secure tenure. Students organized a protest a few years ago when a popular teacher did not receive tenure, but because he lacked the publication record the university was looking for, the dean refused to budge. By all accounts, tenure decisions are based almost exclusively on publications, a trend that does not bode well for the future quality of undergraduate teaching at Washington University. Indeed, the university's teaching reputation took a hit recently when, in an embarrassing moment for both faculty and administration, several of the student-nominated teaching awards in the arts and sciences were given to graduate teaching assistants, not tenured faculty.

Apart from the pressure to publish, Washington University maintains, in general, a high level of academic freedom. Even the one blight on that record — a faculty "sensitivity training" course — is not required and, according to one faculty member, is even "partly defensible" because of past incidents in which faculty have abused female students.

Washington University's Assembly Series, the annual lecture series held in the university's Graham Chapel, hosts predominantly liberal speakers from both mainstream and academic communities, including NPR correspondent Nina Totenberg, Columbia University professor of comparative literature Edward Said, and First Lady Hillary Rodham Clinton. From the other side of the spectrum the university has invited and hosted such speakers as Jack Kemp and George Will. Even so, liberal groups dominate the student sphere. These include Against Discrimination and Hatred on Campus; Gay, Lesbian, and Bisexual Alliance of Washington University; PAC (Progressive Action Coalition); Student Environmental Action Coalition; and Students for Choice.

Campus Life: Meet Me in St. Louis

Washington University's hilltop campus is in a suburban part of St. Louis, just minutes from the downtown area. The main university architecture is neo-Gothic, replete with visually appealing arches, gargoyles, and other attractive features. The university abuts Forest Park, one of the country's largest municipal parks. With over 1,300 acres, Forest Park is home to the St. Louis Zoo, Art Museum, and History Museum. Students and faculty alike use the path that runs along the periphery of the park for jogging, cycling, and rollerblading.

On campus, the Olin Library is the university's main research library; this and twelve other departmental and school libraries hold close to 3 million volumes and fifteen thousand periodicals. The university also has an impressive special collection of the correspondence and manuscripts of several renowned modern authors, including Elizabeth Bishop, Samuel Beckett, and Ford Madox Ford. The university is also home to the impressive Washington University Gallery of Art, opened in 1881, which boasts a permanent collection of nineteenth-century American paintings along with the works of such masters as Picasso and Matisse.

All nonlocal students are required to live in residence halls their first year. Washington University's sixteen residence halls are located in the "South 40," an area at the southern edge of the campus. Most are coed, although a number of "special interest" residence options exist for students, including single-sex living and smoke-free living. Because the Greek system flourishes at the university, many men live in one of several houses along "fraternity row." Upper-level undergraduates and graduate students find rental accommodations in one of the neighboring residential areas, including the exclusive Central West End area near the medical school. The university recently purchased a number of local apartment buildings that will be used to house additional students.

Favorite local eateries include Ted Drew's frozen custard, the St. Louis Bread Company, and various ethnic restaurants on a commercial strip of Delmar Avenue known as "the Loop." Although students from huge metropolises like New York complain that St. Louis is too provincial, the city is, after all, the sixteenth-largest in the nation, and hosts a variety of major-league social and cultural activities. Students can watch the Cardinals, Rams, and Blues or hear the world-renowned St. Louis Symphony Orchestra (made famous by its illustrious former conductor, Leonard Slatkin) at Powell Hall. Upscale shopping at the Galleria Mall is only minutes away by university shuttle. Other attractions include the famous St. Louis Arch, which all but the most weak-kneed should ascend at least once.

There certainly is no dearth of social opportunities at Washington University; indeed, by some accounts the university is well on its way to establishing a reputation as a "party school." Students seem as motivated in their sense of campus spirit as they are in their academic pursuits. Popular events include "Thurtene," an annual carnival on the front lawn of campus complete with fair rides and concessions. There is also the raucous end-of-semester event appropriately called "WILD" (Walk In, Lay Down), which features bands and a daylong list of activities. Students also sponsor a "RegressFest," where they play with Play-Doh and participate in a Twister tournament. The school is home to an active chapter of the Society for Creative Anachronism, and it is not uncommon to see folks in medieval garb engaging in a mock joust on the campus quad. Hopefully, they are learning their medieval history elsewhere.

The Washington University Bears compete in the NCAA Division III and the University Athletic Association, which includes such schools as Carnegie Mellon, Chicago, Emory, and Johns Hopkins. Varsity sports include men's and women's basketball, soccer, track, swimming, and tennis, among others. The women's volleyball team is highly rated, having won, at this writing, six consecutive national championships. There is also a flourishing intramural sports program at Washington University, including such popular pastimes as ultimate Frisbee.

WELLESLEY COLLEGE

106 Central Street
Wellesley, MA 02181-8292
(781) 235-0320
www.wellesley.edu

Total enrollment: 2,320
Undergraduates: 2,320
SAT Ranges (Verbal/Math): V 640-730, M 600-680
Financial aid: 52%
Applicants: 3,310
Accepted: 40%
Enrolled: 45%
Application deadline: Early decision, Nov. 1; regular admissions, Jan. 15
Financial aid application deadline: Feb. 1
Tuition: $22,114
Core curriculum: No

The End of History?

Wellesley is a highly selective college, nearly unparalleled in the types of connections and support it can offer to young women, with an idyllically beautiful campus designed by the architect of New York's Central Park in one of Boston's most pleasant suburbs. By all accounts, Wellesley's faculty are considered competent and rigorous.

"Wellesley is more than any group of people, faculty, and students, gathered at any one time," enthuses Caroline Hazard, who speaks with the reverence that is characteristic of Wellesley College alumnae. "It is the resultant power of the effort, the endeavor, the inspiration of all who have lived in it, and of those who shall live; a stream of life; a continuity of thought which has in it the elements of eternity."

A historical and near-mythical sentiment indeed, but one hard to find in any of the current literature in which Wellesley advertises itself. Although the Wellesley College *Bulletin* does mention that the college was founded by Henry Fowle Durant, "an impassioned believer in educational opportunity for women," the catalogue mentions little else about Wellesley's history or founding, or its status as a preeminent member of the "Seven Sisters," the moniker commonly applied to the nation's most lauded and remarkable (at least historically) colleges for women.

While the college does appear proud of its role as the alma mater of some of the nation's *currently* most powerful and interesting women, all of the college's present communications emphasize only, in rather mechanistic fashion, the contemporary relevance of Wellesley's curricular offerings.

The college does not at first glance appear to be shirking any notion of itself as a liberal arts institution; in fact, the opposite would seem to be the case, from a glance at the college's publication *Voices of Wellesley,* which begins:

> In a time when technology is widely accepted as a substitute for ideas, when action all too often preempts thought, and when instant analysis masquerades as understanding, a liberal arts education has never been more crucial. In such a time, Wellesley College may well offer more to its students than ever before in its history.

But Wellesley's unwillingness to advertise its own history is curious. Most selective colleges with sectarian or patrician roots don't work as hard as Wellesley does to focus so exclusively on present-day achievements.

As at other colleges of its stature, Wellesley's humanities faculty has become increasingly enchanted with multiculturalism and ideologically charged theories. It should be no surprise, then, given such a philosophical bias, that Wellesley's commitment to the liberal arts is ambiguous at best and hypocritical at worst.

Academic Life: Dispatches from the Front

The relentless focus on "diversity" in Wellesley's general presentation of itself is manifested in its notion of a core curriculum. While its departments are, for the most part, acknowledged as the home of excellent teachers, and the general education requirements are fairly intensive, the school is infatuated with the interdisciplinary approach to education to the extent that college literature seems almost to denigrate the concept of a deep and sustained engagement with just one academic discipline.

A recent edition of the *Bulletin* takes pains to state that "central to the curriculum is the concept of diversity, the concept that the student should pursue a number of disciplines during her four years at the College." In practice, what such an emphasis tends to translate to is exemplified in one student's statement about her major: "I wanted to take two majors — sociology and women's studies — and people were absolutely happy to work together with me. I also wanted to write a thesis focusing on Jewish Studies, sociology, and women's studies, and teachers from the different departments made sure I had the resources to pursue it."

There certainly are the resources to pursue it. More than nine hundred courses are available at Wellesley, each designated as introductory, intermediate, or advanced, and not one of them is required "except Writing 125," the *Bulletin* notes. But even this exception is somewhat misleading: there is a Writing Program at Wellesley, in which "many departments cooperate . . . in offering combined sections," so even this requirement is not one all students share.

Having said this, it must also be stated that most Writing 125 courses are serious, solid, and noncontroversial. The philosophy course focuses, amazingly, *only* on Plato and Aristotle; another fine example is Political Science 101, "a study of political conflict and consensus through comparison of democratic and authoritarian systems . . . designed to teach critical writing on political topics," which is taught by acclaimed professor Ed Stettner. Even more "modern" alternatives such as "Writing about Science" and "Great Essays" still require serious reading. There are, however, a couple of lightweight options: in the catalogue note to "Women and Memoir: A Revision of Life," appended to a reading list that includes Mary McCarthy and Alice Walker, is the disturbing addendum that "students will have the opportunity to use their own journal entries as raw material for critical essays," which would seem to lessen greatly the opportunities for learning critical objectivity. Then there are the standard movie courses that have become ubiquitous college fare, in this case given a particularly "Wellesley" spin, such as "Strong Women in Film."

Beyond the Writing 125 requirement are the distribution requirements, which one professor known for rigor notes approvingly as "fairly stiff." In satisfaction of these, students must elect three units "in each of the three academic areas as part of the 32 units required for graduation," the *Bulletin* states. (In Wellesley terminology, one "unit" generally refers to one course, although since the fall of 1993 some particularly challenging courses count for 1.25 units.) The "three academic areas" in question are defined in a slightly more subtle fashion than the usual arts/social science/science triumvirate. Group A consists of literature, foreign languages, art, and music, but extends further to include some courses, the *Bulletin* annotates, from both classical civilization and Africana studies.

Group B, which in its larger manifestation includes "Social Science, Religion, Philosophy, and Education," is actually subdivided into two groups, B^1 and B^2. The B^1 courses center more on the historical, while B^2 courses consist of the more quantitative fields such as psychology, economics, sociology, and anthropology. (Political science is included in this grouping, rather than with the more traditionally "liberal" disciplines, although one faculty member maintains that the department is, on the whole, balanced.) Incidentally, it is possible for one to fulfill *both* Group B requirements in whichever subdivision one wishes, which renders suspect the college's official boast about providing a "broad foundation in the liberal arts."

Group C is the killer. C consists of various departments of science and mathematics. Three units are required in this division, which is not that unusual, given that at many colleges mathematics and sciences are considered separately, but at Wellesley one of these units must be a laboratory science, and these have the reputation for being difficult. Across the departments, the laboratory sciences are strong: "Wellesley's best known for the humanities," one student reveals, "but I've found science wonderful here." In fact, those with a bent toward the sciences should take note: the same student (a biochemistry major) mentions that science graduates are "wanted everywhere" by companies and corporations. "They're snapped up because of their good lab experience."

The language requirement "has been upheld," according to one professor, although not without challenge. One must progress through two units of second-year language courses, which translates into four completed semesters for entering students with no prior language experience. Since many Wellesley students come from rigorous secondary-school backgrounds, these students may fulfill the requirement by completing one "unit of language study above the second year college level"; one can also fulfill the requirement with sufficient scores on either an achievement or advanced placement test.

One means by which freshmen may satisfy several of these distribution requirements is by electing the First-Year Cluster Program, an instance of Wellesley's passion for the interdisciplinary. When first instituted the program "featured a largely historical focus," but has in the past few years "been redesigned to approach the traditional subject matter of the liberal arts in an interdisciplinary format that is more theme-oriented." During the fall term of their first year, students in the cluster program take "two of the Specialty courses offered by the Cluster faculty," then in the spring semester they take their required Writing 125 class in a specially designated cluster section. What makes the cluster experience even more intensive is the fact that students live together in the same dorm.

Imagine the intensity of sharing dormitory space with a group of students, all of whom happen to be taking a cluster entitled "Constructions of the Self: Gender, Reproduction, Sexuality" — the actual cluster topic for 1993-94. Underlying all of the courses offered was "the central question of how gender and sexuality are socially constituted despite cultural assumptions that they are natural phenomena." Available for the two elective courses that students must take as part of the cluster were such courses as "Sexuality and Literary Identity," "The Biology and Technology of Human Reproduction," and a particularly curious one entitled "The Intersection of Sexuality, Gender, and Culture," which promised that "sexuality will be examined within a social constructionist perspective . . . the multicultural perspective on sexuality and its cultural determination will be explored with a particular emphasis on Asian-American women."

Far and away, though, the most controversial part of the distribution requirements is the "multicultural" requirement, which was instituted in 1990 — around the time Stanford was beset by marchers chanting that Western culture "had to go." Wellesley's "multicultural" requirement has since undergone a major overhaul. The original requirement stated that students had to take one course (or unit) primarily concerned with "1) the peoples, cultures, and societies of Africa, Asia, Middle East, Oceania, or Latin America and the Caribbean; or 2) the peoples, cultures and societies of North America that trace their historical origins to these areas; or 3) Native American peoples, cultures, and societies." Several additional stipulations regarding course content were attached to the requirement, but their purpose was "to allow the student to see the people, culture, or society through its own eyes."

In practice, the way the original requirement was phrased tended to bother members of the Wellesley community across the spectrum, left to right, and the resulting disgruntlement lasted for years. For one thing, an enormous number of courses fulfilled the requirement, including such unlikely offerings as "Introduction to the Hebrew Bible/Old Testament." Furthermore, as a 1996 article about the issue in the *Chronicle of Higher Education* noted, some professors were not satisfied with the spectacle of students "taking courses about their own cultures." "People from Asia didn't need to be taking courses on Asia," stated one professor involved in the "big curricular revision" a couple of years ago. Now the multicultural requirement is in a form where it's almost acceptable: as of fall 1997 a student must choose a course from roughly the same areas as before, though also including "minority American cultures . . . defined by race, religion, ethnicity, sexual orientation, or physical ability." Having done so, the student must then, states the *Chronicle,* "write a statement justifying her choice."

Even this compromise hasn't been popular across the board — faculty members with varying ideologies spoke against it, both because it is politically correct and also because, given the vast increase in multicultural approaches in most departments, it simply isn't needed anymore.

Politicization among the various departments at Wellesley is widespread but, surprisingly, not extreme, according to most reports. Even Africana studies, which produces "some absolutely radicalized nonsense," according to one longtime Wellesley observer, still has "some good courses." In English, a hotbed of trendiness at many colleges, "most of the courses are on the usual stuff," a faculty member notes; indeed, Wellesley, unlike many colleges today, still requires a Shakespeare course of its majors. Political science is known for having some politicized faculty members, but as a whole the department lacks a radical tone. "There are certainly plenty of moderates," a faculty member assures, if not exactly conservatives, beyond Mary Lefkowitz, the Andrew W. Mellon Professor in the Humanities and an esteemed faculty member in the departments of Greek and Latin. Lefkowitz is widely acknowledged to be one of the most respected classics scholars in the world, and in recent years her efforts as a classicist have placed her in combat against spurious scholarship from Afrocentric scholars. This culminated in the writing of Lefkowitz's critically acclaimed 1996 book *Not out of Africa: How Afrocentrism Became an Excuse to Teach Myth as History.*

At the other end of the scale is, for example, Professor of Africana Studies Tony Martin, who has his students read a book entitled *The Secret Relationship between Blacks and Jews,* which purports to uncover the major role that Jews had in promoting the African slave trade, and which is published by the Nation of Islam. According to the *Chronicle of Higher Education,* "many critics view [the book] as anti-Semitic." And National Public Radio commentator Anthony Brooks pointed out that, while "the college upheld Martin's right to use the text, several of his colleagues criticized the book." The chairman of the Africana studies department has been quoted as saying that "the book is both anti-Semitic and bad scholarship, not because it suggests Jews had a role in the slave trade, but because its conclusions about Jews are politically driven." Martin's own experience culminated in his writing *The Jewish Onslaught: Dispatches from the Wellesley Battlefront,* which details his own experiences regarding the controversy and, in particular, attacks he feels have been aimed at him by Lefkowitz.

The official attitude of Wellesley to all this instability has been embarrassment, and a recognition that, as Wellesley president Diana Chapman Walsh said, "this is the kind of challenge facing many American colleges and universities as they start down the road to multiculturalism."

Outstanding professors at Wellesley include Jonathan Imber in sociology, William Kane in English, Marshall Goldman in economics, Edward Stettner and Marion Just in political science, Andrew Webb in biology, and Mary Lefkowitz in Greek and Latin. The strongest departments are said to be art, biology, chemistry, economics, and political science.

Wellesley has two major assets that enhance her special programs: a distinguished alumnae network that is nonpareil among American colleges, and access to seemingly unlimited funding sources, both internal and external. Among the many programs for students is the Washington Public Service Summer Internship Program for junior-year students, which offers "ten-week internships, including a living expense stipend and housing in local university dormitories." Given that both the first lady of the United States (Hillary Rodham Clinton) and the secretary of state (Madeleine Albright) are both Wellesley alumnae, it would seem that the internship offers a likely lead-in to a first job, and certainly a plethora of networking opportunities.

For those students interested less in personal advancement and more in community outreach and service, Wellesley has "a long-standing tradition of reaching out into the world beyond the College," and even offers Service Opportunity grants so that they can afford to spend summers taking advantage of "unpaid community and public service positions."

Political Atmosphere: Cracked Mosaic?

As at most other elite colleges today, campus debate is dominated, a source close to the Wellesley community complains, by "perceived issues of racism or sexism, which sometimes I think are overreactions to people's stupid mistakes." Last year someone on campus wrote a racist graffito on the dry-erase board of an African-American student, which led to escalating campus controversy over the issue, rather than, one faculty member complained, just "saying 'this is stupid.'" This same faculty member spoke approvingly of how the faculty group enlisted to look into the issue handled it. The group was chaired by Marcellus Andrews, an African-American economist, who rendered the very reasonable conclusion that, in the words of another faculty member, "You can't infringe upon free speech." The graffito may have been "a very senseless response . . . it's quite obnoxious, but it's not physically dangerous."

Most of all, it appears, members of the Wellesley community would like to maintain the fragile peace that has been effected in the past years, and are amenable to reasonable dialogue — for the most part. Unlike at other institutions, where grand-standing and publishing put one on the fast track, tenure at Wellesley is based on good teaching as much as research. Faculty from across the political spectrum tend to respect the scholarship and teaching of others, even when they do not agree with them. There is sensitivity training at Wellesley, but even here, one faculty member claims, "people are getting impatient" with that kind of thing.

True to its multicultural mission, though, Wellesley does manage to present all the appropriate resources to its "mosaic of faces." The Slater International/Multicultural Center sponsors programs that focus on a number of groups, while specific groups target African-American, Latina, and Asian students. African-American students are headquartered at their own Harambee House, whose name, *Voices of Wellesley* notes, comes from "the Swahili word for 'working together.'" The student organization for African-American students, though, is called Ethos, which has its own choir, dance troupe, and black theater. There is a chapter of the historic black sorority Alpha Kappa Alpha, which includes students from MIT and Harvard. Among the religious organizations, there is a Ministry to Black Women. As might be expected, Mezcla and Alianza center on the Latina communities and give particular attention to human rights issues, both in the United States, as in the case of migrant workers, and "in Central and Latin America."

There are even a couple of conservative organizations. There's the Wellesley Republicans, and even the Wellesley Alliance for Life, a companion group to the Wellesley Women for Choice. But while accepted, conservative organizations tend to have a harder time of it than their more progressive peers because "they have a great deal of trouble finding faculty willing to be their advisors," one faculty member remarks. An alternative student publication is put out as a joint venture between Wellesley and MIT, called *Counterpoint,* but while it tends to be more open than the

Wellesley News (the official newspaper), it plays the role of general gadfly rather than a forum of specifically conservative opinion.

Student Life: Sisterly Support

From all reports, life is peaceful and safe in the college's twenty-one residence halls, or, as *Voice of Wellesley* puts it, "casual and welcoming." One of the features of Wellesley about which both faculty and students seem to agree enthusiastically is the availability of support networks for the students, and the unusually close relationships that students appear to have with faculty members. Whereas the atmosphere at many colleges, even selective ones, can be somewhat fearsome and alienating, Wellesley faculty and students alike maintain a sisterly watch over one another. Each dormitory has its own governing structure and a "house associate, generally a faculty or staff member." One faculty member fondly recalls being amazed recently when a student was in the hospital for surgery, "at how well the machine worked" in people's willingness to get the student's assignments to her and help out in any way they could. "When I've taught elsewhere," the same faculty member maintains, "if students are in trouble, there's no one to call."

A number of campus traditions are localized in the dormitories. "Each dorm has a long tradition of parties and get-togethers with students from other Boston-area colleges," states *Voices of Wellesley*. A small community atmosphere is preserved as well, with first-year students sharing both dorms (if not rooms) and meals with members of the other classes. Despite the fact that the college is single-sex, Wellesley women are reported to have an extensive social life with men from the plethora of colleges around Boston, and men are welcome visitors on campus. And, unlike almost every other college in America, one faculty member notes incredulously, "There's no drinking problem. It's the most *sober* campus."

As for student organizations, Wellesley has a plethora: more than 130 are listed, including such unlikely options as a Rugby Club and the amusingly named Archeologists Anonymous. Musical options abound: there are three a cappella music groups, one of which is combined with students from MIT; a glee club; an orchestra; and choirs and jazz groups. Also available are the Dead Serious Improvisational Comedy Troupe, a student-run radio station, and a college dance troupe.

A full range of opportunities exists for students to get involved in college government, and, in a similar vein, a number of political and preprofessional societies help them tap into Wellesley's alumnae network. There are fewer community service options that one might expect, though the fact that Wellesley is located in one of the most prosperous suburbs in the United States might have something to do with that. There's a surfeit, however, of organizations under the heading of "ethnic/cultural awareness."

One persistent but compelling feature of extracurricular life at Wellesley is the "society houses," not advertised at all in *Voices of Wellesley* but deeply wed to college traditions. Rather like intellectual sororities, these societies have their own houses, with kitchens and dining and social spaces. Shakespeare House, obviously, is for "students interested in Shakespearean drama," and there are three others with Greek names that focus, respectively, on art and music, "modern drama," and "intelligent interest in cultural and public affairs." While careful to note that students can enter society houses as early as the second semester of their freshman year, the *Bulletin* does not note whether these organizations have selective admissions policies.

Wellesley provides a full range of standard athletic options, such as NCAA Division III basketball, cross-country, and tennis. The college is especially proud of its crew team — one historic aspect of Wellesley of which the college is forthright and proud. Notes *Voices of Wellesley:* "Wellesley's strength in crew is legendary on the East Coast, a reputation that is nearly as old as the College itself, since Wellesley established its crew team in 1876." Wellesley's crew team has even distinguished itself mightily at the time-honored Head of the Charles Regatta, held every fall in Boston, with dozens of the nation's most noted college teams in attendance.

WESLEYAN UNIVERSITY

Office of Admissions
Middletown, CT 06457
(860) 653-3000
www.wesleyan.edu

Total enrollment: 2,950
Undergraduates: 2,730
SAT Ranges (Verbal/Math): V 610-720, M 610-700
Financial aid: 50%
Applicants: 5,724
Accepted: 32%
Enrolled: 38%
Application deadline: Early decision, Nov. 15, Jan. 1; regular, Jan. 1
Financial aid application deadline: Nov. 15, Feb. 1; guarantees to meet demonstrated need
Tuition: $22,980
Core curriculum: No

A Methodism to the Madness

Wesleyan was founded in 1831 by the Methodist church as a means of educating men for the ministry. It was the first school in the United States to be named in honor of John Wesley — the school's teams were known as the Methodists until the 1930s. Recruitment of non-Methodist professors began in 1888 when Woodrow Wilson, a Presbyterian, came for two years before leaving to become president of Princeton University. Wesleyan is proud of the fact that it adopted the research model of the modern university at this time, long before many schools of similar size jettisoned the classical curriculum for the German model.

What Wesleyan did not do was grow into a larger research-oriented institution on the model of Princeton or Johns Hopkins. When Edwin Etherington, president of the American Stock Exchange and Wesleyan alumnus, became president in 1967, the university, according to its own literature, "plunged immediately into a variety of new programs as the trustees voted to admit women, as recruitment of minority students was intensified, as the faculty liberalized the general requirements for graduation, and as new buildings were planned and approved." Thus it was a businessman, rather than a scholar, who led Wesleyan to loosen its curricular standards and abandon many of its traditions. (The current president, Douglas J. Bennet, is an alumnus and former president of National Public Radio.)

Today the student body numbers some 3,000, about half men and half women. Only 6 percent hails from Connecticut, with the largest portion of the remainder coming from New England and the Northeast. It is impressive, however, that at such a small school 43 states and 25 foreign countries are represented in the student body.

Wesleyan employs many very good scholars who are no doubt dedicated teachers as well. Its library, with some 1.3 million volumes, is larger than that found at most comparably sized schools. Nevertheless, the administration has made no secret of the fact that it has jumped onto the multicultural bandwagon that is tearing through academia today.

Wesleyan can draw on the intellectual capital it built up before political ideologies became so deeply entrenched in higher education, however, so it remains a place where an outstanding liberal education can still be found. It would seem that the school must be doing something right: over the past five years it has witnessed a 22 percent increase in applications.

Academic Life: Do Your Own Thing

In keeping with decisions made a century ago to become a center of research as well as liberal learning, the curriculum at Wesleyan emphasizes research skills in a student's chosen field of study rather than the absorption of a large body of knowledge in the liberal arts and sciences. This vision of education assumes that questions of methodology are more important than questions of content. Thus, like many institutions of higher learning today, Wesleyan refuses to define what an educated person should know. According to a report by the administration, "The opportunity for students to engage in research and discovery becomes all the more valuable when learning capabilities rather than content will be the most abiding legacy of a liberal education." Or, as the report later puts it: "By engaging directly the most challenging and important developments in current scholarship, Wesleyan scholar-teachers can help students participate in shaping knowledge rather than being mere consumers of established views."

In light of these assertions, Wesleyan's curriculum is very open and does not demand that students master any particular body of knowledge. To obtain a truly liberal education at Wesleyan, students must seek the help of older peers and trusted professors.

The university's official literature explains the curriculum in this way: "Unlike many colleges and universities, Wesleyan does not have a core curriculum, nor does it systematically limit first- or second-year students to certain classes or levels of instruction. No single set of courses is required for graduation." All students must, in their first two years, take two courses in each of three areas, all from different departments: social and behavioral sciences, humanities and the arts, and natural and mathematical sciences. Over the following two years one more course in each of these three areas must also be completed. Freshmen take special classes in the First-Year Initiative Program (FYI) that are designed to improve students' writing and rhetorical skills. Taught in small seminars, most of which contain fewer than twenty students, FYIs are "entirely optional," although "students are advised to consider taking at least one of these courses during their first year," according to the catalogue. There is no English composition requirement because, again according to the catalogue, "writing skills are emphasized and developed throughout the curriculum."

The Wesleyan faculty numbers 353, every one of whom teaches undergraduates. At least 285 teach full-time, and the student-faculty ratio is eleven-to-one. These are outstanding numbers, signaling an authentic commitment to teaching of the highest quality.

Some of the better departments include history, medieval studies, art history and architectural history, theater, classics, molecular biology and biochemistry, biology, and physics. Wesleyan also claims a strong literary tradition, something that is embodied in the university press and the prestigious summer workshop for writers. The school's most famous literary figure is Pulitzer Prize winner Annie Dillard, who teaches an occasional course in the English department. Other outstanding faculty members include Martha Crenshaw, Marc Allen Eisner, and John E. Finn in government; Stephen Crites in philosophy; John Bonin in economics; and Joseph Reed and Richard Slotkin in English.

Wesleyan offers two interdisciplinary programs that derive their excellence from the seminar/colloquia setting of the classes and the dedication of the professors.

Indeed, the College of Letters and the College of Social Sciences offer such good programs that one might call them the true intellectual heart of the university. Although not immune to political correctness, the former is an excellent choice for the ambitious student who wishes to pursue studies in the humanities. It is "an interdisciplinary major program for the study of Western literature, history, and philosophy. The core of the program is a series of five colloquia designed to acquaint students with works of literature, history, and philosophy in the ancient world, the Middle Ages and Renaissance, the 17th and 18th centuries, the 19th century, and the 20th century." The catalogue description continues: "Our general goal is cultivation of 'the educated imagination.'" Sophomores who have completed at least two years of work or its equivalent in a foreign language may apply, and all students must spend a semester abroad studying the language in which they choose to become proficient.

The College of Social Sciences (CSS) is also a very attractive major. Much like the College of Letters in that it requires students to pursue their studies in a structured academic setting, CSS, founded in 1959, is a good alternative to many of the more politicized traditional departments.

Both of these colleges deserve close examination by serious students and go a long way toward maintaining true academic integrity at Wesleyan. They offer small classes, intense interaction with faculty, and a coherent approach to the subjects under study. They are indeed colleges within a college.

Despite the administration's fondness for chic studies, many Wesleyan faculty members offer rigorous coursework in traditional and important areas of study. Students wishing to avoid the more politicized elements of intellectual life should peruse the course offerings, find a trusted faculty member upon whom they can rely for advice at registration, and look to their more level-headed peers for knowledge gained through experience. Wesleyan has a great deal to offer the serious student in spite of the best efforts of the administration and its favored faculty members: excellent facilities, dedicated professors, a very good library, and a small and friendly student body.

Departments and programs with a large number of politicized courses include African-American studies, American studies, Queer Studies (a subunit of American studies), and women's studies. Also politicized is the Center for the Humanities, an interdisciplinary program that offers a collection of the most politicized courses from departments across campus, most of which treat their subjects from a Marxist or gender perspective.

Among the most politicized (or just plain bizarre) courses are these:

■ American Studies 180, "Critical Issues in Contemporary Society: Approaches to Radical Change." "A collectively taught and student-organized course, it confronts the traditional character of teacher-student relations by rotating teaching responsibilities. The course challenges the hierarchy, oppression, and exploitation in modern American culture with a variety of critical analyses and alternative proposals. With the guidance of two student facilitators, groups of eight to 12 students will plan and read the course's agenda: They will educate themselves. Topics cover an introduction to current trends in leftist thought, including anarchism, ecology, feminism, Marxism, and ethnic perspectives. The class will deepen its understanding of these views with an analysis of sexuality, heterosexuality, gender, family, race, community, society, and liberalism. This course integrates the personal with the political. Projects have included guerrilla theater, community organizing, and campus activism."

■ College of Letters 290, "Pornography: Writing of Prostitutes." "This course investigates pornographic literature as a body of discursive practices whose 'materials,' according to the cultural critic Susan Sontag, comprise 'one of the extreme forms of human consciousness.' The pornography we study is an art of transgression which impels human sexuality toward, against, and beyond the limits which have traditionally defined civil discourses and practices. . . . Our examination . . . includes the implication of pornography in so-called perverse practices such as voyeurism, bestiality, sadism, and masochism, and considers the inflections of the dominant white-heterosexual tradition by alternative sexualities and genders, as well as by race, class, age, mental and physical competence."

■ Women's Studies 248, "Race, Sex and the History of Normal People." " 'Normal People' have existed only since the last century. This course considers how scientists have historically related the idea of 'normal' to notions of the superior, good, beuatiful [*sic*], healthy and natural in the context of struggles for power by dominant and marginalized communities. Themes, involving questions of equality and inequality, inclusion and exclusion, include: scientific theories of essential 'race,' 'sex,' and 'culture'; conceptions of the body as physically or mentally healthy or diseased; and classifications of normality and abnormality concerned with sexual behavior."

Political Atmosphere: "Get Involved!"

The degree to which multicultural ideologies permeate life at Wesleyan is surprising, even by the standards of today's academy. While there remain many excellent courses taught by accomplished professors, many others, as shown in the brief sampling above, carry a heavy ideological load. Beyond this, the cultural life of the campus is laden with multicultural programs, publications, and various forms of propaganda.

Two areas that are particularly politicized at Wesleyan, as they are at many other universities, are race relations and homosexuality. In both cases Wesleyan stands out not only for the amount of attention accorded these matters, but for the fact that all of this goes on in a university of only 2,900 students. Some state universities with tens of thousands of students produce fewer special programs, housing arrangements, or publications for these groups than does Wesleyan.

Anyone who examines the university's website will come across the "Student of Color Guide," an eleven-page manual for those curious as to how Wesleyan instructs its students on the delicate matter of race relations. On the first page of this guide, in "An Inside Look at Student Thoughts," the following advice is dispensed: "Persistence overcomes resistance," "Always remember to think before you act or speak," "Budget Your Time!," "Get involved," and "Be respectful of other people's race, culture, and beliefs."

One will also find information on segregated financial assistance, fellowships, scholarships, and career opportunities. There are five special-interest, i.e., ethnic, residential houses at Wesleyan, including the Asian/Asian-American House, the Intercultural House, Malcolm X House, and the Women of Color House. No fewer than 23 "Student of Color Organizations" are listed, including Ajua Campos, the "major support group for Latino students on campus"; Ankh, a "creative, political and educational publication produced by and about people of color"; the Black Women's Collective; GBLOC (Gay, Bi-sexual, Lesbians of Color), "an informal soil space for Queer Students of Color to meet and discuss issues regarding our dual identities"; Ujamaa, founded in 1969 to serve the black community; and Women of Color Collective, which believes "Women of Color should not be asked to choose between race or gender."

One recent controversy took place over the Malcolm X House. In the spring of 1996 very few students showed an interest in selecting the Malcolm X House as their dormitory. The university administration allowed nine rooms to be entered in the campuswide housing lottery, and they were filled with white students. Over four hundred students launched a protest, wherein students observed ten minutes of silence "to symbolize the silencing of the students of color community," according to a flyer. The *Chronicle of Higher Education* reported that "The protesters . . . asked for an explicit policy reserving the house for black students. Administrators told them that such a rule would violate campus anti-discrimination guidelines. But they agreed to let the students draft guidelines over the summer for determining who can live in the house."

Student Life: Blue Collars, White T-shirts

Middletown is a mostly blue-collar community of about forty-three thousand. It is less a college town than one could hope for, although there are shops aplenty for the average student. New Haven and Hartford are about thirty minutes away, and New York and Boston are each about two hours by car. There is no public transportation to the big cities, however.

Over 125 student organizations call Wesleyan home, a number that insures there will be something to match almost any student's interests. Among the more interesting: Christian Fellowship; Community Tutorial, which works in the Middletown area; the Equestrian Team; the Cardinal Singers, a women's a cappella group; Green Eggs and Jam, another a cappella group; the Medieval House; several student theater and dance groups; Wesleyan for Life, a pro-life group; the *Wesleyan Review,* a "right of center" newspaper; and the Outing Club.

Freshmen are housed in residence halls and houses. Some housing is single-sex, although most is coed. Clark Residence Hall, next to the Olin Library, is reserved exclusively for freshmen. Each hall in Clark "is equipped with three bathrooms (one for men, one for women, and one coed)." In addition to Malcolm X House for black students, there are several other theme houses, including the Intercultural House, in which "each house member is encouraged to make the house free from prejudice and discrimination and to create opportunities for an active exchange and interaction among people of different backgrounds." About 95 percent of the undergraduate student body lives on campus, and housing is guaranteed for all four years.

One of the most admirable features of Wesleyan is its pledge to meet the demonstrated financial needs of anyone it admits.

Athletic facilities at the school are quite good thanks to the Freeman Athletic Center, completed in 1990. The $22 million complex offers just about any diversion one could imagine, including a 25-yard pool, a 5,000-square-foot multi-exercise room, and an ice-skating arena. About 700 of the university's 2,900 students participate in intercollegiate competition on Wesleyan's Division III varsity teams — fourteen for men, fourteen for women, and one coed (golf). These include baseball, basketball, football, ice hockey, lacrosse, squash, and tennis. Among the intercollegiate club sports are cycling (men and women), sailing (men and women), and water polo (men and women). Intramural sports include badminton, floor hockey, and racquetball.

WHEATON COLLEGE (ILLINOIS)

Office of Admissions
Wheaton, IL 60187-5593
(708) 752-5005
www.wheaton.edu

Total enrollment: 2,500
Undergraduates: 2,200
SAT Ranges (Verbal/Math): V 550-640, M 510-600

Financial aid: 66%
Applicants: 1,920
Accepted: 75%
Enrolled: 31%
Application deadline: Jan. 15
Financial aid application deadline: Mar. 1
Tuition: $14,360
Core curriculum: No

The Intellectual Capital of Evangelicalism

What Notre Dame used to be to American Catholicism, Wheaton College in Illinois remains to this country's evangelicals: a bastion of the faith and an intellectual center for a large community of like-minded believers. Unlike Notre Dame, Wheaton so far has refused to cave in to outside pressures, and today rests on the same intellectual and spiritual foundations upon which it was founded in the mid–nineteenth century.

The challenge for Wheaton today is similar to that which the college faced in earlier decades: staying true to its beliefs and therefore staying somewhat separate from the rest of the world, but at the same time remaining fully engaged with the world. Though Wheaton is not only for evangelicals, its rules for campus life will drive away many who can't abide by them. Evangelical beliefs have engendered strict prohibitions on alcohol and tobacco, but the same beliefs have kept the college clear, for the most part, of many of the detrimental trends — both academic and social — found on many other campuses today. However, according to its administration's policy statements, Wheaton is seeking ways to accommodate some of the prevailing trends in academia. The college continues to experiment with a mixture of multicul-turalism and conservative Christianity, but has so far come out on the traditional side of the spectrum.

One doesn't go to Wheaton for the parties, or for disco night at the student union, or to meet potential fraternity brothers-for-life. A student enrolling at Wheaton must have a good religious and liberal arts education as his specific purpose, and must believe that whatever is lost at a somewhat insular church school is made up for in a strengthening of his beliefs and commitment to the evangelical mission. Of course, many students find such an environment liberating and manage to have plenty of fun in the bargain.

Academic Life: Reformed, Not Relativist

Among Wheaton's several famous alumni, the best known is evangelist Billy Graham. The campus is home to the Billy Graham Center, which is used for art exhibits, student gatherings, and several evangelical institutes. And, as befits the alma mater of such a widely revered preacher, the distribution requirements at Wheaton include fourteen credit hours (in a semester system) of Bible and theology.

Overall, the distribution requirements at Wheaton are fairly broad, yet they include numerous courses in the liberal arts and sciences. All students must take two courses in a foreign language. There is a world civilization requirement, and, unlike some other colleges in this book, Wheaton does consider the West to be part of the world; however, there is no Western civilization requirement per se. While the distribution requirements at Wheaton are not sufficient to compose a true core curriculum, the school's basic course requirements do surpass those at many state universities and some private schools with a more professional orientation. "The core is excellent and is based on a broad liberal arts education," says one faculty member. "Most students study Western civilization through various departments."

The strongest departments at Wheaton include several disciplines from the humanities — music and history — and several sciences, such as chemistry, biology, mathematics, and economics. Students and faculty name a handful of outstanding professors, including Peter J. Hill and Seth Norton in economics; Roger Lundin, Jill Baumgaertner, and Sharon Ewert Coolidge in English; Mark Noll in history; and art professors Joel Sheesley and John Walford. English is the most popular major on campus, followed by the social sciences and history. Almost 10 percent of the student body majors in religious studies, a statistic that reflects Wheaton's mission and strong emphasis on biblical studies.

By all accounts, the most politicized department is sociology, which, in the words of a professor in another department, "would like to be politically correct but which has no strength." Another professor says most of the liberalism on campus manifests itself in "an antipathy for the free market. Our concern is that Western missionaries are ethnocentric, so there is some cultural relativism. It can be an underlying theme at times."

The college offers several off-campus programs that place students in unique and interesting situations. Overseas programs are based in Europe, Asia, and the Middle East, and the Black Hills Science Station in South Dakota runs an academic program that may count toward fulfillment of the science requirements. On campus, the Center for Applied Christian Ethics sponsors forums and promotes discussions on the role and nature of Christian ethics in a pluralistic world. The center, whose national advisory board is chaired by former surgeon general C. Everett Koop, has in recent years discussed welfare reform, "Competition and Success," "Secrecy, Lying, and Censorship," "Greed and Generosity," as well as education, health care, and medical research.

Wheaton is also strengthened by its library holdings, which include many of the private papers of some of the greatest Christian apologists of the last century. Among those represented are Malcolm Muggeridge, C. S. Lewis, J. R. R. Tolkien, Dorothy Sayers, and G. K. Chesterton. The presence of the papers of the latter may surprise some, since Chesterton's love of cigars and drink (both forbidden to Wheaton faculty and students) is well known. But it is to Wheaton's credit that Chesterton and the other luminaries mentioned are indeed loved and appreciated — that is, read — at Wheaton, which is more than can be said of several such writers at places considered more prestigious.

Political Atmosphere: Into All the World

Since the political climate at Wheaton might best be described as evangelical, it may be of help to explain the college's take on that word. The college's web pages, citing David Bebbington, list four "hallmarks of evangelical religion: *conversionism,* the belief that lives need to be changed; *activism,* the expression of the gospel in effort; *biblicism,* a particular regard for the Bible; and *crucicentrism,* a stress on the sacrifice of Christ on the cross." This same web page adds that "the overall political tenor of the movement could be described as mildly conservative and more likely to be Republican." Not coincidentally, the National Association of Evangelicals is headquartered in the city of Wheaton.

The conservative evangelical Christianity of Wheaton faculty has been a major factor in constraining the more radical versions of multiculturalism on campus. One professor says the faculty's beliefs set "the parameters so that the more obnoxious stuff of some campuses is less present here," resulting in a political atmosphere that is "not great but better than most places." But, as on many other campuses, there is some fear of the future.

Wheaton will hire strong multicultural-type professors who "fit other criteria," says one faculty member. "We're open to all, but we don't lower our standards," says another. Given this, students cannot assume that by coming to Wheaton they will find only traditionalist faculty. A student may assume, however, that virtually all professors will possess more than a little evangelical fervor, and that the faculty will not be a collection of secularists bent on convincing students that their religious beliefs are mere cultural constructs or primitive notions. "There is no pro-choice position on campus, and no one says that spreading Christianity abroad is a bad thing," says a professor. "There are some radical feminists here, but it's much more constrained than at other places. There's a genuine sense of collegiality."

Enrolling at Wheaton involves more than just taking classes: it takes a commitment to the clean-living standards required of all members of the Wheaton community. Students and faculty members must pledge that they will not smoke nor will they drink alcohol while they are at Wheaton. Also, dancing (other than square dancing) is banned, and everyone is expected to keep the Sabbath. Chapel services are mandatory, and the college's application for admission asks whether the applicant has accepted Jesus Christ as his or her Savior. While many denominations are represented at Wheaton, this evangelical Christianity pervades life on campus, and any student not comfortable with this form of Christianity might feel out of place. However, the college has not adopted any sort of speech code (despite some soft rumblings about one), and it is one professor's feeling that such a code is not needed. "We don't need it given our efforts to treat each other with respect," the professor says.

To maintain this atmosphere, new faculty are carefully screened. "The Christian commitment from all faculty must be done very seriously, not in a liberal wishy-washy way," a professor says. "Every department does their own recruiting, but there is a faculty personnel committee which screens for the Wheaton community. So, if someone had great academic credentials but no agreement with the mission statement of the college, they wouldn't be hired." Potential faculty members are also interviewed by the president and provost.

In its literature, Wheaton makes no apologies for its evangelical identity, and most faculty members seem determined to keep the college on track. Yet some at Wheaton notice what one professor calls "a temptation — a tension — over how to be both a good college yet a Christian one. There is a very real feeling that Wheaton can go down" if this balance is not kept in the forefront by the college's administrators. Another professor is cautiously optimistic about the college's future, but says: "The administration and Board of Trustees are behind us, but they're naive sometimes, and that worries me a great deal." Notes another professor: "Wheaton is an island, and some don't understand just how radical and alienated many faculty members are."

So, while Wheaton remains a strong voice for evangelical Christianity, maintaining that witness into the coming century is going to require diligence and perhaps a bit of worldly wisdom on the part of those to whom its future is entrusted. Examples abound of colleges that began as straitlaced church-related institutions but then took drastic turns — recently or decades ago — toward secularization when those whose mission it was to oversee the traditions and foundations of the colleges somehow failed.

Wheaton does seem prepared to resist at least one trend — the push for increased diversity and multiculturalism. This subject was addressed by the college's president in remarks entitled "Wheaton College Initiatives, a Vision for the Future," a plan to improve the college as it enters the new century. "In recent years, the Biblical notion of diversity has sometimes been overshadowed by distorted notions of political correctness," the president wrote. "Through our Diversity Initiative we want to recover the important biblical idea of diversity as 'an earthly reflection of the body of Christ.' Because we celebrate the diversity of Christ's church, we are making intentional efforts to enhance the heterogeneity of our community." As an evangelical church school, Wheaton sees spreading the gospel to the entire world — not just to the generally white, Midwestern constituency it has traditionally attracted — as an important part of its mission, perhaps the central part. This is a noble goal, but it must be sought with wisdom.

Another threat to traditional institutions has been the pressure placed on faculty to research and publish. At Wheaton, teaching has traditionally taken first place, although many Wheaton scholars have long been accomplished researchers. The "Wheaton Initiative" calls for a continued emphasis on both teaching and scholarly research. It states: "Wheaton College has always focused on the teaching and mentoring of students. Thus our faculty stand at the very core of our mission." At this time it seems unlikely that Wheaton will do anything to upset this balance, and students should be able to find many professors who are willing to spend a great deal of time with them.

In short, Wheaton seems to be well insulated against the passing trends of academia. Again, the college president has addressed this issue. "As a pervasive relativism continues to erode the foundations of our society, leaching away the very notions of truth and meaning, our generation is discovering with alarm the bankruptcy of its own secularism," he recently stated. "Meanwhile, the academic world, long considered a source for truth, lies fragmented, both an instigator and a reflector of these societal trends. While disallowing any idea of absolute Truth, our universities struggle to rediscover some substitute center, something to unify and make sense of the explosion of information and data. In short, most of us have never known a time when our world was more intellectually and morally confused, or the product of Christian higher education more relevant."

Student Life: *In Loco Parentis*

The rules for living in the Wheaton community pretty much eliminate some pastimes commonly found on other campuses: beer, tobacco, drugs, dancing, and fraternities and sororities, to name a few. Most college and university students would think there was nothing left to do at the place. But Wheaton students (known as "Wheaties") engage in different kinds of fun, much of it based on trips to nearby Chicago, only 25 miles to the east. There they find the myriad attractions of this great city, including museums, bookstores, plays, movies, restaurants, and shopping. Several programs on campus allow Wheaton students to aid the poor in Chicago, and they take this very seriously as part of their Christian obligation to serve those less fortunate than themselves.

Still taken seriously on campus is the once-dominant belief that a college should act *in loco parentis*. All Wheaton students are required to live in college-owned housing, and freshmen must live in dormitories. Upperclassmen may live in dorms or in college-owned houses or apartments. There is a midnight curfew (2 A.M. on Friday and Saturday nights) for freshmen; students must sign out when leaving for the night; and all areas have quiet hours overnight and in the early mornings. All residence halls are served by residence directors, professionally educated adults who live in the halls and provide guidance and assistance to the residents.

Wheaton fields several men's and women's sports teams, including men's soccer and swimming and diving teams of both sexes, all of which usually post winning and even championship seasons. Football and basketball are also popular, as are the 24 intramural teams which offer a sport for just about everyone.

The college, with refreshing candor, admits on its own home page that its facilities, "including a student center built more than 45 years ago for a student body half our present size, are inadequate for today's needs." Plans are under way, however, to convert two buildings, including the present gymnasium, into "a true campus center" that will house an arena and multicourt indoor recreation facility. Facilities are good enough, in any case, to have hosted in the college's Artist Series several well-known musicians, including Yo Yo Ma, Leontyne Price, and James Galway.

COLLEGE OF WILLIAM AND MARY

Office of Undergraduate Admission
P.O. Box 8795
Williamsburg, VA 23187-8795
(757) 221-4223
www.wm.edu

Total enrollment: 7,700
Undergraduates: 5,480
SAT Ranges (Verbal/Math): V 600-710, M 590-690
Financial aid: 30%
Applicants: 7,420
Accepted: 43%
Enrolled: 41%
Application deadline: Jan. 15
Financial aid application deadline: Feb. 15
Tuition: in-state, $5,148; out-of-state, $15,378
Core curriculum: No

Academic Royalty

The College of William and Mary (W&M) is the second-oldest institution of higher learning in the United States, and is the only institution in the country to have a Royal Charter (granted in 1693 by namesakes King William III and Queen Mary II). Phi Beta

Kappa was founded there the same year as the United States, and the largely honorary title of college chancellor has been held by George Washington, John Tyler, Warren Burger, and, currently, Margaret Thatcher. The school has scores of reasons to be proud of its past — and unlike a lot of other colleges, it is.

But W&M has ample reason to be proud of its present, too. The college, private until 1906, is one of best state schools in the country, and its faculty is famously dedicated to undergraduate teaching. State funding has gone down in recent years, but the college continues to improve. "It really is a great bargain — one of the eminent state universities, and it has the ambiance of a small college even though it's a university," a professor says.

The college attracts an excellent student body, well rounded and focused on its studies. The 7,700 students (5,500 undergraduates) enjoy a student-faculty ratio of twelve-to-one. The beautiful campus includes the oldest academic building in continual use in the country, and it is thought to have been designed by none other than Christopher Wren.

Academic Life: A Glorious Revolution

William and Mary uses distribution requirements rather than a core curriculum. A revised general education curriculum went into effect in 1996, and while at other schools that might have meant a looser, more politicized set of requirements, faculty say the new standards actually closed some gaps in the old curriculum. They "make it more likely that all undergraduate students get a taste of a broad range of intellectual experiences, including creative endeavors, before they leave," a professor says. "The older system was good, but left some loopholes through which many students could slip if carelessly advised, whereas the new system specifies in more detail what a good adviser and well motivated student would have come up with under the old system."

The revised curriculum requires 11 courses distributed among mathematics and quantitative reasoning; natural sciences (including a laboratory course); social sciences; world cultures and history; literature and history of the arts; creative and performing arts; and philosophical, religious, and social thought. Students must also demonstrate proficiency in a foreign language, writing, and physical education. Each entering freshman must take one freshman seminar; these are offered in most of the college's departments. There is also a Western civilization requirement.

While the general education classes are mostly solid liberal arts courses, enough is left up to the instructor that someone so inclined could taint the course with the ideology of his choice. "The only risk [under the new system] is that, under our system of classroom freedom, some instructors will deviate from catalogue descriptions of courses far enough to make a course inappropriate for the requirement that it supposedly fulfills," a professor says.

A student says advisers encourage students to take a range of classes, and especially ask them to explore areas outside their majors. "They don't usually have an agenda — my advisor is a campaign manager of the Democratic Party, but he doesn't try to steer me toward liberal professors," the student says. "And they try to get students to take courses from a wide variety of departments, so that if you're a humanities major you're encouraged to take science courses."

Although some professors and administrators would like to see W&M become more politicized in both its course offerings and faculty makeup, it has resisted the onslaught of politicization more adamantly than many other schools of comparable quality. "The issue here is well under control at present," a professor says. "Students are made aware of the real injustices which have been done in the past, but none of this has been done in such a way as to disrupt the process of true liberal education; attempts to do that have failed quite quickly because the many women and minorities in the administration are, for the most part, realists who know how to work within the system." In general, administrators have no radical agenda or PC bias, a student says.

The professors who teach some of the best courses at W&M are George Grayson and Clayton Clemens in government, Robert E. Welsh and Hans C. von Baeyer in physics, Dale Hoak and James Lewis Axtell in history, Kim Wheatley and John Conlee in English, Lewis Leadbeater and James Baron in classical studies, James Livingston and Thomas Finn in religion, Gerald Johnson in geology, and Lawrence Wiseman in biology.

According to faculty and students, the college's strongest departments are biology, classical studies, economics, geology, physics, and religion. Government has some excellent professors, but has become increasingly politicized in recent years.

Despite the college's best efforts, ideological teaching has crept into several departments. These, according to faculty and students, include public policy, English, and the department of literary and cultural studies.

In addition, several of the freshman seminars reveal an agenda beyond merely expanding the intellectual horizons of students. One example is "Gender and Power in Africa," wherein, the catalogue states, "the gendered dimensions of ritual symbolism, social institutions, and political power will be of particular importance." Other politicized seminars include "Recycling Technology"; an English department offering called "Language, Race and Gender," which focuses on "racial, ethnic and sex differences in American English, and thus American society"; "Gender, Regime, Transitions, War and Revolution," a government department seminar; "Multicultural Musics of America"; sociology's "Gender Nonwestern"; and women's studies' "Gender and Science."

The idea of the freshman seminar is perfectly valid: give new students the opportunity to learn in a small setting from an experienced faculty member. And many of W&M's seminars do just that. Students must pay attention, read the material, and be ready to contribute to class discussions — even in the politicized offerings.

645

Yet the radical seminars listed above miss out on another educational chance: the pursuit of broad knowledge rather than narrow ideology. This lack is especially unfortunate when the participants are freshmen and still in the process of training their minds toward the manner in which they will be educated for the rest of their lives.

There are also some radical classes beyond the freshman seminars, though these are more rare than at similar institutions. The English department teaches "Modern Black American Literature," which addresses "the problem of patronage, the 'black aesthetic,' and the rise of black literary theory and 'womanist' criticism." The literary and cultural studies department offers an introductory course whose topic varies each year. Recently the topic was "Literary and Cultural Constructions of Crime," in which students covered works that ranged from "Greek tragedy and Dante to the detective novel and gangster rap."

Political Atmosphere: Teaching Fit for a King

Faculty at William and Mary value the teaching role of the college, and those who want it to remain true to its original mission have kept the institution from the problems that arise in trying to become a major research university. According to a faculty member, during the 1980s and into the early 1990s the administration wanted the college to become a research institute along the lines of a Johns Hopkins. "They encountered considerable resistance from most of the faculty, although the chemistry, physics, and history departments always have been dominated by people who thought that way," the professor says.

Other factors beyond the school's control have played a part as well. "What really saved us during those years was the tight budget," a professor says. With no money to escape its tradition, W&M did its best to keep alive the better portions of its rich past. Another benefit came from a new post-tenure review procedure demanded by the Virginia Council of Higher Education. This directive "made it very clear that research was third behind teaching and service in what the state expected to have reviewed," a professor says.

Typical professors at W&M teach a heavier load than do their counterparts at similar schools, although full professors often teach less — "often for good reason," a professor says. A few years ago the college eliminated eight graduate programs, including the popular M.A. in English, so fewer teaching assistants are available, those on campus say. But since professors no longer had to spend as much time with graduate students, there was increased pressure to produce research. However, the steps taken by W&M to emphasize teaching prevented the situation from becoming unbalanced.

The college has also tamed the growth of business and other professional programs that sometimes overshadow the liberal arts departments. Part of this was by design, part by accident: "Business deans have had a talent for shooting themselves in the foot," a professor says. But the professional programs still attract the largest donations, mostly because alumni of those programs are in better financial shape to dispense their largesse.

Although Virginia, home to about two-thirds of the students, is a conservative state, the student body is less conservative than the college administration and more similar politically to the faculty. "The general ideology is liberal," a professor says. "Most students are knee-jerk liberals, and there are more leftist groups on campus that do a lot of programs, but they're no more favored by the administration than conservative groups."

W&M does have several well-promoted "diversity weeks," and the administration seems solidly in favor of these. However, according to a student, "no one pays attention to [multicultural groups] beyond these weeks. This is not so much a conservative school as one where everyone on both sides is relaxed and less vocal."

The diversity weeks are organized by the college's Office of Multicultural Affairs, whose other events range from ethnic dinners to entire months dedicated to selected groups. Some examples include Hispanic Heritage Month, Chusok Festival, Expressions of India, Pre-Kwanzaa Celebration, Lunar New Year Celebration, Black History Month, Women's History Month, and Taste of Asia. The college sponsors the Multicultural Leadership Retreat each August for presidents of cultural organizations like the African American Male Coalition, Global Nomads, ESSENCE — Women of Color, Empowerment Network, and the Latin American Club.

The Office of Multicultural Affairs also offers such services as "Multicultural Student Advocacy," through which "professional staff are available to provide information and advice on personal and social matters, to make referrals to other campus and community resources as appropriate . . . and to serve as a catalyst if you feel you have been offended or the victim of discrimination." The office also runs "Diversity Training," designed to "break down barriers, challenge the stereotypes, and strive to learn from differences in people, cultures, and the global community." According to the office, topics include "building community through target/non-target group exercises, stand and declare, and a cultural simulation entitled 'In Each Others [*sic*] Eyes.'"

The college has no formal speech code, and freshmen face only a light dose of instruction upon arriving on campus: a one-hour seminar preaches the merits of safe sex, getting plenty of sleep, and eating well. After this, according to a student, "there is no more propaganda."

Student Life: Life in a Museum

William and Mary stands at one end of Duke of Gloucester Street, the heart of exquisitely and meticulously restored Colonial Williamsburg. Essentially a large, open-air museum, Colonial Williamsburg includes scores of period houses, shops, mansions, and buildings used by the colonial government, all explained by costumed guides and craftsmen. Some W&M students work in the shops and museums, and the restored buildings of the colonial town are architecturally similar to the college's oldest buildings. The 1,200-acre W&M campus has the oldest continually used academic building in the nation; built in 1697, the Christopher Wren Building is named for its presumed architect. Even the more recent additions to the campus reflect the influence of colonial brickwork and proportions.

The Tidewater region of Virginia includes many other historical attractions such as Yorktown and Jamestown, but also offers beaches and the Chesapeake Bay. The Outer Banks of North Carolina are only three hours away. Williamsburg is about 150 miles south of Washington, D.C., and 50 miles from both Richmond and Norfolk, Virginia.

The student body is mostly Virginian, with about two-thirds hailing from that state. Recent statistics show that 54 percent of in-state applicants were accepted, while only 32 percent of out-of-staters made it in. Students appreciate the atmosphere and the quality of teaching at W&M. "I visited campus and really liked it," a student says. "It's moderately sized, mostly an undergraduate school, and there are good professors. I like the lower key atmosphere here. It isn't an all-consuming school." For the quality of education offered, W&M is a bargain for in-state students, who paid around $5,000 in tuition for the 1997-98 academic year. Out-of-state students pay just over $15,000.

The Earl Gregg Swem Library holds more than 1 million volumes and houses special collections of documents from a number of historical figures, including former chief justice Warren Burger.

W&M was the first school in the country to institute an honor code, and this code survives today. Students are also responsible for governing their own residence halls, deciding open hours, smoking policies, and quiet times. Both coed and single-sex dorms are available, and all freshmen are required to live on campus unless they reside with their family within thirty miles of the school. Housing is guaranteed for three out of four years, but most upperclassmen who want rooms can get them. Only juniors and seniors are allowed to keep cars on campus.

There are 260 student groups at W&M, ranging from performing ensembles to religious and service organizations. The college says that about two-thirds of students participate in some form of community service, and President George Bush once praised the students' commitment, saying they were "what I call points of light in action." The campus also has 15 national social fraternities and 13 sororities.

The largest group on campus, however, is the College Republicans. Other conservative groups include the Thatcher Society, which sponsors debates, and the *Remnant,* an alternative student newspaper.

W&M has 23 intercollegiate sports teams, and its student-athletes are noted as students as frequently as they are as athletes. The graduation rate for W&M athletes is in the top 3 percent of all NCAA Division I programs. There are also 29 student-run club teams, including, in a nod to the college's English roots, cricket. Almost 90 percent of students participate in a sport, including intercollegiate, club, or intramural activities.

WILLIAMS COLLEGE

Office of Admissions
Director of Admissions
Williams College
P.O. Box 487
Williamstown, MA 01267
(413) 597-2211
www.williams.edu

Total enrollment: 2,024
Undergraduates: 1,981
SAT Ranges (Verbal/Math): V 650-770, M 660-750
Financial aid: 50%
Applicants: 4,540
Accepted: 25%
Enrolled: 45%
Application deadline: Jan. 1
Financial aid application deadline: Feb. 1
Tuition: $29,350 (conprehensive)
Core curriculum: No

Traditions Reconsidered

Nestled in the beautiful Berkshire Hills, Williams College has a long and distinguished history as one of the nation's top liberal arts schools. Chartered in 1793, the college began by educating "young gentlemen from every part of the Union . . . in all branches of useful and polite literature." But Williams College is now vastly different than it was 200 — or even 40 — years ago.

The Williams administration attributes some changes at the college to more competitive admissions since World War II — a rather odd place to lay the credit or blame for alterations to an august tradition. In the college catalogue, the school claims that these changes have meant "a quickening of the intellectual life of the college and a reconsideration of traditions and emphases no longer considered appropriate for an institution of higher learning." The catalogue lists an all-male student body, compulsory religious services, and fraternities as things Williams has abandoned under this rationale. The number of majors has also expanded — at the expense of the core curriculum. And though Williams remains a very good school, its commitment to the traditional liberal arts has waned.

In relative terms, however, Williams still has much to boast about: its location is stunning, its facilities are outstanding, and its alumni are still highly loyal. It is not, however, all its reputation would suggest.

Academic Life: Long Divisions

There is no core curriculum at Williams, only a very broad set of distribution requirements. In order to graduate, students must take at least three courses in each of three divisions: language and the arts, social studies, and science and mathematics. These divisions do little to limit students' options — virtually any course satisfies one requirement or another. Under each division, the college catalogue lists whole departments rather than specific courses. For instance, students could get the same language and the arts credit from taking "Samuel Johnson and the Literary Tradition" or "Latina Feminisms in the United States," or for that matter "Traditional Chinese Literature in Translation."

"It is very easy for a student to graduate with no understanding of the Constitution, the tradition of ideas that shaped the American founding, Plato, Aristotle, Aquinas, and so on," says one Williams student. Yet while students can graduate without courses on Shakespeare, *The Federalist Papers,* or ancient Greece and Rome, they cannot receive a degree without taking a course in non-European history and thought. That is because Williams also has a one-course "requirement in peoples and cultures," intended to "ensure that all students graduate with at least some basic understanding of the cultural pluralism of American society and the world at large." The course used to fulfill the requirement must be "primarily concerned with peoples and culture of North America that trace their origins to Africa, Asia, Latin America, Oceania, or the Caribbean; Native American peoples and cultures; or the peoples and cultures of Africa, Asia, Latin America, Oceania, or the Caribbean." This means that a course in Japanese or the history of blacks in the American South would count toward the "peoples and cultures" credit, for instance, while one in the history of Irish immigration would not. The class used to meet the diversity requirement may also count as one of the nine required from the distribution list.

The "peoples and cultures" requirement is affectionately referred to as the "PC requirement" by some undergraduates. Nearly 100 courses fulfill the requirement —

courses that, according to one student, "are tied together primarily by their common focus on identity politics and victimization studies." Because it is only one course and because many courses fit the criteria, one professor says the requirement is "so minimal and unobtrusive" that it should not be particularly bothersome to students. But a student laments that there are not "very many courses which focus on the traditions and ideas which have shaped the Western consciousness and social, political, and economic reality." Many Williams students with interests in the traditional humanities would like to see a reform of the curriculum, and wish the college president would "consider at least an optional core curriculum or a Great Books course," the student says. Others say it might be better that there is no core, since those in charge of drafting and implementing it would surely have a radical agenda to promote. There was extensive faculty debate about a core at Williams nearly a decade ago, but nothing came of it, and since there "is no common agreement" among faculty as to what such a core would look like, implementing one would be "unrealistic at this point," one professor says. Consequently, the four-course requirement in physical education (which includes a swim test for all freshmen) might be the portion of the general education plan with the most support across campus.

Credit is also available for skiing. The Williams academic calendar contains a January term that sometimes is more of a winter break for credit than a true learning experience, according to faculty and students. One student says that instead of taking an academic course, students can go to Vail, Colorado, and ski for a month. Grading is on a pass/fail basis and is often based on a single ten-page paper due at the end of the term. Some of the January courses — "Science Fiction," "Introduction to Dutch" — would not otherwise be available to students, but as a student says, the term mainly "allows you to be on campus and have more free time."

More rewarding is an enticing program called "Semester on the Sea," in which students study the history and literature of the oceans, along with practical marine skills, while living in historic cooperative houses at the Mystic (Conn.) Seaport Museum. In addition to learning boatbuilding, shipsmithing, sailing, and celestial navigation, students enrolled in this program take courses in maritime history, literature of the sea, oceanography or marine ecology, and marine policy.

According to students, the strongest professors at Williams include Gary Jacobsohn in political science, Richard DeVeaux in mathematics, Michael Lewis in art history, Robert Johnson in history, and Robert Jackall in sociology/anthropology.

Williams's programs in the sciences are still extremely good, according to students. Biology, chemistry, physics, geology, mathematics, and a rare undergraduate neuroscience program are all recommended. The premed program is highly rated, and Williams graduates enjoy consistent high placement in medical schools. The Science Center is undergoing a massive renovation of its quad and laboratories, which will further improve the science facilities at the college. The joint anthropology/sociology program is also very good; according to one student, it has "maintained its intellectual core through required sequence courses and largely resisted the holy trinity of race, class, and gender that has all but taken over history, English, political science, and economics." The art history department, which works closely with the nearby Clark Institute of Art, is also widely praised.

As for politicized departments, the worst offenders are, not surprisingly, women's studies and African-American studies. The college catalogue lists several courses under the heading of gay, lesbian, and bisexual studies, but there is as yet no formal concentration in that area.

Course listings in the humanities are also particularly illustrative of the light-weight nature or political tenor of some Williams instruction. In the anthropology course "Witchcraft, Sorcery, and Magic," students will answer such questions as "Are witches self-aware agents who believe in the malign magic they practice, or are they innocent, marginalized victims of hegemonic powers?" And then there's a political science course called "Practicing Feminism: A Study of Political Activism," which not only indoctrinates students but hopes to spread its gospel through "fieldwork at community agencies" where students work on "projects that might raise awareness of feminist issues in the community," according to the college catalogue.

Feminism and New Age spirituality merge in many religion department courses. In "Christ and Isis" students discuss "issues of self, sexuality, ethics, and politics." "Theologies of Liberation" includes an examination of the writings of the feminist witch Starhawk. And the goal of "Eve and the Snake," according to the catalogue, "is to understand and analyze the relationship between contemporary feminist spiritual movements and the search for inclusive self-identity."

In the good departments, students encounter a broad range of views in the classroom — some worthwhile, some harmless, and some decidedly nonacademic. A professor of anthropology and Latin American studies recently published a book on the New Age practice of channeling that, according to a college press release, "examines the phenomenon of channeling, the practice of serving as a vessel for the voices of ancient or other worldly beings." The chair of the German and Russian departments has published award-winning cookbooks. And Professors Jacobsohn (political science) and Susan Dunn (Romance languages) recently coedited a collection of essays entitled *Diversity and Citizenship: Rediscovering American Nationhood* (Rowman and Littlefield, 1997), which examines "the connection between citizenship and nationhood and the relationship between individual and collective identities."

As one professor notes, there is a "strong research element at Williams for an undergraduate liberal arts college." The professor who wrote the book on channeling goes so far as to argue, in a letter to the editor of the *Williams Observer*, a student newspaper, that the college would still exist without any students so long as faculty continued their distinguished contributions to the publishing world. "The education of undergraduates is an important part of our work, and one in which we take justifiable pride," the professor writes. "But it is not the reason why Williams exists or why we do what we do." The professor also maintains that students' tuition money does not pay faculty salaries — rather, much of that money comes from research grants and the school's endowment. The editor of the paper responded that while one of the fundamental tasks of a university "is to increase human knowledge," it must also take at least equal pains to see that "this knowledge, once acquired, is imparted." To tell the truth, we're not sure we want all the channeling stuff handed on.

For the record, faculty at Williams do most of their research on their own, and student participation is only "idiosyncratic," according to a professor. Each department does offer at least one course taught as a tutorial, in which pairs of students meet weekly with a professor "to discuss a paper, problem set, or work of art produced by one of the students," according to the catalogue.

The research element would be more palatable if faculty advising were better than poor to fair. During freshman year, "advisors more or less rubber stamp anything you want to take," a student says. "After that, you're pretty much on your own." According to both students and faculty, individual initiative is the key to obtaining good advice from faculty. One professor says "some students get inadequate advising after the first year . . . it all depends on what the student wants." In order to combat complaints about poor freshman advising, the college recently decided that an individual faculty member can serve as adviser for no more than five freshmen.

The current and recent presidents of Williams all enjoyed prior lives as humanities professors — a refreshing fact in an age when so many high-ranking college officials are career administrators. President Harry Payne, inaugurated in 1994, is a respected scholar of European intellectual history and has served as the president of the American Society for Eighteenth-Century Studies.

Political Atmosphere: Militia, Not Minutemen

Williams made the front page of the *New York Times* in 1997 after a radical, armed, left-wing organization recruited members on the college's campus. And not just in dorms and abandoned buildings: members of the Provisional Communist Party, a paramilitary organization planning a takeover of the United States, not only recruited, but spoke in political science classes under the auspices of a local labor organization. Some Williams students joined the organization, and one was arrested in Brooklyn when a cache of weapons was discovered in an apartment there.

Overall, though, students and faculty report that the majority of the student body is not very active politically. Student activism is a regular part of the campus atmosphere, but only a small percentage of the student body does the talking. An increasing number of students are conservative or Republican, but one student remarks that "most students could be labeled apathetic . . . they do not have much interest in campus politics . . . few see the stakes in the ideological battles, choosing instead to have a good time." The faculty at Williams is predominantly liberal, and President Payne, while not conservative, is described by one conservative student as in most respects "a fair and decent man."

One professor notes that ideological views on campus "express themselves in majoritarian ways," and that there is consequently an atmosphere of "routine political correctness" at Williams. There is also a "fairly vocal and verbal expression on the right," which articulates itself most concisely in the pages of the *Williams Free Press*. The paper began in 1994 when several Williams students and concerned alumni established a nonprofit corporation called the Zenger Foundation (after printer John Peter Zenger, acquitted in 1735 in the most prominent libel trial of the colonial days) to raise money for the paper and fund a conservative speakers bureau on campus.

According to one professor, the *Free Press* has "raised some very good issues, though sometimes in a gratuitously provocative way." The newspaper regularly runs afoul of the faculty and administration at Williams. During the spring semester of 1997, for instance, 36 professors signed a letter of complaint to the *Free Press* editorial board, contending that critiques of faculty and administrators were becoming too personal. Yet some faculty continue to support the premise of the publication. "The issues they raise are entirely appropriate," one says.

Although it may offend the sensibilities of certain faculty members, the *Free Press* does have widespread support off campus, including from a large number of Williams alumni: of roughly 20,000 graduates, 700 are subscribers. Well-known conservative writers like William Bennett (class of 1965), George Gilder, and Dinesh D'Souza all serve on the paper's advisory board.

The college itself funds all types of student groups. However, one student says the Black Student Union; the Bisexual, Gay, and Lesbian Union; and the Williams Feminist Alliance "all get special funding, channeled through the Williams College Multicultural Center." The views expressed by these groups are sometimes extreme, but they have widespread administrative support. The campus homosexual group, for instance, routinely chalks the campus with offensive slogans that are tolerated by the university in the name of "diversity."

The James A. Garfield Republican Club, also funded by the college, has sponsored numerous conservative speakers on campus in recent years, including Charles Murray, William Buckley, Robert Novak, Michael Medved, and Christina Hoff Sommers.

Campus Life: One Sex Fits All

The vast majority of Williams students live on campus. Certain dormitories are set aside for freshmen, while other housing is assigned by lottery. Several of the old fraternity houses (fraternities were banned in the 1960s) are considered the most pleasant and attractive places to live, while there are also "some monstrous 60s and 70s buildings," according to one student.

Students wishing for some measure of privacy in Williams's residential system will be disappointed to learn that the college has a unisex residential bathroom policy.

This policy made headlines a couple of years ago when a student journalist, Wendy Shalit, excoriated Williams in the pages of *U.S. News and World Report* and several other magazines with an article entitled "A Ladies Room of One's Own."

The policy seems out of place, since President Payne waged war on fraternities and alcohol when he was at Hamilton College. While frats no longer exist at Williams, Payne has instituted a number of "party policies" since arriving. Many students contend that these steps have dampened student initiative in social events. "The campus is a gloomy place," reports one student. "Student social life revolves around large campus events (which are too crowded and guarded by campus security) and the two local bars — the Purple Pub and Canterbury's. There is a new place in town, called Mezze, which has attracted a bit of an avant-garde clientele."

Outdoor activities are an integral part of the average Williams student's life, due to the college's pristine western Massachusetts location. "There is a definite sense of insularity here," notes one professor. The campus is certainly more rural than cosmopolitan, and consequently, "people get their sustenance from the surrounding landscape," the professor says.

Both intramural and varsity sports are big at Williams, and a large portion of the student body participates in this athletic life of the college. There are 31 varsity and 15 junior varsity teams, as well as seven club teams. In both 1996 and 1997 the Williams Ephs won the Sears NCAA Division III Directors' Cup, a competition which honors the nation's best athletic department by assigning points based on the achievements of all the sports teams from a college. Williams is extremely proud of the high academic performance of many of its athletes, and annually honors those carrying strong academic records. In one recent academic year, 137 students were named Eph Scholar-Athletes (with GPAs better than 3.2), among them one Rhodes scholar. The athletic facilities are excellent, and the Taconic Golf Course is one of the best in the region, recently hosting the U.S. Senior Amateur Open. "In many respects, the school is more of a paradise or country club than a college," notes one student.

A Williams education also carries a price tag in keeping with this elite aura; the cost of tuition, room, board, and fees hovers just under $30,000, though Williams continues its "need-blind admissions policy" and offers an average financial aid package of $19,400. Williams has approximately 2,000 undergraduates, and the entering class for the 1996-97 academic year was the largest ever, with 554 students. New York, Massachusetts, New Jersey, and California send the greatest number of students to Williams.

Although Williams has dumped several of its grand traditions, some remain strong. For instance, the bitter rivalry between Williams and Amherst College, still a vital part of the Williams atmosphere, began in the nineteenth century when some members of the Williams community petitioned to move the college into the Connecticut Valley because of the remoteness of Williamstown. In 1821 Williams president Zephaniah Swift Moore left with a group of students to found Amherst, which to this day serves as Williams's archrival. The Hopkins Observatory at Williams, the oldest astronomical observatory in the country, dates from 1838. There is also a beautiful chapel, and, unlike at Swarthmore, where the chapel has been transformed into a student center, at Williams it still operates as a chapel (though attendance is no longer mandatory), and the student-played bell tower chimes can be heard daily (though often, according to one student, the campus is treated to the less-than-reverent *Flintstones* theme or the *Star Wars* "Death March").

UNIVERSITY OF WISCONSIN AT MADISON

Office of Admissions
Director of Admissions
University of Wisconsin at Madison
750 University Avenue
Madison, WI 53706
(608) 262-3961
www.wisc.edu/

Total enrollment: 40,196
Undergraduates: 27,533
SAT Ranges (Verbal/Math): V 520-650, M 550-670
Financial aid: 55%
Applicants: 16,500
Accepted: 72%
Enrolled: 45%
Application deadline: Feb. 1
Financial aid application deadline: Mar. 1
Tuition: in-state, $3,189; out-of-state, $10,750
Core curriculum: No

Progressive Hotbed

One of the nation's first land-grant colleges, the University of Wisconsin at Madison still proclaims loyalty to its original mission: under the terms of the "Wisconsin Idea," the university "through teaching, research, and community service, is an asset with offerings for every corner of the state." The university can make strong claims to having a salutary impact on the state, with roughly a third of its nearly 300,000 alumni living in-state and a number of programs of study, such as dairy science and rural sociology, that have obvious applications to the region.

But observers of UW-Madison's increasingly radical political tenor contend that the school has merely become a haven for activism and a laboratory for social engineering. The university competed with Berkeley in the 1960s for campus protests, and has been a breeding ground for left-wing activism ever since. Also, the city of Madison, because of the presence of the university and a staunchly Democratic state legislature, has developed a reputation as a liberal town, despite the recent gubernatorial successes of conservative Tommy Thompson. Dubbing it "The Heartland's Progressive Hotbed," the *Utne Reader* recently selected the city as one of the nation's "10 most enlightened towns," a place where individuals can "sip latte, watch foreign films, visit naturopaths, join kayak clubs, browse used-book shops, buy organic chevre, or find meditation centers."

In recent years the Wisconsin Idea has yielded to the "Madison Plan," an aggressive multicultural initiative designed to increase the number of minority students and faculty and to raise "diversity" awareness among the student population. But politics is not everything at UW-Madison. Thanks to the sheer size of the institution, the university still harbors pockets of traditional academic excellence, and pursuing a program of solid liberal studies remains a possibility for the determined student.

Academic Life: Appearance versus Reality

The University of Wisconsin at Madison is made up of nine separate colleges: the College of Agricultural and Life Sciences, the School of Business, the College of Engineering, the School of Education, the School of Family Resources and Consumer Sciences, the College of Letters and Science, the School of Medicine, the School of Nursing, and the School of Pharmacy. The university enrolls nearly 28,000 undergraduates, two-thirds of whom pursue studies in the College of Letters and Science.

In its undergraduate bulletin, the university sets out the components of a liberal education in a remarkably traditional fashion, admirably free from the political and utilitarian emphasis given at most state universities. A degree from the College of Letters and Science will provide students with four things: (1) education of the complete person (including "the capacity to think critically"); (2) education for citizenship (echoing the Wisconsin Idea's call to state service); (3) education for a productive life (emphasizing not just a formal work setting, but such activities as "participation in the arts" and "community service"); and (4) education for the love of learning (considered the "cornerstone of liberal arts"). The guide continues in words that would make John Henry Newman proud: "Although this may appear to go against the practical, bottom-line grain that is often so prevalent, in truth the practical world is shaped by the ideas and devices whose origins were in the love of learning for its own sake. The students of the liberal arts benefit from, and pass on, this legacy."

Turning from this elevated rhetoric to the general education requirements is a rather disappointing experience. Students are required to take from three to six credits in both communication and quantitative reasoning, from four to six in natural science, six in humanities/literature/arts, three in social studies, and three in ethnic studies. The latter requisite, recently instituted, is essentially a "diversity require-ment." There is no Western civilization requirement and no foreign language require-ment.

Still, students can piece together their own course of liberal studies from the numerous offerings at the university. According to one undergraduate, academic programs at UW-Madison offer "something for everyone." Courses in forty foreign languages are offered, and students can major in such fields as Greek, Hebrew, Polish, Portuguese, Russian, and Scandinavian Studies. One student complains that most political science courses are skewed to the left, and that the economics department is overly Keynesian. English and history still have some solid offerings, but by far the most impressive course of studies is a certificate program in Integrated Liberal Studies (ILS).

The ILS program does not dismiss the vast intellectual contributions of West-ern culture, but was established as an alternative to the "scattered electives" offered by the university. "The purpose of the program," according to the course description, "is to counter the fragmentation of undergraduate education by providing a common ground of learning." All students take two courses in the history of Western culture, as well as numerous interdisciplinary classes that encourage them to make connec-tions between "literature and the arts; science, technology, and philosophy; and political, economic, and social thought." Courses are organized historically and pro-vide "a comprehensive introduction to the achievements of Western culture." ILS professors volunteer for the program, and are selected "on the basis of their commit-ment to general education and their interest in undergraduate teaching." Faculty-student contact is encouraged.

The ILS program exists as an oasis in a desert of disparate and frequently vapid courses and programs. Indeed, the university certainly suffers from both the intel-lectual fluffiness and the politicization that are plaguing higher education in general. It is a sad day in academe when a student can receive course credit for "Daytime Serials: Family and Social Roles." The course, offered through the pseudodiscipline of Family and Consumer Communications, bears the following description: "Analysis of the themes and characters that populate television's daytime serials and investiga-tion of what impact these portrayals have on women's and men's roles in the family and in the work place. The course will compare and contrast prime-time programs with daytime serials for these themes."

Despite their predominant interest in research, professors do make themselves available to students, and one student describes them as "pretty accessible." Advising is said to be virtually nonexistent: "I've never been contacted by an advisor," notes one student. The numerous academic clubs for students help alleviate the feeling of anonymity on such a large campus. One student recommends the International Business Club; others groups include the Entrepreneur Club, the Economics Student Association, and numerous honorary societies.

Political Atmosphere: The Fluffy and the Political

Fashionable views dominate the political landscape at UW-Madison, and there is seldom a quiet moment in campus politics. The campus is "prone to demonstrations," in the words of one student, and the hillside leading up to campus is perennially chalked with slogans of every variety. Campus lecturers tend to be "very liberal," according to one student; a recent sampling of topics reveals several with decidedly trendy political or theoretical overtones: "Framing the Other: Ethnic Outsiders in Swedish Film," "Racial Histories and Their Regimes of Truth: On the Politics of Epistemology," and "To Be a Jewish Woman Is to Be an Activist."

Political, social, and environmental groups on campus are numerous and vocal. The university is home to chapters of such groups as Hooked on Ebonics, Bi?Shy?Why?, Alliance for Animals, the Progressive Student Network, and Students of Objectivism. There is also a host of groups comically paired on opposite sides of the political spectrum: the Ten Percent Society and the Ninety Percent Society, the International Capitalism Society and the International Socialist Organization, the Alliance for a Corporate-Free University and the Students for a Corporate Run University, the Students Addressing Multiethnicity (SAME) and the Madisonians against Diversity (MAD), and the Students for an Independent Quebec and the Students against an Independent Quebec.

On most political issues, however, the administration "comes down in support of radical groups," complains one student. The university recently became embroiled in a student fees controversy after several students went to court contending that their student fees shouldn't be used to fund certain groups with whose views they disagree. The Wisconsin State Supreme Court ruled in favor of the students.

When it comes to multiculturalism, diversity, and campus life, "sensitivity" is all the rage at UW-Madison. The university sponsors a Race Relations Education Program (RREP) under the guidance of a Race Awareness Committee composed of faculty, staff, and students. The committee conducts workshops "that provide a critical understanding of how racism works in U.S. society, challenges participants to recognize their own racial biases and misinformation, and facilitates healthy awareness of racial and cultural differences."

In addition, the university has an Interim Multicultural Center (IMCC) focusing on five American ethnic groups — African-Americans, Native Americans, Chicanos/Chicanas, Asian-Americans, and Puerto Ricans — as well as a Disability Resource Center that provides advocacy, information, and referral services. Recently a campus student group sponsored a program as part of Disabilities Awareness Week that involved students performing routine tasks while sitting in wheelchairs or having their eyes covered. One student describes the university's numerous awareness weeks as "fluffy" and "pretty political."

The university recently issued a report from the Committee on Gay, Lesbian, and Bisexual Issues containing numerous recommendations expanding the privileges and programs available to homosexuals at the university. The report recommends "establishing a certificate program in gay, lesbian, and bisexual studies, possibly leading to a full major in five years." Other recommendations include extending health insurance to domestic partners of gay, lesbian, and bisexual faculty, staff, and students and establishing a gay, lesbian, and bisexual campus center. But perhaps the most egregious element of the committee report is the proposal to create a full-time gay, lesbian, and bisexual university liaison and to provide "sensitivity training" that would "encourage faculty and staff to examine the 'assumption of heterosexuality.'" No final decisions on any of the committee recommendations have yet been made.

Because of the large number of graduate students on campus, many campus political issues revolve around their concerns. A significant number of graduate students act as teaching assistants, and their concerns over inadequate pay and benefits have erupted in protest in recent years. In the spring of 1997, for instance, a group of students carrying a replica of the administration building demonstrated in front of that building in a gesture intended to symbolize "that our work carries the university," according to a member of the Wisconsin Teaching Assistants' Association, as quoted in the *Chronicle of Higher Education*.

During her tenure as chancellor of the university, Clinton Administration cabinet member Donna Shalala vigorously pursued the "Madison Plan." Competing with other, similar race-based admission programs, the university has continually failed to meet its minority enrollment goals, in no small part because of the small number of minorities living in the state of Wisconsin. But the Madison Plan has been effective in introducing a politicized multicultural component to the undergraduate curriculum, in the form of the ethnic studies requirement.

Current chancellor David Ward has recently reaffirmed the university's emphasis on undergraduate education, issuing a letter entitled "Returning to Our Roots: The Student Experience" at a gathering of land-grant college presidents in Washington, D.C., in the spring of 1997. But the way in which this commitment translates into action at the curricular level is unlikely to be beneficial to those seeking a traditional liberal education. Although priorities of the initiative include a "commitment to undergraduate education," for a public university the size of UW-Madison, such changes include a diminishment of general education requirements, expanded use of computers in the classroom, and an emphasis on diversity.

Student Life: Always Something to Do in "Mad City"

One thing the University of Wisconsin definitely has going for it is its vibrant and pristine location on the edges of two large, glacial lakes, Mendota and Monona. Although some students complain about the long, harsh winters, most find the inclement weather offset by the myriad social opportunities Madison has to offer. State Street is a popular student venue, with shops, cafes, bookstores, and plenty of opportunities to hear live music. From May to September the town hosts an impressive Saturday morning farmers market. As one undergraduate remarks of the town, "It's really student-oriented — there's always something to do."

Housing in Madison does not appear to be a major problem, despite the fact that the university has room for only one-sixth of its total student population. Undergraduates are not required to live on campus, although most freshmen choose to live in residence halls. Single-sex housing is available, as is housing with limited visitation privileges. Other options include special-interest housing such as honors houses for honors program students, fraternity and sorority houses, and off-campus apartments or homes. Crime does not appear to be a major problem in this midwestern city: "I just feel safe everywhere I go," notes one student.

With upwards of six hundred student organizations available, students will find no shortage of extracurricular opportunities. Groups range from the American Association of Bovine Practitioners and the Porcine Interest Group (PIG) to the Secret Organization of Linguistic Undergrads and the Future Housepersons of Madison. Students with less esoteric tastes will find a variety of mainstream social, academic, and athletic clubs. Panhellenic organizations also offer students a sense of community in what can be an overwhelming social environment. The Greek system is strong, and about 10 percent of undergraduates are members of fraternities or sororities.

As a member of the Big Ten, the university fields several high-profile athletic programs. Fans from the university and around the state are extremely loyal to the Wisconsin Badgers football team, and thousands traveled to Pasadena in 1994 to watch them beat UCLA in the Rose Bowl. Other high-performing sports include men's hockey, soccer, and track, and women's cross-country. Because of its location between two lakes, crew is also a popular sport. In the coming year the university is slated to open a new, impressive $45 million athletic facility.

Although excessive drinking among undergraduates is a continual concern for the UW-Madison community, some students are upset with what they consider excessive measures on the part of the local community to clamp down on student parties. Last year the Associated Students of Madison banded together for a "Stop the Sting" effort. Designed to pressure the Madison City Council to rescind a grant to the police department that was earmarked to cut down on drunk driving, the student protest charges that police have misused the funds to go undercover at large, off-campus student parties. One sophomore complained that most students walk to the parties, and that the police effort unfairly targeted UW-Madison undergraduates, according to the *Chronicle of Higher Education.*

YALE UNIVERSITY

P.O. Box 208234
New Haven, CT 06520
(203) 432-1900
www.yale.edu

Total enrollment: 10,982
Undergraduates: 5,315
SAT Ranges (Verbal/Math): V 670-770, M 670-760
Financial aid: 41%
Applicants: 12,046
Accepted: 18%
Enrolled: 62%
Application deadline: Dec. 31
Financial aid application deadline: Feb. 1
Tuition: $23,780
Core curriculum: No

Genteel yet Unpretentious?

Yale University shares with Harvard the prestige that comes from centuries of tradition and excellence. Its graduates have played a huge role in the history of the United States and the rest of the world, and its name has long been synonymous with the old established order of privileged leaders in all walks of life. Founded by Congregationalist ministers in 1701 as the Collegiate School, Yale moved to New Haven in 1716 and was named for its benefactor, Elihu Yale, two years later. It is thus the third-oldest institution of higher learning in America — Harvard and William and Mary being the only schools that can claim a longer lineage. Today Yale's size and research budget place it somewhere between those two illustrious predecessors.

In fact, Yale has long prided itself on its genteel yet unpretentious status among the elite institutions in this country. Whereas the graduates of Harvard and many other top schools have tended to be professionally oriented types — lawyers, doctors, bankers, Wall Street heavyweights — Yale alumni are often found in the less lucrative fields of the humanities and social sciences teaching at colleges and universities across the country. Yale's law school accepts only a hundred or so students each year, and the business school does not have the reputation of a Wharton or a Stanford. Instead, Yale has emphasized the liberal arts as a venture worthy of serious and sustained support. This path has insulated Yale from the negative effects that tend to come with large professional schools: the dominance of pragmatism and professionalism. Taking this path has required some courage because it means that the university has also lost out on some of the big money that comes with thriving professional schools. In the long run, however, Yale's commitment to the liberal arts has enabled it to preserve a deeper and more enduring vision of a university education.

So, while Yale has hardly been immune from the plagues of political ideology and narrow specialization, it retains a battered but still living tradition of liberal education. That's more than can be said of some of Yale's closest competitors.

Academic Life: Directed and Undirected Studies

Yale has no core curriculum; instead, all students must complete a set of requirements from four distribution groups: foreign languages, humanities, social sciences, and the natural sciences. Students must take three courses in each of the first three areas and two natural sciences. There is no lab requirement, and students may be exempted from the language requirement with high advanced placement scores. Students have access to the *Yale College Programs of Study,* known locally as the *Blue Book,* which lists the courses at Yale College, the largest and oldest unit of the university.

One student says these requirements are "weak and [offer] little direction. I came here when I was 17, and I wasn't prepared to find the best classes and study the canon. I feel kind of embarrassed that there are important books I've never read: I've never read Plato and Aristotle, but spent much time in so many other classes and requirements. There's a disincentive to take those classes" that would teach the classic works, because so much time is required to fulfill the distribution requirements. A professor offers a more positive review, although he, too, would prefer a core. "The distribution requirements aren't all that bad, given the absence of a core, which we haven't had since the 1960s. It does force students to get some general background in some of the areas of study. Few of the kids who come here know what they want to do, and at least this gives them the chance to sample around a bit and see where their interests lie. Some come wanting to do pre-med or pre-professional, and they discover they don't like it after all." Another faculty member says: "They do a pretty good job at it, although if you wanted to get away with bad classes, you could." Yet another professor has a less sanguine view: "The core has become the periphery, and the periphery has become the core."

A praiseworthy element of Yale's curriculum is the absence of any professional undergraduate degree. There is no major in either education or business, for example — concentrations that grab a very large share of the undergraduate student body at most universities.

Yale has long been known as a university that tries to take care of undergraduates to a much greater degree than most other elite schools. Advising is centered around the residential college system. "We look after the intellectual progress of the students," says one professor. Yet a student says "there is no one to help you choose which classes to take to get a degree. My undergraduate advisor is a nice guy, but he's not much help. The freshman counselors warn you not to over-burden yourself. They're really support counselors." Another professor says an attempt is under way to improve the advising system. "Advising is centered around the college system, so it's hit or miss as to whether or not they get an advisor in their field," this professor says. "In their sophomore year they're likely to be told to go find someone to advise them, but it's really up to them."

Yale employs many outstanding professors who are not only leading scholars in their fields but are also very dedicated teachers who take seriously the intellectual nurturing of their students. Among them are: Steven Smith, Norma Thompson, H. Bradford Westerfield, Shelley Burtt, and Allan Stam in political science; Louis Dupre, Wayne Meeks, Richard Fern, Jaroslav Pelikan, Brevard Childs, and Harry Stout in religious studies; David Brian Davis, Gaddis Smith, Henry Turner, Jonathan Spence, Paul Freedman, John Gaddis, Paul Kennedy, P. Squatriti, Donald Kagan, and Frank Turner in history; Creighton Gilbert, Vincent Scully, and Walter Cahn in art history; Sarah Winter, Laura Green, Ruth Yeazell, Alexander Welsh, Tyrus Miller, and Annabel Patterson in English; Guiseppe Mozzotta in Italian; Dan Soloman and Patrice Rankine in classics; Vladimir Alexandrov in Russian; Edwin McClellan in Japanese Studies; Karsten Harries in philosophy; Peter Schultheiss and Serge Lang in mathematics; David Gelertner in computer science; Sidney Altman in biology; and Eric Denardo in operations research.

As is the case at many schools, even the better departments at Yale contain some politicized faculty members. Nevertheless, the following departments are deemed by faculty and students to be quite strong, and all contain scholars and teachers of the highest caliber: history, art history, English, biology, biochemistry, genetics, mathematics, music, neuroscience, physiology, political science, and a specialized major known as Ethics, Politics, and Economics, or EPE, that admits only forty students each year. According to one professor, EPE "attracts the best students," often produces the winning senior essay, and has a wonderful intellectual coherence.

Of the political science department, one professor says, "It's a really strange conglomerate. The political theorists there have almost nothing in common with the folks in international relations. It's not a coherent major, but it's an affable department because everyone in it does something different." Another professor notes, "Political science is in better shape than history, because it gives people the freedom to flourish." A student says the offerings in American government "are being brushed aside in favor of those focusing upon various oppressed segments of society."

Regarding the English department, a professor comments: "English retains a sense of its teaching mission, and is getting over its 'deconstructionist' phase. There are many there who are into the New Historicism, but what goes on in the classroom is not as bad as what you might see elsewhere."

"There are some really serious scholars in the history department," says an undergraduate. A faculty member adds, less optimistically, "History has problems because there are lots of social historians [a politicized school of historiography], but there are huge gaps in their offerings, such as in the American Revolution. Important time periods are frequently overlooked in favor of social history." History is included in the best-departments list despite these obvious drawbacks because a student can still take superb classes there if he chooses his courses with care.

One of the most attractive options for students of the highest caliber is the Program in Directed Studies for freshmen. Those wishing to take part in it must apply the summer after they are accepted at Yale. The university allows 120 persons into Directed Studies, up from 80 two years ago. Somewhat over 200 apply out of the freshman class of 1,100. The curriculum consists of close reading of primary sources of the West from the Greeks to the modern world in seminars of 18 students or fewer. It is, in the words of one professor, an "elite course." "Directed Studies is a good choice," this professor continues, "because it is the only chance these students have at Yale to immerse themselves in a coherent syllabus. They do have the opportunity later on to fashion a coherent discipline, but often even the majors are very wide. Directed Studies gives them a broad base they don't get elsewhere except for certain areas of math and science." The program requires a great deal of writing from the students, and is, according to another faculty member, the "crown jewel of Yale College. It is a truly outstanding program — there is no matching its quality. Professors can pick out these students later because they are better writers and speakers."

How can such a program thrive at a modern university? In part, faculty who might be hostile to the authors taught — Homer, Herodotus, St. Augustine, Machiavelli, and Mill, among others — know it is but one option among many, professors favorably disposed to the program say. The administration, say sources on campus, know many alumni favor such offerings, and they can point to Directed Studies as proof of the vitality of studies in Western civilization without having to require it of every student.

At least some students who didn't make it into the program wish it were available to the general student body. "It would have been a great deal," says a student who was rejected. "Everyone who wants to take it should be able to. But it's taught by professors rather than teaching assistants, so it is expensive. Only so many professors are willing to teach it." Speaking on that matter, a professor says: "Those students who aren't in Directed Studies can fare very well by choosing good courses that duplicate much of the same reading. They won't get the coherence or the seminars, however."

Among the most politicized departments is a new creation, Ethnicity, Race, and Migration, or ERM. Other departments where ideology tends to hold sway are economics, Latin American studies, women's studies, sociology, and American studies. Of ERM, a professor says: "ERM is trying to model itself on EPE (Ethics, Politics, and Economics), which is very solid. EPE attracts the best students, and requires a senior essay. They produce most of the winners of the senior essay contests. It has an obvious coherence and is modeled on an Oxford program. So, ERM, which is pure leftist propaganda, has tried to ride on the success of EPE." A graduate student says ERM is "a political correctness factory and a haven for folks who want to do nothing but major in race, class, and gender."

A professor says American studies is "notoriously easy. Students there don't have to know anything" to get good grades; they need only "swallow a very big political pill" to move along. It is, this professor adds, Yale's "worst department." And, although the history department contains several excellent scholar-teachers, a professor notes that the stylishness of social history means that they "have people who under the guise of social history are really teaching ethnic and feminist studies."

Of women's studies, a faculty member says: "It's so predictable. It's the same old bunch you'd expect." A student says the economics department "is the biggest disappointment I've experienced here. It is very Keynesian. A poll revealed that a third of the graduating seniors in economics couldn't identify Adam Smith with his famous line about the invisible hand. And almost no one could identify [free-market economists] von Mises or Hayek."

It is generally agreed that the teaching assistants at Yale are more likely to be radical than the professoriate. Says a student: "T.A.s are highly politicized. I never sign up for the sections [taught by T.A.s rather than faculty] if I have a chance." Notes a graduate student: "People feel very pressured to agree with their T.A. lest their grades suffer. And this influences the students, because there are also many faculty members who are unashamed to politicize their classrooms."

Political Atmosphere: Western Civ Has Got to Go?

The most spectacular episode in the struggles over multiculturalism at Yale began in 1991, when alumnus Lee Bass gave the university $20 million for a program in Western civilization studies. In what became a major embarrassment to the Yale community, the university refused to use the money in ways that conformed to the original agreement with Mr. Bass. After Yale had spent time stonewalling and generating misinformation about the situation, it was eventually forced to return the gift. This fiasco is a sign of the degree to which the administration, in conjunction with the more radicalized elements of the Yale community, is hostile to courses that emphasize the Western heritage (of which the modern university itself is a part). In this particular case, Yale was perfectly happy to take the money and use it for the creation of politicized courses, but it preferred to return the money rather than offer the same kind of education that generations of Yale alumni have enjoyed. The Bass affair caused an uproar among many loyal alumni who were outraged at the administration's arrogance and dishonesty.

One of the more troubling developments on many campuses has been the preferential treatment administrations have given to radical student groups. Despite their generally low membership rolls, this official imprimatur emboldens these organizations and amplifies their voices on campus. At Yale, such groups include Mecha, a militant Mexican group that celebrates Columbus Day by chalking the campus with such phrases as "Columbus raped my mother." In solidarity with migrant workers in California, Yale has been grapeless for years now. The local homosexual group sponsors a co-op dance every semester, at which time they display posters around campus that one student calls "pornographic. They depict S & M and explicit sexual acts." This student continues: "Most people are afraid to speak out against them."

Says a student: "If Yale listens to its alumni, it can make the right decisions. But many in the administration just want to please everyone. They should listen to the voice of reason." Another student adds: "The left here is sort of sleepy. Most people are liberal, but not fanatics — it's just the accepted wisdom. But Yale offers the highest quality of life for traditional students in the Ivy League. You aren't hunted down."

"You hear the same sort of diversity rhetoric here that you hear everywhere," says a graduate student. "But because there's an aggressive conservative force on campus, the administration is becoming more sensitive to press criticism." And students who insist on obtaining an authentic liberal arts education can do so if they are persistent. Says a senior: "Faculty who aren't politicized are here in adequate numbers. For the most part professors try to be fair. I'm satisfied."

There is no speech code at Yale. "Yale escaped the whole speech code trend of the '90s," says a student. "There's a lot of free-wheeling debate here. You can say almost anything" if you're willing to stand up for what you believe and can withstand the peer pressure to conform. "The orientation sessions are forceful, but classes and peer pressure do the most damage. There's always subtle pressure, and everyone knows the PC thing to say." According to another student, "The main thing is to have courage. If you're courageous, you can be pretty happy at Yale. Life can be very rich here, and I don't mean just activism, but the intellectual life."

As for sensitivity training, a senior says freshmen must attend three seminars that cover security, safe sex, and "after the party." The first is innocuous enough, says the student, but the "safer sex" seminar was "graphic and explicit." Although abstinence is also taught at this seminar, according to a student journalist, "Information on a variety of nonstandard sexual practices may be discussed. Several students recall explicit instructions regarding sexual activities being provided at this meeting in previous years." Condoms are given away after the session. The third part of the orientation deals with the dangers of date rape. While this threat is to be taken seriously, a female undergraduate says the administration has accepted the current trends on the subject. "If a couple gets drunk and has sex, it's obviously rape! All of this is encouraged. Promiscuity is old news, but now women want to have it both ways by having sex and then retroactively withdrawing consent, and it's done anonymously. It can destroy a guy's life."

Regarding tenure at Yale, a professor comments that "You see strange customs of tenure here." Noting that a female professor with an "incredible record" but "fairly conservative politics" was recently "sacked by her tenure committee," this source says this practice has occurred several times over the past few years. From these observations, and from the number of ideologized courses in the politicized departments noted above, it is clear that no small number of professors at Yale are only too happy to politicize the hiring/tenure process, thereby reducing the true diversity of the Yale faculty.

Student Life: A Haven within New Haven

Student life at Yale College revolves around the residential college system, installed in 1932. There are twelve such colleges for the undergraduates, who move into them at the beginning of their sophomore year after spending their freshman year in Old Campus, a beautiful quadrangle built in the last century. Each college has its own personality, developed over the decades, and graduates are almost as loyal to their college as to their school. Headed by a residential master and a dean, colleges have their own dining hall, library, common rooms, and courtyard. This historic element of student life is one of the most distinctive and beneficial experiences for Yale undergraduates, because it creates a much smaller circle in which students can live than would be possible in an 11,000-student university with no unifying infrastructure. The master and dean also advise students. A professor notes that the level of civility in the colleges is higher than would be the case in most dorms, both because of the presence of the master, which assures that students live with "a measure of adult supervision," and because of the degree of responsibility expected of the students themselves.

Yale has a very active intellectual and social life, both of which are nurtured through the Yale Political Union, the largest undergraduate organization at Yale with over 1,400 members, or some 25 percent of the undergraduate body, and the only group of its kind in the country. It is modeled on the Oxford and Cambridge Union Societies, and it sponsors debates among the six student-run political parties as well as speeches by invited guests (along with student responses) from the worlds of politics, academe, public policy, and journalism. The Political Union is nonpartisan and invites guests from across the philosophical spectrum. It accomplishes today the same mission its founder, A. Whitney Griswold, professor and later president of Yale, hoped it would when he founded it in 1934: "To combat the insular and apathetic Yale political culture of the 1930s," according to campus literature.

Each of the six parties — Liberal, Progressive, Independent, Conservative, Tory, and the Party of the Right (POR) — enacts a wide range of programs throughout the semester, including weekly debates; traditional toasting sessions at Mory's, a local private club; and other activities aimed at promoting both fellowship and serious discussion. For the student who is unwilling to conform to campus orthodoxies, the Conservative Party, the Tory Party, and the POR offer opportunities to find other traditionalist students. "Conservative students at Yale are a lot better off than at Harvard, MIT, Wellesley, or other such schools," says a graduate student. "The Political Union does a lot to insure that conservative voices are heard. It gives them a platform absent at many other places. It's the highest quality of life for the traditional student in the Ivy League." Says a student: "The conservative groups compete with one another like frats during rush. There's plenty of room for conservatives of different stripes. None are overtly libertarian. The Tories are more moderate, and the Conservative Party and the POR both have a mix of traditionalists and libertarians." The debates cover serious topics. According to one member, the Conservative Party is "a fraternal order that is intellectually stimulating. We have dinner together most nights." After meals this party holds a Sir Thomas More lecture on a topic of interest in arts and literature. A local institution to which these parties and others have recourse is Mory's, a private club described by one student as "a gentleman's club from way back. It's very traditional."

The presence of these parties under the auspices of the Yale Political Union speaks of the vibrant social life available for those willing to put in the time to enjoy this bounty. Also available are numerous organizations with interests that range from the ridiculous to the sublime. The Society of Orpheus and Bacchus, for example, is an a cappella male singing group founded in 1939 and known locally as the SOBs. There are many other groups devoted to music and theater; professional associations organized by academic discipline; religious groups such as the Episcopal Church at Yale, St. Thomas More House (the Catholic center and chapel at Yale), and Yale Hillel; and numerous others that cover a huge range of interests.

The number of highly politicized groups is small but, as is usually the case, quite loud. Among the more radical groups, students and professors mention the Lesbian, Gay, Bisexual Cooperative at Yale, which sponsors a co-op dance every semester and chalks the sidewalk liberally.

Yale fields intercollegiate teams in all of the major sports. Like other Ivy League schools, it requires that its athletes maintain high academic standards and does not award athletic scholarships. Among the many intramural sports, organized by residential college, are golf, soccer, football, tennis, basketball, swimming, squash, softball, and billiards.

Student publications include *Light and Truth,* an alternative student magazine; the Yale *Record,* a humor monthly published since 1872; the *Yale Free Press,* another alternative paper; and the *Yale Daily News,* Yale's so-called mainstream student daily.

Yale brims with cultural institutions, including the Center for British Art, one of the finest of its kind in North America; the University Art Gallery; the Peabody Museum of Natural History; and the huge library system. Centering around the Sterling Memorial Library, Yale's collection of some 10 million volumes is second in size only to Harvard's and is one of the great collections in the world. It is the kind of research facility scholars from other schools travel long distances to use.

Yale is now engaged in a massive effort to improve its physical plant. Fifteen architectural firms were retained to help renovate 100 of the 224 buildings — a project that will take $500 million to complete. This is very welcome news, since one of the glories of Yale is its beautiful Gothic and Colonial buildings that make it one of the most photogenic campuses anywhere. More than $120 million will be spent on the Sterling and Law Libraries alone. In carrying out this mammoth project, Yale is finally catching up on long-delayed renovations and even simple maintenance that have worried its alumni for many years.

A final word about beleaguered New Haven, described by one professor as "an industrial city with no industry." An alum warns students not to stray too far from campus "or they'll take a stray bullet." "There have been shootings along the Main Line," says another. While the area immediately around campus is generally safe, crime at Yale is significantly higher than at most other universities in the country, and students love Yale in spite of, not because of, its environs. Many Yale students volunteer their time to help tutor area youngsters or to do what they can to improve New Haven's housing.

Intercollegiate Studies Institute

The Intercollegiate Studies Institute (ISI) was founded in 1953 by citizens deeply concerned about the preservation and extension of individual liberty in order to further in successive generations of American college youth a better understanding of the economic, political, and spiritual values that sustain a free society. ISI believes that freedom in any society is diminished or extended according to the quality and scope of the education of the individual. This education must provide the broad knowledge and understanding essential for good judgment.

Traditionally this level of knowledge has been attained through liberal arts education involving an understanding of the principles of various disciplines as they have been gleaned from Western thought and experience. ISI believes that a lack of this proper education leaves men prey to panaceas which offer utopia but inevitably lead to despotism. Hence, the ISI motto: *To Educate for Liberty.*

With ISI's volunteer representatives at over 1,100 colleges and universities, and with more than 60,000 ISI student and faculty members on virtually every campus in the country, ISI directs thousands of young people each year to a wide array of educational programs that deepen their understanding of the American ideal of ordered liberty. These include over 300 yearly lectures at colleges nationwide, as well as a prep school lecture series; an Honors Fellows program for outstanding under-graduates seeking faculty mentors who share their intellectual interests; a Campus Leaders program for active and intellectually serious undergraduates and graduate students; a conference program that sponsors student and faculty events, ranging from regional Leadership Conferences to weekend colloquia to a summer Western Civilization Summit; and three lucrative and prestigious fellowships for graduate study.

ISI also publishes an array of materials offering both students and professors timely writing on perennially important themes. All members receive free-of-charge *Campus: America's Student Newspaper* and *The Intercollegiate Review. Campus,* the only national student-written collegiate newspaper, offers lively coverage of the intellectual and political trends that drive college life. *The Intercollegiate Review,* ISI's biannual flagship journal, publishes essays and reviews by some of America's most distinguished authors. Our other journals include *Modern Age,* a quarterly journal of scholarship in the liberal arts that just celebrated its fortieth year of publication, and *The Political Science Reviewer,* one of the leading journals in its discipline. ISI distributes nationally three other journals of scholarship and opinion, *The Chesterton Review, The Salisbury Review,* and *The University Bookman.*

Under its imprint, ISI Books, the Institute also publishes a growing number of serious nonfiction titles, monographs, and other educational resources meant to advance an understanding of liberty and aid concerned citizens in the renewal of America's cherished political and cultural traditions. ISI Books appeal to general audiences and are suitable for classroom use as well. Forthcoming ISI resources designed to advance the study of our cultural heritage include ISI's *Core Curriculum Self-Study Guide,* which will enable students at any university to use their electives to achieve a genuine education; ISI's Bibliographies of Freedom, a series of publications that will introduce students to authors and ideas, in six major fields of study, that are absent from today's politicized syllabus; and our Modern Thinkers series, which consists of short, accessible intellectual biographies of this country's leading minds.

In recognition of its preeminent status among organizations concerned with higher education. ISI was selected by the John Templeton Foundation to administer the *Templeton Honor Rolls for Education in a Free Society.* ISI also administers the Collegiate Network (CN), a voluntary membership association that offers technical and financial support to more than 65 alternative college newspapers.

All of the elements of ISI's national effort work together, at different levels and in different ways, to identify the best and brightest students — America's future leaders — and to nurture them in an allegiance to the American tradition of ordered liberty.

To learn more about ISI, visit our website at www.isi.org. You may call us at 1-800-526-7022, or send e-mail inquiries to isi@isi.org.

Choosing the Right College Reply Card

ISI values your opinion of its college guide and hopes you will help it better determine the effectiveness of this book by completing and returning this **reply card**. ISI will in turn send you a free subscription to *Campus: America's Student Newspaper*, edited and written entirely by students.

Name: _____   E-mail Address: _____

Address: _____

Schools in which you are most interested: _____

Check all that apply: I am a   student   parent   professor   journalist   college donor   other

Please circle your answer from 1 to 5, with 1 being of no help and 5 being extremely helpful.

1. How helpful was this guide in choosing your school?   1   2   3   4   5

2. Did the use of this guide change your mind about a given institution?   1   2   3   4   5

3. How satisfied were you with the range and number of schools considered?   1   2   3   4   5

4. How strongly would you recommend this guide to others?   1   2   3   4   5

5. Please rate the following features of each essay, from 1 to 5:   Academic Life _____   Political Atmosphere _____   Student Life _____

BUSINESS REPLY MAIL
PERMIT NO. 44 WILMINGTON, DE

INTERCOLLEGIATE STUDIES INSTITUTE, INC.
PO BOX 4431
WILMINGTON, DE 19807-9957